# POLYBIUS
## BOOK 8

EDITED BY

G. O. HUTCHINSON

*Regius Professor of Greek Emeritus, University of Oxford*

## CAMBRIDGE
UNIVERSITY PRESS

Shaftesbury Road, Cambridge CB2 8EA, United Kingdom
One Liberty Plaza, 20th Floor, New York, NY 10006, USA
477 Williamstown Road, Port Melbourne, VIC 3207, Australia
314–321, 3rd Floor, Plot 3, Splendor Forum, Jasola District Centre,
New Delhi – 110025, India
103 Penang Road, #05–06/07, Visioncrest Commercial, Singapore 238467

Cambridge University Press is part of Cambridge University Press & Assessment,
a department of the University of Cambridge.

We share the University's mission to contribute to society through the pursuit of
education, learning and research at the highest international levels of excellence.

www.cambridge.org
Information on this title: www.cambridge.org/9781009265881
DOI: 10.1017/9781009265843
© Cambridge University Press & Assessment 2025

This publication is in copyright. Subject to statutory exception and to the provisions
of relevant collective licensing agreements, no reproduction of any part may take place
without the written permission of Cambridge University Press & Assessment.

When citing this work, please include a reference to the DOI 10.1017/9781009265843

First published 2025

*A catalogue record for this publication is available from the British Library*

Library of Congress Cataloging-in-Publication Data
NAMES: Polybius author | Hutchinson, G. O. editor
TITLE: Book 8 / Polybius ; edited by G. O. Hutchinson, Regius professor of
Greek emeritus, University of Oxford.
OTHER TITLES: Historiae. Liber 8. Greek. | Cambridge Greek and Latin classics
DESCRIPTION: Cambridge, United Kingdom ; New York, NY : Cambridge
University Press, 2025. | Series: Cambridge Greek and Latin classics |
Includes bibliographical references and index.
IDENTIFIERS: LCCN 2025009234 | ISBN 9781009265881 hardback | ISBN
9781009265850 paperback | ISBN 9781009265843 ebook
SUBJECTS: LCSH: Polybius. Historiae. Liber 8 | Punic War, 2nd, 218–201
B.C. – Early works to 1800 | Macedonian War, 1st, 215–205 B.C. – Early
works to 1800 | Rome – History – Republic, 265-30 B.C. – Early works to
1800 | Greece – History – 281–146 B.C. – Early works to 1800
CLASSIFICATION: LCC PA4391 .A3 2025 | DDC 937/.04–dc23/eng/20250502
LC record available at https://lccn.loc.gov/2025009234

ISBN 978-1-009-26588-1 Hardback
ISBN 978-1-009-26585-0 Paperback

Cambridge University Press & Assessment has no responsibility for the persistence
or accuracy of URLs for external or third-party internet websites referred to in this
publication and does not guarantee that any content on such websites is,
or will remain, accurate or appropriate.

# CAMBRIDGE GREEK AND LATIN CLASSICS

GENERAL EDITORS

P. E. EASTERLING
*Regius Professor Emeritus of Greek, University of Cambridge*

PHILIP HARDIE
*Fellow, Trinity College, and Honorary Professor of Latin Emeritus,
University of Cambridge*

† NEIL HOPKINSON

RICHARD HUNTER
*Regius Professor of Greek Emeritus, University of Cambridge*

S. P. OAKLEY
*Kennedy Professor of Latin, University of Cambridge*

OLIVER THOMAS
*Associate Professor in Classics, University of Nottingham*

CHRISTOPHER WHITTON
*Professor of Latin Literature, University of Cambridge*

FOUNDING EDITORS

P. E. EASTERLING
† E. J. KENNEY

*IN MEMORY OF PAUL HUTCHINSON*
*9.10.1959–8.3.2024*

# CONTENTS

| | |
|---|---|
| List of Maps and Figures | page viii |
| Preface | ix |
| List of Abbreviations | xi |
| Introduction | 1 |
| Part I: Polybius | 1 |
| 1  Tasters and Texture | 1 |
| 2  General and Particular | 4 |
| 3  Literary Context | 5 |
| 4  Historiographical Art | 10 |
| 5  Style | 12 |
| 6  Design | 15 |
| 7  Greeks and Romans | 19 |
| 8  Methodology | 24 |
| Part II: Book 8 | 27 |
| 9  Summary | 27 |
| 10  Cohesion | 28 |
| 11  Structures of Places and People | 31 |
| 12  Context of Events | 33 |
| 13  Language | 40 |
| 14  Transmission and Reception | 44 |
| Sigla, Abbreviations and Order of Chapters | 53 |
| POLYBIUS BOOK 8 | 55 |
| Commentary | 86 |
| Works Cited | 243 |
| Indexes | 266 |
| 1  Passages | 266 |
| 2  Greek Words | 278 |
| 3  General | 284 |

# MAPS AND FIGURES

## MAPS

| | | |
|---|---|---|
| 1 | Mediterranean | *page* xiv |
| 2 | Syracuse | 105 |
| 3 | Tarentum | 193 |

The maps essentially include only places mentioned in this book.

## FIGURES

1. Musician with sambuca; wall-painting (detail), Museo Archeologico Nazionale di Napoli, inv. 9023 (AD 30–40); from Pompeii (Third Style), further provenance unknown. © Alamy — 113
2. Lissus and Acrolissus; image (colour) by Shkelzen Rexha; licence https://creativecommons.org/licenses/by-sa/4.0/deed.en; see https://commons.wikimedia.org/wiki/File:Varri_i_Sk%C3%ABnderbeut_%26_Kalaja_-_Lezh%C3%AB.jpg — 149
3. Achaeus, silver tetradrachm, *CH* 2010.277 no. 74; image as in *Coin Hoards* 2010, by kind permission of Professor Andrew Meadows — 159
4. Acropolis, Sardis, south side; ©Archaeological Exploration of Sardis/President and Fellows of Harvard College — 160

# PREFACE

This edition aims to introduce new readers to a major author, and to offer those who know him a fuller insight. Polybius is not only a crucial historical source but an impressive writer; a commentary offers a good way of getting to grips with his words. Book 8 has been chosen, rather than a completely preserved book: the limits of the series would have left inadequate room for comment on a complete book, and for someone new to Polybius a complete book would be a more daunting start. Book 8 graphically displays Polybius' range; its two longest episodes show Polybius at his most tragic (Sardis) and his most entertaining (Tarentum).

In accordance with the aim of the edition, the Introduction is to Polybius in general (Part I) as well as to book 8 in particular (Part II) – with some overlap. The text includes new suggestions on an author who has been read too cursorily; the circumstances of transmission require a larger apparatus than is usual in the series.[1] The commentary seeks to analyse Polybius' words, and to show the historical and archaeological context of the various sections. The scholarly literature referred to is mostly recent; from it, earlier literature can easily be found. The laws of the series have constrained the amount of scholarship referred to, and especially the number of images and maps (I would have liked many more, but I am grateful for a larger than usual allowance). The laws of the series further prescribe the explanation of my own view first, rather than last after exposition of the problem and consideration of other possibilities.

I have long been fond of Polybius; but the impetus to write on him came from a seminar which I suggested to Professor Nino Luraghi that we should run together. The seminar showed hearteningly how literary graduates and scholars could come to appreciate Polybius, and how historians could appreciate wider views of him. Professor Luraghi has read some of the commentary, lent books and given encouragement. Professor Peter Thonemann has kindly read the Introduction. The Greek series editors Professor Richard Hunter and Dr Oliver Thomas have been extremely helpful; I add most grateful thanks to Professor Stephen Oakley, who generously volunteered to read my drafts too. The Craven Committee and Christ Church paid for trips to Sardis and Taranto. My hopes of ascending the acropolis at Sardis were rather dramatically cut short by sunstroke; but Professor Nicholas Cahill, Dr Baha Yıldırım and the whole excavation team made my stay in Türkiye valuable. Images of manuscripts have

---

[1] I should mention that I seem to have embarked on an Oxford Classical Text of Polybius.

been kindly supplied by the Bayerische Staatsbibliothek, Munich, the Biblioteca Nazionale Marciana, Venice (thanks to Dr Alessandro Moro), and the Biblioteca Apostolica Vaticana (special thanks to Dr András Németh). I am grateful to Professor Andrew Meadows for images of a coin. I have other debts to Dr Victoria Fendel, Professor Anna Magnetto, Dr Michael McOsker, Professor Chris Pelling, Professor Michael Reeve, Dr Jonas Schollmeyer, the Art Library and the Old Bodleian Library, Oxford, the libraries of Christ Church, Corpus Christi, Exeter and New College, Oxford. Much help has been given in and before production by Joanna Berry, Dr Jane Burkowski (who has copyedited me sympathetically and astutely), Katie Idle, Bethany Johnson, Joe LeMonnier (who has miraculously transformed my scruffy sketches for maps) and, constantly, Dr Michael Sharp. My wife's kindness and understanding have made all the difference.

The book was practically finished in rough before my retirement at the end of September 2023. My gratitude to colleagues and students at Oxford is immense; to talk about Greek and Latin with them has been such a privilege.

The book is dedicated to the memory of my brother Paul, so brave and so clever.

# ABBREVIATIONS

Abbreviations for ancient authors are roughly as in *LSJ*, *OLD*² and *Thesaurus Linguae Latinae*; for inscriptions they are as at https://aiegl.org/grepi-abbr.html (additions below), for papyri as at https://papyri.info/docs/checklist#Papyri. Journals are roughly as in *L'Année philologique*.

| | |
|---|---|
| *ACT* | *Atti del Convegno Internazionale di Studi sulla Magna Grecia* (Taranto 1961–). |
| Anon. *Obs.* | Anonymus, *De obsidione toleranda* (ed. H. van den Berg, Leiden 1947). |
| *Barrington* | R. J. A. Talbert (ed.), *Barrington atlas of the Greek and Roman world* (Princeton 2000). |
| *BDAG* | F. Montanari, *The Brill dictionary of ancient Greek* (Leiden 2015). |
| *CAG* | *Commentaria in Aristotelem Graeca*, 23 vols (Berlin 1882–1909). |
| *CCL* | *Corpus Christianorum: Series Latina* (Turnhout 1953–). |
| *CGL* | J. Diggle et al., *The Cambridge Greek lexicon*, 2 vols. (Cambridge 2021). |
| *CIL* | *Corpus inscriptionum Latinarum* (Berlin 1863–). |
| *CMG* | *Corpus medicorum Graecorum* (Leipzig and Berlin 1904–). |
| *DNP* | H. Cancik and H. Schneider, eds, *Der neue Pauly: Enzyklopädie der Antike* (Stuttgart 1996–). |
| *Exc. Const.* | (eds) U. Ph. Boissevain, C. de Boor, Th. Büttner-Wobst and A. G. Roos, *Excerpta historica iussu Imp. Constantini Porphyrogeniti confecta*, 4 vols (Berlin 1903–10). |
| *FGrHist* | (eds) F. Jacoby and others, *Fragmente der griechischen Historiker* (Berlin 1923–); new version, ed. I. Worthington, in *Brill's New Jacoby*, https://scholarlyeditions.brill.com/bnjo/. |
| *FHG* | (ed.) C. Müller et al., *Fragmenta historicorum Graecorum* (Paris 1848–70). |
| *FRHist* | (ed.) T. J. Cornell (ed.), *The fragments of the Roman historians*, 3 vols (Oxford 2013). |
| *GGM* | (ed.) C. Müller, *Geographi Graeci minores*, 2 vols (Paris 1855–82). |
| *GLK* | (ed.) H. Keil, *Grammatici Latini*, 8 vols (Leipzig 1857–70). |
| *ILLRP* | (ed.) A. Degrassi, *Inscriptiones Latinae liberae rei publicae*, 2nd edn, 2 vols (Florence 1963–5). |

| | |
|---|---|
| *IMT* | (eds) M. Barth and J. Stauber, *Inschriften Mysia und Troas* (Munich 1993). |
| K–G | R. Kühner and B. Gerth, *Ausführliche Grammatik der griechischen Sprache*. 2. *Teil: Satzlehre*, 3rd edn, 2 vols (Hanover 1898–1904). |
| *LGPN* | P. M. Fraser, E. Matthews et al., *A lexicon of Greek personal names* (Oxford 1987–). |
| LSJ | H. G. Liddell and R. Scott, *A Greek–English lexicon*, 9th edn, rev. H. S. Jones, revised Supplement P. G. W. Glare (Oxford 1996). |
| *MRR* | T. R. S. Broughton and M. L. Patterson, *The magistrates of the Roman Republic*, 3 vols (New York 1951–86). |
| *OLD*² | P. G. W. Glare, *Oxford Latin dictionary*, 2nd edn (Oxford 2012). |
| *PL* | A. Mauersberger, Chr.-Fr. Collatz, H. Helms et al., *Polybios-Lexikon*, 2nd edn, 3 vols in 8 (Berlin 1998–2006). |
| *PP* | W. Peremans et al., *Prosopographia Ptolemaica*, 10 vols (Leuven 1950–2002); and see now https://www.trismegistos.org. |
| *RE* | A. Pauly, G. Wissowa and W. Kroll, eds, *Real-Enzyklopädie der classischen Altertumswissenschaft* (Stuttgart 1893–1980). |
| *SC* | A. Houghton and C. Lorber, *Seleucid coins. Part I*, 2 vols (New York 2002). |
| *SH* | (eds) H. Lloyd-Jones and P. J. Parsons, *Supplementum Hellenisticum* (Berlin 1983). |
| *SVF* | (eds) H. von Arnim and M. Adler, *Stoicorum veterum fragmenta*, 4 vols (Leipzig 1905–24). |
| *TIR* | *Tabula imperii Romani* (Rome etc. 1931–). |

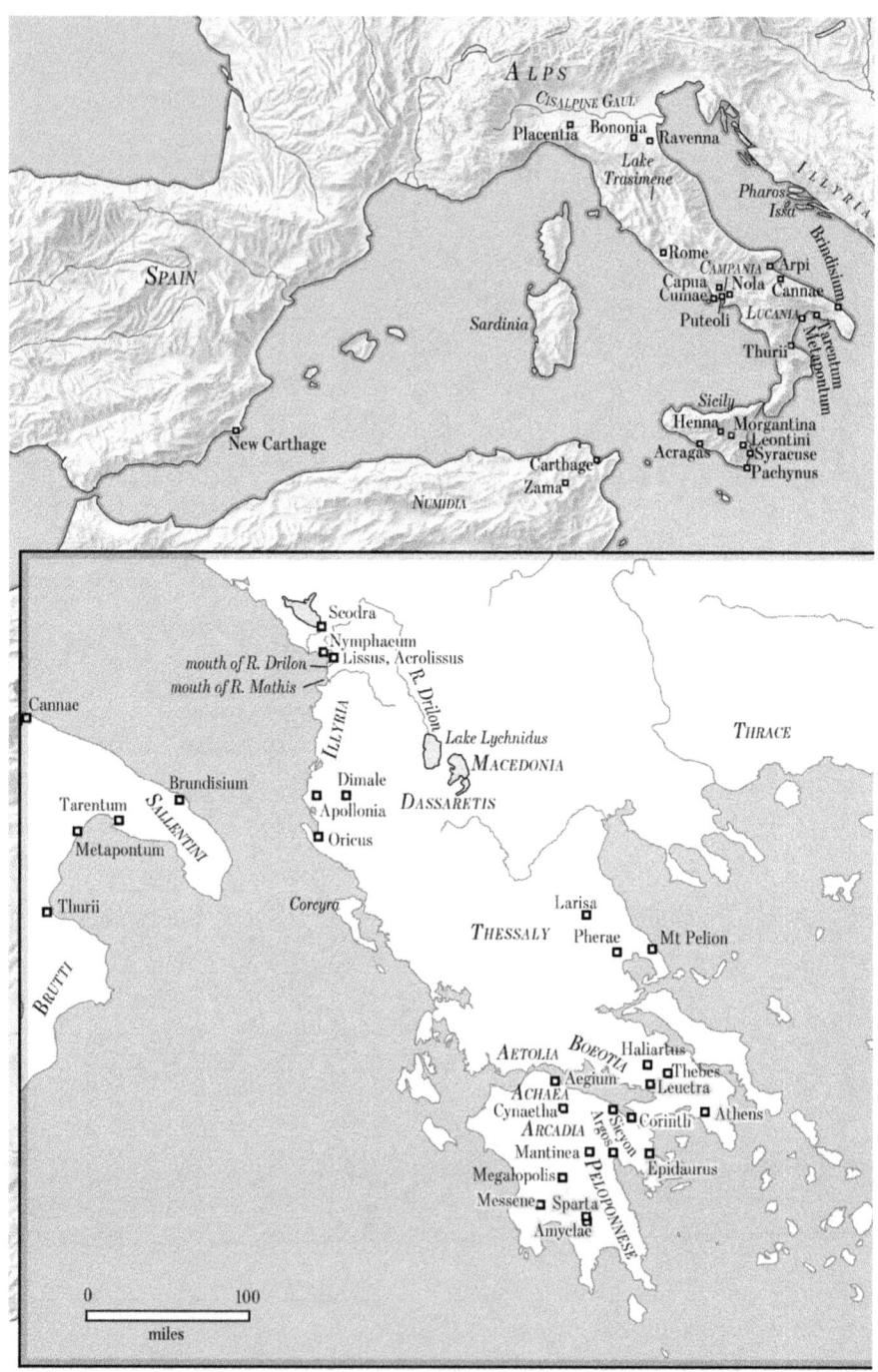

Map 1  Mediterranean  (Joe LeMonnier, https://mapartist.com/)

MAP 1

# INTRODUCTION

## Part I: Polybius
### 1 TASTERS AND TEXTURE

*(a) Medley*

To start, six passages which give a flavour of Polybius (P.). Moeragenes, a courtier at Alexandria, has been stripped naked, and is about to be whipped; but, extraordinarily, after whisperings and glances, all present steal away. Agathocles' coup is going wrong (15.27.7–28.4). – Though some say that people's true natures are brought out by circumstances, I think (P. says) that friends and tricky situations usually force people to go against their chosen approach to life, their προαίρεσις (9.22.9–10). – Two grown sons of Queen Apollonis visit her; all three holding hands, they walk round the sights of Cyzicus, admired by onlookers for their affection (22.20.4–7). – Gauls' swords bend after the first downward blow; the Romans, fighting the Insubres, prevented them from straightening their swords, and so inflicted blow upon blow (2.33.2–6). – If you only do history from books, like Timaeus, you just need a neighbouring library and you can lie at your ease comparing earlier sources (12.27.3–6). – The scene was strange and spectacular (τραγική): together with those desperately swimming in the river were borne along horses, beasts of burden, weapons, dead bodies, baggage of all kinds (5.48.7–9).[1]

*(b) Readers*

That assortment gives a taste of P., the graphic, contentious, discursive, practical, intelligent writer. One can see how he both resembles and differs from other extant historiography. His intensely involving and picturable scenes and sequences make him more like other ancient historiographers than is often realized. But he is unlike them in the abundance of his movement beyond the story in hand and the narrative mode. Readers, usually a plural entity rather than our more intimate 'the reader', have much more of an explicit presence in P.'s text than in other historians' (typical terms: 1.3.10 τοῖς ἐντυγχάνουσιν, 1.5.5 τοῖς ἀκούουσιν, 3.9.5 τοὺς ἀναγινώσκοντας). They are not merely 'narratees', the recipients

---

[1] No knowledge of the characters or events is required here or in most of Part I. Book 8 is summarized in Part II, Section 9.

of narrative in classic narratology; they have much thinking to be doing beyond immersion in the story.[2]

Indeed, P. plays down emotional reactions in his readers, save for wonder (so 8.1.4) and the emotion implied by approval or disapproval. Of course, actual readers will feel much engaged in P.'s account of Achaeus' fate (8.15.1–21.11), especially the later parts of it. But only through the pity and hatred aroused in people at the time does P. even hint at readers' related reactions – and he does so outside the narrative itself (8.36.9). Strabo describes P. as telling ἐν οἴκτου μέρει 'in piteous, lamenting vein' what happened at the sack of Corinth (Strabo 8.6.23 (II 520.7–8 Radt); P. 39.2.1). But P. says that overwhelming impact is rather for tragedy or historians misguidedly emulating it (2.56.10–12).[3]

We can see three connected worlds in which readers should have at any rate a keen interest: that of the historical events, that of their own lives and that of the historian judging events, guiding readers and doing battle with his competitors. Thus at 2.55.1–63.6, while reproaching the historian Phylarchus for arousing pity (2.56.7, etc.), P. inculcates strong responses to events, suggests inspiration for readers' own conduct (2.61.11) and captivates them, as an orator would, by his eloquent combat with his adversary. All these reactions of feeling are connected to thinking and argument. Reading P. is a challenging and complicated matter, in his presentation of it, and still more in actuality.

*(c) Plot and Digression*

P.'s work has a firm and imposing plot. His work was originally planned to cover events all over the known world from 220/19 to 168/7 BC; in these years that world is rapidly mastered by Rome. In its final form, with books 30–40, the work examines Rome in charge, and extends to the Roman destruction of Carthage and Corinth in 146 BC. (P. himself seems to have lived until 118 or later, and may have been born around 200.) The implications of the plot will be discussed later; the immediate point is that

---

[2] P.'s readers as narratees: Miltsios (2013) 140–6.

[3] ἐκπλήττειν is to be avoided by the historian at 2.56.10, but seems quite close to P.'s aim of making the narrative καταπληκτική at 4.28.6; there, however, προσέχουσιν ('giving their attention') emphasizes the intellectual effort involved. As to the phrase ἐν οἴκτου μέρει, cf. Arist. *EN* 4.1128a19–20, Liban. *Or.* 56.6. For suggestions of readers' emotions, especially pity, in P., see Loehr (2017) 226–36. See also Rutherford (2007); Marincola (2003 and 2013); Eckstein (2013). The new fragment (Németh (2022 and 2023)) offers a forcefully emotional scene on the suicide of Hasdrubal's wife; but it is also part of an ethical argument, and Fortune, not P., is made the dramatist (ὡς ἐν δράματι ... ἐπεισαγαγούσης).

the execution of the plot is complicated by very numerous digressions. Excursions from the main story are both narrative and non-narrative; but non-narrative elements are basic to the work and its whole texture.[4]

Our grasp of that texture is impeded by the state of the text's preservation. After book 5, we have only copious extracts (3½ of the Loeb's six volumes); for books 6–40 we can merely say there were a great many excursive passages, and a few books which were all excursion (6 on the Roman πολιτεία, 12 on faults of P.'s predecessor Timaeus, 34 on geography). The books that we have entire set out the plan with much emphasis; explaining and fulfilling authorial plans is important to much Hellenistic prose, and fulfilling plans is central to the values of P.'s work on every level. But by the end of book 6 the promised integration of events in Italy, Asia etc. has still not reached its full form.[5]

This delay is planned: books 1–2 have been announced as a prelude covering the years from 264. But those books treat in detail not only the First Punic War (264–241) but wars of which detailed knowledge might not seem essential for what follows. So P. tells of the Romans' war with the Celts in 225–222, and maintains it is 'absolutely necessary' to go back to 387/6 (2.14.2), with first some quick geography (2.14.4–17.2). Now this geography is actually important for the work as a whole. The digressions from the plot, though salient interruptions of the story, all contribute to the total vision which the work presents.[6]

After books 1 and 2, P. further defers the planned structure, that is parallel sections on events in different regions over the same year (cf. 4.28.1–6; 5.31.4–5). In the meantime, there is much divagation. Book 4 includes digressions on music in Arcadia (20.1–21.12) and a long one (38.11–45.8) on the site of Byzantium (and Chalcedon). That digression is interrupted by another on silting, and itself forms part of recounting a war between Byzantium and Rhodes; that war, together with an account of Cretan affairs, interrupts the narrative of the Social War. The account of the Fourth Syrian War in book 5, before the structure by sections from book 7 onwards, both treats a main topic (1.3.1) and produces a digression from the Social War (5.91.1 ἐκτροπή). The moment of return to the Social War is blurred by a digression on gifts to Rhodes, which extends to present morality (5.88–90); the narrative of the Syrian War includes

---

[4] Digressions in P.: Khellaf (2018). On the dates of P.'s life see Walbank (1957–79) I 1, 373.
[5] Plans in Hellenistic prose: Hutchinson (2008) 229–32.
[6] The preliminary section books 1–2 has its own forerunner to continue from, Timaeus (1.5.1, 39.8.4); the continuity is slightly vague. The main account more closely runs on from the end of Aratus' Ὑπομνήματα (1.3.2).

long analepses (flashbacks) on the two kings in conflict, Ptolemy IV and Antiochus III (31.8–57.8), with an inset digression on Media (43.8–44.11). Book 6 was entirely an excursion on the Roman state, including much excursion within excursion on other constitutions.[7]

The essentially non-narrative book 6 had been carefully prepared for readers: P. says he will 'stop the narrative' for book 6 (3.2.6). Other excursions in books 4–6 (see above) are more surprising. The books illustrate how P. unites a strong plan, known from the beginning, with unexpected movements of apparent spontaneity. But these movements too show careful design – P.'s mind is always organizing – and link with his large themes and concerns. An expressive sentence is 10.47.12, after a digression on fire-signals: ταῦτα μὲν οὖν κατὰ τὴν ἐξ ἀρχῆς ἐπαγγελίαν προήχθημεν εἰπεῖν, 'I have been drawn on to say all this [so unplanned spontaneity] in accordance with my original promise [so part of a plan].'[8]

Such frequent divergence from the straight path of story clearly continued throughout the work. This makes the work quite unlike that of, say, Thucydides. It was probably a feature of other Hellenistic historians, such as P.'s official predecessor Timaeus. Historiography was breaking away from straight narrative; this Hellenistic experimentalism is curtailed in the Imperial period (save for Lucan's historical epic, and to some extent Plutarch's historical biography).[9]

## 2 GENERAL AND PARTICULAR

### (a) Argument

P.'s work cannot even be neatly separated into passages which tell a story and passages which reflect. A narrative impulse and an argumentative impulse run through the work; the general and the particular are much entangled, and P. likes to argue about specific events and people as well as general ideas. The argument on character at 9.22.9–10, paraphrased in the first paragraph of this Introduction, comes from a consideration of Hannibal's failings. The generalizing thought on character and other factors is variously illustrated by examples, and leads off into ideas about cities and leaders, also exemplified. Some of the examples sketch a narrative; there is then an extended anecdote on advice to Hannibal (9.24.3–7).

---

[7] For analepsis in historiography see Grethlein and Krebs (2012).
[8] Cf. 9.2.3–7 for the 'promise'.
[9] Explicit digression naturally precedes the Hellenistic period; cf. e.g. Hdt. 7.137.1, Xen. *Hell.* 6.5.1, Ephor. *FGrHist* 70 F191.37 (randomly preserved) παρεξ[έβ]ημεν.

At 18.13–15 P. wants to talk generally about the folly of being a traitor; but he starts with the point that not everyone thought to be a traitor is so, which leads him on to specific people: Demosthenes and the individuals Demosthenes wrongly called traitors (notably Peloponnesians). P. finally returns to his main point, which is enlarged into thoughts on mistakes in animals and humans. This is not mere purposeless prolixity. The time of Philip II, and the Peloponnese within it, are important to P., in themselves and for comparison with the time of Philip V. P. further wants to show himself making subtle distinctions, and being reasonable on the particulars, by contrast with Demosthenes and his 'most bitter' (πικρότατον) abuse. In introducing Demosthenes himself, P. is balanced: 'one would praise him for many things but blame him for this' (18.14.1).

### (b) Narrative

As P.'s arguments lead to specifics, so P.'s ordinary narrative is run through with argument. Thus at 30.20 P. contends that the Athenians' embassy to Rome behaved badly by seeking to acquire the territory of Haliartus in Boeotia. P. again marks his reasonableness by allowing that the Athenians' other claims, though they did not work out well (8–9), did not deserve criticism (3). His grounds for criticizing and not criticizing rest on consistency, with Athens' past policy and known character. The description of Flaminius' emotions, behaviour and speech on approaching Lake Trasimene (3.82) follows through the universal argument (3.81) that a general must know his opposite number's failings, as Hannibal knew Flaminius'.[10]

## 3 LITERARY CONTEXT

### (a) Historiography

Important to P.'s presentation of his work is an idea that mingles general and particular. The work offers universal history: it deals, in its chosen period, with all events everywhere, not merely with one city, region or individual, or one set of events. But this unlimited sort of history makes special sense for precisely this period, where for the first time events everywhere are connected and 'woven together'. (On this συμπλοκή see Section 6 below.)

---

[10] For P. and Athens, cf. Perrin-Saminadayar (1999).

P. enhances the drama and the plot of his own activity by setting himself in a context of literary history. The context created has little to do with Herodotus or Thucydides, though Herodotus in particular might seem to write about every region, τὰ ὅλα. Rather, P. gives himself a model in Ephorus (5.33.2), who died *c*.330; he classes him among 'ancient writers', οἱ ἀρχαῖοι συγγραφεῖς (6.45.1). Ephorus first and alone sought to write about every place, τὰ καθόλου (5.33.2). Since him, there have just been writers like Timaeus, who confined himself to Italy and to Sicily, that little saucer (ὀξύβαφον, 12.23.7). Timaeus vainly hoped to match those who wrote about the whole world and deeds everywhere (i.e. Ephorus and perhaps Callisthenes). Admittedly, some of P.'s contemporaries, whom he scorns to name, have claimed to encompass all deeds in Greece and barbarian lands (5.33.5). But their small scale makes their claim absurd, three or four papyrus columns – he colourfully alleges – for the Second Punic War (5.33.3). The massive size of P.'s universal history is part of the point. Since Ephorus, he stands alone.[11]

The student of historiography will regard P.'s picture of others with scepticism; but to give his writing a fuller context, and to seize its character, we need to look more widely in Hellenistic culture.

*(b) Rhetoric*

Rhetoric and oratory play a critical part in P.'s work, even if he is relatively sparing in his use of speeches, and accepts that historiography is distant from epideictic, i.e. oratory of praise and blame with no practical purpose (12.28a.6). But rhetoric played a primary role in education, as he himself attests (e.g. 12.25k.8–11, 26.9, 26b.5) and as rhetorical exercises on papyri confirm (e.g. P. Berol. 9781 (iii BC), PSI Laur. inv. 22013 (ii–i BC)). P. himself made public speeches (cf. e.g. 29.24.6–9), and offered himself to the Younger Africanus as a top-quality coach in speaking (31.23.11, 24.5–8). The oratorical frame of mind and form of expression is seen everywhere in his own discourse. He wishes to persuade and to seem a persuasive figure; he deploys all the orator's arts. We have already seen him subtly refining his argument so as to seem reasonable – for him an essential stance. At 28.9.5–6 he explicitly says 'I think no one with sense

---

[11] The converse of writing universal history is writing κατὰ μέρος, e.g. 1.4.6. The limitation implied in the phrase is primarily geographical: Weaire (2021) answers effectively the claim of Tully (2014) that it refers to limited interpretation; Tully's thoughts on Ephorus remain of interest. On Ephorus books 4 and 5, see Luraghi (2014) 137; Parmeggiani (2024) 191–204, and more widely 332–61 and Marincola (2007*b*). On P.'s relation to local history, cf. Thomas (2019), esp. 43–5.

3 LITERARY CONTEXT 7

would disagree with me on these things' (δοκῶ μηδένα τῶν νοῦν ἐχόντων πρός με διαμφισβητῆσαι περὶ τούτων). He has just engaged in the orator's complicated layers of thought: if Perseus had given kings and others money, 'I do not say (οὐ λέγω) lavishly, as he could have done, but just moderately', then 'all Greeks and all Greek kings, or if not all, then most' would have been shown up.[12]

The rhetorical character of P.'s exposition is well seen in the abundance of his rhetorical questions – a device also deployed in his speeches. Sometimes such questions are piled up, as at 29.9.2–13: who would not observe the stupidity of both kings, Eumenes and Perseus (τίς γὰρ οὐκ ἂν ἐπισημήναιτο; Cf. e.g. Dem. *Cor.* 204 τίς γὰρ οὐκ ἂν ἀγάσαιτο ...;)? How did Eumenes think the Romans would not notice? Whatever would he have suffered if he had succeeded? Who would not be amazed at how Perseus failed to trick Eumenes? What was the cause (τίς οὖν αἰτία τῆς ...; Cf. e.g. Dem. *Phil.* 3.36 τί οὖν αἴτιον τουτωνί;)? The love of money. What else could one say? (τί γὰρ ἂν ἄλλο τις εἴπειεν; Cf. e.g. Dem. 23.63 τί ἂν ἄλλο τις εἴποι;). The combination of intensity and discernment makes P. a formidable persuasive force.[13]

*(c) Technical Writing*

Technical elements in P. are part of a mindset as well as a way of writing; they display the importance of expertise, of knowing how things work. The Hellenistic period had seen a great growth in works on technical subjects, military, mathematical, geographical and so forth. This embodied a growth in knowledge and know-how which P. saw as a primary reason for writing the history of real and recent πράξεις, rather than mythology or genealogy. Sciences and skills had made such progress that most of them had become μεθοδικαί, i.e. organized into a satisfactory system; hence studious readers of history could handle the upshot of events μεθοδικῶς

---

[12] I.e. would have accepted the money; the contrast with 8 ἠλογήθησαν (ἠλέγχθησαν Reiske) suggests this understanding rather than 'have been under pressure' for ἐξελεγχθῆναι (cf. *PL* II). In δοκῶ κτλ. one should perhaps read μηδέν' ἂν (cf. 14.10.2) and πρὸς ἐμὲ (cf. 11.28.6). Epideictic: Pernot (2015). Just as P. implicitly contemns the fictional aspects of oratory in education (12.25i.5), so he spurns unreality and paradox in philosophy, with which he is well acquainted (12.26c). For a valuable list of rhetorical papyri and themes see Stramaglia (2015) 167–71. For the fragments of Hellenistic oratory, see Berardi (2020). Thornton (2013a) 33–8 touches on rhetorical elements in P.; cf. also Farrington (2015). Scholars could go further on rhetorical style and argument in P.
[13] τίς οὖν αἰτία is not what we would call a rhetorical question. For questions in oratory cf. Quint. *Inst.* 9.2.6–16, with Cavarzere and Cristante's notes.

(9.2.4–6, 10.47.12–13). P. is intently concerned with practicality, a matter of knowing relevant areas of study as well as of hands-on experience. This includes a willingness to use the language of technical writing, to pursue technical questions, to sound, fleetingly or at length, something like a technical writer.[14]

The long excursus on fire-signals (10.43–7) begins with significant emphasis (43.1–2): fire-signals have the greatest (πλείστην) power in contributing to acting at the right moment, which is of particular (μεγίστην) importance in warfare. P. shows the problem of imprecision in this art, and how the earlier writer Aeneas Tacticus met it slightly (βραχύ τι 44.1, 45.1), and then how finally, thanks to others and himself, the system became definite and accurate. He sets it out in detail. When Philip V arrives to take a city with ladders that are much too short for the walls, P. explodes with rhetorical questions on the failure to consider, measure and construct (5.98.1–3). He explains that the method of making suitable ladders is infallible, if approached μεθοδικῶς. But he saves the detailed exposition for later (9.19.5–9). There it is wrapped up in a lengthy disquisition on the indispensability to the general of knowing at least some astronomy, geometry and so forth (9.12–20).[15]

P. had himself written a technical work on tactics (9.20.4); he alludes to it, but indicates that in that technical treatise the matter had been handled ἀκριβέστερον, with more precision on spatial proportion. The idea and the practice of technical writing are vital to P.'s historiography; but as with oratorical elements, the nature of the work determines how they are employed.

*(d) Use of Other Texts*

A broad feature can be discerned in various areas of Hellenistic prose: close and explicit engagement with other texts and authors. This period sees the evolution of detailed commentaries, particularly on poets; of special interest is Hipparchus' negative astronomical commentary on the poet Aratus. From the first century BC we have Apollonius of Citium's medical commentary on Hippocrates, *On Limbs* (*CMG* xi.1.1). The works of the philosopher Philodemus contain much detailed paraphrase and quotation of writings which he proceeds to attack (so *Sign.* col. vii.5–xix.11,

---

[14] For technical writing see e.g. Fögen (2005); Asper (2007); Formisano and Van der Eijk (2017). An important passage is Philo, *Bel.* 50.14–51.7 (107–8 Marsden): restless experiment has led to accuracy in both artillery and architecture; later people (οἱ ὕστεροι) have improved decisively on those of old (οἱ ἀρχαῖοι).

[15] For P. on fire-signalling see D. Moore (2017).

## 3 LITERARY CONTEXT

where both exposition and refutation are based on Zeno of Sidon, ii–i BC). Aristotle had disagreed with Plato and others; but there is not nearly such close textual engagement. In historiography, Herodotus and Thucydides had made the odd disagreeable remark on Hecataeus and Hellanicus (Hdt. 2.143.1–4, *al.*, Thuc. 1.97.2); but their polemic, keen as we are to see it, for the most part lies beneath the surface. P. often assails other historians in the plural without naming them, both for their general approach and for their handling of specific moments (e.g. 3.47.6–48.12, 'some', ἔνιοι, on Hannibal crossing the Alps). But his work also abounds in direct encounters with other texts, their mistaken remarks and stances and the larger implications.[16]

The whole twelfth book is devoted to the author whom he continues, Timaeus. So Timaeus' own specific criticisms of specific passages in Theopompus and Ephorus are themselves criticized (12.4a.1–6). Timaeus' sentence abusing Demochares is abused as beyond the utterances even of the brothel (12.13.1–2). P. attacks a specific passage of the prologue to Timaeus' sixth book (so identified), a passage attacking Ephorus; in doing so, he takes on general questions of how a historian should gather his material (12.28–28a).[17]

P. points out various particular errors by Zeno and Antisthenes, both of Rhodes. On the one hand, P. shows readers he cared so much about some of these errors that he wrote to Zeno (16.20.5–7; Zeno politely replied with professed gratitude). On the other hand, P. connects this excursus with wider points, how far historians should favour their own cities (16.14.5–10), how important style is in the writing of history (16.17.9–11). On both topics, P. aims to strike a position of reasonable balance. A chief purpose of this overt interaction with other texts is for P. to display and define his own approach, and through attacking others to defend and (obliquely) praise himself.

---

[16] For polemic in P. cf. Marincola (1997) 217–36; Prandi (2005); Eckstein (2013); Burton (2022); Stropp (2023) 159–62. On Herodotus and Hecataeus, cf. Dillery (2018). Hdt. 2.5.1 may point at a phrase of Hecataeus (*FGrHist* 1 F301), but even so the passage does not name him (and does not ποιήματα mean 'verses'?); the writer Hecataeus appears explicitly in Herodotus' work as a character, not a text.

[17] For attacks on Timaeus by other authors, some in separate works, see *FGrHist* 566 T11, 16, 17, 25–7; Polemon's had more than one book.

## 4 HISTORIOGRAPHICAL ART

*(a) Narrative and Detail*

P., as has now been illustrated, draws on many areas of contemporary culture to produce his sort of writing; there is much more to his work than the creation of an absorbing narrative. Not that P.'s narrative should be underrated either. Some of the features that have been discussed can also be regarded from a narratological perspective. So digressions can be seen as promoting the slow and ample pace with which the total plot is unfolded, and as producing, in particular contexts, an effective retardation. But such abstraction will only take us so far. Within particular pieces of narrative, the fullness of detail affects the narrative pace or 'narrative rhythm'; but the actual pointed details contribute much more to the narration. Detail can intensify the moment, suggest multiple perspectives, and help the structuring and significance of a whole sequence.[18]

In the passage from which we started, Moeragenes has been humiliatingly stripped; the men with whips are taking off their cloaks to undertake their task (15.27.9). The differentiated removal of clothing contrasts the would-be agents and their victim. When Moeragenes flees to a tent of Macedonian soldiers, he is naked (15.28.4): a proof of his tale (6), but also a startling visual scene. The scene is made the more arresting because the men are having their breakfast, 'by chance'. This is a reason for lots of men to be in the tent; but the breakfast is also an ordinary and harmless happening for Moeragenes' surprising entrance to interrupt. If readers had just been told there were many soldiers in the tent, they would not have wondered why. Earlier, immediately Moeragenes is stripped, P. puts into effect the combination of unpredictable (for Moeragenes) and comprehensible (for readers): readers have more idea of the way the coup is going. A slave arrives and whispers ἄττα δήποτ' οὖν 'something or other' to Nicostratus, who is in charge of the torture; Nicostratus leaves 'saying nothing but constantly beating his thigh' (15.27.10–11). Both are seen through readers' eyes, through Moeragenes', and through those of Nicostratus' subordinates. Puzzles and surprise for the characters mix with surprise and intelligibility for readers.[19]

Agathocles, who had instigated the coup, hides behind three doors; the number and the scene are made more striking when it is said, with unexpected fullness, that the doors are made of lattice and can be seen

---

[18] For narrative rhythm see De Jong (2014) 92–8. On description and specific detail cf. Wanlin (2007).

[19] For focalization and its complications, see De Jong (2004); Fowler (2000) 40–63.

through (15.30.8). The mention prepares humiliating nakedness for the conspirators: Agathocles' sister, the late king's mistress, bizarrely puts her breasts through the lattice-work of the third door, pleading that she had nursed the new king (the infant Ptolemy V, 15.31.13). She and others are stripped naked before the mob kills them (15.33.7–8, 12). The details, then, form part of the practicality, but also of the pragmatic, ethical and purposeful shaping of events. P. actually claims to have made his account less shocking and less laboriously didactic than other writers' (15.34–5); he is deliberately eschewing grandeur. This eschewal further marks out the impact of the narrative: shaped, but expressive of P.'s scorn.[20]

*(b) Aesthetics and History*

Is the artistry which is here being attributed to P. at odds with his own remarks about his work, and with his reputation for stylelessness? As to the first, there is not necessarily a clash; but ancient authors' statements about their works need to be treated as rhetoric and skilled self-presentation rather than as straightforward truth. Tacitus writes of the conspicuous and wearisome sameness of events in his *Annals* (*obuia rerum similitudine et satietate*, 4.32.3, with 'I am not unaware' at 4.32.1); modern readers take this self-deprecation with a pinch of salt. P. writes 'I am not unaware (οὐκ ἀγνοῶ) that my history has something austere about it ... the unvarying uniformity of the work' (τὸ μονοειδὲς τῆς συντάξεως, 9.1.2); we should take the negative side of this no less gingerly. P. claims to write only for serious students of history: his work is ἀψυχαγώγητος, 'unattractive', for most readers (9.1.5). There is some pride at this professed exclusiveness of audience, as there is in the actually very popular Callimachus; but even from P.'s own remarks elsewhere the pleasure of history emerges, and the importance of expression. To be sure, these things are made subordinate to utility; but that is very common when ancient authors present their work. P. says that his universal type of history is the only one that enables readers to get 'both the useful and the delightful' (τὸ τερπνόν) from history (1.4.11). One might suppose that the partial sort of history, of single wars, cities, individuals, at least had τὸ τερπνόν; yet partial history is like dissecting a beautiful animal's body, and losing its beauty (1.4.7; cf. 8). Universal history alone presents to readers 'the most beautiful and at the same time most useful work of Fortune' (τῆς τύχης, 1.4.4). The author does not boast of the beauty of his work; the creation of beauty is shifted

---

[20] Agathocleia's gesture in P. presents a distorted version of the μαστῶν ἐκβολαί which Phylarchus is said to resort to for pathos (2.56.7).

to the unconscious craftswoman Fortune. But the aesthetic dimension of the work is made clear.[21]

P. writes of Ephorus, his ostensible model for universal history, as wonderful in style (φράσις, 12.28.10). Certainly he classes Ephorus among 'the writers of old' (6.45.1), including Callisthenes (d. 327 BC); but it is improbable that, like Dionysius, he thinks of old writers as devoted to beauty of language and of himself and his period as completely indifferent to it (cf. DH *Comp.* 4.14–15). In his own time, Zeno of Rhodes, he says, gives too primary a place to 'crafting his style' (ἡ τῆς λέξεως κατασκευή), and prides himself on doing so, like other famous writers (16.17.9). P. himself regards fitting expression as clearly contributing much to history (16.17.10).

## 5 STYLE

### (a) Hiatus

The care P. himself gives to his writing can be seen in his scrupulous approach to hiatus – where final vowel meets initial vowel without punctuation. In P.'s first three books, quoted treaties etc. apart, there are no instances not involving ὁ, μή, ὅσος, καί, περί, πρό, ὦ or numerals. By way of comparison, the quoted treaties and oath in 3.22 and 24–5 show 12 examples. Diodorus seeks to avoid hiatus, but instances are easily found in his first three books, including instances where the first element is a long vowel or a diphthong, so 1.2.1 αἰτίαι ἱστορίαι, 16.1 ἱερογραμματέα ἅπαντας. In Dionysius' history instances abound, so *AR* 1.46.1 δουρείου ἵππου, ἐπιστῆναι ἔοικεν, 46.2 ἤδη ἐκρατεῖτο, 47.2 συνεσκευασμένοι ἔτυχον. Apart from Theopompus and possibly Timaeus, fragmentary historians readily provide examples, such as Ephor. *FGrHist* 70 F96 θεοῦ ἐξεκόμισαν, σκυθρωπὴ οὖσα, Phylarch. *FGrHist* 81 F24 πιστευομένη ὑπ'.[22]

---

[21] See Thomas (2019) 43–5 on P.'s 'mock apology' in book 9. Lucr. 1.935–50 is a familiar instance of subordinating aesthetic to pragmatic considerations; the passage is usually taken entirely at face value, and the aesthetic element underrated. The two passages belong in the same sphere of discussion. In Lucretius too austerity in the thought puts common readers off (but he is dealing with that); beauty, though present in the work, is finally assigned to nature (950 *qua constet compta figura*). On τὸ τερπνόν cf. Avenarius (1956) 26–9.

[22] For hiatus in P. see Hultsch (1859); Brief (1907); Foucault (1972) 277–87. P. generally avoids elision too, except where very common words are involved and with certain other categories. In general see Reeve (1971); Dr J. Schollmeyer is working on the subject. It is hard to be sure how far particular choices of P. are motivated by the wish to avoid hiatus. In effective prose other factors are usually involved too; so they are in rhythmic prose when words are arranged partly to

5 STYLE    13

*(b) Repetition*

At 36.12.2 P. explains that he sometimes speaks of himself as historical agent in the first person, to avoid annoying repetition of the name: ταυτολογοῦντες shows that the annoyance is in the repetition not the particular name. The principle indicated here is seen in practice throughout P., where he takes constant pains to vary a word previously used, as will be seen in the commentary. The means of variation include ὁ προειρημένος ἀνήρ, 'the man mentioned above'; this, with other cases and numbers, comes 33 times in P., and not in Diodorus or Dionysius. (The larger-scale repetition it involves matters less to P.)[23]

*(c) Word Order*

A more expressive aspect of style is P.'s exploitation of word order. Thus he very frequently separates adjectives etc. from the nouns they belong with, so as to throw them into relief. Sometimes he does this twice in the same sentence. At 11.19.3 he says that Hannibal, 'though fighting' the Romans 'for 16 years', kept his army together without discord, 'although using units that not only were not from the same people, but were not even from the same group of peoples'. ἑκκαίδεκα πολεμήσας ἔτη underlines the remarkable number. At the end of the sentence the diversity is highlighted with καίπερ οὐχ οἷον ὁμοεθνέσιν, ἀλλ' οὐδ' ὁμοφύλοις χρησάμενος στρατοπέδοις. The highlighting is confirmed by what immediately follows: a string of seven ethnic groups in asyndeton; then a series of four words or phrases in asyndeton for what they did not share, οὐ νόμος, οὐκ ἔθος, κτλ. 'not law, not custom', etc.

At 12.25b.4 P. is criticizing the inauthenticity of Timaeus' speeches, the wordiness of his speeches and narrative, his failure to address causation.

---

secure rhythmic closes (P. himself is not clearly rhythmic). At DS 1.36.1 and 56.1, it should be noted, there are MSS variants. DS 1.27.3–5 shows, like the treaties in P., numerous examples in inscriptions quoted verbatim (at second hand), cf. *I.Kyme* 41 (i BC), *IG* XII.5.1.14 (Ios, ii–iii AD). At Theop. *FGrHist* 115 F171 πολέμωι οἱ, punctuation would be possible; F248 is from a different work, and the quotation may be abbreviated. Verbatim quotations from Timaeus are limited; Tim. *FGrHist* 566 F158 πρώτωι ἐκπιόντι, χοᾶ ἆθλον may not be verbatim. P. seems to allow hiatus after καί more rarely than Theopompus. Theopompus', and Ephorus', supposed teacher Isocrates was the most important antecedent for eschewing hiatus (so Demetr. *Eloc.* 68, 299), though the reality is more complicated (Whitehead (2022) I 16–18). See also McOsker (forthcoming).

[23] With other nouns cf. e.g. DS 1.37.5 τοῦ δὲ προειρημένου βασιλέως, *I.Olympia* 52 (*c.*138 BC) col. ii.50 τοῦ προειρημένο[υ] στρατηγοῦ. For instances of variation see 35.6, 7.3, 7.4, 8.9, 9.1, 9.5, 13.4, 21.8, 25.11, 28.7–8, 29.7, 31.3nn.

P. talks of things 'transferred' by readers of history 'to their own circumstances from similar ones', ἐκ τῶν ὁμοίων ἐπὶ τοὺς οἰκείους μεταφερομένων καιρούς: οἰκείους, vital to the argument, is dwelt on and joined with ὁμοίων. Shortly afterwards he says that Timaeus keeps quiet on causation and speeches actually delivered; instead he delivers untrue efforts, pointlessly elaborate speeches, and he thereby destroys what is special about history, ψευδῆ δ' ἀντὶ τούτων ἐπιχειρήματα καὶ διεξοδικοὺς λέγων λόγους ἀναιρεῖ τὸ τῆς ἱστορίας ἴδιον. The separated adjectives in the participial clause drive home the charges, before, at the end, the pithy and devastating result. ψευδ- runs through book 12 like a refrain; the choicer διεξοδικός is deployed again at 12.26d.6. The emphasis in the second separation is confirmed at 36.1.6: politicians do not need 'to show rhetorical inventiveness and deliver elaborate speeches' on every subject, εὑρησιλογεῖν καὶ διεξοδικοῖς χρῆσθαι λόγοις; rather they should use λόγοι that fit the particular moment. P.'s word order is highly expressive, then, and strongly related to his line of thought. The present device (hyperbaton) clusters in some passages more than others: it is not a casual mannerism. Overall, investigation suggests that P. uses it more often than Demosthenes.[24]

*(d) Shaping of Sentences*

Basic to the work is the shaping and vitality of P.'s sentences. Each sentence is worked into a context; but even if one takes sentences from P. at random, one always alights on a carefully organized structure, and most times on utterance full of Polybian energy and thought. So at 38.1.6 P. is arguing that in 146 BC the Greeks were more unfortunate than the Carthaginians:

καὶ Καρχηδόνιοι μὲν ἅμα ταῖς περιπετείαις ἄρδην ἀφανισθέντες ἀνεπαίσθητοι τῶν σφετέρων εἰς τὸ μέλλον ἐγένοντο συμπτωμάτων, οἱ δ' Ἕλληνες ἐφορῶντες τὰς αὐτῶν ἀτυχίας παισὶ παίδων παραδόσιμον ἐποίησαν τὴν ἀκληρίαν.

The Carthaginians were utterly destroyed at the moment of their disasters, and so were unable to perceive their own catastrophes coming in the future; the Greeks looked upon their own calamities and bequeathed their misfortune to their children's children.

[24] Foucault (1972) 257, cf. 255–60, thinks that the device is used too often to have meaning in P.: it is just a 'tic'. He suggests that P. has drawn it from Isocrates, but it is used elsewhere in the period, cf. e.g. Philo, *Bel.* 50.25–6 (108 Marsden) μεγάλην ἐσχηκότας χορηγίαν διὰ τὸ φιλοδόξων καὶ φιλοτέχνων ἐπειλῆφθαι βασιλέων. For examples in book 8 see 36.5, 1.4, 2.1, 7.10, 13.9, 18.6, 24.7, 27.1, 29.7, 31.3, 33.3, 22.2nn.

The sentence balances many elements in its two halves: Carthaginians and Greeks, not perceiving and perceiving, their own misfortunes (twice), time present and future (twice). The wish to vary is apparent in τῶν σφετέρων ... συμπτωμάτων and τὰς αὐτῶν ἀτυχίας, and in the other words for 'misfortune'. But the two halves are cunningly related: ἀνεπαίσθητοι applies to the future, ἐφορῶντες to the time of the disaster (presumably the Carthaginians, like the Greeks, perceived their present misfortune, but the structure hides this). Each half is itself forcefully organized: the first turns total destruction into a good thing, through the oblivion it brought; the second creates a long line from original seeing to an extended legacy of misfortune, and perverts the ideas of literal succession and metaphorical passing down of glory; cf. 6.54.2 παραδόσιμος τοῖς ἐπιγινομένοις ... δόξα. Words are strikingly combined in ἅμα ταῖς περιπετείαις ... ἀφανισθέντες; the sentence ends with a flourish in τὴν ἀκληρίαν after the build-up of inheritance in παισὶ παίδων παραδόσιμον ἐποίησαν. In the first half of the sentence, the separation of συμπτωμάτων from σφετέρων makes paradoxical the idea of not perceiving what is one's own, and adds stress to εἰς τὸ μέλλον. The sentence shows how P.'s artistic and historiographical intelligence go together.[25]

## 6 DESIGN

*(a) Extension of Plan*

Now that we have seen P. intensely organizing on every level, we can turn back to the total design. The most immediately arresting feature is the decision to go on beyond 168/7 BC. In a notable passage, P. stresses that his plan as originally conceived marks the end of the growth of Roman power – ἐτετελείωτο (3.4.2). But conceptions of the successful Romans cannot be utterly final, αὐτοτελεῖς, without considering how they ruled, and what those ruled thought of them, both for present practical choices on Roman rule and for subsequent views on whether it should be praised or blamed (3.4.4–7). Achieving conquest is not a τέλος in action any more than sailing is an end in itself, he wittily puts it (3.4.9–11). With the expansion, his work too can accomplish its final task, its τελεσιούργημα (3.4.12). At the same time, he has been lured on (προήχθην, 3.4.13), after his original intentions, and will make as it were another start (οἷον ἀρχὴν

---

[25] For the shaping of sentences in book 8, see 35.3, 1.2, 2.8, 2.9–10, 4.2, 9.1, 10.2, 11.3nn., etc. The genre allowed a wide range of possibilities; so one may contrast with P.'s elaborate structures the short sentences of *FGrHist* 148 (history of Alexander, P. Oxy. xv 1798), esp. fr. 44. Cf. Purcell (1995) on how the sacking of Carthage relates to that of Corinth, the most terrible event for the Greeks in 146.

ποιησάμενος ἄλλην). With skilful presentation, he conveys both the satisfying shape of 'the whole narrative' (τὴν ὅλην διήγησιν, 3.3.7) up to 168/7 and the deeper conception involved in going on to 146. The action may be complete by 168/7, but not the conception of that action, or the agents' larger aim in carrying it out. The change in his thought, the freshness of his invention, is marked out, and a new beginning is acknowledged. This is, then, a supreme example of what we saw earlier, the mixture of design, spontaneity and restless thinking.[26]

*(b) συμπλοκή and Minds*

To the whole design the concept of συμπλοκή is essential: the historian weaving together events in different parts of the world, but still more the events entangling with each other. The concept is more elusive than it may seem. P. holds that from the years 220/19–217/16 onwards historical writing becomes σωματοειδής in its content, like a single unified body; previously events were scattered (1.3.4). The συμπλοκή of events happened in a particular year, 218/17, as wars which began in separate regions became common to all in their end (4.28.3, 5): Roman victories resulted in Roman domination of the world. This although by 146 Rome did not really rule over Asia; of Gaul and of Spain (Iberia) only part was in the power of Rome. But Rome had prevailed over powerful individuals, to whom are ascribed plans to master the world (Hannibal, Philip V); the Romans themselves, at a point not fixed with precision, are held to have nursed such ambitions.[27]

The intentions which generate the events make the συμπλοκή real and dynamic; so do the wide-ranging actions of individuals. The single individual Hannibal, though in part through intermediaries, arranged events in Italy, Spain, Sicily, Greece, Illyria (9.22.1–6); Hannibal's plans involved

---

[26] Ennius' justification of his expansion at *Ann.* 403 Skutsch (if such it is) has more to do with keeping up to date; P. does emphasize his own involvement in the later events as a reason for treating them (3.4.13). Thuc. 5.26 argues for the unity of his subject – a single war, despite an apparent interruption; autobiography comes in too (5.26.4–6), as in P. (cf. also 3.5.7–8) and Ennius (401; 402?).

[27] See 1.3, 2.6nn. The idea starts from Alexander and then the Diadochi; cf. P. Köln VI 247 col. i.24–8: Antigonus is convinced he will rule (ἡγήσεσθαι) [τῆς οἰκο]υμένης ἁπάσης, following Alexander. Cf. J. Hornblower (1981) 167–71. On P.'s choice of date cf. e.g. Vollmer (1990) 1–14, 152–5. For ἱστορία at 1.3.4 cf. *PL* II2b; for the extensiveness of ἡ οἰκουμένη in P. cf. 3.1.4 ('all known parts' of it indicates it is not just the civilized world), 59.1–8, 8.2.4. συμπλέκω can denote the weaving together of separate narrative strands, cf. 5.31.4; but, in regard to events, we should remember συμπλοκή and συμπλέκεσθαι of enemy ships that crash into each other and join combat (1.23.6, 16.3.10 etc.).

the whole οἰκουμένη, not just the Romans, who thwarted him (11.19.6). Demetrius persuades Philip to think of a crossing to Italy as the start of an attempt to conquer the world (ἀρχὴν εἶναι τῆς ὑπὲρ τῶν ὅλων ἐπιβολῆς), now that the Romans are out of the picture (5.101.9–102.1). Scipio's conquests for Rome are suggested, with cunning rhetoric, to encompass Spain, Asia, Syria and the greater part of Africa (10.40.7); but he avoids kingly power for himself. Rome's ambition is already discernible as the Romans begin the final battle of the Second Punic War (15.9.2–5, 10.2: τὰ ὅλα, all the οἰκουμένη, the parts of the οἰκουμένη subject to ἱστορία). The constructed minds, and the carefully packaged actions, of mighty individuals and cities help to carry the weight of P.'s idea, and to give it narrative impetus.

*(c) συμπλοκή and Structure*

For the most part, the history is split into separate strands: Spain, Italy, Sicily etc. get a section each every year. The constant changes of scene continually refresh the excitement of the thought that these different areas are conjoined. The events as narrated are κατάλληλος (39.8.6 etc.), that is, they occur at the same time; but they are still narrated separately. So at 28.16.9, in a section on Greece, P. says he has already mentioned the outcome of a Rhodian embassy ἐν τοῖς Ἰταλικοῖς, in his Italian section. He explains that he narrates αἱ κατάλληλοι πράξεις year by year. Within each year what has happened παρ' ἑκάστοις 'among each group' – people in Italy, etc. – is drawn together as a unit (συγκεφαλαιοῦσθαι), i.e. the narrative for each region is separate (12). At 4.28.2 he says that he would have recounted events in Greece ἐναλλάξ ... καὶ κατὰ παράθεσιν τοῖς Ἰβηρικοῖς 'in alternation with, and putting them side by side with, those in Spain', if they had been linked together then (ἐπιπεπλέχθαι). The formal arrangement in sections does not actually begin until 216/15 and the 141st Olympiad (cf. 5.31.4–5).

*(d) συμπλοκή and Building Up*

This arrangement is built up to. Particularly with regard to Greece, the real centre of P.'s concerns, portentous warnings in speeches point the way. 'Clouds from the west', that is from Rome, are feared by a speaker who urges Philip to lay claim to rule over τὰ ὅλα, the world (5.104.7, 10). Later too, Roman invasion of Greece is warned of, once the Romans have finished off the war in Italy (11.6.1–2); the κακὰ μεγάλα of 146 might here seem to be envisaged by P. (11.5.9, 6.3). It is the separated geographical areas which make physical crossing between them such potent moments in the move towards συμπλοκή, as in its later development. At 2.2.1 the Romans seek to make τὴν πρώτην διάβασιν εἰς τὴν Ἰλλυρίδα καὶ ταῦτα τὰ μέρη τῆς Εὐρώπης ('their first crossing into Illyria and that part of Europe') – a significant addition. P. stresses that the crossing is crucial to his plan, to the growth of Roman power and to ἐπιπλοκή with Greece (2.2.2, 12.7). Scipio begins his reply to Hannibal before Zama with the crossing of the Romans into Africa (15.8.4).[28]

In book 8 (see the summary in Section 9), an excursus shows the value of looking at the total picture, τὰ ὅλα, as regards Roman and Carthaginian actions in Spain and Sicily (1–2). But Antiochus III and even Philip V still seem to be acting in spheres detached from Rome. Yet Illyria (Lissus) is close to Roman action and ships, and both monarchs will in the end be defeated by the Romans (Philip at Cynoscephalae in 197 BC, Antiochus at Magnesia ad Sipylum in 189, not far from Sardis). A long plot unfolds: the change is not as abrupt as P.'s assertions suggest. In the *Odyssey*, action in different locales is slowly brought together into one house; in P. these areas will all gradually become connected.[29]

From another angle, the stimulation of organized variety is offered by the distance in space, and the difference in content (in book 8 kings, Romans; ships, land ...). So at 38.5.4–6.6 P. compares his alternations to the pleasure of varied tastes, sounds, sights, but emphasizes that he, unlike other historians, follows this practice uniformly and τεταγμένως (6.3). Even here, then, the structuring is emphasized; and the historical vision of a connected world underlies the whole conception.[30]

*(e) Years*

P.'s design is based on years. The Polybian year is a loose entity, mainly aimed to keep units of campaigning together – campaigns mostly stop in the winter months. The year forms part of a structure by Olympiads, sets of four years. An initial προέκθεσις summarized the events of each Olympiad (11.1a) and drew great and numerous events from the whole world into a single σύνοψις (14.1a.1). In book 8, P. is still early on in his pattern of

---

[28] Key crossings in past history, with foreshadowing of συμπλοκή: Xerxes 6.11.1, Alexander 3.6.14, Pyrrhus 2.41.11, etc. Cf. *FGrHist* 255 (P. Oxy. I 12) col. vi 15–16: Antipater crossing into Asia.

[29] For the build-up, cf. Dreyer (2007) 127–9. See also Meadows (2013) 111–12, for interweaving in practice in books 4 and 5. In 214 Philip shows a broad and thoughtful interest in Roman society: *IG* IX.2.517.29–34.

[30] For variety, cf. Pausch (2011) 79–81. P. takes a distinctive position on the relation between nature, variety and human taste; cf. Fitzgerald (2016) 36–7.

covering one Olympiad in two books, and having each year run through different regions in order. As will be seen, significant contrasts result.[31]

As ever, P. breaks free of his own tight structures for expressive and significant effect. In book 14, approaching the climax of the Roman victory over the Carthaginians at Zama, P. says he will stop his previous practice and give 204/3 and 203/2 one book each, so that he can narrate the deeds as they deserve, κατ' ἀξίαν (14.1a.5). Later in book 14 itself, with pointed difference, he runs together the inglorious deeds of Ptolemy IV over many years in a continuous narrative (14.12.1–5). The events, even the war with the Egyptians (5.107.1–3), contained nothing μνήμης ἄξιον ('worthy of mention', 14.12.4). At the same time, there is the positive advantage of displaying the dissolute king's chosen approach to life, his προαίρεσις (14.12.5) – another concern of P.'s.[32]

## 7 GREEKS AND ROMANS

### (a) Life of Polybius

At this point, we may turn to P.'s life, working methods and apparent sympathies. His city matters greatly. He was a leading citizen of Megalopolis in Arcadia, near the centre of the Peloponnese. Brick-stamps show P. contributing to rebuilding in Megalopolis, perhaps after his return from Rome (Lauter (2002)). Megalopolis was a relatively recent foundation (371 or slightly later); it was an important city in the region, with enemies and rivals. Mainland Greece, especially the Peloponnese, plays an outsize part in P.'s work, in that his major theme is Rome's conquest of the οἰκουμένη. The work ends with P. returning from Rome to Megalopolis, a symbolic close (39.8.1); P. had been given the task of visiting cities in Greece, and smoothing acceptance of the Roman settlement (39.5.2–3). The fate of Greece in 146 is made the work's tragic climax, still more than that of Carthage (38.1.1–3.13). The Peloponnese (not, say, Athens) is important in the early part of the work, in books 2 and 4. P. expresses a wish for the Peloponnese (4.32.9), offers advice to Messene

---

[31] On P.'s year see De Sanctis (1916) 219–23; Walbank (1957–79) I 35–7, III 239; Pédech (1964) 449–67. The Olympic festival took place, awkwardly for P.'s military structuring, in the summer. For some events in book 8 (Syracuse and Sardis), contemporary inscriptions indicate the absolute chronology: see introductions to 3a and 1–7 and to 24–34.

[32] The pattern of two years to a book (14.1a.5) changes more often after book 18.

and Megalopolis (4.32.10), and lectures the Arcadians, particularly the deplorable Cynaetheans (4.21.10–11).³³

P. was the son of Lycortas; Lycortas was *strategos* (leader) of the Achaean League at some point in the 180s and a prominent Achaean politician. His and P.'s cautious approach to Rome led to them being transported there after the Roman defeat of the Macedonians in 168. The Romans wished to keep an eye on him and other dubious Achaeans; but the terms of this exile did not stop him forming a rather didactic friendship with the young Scipio Aemilianus, afterwards Africanus the Younger. The start of their closeness is compellingly described at 31.23.6–25.1: Scipio wants the Greek intellectual to be his devoted friend so that he himself can be worthy of Scipiones and Aemilii. On the other hand, P. is quite willing to help his friend Demetrius I of Syria escape from Rome in 163/2, in contravention of the Senate's wishes (31.11–15 – exciting homodiegetic narrative).³⁴

*(b) Readers*

The question of P.'s approach to Rome is not a purely literary one. Roman attitudes to him seem to change between his original deportation and his diplomacy after the sack of Corinth; it might well be that his attitudes changed too. Within his work, P. admires Rome as a political and military structure and is amazed at Rome's triumph. He certainly imagines that Romans will read his work; but the very passages where he mentions Roman readers show he has other readers in view as well or primarily, especially readers in mainland Greece. In 6.11.3–8 he counters possible Roman criticism of his account of the Roman state. He makes it evident that the account is not primarily for Roman readers, since they know it all; the book's treatment of army, camp, funerals bears this out. At 31.22.8–10 he points out that Romans in particular (μάλιστα 'Ρωμαίους) will pick up his works (ἀναληψομένους εἰς τὰς χεῖρας); but he is here making an argument for his credibility on Roman matters, for the benefit of sceptical, non-Roman readers. It suits the rhetoric to stress the Roman readers, but different readers are aimed at even here.

---

³³ P.'s advice to Roman and Carthaginian leaders in 9.9.9–10 quickly moves to leaders in general; cf. 23.14.12. For the brick-stamps, see also Lauter (2005) 239. On Megalopolis see Østby (2005) 223–70 (S. Hornblower (1990) for the foundation), and Luraghi and Magnetto (2012) for an important inscription. On P.'s dates (200–118 or later?), see n. 4 above.

³⁴ At any rate, P. is a character in the story, though in the third person; cf. 36.12.1–5. On the relationship with Scipio, cf. Sommer (2013); it is favourably viewed at DS 31.26.5 and elsewhere.

As with most Greek writing that was accessible to Romans, a degree of judicious politeness is probable; one may contrast the robust rudeness on Roman literature that Aulus Gellius reports or alleges from Greeks at a party (19.9.7). This only makes it the more striking that on the fundamental issues of the Second and Third Punic Wars P. evades any straightforward support for Rome. On the causes of the Second War, he diplomatically (3.9.5) but firmly (3.8.9–10) places what the events themselves show above the authority of Fabius Pictor. For an account of the causes hostile to Carthage (3.6.1–2) he substitutes an account where Rome's harshness plays a crucial role (3.10.1–6). On the causes of the Third, he employs a device later used by Tacitus on Augustus (*Ann.* 1.9.3–10.7). Two pairs of opposed groups in mainland Greece voice discordant views on the Romans' destruction of Carthage (P. 36.9.1–17). Whichever case may be thought stronger, the device clearly aims at avoiding a committed utterance – something more notable with P. than with some authors – and probably invites readers to see a complex historical phenomenon.[35]

*(c) Romans: Distanced Stance*

The Greeks are noteworthy commentators on the fate of Carthage, when they have suffered calamity at the same time from the same people. They have suffered it through their own errors, P. stresses (38.1.2–9). As a person, P. wishes to justify his own 'obeying' of Rome (cf. 36.11.2); as a historian, he wishes to display penetrating detachment from his own people. But the Greeks' folly, unexpectedly in P., increases the pitiable tragedy (38.1.3–4, 7). We have seen that, according to Strabo, P.'s first-hand account of the fall of Corinth aimed at arousing pity, among other things through Roman soldiers' indifference to Greek art (39.2). On Greece, more than anywhere, complicated feelings are suggested in the narrator.

P.'s history does not adopt an all-pervading pro-Roman stance, as if he were a Roman writer. We shall see in book 8 how Romans are miserably worsted by Greeks and Carthaginians; both failures are set against

---

[35] P. 36.9.13 has connections to 36.3.9–4.4, but that does little to resolve anything; 36.9.14–17 seem to push the positive case implausibly far. At 38.1.5 τόπον ἔσχατον ἀπολογίας ('a slight [translation disputed] possibility of defence') appears to presuppose a view in favour of Rome, not altogether compatibly with 36.9. P. praises Scipio at the fall of Carthage, but for extrapolating to the fall of Rome – which turns the complexities in a different direction (38.21.1–3, Németh (2023)). For a view of P.'s work as a diplomatic endeavour, see Thornton (2013*b*).

the eventual triumph of Rome at Syracuse. P. greatly praises Hannibal, as a model of planning, energy and people skills (cf. e.g. 11.19.1–6). He does suggest that at Zama Scipio Africanus the Elder was even better than Hannibal (15.16.6); but he minimizes any criticism of Hannibal for the loss (15.16.1–6). At 9.8.1 and 9.9.1–9, P. carefully applauds both Romans and Carthaginians (9.8.1 τε ... καί); he makes his point with a prolonged example from fourth-century Greek history (9.8.2–13). He shows himself looking at both peoples from outside.

### (d) Praise and Prejudice

Two points should be added. P. sees limitations in the Romans' dauntless obstinacy as they persevere with their objectives (1.37.5–10). But this obstinacy yields a narrative pattern of failure then triumph which repeats and embodies Roman success. It shows what makes the Romans tick – something we learn less of with regard to Carthage.

Second, P.'s judicious multiplicity of perspectives is not universal. Perceived groups against whom he voices a generalized prejudice include women (so 2.4.8, 2.8.12) and 'barbarians' (so 38.18.7). Such groups are most conspicuous, however, among the Greeks: so the Cretans (8.16.4, 6nn.) and especially the old enemies of his Achaean League, the Aetolians. The Aetolians in the work highlight human values by lacking them: they ignore the ἔθη καὶ νόμιμα common to mankind (4.67.4). P.'s treatment of the Aetolians conflicts with his more notable position that the genre and job of history requires the highest praise for one's enemies when their deeds demand it (1.14.5). He does allow one Aetolian a more limited praise for daring of a kind which is called Αἰτωλικῆι μὲν ἀλλ' οὐκ ἀνάνδρωι 'Aetolian, but not lacking in bravery' (5.81.1); P. is displaying his broad-mindedness.[36]

It is assumed that the historian should evaluate, should praise and blame (Thucydides and even Herodotus evaluate much less frequently than P.). But praise and blame should not be dictated by one's own fatherland, and the same group can be now praised, now blamed, as the actions not the agents demand (1.14.7–8). P. brings out here his own stance and balance by contrasting himself with both the pro-Roman Roman Fabius Pictor and the pro-Carthaginian Sicilian Philinus (1.14.1–3, 15.1–12),

---

[36] For less damning but still extreme depiction of the Aetolians, cf. Agatharch. *FGrHist* 86 F6. On barbarians in P. cf. Champion (2004), incl. 30–63, 241–53. For individual women whom P. admires, cf. 21.38.7, and the new fragment (Németh (2022 and 2023)).

the admired historians of the First Punic War. One function of beginning with the First Punic War, in all its ups and downs, is to show that P. is free from any single perspective.³⁷

*(e) Human Changeability*

The basis for this position on peoples is a vision of human inconstancy and mixed ability; it applies still more in the treatment of individuals (1.14.7). Even in sketching the φύσις of Aratus, one of the figures he presents most positively, P. stresses that there is a multiplicity in people's souls (τι πολυειδές, 4.8.7); hence Aratus was perfect in some areas of action (4.8.1), but feeble in others (4.8.5). P. presents this as an answer to possible criticism of his own inconsistency by readers (4.8.12). He makes comparisons with the ability of particular groups in warfare; the cavalry even of the Aetolians has its plus and minus points (4.8.10).³⁸

More profoundly, the relation of character to events is intricate. People do not have contradictory dispositions (διαθέσεις) in their natures; but circumstances force rulers to display or seem to display dispositions which are opposite to their nature, and to behave in ways contrary to their προαίρεσις (9.22.10, 23.4). There is a parallel with cities (9.23.5–8).

In practice, P. varies: we hear little ill of the Elder or Younger Africanus, perhaps for reasons of caution; in some large-scale portraits, as especially of Philip V, P. offers big pictures of change, from good to bad. Such large patterns are broken by surprising behaviour, which must be properly valued (16.28.4–7); P. here defends himself from a charge of self-contradiction (4–5). He now sees φύσεις themselves as sometimes varied (7). And the larger patterns can take unexpected turns: so Philip behaves badly when fortunate, but later well when unfortunate (25.3.9).³⁹

---

³⁷ Cf. 10.21.8 on praise and blame in history as against encomiastic biography (but there are problems in the text); Schorn (2014); Stropp (2023) 185. P. and praise: Eckstein (2013) 325–6; Gibson (2018). Praise and blame in historiography: Avenarius (1956) 157–63; Marincola (1997) 6, 173; S. P. Oakley (2005) 57.

³⁸ For πολυειδές cf. Sen. *Ep.* 120.22: apart from the wise man, *multiformes sumus*. There could be philosophical colouring in P. here. P. and Aratus: Meadows (2013) 93–4.

³⁹ Welwei (1963) 38 finds extreme contradictions in P.'s treatment of Philip V. On that treatment see Nicholson (2023).

## 8 METHODOLOGY

*(a) Rivals' Failings*

Evaluation, then, is central to P.'s enterprise, as is independence. This matters in considering P.'s ways of working. He has a picture of these to project; that picture is of great importance for his impact on readers. The picture must to some extent correspond to the reality; but his information is too fleeting, and our external knowledge too slight, for us to gain a detailed impression of how he put his history together – the sort of impression that his own work often enables us to form for Livy. In his picture, P. himself forms a predominant figure, through his power of mind and his practical action; the power of mind partly springs from his practical experience.

In numerous clashes, he takes issue with other historians of the same events over evaluation and practicalities. We have seen instances above of P. at war with his colleagues; their misguided judgements often go back to the primary dichotomy of universal and partial history. Some λογογράφοι produce wild pictures of Hieronymus' tyranny; but they are 'forced' by writing partial history to make small things large (7.7.1–6). Timaeus makes Timoleon greater than the most famous gods, though his achievements were confined to Sicily. This is so that his own limited history of Magna Graecia and Sicily could be compared, as we saw, with works that cover the world and events everywhere (12.23.1–7).

P. produces satirical depictions of bookishness. The point is primarily spatial: writers like Timaeus stay in one place (12.28.6), rather than roaming the world, seeing sights (and sites) and gaining experience. As we saw at the start, the historian who works just from books does his research lying down (κατακείμενον, 12.27.5); at ease, he compares the mistaken accounts of previous writers. Historians are mostly ignorant (12.28.5). Ephorus, P.'s model for universal history, at least knew a bit about naval warfare; but his account of Mantinea is exposed as a sham by true assessment of the terrain, and measurement (12.25f.4–5). Usually, the work of writers without topographical and political experience lacks vividness (ἔμφασις), and is full of falsehoods and absurdities (12.25g.2, 25h.3, 16.20.1). These criticisms indicate the merit of P.'s own methods.[40]

---

[40] Timaeus and bookishness: Burton (2022) 68–9. P.'s journeyings were singled out on the monument to him at the temple of Zeus Lycaeus at Megalopolis, Paus. 8.30.8 (wandering over all earth and sea). Although he claims to avoid local lore (9.2.1–3), P.'s knowledge of places includes knowledge from books (cf. 33.9n.).

## (b) Literary Sources

Whether other historians are sources of information for P. is not often made explicit. His use of Aratus seems a likely instance (2.56.2). Previous writings are certainly implied to be sources for other historians (so 12.27.1–4). P. condemns a limitation to books alone; but equally it is not clear how experience, topography and monuments alone would give him sufficient material for his earlier narratives. We can assume that P. is drawing material from historians and other written sources in circulation.[41]

But we must certainly not assume that P. takes over the bias of those sources without reflection. Scholars frequently imagine that they can spot bias which P. has neither spotted nor created, and so that they can get behind P. to an account written, say, in the court of Antiochus III. P. may well derive some approaches from his predecessors; but we cannot infer with confidence which those approaches are, because of his fierce determination to think for himself. Even in the case of Aratus, he is not blindly transcribing. He has made a decision (2.56.2 προῃρημένοις) to follow Aratus on the war with Cleomenes rather than Aratus' contemporary Phylarchus, who often conflicts with him. P. has read Phylarchus closely and indignantly, and argues his case at length (2.56–63). He thinks he is in a position to pronounce Aratus' ὑπομνηματισμοί extremely truthful (2.40.4); he knows of matters which Aratus kept out of them (2.47.11).[42]

## (c) Interviewing

The good historian's mind and knowledge do not merely control what he receives from books; they also shape what he receives from eyewitnesses. He does not merely write down what he hears from them. His informed questioning is as important as the information of the witness, whom he guides throughout (χειραγωγεῖ, 12.28a.9). That information needs the historian's understanding (8). C. Laelius, the close friend of Scipio Africanus the Elder, was clearly a marvellous source on Scipio for P.; but P. does not simply accept what he said. Rather, he adopts Laelius' view of Scipio because his remarks seemed plausible, and in accord with what Scipio actually did (10.3.2).

---

[41] A new inscription from Cyme in Aeolis (iii BC) speaks of a historian (Mnesiptolemus?) as working ἐκ τῶν ἀρχαίων ὑπομνημάτων (line 13): see Magnetto (2024).

[42] For P. and Aratus' writing see Meadows (2013). For the idea that bias reveals sources see e.g. Schmitt (1964) 175–85, cf. Primo (2009) 126–59; against: Hoyos (1998) 285–8. Still useful is Ziegler (1952) 1560–4. On sources for book 8, see the introductions to 3a and 1–7, 15–21, 24–34, 8.3n.

*(d) Experience*

Beyond speaking to eyewitnesses, there is the historian's own experience of events. After chiding Timaeus for laziness on the questioning of eyewitnesses (ἀνακρίσεις, 12.27.3), P. sets up further contrasts: between bookishness on Celts and others and being an αὐτόπτης of peoples (12.28a.3–4), and between quizzing those present at battles and participating in them oneself (5). Yet even writing from being present demands experience and understanding; the ἄπειρος, the man without experience, could not make sense of what he saw (12.28a.10).[43]

*(e) Inscriptions*

Important too are inscriptions. Timaeus, surprisingly in view of P.'s picture of him, claimed to have visited some Locrians in Greece and seen an inscription (12.9.2–3); he was thought to have attached much significance to studying inscriptions carefully (12.10.3–5). P. supposes he was lying on his actions, but does not contest the principle. Here P. notably portrays inscriptions, especially public ones, as better evidence than that of informants (12.10.7–9). P. himself investigates inscriptions as records of public decisions; he thinks he can assert there is 'not even a stele' from the first cities to form the Achaean League (2.41.12; cf. 3.26.4). Inscriptions may very well be the source of details on treaties more often than they are explicitly quoted from autopsy.

At 3.33.17–18 P. makes great flourish over his discovery of a bronze tablet drawn up by Hannibal: this justifies the exact numbers P. has given. He stresses, as with Aratus, his own decision to follow a source he thought 'trustworthy on such matters'. At 3.26.1–2 he implicitly contrasts his own knowledge of the treaties he has quoted with the ignorance of Philinus and of P.'s contemporaries. He claims to have translated the first of his treaties from archaic Latin, which challenged the experts (3.22.3 – one would guess he had had some help). P. enters into the subsequent discussion of some of the treaties in 22–7 by the parties themselves, and gives his arguments. The inscriptions are made to form part of P.'s historical consideration of who caused the war (3.28.5, 29, so 29.4 with 27.3). Inscriptions too require the historian's masterful mind, and assist the picture of him.

---

[43] The text in 12.28a.7 is very uncertain.

## (f) Polybius Dominates

The image that P. creates is plain: P. puts abundant effort into acquiring material; but the material is rarely self-explanatory. His powerful mind and massive experience form and make sense of what he accumulates. P. almost blends in with his most imposing characters: Hannibal and P. at the Alps resemble each other in their meticulous inquiries and preparation (3.48.10–12). P. has crossed the Alps himself – but for the sake of knowledge (12). Yet as this instance shows, we are left with many questions. The events of book 8 happened before P. was born, and, if he is writing after 168, they happened over 44 years before he actually puts his work together. Those surviving from the time might have had more useful knowledge to contribute on some events than on others: on the capture of Tarentum more than on the secret negotiations at Sardis. Even for Tarentum, it is uncertain how much P. gets from such sources: Tarentum will have been included in earlier historians' accounts of Hannibal's deeds.

P. is not generally concerned to show the specifics of his sources and the transmission of information; we are not in a position to know how far his reshaping of material reached, or whether some of the detail is his own recreation, for instance on the basis of his topographical knowledge. That makes it harder to get from his accounts to the historical actualities; but the picture of his method that he projects has its own historical interest for Hellenistic culture. It is certainly an imposing literary and intellectual construction.

# Part II: Book 8

## 9 SUMMARY

The remains of book 8 offer first a discussion, with examples, of whether one should blame those deceived by treachery (35–6). Then comes the siege of Syracuse by the Romans (1–7). After a fragment on universal history and on the wider activities and ambitions of Rome and Carthage (1–2) comes the Roman attack on Syracuse by sea and land; it is completely worsted by Archimedes' machines (3–7). Also in this year (214/13) P. deals with Philip V of Macedon in the Peloponnese and in Illyria. His treatment of Messenia leads P. to consider historians writing on monarchs, and in particular Theopompus' unrestrained writing on Philip II and his friends (8–11). P. tells of Philip V poisoning his friend the statesman Aratus (12). A separate extract narrates Philip V's capture of Lissus in Illyria (13–14). P. depicts at length how in this year the Cretan Bolis tricks Achaeus, the rival of the Seleucid king Antiochus III, into attempting an escape from the acropolis of Sardis, after Antiochus has taken the main city; Achaeus is captured and horribly killed (15–21). In the following year (213/12), the city of Tarentum in South Italy, which is in Roman control, is taken over by Hannibal; Hannibal and some of the Tarentines trick the unduly relaxed Roman *praefectus* (24–34). The Romans seize Epipolae, the heights within the defences of Syracuse (37). A short fragment tells of Cavarus, a king of the Galatae in Thrace (22), a longer one of King Xerxes of Armenia, who is well treated by Antiochus III (23).

Each episode or segment receives an introduction of its own in the commentary. Relations between parts of the book come into the following two sections of this Introduction.

## 10 COHESION

### (a) Structure and Book

To what extent is it reasonable to see a book as a cohesive entity? P. gives emphasis to his structuring of the work into books; in the complete books he summarizes and looks back explicitly, even when, as with the first two books, they form a pair (2.1.1–3 on book 1). At 8.8.3 he says he was drawn to say more on these actions 'both now and in the previous book': thus, even as he resumes his discussion of Philip from book 7 (7.11, 12, 13–14), he marks the books as distinct entities. Books 7 and 8 form a pair; the break produced by book 6 makes the links the more obvious. Although the four years of an Olympiad seem an arbitrary division to us, P. partly thinks through this grouping, as we do with numbered centuries and decades. Narrations and excursions run across books 7 and 8, as closely connected wholes divided into parts: Antiochus' capture of Sardis (7.15–18) and then his capture of Achaeus and the citadel (8.15–21); discussion of Philip V, centred on his actions at Messene (7.11–14, 8.8–12). Within book 8 itself, there is a cognate divided whole: the Romans are thwarted at Syracuse in the first year (3–7) and succeed in the second (37). Antiochus' relation with his advisers in regard to Achaeus (21.1–3) and to Xerxes in Armenia (23.3–4) shows him developing, as we shall see.[44]

---

[44] The treatment of Syracuse from Hieronymus' flirtation with Carthage (book 7) to the siege and capture carries on into book 9; but connection is felt across the books, thanks not least to the excursus in 7.8.1–9 on past Syracusan rulers. We can see the Olympiad shaping the historical material in the chronographic *FGrHist* 255 col. v 18–23.

## (b) Connections

Trickier is the question of whether episodes with different subject matter should be seen by readers as related in theme and material – and the more related because of their proximity, not just as part of P.'s general concerns. At 8.36.7–8 P., who has started from some unknown event, illustrates a point by the instance of Achaeus, which will be narrated later in the book (same year). There are plenty of older examples; 'but most vivid and closest in time to the present subject will be what happened in the case of Achaeus'. The proximity in time gives this example particular salience. P. is inviting readers to compare items within the book; the connection is thematic and practical.

At 8.2.7–8 P. says that the greatness of Rome's and Carthage's attempts on Sicily (and Spain and Sardinia) can only be properly appreciated if one is aware of these cities' other endeavours at the same time, all the enterprises abroad and wars at home. He has the fighting in Italy especially in mind (cf. 8.1.4), as well as Spain, and the fleet off Greece keeping watch on Philip (8.1.4–6). P.'s general desire that events should not just be considered alone, in a κατὰ μέρος fashion, is strengthened by the forthright declaration at this point. P. is inviting readers of this book to look at the events involving Rome and Carthage all together; the connection here is in historical understanding.

There is, then, broad authorial encouragement to relate items in this book. How far readers go is not fixed, and need not be bound by authorial intention. If connections seem prominent and pointed, and work, that is part of a reasonable reader's experience. Within the same episode, readers are bound to relate Antiochus' and Achaeus' reaction to the bearers of surprising good news. Antiochus is overjoyed (ὑπερχαρής, 8.17.2) but suspicious, and asks lots of questions; he then receives Bolis kindly, φιλοφρόνως (8.18.10). Achaeus in the next sentence receives Bolis φιλοφρόνως (8.19.1), asks lots of questions, and is περιχαρής 'overjoyed', though also anxious (8.19.2). This all contributes to the argument: both Antiochus and Achaeus behave prudently and aptly, despite their emotion. No such emotional reaction had been given when Lagoras told Antiochus his plan for capturing Sardis (7.16.1), after a year's fruitless siege (7.15.2). To go now beyond the episode of Achaeus: Hannibal receives the Tarentine young men and their plan kindly, φιλανθρώπως (8.24.8). He wants time to investigate about these young men (8.24.10); he is overjoyed (περιχαρής, 8.24.11). There are some differences from Antiochus and Achaeus: Hannibal more subtly makes his explorations without the young men there, and so does not dilute his friendly welcome. But the drive for readers to connect this and the earlier behaviour is considerable.

Within the episode of Sardis, the similarity of Antiochus' and Achaeus' behaviour is pointed: the very same man is being treated with cautious and sensible trust, in the one case rightly, in the other wrongly but unavoidably. Hannibal's procedure joins into the pattern, which has received generalizing treatment at the earlier 8.36.1–8 (for the order see introduction to 35–6). The emphasis on receiving proper πίστεις, pledges, at 8.36.2–3 ties in with Hannibal and the young men giving and receiving πίστεις (8.25.1; cf. also 8.18.10, Antiochus to Bolis). In Hannibal's case, everything runs smoothly, while Achaeus is ensnared in a trap. Hannibal like Antiochus gains a lucky break, but unlike Antiochus, who passively awaits results, Hannibal himself is much involved in successful trickery and organization.

Unlike the careful and sceptical Achaeus and Antiochus, the Romans at Tarentum are simple-minded. The guard is taken in by food; the *praefectus* is even more unsuspecting (ἀνύποπτος) when he learns something of the enemy's attack (8.27.2). He too is taken in by gifts of food (8.25.7); his drunken joy, carefree mood and trust of the young Tarentines (8.27.6) is radically different from Achaeus' anxiety and determination not to trust Bolis fully, intelligent and experienced man that Achaeus is (8.19.2–3; cf. 8.19.2 πλήρης ἀγωνίας 'full of anxiety' with 8.27.6 χαρᾶς δὲ πλήρης καὶ ῥαιθυμίας 'full of happiness and ease', and cf. διάνοια at 19.3 and at 27.6). Not trusting anyone easily (8.21.11) is one useful lesson from Achaeus' fate (not that Achaeus trusts anyone easily) – but it leads on to the second, that anything can happen to mortals. On the other hand, meticulous plans like Hannibal's do work.

Connected is the opposition between the two episodes in their colour and character. There is something light-hearted, perhaps comic, about the capture of Tarentum, even if the guard tricked by the hope of eating boar is promptly put to death (8.29.6–8). The capture and fate of Achaeus, even if there are lighter strands to begin with, ends in overwhelming tragedy (8.20.7–21.11). Readers are drawn to take the book cohesively, not just κατὰ μέρος, and gain much from doing so.

Not long in the book after the Carthaginian capture of Tarentum came the Roman capture of Epipolae. That episode clearly reversed the bafflement of the Romans at Syracuse earlier in the book. The contrast with the Romans at Tarentum is also palpable. At Tarentum it had been the Roman commander who rested drunkenly (μεθύων, 8.27.6), after excesses inspired by Greeks; now it is the Greek soldiers who had long been in a drunken sleep (μεθυσκόμενοι, 8.37.9). Marcellus is now a more Hannibal-like figure, tightly organizing his troops; both Hannibal and Marcellus are chary of revealing their plan (26.7 οὐ διεσάφει, 37.4 διασαφῶν οὐδέν), insist on their orders (26.9 τοῖς παραγγελλομένοις, 37.4 τὸ παραγγελλόμενον) and wisely point to rewards (26.7, 37.3, 5).

11 STRUCTURES OF PLACES AND PEOPLE

(a) Cities

The episodes in the book as we have it are connected in the physical and political structures they present: structures for living (cities), political structures (constitutions). What we have particularly concerns four cities, Syracuse in Sicily, Lissus in Illyria, Sardis in Asia Minor and Tarentum in South Italy. Cities occur throughout P., but this group particularly invites contemplation and comparison. The cities share a form: a citadel which is separated physically, and can be defended separately, and the rest of the city. The form itself is ubiquitous in the period; but the nature and degree of the separation are not. Lissus' citadel (in effect) is on a separate hill from the main city, which is on a lower hill. At Sardis the citadel is at the top of the same hill, but particularly hard to reach. In the case of Tarentum and probably Syracuse it is on a near-island; for neither is it significantly higher than the main city. Capture of the city is fully achieved in the book for Lissus and Sardis (in this book the citadel of Sardis is captured; the main city had been captured in book 7). It is starting to be achieved for Syracuse; in Tarentum it is achieved for the main city but not the citadel. At Lissus, Tarentum and Sardis, the citadel forms a separate challenge for the besieger. The means of capture differ: at Syracuse the most modern naval technology is deployed, but defeated by superior technology; eventually low-tech cleverness prevails. At Lissus, ingenious land tactics exploit the topography of city and citadel. Tarentum is captured through careful trickery and knowledge of the occupying individuals. At Sardis personal relationships with the ruler enable small-scale deception; here P. is ethically repelled.[45]

[45] Ortygia (Map 2) joined to the mainland: cf. Gans (2006); Basile (2012) 180–204; Beste and Mertens (2015) 242. Ortygia was crucial in the political narrative before the siege: see Livy 24.21.6, 11, 22.4, 7, 12, 23.4, 24.8, 25.3–4; cf. 25.24.8–10 (fortifications clearly in place). While Ortygia is in practice the citadel from Dionysius I on, DS 14.7.3 uses ἀκρόπολις of a structure on Ortygia; cf. Livy 24.21.6; 21.9n. For the conceptual separation of city and citadel (32.2, etc.) cf. e.g. *FGrHist* 160 (report, 246 BC) col. ii.12–13: we gained καὶ τὴν πόλιν καὶ τὴν ἄκραν (of Seleucia Pieria). The conception adversely affects Hannibal's strategy at Tarentum (introduction to 24–34, 31.1n.). Notably, Lorentzen (2016) 303 deliberately excludes the Hellenistic fortifications of the acropolis in presenting the fortifications of Pergamum; for them cf. W. Radt (2011) 63–8.

Syracuse and Tarentum adjoin the sea, Lissus is very close, Sardis is further inland. Hills are essential to Lissus, Acrolissus and Sardis, which are built on them; the hills that encompass Syracuse are essential to its defence. Syracuse has become a big conglomerate, built up of different 'cities'; Lissus is much smaller. Tarentum too has become a large city by ancient standards, but a lot of the fortified area includes the necropolis. Syracuse's fortified area includes the empty heights of Epipolae. Syracuse and Tarentum are archaic colonizations from mainland Greece; the Spartan basis of Tarentum is important in P.'s account. Tarentum has recently become occupied by a Roman force. The population of Lissus is mainly Illyrian, not Greek. Sardis had been the capital of the Lydian kings, and was then captured by the Achaemenids; there is at least a non-Greek element at the grandest level, the ruler's court. But cultures influence each other: the Romans in Tarentum take to Greek partying and Tarentine drinking; Antiochus' council go for punishments used by Asian non-Greeks.[46]

*(b) Constitutions*

Political forms are an important ingredient of the book, and of P. in general. Monarchy is the predominant form, but rarely uncontested. Antiochus strives with his rival Achaeus, whom P. probably does not elevate quite to the rank of king. Philip's monarchy is secure, but he confronts the guidance and the principles of Aratus. Aratus is in some ways an adviser to the king, and his supposed friend (8.12.1, 5); but he is also the elected leader, for the year, of the Achaean League. Syracuse, after the assassination of the young king Hieronymus, is eventually controlled by elected pro-Carthaginian *strategoi*. Hannibal was elected as general; P. classes his position among the δυναστεῖαι of the time (4.2.9–10). The Roman expedition in Sicily is commanded by Marcellus as consul then proconsul and by Ap. Claudius Pulcher in some post. C. Livius occupies Tarentum with a military command as *praefectus*. Both Carthage and Rome have a mixed constitution, as P. sees it. The book presents us with other monarchs, including Xerxes in Armenia, Cavarus king of the Galatae in Thrace and earlier Archidamus and Cleomenes III of Sparta, still earlier Philip II and Alexander, far earlier Sardanapallus the Assyrian voluptuary. Political forms clash forcefully in the struggles of two fourth-century Thebans for Greek freedom against a Thessalian tyrant (8.35.6–8).[47]

[46] In P. punishment and cruelty are, in principle, an important area of difference between Greeks and 'barbarians'; cf. Rollinger, Lang and Barta (2012).
[47] On Achaeus, cf. Kobes (1996) 29–30, 33 (evasive, but his general criteria suggest he thinks P. sees Achaeus as a king).

P.'s approach to constitutions is mingled, here and elsewhere. He certainly thinks that rule by one person, by a few and by the people are prone to decline into worse forms of the same set-up, and then change into different forms (so 8.24.1); Plato is the basis, though here P.'s psychology is more complex. Kings can confer ἐλευθερία on their own cities and others (5.9.9 Antigonus Doson and Sparta) – though it is often a pretence (15.24.4). Hannibal claims to be bringing ἐλευθερία to Italy (3.77.6, etc.), including Tarentum (8.34.4): the Romans, by imposing their will from outside, remove freedom from others, regardless of their own constitution. Democracy is the form most associated with ἐλευθερία, and with the fairest name, though this can conceal the worst set-up, rule by the mob (6.57.9). P. ardently commends the Achaean League for democracy (2.38.6) and freedom (cf. 2.37.9), and sees the Theban heroes of the fourth century as the champions of those notions (8.35.6).

But he nurses an ideal of kingship too. Kingship, especially by an exceptional individual, is highly valued in Plato (*Politicus*, cf. 301b5–7, 302e10–303b5) and Aristotle (*Pol.* 3.1284b25–34, *EN* 8.1160a31–b9). This valuation grows from fifth-century ideas of great men. P.'s ideals for kings include public acceptance of the sole ruler (6.4.2), but also, less tangibly, dignity, generosity and charm in the monarch (8.23.5, 11.34.3, 9; 8.10.10 βασιλικοί 'in the magnanimity and self-control of their conduct'). P. stands aside, though, from the facile panegyric of certain historians (8.8.5–6). Sole rule has three forms in P. (6.3.9, 6.4.7–8); it is thus particularly complicated among constitutions. The length of some reigns enables P. to portray and examine decline on a large historiographical scale. In Philip we see decline already under way. Antiochus is seen at an earlier point, gaining independence from his advisers, and so rising closer to kingly excellence. P.'s explicitness and passages of generality keep these issues to the fore.[48]

## 12 CONTEXT OF EVENTS

### (a) Second Punic War and Other Wars

The intensely detailed narratives in and around cities are focal points in longer and larger stories, which involve wide regions, big movements of armies and extensive concerns in their leaders. Readers will gain more from book 8 if they are aware of these multiple stories, both as P. sees

---

[48] Monarchy in P.: Welwei (1963); Piérart (2016). For the background see also Haake (2013). On the idea of being worthy of the royal title (11.34.9), cf. P. Köln VI 247 col. ii.28–30.

them and otherwise; they can then perceive how much is involved in the episodes and what drives the immediate plans and conflicts. It will emerge how P. forms his version of the stories to present imposing characters with vast ambitions.[49]

P., despite his concern with Rome's rise to dominate the οἰκουμένη, names three wars as his starting point (1.3.1–2): the Social War in Greece (including Philip), the Syrian War in Asia (including Antiochus) and the Second Punic War (including Hannibal). He begins with book 3 on the start of the Punic War; but books 4 and 5 turn to affairs in the Greek-speaking world. The three wars figure in Fortune's complete remake of the world (ὡσανεὶ κεκαινοποιηκέναι πάντα τὰ κατὰ τὴν οἰκουμένην, 4.2.4). Hannibal's appointment as general accompanies the new reigns of Philip V, Antiochus III (and Achaeus), Ariarathes IV in Cappadocia, Ptolemy IV in Egypt and Lycurgus in Sparta (4.2.4–11). Despite the alleged συμπλοκή of events, P. does not think of the Punic War as all-engulfing. Western affairs, in Syracuse and in Tarentum, are part of that war; Philip in Messenia is only tangentially related to it, and Antiochus at Sardis not at all.

## (b) Hannibal

The causes of the Second Punic War, and P.'s view of those causes, are much debated. In discussing causes (3.9.6–12.7), P. invokes people and places: Hannibal's father Hamilcar, Hasdrubal, Hannibal himself; Sardinia, lost to Carthage in 238/7 (3.27.7–8), and Spain, much of which Carthage had taken over. The Carthaginians, and Hamilcar in particular, were greatly aggrieved by Rome's defeat of them in Sicily, in the twenty-three-year First Punic War (264–241 BC; 3.9.6–7, 3.13.1). P. portrays Hannibal as 'full of irrationality and violent anger' (3.15.9) in his hatred of Rome.[50]

But P. elsewhere seems to see Hannibal, implausibly, as having plans (11.19.6 οὐδὲν ... τῶν προτεθέντων) for world domination; of these plans defeating Rome was only the start (11.19.6–7). However, in the quoted

---

[49] For the history in the episodes themselves, see the introductions to them in the commentary; a little overlap is probably helpful to the reader.

[50] On P. and the causes of the war see e.g. Mantel (1991) 47–104; Hoyos (1998) 150–296; Wiater (2020). Second Punic War (esp. to 211): e.g. Lazenby (1978); Le Bohec (1996) 107–224; Goldsworthy (2000) 143–268; Hoyos (2011) 223–392; Steinby (2014) 121–63; Briscoe and Hornblower (2020) 2–8; S. Hornblower (2024) 80–3. See now the last for Hannibal more generally; earlier, see esp. Seibert (1993a and 1993b).

treaty between Hannibal and Philip success in the war against Rome would entail the Romans being allowed φιλία with both, provided they give up possessions in Illyria (7.9.9–15); it would not mean the Romans being the subjects of the conqueror Hannibal (cf. 3.118.4).

*(c) War in Italy*

The First Punic War had been fought in Sicily, the crucial stepping stone between North Africa and Italy; Sicily, predominantly Greek-speaking, was not thought of as part of Italy. P. says the Romans were expecting war now, but thought that it would be fought in Spain (3.15.13, 16.6). Hannibal surprised them by moving the war to Italy, with speed and, in crossing the Alps, sensational audacity. Placing the war primarily in Italy much increased the pressure on Rome, and then on Hannibal himself. He inflicted catastrophic defeats at the Trebia, near Placentia in Cisalpine Gaul (December 218), at Lake Trasimene in Umbria (June 217) and at Cannae in Apulia (August 216). Hannibal's initial objective was not to capture Rome (cf. 3.118.4, 9.9.2–3); but the terror and humiliation of these defeats were enormous.

Vital to his plans was removing from Rome the Italian cities which were its subordinate allies; this would diminish Rome's base of power and the greater part of its army (cf. 2.24.1–17). The cities were also essential for the supplying of Hannibal's forces. There had been numerous changes in cities' allegiance after Cannae (cf. 3.118.2–3); but such changes in allegiance became harder for Hannibal to achieve when Rome's altered strategy evaded disastrous encounters. The inhabitants of each Italian city nursed diverse views on Rome and Carthage; ambition within the city and the region seems to have played a part, and fear of the force which both Rome and Carthage deployed when they thought necessary. Hannibal's failure to take Nola, Cumae and Tarentum in 215 and 214 was followed by a run of successes in 213 and 212. The capture of Tarentum in late 213 (see 26.1n.) was the result of collaboration with elements inside the city, and did not involve a siege. Roman brutality had played a part in encouraging resentment (Livy 25.7.10–8.2). The Romans had occupied this city with a garrison in 214; its port, wealth and prestige made it an important gain for Hannibal – the port especially (cf. P. 10.1.1–10). P. makes Hannibal's success display the masterly general, and the value of meticulous planning and plotting. Some hitches are smoothed over.[51]

---

[51] See introduction to 24–34. For the Italian cities in this period, see esp. Fronda (2010).

## (d) Sicily

Even in the early years of the Second Punic War, Rome maintained its interests in areas outside Italy – most especially in Sicily, a vital source of grain and income and the scene of Rome's victory over Carthage. The interest, and demands, had intensified in recent years (from 227 a praetor ran the province, Solin. 5.1). Sicily could also have been a means for Carthage to send supplies to Hannibal in Italy (cf. Livy 24.8.14; and Cic. *Verr.* 2.3 for Romans later working in the reverse direction). M. Claudius Marcellus, consul in 214, was sent there in the later part of that year (Livy 24.21.1; see the introduction to 3a and 1–7). Although Carthage had been compelled to leave Sicily after the war, Carthage's cause continued to enjoy support there. Hieron II, ruler of Syracuse and some of eastern Sicily, had eventually opted for Rome (App. *Sic.* 2.6), while attempting to keep Carthage friendly; his son and co-regent Gelon, and much of the Syracusan *demos*, favoured Carthage (cf. Livy 25.32.2). Hieronymus, Hieron's grandson, took over his kingdom in 215; under the influence of the half-Carthaginian Hippocrates and Epicydes, he did not sustain or renew his grandfather's treaty with Rome (P. 7.2.1–5.8). Hieronymus was assassinated (P. 7.7.1–3, DS 26.15.1, Livy 25.7.1–7); tumult ensued, but Hippocrates and Epicydes emerged as *strategoi*, and so as leaders of the city (Livy 24.21.2–33.9, probably based on P.; DS 26.15.2, App. *Sic.* 3.2).[52]

The Romans, angered by the killing of a Roman force, had demanded the city should exile Hippocrates and Epicydes (Livy 24.29.4–5, 10). A siege soon began. Syracuse proved a less easy prospect than Leontini, which Marcellus took *primo impetu* (Livy 24.30.1). The enormous Syracuse had been elaborately fortified by successive rulers; defensive machines had been contrived by Hieron's protégé, the great mathematician and engineer Archimedes.

## (e) Illyria

Land to the east of Italy was of less pressing concern to Rome at present. Of most interest, to Rome as to Philip, was the coast facing Apulia and Calabria. This is the area which Rome had gained control of in 229/8. Specific names in it are mentioned in the treaty between Hannibal and Philip as places which are not to be in the Romans' charge, when the war is

---

[52] See e.g. De Sensi Sestito (1976), esp. 132–5, 178–80; Serrati (2000a) 111–12, (2000b); Soraci (2016) 36–43; S. Hornblower (2024) 145–8. The treaty is taken as still in force after Hieron's death at P. 7.3.4, 5.1, 3, 7, Livy 24.6.6, though in need of renewal (7.3.1, Livy 24.6.4, App. *Sic.* 3.1). Cf. De Sensi Sestito (1976) 126.

won (P. 7.9.13, unique in the version that we have of that treaty). The consuls of 219 had taken Dimale and Pharos (P. 3.18.1–19.13; 19.12 is exaggerated: all Illyria conquered). Philip in 217 had vied with his antagonist the Illyrian ruler Scerdilaidas over the adjoining inland area; but when Scerdilaidas sought Roman aid and the Romans sent ten ships, Philip cautiously retreated (5.109.1–110.11 – P. thinks he imagined a larger force). In 214 Philip engaged more directly with Rome over Corcyra (App. *Mac.* 1.3), Apollonia, Oricus (Livy 24.40.1–17); he was certainly unsuccessful in the last two. His attack on Lissus in 214/13, described in book 8, reverts to a city and area just out of Roman control.[53]

The Romans wanted to keep an eye on Philip (8.1.6), especially after knowledge of his dealings with Hannibal (*Staatsverträge* III.528); but the conflict seems localized in practice. Philip's ambitions of world conquest are not apparent, despite P. (5.104.7, 108.4–5 etc.). The treaty of 7.9 suggests that the Romans might fear Philip helping Hannibal – not Philip conquering them and the world in despite of Hannibal. In 212 or 211, Rome, through M. Valerius Laevinus, long active against Philip, starts to engage with the Aetolian League to act against Philip together (*Staatsverträge* III.536). From Rome's point of view, the action would be characteristically pre-emptive; but Rome's interests are just beginning to spread into Greece proper.[54]

*(f) Philip V in Greece*

Notable in the fragment of the treaty between Rome and the Aetolians (*IG* IX.1².2.241, *Staatsverträge* III.536) is the blunt emphasis on the Romans or Aetolians 'having' (ἔχειν, ἐχόντωσαν, 8, 10, 13) cities that the Romans have captured. Philip's influence or dominance in Greece had initially rested on forms which suggested more consent. He was chosen by Crete as leader, προστάτης, of their island, in its willing alliance (P. 7.12.9). In his letters to Larisa in Thessaly of 217 and 214, the votes of the city matter as well as his authority (*IG* IX.2.517.3–9, 25–39). His relations with the Achaeans, and perhaps the Greeks more widely, were based on alliance, though he was leader, ἡγεμών, of the allies (cf. Moretti, *ISE* I.47.2 (Epidaurus, 217–215)

---

[53] For Philip in these years cf., besides literature cited in the commentary, Worthington (2023) 44–81. For Illyria see Gruen (1984) 368–80; Cavallaro (2004) 201–27; Eckstein (2006) 265–8.

[54] *AP* 9.518 (Alcaeus) claims Philip rules land and sea already: the warning to Zeus could be, not a declaration of Philip's further ambition, but an overstatement of his present achievement. The poem will be earlier than those attacking Philip, unless there is an element of hostile irony. Cf. Dreyer (2007) 134. Acceptance of P. on Philip's plans: Seibert (1995) 239–42.

Ἑλλάνων ἁγ[εμόν']). Initially Aratus and the Achaean League, seen by P. as deeply democratic, had been opposed to the Macedonian monarchy; but a delicate and uneasy rapprochement had been reached. This included the difficult position of Aratus, the most eminent and frequently elected *strategos* of the Achaeans, but also (as we have seen) the friend and counsellor of Philip – a position awkwardly close to the monarchical institution of *philoi*. The Peace of Naupactus (217) had temporarily brought stability to Greece after the Social War, in which the Aetolians, among others, fought Philip and his allies.[55]

Philip's arrival to intervene in the internal discord of Messene appeared to disturb the balance and to upset relations with Aratus. The discord in Messene was connected with social and constitutional divisions; but the factional killings were ascribed to Philip's agency (P. 7.13.6–7, Plut. *Arat.* 49.3–5). Demetrius, the previous ruler of Pharos, who was thought to advise Philip on Illyria, was involved in the action at Messene (P. 3.19.11, 7.14.2–3); that heightened the sense of an entanglement, and tension, between approaches suited to Illyria and to Greece. For P. these events are the crucial turning point as Philip declines into tyranny. Philip could rather be seen, perhaps, as attuning himself with various approaches to politics and power, while he seeks to maintain and expand control in the Illyrian environs of Macedonia and in the complexity of Greece. The Romans and their strife with the Carthaginians add to his problems and chances.[56]

*(g) Asia and Antiochus III*

We can now take a look at structures further east. After the death of Alexander and the ensuing strife, separate monarchical entities formed. By the time of book 8, there is the Antigonid kingdom of Philip V, based in Macedon, and interested in Illyria and in mainland Greece; the Ptolemaic Empire of Ptolemy IV Philopator, based in Egypt but with considerable territory and interest elsewhere; the Seleucid Empire of Antiochus III, with interests and territory spreading from western Asia Minor to Armenia and (shortly after this book) Bactria and beyond; the Attalid kingdom, ruled from 241 by Attalus I, with its centre in Pergamum and

---

[55] For *IG* IX.2.517 see Habicht (2006) 67–73, 134–47, and also Oetjen (2010); translation of the inscription e.g. Austin (2006) 157–9. For Philip's predecessor Antigonus Doson as leader of the allies see P. 2.54.4; cf. Scherberich (2009) 179–81; Le Bohec (1993) 379.

[56] For Messenia, see Luraghi (2008) 256–61; Fröhlich (2008) 203–10; Shipley (2018) 79–82. For Demetrius see Coppola (1993).

interests in Asia Minor more widely. Also involved is Prusias I of Bithynia (not to mention powerful islands and cities like Rhodes and Byzantium). In Asia collaboration, financial and military, is important in the conflicts, so between Antiochus and Attalus in relation to Antiochus' rebellious relative Achaeus (5.107.4), and between Ptolemy IV (and III) and Achaeus in relation to Antiochus.[57]

Antiochus' concerns at this point hardly extend to mainland Greece, and certainly not to Italy or Sicily. The Seleucid Empire was embedded in Asia, and had taken over from the Achaemenid Empire organizational and other features. The enormous Seleucid area was difficult to control simultaneously, especially on both sides of the Taurus Mountains, which separated Asia Minor from Syria. This was particularly hard for Antiochus at the beginning of his reign (223).[58]

Antiochus was in the eastern parts of the empire (cf. P. 5.40.5–6) when he suddenly became king after the killing of his brother Seleucus III. He entrusted Asia Minor to the power of his relative Achaeus, already in the area (4.48.9–11), Media and Persia to Molon and Molon's brother Alexander (5.40.7). The brothers revolted, and hoped that Achaeus would too (5.41.1); but he declined. The revolt apart, Antiochus involved himself in conflict with Ptolemy III and then Ptolemy IV in Coele Syria. He thought, perhaps rightly, that a Ptolemy was urging Achaeus to take over his rule (5.42.7–9); he acted against the Ptolemy rather than Achaeus, still thought to be loyal (cf. 5.42.8).[59]

Achaeus eventually, in 220, declared himself king (4.48.12, 5.57.1–2), with support and perhaps pressure from Ptolemy IV (5.57.2, 67.12; cf. also 4.51.3). Achaeus is seen by P. as having designs on the Seleucid Empire as a whole (5.57.3–8, cf. 4.48.10); but he at least showed his troops a different idea, in which his dominion was limited to west of the Taurus (5.57.5–8). This alone makes sense of their original approval of his kingship (4.48.10; cf. 5.57.6).[60]

---

[57] Chrubasik (2013), esp. 96–7, argues that the independence of the Attalids from the Seleucid Empire was limited, from 216 on. For the Attalids see generally Thonemann (2013). See Kosmin (2014) 122–3 for Seleucid strife with Ptolemaic Egypt.
[58] Coins give some idea of the extent of Antiochus' interests at different points. But coins can seldom be dated precisely; and it is far from clear what level of Seleucid control, involvement or oversight is involved in the minting of a coin with Seleucid types at, say, Aï Khanoum (Afghanistan). Cf. Kritt (2001) 152–62, (2016) 148. For the Seleucid Empire see Ma (1999); SC I 327–469; Capdetrey (2007); Kosmin (2014); Chrubasik (2016).
[59] Antiochus was in Babylon when Seleucus III was killed, according to Jerome, Dan. 3.11.10 (CCL LXXVA 905.995–7, 906.999–1000).
[60] τῶν ὄχλων at 4.48.10 means 'troops'. The conception of a purely western

Antiochus, after ending the brothers' rebellion in 220, proceeded to engage with Ptolemy IV in Syria, where he lost the battle of Raphia in 217. In 216 he finally crosses the Taurus Mountains and wars with Achaeus; he confines him to his capital Sardis, and captures the main city, not the citadel, after a year's siege (7.15.2). Previously, Achaeus had confined Attalus to his capital Pergamum (4.48.11). Attalus had in 226 appropriated the western part of Seleucus III's kingdom (4.48.7) when Seleucus came to the throne in the east (4.48.6). Seleucus with Achaeus had hastened west; Achaeus retook what Attalus had appropriated. Attalus subsequently started taking it back again, through diplomacy and war, while Achaeus was further east and south, in Pisidia (5.77.2–78.6); Achaeus then returned to Sardis and fought Attalus (5.77.1). It was hard to be everywhere at once.

Philip had with Illyria and Greece a related problem to Antiochus'; Rome, with more commanders in a more complex political structure, did not face that situation. In any case, the Seleucid dominions had a very different geographical shape from Italy (with Sicily) and mainland Greece (with Illyria). In those dominions various monarchies were in overlapping competition to form or maintain themselves in the same space. Warfare and politics in Asia have a distinctive texture.[61]

## 13 LANGUAGE

*(a) Attic*

The gradual expansion of Attic Greek to become the main language of literature, administration and to some degree everyday life is of huge importance if we are asking what was spoken where. P. himself probably spoke in non-Attic dialects at Megalopolis and at meetings of the Achaean League, and in Attic for his tuition of Fabius and Scipio (31.23.9, 24.3); he wrote in Attic. This spatially expanded Attic is often called 'the koine'; but the definite article and the separate name are not necessarily helpful to

---

kingship is also needed at 5.57.1–2; there καθόλου πλείω τοῦ δέοντος κινούμενος, 'being generally up to more than he should be', would be ridiculous as part of the second charge if the first is proposing to replace Antiochus. This could be relevant at 5.67.12–13 (Ptolemy wants the deal to involve Achaeus). Cf. also 4.2.6, 5.57.8 τὴν οἰκείαν, 8.20.11. The accommodations with Attalus (5.107.4), and with Xerxes of Armenia (8.23) and Euthydemus of Bactria (11.34.1–10), show a theoretical possibility (for Euthydemus see Kritt (2001) 70–166); but Achaeus' former subordination makes all the difference (note 11.34.2 γεγονέναι γὰρ οὐκ αὐτὸς ἀποστάτης τοῦ βασιλέως, 'he said he had not himself rebelled from the king').

[61] Asia: cf. e.g. Brun, Capdetrey and Fröhlich (2021).

readers of P. There are only limited phonological and morphological differences from the Attic of the fifth and fourth centuries. P. keeps Attic ττ instead of σσ, and usually ρρ instead of ρσ (θαρρέω, ἀναθαρρέω, but εὐθαρσ- as in earlier Attic; see also ταρσός, 4.2n.). γίνομαι and γινώσκω are used, as in Aristotle, rather than γιγν-. Both εἶπον and εἶπα are employed for the first-person aorist; the latter appears in fourth-century Attic comedy (Alex. fr. 2.3 K–A, etc.). This book offers the '-μι verb' forms ἀποδείκνυσι (8.9.2) and συμμιγνύναι (8.25.4); the newer δεικνύω is commoner in P., and is already seen in Xenophon and Demosthenes. Non-interrogative τις can appear first in its clause (8.5.9, 8.6.4), as in Theophrastus (*HP* 8.10.1) and Epicurus (*Hdt.* 76, *Pyth.* 113). ὅς can be used as if it were ὁ (8.35.2 οἷς μέν ... οἷς δέ), as in Aristotle (so *HA* 1.491b12–14). The optative will fade much later, and Ptolemaic papyri already seem limited in their use of it; in P. it is still widely employed.[62]

*(b) Meaning of Words*

Much more challenging to present readers are meanings of words they are not used to. But these are part of the development of Greek already seen in Aristotle or Epicurus. Many instances find examples or at least starting points in the fifth or fourth century. So instances (all from book 8) which have examples before the third century: διαλογισμός 'thought, plan' 18.1; διαφερόντως 'exceptionally, exceedingly' 13.3, 34.10; διότι 'that' with reported statement 3.3; ἐπισημαίνομαι 'approve, applaud' 1.2, 31.4; καταστροφή 'death' 3.1; παράβολος 'daring, bold' 15.1; παρεμβολή 'camp' 7.5 etc.; περίστασις 'circumstance, crisis' 2.9; προσπίπτω 'reach someone's ears' 3.1; προστασία 'standing, rank' 15.1.

With starting points in meanings found before the third century: ἀκάκως 'without suspicion' 29.8 (starting point the earlier 'innocently'); ἀντιφωνέω 'answer in a letter' 16.11 (earlier 'answer in speech'); διάθεσις 'position' of person as such and such 15.9, 'state' of thing 27.1 (earlier 'state, condition' of person); διατροπή 'dismay, turmoil' 5.3 (new noun; earlier διατρέπομαι 'be disturbed'); δυνάμεις 'troops' 20.12 (earlier δύναμις 'army', as at 34.13); ἐπιβολή 'endeavour, undertaking' 17.4, etc. (earlier ἐπιβάλλομαι 'undertake'); οἱ περί X = X, see 7.1, 16.11nn. etc. (earlier

---

[62] For the optative see 5.3, 18.8, 25.3, 26.5nn., and Langslow (2012) 87–9. He and Foucault (1972) and Dubuisson (1985) give larger accounts of P.'s language. On 'the koine' cf. e.g. Browning (1969) 27–58; Rodríguez Adrados (2005) 176–225; Bortone (2010) 171–5. Mayser (1934–70) is a principal work of reference. Although Attic forms are normal in Hellenistic historiography, Ionic dialect is used in the account of the siege of Rhodes in 305–304 BC, P. Berol. 11632.

'those in attendance on, in a group with'); προκοπή 'progress' 15.6 (new noun; earlier προκόπτω 'progress'); πρόληψις 'thought in advance' 27.1 (earlier 'conception'). Other uses, with or without an earlier point of departure: λοιπόν 'hence' 38b.2, 11.2; πλήν 'but' 3.3 etc.; τὸ συνέχον 'the crucial matter' 2.3.

In P. the use of 'support verbs' like ποιέομαι + verbal noun instead of a simple verb is considerably extended in frequency. So: 4.1 ἐποιεῖτο τὸν ἐπίπλουν; 11.5 ποιήσασθαι μετάβασιν; 28.4 ποιεῖσθαι τὴν πορείαν; 34.11 εἴληφει συντέλειαν. Often a predicative adjective accompanies the noun; see 16.6n.[63]

*(c) Period and Other Historians*

Inscriptions and documentary papyri make it clear that P. writes, to put it broadly, in the language of his own time. It would scarcely have occurred to him to do otherwise, as is indicated by the close likeness of his (and the documents') language to that of Diodorus, Dionysius and fragmentary Hellenistic historians. Linguistic Atticism – recurrence to the Attic of the fifth and fourth centuries – had not yet been devised. Even Josephus, Plutarch and Appian are in language much closer to P. than our notions of Atticism might suggest.[64]

One might sometimes wonder, here and there, if we can see P. embracing the language of his time to a still further degree than Diodorus and Dionysius. Occasionally we find a word or usage, before Middle and Late Byzantine literature, only in P. and documents, so πραξικοπέω 'take through treachery, outwit' (9.3; cf. e.g. *I.Pessinous* 1–2.7 (163 BC)) or συντίθημι of giving a messenger a letter (8.17.4; cf. e.g. *PSI* V 524.3–4 (241/0 BC) τὴν ἐπιστολὴν | συντόμως συνθέντες Προθύμωι, LSJ A III.1). Or a word is found in P. and documents and hardly in other pagan writers, so ἐπαύριον, as at 8.13.6 εἰς τὴν ἐπαύριον 'on the next day'. P. uses ἐπαύριον 27 times, in the variations εἰς τὴν ἐπαύριον and τῆι ἐπαύριον. τῆι ἐπαύριον is found in the *Life of Aesop*, the Septuagint, the New Testament and later Christian writers; ἐπαύριον appears in papyri, the earliest P. Lille I 15.2 (242–241 BC) τῆι δ' ἐπαύριον ἡμέραι.

---

[63] Cf. Jiménez López (2016); Fendel (2025).
[64] New inscriptions can add to the evidence for P. using current words; see notably Adak and Thonemann (2022) 24, 33, 40, 48 etc. For particular areas of connection see Mari and Thornton (2013). P., Diodorus and Dionysius occasionally share features which do not seem to be part of the ordinary language, so 8.30.4 κτείνειν instead of ἀποκτείνειν, as e.g. DS 15.91, DH *AR* 1.16.4, P. Berol. 11632.46 (historiography).

## 13 LANGUAGE

It is commoner for words and forms to appear in P., Diodorus, Dionysius and documents but with striking differences of frequency between P. and the other two writers. For an intriguing case take some words and forms for 'immediately'. P., like inscriptions and papyri on present information, greatly prefers εὐθέως (205 times) to εὐθύς (13). Diodorus and Dionysius, like prose literature in general, greatly prefer εὐθύς (181 and 120 times) to εὐθέως (21, 7). On the other hand, P. markedly prefers εὐθέως to παραχρῆμα (100), and Diodorus and Dionysius markedly prefer εὐθύς to παραχρῆμα (88, 24); inscriptions and papyri markedly prefer παραχρῆμα to either. P. seems closer to the documents; but it will be seen that interpretation is not straightforward.[65]

In any case, P. is isolated chronologically: we have only fragments of historiography from the third and second centuries; Diodorus' work is finished c.30 BC. So we cannot properly see P. in the context of contemporary historians. A salutary example is ἀκμήν 'still', which P. employs 54 times, and the medical writer Soranus (i–ii AD), in the form we have his main work, 18 (in 219 pages). It comes, for example, in Philodemus and the New Testament, and in inscriptions, so *I.Egypte prose* 49.34 (5 BC). Diodorus and Dionysius do not employ it. But it is found in a papyrus fragment of Sosylus (*FGrHist* 176 F1.31; late iii BC). Any wider discussion of these questions would need more investigation of Diodorus and Dionysius. A salient example is ἰδιοπραγεῖν, which comes once in P. (8.26.9); it comes 7 times in Diodorus, all in book 18 on the Diadochi.[66]

More important, from a literary point of view, is that P. organizes the words that contemporary language gives him into expressive and forceful structures.

---

[65] Some examples of words much commoner in P. than DS and DH: διαπιστέω '(thoroughly) distrust' (8.17.2, 21.9): P. 26 times, DS once, DH never. The word has a solid pedigree in Dem. 19.324, then Arist. 1, Philo 1, Jos. 1, Plut. 1, and PSI IV 377. 9 (250/49 BC). διάληψις 'view' (main sense; 8.25.6): P. 69 times, DS 4, DH never, Arist. 6, Theophr. 2, Epicur. 6, Philod. 5, Gal. 5, inscriptions e.g. Welles, *RC* 31.17–18 (Magnesia on Maeander, c.205 BC). ἐπὶ ποσόν 'for a bit' (8.11.5), P. 27 times, DS 3, DH never, Hipp. *Epid.* 7.1.3, Chrys. 1 (direct quotation), Philod. 3, Ap. Cit. 4, Strabo 2, Philo 2, Epict. 1, Hero 3 (all proem), Diosc. 5, Soran. 1, Luc. 1, Gal. 5, Ath. 2, Marc. Aur. 1, Sext. 3, PSI x 1160.1 (i BC). ἀναζυγή 'setting off, marching' (8.26.3): P. 23 times, DS 1, DH never, Septuag. 3 (2 2 *Macc.*), Jos. 1, Plut. 5, P. Hamb. 91 *recto* 8 (Heracleopolis, 167 BC).

[66] Philod. 1, Strabo 1, Gal. 2; not in documents. Cf. J. Hornblower (1981) 168–9. For ἀκμήν 'still' see earlier Xen. *Anab.* 4.3.26, and Crat. fr. 408 K-A and Men. fr. 504 K-A with Kassel and Austin's notes.

## 14 TRANSMISSION AND RECEPTION

The complicated transmission of P. is best considered as part of the involved and absorbing story of his reception in the ancient, medieval and early modern world. Different aspects of this many-sided writer, pragmatic, literary, historical, appeal to different people and affect what is preserved; different approaches are taken to him. Only some elements in the story and the transmission will be touched on here. The emphasis will be particularly on things relevant to book 8.[67]

### (a) Reception: Cicero and Livy

Cicero shows us P. held in high regard as a reliable source (*Off.* 3.113 *bonus auctor imprimis*), as assiduous in chronological research (*Rep.* 2.27, Scipio speaking) and as deeply versed in constitutions and politics (*res ciuiles*, *Rep.* 1.34, together with Panaetius; Scipio speaking). Livy likewise describes him as 'no mean authority' (*haud quaquam spernendus auctor*, 30.45.5; cf. 33.10.10). It is part of Livy's stance as a Roman historian that explicitly he engages more with his Roman predecessors, most often antagonistically. But P. is his primary source in many parts of his history, including parts of books 21–30. The most familiar example is Hannibal's crossing of the Alps in Livy 21.29.7–38.9; but the episodes of Syracuse and Tarentum from P. book 8 well demonstrate Livy's closeness to P.'s words, and the skill and resourcefulness with which he adapts them into Latin. He turns them from one potent style into another. At 24.34.8 (after *uariae magnitudinis*) he writes of Archimedes *in eas quae procul erant naues saxa ingenti pondere emittebat; propiores leuioribus eoque magis crebris petebat telis* 'he hurled heavy rocks against the ships at a distance; the nearer ships he attacked with lighter and hence more frequent missiles'. The brief sentence, with one astute insertion (*eoque magis crebris*), is trenchantly and elegantly organized into short units. The original forms part of an elaborate structure (P. 8.5.1–4) which displays the physical and intellectual processes with more searching precision.[68]

---

[67] Much is excluded, for example Diodorus' and Appian's use of P.
[68] On Livy's use of P., see Levene (2010) 126–63; Hutchinson (2013) 166–70 (23–4 on Livy preferring fights with Romans); Baron (2018), esp. 203–4; S. P. Oakley (2018), esp. 157 n. 3, (2019); Briscoe and Hornblower (2020) 10; cf. Briscoe (1978) 268, against Tränkle (1977). Livy boldly takes P. on over the chronology of Scipio's death at 39.52.1–6; see Walbank (1957–79) III 235–8; Briscoe (2008) 395–6. Beyond Cicero and Livy, Brutus writes an epitome of P. while on campaign, Plut. *Brut.* 4.8.

## (b) Reception: Dionysius and Strabo

Dionysius, writing like Livy in the principate of Augustus, shows a quite different approach towards P. He assails P., and Hellenistic historians in general, for indifference to beauty in arranging words: hence no one can bear to read them to the end (*Comp.* 4.14–15). Perhaps already the earlier books of P. were more read than the later. The attack is different from, but related to, Dionysius' attack on the recent Asian decadence in oratory which had until lately superseded the respectable Attic Muse (*Vet. Or.* 1.2–2.2). He also harangues P. and others for sketchiness and inadequate research on the period treated in his own *Antiquitates* (*AR* 1.6.1, 1.7.1), and singles P. out for chronological inadequacy (1.74.1). The significance of P. is indicated, none the less, by Dionysius' choice of P.'s starting year of 264 as his point to stop (Phot. *Bibl.* 83.64b–65a). P.'s own choice of 264 indicates the significance of Timaeus, from whom he follows on; but P. treats Timaeus to extended castigation, as Dionysius does not treat P. For Strabo, P. is an important and respected predecessor, sometimes in the wrong (so 2.4.2–3 (I 254.35–258.26 Radt)), but an ἀνὴρ φιλόσοφος (1.1.1 (I 2.2–3bis Radt)).[69]

## (c) Transmission and Reception: Papyri

Papyri suggest that P. was read at least as much as other historians later than Herodotus (54 papyri), Thucydides (100) and Xenophon (7 of *Hellenica*). The number of P.'s papyri has recently risen from one to four, so that one might wonder if there are more to come (P. Berol. inv. 21129 fr. b (i BC), P. Oxy. LXXXII 5300 (i AD), LXXXI 5267 (ii AD), P. Berol. inv. 9570 + P. Ryl. I 60 (ii–iii AD)). Of Dionysius' *Antiquitates* so far there are two (one a summary), of Appian one, of Dio Cassius one. There are five of Plutarch's *Lives*. In text, P.'s papyri confirm that the medieval extracts are full of corruptions. The papyrus of book 8 may itself come from a collection of extracts (21.11n.). P. Oxy. LXXI 4808 (papyrus i–ii AD), a work, or notes, with brief accounts of Hellenistic historians, shows interest in this period of historiography. P. is said to write with love for truth (φιλα[λήθως, col. ii.27), and called 'extremely knowledgeable, especially in political matters' (πολυμ[αθέστε]ρος [most likely a superlative] ... καὶ μάλισ[τα ἐν τοῖς] πολειτικοῖς, col. ii.28–31). This shares a tradition or source with Cic.

---

[69] For hostility cf. Scylax's Ἀντιγραφή to P.'s history (*FGrHist* 709 T1). This Scylax's date is unknown; the *Suda* has characteristically blended one Scylax with another.

*Rep.* 1.34 (Panaetius and P.) 'most deeply versed in political matters' (*uel peritissimis rerum ciuilium*).⁷⁰

*(d) Reception: Plutarch*

Plutarch naturally uses P. as a source, as he sometimes acknowledges. In his account of the siege of Syracuse, he bases himself on P., but does not mention him. He writes up Archimedes' machines to make the marvels still more graphic, while sacrificing P.'s precision on the mechanisms. A ship raised from the sea and twisting around hither and thither was a 'terrifying spectacle', θέαμα φρικῶδες (*Marc.* 15.4; cf. P. 8.6.3). P. talks of stones no less than 10 talents in weight (8.5.9); Plutarch splits them up to evoke the moment, with first one of 10 talents, then another, then a third, falling μεγάλωι κτύπωι τε καὶ κλύδωνι 'with a mighty noise and surge' (*Marc.* 15.6). Plutarch is much interested in P.'s relationship with the Romans, and especially with Scipio (so *Praec. ger. reip.* 814c–d; *Quaest. conv.* 4 pr. 659e–f). Plutarch shares this interest with others; but it suits the particular concerns he shows in the *Lives* and elsewhere.⁷¹

*(e) Transmission and Reception: Athenaeus and Stephanus*

Athenaeus often refers to P., with book number, and gives direct quotations. He refers to Phylarchus even more frequently (43 times as against 36): P. is not predominating over other Hellenistic historians, at least for Athenaeus' interests in dining and pleasure.⁷²

Stephanus of Byzantium in the sixth century produces a lexicon of names for places and their inhabitants; we have, for the most part, an 'epitome'. P.'s wide and specific geographical concerns mean that Stephanus draws on P. extensively. There are 3 references to book 8. It should be observed that of 92 quotations from known books, 89 are from books 1–20 (out of 40): the later books may already have been less current or less read.⁷³

---

⁷⁰ Cf. Wilcken (1901) 392–5. For P. Berol. inv. 21129 fr. b see Luiselli (2016), who identified the scrap as P. book 8; an image can be found at https://berl-pap.smb.museum/record/?result=1&Alle=21129&lang=en. See also Ioannidou (1996) 39–40 and Taf. 14. On papyri of Plutarch, see Schmidt (2019).
⁷¹ For Plutarch and P. cf. Almagor (2020).
⁷² For Athenaeus' quotations of P., Duris and Phylarchus, see Hau (2021).
⁷³ In fact, there are no quotes from book 17 or 19, which are also missing in the later excerpted tradition (9 quotes from 16, 3 from 18, 2 from 20); but there are none from books 14 or 15 either, and there is one from book 37, later lost (μ 222). Billerbeck and Neumann-Hartmann (2021) 60 take it that Stephanus is using P. directly, not an intermediary source.

*(f) Transmission and Reception: Excerpta Antiqua*

As will be seen, the text of most of P. is likely to have been extant in the tenth century. Books 1–5 are still extant now, complete. Probably in the ninth or tenth century, and certainly by the early eleventh, an abridged version of books 1–18 was produced. This version, usually known as the *Excerpta Antiqua*, is our biggest source for book 8 (35–6, 1–2, 4–7, 12, 13–14, 15–21, 24–34). The version presented some parts of the complete text; it did not, save for the introductory sentence of each part, purposefully change the extract itself. This can be seen from the abridgement of books 1–5, preserved only in the oldest MS of the *Excerpta Antiqua*, F (x–xi AD). Copying errors apart, the abridgement largely agrees with MSS of the complete text. The two main methods for a modern student to get a dissertation down to the word count are to omit paragraphs, or slim down numerous individual sentences; the first is what we see in the *Excerpta Antiqua*, even if they are sometimes called 'epitome(s)' (cf. F fol. 1ʳ, fourteenth century, τῆς Πολυβίου ἐπιτομῆς λόγος πρῶτος; κατ' ἐπιτομήν in D and G; ἐπιτομή of individual items in the margin of D). An abridged version was not necessarily designed to replace the original: Strabo survived entire alongside his abridgement, and books 1–5 of P. continued to circulate. It was rather the abridgement of books 1–5 that disappeared, after our first manuscript F: evidently the abridgement came to be valued as a primary source for books 6–18 when the complete books were lost.[74]

The abridgement of 1–5 shows us the selection in action: the varied interests, the liking for colourful material, the willingness to include substantial chunks of gripping narrative but to ditch less fun preliminaries. In the case of book 8, other material shows that on the siege of Syracuse the *Excerpta Antiqua* go straight for the enticing siege machinery; they omit the strategic and political preliminaries (8.3; Livy 24.21.1–33.8, probably based on P.). In the *Excerpta*, the episode of Achaeus forcefully resumes the moral and anecdotal section 8.35–6, their first item in book 8.

---

[74] See below for details on F, D and G. On the MSS of P., see J. M. Moore (1965) and (1971). https://pinakes.irht.cnrs.fr/ gives an up-to-date list, with invaluable links and bibliography. Apart from MSS of the *Suda*, which have only been consulted occasionally, the relevant MSS have all been collated from images for the present edition, including V and P, of *De obsidione toleranda*, A, C and E of Athenaeus, and R, Q and P (but not the derivative N) of Stephanus. In presenting readings, the apparatus largely ignores incorrect or (from our perspective) missing accents in F and other early MSS, confusion of ο and ω, etc., and gives proper names upper case. Errors common to all MSS are usually noted; errors and variants only found in some are noted where significant or interesting. Quotes from the *Suda* etc. are usually mentioned at the start of the relevant section.

In them, 8.12 on Aratus takes up the encounter of Philip and Aratus in 7.11; the digression on Theopompus and Philip II (8.8–11) is left out.[75]

In book 8, the independent manuscripts for the *Excerpta Antiqua* are **F** (Vat. Urb. gr. 102, late x to very early xi), **D** (Munich, Cod. graec. 388, xiv?) and **G** (Laur. Plut. 69.9, AD 1435). D preceded the *Excerpta* from books 1–18 not, like F, with the *Excerpta* from 1–5 but with 1–5 complete; G has been combined in one volume with an earlier MS of 1–5. The MSS can be seen online: F https://digi.vatlib.it/view/MSS_Urb.gr.102; D www.digitale-sammlungen.de/en/search?query=%28cgm+388%29; G http://mss.bmlonline.it/?search=Plut.69.9. D and G are closely related. G was owned by the famous fifteenth-century scholar Poliziano (Politian, 1454–94), and illustrates Polybius establishing himself in Italy.[76]

*(g) Transmission and Reception: Excerpta Constantiniana*

Large concerns with desirable action were displayed by the emperor Constantine VII Porphyrogenitus (reigned 913–59, sole reign from 945). He organized an extensive series of extracts from historians, arranged by theme; only some parts have survived. A nearly complete text of P. was probably still available to the excerptors.

For our purposes, the most important set is *De uirtutibus et uitiis* (περὶ ἀρετῆς καὶ κακίας), in which the authors most used are Polybius and Cassius Dio. The only extant MS is **P**, Turonensis 980 (x). It can be seen online at https://arca.irht.cnrs.fr/ark:/63955/md021c18fhog. The extracts from book 8 are on fol. 110ʳ–113ʳ, cf. *Exc. Const.* II.2.107–13. They alone give us 22.1 (Cavarus), 23 (Antiochus and Xerxes) and the chapters on Theopompus and the friends of Philip II (8–11), which the *Excerpta Antiqua* did not include; P and FDG overlap for 12.1–7. The set *De sententiis* is preserved only by **M**, Vat. gr. 73 (x). For book 8 see *Exc. Const.* IV 134. M alone gives us the beginning of the passage on trickery by one's enemies (35.1), a short passage on the history of Tarentum (24.1) and some random wisdom (24.2). The *Excerpta Constantiniana* again do not seek to alter the main text of their passages; but the opening sentences, starting with ὅτι, can be summaries which at most borrow phrases from P.

---

[75] F², which writes the titles for excerpts in the margins, also writes the excerpts from book 14; perhaps eleventh century, cf. Vat. Barb. gr. 276 (https://digi.vatlib.it/view/MSS_Barb.gr.276).

[76] J. M. Moore (1965) 16 dates D to the fourteenth century, rather than late fifteenth (Pinakes) or fifteenth to sixteenth (www.digitale-sammlungen.de/en/details/bsb00113933); fourteenth looks plausible. Cf. Turyn (1972) pl. 148 (Ferrara II, 188, AD 1334), (1964) tab. 90 (Vat. gr. 509, AD 1313).

The excerpts will sometimes also omit parts of passages, or make substantial cuts to join passages together.[77]

*(h) Transmission and Reception: Siege Literature*

One angle from which P. attracted interest was his writing on sieges. The interest is literary in part, but also practical: ancient siegecraft was of much importance to Byzantium in confronting its enemies. One MS, **T**, Paris Suppl. gr. 607 (late x), offers in one part a series of extracts from different authors on sieges, including, on fol. 98ʳ–100ᵛ, ἐκ τῶν Πολυβίου Συρακουσῶν πολιορκία. It can be seen online at https://gallica.bnf.fr/ ark:/12148/btv1b8593585j/f205.item. It makes a single narrative out of P. on Syracuse in two separate years. Two MSS, **V** and **P₁**, Vat. gr. 1164 (late x or early xi) and Vat. Barb. gr. 276 (early xi), present a practical work on siegecraft, *De obsidione toleranda*, which includes narrative excerpts, without an indication of sources: chh. 58–9 on the later year at Syracuse, 200–41 on the earlier (the beginning of 58 connects the events). V is online at https://digi.vatlib.it/view/MSS_Vat.gr.1164, P₁ at https://digi.vatlib.it/ view/MSS_Barb.gr.276. The three MSS have omissions and compressions, especially at beginnings and ends. The Polybian material for treatise (VP₁) and collection (T) may derive from the *Excerpta Constantiniana*, as fits with citations by the *Suda* in chh. 3 and 37 (see below). Even if it so derives, extracts from extracts from P. are being deployed to suit particular interests and literary structures.[78]

*(i) Transmission and Reception: Suda*

Lastly, the *Suda* should be mentioned. This large encyclopaedia-cum-dictionary from the tenth century is especially keen to include material from P.; perhaps he is seen as a prestigious author. Some of the *Suda*'s many quotations from P. omit the author's name; these are most commonly to illustrate the use of a word. The *Suda* appears to take its material from the *Excerpta Constantiniana*, if we can extrapolate to lost parts of the

---

[77] Cf. P. Oxy. LXXXI 5267.1–4, which suggests that something had been left out in 28.2.5–7; and see Németh (2022) on the new fragment. For the *Excerpta Constantiniana*, see Delacenserie and Van Nuffelen (2017), esp. Agati *et al.* (2017), and Németh (2018). M is a palimpsest: see Mercati and De' Cavalieri (1923) 68–70, 67–78, Németh (2015). The original page numbers have to be reconstructed; but it is clear that M, like P, followed the order of P.'s text.

[78] J. M. Moore (1965) 134–6 does not seem to be aware of the *De obsidione*. On practicality see e.g. Sullivan (2000) vii.

*Excerpta Constantiniana* from extant parts which the *Suda* clearly uses. It often alters or abbreviates.[79]

*(j) Transmission: Shape*

One may doubt whether the *Excerpta Antiqua* and *Constantiniana* can be blamed for the disappearance of the almost complete text of P. For 1–5 the complete version was clearly preferred to the excerpted, which falls from use. It looks broadly as though earlier books of P. had a better chance of survival than later. The general shape of P.'s preservation is similar to that of, say, Dionysius' *Antiquitates Romanae* and Appian's *Roman History*. Of those some books are preserved complete; there are substantial excerpts from others. In the case of Dionysius, the first ten of twenty books survive entire; most of book 11 survives, but only in MSS of the fifteenth and sixteenth centuries, not in A (x) and B (x–xi). Photius in the ninth century evidently had the two works complete (*Bibl.* 57 and 83); this is especially clear of Appian. Only the earlier books of Appian in Photius' list are used by Constantine's excerptors.[80]

*(k) Reception: Machiavelli*

MSS of books 1–5 multiply in the fifteenth century, and, to a lesser extent, of *Excerpta Antiqua*; MSS of *Excerpta Antiqua* and, to a lesser extent, *Excerpta Constantiniana* multiply in the sixteenth. P. was an author of much significance for political thinkers in the Renaissance. The complete books entered consciousness in Italy earlier than the excerpts. First came Leonardo Bruni, who produced his own version of wars from P. book 1 and the early part of book 2 (*c*.1418–19); books 1–5 were translated into Latin by Niccolò Perotti (1454). Books 1–5 were first printed in Greek in 1530; books 6–18 were first printed in Greek in 1549 (some of book 6 had appeared in 1529).

---

[79] For the *Suda* see De Boor (1912 and 1914–19), esp. (1914–19) 76–8 for citations from book 8; Németh (2018) 238–55.

[80] Constantine's excerptors do not use Appian's *Civil Wars* (13th–17th in Photius' list), though these survive in MSS; there are other complications to the story of Appian. The gap in MSS of P. between the early eleventh century and the fourteenth, and gaps in other historians, suggest that changes in readers' tastes as well as destruction in 1204 could be relevant to the loss of much P. So on the twelfth century and its scholarship see Kaldellis (2009).

Machiavelli (1469–1527) has knowledge of the complete books: so the Mercenary War from book 1 comes in *Il Principe* 12.14 (1513?), *Discorsi sopra la prima deca di Tito Livio* 3.32.5–9 (1519?) and *Dell'arte della guerra* 1.55 (published 1521). Of much greater importance to him is the non-narrative book 6, which he knows about at least by the time of *Discorsi* 1.2.2–36. It engages him both in its account of constitutions and in its depiction of the Roman army (so *Dell'arte della guerra* 6.113–16). He did not know Greek, or have a published translation of book 6; but P., book 6 included, was being discussed in Florence, and he may have seen an unpublished rendering. It is disputed how central P. is to his dramatically new political theorizing; on some accounts P. is fundamental. Machiavelli never names him. Knowledge of book 6 also seems to spread to France early in the sixteenth century. P. appears to be exciting attention, but on a relatively narrow basis.[81]

*(l) Reception: Scholarship*

Only a word can be offered here on P.'s reception in scholarship. Important stages are Casaubon's edition (1609), with ardent preface, Reiske's textual notes (vol. IV of *Animadversiones in auctores Graecos*, 1757–66), Schweighaeuser's edition (1789–95), with substantial commentary. Hultsch and Büttner-Wobst both produced editions (1867–72 (Hultsch first edn), 1882–1904); Büttner-Wobst's, still the standard edition, has no apparatus for book 8. In the later nineteenth and early twentieth centuries, P. was highly regarded as a historical source; but a Greek historian later than the fourth century could not receive the close and loving exegesis of a detailed commentary – such as Herodotus, Thucydides and Livy received. The great commentary of Walbank (1957–79) explicitly concentrates on history rather than P.'s words. There have since been bilingual editions with valuable brief notes; Weil's Budé of 7–9 (1982) has a useful apparatus. In recent years, work on P. has flourished, and has treated his ideas, his approach to history, his narrative techniques. There perhaps

---

[81] Machiavelli's knowledge of P. and his use of it: Marchand (2001) II.1, xxix–xxx; Sciacca (2005) 53–64; Nederman (2016). References to Machiavelli's work are as in Marchand (2001). Marc. gr. VII.4 (B2 + H11), which includes the *Excerpta Antiqua* from book 6, was written in Florence (fol. 245ᵛ) in the late fifteenth century. In general for P. in the early modern period: Momigliano (1980) 103–23, 125–41; Edelstein (2022) (it is argued that the political term 'revolution' comes from translations of P.). For circulation and spread into France, Nederman (2016) 467–9, 472–3. *Princ*. 17.16–18 could be from Livy 28.12.2–5 rather than P. 11.19.3–4; for the start of *Disc*. 1.2 see also Cic. *Inv*. 1.2.

remains room for commentaries which burrow deeper into P.'s words and sentences, and which join this discussion with history and archaeology in the light of more recent work. The hope would be to bring P.'s many sides together and to give some sense of this extraordinary author and the excitement of reading him.[82]

---

[82] On Casaubon and P. see Parenty (2009) 74–7, 183–205. It sounds as if his *Commentarii* had got nearer printing than Parenty (2009) 75 suggests; cf., besides the preface, p. 1026 of the edition. Casaubon detests *ille Etruscus*, i.e. Machiavelli (preface, p. [20]). P. as source: see e.g. Mommsen (1906) [1885] 42 on Zama, Wilamowitz (1903) 28 on Cannae. Weissenborn's introduction to his edition of Livy sees P. as like a modern historian in his research, but not much of a writer (edn 8, 1 23, 33–4; La-Roche (1857) 55–63 is somewhat more sympathetic). A volume on and around Walbank: Gibson and Harrison (2013). Besides Budé, see esp. Loeb and BUR; for book 8 Paton (2011), Musti, Mari and Thornton (2002). Recent work on P. includes, for ideas, e.g. Eckstein (1995); Champion (2004); Maier (2012); Hau (2016), esp. chh. 1 and 3; for historiography: Candau (2003); Clarke (2003); Marincola (2013); Longley (2014); Schorn (2014); Krewet (2017); for narratology: Rood (2007, 2012); Miltsios (2013); Maier (2016); Wiater (2016); Pitcher (2018).

# SIGLA, ABBREVIATIONS AND ORDER OF CHAPTERS

## 1 PAPYRUS

Π   P. Berol. inv. 21129 fr. b (i BC)

## 2 MEDIEVAL MANUSCRIPTS

### Excerpta Antiqua

D   Monacensis gr. 388 (xiv?)
F   Vaticanus Urbinas gr. 102 (late x to very early xi)
G   Laurentianus Plut. 69.9 (AD 1435)

### Excerpta Constantiniana

M   Vaticanus gr. 73, undertext (x)
P   Turonensis 980 (x)

### Collection on Sieges

T   Parisinus Suppl. gr. 607 (late x)

### Anonymous, De obsidione toleranda

$P_1$   Vaticanus Barberianus gr. 276 (early xi)
V   Vaticanus gr. 1164 (late x or early xi)

### Athenaeus

A   Marcianus gr. 447 (late ix)
C   Parisinus Suppl. gr. 841 (xvi) (epitome)
E   Laurentianus Plut. 60.2 (xv) (epitome)

### Stephanus of Byzantium

P   Vaticanus Palatinus gr. 57 (before AD 1492)
Q   Vaticanus Palatinus gr. 253 (before AD 1485)
R   Rehdigeranus 47 (c.AD 1500)

*Suda*

F   Laurentianus 55.1 (AD 1422)
M   Marcianus gr. 448 (xiii)

## ABBREVIATIONS

$F^1$   first hand in F
$F^{mg}$ F in the margin
$F^{ac}$ F before correction
$F^{pc}$ F after correction
$F^{sl}$ F above the line
fol. $102^r$ folium 102, recto
fol. $102^v$ folium 102, verso

Smaller type is used when there is at least reason to doubt that the text is straight P.

## ORDER OF CHAPTERS

38b, 35–6, 3a, 1–21, 24–34, 37, 22–3

# POLYBIUS: BOOK 8

# ΠΟΛΥΒΙΟΥ Η

**38b.1** Ἄγκαρα, πόλις Ἰταλίας, ὡς Ἄντια, Ἄδρια. τὸ ἐθνικὸν Ἀγκαράτης, ὡς Πολύβιος η̄.

**38b.2** λοιπὸν ταῖς ἀδήλοις ἐλπίσι προσανέχων, διὰ τὸ πρόδηλον τῆς τιμωρίας πᾶν ἔκρινεν ὑπομένειν.

**35.1** ὅτι Τιβέριος ὁ Ῥωμαίων στρατηγὸς δόλωι ἐνεδρευθεὶς καὶ γενναίως ὑποστὰς σὺν τοῖς περὶ αὑτὸν τὸν βίον κατέστρεψεν. περὶ δὲ τῶν τοιούτων περιπετειῶν, πότερα χρὴ τοῖς πάσχουσιν ἐπιτιμᾶν ἢ συγγνώμην ἔχειν, καθόλου μὲν οὐκ ἀσφαλὲς ἀποφήνασθαι, διὰ τὸ καὶ πλείους τὰ κατὰ λόγον πάντα πράξαντας ὅμως ὑποχειρίους γεγονέναι τοῖς ἑτοίμως τὰ παρ' ἀνθρώποις ὡρισμένα δίκαια παραβαίνουσιν· **2** οὐ μὴν οὐδ' αὐτόθεν ἀποστατέον τῆς ἀποφάσεως ἀργῶς, ἀλλὰ βλέποντα πρὸς τοὺς καιροὺς καὶ τὰς περιστάσεις οἷς μὲν ἐπιτιμητέον τῶν ἡγεμόνων, οἷς δὲ συγγνώμην δοτέον. ἔσται δὲ τὸ λεγόμενον δῆλον ἐκ τούτων. **3** Ἀρχίδαμος ὁ τῶν Λακεδαιμονίων βασιλεύς, ὑπιδόμενος τὴν Κλεομένους φιλαρχίαν, ἔφυγεν ἐκ τῆς Σπάρτης· μετ' οὐ πολὺ δὲ πάλιν πεισθεὶς ἐνεχείρισεν αὑτὸν τῶι προειρημένωι. **4** τοιγαροῦν ἅμα τῆς ἀρχῆς καὶ τοῦ βίου στερηθείς, οὐδ' ἀπολογίαν αὑτῶι κατέλιπε πρὸς τοὺς ἐπιγινομένους· **5** τῆς γὰρ ὑποθέσεως τῆς αὐτῆς μενούσης, τῆς δὲ Κλεομένους φιλαρχίας καὶ δυναστείας ἐπηυξημένης, ὁ τούτοις ἐγχειρίσας αὑτὸν οὓς φυγὼν πρότερον ἔτυχε παραδόξως τῆς σωτηρίας πῶς οὐκ εὐλόγως ἔμελλε τοῖς προειρημένοις ἐγκυρήσειν; **6** καὶ μὴν Πελοπίδας ὁ Θηβαῖος, εἰδὼς τὴν Ἀλεξάνδρου τοῦ τυράννου παρανομίαν καὶ σαφῶς γινώσκων ὅτι πᾶς τύραννος πολεμιωτάτους αὑτῶι νομίζει τοὺς τῆς ἐλευθερίας προεστῶτας, αὐτὸς οὐ μόνον τῆς Θηβαίων ἀλλὰ καὶ τῆς τῶν Ἑλλήνων δημοκρατίας ἔπειθεν Ἐπαμινώνδαν προεστάναι, **7** καὶ <πρότερον> παρὼν εἰς Θετταλίαν πολέμιος ἐπὶ καταλύσει τῆς Ἀλεξάνδρου μοναρχίας, πρεσβεύειν πρὸς τοῦτον ὑπέμεινε †δεύτερον†. **8** τοιγαροῦν γενόμενος ὑποχείριος τοῖς ἐχθροῖς ἔβλαψε μὲν Θηβαίους μεγάλα, κατέλυσε δὲ τὴν αὑτῶι προγεγενημένην δόξαν, εἰκῆι καὶ ἀκρίτως πιστεύσας οἷς ἥκιστ' ἐχρῆν. **9** παραπλήσια δὲ τούτοις καὶ Γνάϊος ὁ Ῥωμαίων στρατηγὸς ἔπαθε κατὰ τὸν Σικελικὸν πόλεμον, ἀλόγως αὑτὸν ἐγχειρίσας τοῖς πολεμίοις· ὁμοίως δὲ καὶ πλείους ἕτεροι.

[38b.1] Steph. Byz. α 32 Billerbeck    Ἀγκαρία ... Ἀντία, Ἀδρία ... Ἀγκαριάτης Meineke    τὸ ἐθνικὸν Ἀγκαράτης P²: της (post spatium uacuum) RQ: om. P¹ (post spatium uacuum et ',')
[38b.2] M, aut ex septimo aut ex octauo libro
[35] 35.1 ὅτι ... ἔχειν κα M; 35.1 περὶ – 36.9 FDG, post Πολυβίου τοῦ η̄ λόγου (F), Πολυβίου ἐκ τῶν Ἱστοριῶν ὀγδόου λόγου κατ' ἐπιτομήν (G; breuius D)    **1** δόλωι: λόχωι legit Heyse, perperam    **5** καὶ δυναστείας om. DG: δυναστείας D$^{mg}$G$^{mg}$, G$^{mg}$ quidem tamquam δ. pro φιλαρχίας legendum sit    **6** εἰδὼς Ursinus: εἶπὼν FDG    **7** <πρότερον> Hutchinson    ὑπέμεινεν ὕστερον Hutchinson: ὑπέμεινε δεύτερος <γενομενος> Naber (melius <αὐτός>) scripsisset)    **8** αὑτῶν DG
**9** Γνάϊος Casaubon: Γάϊος FDG

**36.1** διὸ καὶ τοῖς μὲν ἀσκέπτως ἑαυτοὺς ἐγχειρίζουσι τοῖς ὑπεναντίοις ἐπιτιμητέον, τοῖς δὲ τὴν ἐνδεχομένην πρόνοιαν ποιουμένοις οὐκ ἐγκλητέον· **2** τὸ μὲν γὰρ μηδενὶ πιστεύειν εἰς τέλος ἄπρακτον, τὸ δὲ λαβόντα τὰς ἐνδεχομένας πίστεις πράττειν τὸ κατὰ λόγον ἀνεπιτίμητον. **3** εἰσὶ δ' ἐνδεχόμεναι πίστεις ὅρκοι, τέκνα, γυναῖκες, <καί>, τὸ μέγιστον, ὁ προγεγονὼς βίος. **4** ἧι καὶ τὸ διὰ τῶν τοιούτων ἀλογηθῆναι καὶ περιπεσεῖν οὐ τῶν πασχόντων ἀλλὰ τῶν πραξάντων ἐστὶν ἔγκλημα. **5** διὸ καὶ μάλιστα μὲν τοιαύτας ζητεῖν πίστεις <δεῖ> δι' ὧν ὁ πιστευθεὶς οὐ δυνήσεται τὴν πίστιν ἀθετεῖν. **6** ἐπεὶ δὲ σπάνιον εὑρεῖν ἐστι τὸ τοιοῦτο, δεύτερος ἂν εἴη πλοῦς τὸ τῶν κατὰ λόγον φροντίζειν, ἵν' ἄν που καὶ σφαλλώμεθα, τῆς παρὰ τοῖς ἐκτὸς συγγνώμης μὴ διαμαρτάνωμεν. **7** ὃ καὶ περὶ πλείους μὲν δὴ γεγένηται τῶν πρότερον· ἐναργέστατον δ' ἔσται καὶ τοῖς καιροῖς ἔγγιστον τοῖς ὑπὲρ ὧν ὁ νῦν δὴ λόγος ἐνέστηκε τὸ κατ' Ἀχαιὸν συμβάν. **8** ὃς οὐδὲν τῶν ἐνδεχομένων πρὸς εὐλάβειαν καὶ πρὸς ἀσφάλειαν παραλιπών, ἀλλ' ὑπὲρ ἁπάντων προνοηθεὶς ἐφ' ὅσον ἀνθρωπίνηι γνώμηι δυνατὸν ἦν, ὅμως ἐγένετο τοῖς ἐχθροῖς ὑποχείριος. **9** τό γε μὴν συμβὰν ἔλεον μὲν τῶι παθόντι καὶ συγγνώμην ἀπειργάσατο παρὰ τοῖς ἐκτός, διαβολὴν δὲ καὶ μῖσος τοῖς πράξασιν.

**3a** οὕτως οἱ πλείους τῶν ἀνθρώπων τὸ κουφότατον ἥκιστα φέρειν δύνανται, λέγω δὲ τὴν σιωπήν.

**1.1** οὐκ ἀλλότριον εἶναί μοι δοκεῖ τῆς ὅλης ἡμῶν ἐπιβολῆς καὶ τῆς ἐν ἀρχαῖς προθέσεως συνεπιστῆσαι τοὺς ἀκούοντας ἐπὶ τὸ μεγαλεῖον τῶν πράξεων καὶ τὸ φιλότιμον τῆς ἑκατέρου τοῦ πολιτεύματος προαιρέσεως, λέγω δὲ τοῦ Ῥωμαίων καὶ Καρχηδονίων. **2** τίς γὰρ οὐκ ἂν ἐπισημήναιτο πῶς τηλικοῦτον μὲν πόλεμον συνεσταμένοι περὶ τῶν κατὰ τὴν Ἰταλίαν πραγμάτων, οὐκ ἐλάττω δὲ τούτου περὶ τῶν κατὰ τὴν Ἰβηρίαν, ἀκμὴν δὲ περὶ τούτων ἀδήλους μὲν ἔχοντες ἐπ' ἴσον ἀμφότεροι τὰς ὑπὲρ τοῦ μέλλοντος ἐλπίδας, ἐφαμίλλους δὲ τοὺς κατὰ τὸ παρὸν ἐνεστῶτας κινδύνους, **3** ὅμως οὐκ ἠρκοῦντο ταῖς προκειμέναις ἐπιβολαῖς, ἀλλὰ καὶ περὶ Σαρδόνος καὶ Σικελίας ἠμφισβήτουν· καὶ πάντα περιελάμβανον, οὐ μόνον ταῖς ἐλπίσιν, ἀλλὰ καὶ ταῖς χορηγίαις καὶ ταῖς παρασκευαῖς. **4** ὃ καὶ μάλιστ' ἄν τις εἰς τὸ κατὰ μέρος ἐμβλέψας θαυμάσειε. δύο μὲν γὰρ Ῥωμαίοις κατὰ τὴν Ἰταλίαν μετὰ τῶν ὑπάτων ἐντελῆ προεκάθητο στρατόπεδα, δύο δὲ κατὰ τὴν Ἰβηρίαν, ὧν τὸ μὲν πεζὸν Γνάϊος εἶχε, τὸ δὲ ναυτικὸν Πόπλιος. **5** ὁμοίως δὲ ταὐτὰ συνέβαινε γίνεσθαι

[36] 3 καί add. Hutchinson    4 ἧι Reiske: ἢ FD: εἰ G    ἀλογηθῆναι Casaubon: ἀναλ. FDG    5 τοιαύτας FD: τὰς τ. D^sl: τοι τὰς αὐτὰς G    δεῖ add. Casaubon
6 κατὰ λόγον D^mgG^mg: κατ' ὀλίγον FDG    που Casaubon: του FDG    7 ἐναργέστατον Reiske: -τερον FDG    9 παρὰ FD^mgG^mg: πᾶσι DG
[3a] F^mg iuxta 36.7-8, fol. 102^v
[1] 1.1-2.11 FDG    1 ad initium ἐπὶ τὸ καὶ G^mg, ex ἐπιτομὴ male lecto (cf. D^mg)    2 τηλικοῦτον μὲν πόλεμον Casaubon: -ούτων μὲν πόλεων FDG    3 post ἠμφισβήτουν lac. stat. Büttner-Wobst    4 ἐντελῆ στρ. ἐκάθητο δύο Ῥωμαϊκά Suda ε 1457    5 Suda οι (post τ) 56    ὁμοίως Reiske: οἰκείως FDG Suda    ταὐτὰ Schweighaeuser: ταῦτα FDG

καὶ παρὰ Καρχηδονίοις. 6 καὶ μὴν τοῖς κατὰ τὴν Ἑλλάδα τόποις ἐφώρμει καὶ ταῖς ἐπιβολαῖς τοῦ Φιλίππου στόλος, ἐφ' οὗ τὸ μὲν πρῶτον Μᾶρκος Οὐαλέριος, μετὰ δὲ ταῦτα Πόπλιος ἐπέπλει Σουλπίκιος. 7 ἅμα δὲ τούτοις Μᾶρκος μὲν Κλαύδιος ἑκατὸν πεντηρικοῖς σκάφεσι, Ἄππιος δὲ πεζικὰς ἔχων δυνάμεις, ἐφήδρευε τοῖς κατὰ τὴν Σικελίαν. 8 τὸ δ' αὐτὸ τοῦτ' Ἀμίλκας ἐποίει παρὰ Καρχηδονίοις.

2.1 δι' ὧν ὑπολαμβάνω τὸ πολλάκις ἐν ἀρχαῖς ἡμῖν τῆς πραγματείας εἰρημένον νῦν δι' αὐτῶν τῶν ἔργων ἀληθινὴν λαμβάνειν πίστιν. 2 τοῦτο δ' ἦν ὡς οὐχ οἷόν τε διὰ τῶν τὰς κατὰ μέρος ἱστορίας γραφόντων συνθεάσασθαι τὴν τῶν ὅλων οἰκονομίαν. 3 πῶς γὰρ ἐνδέχεται ψιλῶς αὐτὰς καθ' αὑτὰς ἀναγνόντα τὰς Σικελικὰς ἢ τὰς Ἰβηρικὰς πράξεις γνῶναι καὶ μαθεῖν ἢ τὸ μέγεθος τῶν γεγονότων ἢ τὸ συνέχον, τίνι τρόπωι καὶ τίνι γένει πολιτείας τὸ παραδοξότατον καθ' ἡμᾶς ἔργον ἡ τύχη συνετέλεσε; 4 τοῦτο δ' ἔστι τὸ πάντα τὰ γνωριζόμενα μέρη τῆς οἰκουμένης ὑπὸ μίαν ἀρχὴν καὶ δυναστείαν ἀγαγεῖν, ὃ πρότερον οὐχ εὑρίσκεται γεγονός. 5 πῶς μὲν γὰρ εἷλον Συρακούσας Ῥωμαῖοι καὶ πῶς Ἰβηρίαν κατέσχον οὐκ ἀδύνατον καὶ διὰ τῶν κατὰ μέρος ἐπὶ ποσὸν γνῶναι συντάξεων· 6 πῶς δὲ τῆς ἁπάντων ἡγεμονίας καθίκοντο, καὶ τί πρὸς τὰς ὁλοσχερεῖς αὐτοῖς ἐπιβολὰς τῶν κατὰ μέρος ἀντέπραξε, καὶ τί πάλιν καὶ κατὰ τίνας καιροὺς συνήργησε, δυσχερὲς καταλαβεῖν ἄνευ τῆς καθόλου τῶν πράξεων ἱστορίας. 7 οὐ μὴν τὸ μέγεθος τῶν ἔργων οὐδὲ τὴν τοῦ πολιτεύματος δύναμιν εὐμαρὲς κατανοῆσαι διὰ τὰς αὐτὰς αἰτίας. 8 τὸ γὰρ ἀντιποιήσασθαι Ῥωμαίους Ἰβηρίας ἢ πάλιν Σικελίας, καὶ στρατεῦσαι πεζικαῖς καὶ ναυτικαῖς δυνάμεσιν, αὐτὸ καθ' αὑτὸ λεγόμενον οὐκ ἂν εἴη θαυμαστόν. 9 ἅμα δὲ τούτων συμβαινόντων καὶ πολλαπλασίων ἄλλων κατὰ τὸν αὐτὸν καιρὸν ἐπιτελουμένων ἐκ τῆς αὐτῆς ἀρχῆς καὶ πολιτείας, καὶ θεωρουμένων ὁμοῦ τούτοις τῶν κατὰ τὴν ἰδίαν χώραν ὑπαρχουσῶν περιστάσεων καὶ πολέμων περὶ τοὺς ἅπαντα τὰ προειρημένα χειρίζοντας, 10 οὕτως ἂν εἴη μόνως σαφῆ τὰ γεγονότα καὶ θαυμαστά, καὶ μάλιστ' ἂν οὕτως τυγχάνοι τῆς ἁρμοζούσης ἐπιστάσεως. 11 ταῦτα μὲν οὖν ἡμῖν εἰρήσθω πρὸς τοὺς ὑπολαμβάνοντας διὰ τῆς τῶν κατὰ μέρος συντάξεως ἐμπειρίαν †ποιήσασθαι† τῆς καθολικῆς καὶ κοινῆς ἱστορίας.

3.1 ὅτε δὴ τὰς Συρακούσας Ἐπικύδης τε καὶ Ἱπποκράτης κατέλαβον, ἑαυτούς τε καὶ τοὺς ἄλλους τῶν πολιτῶν τῆς Ῥωμαίων φιλίας ἀλλοτριώσαντες, οἱ Ῥωμαῖοι, προσπεπτωκυίας αὐτοῖς ἤδη καὶ τῆς Ἱερωνύμου τοῦ Συρακοσίων τυράννου καταστροφῆς, Μᾶρκον Κλαύδιον ἀντιστράτηγον καταστήσαντες, αὐτῶι μὲν τὴν πεζὴν συνέστησαν δύναμιν, τὸν δὲ νηΐτην

[1] 5 παρὰ F Suda: πᾶσι DG   6 τοῦ G: τᾶις FD   Μᾶρκος hic et postea: Μάρκος FDG   7 Μᾶρκος μὲν Κλαύδιος ... Ἄππιος δὲ Hutchinson: Ἄππιος μὲν ... Μάρκος δὲ Κλαύδιος FDG   8 [παρὰ Καρχηδονίοις] Hutchinson
[2] 7 οὐ μὴν <ἀλλὰ> Bekker   9 πολλαπλασίων Casaubon: πολλοι πλ. F: πολυπλ. DG   10 μόνως Schweighaeuser: μόνος F: μόνον DG   11 ποιήσασθαι: <περι>ποιήσεσθαι Naber: πεπορίσθαι Hutchinson (πορίσασθαι iam Bekker)
[3] 3.1–7.12 primum T tantum; tum accedunt $VP_1$, tum FDG, qui soli finem adferunt   1 incipit T, fol. 98$^r$ (ἐκ τοῦ Πολυβίου Συρακουσῶν πολιορκία)   Μᾶρκον ... Ἄππιος: Ἄππιον ... Μάρκος Hultsch, recte quod ad Polybium attinet

αὐτοῖς στόλον ἐπετρόπευσε Ἄππιος Κλαύδιος. 2 οὗτοι μὲν δὴ τὴν στρατοπεδείαν ἐβάλοντο, μικρὸν ἀποσχόντες τῆς πόλεως, τὰς δὲ προσβολὰς ἔκριναν ποιεῖσθαι τῆι μὲν πεζῆι δυνάμει κατὰ τοὺς ἀπὸ τῶν Ἑξαπύλων τόπους, τῆι δὲ ναυτικῆι τῆς Ἀχραδίνης κατὰ τὴν Σκυτικὴν προσαγορευομένην στοάν, καθ' ἣν ἐπ' αὐτῆς κεῖται τῆς κρηπῖδος τὸ τεῖχος παρὰ θάλατταν. 3 ἑτοιμασάμενοι δὲ γέρρα καὶ βέλη καὶ τἆλλα τὰ πρὸς τὴν πολιορκίαν, ἐν ἡμέραις πέντε διὰ τὴν πολυχειρίαν ἤλπισαν <          > καταταχήσειν τῆι παρασκευῆι τοὺς ὑπεναντίους, οὐ λογισάμενοι τὴν Ἀρχιμήδους δύναμιν, οὐδὲ προϊδόμενοι διότι μία ψυχὴ τῆς ἁπάσης πολυχειρίας ἐν ἐνίοις καιροῖς ἀνυστικωτέρα. πλὴν τότε δι' αὐτῶν ἔγνωσαν τῶν ἔργων τὸ λεγόμενον. 4 οὔσης γὰρ ὀχυρᾶς τῆς πόλεως διὰ τὸ κεῖσθαι κύκλωι τὸ τεῖχος ἐπὶ τόπων ὑπερδεξίων, καὶ προκειμένης ὀφρύος, πρὸς ἣν καὶ μηδενὸς κωλύοντος οὐκ ἂν εὐμαρῶς τις δύναιτο πελάσαι πλὴν κατά τινας τόπους ὡρισμένους, 5 τοιαύτην ἡτοίμασε παρασκευὴν ὁ προειρημένος ἀνὴρ ἐντὸς τῆς πόλεως <          >, ὁμοίως δὲ καὶ πρὸς τοὺς κατὰ θάλατταν ἐπιπορευομένους, ὥστε μηδὲν ἐκ τοῦ καιροῦ δεῖν ἀσχολεῖσθαι τοὺς ἀμυνομένους, πρὸς πᾶν δὲ τὸ γινόμενον ὑπὸ τῶν ἐναντίων ἐξ ἑτοίμου ποιεῖσθαι τὴν ἀπάντησιν. 6 πλὴν ὁ μὲν Ἄππιος ἔχων γέρρα καὶ κλίμακας ἐνεχείρει προσφέρειν ταῦτα τῶι συνάπτοντι τείχει τοῖς Ἑξαπύλοις ἀπὸ τῶν ἀνατολῶν.

4.1 ὁ δὲ Μᾶρκος ἑξήκοντα σκάφεσι πεντηρικοῖς ἐποιεῖτο τὸν ἐπίπλουν ἐπὶ τὴν Ἀχραδίνην, ὧν ἕκαστον πλῆρες ἦν ἀνδρῶν ἐχόντων τόξα καὶ σφενδόνας καὶ γρόσφους, δι' ὧν ἔμελλον τοὺς ἀπὸ τῶν ἐπάλξεων μαχομένους ἀναστέλλειν. 2 ἅμα δὲ τούτοις, ὀκτὼ πεντήρεσι, παραλελυμέναις τοὺς ταρσούς, ταῖς μὲν τοὺς δεξιούς, ταῖς δὲ τοὺς εὐωνύμους, καὶ συνεζευγμέναις πρὸς ἀλλήλας σύνδυο κατὰ τοὺς ἐψιλωμένους τοίχους, προσῆγον πρὸς τὸ τεῖχος διὰ τῆς τῶν ἐκτὸς τοίχων εἰρεσίας τὰς λεγομένας σαμβύκας. 3 τὸ δὲ γένος τῶν εἰρημένων ὀργάνων ἐστὶ τοιοῦτο. 4 κλίμακα τῶι πλάτει τετράπεδον ἑτοιμάσαντες, ὥστ' ἐξ ἀποβάσεως ἰσοϋψῆ γενέσθαι τῶι τείχει, ταύτης ἑκατέραν τὴν πλευρὰν δρυφακτώσαντες καὶ

[3] 2 ἐβάλοντο Hultsch: ἐβάλλ- T    a τῆι μὲν πεζῆι incipiunt V (fol. 184ᵛ) et P₁ (fol. 99ʳ) Anonymi De obsidione toleranda    post δ. κατά, τοὺς ... κατὰ om. VP₁    τῆς Ἀχρ. Hultsch: κατασχρ. T: κατὰ τῆς Ἀχρ. Wescher    στοὰν προσαγ. VP₁    3-5 πολιορκίαν, οὐ προϊδόμενοι τὴν Ἀρχιμήδους δύναμιν, ἐν ἡμέραις ... ὑπεναντίους. πλὴν ὁ προειρημένος ἀνὴρ κατὰ ... τοιαύτην ἐπὶ τοῦ τείχους ἧτ. π.· ὁμοίως T, οὐ λογισάμενοι et διότι ... δύναιτο et ἐντὸς τῆς πόλεως omissis    3 οὐ λογισάμενοι ... δύναμιν Suda ε 2907, μία ... ἀνυστικωτέρα α 2797    ἑτοιμασάμενοι δὲ T: περιστοιχίσαντες ἑτοιμασαμένων τε VP₁    post ἤλπισαν lac. stat. Hutchinson (<τοὔργον ἐπιτελέσαντες> exempli causa suppleuit)    ἁπάσης π. Suda: ἁπάσης ἐστὶ π. TVP₁    5 lac. stat. Schweighaeuser, <πρὸς τοὺς κατὰ γῆν> suppleuit    δεῖν om. T    6 Ἄππιος VP₁: Μᾶρκος (μαρκος) T
[4] 1 incipiunt FDG    Μᾶρκος FDGVP₁ (cf. Liu. 24.34.4 Marcellus): Ἄππιος T    2 σάμβυκες (sic) ex Polybio Suda σ 74    παραλελυμέναις TVP₁: παραλελεμμέναις Dˢˡ: παραλεμμέναις FDG    3 δὲ om. FDG    γένος T: γένος τῆς κατασκευῆς FDG: σκεῦος τῆς κατασκευῆς VP₁    4 ἰσοϋψῆ (ει-) T: εἰς ὕψη VP₁: εἰς ὕψει FDG: ἐς ἴσον Dᵐᵍ    γίνεσθαι VP₁

σκεπάσαντες ὑπερπετέσι θωρακίοις, ἔθηκαν πλαγίαν ἐπὶ τοὺς συμψαύοντας τοίχους τῶν συνεζευγμένων νεῶν, πολὺ προπίπτουσαν τῶν ἐμβόλων. **5** πρὸς δὲ τοῖς ἱστοῖς ἐκ τῶν ἄνω μερῶν τροχιλεῖαι προσήρτηνται σὺν κάλοις. **6** λοιπὸν ὅταν ἐγγίσωσι τῆς χρείας, ἐνδεδεμένων τῶν κάλων εἰς τὴν κορυφὴν τῆς κλίμακος, ἕλκουσι διὰ τῶν τροχιλειῶν τούτους ἑστῶτες ἐν ταῖς πρύμναις· ἕτεροι δὲ παραπλησίως ἐν ταῖς πρώιραις ἐξερείδοντες [ταῖς] ἀντηρίσιν ἀσφαλίζονται τὴν ἄρσιν τοῦ μηχανήματος. **7** κἄπειτα διὰ τῆς εἰρεσίας τῆς ἀφ' ἑκατέρου τῶν ἐκτὸς ταρσῶν ἐγγίσαντες τῆι γῆι τὰς ναῦς, πειράζουσι προσερείδειν τῶι τείχει τὸ προειρημένον ὄργανον. **8** ἐπὶ δὲ τῆς κλίμακος ἄκρας ὑπάρχει πέτευρον, ἠσφαλισμένον γέρροις τὰς τρεῖς ἐπιφανείας, ἐφ' οὗ τέτταρες ἄνδρες ἐπιβεβηκότες ἀγωνίζονται, διαμαχόμενοι πρὸς τοὺς εἴργοντας ἀπὸ τῶν ἐπάλξεων τὴν πρόσθεσιν τῆς σαμβύκης. **9** ἐπὰν δὲ προσερείσαντες ὑπερδέξιοι γένωνται τοῦ τείχους, οὗτοι μὲν τὰ πλάγια τῶν γέρρων παραλύσαντες, ἐξ ἑκατέρου τοῦ μέρους ἐπιβαίνουσιν ἐπὶ τὰς ἐπάλξεις ἢ τοὺς πύργους. **10** οἱ δὲ λοιποὶ διὰ τῆς σαμβύκης ἕπονται τούτοις, ἀσφαλῶς τοῖς κάλοις βεβηκυίας τῆς κλίμακος εἰς ἀμφοτέρας τὰς ναῦς. **11** εἰκότως δὲ τὸ κατασκεύασμα τῆς προσηγορίας τέτευχε ταύτης· ἐπειδὰν γὰρ ἐξαρθῆι, γίνεται τὸ σχῆμα τῆς νεὼς †ταύτης† καὶ τῆς κλίμακος ἑνοποιηθὲν παραπλήσιον σαμβύκηι.

**5.**1 οὗτοι μὲν οὖν τὸν τρόπον τοῦτον διηρμοσμένοι προσάγειν διενοοῦντο τῶι τείχει· **2** ὁ δὲ προειρημένος ἀνήρ, παρεσκευασμένος ὄργανα πρὸς ἅπαν ἐμβελὲς διάστημα, πόρρωθεν μὲν ἐπιπλέοντας τοῖς εὐτονωτέροις καὶ μείζοσι λιθοβόλοις καὶ βέλεσι τιτρώσκων εἰς ἀπορίαν ἐνέβαλε καὶ δυσχρηστίαν, **3** ὅτε δὲ ταῦθ' ὑπερπετῆ γίνοιτο, τοῖς ἐλάττοσι κατὰ λόγον ἀεὶ πρὸς τὸ παρὸν ἀπόστημα χρώμενος εἰς τοιαύτην ἤγαγε διατροπὴν ὥστε καθόλου κωλύειν αὐτῶν τὴν ὁρμὴν καὶ τὸν ἐπίπλουν, **4** ἕως ὁ Μᾶρκος δυσθετούμενος ἠναγκάσθη λάθραι νυκτὸς ἔτι ποιήσασθαι τὴν παραγωγήν. **5** γενομένων δ' αὐτῶν ἐντὸς βέλους πρὸς τῆι γῆι, πάλιν ἑτέραν ἡτοιμάκει παρασκευὴν πρὸς τοὺς ἀπομαχομένους ἐκ τῶν πλοίων. **6** ἕως ἀνδρομήκους ὕψους κατεπύκνωσε τρήμασι τὸ τεῖχος ὡς παλαιστιαίοις τὸ μέγεθος κατὰ τὴν ἐκτὸς ἐπιφάνειαν· οἷς τοξότας καὶ σκορπίδια παραστήσας ἐντὸς τοῦ τείχους, καὶ βάλλων διὰ τούτων, ἀχρήστους ἐποίει τοὺς ἐπιβάτας.

[4] 5 τροχιλεῖαι (item 6): -ίαι codd.     προσήρτηνται Τ: -το FDGVP$_1$     6 ἕλκουσι om. Τ     ταῖς del. Hutchinson     ἀσφαλίζουσι FDG     8 ἐπὶ ... πέτευρον om. Τ     εἴργοντας FDGVP$_1$: εἰσρέοντας Τ     πρόσθεσιν FDGT: πρόθ. VP$_1$     11 om. Τ     ἐφ κατ.: κατ. FD     ταύτης (alterum) FDG: τούτης V (signo corruptelae addito) P$_1$: ἑκατέρας Hutchinson
[5] 1-3 παρεσκευάσατο ... μείζοσιν· ὅτε ... ἐλάττοσιν Suda ε 945, λιθ. ... δυσχρ. omissis     1 οὗτοι μὲν οὖν Τ: πλὴν οὗτοι μὲν FDGVP$_1$     προσάγειν διενοοῦντο τῶι τείχει: πρ. διεν. τοῖς πύργοις FDG: πρ. διεν. τῶν πύργων VP$_1$: τῶι τείχει προσέβαλλον Τ     **2** ἐμβελὲς Suda: ἐμβελῆς VP$_1$: ἐμβάλλει Τ: ἐμμελὲς FDG     καὶ δυσχρηστίαν om. VP$_1$     **3** γένοιτο P$_1$     κατὰ λόγον FDGT$^{\text{N}}$VP$_1$: κατ' ἐλάττονα Τ     **4** δυσθετούμενος om. Τ     ἔτι ποιήσασθαι Scaliger: ἐπιποιήσασθαι fere FDGVP$_1$: ποιήσασθαι Τ     **5-6** πάλιν ... ἐπιβάτας Suda σ 669     **6** ἕως Schweighaeuser: ὡς FDGTVP$_1$: ἕως <γὰρ> Hutchinson     καὶ βάλλων om. Suda

7 ἐξ οὗ καὶ μακρὰν ἀφεστῶτας καὶ σύνεγγυς ὄντας τοὺς πολεμίους οὐ μόνον ἀπράκτους παρεσκεύαζε πρὸς τὰς ἰδίας ἐπιβολάς, ἀλλὰ καὶ διέφθειρε τοὺς πλείστους αὐτῶν. 8 ὅτε δὲ τὰς σαμβύκας ἐγχειρήσαιεν ἐξαίρειν, ὄργανα παρ' ὅλον τὸ τεῖχος ἡτοιμάκει, τὸν μὲν λοιπὸν χρόνον ἀφανῆ, κατὰ δὲ τὸν τῆς χρείας καιρὸν ἐκ τῶν ἔσω μερῶν ὑπὲρ τοῦ τείχους ἀνιστάμενα καὶ προπίπτοντα πολὺ τῆς ἐπάλξεως ταῖς κεραίαις· 9 ὧν τινὰ μὲν ἐβάσταζε λίθους οὐκ ἐλάττους δέκα ταλάντων, τινὰ δὲ σηκώματα μολίβδινα. 10 λοιπὸν ὅτε συνεγγίζοιεν αἱ σαμβῦκαι, τότε περιαγόμεναι καρχησίωι πρὸς τὸ δέον αἱ κεραῖαι, διά τινος σχαστηρίας ἠφίεσαν εἰς τὸ κατασκεύασμα τὸν λίθον· 11 ἐξ οὗ συνέβαινε μὴ μόνον αὐτὸ συνθραύεσθαι τοὔργανον, ἀλλὰ καὶ τὴν ναῦν καὶ τοὺς ἐν αὐτῆι κινδυνεύειν ὁλοσχερῶς.

6.1 τινὰ τε τῶν μηχανημάτων πάλιν ἐπὶ τοὺς ἐφορμῶντας καὶ προβεβλημένους γέρρα καὶ διὰ τούτων ἠσφαλισμένους πρὸς τὸ μηδὲν πάσχειν ὑπὸ τῶν διὰ τοῦ τείχους φερομένων βελῶν ἠφίει μὲν καὶ λίθους συμμέτρους πρὸς τὸ φεύγειν ἐκ τῆς πρώιρας τοὺς ἀγωνιζομένους, 2 ἅμα δὲ καὶ καθίει χεῖρα σιδηρᾶν ἐξ ἁλύσεως δεδεμένην, ἧι δραξάμενος ὁ τὴν κεραίαν οἰακίζων, ὅτ' ἐπιλάβοιτο τῆς πρώιρας, κατῆγε τὴν πτέρναν τῆς μηχανῆς ἐντὸς τοῦ τείχους. 3 ὅτε δέ, κουφίζων τὴν πρῶιραν, ὀρθὸν ποιήσειε τὸ σκάφος ἐπὶ πρύμναν, τὰς μὲν πτέρνας τῶν ὀργάνων εἰς ἀκίνητον καθῆπτε, τὴν δὲ χεῖρα καὶ τὴν ἄλυσιν ἐκ τῆς μηχανῆς †ἐξέρεναι† διά τινος σχαστηρίας. 4 οὗ γινομένου τινὰ μὲν τῶν πλοίων πλάγια κατέπιπτε, τινὰ δὲ καὶ κατεστρέφετο, τὰ δὲ πλεῖστα, τῆς πρώιρας ἀφ' ὕψους ῥιφθείσης, βαπτιζόμενα πλήρη θαλάττης ἐγίνετο καὶ ταραχῆς. 5 Μᾶρκος δὲ δυσχρηστούμενος ἐπὶ τοῖς ἀπαντωμένοις ὑπ' Ἀρχιμήδους, καὶ θεωρῶν μετὰ βλάβης καὶ χλευασμοῦ τοὺς ἔνδον ἀποτριβομένους αὐτοῦ τὰς ἐπιβολάς, 6 δυσχερῶς μὲν ἔφερε τὸ συμβαῖνον, ὅμως δ' ἐπισκώπτων τὰς αὐτοῦ πράξεις ἔφη ταῖς μὲν ναυσὶν αὐτοῦ κυαθίζειν ἐκ θαλάττης Ἀρχιμήδην, τὰς δὲ σαμβύκας ῥαπιζομένας ὥσπερ ἐκ πότου μετ' αἰσχύνης ἐκπεπτωκέναι. 7 καὶ τῆς μὲν κατὰ θάλατταν πολιορκίας τοιοῦτον ἀπέβη τὸ τέλος.

7.1 οἱ δὲ περὶ τὸν Ἄππιον εἰς παραπλησίους ἐμπεσόντες δυσχερείας ἀπέστησαν τῆς ἐπιβολῆς. 2 ἔτι μὲν γὰρ ὄντες ἐν ἀποστήματι, τοῖς τε πετροβόλοις καὶ καταπέλταις τυπτόμενοι διεφθείροντο, διὰ τὸ θαυμάσιον εἶναι τὴν τῶν βελῶν

[5] 7 ἀφεστῶτας FDGVP₁: ἀπόντας T  8 ὄργανα ἐξαίρειν FDG  ὑπὲρ FDGVP₁: ἐπὶ T  προπίπτοντα TVP₁: προσ- FDG  10 τότε T: ποτὲ FDGVP₁  καρχησίωι om. T  σχαστηρίας TVP₁: χαστ. FDG^mg: χαριστηρίας G  11 θραύεσθαι T  τὰς ναῦς ... αὐταῖς Hutchinson
[6] 1 ἐφορμῶντας TVP₁: ἐφορμοῦντας FDG  ὑπὸ τῶν διὰ FDGVP₁: ἀπὸ τῶν ἐκ T  2 ὅτ' Hutchinson: ὅθεν FDGTVP₁  κατῆγε T: κατάγε FDGVP₁  3 πτέρνας Valesius: πρώρας fere FDGTVP₁  ἐξέρεναι FVP₁: ἐξέραινε DG: ἐξέρραινε T: ἐξερρίπτει (e.g.) Hutchinson  σχαστηρίας T: χαστ- FDVP₁: χαριστ- G  4 γενομένου DG  ῥιφθείσης TVP₁: ῥηθ- FDG  καὶ ταραχῆς — 7.5 χιλιάρχων om.  6 ταῖς ... ἐκπεπτωκέναι (et 5 δυσχρησούμενος) Ath. 14.634b  Ἀρχιμήδην Ath.: -μήδη FDG: -μήδης VP₁  ῥαπιζομένας (-ους VP₁): ἀκρατιζομένας Kaibel  ἐκ πότου Ath.: ἐκσπόνδους FDGVP₁, edd.

κατασκευήν καί κατά τό πλήθος καί κατά τήν ενέργειαν, ώς άν Ίέρωνος μέν χορηγού γεγονότος, άρχιτέκτονος δε καί δημιουργού τών επινοημάτων Άρχιμήδους. 3 συνεγγίζοντές γε μήν πρός τήν πόλιν, οί μέν ταΐς διά τού τείχους τοξότισιν, ώς επάνω προεΐπον, κακούμενοι συνεχώς είργοντο τής προσόδου· οί δε μετά τών γέρρων βιαζόμενοι ταΐς τών κατά κορυφήν λίθων καί δοκών έμβολαΐς διεφθείροντο. 4 ούκ όλίγα δέ καί ταΐς χερσί ταΐς έκ τών μηχανών εκακοποίουν, ώς καί πρότερον εΐπα· σύν αύτοΐς γάρ τοΐς οπλοις τούς άνδρας έξαιρούντες έρρίπτουν. 5 τό δέ πέρας, άναχωρήσαντες εις τήν παρεμβολήν καί συνεδρεύσαντες μετά τών χιλιάρχων οί περί τόν Άππιον, όμοθυμαδόν έβουλεύσαντο πάσης έλπίδος πεΐραν λαμβάνειν πλήν τού διά πολιορκίας έλεΐν τάς Συρακούσας, ώς καί τέλος έποίησαν· 6 όκτώ γάρ μήνας τήι πόλει προσκαθεζόμενοι τών μέν άλλων στρατηγημάτων ή τολμημάτων ούδενός άπέστησαν, τού δέ πολιορκεΐν ούδέποτε πεΐραν έτι λαβεΐν έθάρρησαν. 7 ούτως εις άνήρ καί μία ψυχή δεόντως ήρμοσμένη πρός ένια τών πραγμάτων μέγα τι χρήμα φαίνεται γίνεσθαι καί θαυμάσιον. 8 έκεΐνοι γούν τηλικαύτας δυνάμεις έχοντες καί κατά γήν καί κατά θάλατταν, εί μέν άφέλοι τις πρεσβύτην ένα Συρακοσίων, παραχρήμα τής πόλεως κυριεύσειν ήλπιζον, 9 τούτου δέ συμπαρόντος ούκ έθάρρουν ούδ' έπιβαλέσθαι, κατά γε τούτον τόν τρόπον καθ' όν άμύνασθαι δυνατός ήν Άρχιμήδης. 10 ού μήν άλλά νομίσαντες μάλιστ' άν ύπό τής τών άναγκαίων ένδείας διά τό πλήθος τούς ένδον ύποχειρίους σφίσι γενέσθαι, ταύτης άντείχοντο τής έλπίδος· καί ταΐς μέν ναυσί τάς κατά θάλατταν έπικουρίας αύτών έκώλυον, τώι δέ πεζώι στρατεύματι τάς κατά γήν. 11 βουλόμενοι δέ μή ποιεΐν άπρακτον τόν χρόνον έν ώι προσεδρεύουσι ταΐς Συρακούσαις, άλλ' άμα τι καί τών έκτός χρησίμων κατασκευάζεσθαι, διεΐλον οί στρατηγοί σφάς αύτούς καί τήν δύναμιν, 12 ώστε τόν μέν Άππιον έχοντα δύο μέρη προσκαθήσθαι τοΐς έν τήι πόλει, τό δέ τρίτον άναλαβόντα Μάρκον έπιπορεύεσθαι τούς τά Καρχηδονίων αίρουμένους κατά τήν Σικελίαν.

8.1 ότι Φίλιππος παραγενόμενος εις τήν Μεσσήνην έφθειρε τήν χώραν δυσμενικώς, θυμώι τό πλεΐον ή λογισμώι χρώμενος· 2 ήλπιζε γάρ, ώς έμοί δοκεΐ, βλάπτων συνεχώς ούδέποτ' άγανακτήσειν ούδέ μισήσειν αύτόν τούς κακώς πάσχοντας. 3 προήχθην δέ καί νύν καί διά τής προτέρας βύβλου σαφέστερον έξηγήσασθαι περί τούτων ού μόνον διά τάς πρότερον ήμΐν είρημένας αίτίας, άλλά καί διά τό τών συγγραφέων τούς μέν όλως παραλελοιπέναι τά κατά τούς Μεσσηνίους, 4 τοΐς

[7] 2 καί κατά τήν ένέργειαν om. VP₁    χορηγού FD^{mg}G^{mg}VP₁: άρχ- DG    3 aut οί μέν <ύπό τών παρεστώτων> aut τοξείαις Hutchinson    4 όπλοις om. VP₁ 4-5 έρρίπτουν. τό δέ VP₁: έρριπτούτο δέ FDG    5-6 οί περί τόν Άππιον ... προσκαθεζόμενοι ita contrahit T (accentibus etc. additis): οί δέ τών 'Ρωμαίων στρατηγοί, τοΐς όλοις άπορούντες τό μηκέτι ποτέ άν έλπίσαι διά πολιορκίας τάς Συρακούσας έλεΐν,; tum 6 τών μέν άλλων ... έθάρρησαν exscribit. deinde ad 37.2 transilit    7 om. VP₁    ψυχή Schweighaeuser: τύχη FDG    8 άφ. τοΐς πρεσβυτέροις ένα Συρακούσιον P₁; Συρακούσιον coniecerat Schweighaeuser    9 post έπιβαλέσθαι desinunt VP₁    12 τά om. FD
[8] 8.1–12.7 P; 12.1–8 FDG    3 βίβλου P hic et 9.5    4 τοΐς Hutchinson: τούς P; aut τούς δέ ... άμ. τεθεικέναι Hutchinson (νενομικέναι uel τεταχέναι iam Reiske)

δὲ καθόλου διὰ τὴν πρὸς τοὺς μονάρχους εὔνοιαν ἢ τἀναντία φόβον οὐχ οἷον ἐν ἁμαρτίαι γεγονέναι τὴν εἰς τοὺς Μεσσηνίους ἀσέβειαν Φιλίππου καὶ παρανομίαν, ἀλλὰ τοὐναντίον ἐν ἐπαίνωι καὶ κατορθώματι τὰ πεπραγμένα διασαφεῖν ἡμῖν. 5 οὐ μόνον δὲ περὶ Μεσσηνίους τοῦτο πεποιηκότας ἰδεῖν ἔστι τοὺς γράφοντας τοῦ Φιλίππου τὰς πράξεις, ἀλλὰ καὶ περὶ τῶν ἄλλων παραπλησίως. 6 ἐξ ὧν ἱστορίας μὲν οὐδαμῶς ἔχειν αὐτοῖς συμβαίνει διάθεσιν τὰς συντάξεις, ἐγκωμίου δὲ μᾶλλον. 7 ἐγὼ δ' οὔτε λοιδορεῖν ψευδῶς φημι δεῖν τοὺς μονάρχους οὔτ' ἐγκωμιάζειν, ὃ πολλοῖς ἤδη συμβέβηκε, τὸν ἀκόλουθον δὲ τοῖς προγεγραμμένοις ἀεὶ καὶ τὸν πρέποντα ταῖς ἑκάστων προαιρέσεσι λόγον ἐφαρμόζειν. 8 ἀλλ' ἴσως τοῦτ' εἰπεῖν μὲν εὐμαρές, πρᾶξαι δὲ καὶ λίαν δυσχερές, διὰ τὸ πολλὰς καὶ ποικίλας εἶναι διαθέσεις καὶ περιστάσεις αἷς εἴκοντες ἄνθρωποι κατὰ τὸν βίον οὔτε λέγειν οὔτε γράφειν δύνανται τὸ φαινόμενον. 9 ὧν χάριν τισὶ μὲν αὐτῶν συγγνώμην δοτέον, ἐνίοις γε μὴν οὐ δοτέον.

9.1 μάλιστα δ' ἄν τις ἐπιτιμήσειε περὶ τοῦτο τὸ μέρος Θεοπόμπωι, ὅς γ' ἐν ἀρχῆι τῆς <περὶ> Φιλίππου συντάξεως [διὰ τὸ] μάλιστα παρορμηθῆναι φήσας πρὸς τὴν ἐπιβολὴν τῆς πραγματείας διὰ τὸ μηδέποτε τὴν Εὐρώπην ἐνηνοχέναι τοιοῦτον ἄνδρα παράπαν οἷον τὸν Ἀμύντου Φίλιππον, 2 μετὰ ταῦτα παρὰ πόδας, ἔν τε τῶι προοιμίωι καὶ παρ' ὅλην δὲ τὴν ἱστορίαν, ἀκρατέστατον μὲν αὐτὸν ἀποδείκνυσι πρὸς γυναῖκας, ὥστε καὶ τὸν ἴδιον οἶκον ἐσφαλκέναι τὸ καθ' αὑτὸν διὰ τὴν πρὸς τοῦτο τὸ μέρος ὁρμὴν καὶ παράστασιν, 3 ἀδικώτατον δὲ καὶ κακοπραγμονέστατον περὶ τὰς τῶν φίλων καὶ συμμάχων κατασκευάς, πλείστας δὲ πόλεις ἐξηνδραποδισμένον καὶ πεπραξικοπηκότα μετὰ δόλου καὶ βίας, 4 ἐκπαθῆ δὲ γεγονότα καὶ πρὸς τὰς ἀκρατοποσίας, ὥστε καὶ μεθ' ἡμέραν πλεονάκις μεθύοντα καταφανῆ γενέσθαι τοῖς φίλοις. 5 εἰ δέ τις ἀναγνῶναι βουληθείη τὴν ἀρχὴν τῆς ἐνάτης καὶ τετταρακοστῆς αὐτῶι βύβλου, παντάπασιν ἂν θαυμάσαι τὴν ἀτοπίαν τοῦ συγγραφέως, ὅς γε χωρὶς τῶν ἄλλων τετόλμηκε καὶ ταῦτα λέγειν – αὐταῖς γὰρ λέξεσιν αἷς ἐκεῖνος κέχρηται κατατετάχαμεν· 6 'εἰ γάρ τις ἦν ἐν τοῖς Ἕλλησιν ἢ τοῖς βαρβάροις', φησί, 'λάσταυρος ἢ βδελυρὸς ἢ θρασὺς τὸν τρόπον, οὗτοι πάντες εἰς Μακεδονίαν ἀθροιζόμενοι πρὸς Φίλιππον ἑταῖροι τοῦ βασιλέως προσηγορεύοντο. 7 καθόλου γὰρ ὁ Φίλιππος τοὺς μὲν κοσμίους τοῖς ἤθεσι καὶ

[9] 1 μάλιστα παρ. ... Φίλιππον Suda π 403    <περὶ> Reiske    [διὰ τὸ] Hutchinson: δια τὸ P: δι' αὐτὸ edd.: δι' αὐτὸν Reiske: διὰ τοῦτο Dindorf    καὶ μάλιστα Suda, fortasse recte    2 μετὰ τ. π. π., ἀκρ. ... γυναῖκας Suda π 417; ὥστε ... προστασίαν, καὶ τὸν ... προστασίαν Suda ε 3239, π 2802    ἀποδείκνυσι Valesius: ἀποδείκνυς (illo accentu) P: δείκνυσι Suda    παράστασιν Ernesti: προστασίαν P Suda: προπέτειαν Reiske    3 ἀδικώτατον ... φίλων κατασκευάς Suda κ 765; πλείστας ... πεπραξικοπηκότα Suda ε 1736, πεπρ. π 1019    4 Suda ε 553, tamquam ex Aeliano    ἀκρατοποσίας Suda: ἀκροπ. P    6 Ath. 4.167b, Suda λ 141    εἰ γάρ: εἰ Ath., Suda    ἢ β. om. P, ἢ β. ἢ θ. om. Suda    σχεδὸν ἅπαντες εἰς Μ. ἀθροισθέντες ἑ. Φιλίππου Ath.    post 6 pleraque om. Polybius; cf. Ath. 4.167b–c    7 Φίλιππος –12 etiam in Ath. 6.260d–f (hic epitome ab A numquam differt)    7 καὶ καθόλου τοὺς μὲν ... προῆγεν Suda α 2978    τοῖς ἤθεσι P Suda: τὰ ἤθη Ath.

τῶν ἰδίων βίων ἐπιμελουμένους ἀπεδοκίμαζε, τοὺς δὲ πολυτελεῖς καὶ ζῶντας ἐν μέθαις καὶ κύβοις ἐτίμα καὶ προῆγε. 8 τοιγαροῦν οὐ μόνον ταῦτ' ἔχειν αὐτοὺς παρεσκεύαζεν, ἀλλὰ καὶ τῆς ἄλλης ἀδικίας καὶ βδελυρίας ἀθλητὰς ἐποίησε. 9 τί γὰρ τῶν αἰσχρῶν ἢ δεινῶν αὐτοῖς οὐ προσῆν; ἢ τί τῶν καλῶν καὶ σπουδαίων οὐκ ἀπῆν; ὧν οἱ μὲν ξυρόμενοι καὶ λεαινόμενοι διετέλουν, ἄνδρες ὄντες, οἱ δ' ἀλλήλοις ἐτόλμων ἐπανίστασθαι πώγωνας ἔχουσι. 10 καὶ περιήγοντο μὲν δύο καὶ τρεῖς τοὺς ἑταιρευομένους, αὐτοὶ δὲ τὰς αὐτὰς ἐκείνοις χρήσεις ἑτέροις παρείχοντο. 11 ὅθεν καὶ δικαίως ἄν τις αὐτοὺς οὐχ ἑταίρους ἀλλ' ἑταίρας ὑπελάμβανεν εἶναι· [οὐδὲ στρατιώτας ἀλλὰ χαμαιτύπας προσηγόρευσεν] 12 ἀνδροφόνοι γὰρ τὴν φύσιν ὄντες, ἀνδρόπορνοι τὸν τρόπον ἦσαν. 13 ἁπλῶς δ' εἰπεῖν, ἵνα παύσωμαι', φησί, 'μακρολογῶν, ἄλλως τε καὶ τοσούτων μοι πραγμάτων ἐπικεχυμένων, ἡγοῦμαι τοιαῦτα θηρία γεγονέναι καὶ τοιούτους τὸν τρόπον τοὺς φίλους καὶ τοὺς ἑταίρους Φιλίππου προσαγορευθέντας οἵους οὔτε τοὺς Κενταύρους τοὺς τὸ Πήλιον κατασχόντας οὔτε τοὺς Λαιστρυγόνας τοὺς τὸ Λεοντίνων πεδίον οἰκήσαντας οὔτ' ἄλλους οὐδ' ὁποίους.'

10.1 ταύτην δὲ τὴν τε πικρίαν καὶ τὴν ἀθυρογλωττίαν τοῦ συγγραφέως τίς οὐκ ἂν ἀποδοκιμάσειεν; 2 οὐ γὰρ μόνον ὅτι μαχόμενα λέγει πρὸς τὴν αὐτοῦ πρόθεσιν ἄξιός ἐστιν ἐπιτιμήσεως, ἀλλὰ καὶ διότι κατέψευσται τοῦ τε βασιλέως καὶ τῶν φίλων, καὶ μάλιστα διότι τὸ ψεῦδος αἰσχρῶς καὶ ἀπρεπῶς διατέθειται. 3 εἰ γὰρ περὶ Σαρδαναπάλλου τις ἢ τῶν ἐκείνου συμβιωτῶν ἐποιεῖτο τοὺς λόγους, μόλις ἂν ἐθάρρησε τῆι κακορρημοσύνηι ταύτηι χρήσασθαι· οὗ τὴν ἐν τῶι βίωι προαίρεσιν καὶ τὴν ἀσέλγειαν διὰ τῆς ἐπιγραφῆς τῆς ἐπὶ τοῦ τάφου τεκμαιρόμεθα. 4 λέγει γάρ· [ἡ ἐπιγραφή]

ταῦτ' ἔχω ὅσσ' ἔφαγον καὶ ἐφύβρισα καὶ μετ' ἔρωτος
τέρπν' ἔπαθον.

[9] 7 βίων P Suda: om. Ath.    μέθαις καὶ κύβοις ἐτίμα καὶ προῆγε(ν) P Suda: κύβοις καὶ πότοις ἐπαινῶν ἐτίμα Ath.    8–9 ἀπῆν Suda α 740, tamquam ex Aeliano, 9 τί γάρ ... ἀπῆν F^mg fol. 107^r    8 τοιγαροῦν Ath., Suda: τοίγαρ P    ταῦτ' ἔχειν αὐτοὺς P Suda: αὐτοὺς τοιαῦτ' ἔχειν Ath.    ἐποίησε P, Ath.: παρεσκεύαζεν Suda 9 ἢ δεινῶν PF^mg Ath.: καὶ δ. Suda    ὧν P: οὐχ Ath.    ξυρούμενοι Ath. 10 ἑταιρουμένους Ath.    παρεῖχον Ath.    11–12 Demetr. Eloc. 27 ἀνδροφ. δὲ τὴν φ. ὄντες, ἀνδρόπ. τὸν τ. ἦσαν [hucusque Eloc. 247 quoque]· καὶ ἐκαλοῦντο μὲν ἕταιροι, ἦσαν δὲ ἕταιραι    11 καὶ om. Ath.    ἀλλ' ἑταίρας om. P    ὑπέλαβεν Ath.    εἶναι om. Ath.    οὐδὲ ... προσηγόρευσεν del. Hutchinson: a Demetrio absunt    στρατιώτας: χαμαικοίτας Meineke    χαμαιτύπας Ath.: -τύπους P    post 12 pleraque om. Polybius; cf. Ath. 260f–261a    13 οἵους ... οἰκήσαντας Suda κ 1330    τοιούτους τὸν τρόπον Reiske: τοιοῦτον τρόπον P; καὶ τοι. τρ. delere possis    κατασχόντας P: ἔχοντας Suda
[10] 1 ἀθυρογλωττία ex hoc nimirum loco Suda α 770    τήν τε πικρίαν Valesius: τὴν ἐπικριαν P    ἀθυρογλωττ- Suda: -σσ- P    οὐκ ἂν Valesius: οὐκεν P    3 ἢ: καὶ Hutchinson    4 γάρ· [ἡ ἐπιγραφή] Hutchinson: γὰρ ἡ [ἐπι]γραφή· Büttner-Wobst    ἔφαγον e.g. Ath. 8.336a (uide SH 335): ἔφαγόν τε P    τέρπν' e.g. Ath.: τερπνῶν P

5 περὶ δὲ Φιλίππου καὶ τῶν ἐκείνου φίλων εὐλαβηθείη τις ἂν οὐχ οἷον εἰς μαλακίαν καὶ ἀνανδρίαν, ἔτι δ' ἀναισχυντίαν λέγειν, ἀλλὰ τοὐναντίον μή ποτ' ἐγκωμιάζειν ἐπιβαλλόμενος οὐ δυνηθῆι καταξίως εἰπεῖν τῆς ἀνδρείας καὶ φιλοπονίας καὶ συλλήβδην τῆς ἀρετῆς τῶν προειρημένων ἀνδρῶν, 6 οἵ γε προφανῶς ταῖς σφετέραις φιλοπονίαις καὶ τόλμαις ἐξ ἐλαχίστης μὲν βασιλείας <τὴν> ἐνδοξοτάτην καὶ μεγίστην Μακεδόνων ἀρχὴν κατεσκεύασαν· 7 χωρὶς δὲ τῶν ἐπὶ Φιλίππου πράξεων αἱ μετὰ τὸν ἐκείνου θάνατον ἐπιτελεσθεῖσαι μετ' Ἀλεξάνδρου πᾶσιν ὁμολογουμένην τὴν ἐπ' ἀρετῆι φήμην παραδεδώκασι περὶ αὐτῶν. 8 μεγάλην γὰρ ἴσως μερίδα θετέον τῶι προεστῶτι τῶν ὅλων Ἀλεξάνδρωι, καίπερ ὄντι νέωι παντελῶς, οὐκ ἐλάττω μέντοι γε τοῖς συνεργοῖς καὶ φίλοις, 9 οἵ πολλαῖς μὲν καὶ παραδόξοις μάχαις ἐνίκησαν τοὺς ὑπεναντίους, πολλοὺς δὲ καὶ παραβόλους ὑπέμειναν πόνους καὶ κινδύνους καὶ ταλαιπωρίας, πλείστης δὲ περιουσίας κυριεύσαντες καὶ πρὸς ἁπάσας τὰς ἐπιθυμίας πλείστης εὐπορήσαντες ἀπολαύσεως, οὔτε κατὰ τὴν σωματικὴν δύναμιν οὐδέποτε διὰ ταῦτ' ἠλαττώθησαν, οὔτε κατὰ τὰς ψυχικὰς ὁρμὰς οὐδὲν ἄδικον οὐδ' ἀσελγὲς ἐπετήδευσαν, 10 ἅπαντες δ', ὡς ἔπος εἰπεῖν, βασιλικοὶ καὶ ταῖς μεγαλοψυχίαις καὶ ταῖς σωφροσύναις καὶ ταῖς τόλμαις ἀπέβησαν, Φιλίππωι καὶ μετ' Ἀλεξάνδρωι συμβιώσαντες. ὧν οὐδὲν ἂν δέοι μνημονεύειν ἐπ' ὀνόματος. 11 μετὰ δὲ τὸν Ἀλεξάνδρου θάνατον οὕτω περὶ τῶν πλείστων μερῶν τῆς οἰκουμένης ἀμφισβητήσαντες παραδόσιμον ἐποίησαν τὴν ἑαυτῶν δόξαν ἐν πλείστοις ὑπομνήμασιν 12 ὥστε τὴν μὲν Τιμαίου τοῦ συγγραφέως πικρίαν ἧι κέχρηται κατ' Ἀγαθοκλέους τοῦ Σικελίας δυνάστου, καίπερ ἀνυπέρβλητον εἶναι δοκοῦσαν, ὅμως λόγον ἔχειν – ὡς γὰρ κατ' ἐχθροῦ καὶ πονηροῦ καὶ τυράννου διατίθεται τὴν κατηγορίαν – τὴν δὲ Θεοπόμπου μηδ' ὑπὸ λόγον πίπτειν.

11.1 προθέμενος γὰρ ὡς περὶ βασιλέως εὐφυεστάτου πρὸς ἀρετὴν γεγονότος, οὐκ ἔστι τῶν αἰσχρῶν καὶ δεινῶν ὃ παραλέλοιπε. 2 λοιπὸν ἢ περὶ τὴν ἀρχὴν καὶ προέκθεσιν τῆς πραγματείας ἀνάγκη ψεύστην καὶ κόλακα φαίνεσθαι τὸν ἱστοριογράφον, ἢ περὶ τὰς κατὰ μέρος ἀποφάσεις ἀνόητον καὶ μειρακιώδη τελείως, εἰ διὰ τῆς ἀλόγου καὶ ἐπικλήτου λοιδορίας ὑπέλαβε πιστότερος μὲν αὐτὸς φανήσεσθαι, παραδοχῆς δὲ μᾶλλον ἀξιωθήσεσθαι τὰς ἐγκωμιαστικὰς ἀποφάσεις αὐτοῦ περὶ Φιλίππου. 3 καὶ μὴν οὐδὲ περὶ τὰς ὁλοσχερεῖς διαλήψεις οὐδεὶς ἂν εὐδοκήσειε τῶι προειρημένωι συγγραφεῖ, ὅς γ' ἐπιβαλόμενος γράφειν τὰς Ἑλληνικὰς πράξεις ἀφ' ὧν Θουκυδίδης ἀπέλιπε, καὶ συνεγγίσας τοῖς Λευκτρικοῖς καιροῖς καὶ τοῖς ἐπιφανεστάτοις τῶν Ἑλληνικῶν ἔργων, τὴν μὲν Ἑλλάδα μεταξὺ καὶ τὰς ταύτης ἐπιβολὰς ἀπέρριψε, μεταλαβὼν δὲ τὴν ὑπόθεσιν τὰς Φιλίππου πράξεις προύθετο γράφειν. 4 καίτοι γε πολλῶι σεμνότερον ἦν καὶ δικαιότερον ἐν

[10] 6 <τὴν> hic Hutchinson, post μεγίστην Reiske    7 ἐπὶ Reiske: ἀπὸ P
8 προεστῶτι Valesius: παρ- P    10 μετ' <αὐτὸν> Reiske    11 ἑαυτῶν Valesius: -οῦ P
[11] 1 ὃ παραλέλοιπε Reiske: ὅπερ ἀπολέλοιπεν P    2 διὰ ... φανήσεσθαι
Suda ε 2387    ἐπικλήτου καὶ ἀλόγου Suda    παραδοχῆς Reiske: παροχης P
3 μεταβαλὼν Valesius

τῆι περὶ τῆς Ἑλλάδος ὑποθέσει τὰ πεπραγμένα Φιλίππωι συμπεριλαβεῖν ἤπερ ἐν τῆι Φιλίππου τὰ τῆς Ἑλλάδος. **5** οὐδὲ γὰρ προκαταληφθεὶς ὑπὸ βασιλικῆς δυναστείας, καὶ τυχὼν ἐξουσίας, οὐδεὶς ἂν ἐπέσχε σὺν καιρῶι ποιήσασθαι μετάβασιν ἐπὶ τὸ τῆς Ἑλλάδος ὄνομα καὶ πρόσωπον· ἀπὸ δὲ ταύτης ἀρξάμενος καὶ προβὰς ἐπὶ ποσόν, οὐδ' ὅλως οὐδεὶς ἂν ἠλλάξατο μονάρχου πρόσχημα καὶ βίον, ἀκεραίωι χρώμενος γνώμηι. **6** καὶ τί δήποτ' ἦν τὸ τὰς τηλικαύτας ἐναντιώσεις βιασάμενον παριδεῖν Θεόπομπον; εἰ μὴ νὴ Δί' ὅτι ἐκείνης μὲν τῆς ὑποθέσεως τέλος ἦν τὸ καλόν, τῆς δὲ κατὰ Φίλιππον τὸ συμφέρον. **7** οὐ μὴν ἀλλὰ πρὸς μὲν ταύτην τὴν ἁμαρτίαν [καθὸ μετέβαλε τὴν ὑπόθεσιν] ἴσως ἂν εἶχέ τι λέγειν, εἴ τις αὐτὸν ἤρετο περὶ τούτων· **8** πρὸς δὲ τὴν κατὰ τῶν φίλων αἰσχρολογίαν οὐκ ἂν οἶμαι δυνηθῆναι λόγον αὐτὸν ἀποδοῦναι, συγχωρῆσαι δὲ διότι πολύ τι παρέπεσε τοῦ καθήκοντος.

**12.1** Φίλιππος δέ, <         > τοὺς μὲν Μεσσηνίους πολεμίους γεγονότας οὐδὲν ἄξιον ἠδυνήθη λόγου βλάψαι, καίπερ ἐπιβαλόμενος κακοποιεῖν αὐτῶν τὴν χώραν, εἰς δὲ τοὺς ἀναγκαιοτάτους τῶν φίλων τὴν μεγίστην ἀσέλγειαν ἐναπεδείξατο. **2** τὸν γὰρ πρεσβύτερον Ἄρατον, δυσαρεστηθέντα τοῖς ὑπ' αὐτοῦ πεπραγμένοις ἐν τῆι Μεσσήνηι, μετ' οὐ πολὺ μετὰ Ταυρίωνος τοῦ χειρίζοντος αὐτῶι τὰ κατὰ Πελοπόννησον ἐπανείλετο φαρμάκωι. **3** παραυτίκα μὲν οὖν ἠγνοεῖτο παρὰ τοῖς ἐκτὸς τὸ γεγονός· καὶ γὰρ ἦν ἡ δύναμις οὐ τῶν παρ' αὐτὸν τὸν καιρὸν ἀπολλυουσῶν, ἀλλὰ χρόνον ἔχουσα καὶ <         > διάθεσιν ἐργαζομένη· **4** τόν γε μὴν Ἄρατον αὐτὸν οὐκ ἐλάνθανε τὸ κακόν. ἐγένετο δὲ δῆλον ἐκ τούτων· **5** ἅπαντας γὰρ ἐπικρυπτόμενος τοὺς ἄλλους, πρὸς ἕνα τῶν ὑπηρετῶν Κεφάλωνα διὰ τὴν συνήθειαν οὐκ ἔστεξε τὸν λόγον, ἀλλ' ἐπιμελῶς αὐτῶι κατὰ τὴν ἀρρωστίαν τοῦ προειρημένου συμπαρόντος καί τι τῶν πρὸς τῶι τοίχωι πτυσμάτων ἐπισημηναμένου δίαιμον ὑπάρχον, εἶπε 'ταῦτα τἀπίχειρα τῆς φιλίας, ὦ Κεφάλων, κεκομίσμεθα τῆς πρὸς Φίλιππον.' **6** οὕτως ἐστὶ μέγα τι καὶ καλὸν χρῆμα μετριότης, ὥστε μᾶλλον ὁ παθὼν τοῦ πράξαντος ἠισχύνετο τὸ γεγονός, εἰ τοσούτων καὶ τηλικούτων κεκοινωνηκὼς ἔργων ἐπὶ τῶι τοῦ Φιλίππου συμφέροντι τοιαῦτα τἀπίχειρα κεκόμισται τῆς εὐνοίας. **7** οὗτος μὲν οὖν καὶ διὰ τὸ πολλάκις τῆς ἀρχῆς τετευχέναι παρὰ τοῖς Ἀχαιοῖς, καὶ διὰ τὸ πλῆθος καὶ διὰ τὸ μέγεθος τῶν εἰς τὸ ἔθνος εὐεργεσιῶν, μεταλλάξας τὸν βίον ἔτυχε πρεπούσης τιμῆς καὶ παρὰ τῆι πατρίδι καὶ παρὰ τῶι κοινῶι τῶν Ἀχαιῶν. **8** καὶ γὰρ θυσίας αὐτῶι καὶ τιμὰς ἡρωϊκὰς ἐψηφίσαντο, καὶ συλλήβδην ὅσα πρὸς αἰώνιον ἀνήκει μνήμην· ὥστ'

---

[11] 5 προβὰς Valesius: προσβὰς P     7 καθὸ ... ὑπόθεσιν del. Hutchinson
[12] 1 pergit P; accedent FDG     uel post δέ uel, ut solitum est, ante Φίλιππος lacuna statuenda     μὲν om. G, add. G^{mg}     ἐπιβαλόμενος P: ἐπίβαλλ- FDG     ἀσέλγειαν: ἀσέβειαν Hutchinson     ἐναπ- FDG: ἀπ- P     2 δυσαρεστηθέντα P: -ος G: -ων FD     ἐν τῆι M. om. P     ἐπανείλετο G: -ατο PFD     3 παρὰ τοῖς P: παρ' αὐτοῖς FDG     lac. stat. Hutchinson     ἐργαζομένη FD: -ομένην P: -όμενοι G     4 κακόν FD: καλόν G     5 τὰ κατὰ FDG     6 ὁ παθὼν om. P     εἰ Casaubon: ἢ PDG: ἡ F
7 παρὰ (bis) om. P     post κοινῶι τῶν Ἀχαιῶν desinit P

εἴπερ καὶ περὶ τοὺς ἀποιχομένους ἔστι τις αἴσθησις, εἰκὸς εὐδοκεῖν αὐτὸν καὶ τῆι τῶν Ἀχαιῶν εὐχαριστίαι καὶ ταῖς ἐν τῶι ζῆν κακοπραγίαις καὶ κινδύνοις. 13.1 πάλαι δὲ τῆι διανοίαι περὶ τὸν Λίσσον καὶ τὸν Ἀκρόλισσον ὤν, καὶ σπουδάζων ἐγκρατὴς γενέσθαι τῶν τόπων τούτων, ὥρμησε μετὰ τῆς δυνάμεως· 2 ποιησάμενος δὲ τὴν πορείαν ἐπὶ δύ' ἡμέρας, καὶ διελθὼν τὰ στενά, κατέζευξε παρὰ τὸν Ἀρδάξανον ποταμόν, οὐ μακρὰν τῆς πόλεως. 3 θεωρῶν δὲ τόν τε τοῦ Λίσσου περίβολον καὶ τὰ πρὸς θαλάττηι καὶ τὰ πρὸς τὴν μεσόγαιον ἠσφαλισμένον διαφερόντως καὶ φύσει καὶ κατασκευῆι, τόν τε παρακείμενον Ἀκρόλισσον αὐτῶι καὶ διὰ τὴν εἰς ὕψος ἀνάτασιν καὶ διὰ τὴν ἄλλην ἐρυμνότητα τοιαύτην ἔχοντα φαντασίαν ὥστε μηδ' ἂν ἐλπίσαι μηδένα κατὰ κράτος ἑλεῖν, τῆς μὲν περὶ τοῦτον ἐλπίδος ἀπέστη τελέως, τῆς δὲ πόλεως οὐ λίαν ἀπήλπισε. 4 συνθεωρήσας δὲ τὸ μεταξὺ διάστημα τοῦ Λίσσου καὶ τοῦ κατὰ τὸν Ἀκρόλισσον πρόποδος σύμμετρον ὑπάρχον πρὸς τὴν ἐπιβολὴν τὴν κατὰ τῆς πόλεως, κατὰ τοῦτο διενοήθη συστησάμενος ἀκροβολισμὸν χρήσασθαι στρατηγήματι πρὸς τὸ παρὸν οἰκείωι. 5 δοὺς δὲ μίαν ἡμέραν πρὸς ἀνάπαυσιν τοῖς Μακεδόσι, καὶ παρακαλέσας ἐν αὐτῆι τὰ πρέποντα τῶι καιρῶι, τὸ μὲν πολὺ μέρος καὶ χρησιμώτατον τῶν εὐζώνων ἔτι νυκτὸς εἴς τινας φάραγγας ὑλώδεις ἔκρυψε κατὰ τὸν ἐπὶ τῆς μεσογαίου τόπον ὑπὲρ τὸ προειρημένον διάστημα, 6 τοὺς δὲ πελταστὰς εἰς τὴν ἐπαύριον ἔχων καὶ τὸ λοιπὸν μέρος τῶν εὐζώνων ἐπὶ θάτερα τῆς πόλεως κατὰ θάλατταν ἐχρῆτο τῆι πορείαι. 7 περιελθὼν δὲ τὴν πόλιν, καὶ γενόμενος κατὰ τὸν προειρημένον τόπον, δῆλος ἦν ὡς ταύτηι ποιησόμενος τὴν πρὸς τὴν πόλιν ἀνάβασιν. 8 οὐκ ἀγνοουμένης δὲ τῆς τοῦ Φιλίππου παρουσίας, ἣν πλῆθος ἱκανὸν ἐξ ἁπάσης τῆς πέριξ Ἰλλυρίδος εἰς τὸν Λίσσον ἠθροισμένον· 9 τῶι μὲν γὰρ Ἀκρολίσσωι διὰ τὴν ὀχυρότητα πιστεύοντες, μετρίαν τινὰ τελέως εἰς αὐτὸν ἀπένειμαν φυλακήν.

14.1 διόπερ ἅμα τῶι συνεγγίζειν τοὺς Μακεδόνας, εὐθέως ἐκ τῆς πόλεως ἐξεχέοντο, θαρροῦντες ἐπί τε τῶι πλήθει καὶ ταῖς τῶν τόπων ὀχυρότησι. 2 τοὺς μὲν οὖν πελταστὰς ὁ βασιλεὺς ἐν τοῖς ἐπιπέδοις ἐπέστησε, τοῖς δὲ κούφοις παρήγγειλε προβαίνειν πρὸς τοὺς λόφους καὶ συμπλέκεσθαι πρὸς τοὺς πολεμίους ἐρρωμένως. 3 ποιούντων δὲ τὸ παραγγελθέν, ἐπὶ ποσὸν μὲν ὁ κίνδυνος πάρισος ἦν· μετὰ δὲ ταῦτα καὶ ταῖς δυσχωρίαις εἴξαντες οἱ παρὰ τοῦ Φιλίππου καὶ τῶι πλήθει τῶν πολεμίων ἐτράπησαν. 4 καταφυγόντων δὲ τούτων εἰς τοὺς πελταστάς, οἱ μὲν ἐκ τῆς πόλεως καταφρονήσαντες προήιεσαν καὶ συγκαταβάντες ἐν τοῖς ἐπιπέδοις προσεμάχοντο τοῖς πελτασταῖς· 5 οἱ δὲ τὸν Ἀκρόλισσον φυλάττοντες, θεωροῦντες τὸν Φίλιππον ἐκ διαδοχῆς ταῖς σπείραις ἐπὶ πόδα ποιούμενον τὴν ἀναχώρησιν, καὶ δόξαντες τοῖς ὅλοις αὐτὸν εἴκειν, ἔλαθον ἐκκληθέντες διὰ τὸ πιστεύειν τῆι φύσει

[13] 13–14 FDG     1 nouum excerptum plane incipiunt F<sup>mg</sup>D, minus plane FG     3 θαλάττηι F: τῆι θ. DG     4 Λίσσου Ursinus: μέσου FDG     ἐπιβολὴν Casaubon: μετα- FDG     5 εὐζώνων Ursinus: εὐσώμων FDG     ἐπὶ Casaubon: ὑπὸ FDG     6 ἐπαύριον FD<sup>mg</sup>: ἐσ- DG
[14] 5 εἴκειν Ursinus: ἥκειν fere FDG     ἔλαθον FD<sup>mg</sup>G<sup>mg</sup>: ἔλθον DG: ἔθεον quoque D<sup>mg</sup>G<sup>mg</sup>     ἐκκληθέντες Casaubon: ἐγ- FDG

τοῦ τόπου, 6 κἄπειτα κατ' ὀλίγους ἐκλιπόντες τὸν Ἀκρόλισσον, κατέρρεον ταῖς ἀνοδίαις εἰς τοὺς ὁμαλοὺς καὶ πεδινοὺς τόπους, ὡς ἤδη τινὸς ὠφελείας ἐκ <τῆς> τροπῆς τῶν πολεμίων ἐσομένης. 7 κατὰ δὲ τὸν καιρὸν τοῦτον, οἱ τὰς ἐνέδρας ἐπὶ τῆς μεσογαίας διειληφότες ἀφανῶς ἐξαναστάντες ἐνεργὸν ἐποιήσαντο τὴν πορείαν καὶ τὴν ἔφοδον· ἅμα δὲ τούτοις ἐκ μεταβολῆς οἱ πελτασταὶ συνεπέθεντο τοῖς ὑπεναντίοις. 8 οὗ συμβάντος διαταραχθέντες οἱ μὲν ἐκ τοῦ Λίσσου σποράδην ποιούμενοι τὴν ἀναχώρησιν διεσωιζοντο πρὸς τὴν πόλιν, οἱ δὲ τὸν Ἀκρόλισσον ἐκλιπόντες ἀπετμήθησαν ὑπὸ τῶν ἐκ τῆς ἐνέδρας ἐξαναστάντων. 9 διὸ καὶ συνέβη τὸ μὲν ἀνέλπιστον, τὸν Ἀκρόλισσον παραχρῆμα ληφθῆναι χωρὶς κινδύνων, τὸν δὲ Λίσσον τῆι κατὰ πόδας ἡμέραι μετὰ μεγάλων ἀγώνων, ποιησαμένων τῶν Μακεδόνων ἐνεργοὺς καὶ καταπληκτικὰς προσβολάς. 10 Φίλιππος μὲν οὖν, παραδόξως ἐγκρατὴς γενόμενος τῶν προειρημένων τόπων, ἅπαντας τοὺς πέριξ ὑποχειρίους ἐποιήσατο διὰ ταύτης τῆς πράξεως, ὥστε τοὺς πλείστους τῶν Ἰλλυριῶν ἐθελοντὴν ἐπιτρέπειν αὐτῶι τὰς πόλεις· 11 οὐδεμία γὰρ ὀχυρότης ἔτι πρὸς τὴν Φιλίππου βίαν οὐδ' ἀσφάλεια τοῖς ἀντιταττομένοις προυφαίνετο, κεκρατημένων μετὰ βίας τῶν προειρημένων ὀχυρωμάτων.

**14b.1** Δασσαρῆται· ἔθνος Ἰλλυρίας. Πολύβιος η̄.

**14b.2** Ὕσκανα· πόλις Ἰλλυρίδος, οὐδετέρως. Πολύβιος η̄.

**15.1** Βῶλις ἦν ἀνὴρ γένει μὲν Κρής, χρόνον δὲ πολὺν ἐν τῆι βασιλείαι διατετριφὼς ἐν ἡγεμονικῆι προστασίαι, δοκῶν δὲ καὶ σύνεσιν ἔχειν καὶ τόλμαν παράβολον καὶ τριβὴν ἐν τοῖς πολεμικοῖς οὐδενὸς ἐλάττω. 2 τοῦτον ὁ Σωσίβιος διὰ πλειόνων λόγων πιστωσάμενος, καὶ παρασκευάσας εὔνουν ἑαυτῶι καὶ πρόθυμον, ἀναδίδωσι τὴν πρᾶξιν, λέγων ὡς οὐδὲν ἂν τῶι βασιλεῖ μεῖζον χαρίσαιτο κατὰ τοὺς ἐνεστῶτας καιροὺς ἢ συνεπινοήσας πῶς καὶ τίνι τρόπωι δύναται σῶσαι τὸν Ἀχαιόν. 3 τότε μὲν οὖν διακούσας ὁ Βῶλις, καὶ φήσας ἐπισκέψεσθαι περὶ τῶν εἰρημένων, ἐχωρίσθη· 4 δοὺς δὲ λόγον ἑαυτῶι, καὶ μετὰ δύ' ἢ τρεῖς ἡμέρας προσελθὼν πρὸς τὸν Σωσίβιον, ἀνεδέξατο τὴν πρᾶξιν εἰς αὐτόν, φήσας καὶ γεγονέναι πλείω χρόνον ἐν ταῖς Σάρδεσι καὶ τῶν τόπων ἐμπειρεῖν, καὶ τὸν Καμβύλον τὸν ἡγεμόνα τῶν παρ' Ἀντιόχωι στρατευομένων Κρητῶν οὐ μόνον πολίτην, ἀλλὰ καὶ συγγενῆ καὶ φίλον ὑπάρχειν αὐτῶι. 5 συνέβαινε δὲ καὶ τὸν Καμβύλον καὶ τοὺς ὑπὸ τοῦτον ταττομένους Κρῆτας πεπιστεῦσθαί τι τῶν φυλακτηρίων τῶν κατὰ τοὺς ὄπισθε τόπους τῆς ἄκρας, οἵτινες κατασκευὴν μὲν οὐκ ἐπεδέχοντο, τῆι δὲ συνεχείαι τῶν

[14] 6 ἐκ G^{mg}: καὶ FDG         τῆς add. Hutchinson         7 οἱ δὲ ἐξαναστάντες ... ἐφοδὸν Suda ε 1252        ἐπὶ Hutchinson: ἐκ FDG        τὴν πορείαν καὶ Suda: om. FDG
9 Λίσσον G^{mg}: μέσον FDG
[14b.1] Steph. Byz. δ 28 Billerbeck         Δασσαρῆται Holste: -ῆται RQP
[14b.2] Steph. Byz. υ 52 Billerbeck et Neumann-Hartmann
[15] 15–21: FDG; 21.4 et fortasse 11 accedit Π, 21.11 accedit M    1 Κρής fere D^{mg}G^{mg}: Κρήτης FDG    3 ἐπισκέψεσθαι Reiske: -ασθαι FDG    4 φήσας ... ἐμπειρεῖν Suda ε 1012         πλείω χρόνον F Suda: χρ. πλ. DG         Σάρδεσι G: ἄρδεσι FD         Ἀντιόχωι: -ωι aut -ου F: -ου DG

ὑπὸ τὸν Καμβύλον τεταγμένων ἀνδρῶν ἐτηροῦντο. 6 τοῦ δὲ Σωσιβίου δεξαμένου τὴν ἐπίνοιαν, καὶ διειληφότος ἢ μὴ δυνατὸν εἶναι σωθῆναι τὸν Ἀχαιὸν ἐκ τῶν περιεστώτων, ἢ δυνατοῦ καθάπαξ ὑπάρχοντος διὰ μηδενὸς ἂν ἑτέρου γενέσθαι τοῦτο βέλτιον ἢ διὰ Βώλιδος, τοιαύτης δὲ συνδραμούσης καὶ περὶ τὸν Βῶλιν προθυμίας, ταχέως ἐλάμβανε τὸ πρᾶγμα προκοπήν. 7 ὅ τε γὰρ Σωσίβιος ἅμα μὲν προεδίδου τῶν χρημάτων εἰς τὸ μηδὲν ἐλλείπειν εἰς τὰς ἐπιβολάς, πολλὰ δ᾽ εὖ γενομένων ὑπισχνεῖτο δώσειν, 8 τὰς δὲ παρὰ τοῦ βασιλέως καὶ παρ᾽ αὑτοῦ τοῦ σωιζομένου χάριτας ἐξ ὑπερβολῆς αὔξων εἰς μεγάλας ἐλπίδας ἦγε τὸν Βῶλιν· 9 ὅ τε προειρημένος ἀνήρ, ἕτοιμος ὢν πρὸς τὴν πρᾶξιν, οὐδένα χρόνον ἐπιμείνας ἐξέπλευσε, συνθήματα λαβὼν καὶ πίστεις πρός τε Νικόμαχον εἰς Ῥόδον, ὃς ἐδόκει πατρὸς ἔχειν διάθεσιν κατὰ τὴν εὔνοιαν καὶ πίστιν πρὸς τὸν Ἀχαιόν, ὁμοίως δὲ καὶ πρὸς Μελαγκόμαν εἰς Ἔφεσον. 10 οὗτοι γὰρ ἦσαν δι᾽ ὧν καὶ τὸν πρὸ τοῦ χρόνου Ἀχαιὸς τά τε πρὸς τὸν Πτολεμαῖον καὶ τὰς ἄλλας ἁπάσας τὰς ἔξωθεν ἐπιβολὰς ἐχείριζε.

16.1 παραγενόμενος δ᾽ εἰς τὴν Ῥόδον καὶ μετὰ ταῦτα πάλιν εἰς τὴν Ἔφεσον, καὶ κοινωσάμενος τοῖς προειρημένοις ἀνδράσι, καὶ λαβὼν αὐτοὺς ἑτοίμους εἰς τὰ παρακαλούμενα, μετὰ ταῦτ᾽ Ἀριανόν τινα τῶν ὑφ᾽ αὑτὸν ταττομένων διαπέμπεται πρὸς τὸν Καμβύλον, 2 φήσας ἐξαπεστάλθαι μὲν ἐκ τῆς Ἀλεξανδρείας ξενολογήσων, βούλεσθαι δὲ τῶι Καμβύλωι συμμῖξαι περί τινων ἀναγκαίων· διόπερ ὤιετο δεῖν τάξασθαι καιρὸν καὶ τόπον ἐν ὧι μηδενὸς συνειδότος αὐτοῖς συναντήσουσι. 3 ταχὺ δὲ τοῦ Ἀριανοῦ συμμίξαντος τῶι Καμβύλωι καὶ δηλώσαντος τὰς ἐντολάς, ἑτοίμως ὁ προειρημένος ἀνὴρ ὑπήκουσε τοῖς παρακαλουμένοις, καὶ συνθέμενος ἡμέραν καὶ τόπον ἑκατέρωι γνωστὸν εἰς ὃν παρέσται νυκτός, ἀπέπεμψε τὸν Ἀριανόν. 4 ὁ δὲ Βῶλις, ἅτε Κρὴς ὑπάρχων καὶ φύσει ποικίλος, πᾶν ἐβάσταζε πρᾶγμα καὶ πᾶσαν ἐπίνοιαν ἐψηλάφα. 5 τέλος δὲ συμμίξας τῶι Καμβύλωι κατὰ τὴν τοῦ Ἀριανοῦ σύνταξιν ἔδωκεν [τὴν] ἐπιστολὴν < >. ἧς τεθείσης εἰς τὸ μέσον ἐποιοῦντο τὴν σκέψιν Κρητικήν· 6 οὐ γὰρ ἐσκόπουν ὑπὲρ τῆς τοῦ κινδυνεύοντος σωτηρίας οὐδ᾽ ὑπὲρ τῆς τῶν ἐγχειρισάντων τὴν πρᾶξιν πίστεως, ἀλλ᾽ ὑπὲρ τῆς αὐτῶν ἀσφαλείας καὶ τοῦ σφίσιν αὐτοῖς συμφέροντος. 7 διόπερ ἀμφότεροι Κρῆτες ὄντες συντόμως κατηνέχθησαν ἐπὶ τὴν αὐτὴν γνώμην· αὕτη δ᾽ ἦν τὰ μὲν παρὰ τοῦ Σωσιβίου προδεδομένα δέκα τάλαντα διελέσθαι κοινῆι, 8 τὴν δὲ πρᾶξιν Ἀντιόχωι δηλώσαντας καὶ συνεργῶι χρησαμένους ἐπαγγείλασθαι τὸν Ἀχαιὸν ἐγχειριεῖν αὐτῶι, λαβόντας χρήματα καὶ τὰς εἰς τὸ μέλλον ἐλπίδας ἀξίας τῆς προειρημένης ἐπιβολῆς. 9 τούτων δὲ κυρωθέντων ὁ μὲν Καμβύλος ἀνεδέξατο χειριεῖν τὰ κατὰ τὸν Ἀντίοχον, ὁ δὲ Βῶλις ἐτάξατο μετά τινας ἡμέρας πέμψειν

[15] 7 προεδίδου Reiske: προσ- FDG    8 παρὰ τοῦ β. Reiske: παρ᾽ αὑτοῦ β. FDG    παρ᾽ αὑτοῦ Casaubon: παρὰ τούτου FDG: παρ᾽ Ἀχαιοῦ Büttner-Wobst    9 ἐπιμείνας Schweighaeuser: ὑπο- FDG    10 ἐπιβολὰς Ursinus: ἐπιβὰς FDG
[16] 2 ὤιετο FD: ἐγένετο ὢι. D^mgG    5 ἔδωκεν [τὴν] ἐπιστολήν < > Hutchinson (suppleri possit e.g. <παρὰ Σωσιβίου>): ἔδωκε τὴν ἐπιστολήν FDG: ἐδήλωσε τὴν ἐπιβολήν Bekker    6 ἐγχειρισάντων cod. rec.: ἐγχειρησ- FDG    8 χρησομένους Hutchinson

ἀκμὴν ἔκρινε μὴ πᾶσαν εἰς τὸν Βῶλιν ἀνακρεμάσαι τὴν πίστιν. 4 διὸ ποιεῖται τοιούτους λόγους πρὸς αὐτόν, ὅτι κατὰ μὲν τὸ παρὸν οὐκ ἔστι δυνατὸν ἐξελθεῖν αὐτῶι, πέμψει δέ τινας τῶν φίλων μετ' ἐκείνου τρεῖς ἢ τέτταρας, ὧν συμμιξάντων τοῖς περὶ τὸν Μελαγκόμαν ἕτοιμον αὐτὸν ἔφη παρασκευάσειν τὶ πρὸς τὴν ἔξοδον. 5 ὁ μὲν οὖν Ἀχαιὸς ἐποίει τὰ δυνατά· τοῦτο δ' ἠγνόει, τὸ δὴ λ̣εγόμενον, πρὸς Κρῆτα κρητίζων, ὁ γὰρ Βῶλις οὐθὲν ἀψηλάφητον εἶχε τῶν ἐπινοηθέντων ἂν εἰς τοῦτο τὸ μέρος. 6 πλὴν παραγενομένης τῆς νυκτὸς ἐν ἧι συνεξαποστελεῖν ἔφη τοὺς φίλους, προπέμψας τὸν Ἀριανὸν καὶ τὸν Βῶλιν ἐπὶ τὴν τῆς ἄκρας ἔξοδον, μένειν προσέταξε μέχρις ἂν οἱ μέλλοντες αὐτοῖς συνεξορμᾶν παραγένωνται. 7 τῶν δὲ πειθαρχησάντων, κοινωσάμενος παρ' αὐτὸν τὸν καιρὸν τῆι γυναικὶ καὶ ποιήσας διὰ τὸ παράδοξον τὴν Λαοδίκην ἔκφρονα, χρόνον μέν τινα λιπαρῶν ταύτην καὶ καταπραΰνων ταῖς προσδοκωμέναις ἐλπίσι προσεκαρτέρει, 8 μετὰ δὲ ταῦτα πέμπτος αὐτὸς γενόμενος, καὶ τοῖς μὲν ἄλλοις μετρίας ἐσθῆτας ἀναδούς, αὐτὸς δὲ λιτὴν καὶ τὴν τυχοῦσαν ἀναλαβὼν καὶ ταπεινὸν αὑτὸν ποιήσας, προῆγε, 9 συντάξας ἑνὶ τῶν φίλων αὐτὸν [ἀεὶ] ἀποκρίνεσθαι πρὸς τὸ λεγόμενον ὑπὸ τῶν περὶ τὸν Ἀριανὸν καὶ πυνθάνεσθαι παρ' ἐκείνων ἀεὶ τὸ κατεπεῖγον, περὶ δὲ τῶν ἄλλων φάναι βαρβάρους αὐτοὺς ὑπάρχειν.

20.1 ἐπεὶ δὲ συνέμιξαν τοῖς περὶ τὸν Ἀριανόν, ἡγεῖτο μὲν αὐτὸς αὐτῶν διὰ τὴν ἐμπειρίαν, ὁ δὲ Βῶλις κατόπιν ἐπέστη κατὰ τὴν ἐξ ἀρχῆς πρόθεσιν, ἀπορῶν καὶ δυσχρηστούμενος ὑπὲρ τοῦ συμβαίνοντος· 2 καίπερ γὰρ ὢν Κρὴς καὶ πᾶν ἄν τι κατὰ τοῦ πέλας ὑποπτεύσας, ὅμως οὐκ ἠδύνατο διὰ τὸ σκότος συννοῆσαι τὸν Ἀχαιόν, οὐχ οἷον τίς ἐστιν, ἀλλ' οὐδὲ καθάπαξ εἰ πάρεστι. 3 τῆς δὲ καταβάσεως κρημνώδους μὲν καὶ δυσβάτου κατὰ τὸ πλεῖστον ὑπαρχούσης, ἔν τισι δὲ τόποις καὶ λίαν ἐπισφαλεῖς ἐχούσης καὶ κινδυνώδεις καταφοράς, ὁπότε παραγένοιντο πρός τινα τοιοῦτον τόπον, τῶν μὲν ἐπιλαμβανομένων, τῶν δὲ πάλιν ἐκδεχομένων τὸν Ἀχαιόν, 4 οὐ δυναμένων [γὰρ] καθόλου τὴν ἐκ τῆς συνηθείας καταξίωσιν στέλλεσθαι πρὸς τὸν παρόντα καιρόν· ταχέως ὁ Βῶλις συνῆκε τίς ἐστι καὶ ποῖος αὐτῶν ὁ Ἀχαιός. 5 ἐπεὶ δὲ παρεγένοντο πρὸς τὸν τῶι Καμβύλωι διατεταγμένον τόπον, καὶ τὸ σύνθημα προσσυρίξας ὁ Βῶλις ἀπέδωκε, τῶν μὲν ἄλλων οἱ διαναστάντες ἐκ τῆς ἐνέδρας ἐπελάβοντο, 6 τὸν δ' Ἀχαιὸν αὐτὸς ὁ Βῶλις ὁμοῦ τοῖς ἱματίοις, ἔνδον τὰς χεῖρας ἔχοντα, συνήρπασε, φοβηθεὶς μὴ συννοήσας τὸ γινόμενον ἐπιβάλοιτο διαφθείρειν αὑτόν· καὶ γὰρ εἶχε μάχαιραν ἐφ' αὑτῶι παρεσκευασμένος. 7 ταχὺ δὲ καὶ πανταχόθεν κυκλωθεὶς ὑποχείριος ἐγένετο τοῖς

[19] 4 οὐκ ἔστι FG^mg: οὐκέτι DG    5 ἠγνόει ... κρητίζων Suda π 2745    τὸ δὴ F Suda: τὸ δὴ τὸ DG    6 συνεξαποστελεῖν Schweighaeuser: -στέλλειν FDG    μένειν F: μένειν ἔφη DG    9 [ἀεὶ] Hutchinson: ἀεὶ D^mgG^mg: εἶεν FDG: αἰὲν Büttner-Wobst    ἀποκρίνεσθαι FD: ἀποκρίνασθαι G
[20] 1 αὐτός: οὗτος Hultsch    3 παραγένοιντο Reiske: -γένοιτο FDG    4 [γὰρ] Hutchinson: γὰρ FD: δὲ G; (οὐ ... καιρὸν) in παρενθέσει G    5 προσσυρίξας Reiske: προσυρίξας FDG    ἀπέδωκε Reiske: ἐπ- FDG    6 ἐπιβάλοιτο Scaliger: ἐπιλάβοιτο FDG    ἐφ' αὑτῶι Büttner-Wobst: ὑφ' αὑτῶι FDG    7 δὲ καὶ FDG^sl: δὲ G

ἐχθροῖς, καὶ παρα**χρῆμα** μετὰ τῶν φίλων ἀνήγετο πρὸς τὸν Ἀντίοχον. **8** ὁ δὲ βασιλεύς, πάλαι μετέωρος ὢν τῆι διανοίαι καὶ καραδοκῶν τὸ συμβησόμενον, ἀπολύσας τοὺς ἐκ τῆς συνουσίας ἔμενε μόνος ἐγρηγορὼς ἐν τῆι σκηνῆι μετὰ δυεῖν ἢ τριῶν σωματοφυλάκων. **9** παρεισελθόντων δὲ τῶν περὶ τὸν Καμβύλον καὶ καθισάντων τὸν Ἀχαιὸν ἐπὶ τὴν γῆν δεδεμένον, εἰς τοιαύτην ἀφασίαν ἦλθε διὰ τὸ παράδοξον ὥστε πολὺν μὲν χρόνον ἀποσιωπῆσαι, τὸ δὲ τελευταῖον συμπαθὴς γενέσθαι καὶ δακρῦσαι. **10** τοῦτο δ' ἔπαθεν ὁρῶν, ὡς ἔμοιγε δοκεῖ, τὸ δυσφύλακτον καὶ παράλογον τῶν ἐκ τῆς τύχης συμβαινόντων. **11** Ἀχαιὸς γὰρ ἦν Ἀνδρομάχου μὲν υἱὸς τοῦ Λαοδίκης ἀδελφοῦ τῆς Σελεύκου γυναικός, ἔγημε δὲ Λαοδίκην τὴν Μιθριδάτου τοῦ βασιλέως θυγατέρα, κύριος δ' ἐγεγόνει τῆς ἐπὶ τάδε τοῦ Ταύρου πάσης. **12** δοκῶν δὲ τότε καὶ ταῖς αὑτοῦ δυνάμεσι καὶ ταῖς τῶν ὑπεναντίων ἐν ὀχυρωτάτωι τόπωι τῆς οἰκουμένης διατρίβειν, ἐκάθητο δεδεμένος ἐπὶ τῆς γῆς, ὑποχείριος γενόμενος τοῖς ἐχθροῖς, οὐδέπω γινώσκοντος οὐθενὸς ἁπλῶς τὸ γεγονὸς πλὴν τῶν πραξάντων.

**21.1** οὐ μὴν ἀλλ' ἅμα τῶι φωτὶ συναθροιζομένων τῶν φίλων εἰς τὴν σκηνὴν κατὰ τὸν ἐθισμόν, καὶ τοῦ πράγματος ὑπὸ τὴν ὄψιν θεωρουμένου, τὸ παραπλήσιον τῶι βασιλεῖ συνέβαινε πάσχειν καὶ τοὺς ἄλλους· θαυμάζοντες γὰρ τὸ γεγονὸς ἠπίστουν τοῖς ὁρωμένοις. **2** καθίσαντος δὲ τοῦ συνεδρίου, πολλοὶ μὲν ἐγίνοντο λόγοι περὶ τοῦ τίσι δεῖ κατ' αὐτοῦ χρήσασθαι τιμωρίαις· **3** ἔδοξε δ' οὖν πρῶτον μὲν ἀκρωτηριάσαι τὸν ταλαίπωρον, μετὰ δὲ ταῦτα τὴν κεφαλὴν ἀποτεμόντας αὐτοῦ καὶ καταρράψαντας εἰς ὄνειον ἀσκὸν ἀνασταυρῶσαι τὸ σῶμα. **4** γενομένων δὲ τούτων, καὶ τῆς δυνάμεως ἐπιγνούσης τὸ συμβεβηκός, τοιοῦτος ἐνθουσιασμὸς ἐγένετο καὶ παράστασις τοῦ στρατοπέδου παντὸς ὥστε τὴν Λαοδίκην ἐκ τῆς ἄκρας, μόνον συνειδυῖαν τὴν ἔξοδον τἀνδρός, τεκμήρασθαι τὸ γεγονὸς ἐκ τῆς περὶ τὸ στρατόπεδον ταραχῆς καὶ κινήσεως. **5** ταχὺ δὲ καὶ [τοῦ] κήρυκος παραγενομένου πρὸς τὴν Λαοδίκην καὶ διασαφοῦντος τὰ περὶ τὸν Ἀχαιόν, καὶ κελεύοντος τίθεσθαι τὰ πράγματα καὶ παραχωρεῖν τῆς ἄκρας, **6** τὸ μὲν πρῶτον †ἀναπόκριτος† οἰμωγὴ καὶ θρῆνοι παράλογοι κατεῖχον τοὺς περὶ τὴν ἀκρόπολιν, οὐχ οὕτως διὰ τὴν πρὸς τὸν Ἀχαιὸν εὔνοιαν ὡς διὰ τὸ παράδοξον καὶ τελέως ἀνέλπιστον ἑκάστωι φαίνεσθαι τὸ συμβεβηκός, **7** μετὰ δὲ ταῦτα πολλή τις ἦν ἀπορία καὶ δυσχρηστία περὶ τοὺς ἔνδον. **8** Ἀντίοχος δὲ διακεχειρισμένος τὸν Ἀχαιὸν ἐπεῖχε τοῖς κατὰ τὴν ἄκραν ἀεί, πεπεισμένος ἀφορμὴν ἐκ τῶν ἔνδον αὐτῶι παραδοθήσεσθαι, καὶ μάλιστα διὰ τῶν στρατιωτῶν. **9** ὃ καὶ τέλος ἐγένετο· στασιάσαντες γὰρ πρὸς σφᾶς ἐμερίσθησαν, οἱ μὲν πρὸς Ἀρίβαζον, οἱ δὲ πρὸς τὴν Λαοδίκην. οὗ γενομένου, διαπιστήσαντες ἀλλήλοις ταχέως ἀμφότεροι παρέδοσαν αὑτοὺς καὶ τὰς ἀκροπόλεις.

[21] 4 ἐνθ]ου|[σιασμὸς ... παράστ]ασις |... συν|[ Π col. i   τὴν [Λαοδίκην] Π, ut coniecerat Scaliger: τῆς Λαοδίκης FDG   συνειδυῖαν F: -δυίας DG: συν|[ tantum Π 5 τοῦ del. Hutchinson   6 †ἀναπόκριτος†: ἦν ἄκριτος Hutchinson: <ἢν> ἀνυπόκριτος noluit Hutchinson: ἀδιάκριτος Wunderer   9 Ἀρίβαζον Schweighaeuser: Ἀριό- FDG

10 Ἀχαιὸς μὲν οὖν πάντα τὰ κατὰ λόγον πράξας, ὑπὸ δὲ τῆς τῶν πιστευθέντων ἡττηθεὶς ἀθεσίας, κατεστρέψατο τὸν βίον, κατὰ δύο τρόπους οὐκ ἀνωφελὲς ὑπόδειγμα γενόμενος τοῖς ἐσομένοις, 11 καθ᾿ ἕνα μὲν πρὸς τὸ μηδενὶ πιστεύειν ῥαιδίως, καθ᾿ ἕτερον δὲ πρὸς τὸ μὴ μεγαλαυχεῖν ἐν ταῖς εὐπραγίαις, πᾶν δὲ προσδοκᾶν ἀνθρώπους ὄντας.

**24.0** κρατούσης γὰρ τῆς ἄκρας τῶν κατὰ τὸν εἴσπλουν τόπων, ὡς ἐπάνω προεῖπον [= 8.34.3 infra]

1 ὅτι οἱ Ταραντῖνοι διὰ τὸ τῆς εὐδαιμονίας ὑπερήφανον ἐπεκαλέσαντο Πύρρον τὸν Ἠπειρώτην. πᾶσα γὰρ ἐλευθερία μετ᾿ ἐξουσίας πολυχρονίου φύσιν ἔχει κόρον λαμβάνειν τῶν ὑποκειμένων, κἄπειτα ζητεῖ δεσπότην· τυχοῦσά γε μὴν τούτου ταχὺ πάλιν μισεῖ διὰ τὸ μεγάλην φαίνεσθαι τὴν πρὸς τὸ χεῖρον μεταβολήν· ὃ καὶ τότε συνέβαινε τοῖς Ταραντίνοις.

2 ὅτι πᾶν τὸ μέλλον κρεῖττον φαίνεται τοῦ παρόντος ὑπάρχειν.

3 προσπεσόντων: ἀγγελθέντων. Πολύβιος· προσπεσόντων δὲ τούτων εἰς Τάραντα καὶ τοὺς Θουρίους, ἠγανάκτει τὰ πλήθη.

4 τὸ μὲν οὖν πρῶτον ὡς ἐπ᾿ ἐξοδείαν ὁρμήσαντες ἐκ τῆς πόλεως καὶ συνεγγίσαντες τῆι παρεμβολῆι τῶν Καρχηδονίων νυκτός, ἄλλοι μὲν συγκαθέντες εἴς τινα τόπον ὑλώδη παρὰ τὴν ὁδὸν ἔμειναν, ὁ δὲ Φιλήμενος καὶ Νίκων προσῆλθον πρὸς τὴν παρεμβολήν. 5 τῶν δὲ φυλάκων ἐπιλαβομένων αὐτῶν, ἀνήγοντο πρὸς τὸν Ἀννίβαν, οὐδὲν εἰπόντες οὔτε πόθεν οὔτε τίνες ἦσαν, αὐτὸ δὲ μόνον τοῦτο δηλοῦντες, ὅτι θέλουσι τῶι στρατηγῶι συμμῖξαι. 6 ταχὺ δὲ πρὸς τὸν Ἀννίβαν ἐπαναχθέντες ἔφασαν αὐτῶι κατ᾿ ἰδίαν βούλεσθαι διαλεχθῆναι. 7 τοῦ δὲ καὶ λίαν ἑτοίμως προσδεξαμένου τὴν ἔντευξιν, ἀπελογίζοντο περί τε τῶν καθ᾿ αὑτοὺς καὶ περὶ τῶν κατὰ τὴν πατρίδα, πολλὰς καὶ ποικίλας ποιούμενοι κατηγορίας Ῥωμαίων, χάριν τοῦ μὴ δοκεῖν ἀλόγως ἐμβαίνειν εἰς τὴν ὑποκειμένην πρᾶξιν. 8 τότε μὲν οὖν Ἀννίβας ἐπαινέσας καὶ τὴν ὁρμὴν αὐτῶν φιλανθρώπως ἀποδεξάμενος, ἐξέπεμψε, συνταξάμενος παραγίνεσθαι καὶ συμμιγνύναι κατὰ τάχος αὐτῶι πάλιν. 9 κατὰ δὲ τὸ παρὸν ἐκέλευσε τὰ πρῶτα τῶν ἐξελασθέντων πρωῒ θρεμμάτων καὶ τοὺς ἅμα τούτοις ἄνδρας, ἐπειδὰν ἱκανὸν ἀπόσχωσι τῆς παρεμβολῆς, περιελασαμένους εὐθαρσῶς ἀπαλλάττεσθαι· περὶ γὰρ τῆς ἀσφαλείας αὐτῶι μελήσειν. 10 ἐποίει δὲ τοῦτο βουλόμενος αὐτῶι μὲν ἀναστροφὴν δοῦναι πρὸς τὸ πολυπραγμονῆσαι τὰ

[21] 10 ἐσομένοις DG: ἐπεσομένοις F    11 πιστεύειν ... ὄντας M quoque praebet. Π col. ii: α[ (§ minus simile ueri; uix λ) | θ[ aut ε[; haec littera est magna. ἔ[τος δ aut ἐ[κ τῆς θ βύβλου aut θ (i.e. ix) Hutchinson
[24.1] ὅτι ... Ταραντίνοις M; πᾶσα ... μισεῖ F^{mg}, ultimis uersibus iuxta initium excerpti antiqui (24.4) collocatis    ἔχειν F^{mg}
[24.2] M
[24.3] Suda π 2786    τὰ πλήθη om. V
[24.4–13] 24.4–34.13 FDG    4 Φιλήμενος, ut F 26.10, 29.4, 6, et Liu. 25.8.3, etc. *Philemenus*: Φιλίμενος FDG hic, ut solent    9 πρωῒ θρεμμάτων Schweighaeuser: πρωθρ. F: προθρ. DG    μελήσειν Casaubon: μελλ- FDG    10 τοῦτο: ταῦτα Hutchinson

κατά τους νεανίσκους, έκείνοις δε πίστιν παρασκευάζειν προς τους πολίτας ως από του κρατίστου ποιουμένοις τας επί τας ληστείας εξόδους. 11 πραξάντων δε των περί τον Νίκωνα το παραγγελθέν, ό μεν Άννίβας περιχαρής ην διά το μόλις αφορμής επειλήφθαι προς την προκειμένην επιβολήν, 12 οί δε περί τον Φιλήμενον έτι μάλλον παρώρμηντο προς την πράξιν διά το και την έντευξιν ασφαλώς γεγονέναι και τον Άννίβαν ηύρηκέναι πρόθυμον, έτι δε την της λείας δαψίλειαν ικανήν αύτοΐς πίστιν παρεσκευακέναι προς τους ιδίους. 13 †τότε† τα μεν αποδόμενοι, τα δ' ευωχούμενοι της λείας, ού μόνον έπιστεύοντο παρά τοΐς Ταραντίνοις, αλλά και ζηλωτάς έσχον ούκ ολίγους.

25.1 μετά δε ταύτα ποιησάμενοι δευτέραν έξοδον, και παραπλησίως χειρίσαντες τα κατά μέρος, αυτοί τε τοις περί τον Άννίβαν έδοσαν πίστεις και παρ' εκείνων έλαβον έπι τούτοις, 2 εφ' ώι Ταραντίνους ελευθερώσειν και μήτε φόρους πράξεσθαι κατά μηδένα τρόπον μήτ' άλλο μηδέν έπιτάξειν Ταραντίνοις Καρχηδονίους, τάς δε των Ρωμαίων οικίας και καταλύσεις, επειδάν κρατήσωσι της πόλεως, έξεϊναι Καρχηδονίοις διαρπάζειν. 3 έποιήσαντο δε και σύνθημα του παραδέχεσθαι σφας τους φύλακας ετοίμως εις την παρεμβολήν ότ' έλθοιεν. 4 ών γενομένων έλαβον έξουσίαν εις το και πλεονάκις συμμιγνύναι τοις περί τον Άννίβαν, ποτέ μεν ως έπ' έξοδείαν, ποτέ δε πάλιν ως επί κυνηγίαν ποιούμενοι τας εκ της πόλεως εξόδους. 5 ταύτα δε διαρμοσάμενοι προς το μέλλον, οι μεν πλείους έπετήρουν τους καιρούς, τον δε Φιλήμενον άπέταξαν επί τας κυνηγίας· 6 διά γαρ την ύπερβάλλουσαν επί τούτο το μέρος έπιθυμίαν ην υπέρ αυτού διάληψις ως ουδέν προυργιαίτερον ποιουμένου κατά τον βίον του κυνηγετεϊν. 7 διό τούτωι μεν έπέτρεψαν εξιδιάσασθαι διά των άλισκομένων θηρίων πρώτον μεν τον επί της πόλεως τεταγμένον Γάϊον Λίβιον, δεύτερον δε τους φυλάττοντας τον πυλώνα [τον υπό τας Τεμενίδας προσαγορευομένας πύλας]. 8 ός παραλαβών την πίστιν ταύτην, και τα μεν αυτός κυνηγετών, των δ' ετοιμαζομένων αύτωι δι' Άννίβου, συνεχώς είσέφερε των θηρίων, ων τα μεν έδίδου τωι Γαϊωι, τα δε τοΐς έπι του πυλώνος χάριν του την ρινοπύλην ετοίμως άνοίγειν αύτωι· 9 το γαρ πλεΐον έποιεϊτο τας εισόδους και τας εξόδους νυκτός, προφάσει μεν χρώμενος τώι φόβωι των πολεμίων, άρμοζόμενος δε προς την υποκειμένην πρόθεσιν. 10 ήδη δε κατεσκευασμένου τοιαύτην συνήθειαν του Φιλημένου προς τους επί της πύλης ώστε μή διαπορεΐν τους φυλάττοντας, αλλ' όπότε προσεγγίσας τώι τείχει προσσυρίξαι νυκτός, ευθέως άνοίγεσθαι την ρινοπύλην αύτωι, 11 τότε παρατηρήσαντες τον επί της πόλεως άρχοντα [των Ρωμαίων], άφ' ημέρας μέλλοντα γίνεσθαι μετά πλειόνων

[24.4–13] 13 τότε: το δε <πέρας> Hutchinson: τότ' ούν Schweighaeuser: διόπερ Weil   αποδόμενοι F: σπενδόμενοι DG
[25] 2 πράξεσθαι Casaubon: -ασθαι FDG   τρόπον Scaliger: τόπον FDG   7 τον ... πύλας del. Hutchinson   υπό: κατά Reiske: υπέρ Bekker   9 ό δε νυκτός έποίει τας εισόδους, άρμ. προς την ύπ. πρ. Suda α 3976   10 προσσυρίξαι FD: προσυρίξαι fere G, quod coniecerat Schweighaeuser   11 πόλεως Casaubon: πύλης FDG   των Ρωμαίων del. Hutchinson   άφ' Reiske: έφ' FDG

τὸν Ἀριανὸν πρὸς τὸν Ἀχαιόν, ἔχοντα παρά τε τοῦ Νικομάχου καὶ Μελαγκόμα συνθηματικὰ γράμματα. 10 περὶ δὲ τοῦ παρεισελθεῖν τὸν Ἀριανὸν εἰς τὴν ἄκραν ἀσφαλῶς καὶ πάλιν ἀπελθεῖν ἐκεῖνον ἐκέλευε φροντίζειν. 11 ἐὰν δὲ προσδεξάμενος τὴν ἐπιβολὴν Ἀχαιὸς ἀντιφωνήσηι τοῖς περὶ τὸν Νικόμαχον καὶ Μελαγκόμαν, οὕτως ἔφη δώσειν ὁ Βῶλις αὐτὸν εἰς τὴν χρείαν καὶ συμμίξειν τῶι Καμβύλωι. 12 τῆς δὲ διατάξεως γενομένης τοιαύτης χωρισθέντες, ἔπραττον ἑκάτεροι τὰ συντεταγμένα.

17.1 καὶ λαβὼν καιρὸν πρῶτον ὁ Καμβύλος προσφέρει τῶι βασιλεῖ τὸν λόγον. 2 ὁ δ' Ἀντίοχος, †πρὸς τρόπον† αὐτῶι καὶ παραδόξου γενομένης τῆς ἐπαγγελίας, τὰ μὲν ὑπερχαρὴς ὢν πάνθ' ὑπισχνεῖτο, τὰ δὲ διαπιστῶν ἐξήταζε τὰς κατὰ μέρος ἐπινοίας καὶ παρασκευὰς αὐτῶν. 3 μετὰ δὲ ταῦτα πιστεύσας, καὶ νομίζων ὡς ἂν εἰ σὺν θεῶι γίνεσθαι τὴν ἐπιβολήν, ἠξίου καὶ πολλάκις ἐδεῖτο τοῦ Καμβύλου συντελεῖν τὴν πρᾶξιν. 4 τὸ δὲ παραπλήσιον ὁ Βῶλις ἐποίει πρὸς τὸν Νικόμαχον καὶ Μελαγκόμαν. οἱ δὲ πιστεύοντες ἀπὸ τοῦ κρατίστου γίνεσθαι τὴν ἐπιβολήν, καὶ παραυτίκα τῶι Ἀριανῶι συνθέντες τὰς πρὸς τὸν Ἀχαιὸν ἐπιστολάς, γεγραμμένας συνθηματικῶς, καθάπερ ἔθος ἦν αὐτοῖς, 5 ἐξαπέστειλαν, παρακαλοῦντες πιστεύειν τοῖς περὶ τὸν Βῶλιν καὶ τὸν Καμβύλον [οὕτως ὥστε τὸν κυριεύσαντα τῆς ἐπιστολῆς μὴ δύνασθαι γνῶναι μηδὲ τῶν ἐν αὐτῆι γεγραμμένων]. 6 ὁ δ' Ἀριανὸς διὰ τοῦ Καμβύλου παρελθὼν εἰς τὴν ἄκραν τὰ γεγραμμένα τοῖς περὶ τὸν Ἀχαιὸν ἀπέδωκε, καὶ συμπαρὼν ἀπὸ τῆς ἀρχῆς τοῖς γινομένοις, ἀκριβῶς τὸν κατὰ μέρος ὑπὲρ ἑκάστων ἀπεδίδου λόγον, πολλάκις μὲν καὶ ποικίλως ὑπὲρ τῶν κατὰ τὸν Σωσίβιον καὶ Βῶλιν ἀνακρινόμενος, πολλάκις δὲ περὶ Νικομάχου καὶ Μελαγκόμα, μάλιστα δὲ περὶ τῶν κατὰ τὸν Καμβύλον. 7 οὐ μὴν ἀλλ' αὐτοπαθῶς καὶ γενναίως ὑπέμενε τοὺς ἐλέγχους, καὶ μάλιστα διὰ τὸ μὴ γινώσκειν τὸ συνέχον τῶν τῶι Καμβύλωι καὶ Βώλιδι δεδογμένων. 8 Ἀχαιὸς δὲ καὶ διὰ τῶν ἀνακρίσεων τῶν τοῦ Ἀριανοῦ καὶ μάλιστα διὰ τῶν παρὰ τοῦ Νικομάχου καὶ Μελαγκόμα συνθημάτων πιστεύσας ἀντεφώνησε, καὶ παραχρῆμα πάλιν ἐξέπεμψε τὸν Ἀριανόν. 9 πλεονάκις δὲ τούτου γενομένου παρ' ἑκατέρων, τέλος οἱ περὶ τὸν Ἀχαιὸν ἐπέτρεψαν περὶ σφῶν τοῖς περὶ τὸν Νικόμαχον, ἅτε μηδεμιᾶς ἄλλης ἐλπίδος ἔτι καταλειπομένης πρὸς σωτηρίαν, καὶ πέμπειν ἐκέλευον ἅμα τῶι Ἀριανῶι τὸν Βῶλιν ἀσελήνου νυκτός, ὡς ἐγχειριοῦντες αὐτούς. 10 ἦν γάρ τις ἐπίνοια περὶ τὸν Ἀχαιὸν τοιαύτη, πρῶτον μὲν διαφυγεῖν τοὺς ἐνεστῶτας κινδύνους, μετὰ δὲ ταῦτα ποιήσασθαι †διὰ προόδου† τὴν ὁρμὴν ἐπὶ τοὺς κατὰ Συρίαν τόπους· 11 πάνυ γὰρ εἶχε μεγάλας ἐλπίδας ἐπιφανεὶς ἄφνω καὶ παραδόξως τοῖς κατὰ Συρίαν ἀνθρώποις, καὶ ἔτι διατρίβοντος Ἀντιόχου περὶ τὰς Σάρδεις, μέγα ποιήσειν κίνημα καὶ μεγάλης

[16] 9 συνθηματικὰ Reiske: σύνθημά τι καὶ FDG: συνθήματα καὶ D^sl
[17] 2 πρός ... ὑπισχνεῖτο Suda π 2831     πρὸς τρόπον FDG Suda (-ων Sudae M^pc, κατὰ τὸν ἑαυτοῦ τρόπον Sudae F): προσφάτου τ' Hutchinson: προσφόρου Naber: πρὸς τρόπου Schweighaeuser     4–5 ἐπιστολὰς ἔγραψε ... αὐτοῖς ὥστε ... γεγραμμένων Suda σ 1592     5 οὕτως ὥστε ... γεγραμμένων suspecta habuit Schweighaeuser: post 4 αὐτοῖς transp. Büttner-Wobst (ut iam Gronovius, οὕτως omisso), cf. Sudam
9 γινομένου F     10 διὰ προόδου: δίχα περιόδου Hutchinson: δίχα προόδου Reiske: διὰ περιόδου Schweighaeuser

ἀποδοχῆς τεύξεσθαι παρά τε τοῖς Ἀντιοχεῦσι καὶ τοῖς κατὰ Κοίλην Συρίαν καὶ Φοινίκην.

18.1 ὁ μὲν οὖν Ἀχαιὸς ἐπί τινος τοιαύτης προσδοκίας καὶ διαλογισμῶν ὑπάρχων ἐκαραδόκει τὴν παρουσίαν τοῦ Βώλιδος· 2 οἱ δὲ περὶ τὸν Μελαγκόμαν ἀποδεξάμενοι τὸν Ἀριανὸν καὶ τὰς ἐπιστολὰς ἀναγνόντες, ἐξέπεμπον τὸν Βῶλιν, παρακαλέσαντες διὰ πλειόνων καὶ μεγάλας ἐλπίδας ὑποδείξαντες, ἐὰν καθίκηται τῆς ἐπιβολῆς. 3 ὁ δὲ προδιαπεμψάμενος τὸν Ἀριανόν, καὶ δηλώσας τῶι Καμβύλωι τὴν αὑτοῦ παρουσίαν, ἧκε νυκτὸς ἐπὶ τὸν συντεθέντα τόπον. 4 γενόμενοι δὲ μίαν ἡμέραν ἐπὶ ταὐτό, καὶ συνταξάμενοι περὶ τοῦ πῶς χειρισθήσεται τὰ κατὰ μέρος, μετὰ ταῦτα νυκτὸς εἰσῆλθον εἰς τὴν παρεμβολήν. 5 ἡ δὲ διάταξις αὐτῶν ἐγεγόνει τοιαύτη τις· εἰ μὲν συμβαίη τὸν Ἀχαιὸν ἐκ τῆς ἄκρας ἐλθεῖν μόνον ἢ καὶ δεύτερον μετὰ τοῦ Βώλιδος καὶ Ἀριανοῦ, τελέως εὐκαταφρόνητος, ἔτι δ' εὐχείρωτος ἔμελλε γίνεσθαι τοῖς ἐνεδρεύουσιν· 6 εἰ δὲ μετὰ πλειόνων, δύσχρηστος ἡ πρόθεσις ἀπέβαινε τοῖς πεπιστευμένοις, ἄλλως τε καὶ ζωγρίαι σπεύδουσι κυριεῦσαι διὰ τὸ τῆς πρὸς τὸν Ἀντίοχον χάριτος τὸ πλεῖστον ἐν τούτωι κεῖσθαι τῶι μέρει. 7 διόπερ ἔδει τὸν μὲν Ἀριανόν, ὅταν ἐξάγηι τὸν Ἀχαιόν, ἡγεῖσθαι διὰ τὸ γινώσκειν τὴν ἀτραπόν, ἧι πολλάκις ἐπεποίητο καὶ τὴν εἴσοδον καὶ τὴν ἔξοδον, 8 τὸν δὲ Βῶλιν ἀκολουθεῖν τῶν ἄλλων κατόπιν, ἵν' ἐπειδὰν παραγένωνται πρὸς τὸν τόπον ἐν ὧι τοὺς ἐνεδρεύοντας ἑτοίμους ὑπάρχειν ἔδει διὰ τοῦ Καμβύλου, τότ' ἐπιλαβόμενος κρατοίη τὸν Ἀχαιόν, καὶ μήτε διαδραίη κατὰ τὸν θόρυβον νυκτὸς οὔσης διὰ τόπων ὑλωδῶν, [καὶ] μήθ' αὑτὸν ῥῖψαι κατά τινος κρημνοῦ περιπαθὴς γενόμενος, πέσοι δὲ κατὰ τὴν πρόθεσιν ὑπὸ τὰς τῶν ἐχθρῶν χεῖρας ζωγρίαι. 9 τούτων δὲ συγκειμένων, καὶ παραγενομένου τοῦ Βώλιδος ὡς τὸν Καμβύλον, ἧι μὲν ἦλθε νυκτί, ταύτηι παράγει πρὸς τὸν Ἀντίοχον τὸν Βῶλιν ὁ Καμβύλος μόνος πρὸς μόνον. 10 ἀποδεξαμένου δὲ τοῦ βασιλέως φιλοφρόνως, καὶ δόντος πίστεις ὑπὲρ τῶν ἐπαγγελιῶν, καὶ παρακαλέσαντος ἀμφοτέρους διὰ πλειόνων μηκέτι μέλλειν ὑπὲρ τῶν προκειμένων, τότε μὲν ἀνεχώρησαν εἰς τὴν αὑτῶν παρεμβολήν, 11 ὑπὸ δὲ τὴν ἑωθινὴν Βῶλις ἀνέβη μετὰ τοῦ Ἀριανοῦ, καὶ παρεισῆλθεν ἔτι νυκτὸς εἰς τὴν ἄκραν.

19.1 Ἀχαιὸς δὲ προσδεξάμενος ἐκτενῶς καὶ φιλανθρώπως τὸν Βῶλιν ἀνέκρινε διὰ πλειόνων ὑπὲρ ἑκάστου τῶν κατὰ μέρος. 2 θεωρῶν δὲ καὶ κατὰ τὴν ἐπιφάνειαν τὸν ἄνδρα καὶ κατὰ τὴν ὁμιλίαν ἕλκοντα τὸ τῆς πράξεως στάσιμον, τὰ μὲν περιχαρὴς ἦν διὰ τὴν ἐλπίδα τῆς σωτηρίας, τὰ δὲ πάλιν ἐπτοημένος καὶ πλήρης ἀγωνίας διὰ τὸ μέγεθος τῶν ἀποβησομένων. 3 ὑπάρχων δὲ καὶ κατὰ τὴν διάνοιαν οὐδενὸς ἥττων καὶ κατὰ τὴν ἐν πράγμασι τριβὴν ἱκανός, [ὅμως]

[18] 5 συμβαίη Hultsch: συμβαίνει FDG    6 δύσχρηστος <ἂν> ἡ πρ. ἀποβαίνοι Hutchinson; ἀπέβαινε om. G    8 μήθ'... γενόμενος Suda π 1230    παραγένωνται Hutchinson: -ηται FDG    καὶ del. Casaubon
[19] 1 Ἀχαιὸς ... μέρος Suda ε 637    φιλανθρώπως Suda: φιλοφρόνως FDG    3 ὅμως del. Hutchinson

ἐν τῶι προσαγορευομένωι Μουσείωι σύνεγγυς τῆς ἀγορᾶς, ταύτην ἐτάξαντο τὴν ἡμέραν πρὸς τὸν Ἀννίβαν. 26.1 ὁ δὲ πάλαι μὲν ἐπεπόριστο σκῆψιν ὡς ἀρρωστῶν, χάριν τοῦ μὴ θαυμάζειν ἀκούοντας τοὺς Ῥωμαίους ὡς καὶ πλείω χρόνον ἐπὶ τῶν αὐτῶν τόπων ποιεῖται τὴν διατριβήν· τότε δὲ καὶ μᾶλλον προσεποιεῖτο τὴν ἀρρωστίαν. 2 ἀπεῖχε δὲ τῶι στρατοπέδωι τριῶν ἡμερῶν ὁδὸν τοῦ Τάραντος. 3 ἥκοντος δὲ τοῦ καιροῦ, παρεσκευακὼς ἔκ τε τῶν ἱππέων καὶ τῶν πεζῶν τοὺς διαφέροντας εὐκινησίαι καὶ τόλμηι, περὶ μυρίους ὄντας τὸν ἀριθμόν, παρήγγειλε τεττάρων ἡμερῶν ἔχειν ἐφόδια. 4 ποιησάμενος δὲ τὴν ἀναζυγὴν ὑπὸ τὴν ἑωθινήν, ἐχρῆτο τῆι πορείαι συντόνως. τῶν δὲ Νομαδικῶν ἱππέων εἰς ὀγδοήκοντα προχειρισάμενος, ἐκέλευε προπορεύεσθαι τῆς δυνάμεως εἰς τριάκοντα σταδίους καὶ τοὺς παρὰ τὴν ὁδὸν τόπους ἐξ ἑκατέρου τοῦ μέρους ἐπιτρέχειν, 5 ἵνα μηδεὶς κατοπτεύσηι τὴν ὅλην δύναμιν, ἀλλ' οἱ μὲν ὑποχείριοι γίνοιντο τῶν διεμπιπτόντων, οἱ δὲ διαφυγόντες ἀναγγέλλοιεν εἰς τὴν πόλιν, ὡς ἐπιδρομῆς οὔσης ἐκ τῶν Νομάδων. 6 ἀποσχόντων δὲ τῶν Νομάδων ὡς ἑκατὸν εἴκοσι σταδίους, ἐδειπνοποιήσατο παρά τινα δυσσύνοπτον καὶ φαραγγώδη ποταμόν. 7 καὶ συναθροίσας τοὺς ἡγεμόνας, κυρίως μὲν οὐ διεσάφει τὴν ἐπιβολήν, ἁπλῶς δὲ παρεκάλει πρῶτον μὲν ἄνδρας ἀγαθοὺς γίνεσθαι πάντας, ὡς οὐδέποτε μειζόνων αὐτοῖς ἄθλων ὑποκειμένων, 8 δεύτερον δὲ συνέχειν ἕκαστον τῆι πορείαι τοὺς ὑφ' αὑτὸν ταττομένους καὶ πικρῶς ἐπιτιμᾶν τοῖς καθόλου παρεκβαίνουσιν ἐκ τῆς ἰδίας τάξεως, 9 τελευταῖον δὲ προσέχειν τὸν νοῦν τοῖς παραγγελλομένοις καὶ μηδὲν ἰδιοπραγεῖν πάρεξ τῶν προσταττομένων. 10 ταῦτ' εἰπὼν καὶ διαφεὶς τοὺς ἡγεμόνας, ἐκίνει τὴν πρωτοπορείαν, κνέφατος ἄρτι γενομένου, σπουδάζων συνάψαι τῶι τείχει περὶ μέσας νύκτας, καθηγεμόνα τὸν Φιλήμενον ἔχων καὶ παρεσκευακὼς ὗν ἄγριον αὐτῶι πρὸς τὴν διατεταγμένην χρείαν. 27.1 τῶι δὲ Γαΐωι τῶι Λιβίωι, γενομένωι μετὰ τῶν συνήθων ἀφ' ἡμέρας ἐν τῶι Μουσείωι κατὰ τὴν τῶν νεανίσκων πρόληψιν, καὶ σχεδὸν ἤδη τοῦ πότου τὴν ἀκμαιοτάτην ἔχοντος διάθεσιν, προσαγγέλλεται περὶ δυσμὰς ἡλίου τοὺς Νομάδας ἐπιτρέχειν τὴν χώραν. 2 ὁ δὲ πρὸς μὲν αὐτὸ τοῦτο διενοήθη, καὶ καλέσας τινὰς τῶν ἡγεμόνων, συνέταξε τοὺς [μὲν] ἡμίσεις τῶν ἱππέων ἐξελθόντας ὑπὸ τὴν ἑωθινὴν κωλῦσαι τοὺς κακοποιοῦντας τὴν χώραν τῶν πολεμίων, τῆς γε μὴν ὅλης πράξεως διὰ ταῦτα καὶ μᾶλλον ἀνύποπτος ἦν. 3 οἱ δὲ περὶ τὸν Νίκωνα καὶ Τραγίσκον, ἅμα τῶι σκότος γενέσθαι συναθροισθέντες ἐν τῆι πόλει πάντες, ἐτήρουν τὴν ἐπάνοδον τῶν περὶ τὸν Λίβιον. 4 τῶν δὲ ταχέως ἐξαναστάντων διὰ τὸ γεγονέναι τὸν

[26] 5 κατοπτεύσηι Reiske: -ευθῆι FDG    διεμπιπτόντων Bothe: διαπ- FDG   ἀναγγέλλοιεν G: ἀναγγέλοιεν FD    6 ποταμόν: τόπον Reiske    7 οὐ Ursinus: οὖν FDG    9 καὶ ... προσταττομένων Suda δ 1068    μηδὲν ἰδιοπραγεῖν $D^{mg}G^{mg}$: μηδενὶ δικαιοπραγεῖν FDG Suda    10 διαφεὶς ... πρωτοπορείαν Suda δ 822, διαφεὶς ... γενομένου κ 1859    διαφεὶς τοὺς ἡγεμόνας DG Suda, bis: διασαφεὶς τοὺς ἡγεμόνας F: διασαφήσας τοῖς ἡγεμόσι $D^{mg}G^{mg}$    ὗν Schweighaeuser: σῦν FDG
[27] 1 πότου $D^{mg}G^{mg}$: τόπου FDG    2 μὲν del. Bekker    τὴν χώραν om. DG

πότον ἀφ' ἡμέρας, οἱ μὲν ἄλλοι πρός τινα τόπον ἀποστάντες ἔμενον, τινὲς δὲ τῶν νεανίσκων ἀπήντων τοῖς περὶ τὸν Γάϊον, διακεχυμένοι καί τι καὶ προσπαίζοντες ἀλλήλοις, ὡς ἂν ὑποκρινόμενοι τοὺς ἐκ συνουσίας ἐπανάγοντας. 5 ἔτι δὲ μᾶλλον ἠλλοιωμένων ὑπὸ τῆς μέθης τῶν περὶ τὸν Λίβιον, ἅμα τῶι συμμῖξαι γέλως ἐξ ἀμφοῖν ἦν καὶ παιδιὰ πρόχειρος. 6 ἐπεὶ δὲ συνανακάμψαντες ἀποκατέστησαν αὐτὸν εἰς οἶκον, ὁ μὲν Γάϊος ἀνεπαύετο μεθύων, ὡς εἰκός ἐστι τοὺς ἀφ' ἡμέρας πίνοντας, οὐδὲν ἄτοπον οὐδὲ δυσχερὲς ἔχων ἐν τῆι διανοίαι, χαρᾶς δὲ πλήρης καὶ ῥαιθυμίας. 7 οἱ δὲ περὶ τὸν Νίκωνα καὶ Τραγίσκον, ἐπεὶ συνέμιξαν τοῖς ἀπολελειμμένοις νεανίσκοις, διελόντες σφᾶς εἰς τρία μέρη παρεφύλαττον διαλαβόντες τῆς ἀγορᾶς τὰς εὐκαιροτάτας εἰσβολάς, ἵνα μήτε τῶν ἔξωθεν προσπιπτόντων μηδὲν αὐτοὺς λανθάνηι μήτε τῶν ἐν αὐτῆι τῆι πόλει γινομένων. 8 ἐπέστησαν δὲ καὶ παρὰ τὴν οἰκίαν τοῦ Γαΐου, σαφῶς εἰδότες ὡς ἐὰν γίνηταί τις ὑπόνοια τοῦ μέλλοντος, ἐπὶ τὸν Λίβιον ἀνοισθήσεται πρῶτον, καὶ πᾶν τὸ πραττόμενον ἀπ' ἐκείνου λήψεται τὴν ἀρχήν. 9 ὡς δ' αἱ μὲν ἀπὸ τῶν δείπνων ἐπάνοδοι καὶ συλλήβδην ὁ τοιοῦτος θόρυβος ἤδη παρωιχήκει, τῶν δὲ δημοτῶν ἡ πληθὺς κατακεκοίμητο, προύβαινε δὲ τὰ τῆς νυκτός, καὶ τὰ τῆς ἐλπίδος ἀκέραια διέμενε, τότε συναθροισθέντες προῆγον ἐπὶ τὴν προκειμένην χρείαν.

28.1 τάδε <δὲ τὰ> συγκείμενα τοῖς νεανίσκοις ἦν πρὸς τοὺς Καρχηδονίους· 2 τὸν μὲν Ἀννίβαν ἔδει συνάψαντα τῆι πόλει κατὰ τὴν ἀπὸ τῆς μεσογαίου, πρὸς ἕω δὲ κειμένην πλευράν, ὡς ἐπὶ τὰς Τημενίδας προσαγορευομένας πύλας, ἀνάψαι πῦρ ἐπὶ τοῦ τάφου τοῦ παρὰ μέν τισιν Ὑακίνθου προσαγορευομένου, παρὰ δέ τισιν Ἀπόλλωνος Ὑακίνθου, 3 τοὺς δὲ περὶ τὸν Τραγίσκον, ὅταν ἴδωσι τοῦτο γινόμενον, ἔνδοθεν ἀντιπυρσεῦσαι. 4 τούτου δὲ συντελεσθέντος, σβέσαι τὸ πῦρ ἔδει τοὺς περὶ τὸν Ἀννίβαν καὶ βάδην ποιεῖσθαι τὴν πορείαν ὡς ἐπὶ τὴν πύλην. 5 ὧν διατεταγμένων, οἱ μὲν νεανίσκοι, διαπορευθέντες τὸν οἰκούμενον τόπον τῆς πόλεως, ἧκον ἐπὶ τοὺς τάφους. 6 τὸ γὰρ πρὸς ἕω μέρος τῆς τῶν Ταραντίνων πόλεως μνημάτων ἐστὶ πλῆρες, διὰ τὸ τοὺς τελευτήσαντας ἔτι καὶ νῦν θάπτεσθαι παρ' αὐτοῖς πάντας ἐντὸς τῶν τειχῶν κατά τι λόγιον ἀρχαῖον. 7 φασὶ γὰρ χρῆσαι τὸν θεὸν τοῖς Ταραντίνοις ἄμεινον καὶ λῶιον ἔσεσθαί σφισι ποιουμένοις τὴν οἴκησιν μετὰ τῶν πλειόνων. 8 τοὺς δὲ νομίσαντας [ἂν] οἰκήσειν οὕτως ἄριστα κατὰ τὸν χρησμόν, εἰ καὶ τοὺς μετηλλαχότας ἐντὸς τοῦ τείχους ἔχοιεν, διὰ ταῦτα θάπτειν ἔτι καὶ νῦν τοὺς μεταλλάξαντας ἐντὸς τῶν πυλῶν. 9 οὐ μὴν ἀλλ' οἵ γε προειρημένοι παραγενόμενοι πρὸς τὸν τοῦ Πυθιονίκου τάφον ἐκαραδόκουν τὸ μέλλον. 10 συνεγγισάντων δὲ τῶν περὶ τὸν Ἀννίβαν καὶ πραξάντων τὸ συνταχθέν, ἅμα τῶι τὸ πῦρ ἰδεῖν οἱ περὶ τὸν Νίκωνα καὶ Τραγίσκον ἀναθαρρήσαντες ταῖς ψυχαῖς καὶ τὸν παρ' αὐτῶν πυρσὸν ἀναδείξαντες, ἐπεὶ τὸ παρ' ἐκείνων πῦρ πάλιν

[27] 4-5 τινὲς ... ἀλλήλοις Suda δ 582, τινὲς ... μέθης υ 526, ὡς ... μέθης σ 1601 4 τι καὶ F: καὶ om. DG, Suda δ 582    5 ἠλλοιωμένων Ursinus: -οι FDG Suda (-ους σ 1601)    6 μὲν Reiske: δὲ FDG    9 αἱ Ursinus: ἀεὶ FDG
[28] 1 τάδε <δὲ τὰ> Hutchinson: τὰ δὲ FDG    2 παρὰ δέ ... Ὑακίνθου om. F¹, add. F² mg (περὶ δέ ...)    8 [ἂν] οἰκήσειν Dindorf: ἂν οἰκῆσ' Büttner-Wobst

ἑώρων ἀποσβεννύμενον, ὥρμησαν ἐπὶ τὴν πύλην μετὰ δρόμου καὶ σπουδῆς, 11 βουλόμενοι φθάσαι φονεύσαντες τοὺς ἐπὶ τοῦ πυλῶνος τεταγμένους, διὰ τὸ συγκεῖσθαι [καὶ] σχολῆι καὶ βάδην ποιεῖσθαι τὴν πορείαν τοὺς Καρχηδονίους. 12 εὐροήσαντος δὲ τοῦ πράγματος, καὶ προκαταληφθέντων τῶν φυλαττόντων, οἱ μὲν ἐφόνευον τούτους, οἱ δὲ διέκοπτον τοὺς μοχλούς. 13 ταχὺ δὲ τῶν πυλῶν ἀνοιχθεισῶν, πρὸς τὸν δέοντα καιρὸν ἧκον οἱ περὶ τὸν Ἀννίβαν, κεχρημένοι τῆι πορείαι συμμέτρως, ὥστε μηδεμίαν ἐπίστασιν γενέσθαι παρ' ὁδὸν ἐπὶ τὴν πόλιν. 29.1 γενομένης δὲ τῆς εἰσόδου κατὰ τὴν πρόθεσιν ἀσφαλοῦς καὶ τελέως ἀθορύβου, δόξαντες ἠνύσθαι σφίσι τὸ πλεῖστον τῆς ἐπιβολῆς, λοιπὸν αὐτοὶ μὲν εὐθαρσῶς ἤδη προῆγον ἐπὶ τὴν ἀγορὰν κατὰ τὴν πλατεῖαν τὴν ἀπὸ τῆς Βαθείας ἀναφέρουσαν· 2 τούς γε μὴν ἱππεῖς ἀπέλιπον ἐκτὸς τοῦ τείχους, ὄντας οὐκ ἐλάττους δισχιλίων, θέλοντες ἐφεδρείαν αὑτοῖς ὑπάρχειν ταύτην πρός τε τὰς ἔξωθεν ἐπιφανείας καὶ πρὸς τὰ παράλογα τῶν ἐν ταῖς τοιαύταις ἐπιβολαῖς συμβαινόντων. 3 ἐγγίσαντες δὲ τοῖς περὶ τὴν ἀγορὰν τόποις τὴν μὲν δύναμιν ἐπέστησαν κατὰ πορείαν, αὐτοὶ δὲ <τὰ> κατὰ τὸν Φιλήμενον ἐκαραδόκουν, δεδιότες πῶς σφίσι προχωρήσει καὶ τοῦτο τὸ μέρος τῆς ἐπιβολῆς. 4 ὅτε γὰρ ἀνάψαντες τὸ πῦρ ἔμελλον πρὸς τὰς πύλας ὁρμᾶν, τότε καὶ τὸν Φιλήμενον, ἔχοντα τὸν ὗν ἐν φερέτρωι, καὶ Λίβυας ὡς εἰς χιλίους ἐξαπέστειλαν ἐπὶ τὴν παρακειμένην πύλην, βουλόμενοι κατὰ τὴν ἐξ ἀρχῆς πρόθεσιν μὴ ψιλῶς ἐκ μιᾶς ἐλπίδος ἐξηρτῆσθαι τὴν ἐπιβολὴν αὐτῶν ἀλλ' ἐκ πλειόνων. 5 ὁ δὲ προειρημένος ἐγγίσας τῶι τείχει κατὰ τὸν ἐθισμόν, ἐπεὶ προσεσύριξε, παρῆν ὁ φύλαξ εὐθέως, καταβαίνων πρὸς τὴν ῥινοπύλην. 6 τοῦ δ' εἰπόντος ἔξωθεν ἀνοίγειν ταχέως, ὅτι βαρύνονται – φέρουσι γὰρ ὗν ἄγριον – ἀσμένως ἀκούσας ὁ φύλαξ ἀνέωιξε μετὰ σπουδῆς, ἐλπίζων καὶ πρὸς αὑτόν τι διατείνειν τὴν εὐαγρίαν τῶν περὶ τὸν Φιλήμενον, διὰ τὸ μερίτην ἀεὶ γίνεσθαι τῶν εἰσφερομένων. 7 αὐτὸς μὲν οὖν ὁ προειρημένος τὴν πρώτην ἔχων χώραν τοῦ φορήματος εἰσῆλθε, καὶ σὺν αὐτῶι νομαδικὴν ἔχων διασκευὴν ἕτερος, ὡς εἷς τις ὢν τῶν ἀπὸ τῆς χώρας, μετὰ δὲ τοῦτον ἄλλοι δύο πάλιν [οἱ] φέροντες ἐκ τῶν ὄπισθεν τὸ θηρίον. 8 ἐπεὶ δὲ τέτταρες ὄντες ἐντὸς ἐγένοντο τῆς ῥινοπύλης, τὸν μὲν ἀνοίξαντα θεώμενον ἀκάκως καὶ ψηλαφῶντα τὸν ὗν αὐτοῦ πατάξαντες ἀπέκτειναν, τοὺς δ' ἑπομένους μὲν αὐτοῖς, προηγουμένους δὲ τῶν ἄλλων, Λίβυας, ὄντας εἰς τριάκοντα, σχολῆι καὶ μεθ' ἡσυχίας παρῆκαν διὰ τῆς πυλίδος. 9 γενομένου δὲ τούτου, κατὰ τὸ συνεχὲς οἱ μὲν τοὺς μοχλοὺς διέκοπτον, οἱ δὲ τοὺς ἐπὶ τοῦ πυλῶνος ἐφόνευον, οἱ δὲ τοὺς ἔξω Λίβυας ἐκάλουν διὰ συνθημάτων. 10 εἰσελθόντων δὲ καὶ τούτων ἀσφαλῶς, προῆγον ὡς ἐπὶ τὴν ἀγορὰν κατὰ τὸ συντεταγμένον. 11 ἅμα δὲ τῶι

[28] 11 καὶ del. Reiske    12 εὐροήσαντος Scaliger: εὐρώ- FDG (-ες G)    13 <τῆς> (Hutchinson) παρόδου (Scaliger) <τῆς> (Bothe) possis
[29] 2 ἀπέλιπον DG    3 <τὰ> κατὰ Casaubon: καὶ Scaliger    4–6 τότε ... εὐαγρίαν Suda φ 233, adumbratis tantum multis    4 ὅτε Casaubon: οὔτε FDG    ὡς εἰς Hultsch: ὡσεὶ FDG    5–6 ὁ δέ φύλαξ εὐθὺς ἀνοίγει, ἐλπίζων ... εἰσφερομένων Suda μ 632    5 προσεσύριξε Scaliger (προεσύριξε), Leopardi: προσέρισε fere FDG, G[mg]    6 τῶν περὶ τὸν Φ. om. Suda    7 οἱ del. Hutchinson    8 αὑτοῦ FD: αὐτὸν G    10 ἀσφαλῶς G: -ῶν FD

συμμΐξαι και τούτους, περιχαρής γενόμενος Ἀννίβας ἐπὶ τῶι κατὰ νοῦν αὑτῶι προχωρεῖν τὴν πρᾶξιν εἴχετο τῶν προκειμένων. 30.1 ἀπομερίσας δὲ τῶν Κελτῶν εἰς δισχιλίους, καὶ διελὼν εἰς τρία μέρη τούτους, συνέστησε τῶν νεανίσκων δύο πρὸς ἕκαστον μέρος τῶν χειριζόντων τὴν πρᾶξιν. 2 ἀκολούθως δὲ καὶ τῶν παρ' αὑτοῦ τινας ἡγεμόνων συνεξαπέστειλε, προστάξας διαλαβεῖν τῶν εἰς τὴν ἀγορὰν φερουσῶν ὁδῶν τὰς εὐκαιροτάτας. 3 ὅταν δὲ τοῦτο πράξωσι, τοῖς μὲν ἐγχωρίοις νεανίσκοις ἐξαιρεῖσθαι παρήγγειλε [δὲ] καὶ σώιζειν τοὺς ἐντυγχάνοντας τῶν πολιτῶν, ἀναβοῶντας ἐκ πολλοῦ μένειν κατὰ χώραν Ταραντίνους, ὡς ὑπαρχούσης αὐτοῖς τῆς ἀσφαλείας· 4 τοῖς δὲ παρὰ τῶν Καρχηδονίων καὶ τῶν Κελτῶν ἡγεμόσι κτείνειν διεκελεύσατο τοὺς ἐντυγχάνοντας τῶν Ῥωμαίων. οὗτοι μὲν οὖν χωρισθέντες ἀλλήλων ἔπραττον μετὰ ταῦτα τὸ προσταχθέν. 5 τῆς δὲ τῶν πολεμίων εἰσόδου καταφανοῦς ἤδη γενομένης τοῖς Ταραντίνοις, πλήρης ἡ πόλις κραυγῆς ἐγίνετο καὶ ταραχῆς παρηλλαγμένης. 6 ὁ μὲν οὖν Γάϊος, προσπεσούσης αὐτῶι τῆς εἰσόδου τῶν πολεμίων, συννοήσας ἀδύνατον αὑτὸν ὄντα διὰ τὴν μέθην, εὐθέως ἐξελθὼν ἐκ τῆς οἰκίας μετὰ τῶν οἰκετῶν, καὶ παραγενόμενος ἐπὶ τὴν πύλην τὴν φέρουσαν ἐπὶ τὸν λιμένα, καὶ μετὰ ταῦτα τοῦ φύλακος ἀνοίξαντος αὐτῶι τὴν ῥινοπύλην, διαδὺς ταύτηι καὶ λαβόμενος ἀκατίου τῶν ὁρμούντων, ἐμβὰς μετὰ τῶν οἰκετῶν εἰς τὴν ἄκραν παρεκομίσθη. 7 κατὰ δὲ τὸν καιρὸν τοῦτον οἱ περὶ τὸν Φιλήμενον, ἡτοιμασμένοι σάλπιγγας Ῥωμαϊκάς, [καὶ] τινῶν αὐταῖς χρῆσθαι δυναμένων διὰ τὴν συνήθειαν, στάντες ἐπὶ τὸ θέατρον ἐσήμαινον. 8 τῶν δὲ Ῥωμαίων βοηθούντων ἐν τοῖς ὅπλοις κατὰ τὸν ἐθισμὸν εἰς τὴν ἄκραν, ἐχώρει τὸ πρᾶγμα κατὰ τὴν πρόθεσιν τοῖς Καρχηδονίοις. 9 παραγενόμενοι γὰρ ταῖς πλατείαις ἀτάκτως καὶ σποράδην, οἱ μὲν εἰς τοὺς Καρχηδονίους ἐνέπιπτον, οἱ δ' εἰς τοὺς Κελτούς· καὶ δὴ τῶι τοιούτωι τρόπωι φονευομένων αὐτῶν πολύ τι πλῆθος διεφθάρη. 10 τῆς δ' ἡμέρας ἐπιφαινομένης οἱ μὲν Ταραντῖνοι τὴν ἡσυχίαν εἶχον κατὰ τὰς οἰκήσεις, οὐδέπω δυνάμενοι †τάξασθαι† τὸ συμβαῖνον. 11 διὰ μὲν γὰρ τὴν σάλπιγγα καὶ τὸ μηδὲν ἀδίκημα γίνεσθαι μηδ' ἁρπαγὴν κατὰ τὴν πόλιν, ἔδοξαν ἐξ αὐτῶν τῶν Ῥωμαίων εἶναι τὸ κίνημα. 12 τῶι δὲ πολλοὺς αὐτῶν ὁρᾶν πεφονευμένους ἐν ταῖς πλατείαις, καί τινας τῶν Γαλατῶν θεωρεῖσθαι σκυλεύοντας τοὺς τῶν Ῥωμαίων νεκρούς, ὑπέτρεχέ τις ἔννοια τῆς τῶν Καρχηδονίων παρουσίας.

31.1 ἤδη δὲ τοῦ μὲν Ἀννίβου παρεμβεβληκότος τὴν δύναμιν εἰς τὴν ἀγοράν, τῶν δὲ Ῥωμαίων ἀποκεχωρηκότων εἰς τὴν ἄκραν διὰ τὸ προκατεσχῆσθαι φρουρᾶι ταύτην ὑπ' αὐτῶν, ὄντος δὲ φωτὸς εἰλικρινοῦς, ὁ μὲν Ἀννίβας ἐκήρυττε

[30] 3 δὲ del. Casaubon    6 λαβόμενος G^mg: λίβανος FDG    7 κατὰ Schweighaeuser: μετὰ FDG    καὶ del. Hutchinson; καί τινας τῶν Casaubon    ἐπὶ F: περὶ DG    9 παραγενόμενοι G: -ος FD    γὰρ F: δὲ DG    10 τάξασθαι pro corrupto habuit Hutchinson; e.g. <κα>ταλαβέσθαι possis    12 τῶι Casaubon: τὸ FDG

τούς Ταραντίνους ἄνευ τῶν ὅπλων ἀθροίζεσθαι πάντας εἰς τὴν ἀγοράν· 2 οἱ δὲ νεανίσκοι περιπορευόμενοι τὴν πόλιν ἐβόων ἐπὶ τὴν ἐλευθερίαν, καὶ παρεκάλουν θαρρεῖν, ὡς ὑπὲρ ἐκείνων ‹ὁρῶντας› παρόντας τοὺς Καρχηδονίους. 3 ὅσοι μὲν οὖν τῶν Ταραντίνων προκατείχοντο τῆι πρὸς τοὺς Ῥωμαίους εὐνοίαι, γνόντες ἀπεχώρουν εἰς τὴν ἄκραν, οἱ δὲ λοιποὶ κατὰ τὸ κήρυγμα συνηθροίζοντο χωρὶς τῶν ὅπλων· πρὸς οὓς Ἀννίβας φιλανθρώπους διελέχθη λόγους. 4 τῶν δὲ Ταραντίνων ὁμοθυμαδὸν ἐπισημηναμένων ἕκαστα τῶν λεγομένων διὰ τὸ παράδοξον τῆς ἐλπίδος, τότε μὲν διαφῆκε τοὺς πολλούς, συντάξας ἕκαστον εἰς τὴν ἰδίαν οἰκίαν ἐπανελθόντας μετὰ σπουδῆς ἐπὶ τὴν θύραν ἐπιγράψαι 'Ταραντίνου'. 5 τῶι δ' ἐπὶ [τὴν] Ῥωμαϊκὴν κατάλυσιν ἐπιγράψαντι ταὐτὸ τοῦτο θάνατον ὥρισε τὴν ζημίαν. 6 αὐτὸς δὲ διελὼν τοὺς ἐπιτηδειοτάτους ‹τῶν› ἐπὶ τῶν πραγμάτων ἐφῆκε διαρπάζειν τὰς τῶν Ῥωμαίων οἰκίας, σύνθημα δοὺς πολεμίας νομίζειν τὰς ἀνεπιγράφους, τοὺς δὲ λοιποὺς συνέχων ἐν τάξει τούτοις ἐφέδρους.

**32.**1 πολλῶν δὲ καὶ παντοδαπῶν κατασκευασμάτων ἀθροισθέντων ἐκ τῆς διαρπαγῆς, καὶ γενομένης ὠφελείας τοῖς Καρχηδονίοις ἀξίας τῶν προσδοκωμένων ἐλπίδων, 2 τότε μὲν ἐπὶ τῶν ὅπλων ηὐλίσθησαν, εἰς δὲ τὴν ἐπιοῦσαν ἡμέραν Ἀννίβας, συνεδρεύσας μετὰ τῶν Ταραντίνων, ἔκρινε διατειχίσαι τὴν πόλιν ἀπὸ τῆς ἄκρας, ἵνα μηδεὶς ἔτι φόβος ἐπικάθηται τοῖς Ταραντίνοις ἀπὸ τῶν κατεχόντων τὴν ἀκρόπολιν Ῥωμαίων. 3 πρῶτον μὲν οὖν ἐπεβάλετο προθέσθαι χάρακα παράλληλον τῶι τείχει τῆς ἀκροπόλεως καὶ τῆι πρὸ τούτου τάφρωι. 4 σαφῶς δὲ γινώσκων οὐκ ἐάσοντας τοὺς ὑπεναντίους, ἀλλ' ἐναποδειξομένους τῆιδέ πηι τὴν αὑτῶν δύναμιν, ἡτοίμασε χεῖρας ἐπιτηδειοτάτας, νομίζων πρὸς τὸ μέλλον οὐδὲν ἀναγκαιότερον εἶναι τοῦ καταπλήξασθαι μὲν τοὺς Ῥωμαίους, εὐθαρσεῖς δὲ ποιῆσαι τοὺς Ταραντίνους. 5 ἅμα δὲ τῶι τίθεσθαι τὸν πρῶτον χάρακα θρασέως τῶν Ῥωμαίων καὶ τετολμηκότως ἐπιχειρούντων τοῖς ὑπεναντίοις, βραχὺ συμμίξας Ἀννίβας καὶ τὰς ὁρμὰς τῶν προειρημένων ἐκκαλεσάμενος, ἐπεὶ προέπεσον οἱ πλείους ἐκτὸς τῆς τάφρου, δοὺς παράγγελμα τοῖς αὑτοῦ προσέβαλε τοῖς πολεμίοις. 6 γενομένης δὲ τῆς μάχης ἰσχυρᾶς, ὡς ἂν ἐν βραχεῖ χώρωι καὶ περιτετειχισμένωι τῆς συμπλοκῆς ἐπιτελουμένης, τὸ πέρας ἐκβιασθέντες ἐτράπησαν οἱ Ῥωμαῖοι. 7 καὶ πολλοὶ μὲν ἔπεσον ἐν χειρῶν νόμωι, τὸ δὲ πλεῖον αὐτῶν μέρος ἀπωθούμενον καὶ συγκρημνιζόμενον ἐν τῆι τάφρωι διεφθάρη.

[31] 2 ὁρῶντας add. Hutchinson     4 διαφῆκε Benseler: δὴ ἀφῆκε fere FDG
5 τῶι ... ζημίαν Suda κ 638     τὴν del. Hutchinson     6 ‹τῶν› ἐπὶ τῶν πραγμάτων
Campe: ἐκ τῶν ταγμάτων Madvig
[32] 3 τῆι Ursinus: τῶι FDG     4 δὲ γινώσκων Hultsch: δὲ διαγινώσκων G: διεγίνωσκον FD     ἐναποδειξομένους Ursinus: -αμένους FDG     5 προέπεσον Reiske: προσ- FDG     7 χειρῶν νόμων G: χερσὶ Νομάδων G$^{mg}$

33.1 τότε μὲν οὖν Ἀννίβας, προβαλόμενος ἀσφαλῶς τὸν χάρακα, τὴν ἡσυχίαν ἔσχε, τῆς ἐπιβολῆς αὐτῶι κατὰ νοῦν κεχωρηκυίας. 2 τοὺς μὲν γὰρ ὑπεναντίους συγκλείσας ἠνάγκασε μένειν ἐντὸς τοῦ τείχους, δεδιότας οὐ μόνον περὶ σφῶν, ἀλλὰ καὶ περὶ τῆς ἄκρας, 3 τοῖς δὲ πολιτικοῖς τοιοῦτο παρέστησε θάρσος ὥστε καὶ χωρὶς τῶν Καρχηδονίων ἱκανοὺς αὑτοὺς ὑπολαμβάνειν ἔσεσθαι τοῖς Ῥωμαίοις. 4 μετὰ δὲ ταῦτα μικρὸν ἀπὸ τοῦ χάρακος ἀποστήσας ὡς πρὸς τὴν πόλιν, τάφρον ἐποίει παράλληλον τῶι χάρακι καὶ τῶι τῆς ἄκρας τείχει· 5 παρ' ἣν ἐκ μεταβολῆς ἐπὶ τῶι πρὸς τῆι πόλει <χείλει> τοῦ χοῦς ἀνασωρευομένου, προσέτι δὲ καὶ χάρακος ἐπ' αὐτῆς τεθέντος, οὐ πολὺ καταδεεστέραν τείχους συνέβαινε τὴν ἀσφάλειαν ἐξ αὐτῆς ἀποτελεῖσθαι. 6 παρὰ δὲ ταύτην, ἐντὸς ἔτι πρὸς τὴν πόλιν, ἀπολιπὼν σύμμετρον διάστημα, τεῖχος ἐπεβάλετο κατασκευάζειν, ἀρξάμενος ἀπὸ τῆς Σωτείρας ἕως εἰς τὴν Βαθεῖαν προσαγορευομένην, 7 ὥστε καὶ χωρὶς ἀνδρῶν τὰς δι' αὐτῶν τῶν κατασκευασμάτων ὀχυρότητας ἱκανὰς εἶναι τοῖς Ταραντίνοις τὴν ἀσφάλειαν παρασκευάζειν. 8 ἀπολιπὼν δὲ τοὺς ἱκανοὺς καὶ τοὺς ἐπιτηδείους πρὸς τὴν τῆς πόλεως φυλακὴν καὶ τὴν τοῦ τείχους παρεφεδρεύσοντας ἱππεῖς, κατεστρατοπέδευσε, περὶ τετταράκοντα σταδίους ἀποσχὼν τῆς πόλεως, παρὰ <τὸν> ποταμὸν τὸν παρὰ μέν τισι Γάλαισον, παρὰ δὲ τοῖς πλείστοις προσαγορευόμενον Εὐρώταν, ὃς ἔχει τὴν ἐπωνυμίαν ταύτην ἀπὸ τῆς τοῦ παρὰ Λακεδαίμονα ῥέοντος Εὐρώτα. 9 πολλὰ δὲ τοιαῦτα κατὰ τὴν χώραν καὶ κατὰ τὴν πόλιν ὑπάρχει τοῖς Ταραντίνοις διὰ τὸ καὶ τὴν ἀποικίαν καὶ τὴν συγγένειαν ὁμολογουμένην αὐτοῖς εἶναι πρὸς Λακεδαιμονίους. 10 ταχὺ δὲ τοῦ τείχους λαμβάνοντος τὴν συντέλειαν διά τε τὴν τῶν Ταραντίνων σπουδὴν καὶ προθυμίαν καὶ τὴν τῶν Καρχηδονίων συνεργίαν, μετὰ ταῦτα διενοήθη καὶ τὴν ἄκραν ἐξελεῖν Ἀννίβας.

34.1 ἤδη δ' ἐντελεῖς αὐτοῦ συνεσταμένου τὰς πρὸς τὴν πολιορκίαν παρασκευάς, παραπεσούσης ἐκ Μεταποντίου βοηθείας εἰς τὴν ἄκραν κατὰ θάλατταν, βραχύ τι ταῖς ψυχαῖς ἀναθαρρήσαντες οἱ Ῥωμαῖοι νυκτὸς ἐπέθεντο τοῖς ἔργοις, καὶ πάσας διέφθειραν τὰς τῶν ἔργων καὶ μηχανημάτων κατασκευάς. 2 οὗ γενομένου τὸ μὲν πολιορκεῖν τὴν ἄκραν Ἀννίβας ἀπέγνω, τῆς δὲ τοῦ τείχους κατασκευῆς ἤδη τετελειωμένης, ἀθροίσας τοὺς Ταραντίνους ἀπεδείκνυε διότι κυριώτατόν ἐστι πρὸς τοὺς ἐνεστῶτας καιροὺς τὸ τῆς θαλάττης ἀντιλαμβάνεσθαι. 3 κρατούσης γὰρ τῆς ἄκρας τῶν κατὰ τὸν εἴσπλουν τόπων, ὡς ἐπάνω προεῖπον, οἱ μὲν Ταραντῖνοι τὸ παράπαν οὐκ ἠδύναντο χρῆσθαι ταῖς ναυσὶν οὐδ' ἐκπλεῖν ἐκ τοῦ λιμένος,

[33] 1 προβαλόμενος Reiske: προβαλλ- FDG   5 τῶι FD: τὸ D^dG   <χείλει> Hutchinson (τὸ ... <χεῖλος> iam Gronovius)   τοῦ χοῦς ἀνασωρευομένου Schweighaeuser (χοὸς ille): τεῖχος -όμενος FDG   τεθέντος Reiske: τιθ- FDG   6 ἐπεβάλετο Gronovius: ἐπελάβετο FDG   8 τείχους <καὶ> Hutchinson   παρεφεδρεύσοντας Reiske: -εύοντας FDG   τὸν add. Bekker   Γάλαισον Hutchinson (Γαλαῖσον iam Schweighaeuser): γαλαῖον fere FDG   ταύτην Casaubon: αὐτὴν FDG
[34] 1 συνεσταμένου Casaubon: συνιστ- FDG   3 τόπων Ursinus: τόπον FDG

τοῖς δὲ Ῥωμαίοις κατὰ θάλατταν ἀσφαλῶς παρεκομίζετο τὰ πρὸς τὴν χρείαν· 4 οὗ συμβαίνοντος οὐδέποτε δυνατὸν ἦν βεβαίως ἐλευθερωθῆναι τὴν πόλιν. 5 ἃ συνορῶν ὁ Ἀννίβας ἐδίδασκε τοὺς Ταραντίνους ὡς, ἐὰν ἀποκλεισθῶσι τῆς κατὰ θάλατταν ἐλπίδος οἱ τὴν ἄκραν τηροῦντες, παρὰ πόδας αὐτοὶ δι' αὑτῶν ἐίξαντες λείψουσι ταύτην καὶ παραδώσουσι τὸν τόπον. 6 ὧν ἀκούοντες οἱ Ταραντῖνοι, τοῖς μὲν λεγομένοις συγκατετίθεντο, ὅπως δ' ἂν γένοιτο τοῦτο κατὰ τὸ παρὸν οὐδαμῶς ἐδύναντο συννοῆσαι, πλὴν εἰ παρὰ Καρχηδονίων ἐπιφανείη στόλος· τοῦτο δ' ἦν κατὰ τοὺς τότε καιροὺς ἀδύνατον. 7 διόπερ ἠδυνάτουν συμβαλεῖν ἐπὶ τί φερόμενος Ἀννίβας τοὺς περὶ τούτων πρὸς σφᾶς ποιεῖται λόγους. 8 φήσαντος δ' αὑτοῦ φανερὸν εἶναι χωρὶς Καρχηδονίων αὐτοὺς δι' αὑτῶν ὅσον ἤδη κρατῆσαι τῆς θαλάττης, μᾶλλον ἐκπλαγεῖς ἦσαν, οὐ δυνάμενοι τὴν ἐπίνοιαν αὐτοῦ συμβαλεῖν. 9 ὁ δὲ συνεωρακὼς τὴν πλατεῖαν εὐδιακόσμητον οὖσαν τὴν ὑπάρχουσαν μὲν ἐντὸς τοῦ διατειχίσματος, φέρουσαν δ' [παρὰ τὸ διατείχισμα] ἐκ τοῦ λιμένος εἰς τὴν ἔξω θάλατταν, ταύτηι διενοεῖτο τὰς ναῦς ἐκ τοῦ λιμένος εἰς τὴν νότιον ὑπερβιβάζειν πλευράν. 10 διόπερ ἅμα τῶι τὴν ἐπίνοιαν ἐπιδεῖξαι τοῖς Ταραντίνοις, οὐ μόνον συγκατέθεντο τοῖς λεγομένοις, ἀλλὰ καὶ διαφερόντως ἐθαύμασαν τὸν ἄνδρα, καὶ διέλαβον ὡς οὐδὲν ἂν περιγένοιτο τῆς ἀγχινοίας τῆς ἐκείνου καὶ τόλμης. 11 ταχὺ δὲ πορείων ὑποτρόχων κατασκευασθέντων, ἅμα τῶι λόγωι τοὔργον εἰλήφει συντέλειαν, ἅτε προθυμίας καὶ πολυχειρίας ὁμοῦ τῆι προθέσει συνεργούσης. 12 οἱ μὲν οὖν Ταραντῖνοι τοῦτον τὸν τρόπον ὑπερνεωλκήσαντες τὰς νῆας εἰς τὴν ἔξω θάλατταν, ἐπολιόρκουν ἀσφαλῶς τοὺς ἐκ τῆς ἄκρας, ἀφηιρημένοι τὰς ἔξωθεν αὐτῶν ἐπικουρίας. 13 Ἀννίβας δὲ φυλακὴν ἀπολιπὼν τῆς πόλεως ἀνέζευξε μετὰ τῆς δυνάμεως, καὶ παρεγένετο τριταῖος ἐπὶ τὸν ἐξ ἀρχῆς χάρακα, καὶ τὸ λοιπὸν τοῦ χειμῶνος ἐνταῦθα διατρίβων ἔμενε κατὰ χώραν.

37.1 ἐξηριθμήσατο τοὺς δόμους· ἦν γὰρ ἐκ συννόμων λίθων ὠικοδομημένος, ὥστε καὶ λίαν εὐσυλλόγιστον εἶναι τὴν ἀπὸ γῆς τῶν ἐπάλξεων ἀπόστασιν. 2 μετὰ δέ τινας ἡμέρας αὐτομόλου διασαφήσαντος ὅτι θυσίαν ἄγουσι πάνδημον οἱ κατὰ τὴν πόλιν ἐφ' ἡμέρας ἤδη τρεῖς Ἀρτέμιδι καὶ τοῖς μὲν σιτίοις λιτοῖς χρῶνται διὰ τὴν σπάνιν, τῶι δ' οἴνωι δαψιλεῖ, πολὺν μὲν Ἐπικύδους δεδωκότος, πολὺν δὲ Συρακοσίων, τότε προσαναλαβὼν ὁ Μᾶρκος τὸ τεῖχος καθ' ὃ μέρος ἦν ταπεινότερον καὶ νομίσας εἰκὸς εἶναι τοὺς ἀνθρώπους μεθύειν διὰ τὴν ἄνεσιν καὶ τὴν ἔνδειαν τῆς ξηρᾶς τροφῆς, ἐπεβάλετο καταπειράζειν τῆς ἐλπίδος.

[34] 5 αὐτοὶ Schweighaeuser: αὐτοῖς FDG    9 δ' [παρὰ τὸ διατείχισμα] Hultsch: δὲ π. τ. δ. FDG    13 φυλακὴν <ἱκανὴν> Naber
[37.1] Suda σ 1597
[37.2–11] 2–11 T (fol. 100ʳ); breuiata exscribunt 2 Suda λ 625 (αὐτομόλου ... δαψιλεῖ), α 1974, π 2593 (προσαν. ... ἐλπίδος), et 2 (αὐτομόλου ... δαψιλεῖ), 3 (ταχὺ ... συντεθεισῶν), 9–10 (εἰς ... ἀποκτείναντες) V (fol. 179ʳ) P₁ (fol. 93ʳ)    2 θυσίαν TVP₁: ἑορτὴν Suda    πανδημεὶ VP₁    λιτοῖς T Suda: ὀλίγον fere VP₁    προσαναλαβὼν ... ταπεινότερον T: προσανανεωσάμενος [etiam ut lemma] τὴν τοῦ τείχους ταπεινότητα Suda, bis    ἦν T: εἴη Hutchinson

3 ταχὺ δὲ κλιμάκων δυεῖν συντεθεισῶν εὐαρμόστων πρὸς τὸ τεῖχος, ἐγένετο περὶ τὰ συνεχῆ τῆς πράξεως, καὶ τοῖς μὲν ἐπιτηδείοις πρὸς τὴν ἀνάβασιν καὶ τὸν ἐπιφανέστατον καὶ πρῶτον κίνδυνον ἐκοινολογεῖτο, περὶ τοῦ μέλλοντος μεγάλας ἐλπίδας αὐτοῖς ἐνδιδούς. 4 τοὺς δὲ τούτοις ὑπουργήσοντας καὶ προσοίσοντας κλίμακας ἐξέλεξε, διασαφῶν οὐδὲν πλὴν ἑτοίμους εἶναι πρὸς τὸ παραγγελλόμενον. πειθαρχησάντων δὲ κατὰ τὸ συνταχθέν, λαβὼν τὸν ἁρμόζοντα καιρὸν νυκτὸς ἤγειρε τοὺς πρώτους. 5 προπέμψας δὲ τούτους ἅμα ταῖς κλίμαξι μετὰ σημείας καὶ χιλιάρχου καὶ προσαναμνήσας τῶν ἐσομένων δωρεῶν τοῖς ἀνδραγαθήσασι, μετὰ [δὲ] ταῦτα πᾶσαν τὴν δύναμιν ἐξεγείρας τοὺς μὲν πρώτους ἐν διαστήμασι κατὰ σημείαν ἐξαποστέλλει· 6 γενομένων δὲ τούτων εἰς χιλίους, βραχὺ διαλιπὼν αὐτὸς εἵπετο μετὰ τῆς ἄλλης στρατιᾶς. 7 ἐπεὶ δ' οἱ φέροντες τὰς κλίμακας ἔλαθον ἀσφαλῶς τῶι τείχει προσερείσαντες, ἐξ αὐτῆς ὥρμησαν ἀπροφασίστως οἱ πρὸς τὴν ἀνάβασιν ἀποτεταγμένοι. 8 λαθόντων δὲ καὶ τούτων καὶ στάντων ἐπὶ τοῦ τείχους βεβαίως, οὐκέτι κατὰ τὴν ἐξ ἀρχῆς τάξιν, ἀλλὰ κατὰ δύναμιν ἅπαντες <ἀν>έβαινον διὰ τῶν κλιμάκων. 9 κατὰ μὲν οὖν τὰς ἀρχὰς ἐπιπορευόμενοι τὴν ἐφοδείαν ἔρημον εὕρισκον· οἱ γὰρ <    >, εἰς τοὺς πύργους ἠθροισμένοι διὰ τὴν θυσίαν, οἱ μὲν ἀκμὴν ἔπινον, 10 οἱ δ' ἐκοιμῶντο πάλαι μεθυσκόμενοι. διὸ καὶ τοῖς μὲν πρώτοις καὶ τοῖς ἑξῆς ἐπιστάντες ἄφνω καὶ μεθ' ἡσυχίας, ἔλαθον τοὺς πλείστους αὐτῶν ἀποκτείναντες. 11 ἐπειδὴ δὲ τοῖς Ἑξαπύλοις ἤγγιζον καταβαίνοντες, ἐνωικοδομημένην τὴν πρώτην πυλίδα διεῖλον, δι' ἧς τόν τε στρατηγὸν καὶ τὸ λοιπὸν ἐδέξαντο στράτευμα. οὕτω δὴ τὰς Συρακούσας εἷλον Ῥωμαῖοι.

12 οὐδενὸς ἐπεγνωκότος τῶν πολιτῶν τὸ συμβαῖνον διὰ τὴν ἀπόστασιν, ἅτε μεγάλης οὔσης τῆς πόλεως.

13 τοὺς δὲ Ῥωμαίους θαρρεῖν συνέβαινε, κρατοῦντας τοῦ περὶ τὰς Ἐπιπολὰς τόπου.

22.1 ὅτι Καύαρος ὁ βασιλεὺς τῶν ἐν τῆι Θράικηι Γαλατῶν βασιλικὸς ὑπάρχων τῆι φύσει καὶ μεγαλόφρων, πολλὴν μὲν ἀσφάλειαν παρεσκεύαζε τοῖς προσπλέουσι τῶν ἐμπόρων εἰς τὸν Πόντον, 2 μεγάλας δὲ παρείχετο χρείας τοῖς Βυζαντίοις ἐν τοῖς πρὸς τοὺς Θρᾶικας καὶ Βιθυνοὺς πολέμοις.

3 Πολύβιος δ' ἐν ὀγδόηι ἱστοριῶν 'Καύαρος', φησίν, 'ὁ Γαλάτης, ὢν τἆλλα ἀνὴρ ἀγαθός, ὑπὸ Σωστράτου τοῦ κόλακος διεστρέφετο, ὃς ἦν Χαλκηδόνιος γένος.'

[37.2–11]  3 δυεῖν Hultsch: δυοῖν T: δύο VP₁    5 τούτους C. Müller: τοὺς T    ἀνδραγαθήσασι Hultsch: -μασι T    δὲ del. Hutchinson    διαστήμασι Hutchinson: διαστήματι T    8 <ἀν>έβαινον Hultsch: ἔμελλον T: <ἀν>έθεον Büttner-Wobst    9 οἱ γὰρ <    > εἰς Hutchinson, qui <φυλάττοντες> (e.g.) suppleuit: οἱ γὰρ ἐς T: εἰς γὰρ VP₁    μὲν ἀκμὴν VP₁: μὲν ἐς ἀκμὴν T
[37.12] Suda α 3546 Πολύβιος
[37.13] Suda ε 2525
[22.1–2] P    2 πρὸς Valesius: περὶ P    πολέμοις Valesius: -ους P
[22.3] Ath. 6.252c–d    τἆλλα ὢν CE (epit.)    ἀνὴρ ἀγαθός CE: ἀγαθός A

**23.**1 ὅτι Ξέρξου βασιλεύοντος πόλεως Ἁρμόσατα, ἣ κεῖται πρὸς τῶι Καλῶι πεδίωι καλουμένωι, μέσον Εὐφράτου καὶ Τίγριδος, ταύτηι τῆι πόλει παραστρατοπεδεύσας Ἀντίοχος ὁ βασιλεὺς ἐπεβάλετο πολιορκεῖν αὐτήν. **2** θεωρῶν δὲ τὴν παρασκευὴν τοῦ βασιλέως ὁ Ξέρξης, τὸ μὲν πρῶτον αὐτὸν ἐκποδὼν ἐποίησε, μετὰ δέ τινα χρόνον δείσας μὴ τοῦ βασιλείου κρατηθέντος ὑπὸ τῶν ἐχθρῶν καὶ τἄλλα τὰ κατὰ τὴν ἀρχὴν αὐτῶι διατραπῆι, μετεμελήθη καὶ διεπέμψατο πρὸς τὸν Ἀντίοχον, φάσκων βούλεσθαι συνελθεῖν εἰς λόγους. **3** οἱ μὲν οὖν πλεῖστοι τῶν φίλων οὐκ ἔφασκον δεῖν προΐεσθαι τὸν νεανίσκον λαβόντ' εἰς χεῖρας, ἀλλὰ συνεβούλευον κυριεύσαντα τῆς πόλεως Μιθριδάτηι παραδοῦναι τὴν δυναστείαν, ὃς ἦν υἱὸς τῆς ἀδελφῆς αὐτοῦ κατὰ φύσιν. **4** ὁ δὲ βασιλεὺς τούτων μὲν οὐδενὶ προσέσχε, μεταπεμψάμενος δὲ τὸν νεανίσκον διελύσατο τὴν ἔχθραν, ἀφῆκε δὲ τὰ πλεῖστα τῶν χρημάτων ἃ συνέβαινε τὸν πατέρα προσοφείλειν αὐτῶι τῶν φόρων. **5** λαβὼν δὲ παραχρῆμα τριακόσια τάλαντα παρ' αὐτοῦ καὶ χιλίους ἵππους καὶ χιλίους ἡμιόνους μετὰ τῆς ἐπισκευῆς, τά τε κατὰ τὴν ἀρχὴν ἅπαντ' ἀ<πο>κατέστησε, καὶ συνοικίσας αὐτῶι τὴν ἀδελφὴν Ἀντιοχίδα πάντας τοὺς ἐκείνων τῶν τόπων ἐψυχαγώγησε καὶ πρὸς ἑ<αυτὸν προε>καλέσατο, δόξας μεγαλοψύχως καὶ βασιλικῶς τοῖς πράγμασι κεχρῆσθαι.

[23] P  1 Ἁρμόσατα: Ἀρσαμοσάτων Hutchinson  2 διατραπῆι: διαρπαγῆι aut διαστραφῆι Hutchinson  3 πλεῖστοι Habicht: πιστοὶ P  λαβόντ' (λαβόντα) Reiske: λαβόντας P  5 ἅπαντ' ἀ<πο>κατέστησε Hultsch: ἅπαντα κατέστησε P  πρὸς ἑ<αυτὸν προε>καλέσατο Hutchinson: προσεκαλέσατο P

# COMMENTARY

## 38b.1 A CITY IN ITALY (OR CISALPINE GAUL)

Ἀγκαράτης: Stephanus gives the ethnic in the singular, as usual, but it is the plural that P. is likely to have employed. Cf. e.g. 2.39.6 Κροτωνιᾶται κτλ., 3.24.16 Ἀρδεάτας κτλ. His only singular ethnics in -της are Σπαρτιάτης, Μεγαλοπολίτης and (29.25.6) Αἰγειράτης. The city, if Stephanus' form is right, could be the same as Ἄκαρα (Strabo 5.1.10 (II 20.34 Radt)), near Bononia (Bologna) and Ravenna; these are Italian cities for Stephanus (β 111 Billerbeck, p 4). The context for the Ἀγκαρᾶται could then be the activity in Cisalpine Gaul of P. Sempronius Tuditanus, praetor in 213 (Münzer (1923*b*) 1443); that would suggest the second half of the book. The Etruscan gentile name Ancari is probably derived from the praenomen Ancar rather than a place (Rix (1963) 258).

## 38b.2 HOPE AND ENDURANCE

What this fragment refers to is unknown. It is item 45 in *Exc. Const.* IV 134, and could come from book 7, like item 44, rather than book 8, like item 46 (start of 8.35.1). Items 44–6 are all on the same page of the palimpsest, so their order is guaranteed; see Introduction §14 g n. 77.

The sentence as it stands suggests that someone held onto a hope, though uncertain, because the punishment for not doing so was certain. There is witty paradox, since the hope is not in fact very firmly entertained. More straightforward is 5.72.2 εὐθαρσῶς ὑπέμενον [cf. ὑπομένειν here] τὴν πολιορκίαν, προσανέχοντες ταῖς ἐλπίσι τῆς βοηθείας. For τὸ πρόδηλον τῆς τιμωρίας cf. 1.84.11, 15.4.7, for πᾶν ὑπομένειν 21.23.7. 5.72.2 makes against reading, say, ἐλπίσιν <οὐκέτι>.

λοιπόν 'hence': cf. *CGL* 2; Cavallin (1941); Blomqvist (1969) 100–3.

## 35–6 ASSESSING THE DECEIVED

P. here offers something characteristic of him: a carefully structured mini-essay, which organizes its material by a refined distinction (35, censure deserved; 36, sympathy deserved). His purpose is, notionally, pragmatic as well as evaluative: readers, if they encounter a parallel fate, will wish to earn συγγνώμη (36.6).

συγγνώμη has an emotional component: it is accompanied by ἔλεος at 36.9; cf. 1.88.2, 2.7.3, 15.7.6. It should not be automatically granted upon disaster; wrongdoing disqualifies one from it, as does folly. Similarly at

2.7.1–3 ἀβουλία incurs ἐπιτίμησις, not συγγνώμη, from the wise. If one at least acts κατὰ λόγον, the quasi-criminal charge (36.4) and people's negative thoughts (36.9) shift from οἱ πάσχοντες to οἱ πράξαντες (cf. 2.7.1–2); otherwise, their attention is focused on the foolish.

The first part (35, censure) looks at two examples in detail and adds a third; the second part (36, sympathy) is more general and argumentative, with the proof resting on an example yet to be narrated – Achaeus. The structure suggests that pity might seem the obvious response to any calamity; but, once that view has been undermined, subtle argument is needed to show how deceit can happen without folly. The second part is aimed at a higher level, at the pragmatically expert. The first half-sentence (from 35.1 περί), in setting up the discussion, anticipates the total argument.

The context was probably something like this: in P.'s narrative someone other than Ti. Gracchus was the victim of trickery. The episode suggested a thought on some wider aspect of such trickery – for example on the means of achieving it. That aspect was illustrated with an example or examples; Gracchus came last. The discussion then shifted – here we come to our passage – to evaluation of the victims. The excerptor for the Constantinian version (M), heedless of the chronology, took the starting point of this new discussion to be Gracchus, who died in 212.

Such elaborate developments from the narrative can be seen, for instance, at 4.31–3. In talking of a Messenian decision, P. first speaks about peace, with one example (cf. e.g. 27.9–10); he then discusses the relations of Messenians with Arcadians and Spartans, giving two examples. In the present section, the event from which P. originally started will have been the καιροί of 36.7, ὑπὲρ ὧν ὁ νῦν δὴ λόγος ἐνέστηκε, not the fall of Gracchus; the καιροί can be a single moment or event (cf. 3.108.5). To this event the fall of Achaeus will be closer in the narrative (the same year) than Archidamus, Pelopidas, Cn. Cornelius (35.3–9). The opening sentence, which appears only in M, shows as often that it is not a sentence by P., but rather an attempt to give the context which draws on P. (see 35.1n.).

The *Excerpta Antiqua* and the *Excerpta Constantiniana* both have the passage in the first half of book 8, so in 214/13 (Achaeus, from the first year, came later in M). But the death of Gracchus cannot have appeared in P.'s ordinary narrative of this year. Livy 25.15.20–17.7 places the death in 212, well into the campaigning season; he reports different versions but indicates no divergence on the year (contrast Tarentum, 25.11.20). Sil. It. 12.473–82 likewise gives 212. So too App. *Hann.* 150–2; cf. 150, 152 ἀνθύπατος/ν: in 213 Gracchus was consul. Val. Max. 1.6.8 does call him consul when killed; but that is a mistake or a corruption. If the consul had been killed mid-year, we would expect to hear of a replacement. It would be straining the Polybian year even to transpose the passage into P.'s narrative of 213/12: P. does not usually run over into a new campaigning year. Have the MSS gravely misplaced the passage? It would have to have been misplaced in both sets of *Excerpta*. In the 46 *Excerpta Antiqua* from books 1–5, there is only one slight misplacement (Walbank (1957–79) II 1); the *Excerpta Constantiniana* stick to the order in authors fully preserved. (We cannot argue, however, that ἔσται in 36.7 shows P. has not yet told Achaeus' story; the future could be used because he is about to explain the point, cf. 8.35.2 and e.g. 18.13.7.) Nor can we suppose a big lacuna after M's first sentence: Gracchus suits the discussion (cf. Livy 25.16.15). Nor will the excerptor have inserted him from thin air.

Ti. Sempronius Gracchus (cos. 215, 213) had his command in Lucania continued in 212 (Livy 25.3.5); the Lucanians were divided between allegiance to Rome and Carthage (25.16.5, etc.). According to Livy, Gracchus had a guest-friendship with Flavus, a Lucanian with high office and leader of the Lucanian pro-Roman element (25.16.5, 15, 23). Livy minimizes Gracchus' recklessness in believing Flavus, who suddenly (25.16.6) switched to a treacherous deal with the Carthaginians. An alternative account placed the killing in Campania, and removed the treachery (25.17.1). On the event and its context see Münzer (1923*a*); Pontrandolfo (1994); Pareti (1997) 405–7; Isayev (2007) 130–1; Fronda (2010) 204–7, 340–1; Wonder (2018).

## 35 EXAMPLES OF RASHNESS

**35.1 ὅτι ... κατέστρεψεν:** the first sentence shows that it is not actual P.; see Introduction §14 h. δόλωι ἐνεδρευθείς is serious hiatus; Τιβέριος is written, not Τεβέριος. P. elsewhere has the order κατέστρεψε/κατεστρέψατο τὸν βίον; ὁ Ῥωμαίων στρατηγός was not needed by P.'s readers now, cf. 25.11n. **περιπετειῶν:** surprising, disastrous events (see 15.36.4 for surprise). **καθόλου:** for all his structural interest in τὰ καθόλου, P. also welcomes an avoidance of sweeping generalization (cf. e.g. 16.28.3). **τὰ παρ' ἀνθρώποις ὡρισμένα δίκαια:** the scope makes the violation the more surprising. One might wonder if such breaches are none the less to be anticipated by someone acting κατὰ λόγον; the complications will be explored in 36.1–6.

**35.2 αὐτόθεν** 'instantly', from the first; cf. *PL* 2. **βλέποντα πρός:** carefully considering; cf. e.g. 15.8.3 βλέπειν τὰ τῆς τύχης, 18.45.10. **τοὺς καιροὺς καὶ τὰς περιστάσεις** 'the times and the circumstances'. But both can suggest a pressing situation rather than something colourlessly abstract.

COMMENTARY: 35.2–35.5    89

Cf. for περιστάσεις e.g. 3.112.9: Roman behaviour ἐν ταῖς περιστάσεσι; Moretti, *ISE* I.59.10–11 (Actium, *c*.216 BC) μεγάλων περιστάντων τὰν Ἀκαρν|ανίαν πολέμων.    **δῆλον:** proof is offered, not just clarification.

**35.3–5** According to P., Archidamus, brother of the murdered Agis IV, fled from Sparta to Messenia in fear of Cleomenes, king from *c*.235 (5.37.2). Sparta usually had two kings at once, from different royal houses, but the φιλαρχία of Cleomenes III made him wish to rule alone or with his brother (cf. Plut. *Ag. Cl.* 32.5). P. might place the killing around the time Cleomenes killed four ephors (227 BC). Plutarch makes Archidamus flee rather from Cleomenes' father Leonidas, at the death of Agis in 241 (*Ag. Cl.* 22.1); Phylarchus thought Cleomenes did not want Archidamus killed (*FGrHist* 81 F51). Thus P.'s view of Archidamus' folly depends on a conception of events to which he knew alternatives; he was a reader of Phylarchus (2.56.1, 60.7, 61.11). His own account of the killing at 5.37.1–6 does not indicate Archidamus' folly; Nicagoras, who brokers the reconciliation, clearly does not expect treachery from Cleomenes (5.37.2–6). P. shapes his account to suit his present purpose. On the history see Stern (1915); Jacoby on *FGrHist* 81 F51; Oliva (1971) 234–41; Piper (1986) 40, 51–2; Richer (1998) 426 n. 239; Cartledge and Spawforth (2002) 49–53; Hoffmann (2014) 118, 120; for Phylarchus see Pédech (1989) 394–493.

**35.3 Ἀρχίδαμος:** there is asyndeton; the τούτων at the end of §2 suffices for connection.    **ὁ τῶν Λακεδαιμονίων βασιλεύς** implies that Archidamus has assumed power, not fled at his brother's death; cf. §4 ἀρχῆς. The half-sentence ends with the contrasting ἔφυγεν ἐκ τῆς Σπάρτης.    **μετ' οὐ πολύ** would not fit the chronology seen in Plutarch; the phrase heightens Archidamus' foolishness in expecting rapid change.    **πεισθείς:** by Nicagoras (5.37.3).    **τῶι προειρημένωι:** P. very often uses this phrase to avoid repeating a name too soon. Cf. Introduction §5 b.

**35.4 ἅμα τῆς ἀρχῆς καὶ τοῦ βίου στερηθείς:** wittily compact, at Archidamus' expense.    **οὐδ':** a defence could not even get started.

**35.5 ὑποθέσεως** 'situation', 'set-up'.    **τῆς αὐτῆς:** not compatible with Leonidas ruling when Archidamus flees. With rhetorical flair, the next clause goes beyond 'the same' in ἐπηυξημένης.    **δυναστείας** is now added to φιλαρχίας (cf. §3 φιλαρχίαν). The accumulation makes the argument better than would replacement, as in G. (D^mg does not add καί, as has been asserted: in the main text the ἕ of the next line seems to be anticipated, as T at 4.1 has εεκαστον.)    **τούτοις:** ἐγχειρίσας αὐτόν picks up §3 ἐνεχείρισεν αὐτόν, but the dative is now not the colourless τῶι προειρημένωι; with οὕς it makes an argumentative point. The plural means much the same as the singular. **παραδόξως** leads to εὐλόγως: if contrary to expectation at that time (something P. has fed into the account), his death now accords with λόγος. **πῶς:** the subject is ὁ ἐγχειρίσας, but the interrogative is delayed to give the question energy after all the irrationality has been set out. **τοῖς προειρημένοις** 'the outcome spoken of', not Cleomenes. ἐγκυρέω takes the dative of things, not people, in P.

**35.6–8** In 369, Pelopidas led a successful Boeotian or Theban expedition against Alexander the new ruler of Pherae (DS 15.67.3–4; Plut. *Pel.* 26.1–4); in 368 he was sent as an envoy, or simply went, to Thessaly, with no military force, and was captured by Alexander (DS 15.71.2–3, Plut. *Pel.* 27.1, 6–7; Nep. *Pel.* 5.1). P.'s presentation requires the same sequence, and fits into the historiographical discussion. Cf. esp. §6 εἰδὼς τὴν Ἀλεξάνδρου τοῦ τυράννου παρανομίαν with Plut. *Pel.* 27.6 (Pelopidas and his fellow envoy) ἐξώλη μὲν ὄντα (Alexander) καὶ μιαιφόνον εἰδότες (but ...), cf. 26.2–3; DS 15.71.2 καταντήσας δὲ πρὸς Ἀλέξανδρον τὸν Φερῶν τύραννον ἀλόγως (punctuate thus, and cf. §9 ἀλόγως); Nep. *Pel.* 5.1 *cum ... legationis ... iure satis tectum se arbitraretur*; Theop. *FGrHist* 115 F409 (actually anonymous), cf. 36.1n. On the history see Buckler (1980) 110–29; Gehrke (1985) 189–94; Beister (1989) 146–7; Sprawki (2006) 137, 140–2; Buckler and Beck (2008) 83–4, 134; Schachter (2016) 195.

εἰδὼς ... παρανομίαν (§6) counters the line of defence indicated in 35.1, and applied to this event by Nep. *Pel.* 5.1: Pelopidas thought himself adequately protected *legationis ... iure ..., quod apud omnes gentes sanctum esse consuesset* (cf. 35.1 παρ' ἀνθρώποις). παρανομίαν shows Alexander is not concerned by any sort of law. The next clauses give general and particular reasons why Alexander would treat Pelopidas as a πολέμιος, not a πρεσβευτής (§6 πολεμιωτάτους, §7 πολέμιος, πρεσβεύειν, all effectively placed).

**35.6 σαφῶς γινώσκων** varies and advances on εἰδώς, πᾶς τύραννος expands on τυράννου. **τοὺς τῆς ἐλευθερίας προεστῶτας:** Pelopidas is not made directly a champion of freedom, but indirectly, as persuading Epaminondas to be one; προεστάναι takes up προεστῶτας at the end of the next clause. αὐτός, though, emphasizes his crucial role. **τῶν Ἑλλήνων:** Epaminondas championed δημοκρατία among the Greeks in general, especially by winning the battle of Leuctra (371 BC). So Nep. *Epam.* 8.3 *uno proelio non solum Thebas* [cf. οὐ μόνον τῆς Θηβαίων] *ab interitu retraxit sed etiam uniuersam Graeciam in libertatem uindicauit*, P. 8.11.3 below. δημοκρατία and ἐλευθερία go closely together for P., as the argument implies; cf. 6.57.9. Epaminondas is more important for P. than Pelopidas: he mentions Epaminondas much more often, and puts him first when he and Pelopidas are paired (6.43.6, fr. 160 Olson). ἔπειθεν: the imperfect is here a general past, not referring to the specific time of the embassy.

**35.7 <πρότερον>:** in the suggested text πρότερον and ὕστερον contrast in chiasmus; for the two words in a pointed contrast cf. 9.9.11. Pelopidas' previous attack as a literal enemy made his later embassy unwise. πρότερον can remove the need for a past participle, especially but not only when the verb has none. Cf. e.g. DS 13.24.1 (ὤν); 36.11.2 (πρωτεύοντες); Plut. *Flamin.* 22.6 Λακεδαιμονίων μὲν γὰρ εὐεργέτης πρότερον ὤν, ὕστερον καὶ τὰ τείχη κατέσκαψε. Pelopidas' leading an assault and going as an ambassador would not combine well on a single occasion (cf. Plut. *Pel.* 27.1, Pelopidas πρεσβεύων, with no military force; Theop. *FGrHist* 115 F409 σπονδάς). The pattern of two encounters fits well with Archidamus and the argument (cf. §5 πρότερον). ἐπὶ καταλύσει τῆς Ἀλεξάνδρου μοναρχίας is pretty well the same phrase as used by DS 15.67.3 of the first expedition, ἐπὶ ... καταλύσει δὲ τῆς Ἀλεξάνδρου τοῦ Φεραίου τυραννίδος. P. would not use the adverb δεύτερον as in the MSS, not making the first item clear (*PL* III; clear at 2.43.4). δεύτερος γενόμενος (Naber (1857) 132), in an embassy with only one other person, produces an awkward repetition of γενόμενος (§8). δεύτερος αὐτός would involve a milder repetition of αὐτός; the phrase would mean 'with one other person'.

**35.8 τοιγαροῦν** again leads to the disastrous result (cf. §4); but this time narrative and argument are joined together, and the consequence is dealt with more briefly than the act. The difficulty with this example for P. is not the folly but the disaster: Pelopidas was actually rescued, on the second attempt (Plut. *Pel.* 28.1, 29.1–12). P. has to stress the initial harm to Thebes and the damage to Pelopidas' reputation. **κατέλυσε** takes up §7 καταλύσει: it was not his good fame that he intended to undo. **προγεγενημένην:** consistency is important for one's reputation in P.; cf. e.g. 2.1.7, and Welles, *RC* 44.7–8 (Antiochus III) ἀγόμενον ἀξίως τῶν προυπηργμένων ἐξ αὐτοῦ. **εἰκῇ καὶ ἀκρίτως:** same pair 18.14.1, εἰκῇ καὶ ἀλόγως 6.56.12, 9.18.3.

**35.9 Γνάϊος:** Cn. Cornelius Scipio Asina (cos. 260, 254; *MRR* I 205; *RE* Cornelius 341). The bare *praenomen* here is remote from Roman usage. In 1.21.4–22.1, this Scipio's capture in 260 is due not to Carthaginian deceit but to his own tactics. Now P. needs to follow the version seen in e.g. Livy, *Per.* 17 (*per fraudem*), App. *Lib.* 279, Polyaen. 6.16.5 (πεισθείς). **ἔπαθε:** part of a thread; cf. 35.1 πάσχουσιν, 36.4 πασχόντων, 9 παθόντι.

## 36 CAUTION IN VAIN

**36.1 ἀσκέπτως:** rarer, and seemingly more forceful, than ἀλόγως (35.9). In P. ἀσκέπτως comes here and at 5.98.2, never in papyri; ἀλόγως comes 20 times in P., often in papyri. **ὑπεναντίοις:** broader than πολεμίοις (35.9, with αὐτὸν ἐγχειρίσας); so it would encompass Archidamus, though perhaps ἑαυτοὺς ἐγχειρίζουσι does not suit Pelopidas so well. **ἐπιτιμητέον:** variation appears in οὐκ ἐγκλητέον, §2 ἀνεπιτίμητον, §4 ἔγκλημα. ἐγκλη- is stronger, with its legal image. **ἐνδεχομένην:** here 'all possible', cf. 1.68.13 πρόνοιαν τὴν ἐνδεχομένην, 3.76.2, LSJ III.2; in §2 more like 'the best available', cf. §3, §§5–6. **πρόνοιαν** often appears in P. with ποιέομαι; in many cases, as here, the construction enables the addition of an adjective.

**36.2 ἄπρακτον:** a penetrating point, related to the philosophical problems of combining Scepticism with practical action (so Sext. *Math.* 7.30).

**36.3 ὅρκοι, τέκνα, γυναῖκες:** an asyndetic trio, though the second and third items belong more closely together; the sentence moves onto something quite different, not a formal surety at all. 'Theop.' *FGrHist* 115 F409 talks of Alexander τοὺς ὅρκους παρ' οὐδὲν θέμενος in capturing Pelopidas. At App. *Lib.* 279, the Carthaginians capture Cn. Scipio ὅρκοις ἀπατήσαντες. Oaths pervade inscriptions, e.g. *Syll.*³ 1 527 (Dreros *c.*220), with fearsome consequences for perjury (75–90). For children and wives as hostages cf. e.g. 1.68.3, 10.35.1, 6. **τὸ μέγιστον:** <καί> adds an element to the whole trio, not to the preceding item. The appositional τὸ μέγιστον always has a καί or δέ in P., 'and, the most important thing,' (27 times); cf. K–G I 285. It would in any case be clumsy to conflate continuing asyndeton for a list and a pause for apposition. For καί cf. 3.34.2–3: excellence of land, size of population and courage of men, καί, τὸ μέγιστον, their hatred of the Romans; 6.14.10, 28.7.10. **βίος:** that of the person one is trusting.

**36.4 ᾗ καί** 'hence'; cf. e.g. 5.67.3. **ἀλογηθῆναι** 'make a mistake'; cf. 28.9.8, and ἀλόγημα. A forceful word to use after §2 πράττειν τὸ κατὰ λόγον. **οὐ τῶν πασχόντων ἀλλὰ τῶν πραξάντων:** pithier and with more moral point from the context than 2.7.1 οὐ τῶν παθόντων, τῆς τύχης δὲ καί τῶν πραξάντων ἐστὶν ἔγκλημα.

**36.5 τοιαύτας ζητεῖν πίστεις <δεῖ> δι' ὧν:** the hyperbaton gives emphasis to τοιαύτας and the thought.

**36.6 δεύτερος ... πλοῦς:** a standard phrase for a Plan B; cf. e.g. Plato, *Phaedo* 99c6–d2, Arist. *EN* 2.1109a33–5 (with φασί). Men. fr. 183 K–A suggests πλοῦς is a second means of motion, oars rather than sails. **που**

softens the failure; in 'if we are deprived of something' (τοῦ FDG), the 'something' would be too weak for the context. **σφαλλώμεθα:** the first person includes the speaker in the generalization, for tactful effect.

**36.7 ἐναργέστατον:** vivid as an example of what P. has been saying; cf. 4.8.4 ἐναργῆ δὲ τῶν τοιούτων μαρτύρια, 38.5.5 εἴη δ' ἂν τὸ λεγόμενον ἐναργὲς πρῶτον μὲν ἐκ τῆς ἀκοῆς, ἥτις κτλ. **τοῖς ὑπὲρ ὧν:** article as antecedent to relative clause; cf. 1.5.1 τοῖς ἀφ' ὧν Τίμαιος ἀπέλιπεν, 21.27.9 τὰ ἐν οἷς διέτριβε πράγμασιν.

**36.8 ἀνθρωπίνηι:** the same near-religious sense of human limitations as in the close on Achaeus at 21.11 below; cf. 2.7.1 ἀνθρώπους ὄντας, 3.31.3, 11.6.6 (speech): many things escape τὴν ἀνθρωπίνην πρόνοιαν, 23.12.4.

**36.9 μῖσος:** an extreme moral response; cf. 30.29.1–2, Plut. *Ag. Cl.* 21.1. Here it is from οἱ ἐκτός, those not involved; cf. 32.6.6 τὸ μισοπόνηρον τῶν Ῥωμαίων.

## 3a AND 1–7: THE SIEGE OF SYRACUSE

P. takes up a subject from book 7 (7.2–9). Hieron II's teenage grandson Hieronymus succeeded him in 215; Hieronymus shifted Syracusan policy towards alliance with Carthage. Tumult after his assassination (214) ended with pro-Carthaginian *strategoi* leading Syracuse. A large part of Sicily had become a Roman province after the First Punic War; much of the rest had remained in the power of the friendly Hieron (Le Bohec (1996) 104; Guido (2010) 127–8). But Carthage had retained support. For it to regain a foothold in Sicily would have meant to the Romans the threat of losing the much-contested island (Plut. *Marc.* 13.2), and perhaps the threat of losing increased revenues from Syracuse itself (Guido (2010) 127–34). In the course of 214 (see below), the Roman siege of Syracuse began. It was rendered harder by the structure of Syracuse, which was divided into separate 'cities', some separately fortified (see §3.2n.). (On the events, context and cityscape see Introduction §11 a, b, §12 d; Marchetti (1972); Lehmler (2005) 97–155; Levathan (2013) 107–9; Beste and Mertens (2015) 294–5.)

P.'s account of the siege exhibits his large designs and his range as a writer. Thucydides (cf. 9.19.1–4), Philistus (*FGrHist* 556 F51–6) and Timaeus on Athens and Syracuse may well be in readers' minds; but the connections are most evident later, on Epipolae (37.11, 13nn.). The first part that we have (1–2) sets the Roman assault on Syracuse in a big context, not of Sicilian history, but of simultaneous activity by Rome and

Carthage. Significant as the event is itself, its grandeur and the greatness of Roman ambition only emerge in the context of Rome and Carthage's total deeds and plans at this point (1.1 τὸ μεγαλεῖον τῶν πράξεων, 2.7 τὸ μέγεθος τῶν ἔργων). Rome as a political structure and as an entity with purpose are fundamental to this picture (1.1 τῆς ἑκατέρου τοῦ πολιτεύματος προαιρέσεως, 2.7 τὴν τοῦ πολιτεύματος δύναμιν). The vast historical point of how Rome's structure led to its conquest of the world is not visible to one merely reading of Sicilian events (2.3 ψιλῶς).

After this imposing lead-in, what we have of the main account (3–7) presents a closely technical description of warfare, closer than those in Livy and Plutarch (cf. Culham (1992)). Ironically, after 1–2, 3–7 show Roman confidence being crushed, and not by a rival political structure but by one individual, a Greek and an old man (7.8). It is Archimedes who has the δύναμις (3.3; cf. 7.9). Large numbers of troops are nothing (3.3 πολυχειρία, twice). Roman over-confidence, especially at sea, has been a theme from the first (so 1.37.3–10). Ultimately, in these events, Roman cunning will triumph, Roman assurance will return (37.2, 13). But the narrative pattern and the change of writing manner draw us into the unpredictability of events and into the challenging interval between vast and small-scale historical vision.

A technical mode in writing is important to P., as was seen in the Introduction §3 c; it draws on the Hellenistic expansion in technical works, not least works on war. P. himself wrote a work on tactics (9.20.4). As technology advanced, machinery and sieges were popular subjects (cf. Wheeler (2022) 706–7). Extant before P. are Philo (*c.*200 BC?), with two or three books from a work on engineering, and Biton (ii BC); for texts see Marsden (1971) and Whitehead (2016). A Ctesibius (iii BC or else ii BC) was closely followed by Hero (i–ii AD?). Works vary in precision and technical detail (on which cf. Schiefsky (2005)). In this episode, P. is concerned with machines throughout; but formally closest to a technical treatise is 4.3–11, where he explains at length how σαμβῦκαι work. Livy 24.34.6–7 drastically compresses, and gives no idea of a specific device; Plut. *Marc.* 15.5 names but does not describe it. Yet there is a considerable interval between P.'s and Biton's accounts of their σαμβῦκαι (Marsden (1971) 72–4). Biton is full of measurements and intricate design, and he includes a diagram: see T fol. 29ᵛ, https://gallica.bnf.fr/ark:/12148/btv1b8593585j/f68.item. P. has only one measurement (4.3), and describes people in action. This YouTube video of smooth operation is designed for contrast with the historical narrative in which the σαμβῦκαι are destroyed by Archimedes' superior machines (5.8–11; cf. 6.6). The description of all Archimedes' machines and arrangements gives a clear idea of how they worked, but without details of construction and with a restricted amount of technical vocabulary (so 5.9–10, 6.3); graphic narrative is vital. Types of writing, technical and historiographical, blend and clash.

P. portrays Archimedes as intensely involved in the defence of Syracuse (cf. 5.2, 6nn.). His mathematical pre-eminence goes far beyond the 'necessary' parts of geometry, which are all P. inculcates in generals, with a typical display of balance (9.20.5–6); but Archimedes forms an emblem for the military power of knowledge. His works add a weighty literary context. Though engineering can provide an impetus (cf. e.g. Archim. *Meth.* Netz *et al.* (2011) 71 col. i.32–73 col. i.22), the works were written largely for οἱ οἰκεῖοι τῶν μαθημάτων, 'those familiar with [rather than 'friendly towards'] mathematics' (*Sph. Cyl. pr.*, Netz *et al.* (2011) 191 col. ii.8–9 (I 4.18–19 Heiberg), cf. *Spir. pr.* II 2.9–10 Heiberg, *Aren.* 20 II 258.5–10, *Quadr. pr.* II 262.5; Netz (2004) 32, 34). P.'s narrative creates the impression that the machines are Archimedes' instant response to the Romans' contrivances, just before the Romans put them to use (implausible, but modern historians write similarly). However, it emerges near the end of the account (7.2) that the remarkable devices had been created earlier, under Hieron II (cf. Livy 24.34.13: machines prepared *per multos annos*; Plut. *Marc.* 14.7–15, earlier than P. in the narrative sequence). They had been part of Hieron's lavish and imposing work to defend the city. Archimedes' own displays were connected with the kings; so he devised the enormously powerful stone-thrower aboard Hieron's huge ship (Moschion *FGrHist* 575 (iii BC) F1.4.3). The seeming disproportion in P. between mighty effects and small origin – Archimedes himself, 7.8–9 – is part of the Archimedes myth (cf. Moschion *FGrHist* 575 F1.2.4, Sil. It. 14.351–2, Plut. *Marc.* 14.12–13, etc.). Plutarch relates Archimedes' belated practicality to the history of philosophy (*Marc.* 14.8–14); P. makes Archimedes' fitness to these circumstances part of his own thought on power through the mind and on supreme individuals. (For Archimedes, see Heiberg (2013 [1879]); Dijksterhuis (1987); Netz (2009), (2013), (2022) 107–220 (203–4 for these events; and 221–51 for P., mathematics and warfare).)

We can say little about P.'s sources. See the introduction to 24–34 on sources for the Second Punic War. Since Hannibal is not directly involved, some writers on his deeds may have been less concerned. But 7.7.1–2 suggest an ample tradition for P. to use and differ from. It would be good to know more about Sicilian local historians for this time; Heraclides' biography of Archimedes is of interest too (*FGrHist* 1108).

Finally, it is important to see that the siege of Syracuse probably begins in 214, not, as is usually supposed, 213. Although Livy compresses events of 214 and 213 into 214, he will not have altered P.'s sequence. In Livy the capture of Henna firmly follows Marcellus' conflict with Archimedes;

and *CIL* I².608 shows that Marcellus, consul in 214 and not 213, took Henna as consul. *consol* there does not refer to a later time of dedication, as *CIL* I².615–16 make clear (Fulvius has no later consulship). Marcellus' consulship extends to February, but the intense fighting at sea should not happen in the winter; a winter pause in fighting is normal. The eight months of P. 8.7.6, which follow defeat by Archimedes, must finish by the end of summer 213 (7.6n.). If the sea-fighting is to be in 213, it would again have to take place in the winter. Chh. 1–2 below, which precede the siege, fit 214 rather than, as is usually thought, 213. (De Sanctis (1968) 319 has normally been followed, though cf. Seibert (1993*b*) 290; the view goes back to Tuzi (1891) 86–8.)

## 3a THE BURDEN OF SILENCE

This passage comes in the margin of F shortly before 1–2. A plausible context is Adranodorus giving away his conspiracy, a secret which he incautiously revealed to a confidant (Livy 24.24.2). This will be in 214, after the killing of Hieronymus; Adranodorus had encouraged Hieronymus towards Carthage and against Rome (P. 7.2.1, 5.4–5). His plans were now to seize control (Livy 24.24.1, 6–7; 26.5); he in his turn is killed (24.4). It is apparent from P. 7.2.1–5.8 that Livy's account draws heavily on P.

οὕτως: see 7.7n. for the characteristic generalization opening out from narrative. οἱ πλείους τῶν ἀνθρώπων: οἱ πλεῖστοι τῶν ἀνθρώπων is similarly scornful at 9.26a.1, 10.17.1. τὸ κουφότατον ἥκιστα φέρειν δύνανται: P. creates witty paradox from φέρω literal and metaphorical. κουφότατον plays with the metaphor; silence has no literal weight. The metaphor is similar at Thgn. 295 κωτίλωι ἀνθρώπωι σιγᾶν χαλεπώτατον ἄχθος; the paradox builds up riddle-like suspense. Likewise at 6.56.7, where λέγω δὲ τὴν δεισιδαιμονίαν reveals the surprising answer. P. advises keeping plans quiet at 9.13.2–5.

## 1–2 THE EVENTS PART OF A WHOLE

**1–2** Chronological footholds are offered by 1.6–8: after Marcellus' arrival in Sicily (later 214), and Valerius' arrival at Oricus (summer 214), before the Romans' siege and initial failure (later 214). The first takes us after the excerptor's résumé in 3.1; cf. Livy 24.21.1. The occasion for 1–2 is not events in Spain: 1–2 precede 3–7 in FDG; Spain would follow Sicily in P.'s usual order, so 3–7 would be in the wrong year.

The protagonists' breadth of vision (ch. 1) leads onto P.'s breadth of vision (2). For all the importance of συμπλοκή in P.'s design (Introduction §6 b–d), and pointers in speeches (so 5.104.2–3, 9.37.10, 39), most of the time the narrative seems to have left the connection of different spheres to readers. This moment will stand out.
P. is shaping events for a particular purpose, in a broad way. Contention over Sardinia (1.3) seems exaggerated. The Romans' motivation in Spain is earlier seen as less ambition than anxiety for Italy (3.97.2–4). Some looseness and legerdemain is characteristic of P.'s more expansive passages; it is unlikely he would turn to a separate source for 1–2 (Walbank (1957–79) II 68), not noticing its divergences from his other sources. P.'s grand design distorts his specific interpretation.

## 1 THE GREATNESS OF ROMAN AND CARTHAGINIAN UNDERTAKINGS

**1.1 οὐκ ἀλλότριον εἶναί μοι δοκεῖ:** justification of apparent excursus. The phrasing spreads from oratory (Isocr. *Antid.* 104); cf. e.g. Caes. *BG* 6.11.1 (*non alienum esse uidetur*), Cels. 2 *pr.* 2, Sext. *Math.* 7.190. P. is suspending his narrative, but is doing so to show the thought that underlies it.   **τῆς ὅλης ἡμῶν ἐπιβολῆς καὶ τῆς ἐν ἀρχαῖς προθέσεως:** both the entirety and the initial plan (cf. 2.1 below) are important for the relevance. P.'s ἐπιβολή 'endeavour, undertaking' matches the Romans' and Carthaginians' ἐπιβολαί (§3).   **συνεπιστῆσαι** 'alert them to, focus their attention on'. Cf. e.g. 10.41.6 (τοὺς ἀναγινώσκοντας).   **τοὺς ἀκούοντας** here, ἀναγνόντα 2.3: the different expression for recipients does not matter.   **τὸ μεγαλεῖον:** μεγαλεῖος is often used of grandiose utterance (Plato, *Hipp. Maj.* 291e3–4, etc.); P. uses it of grand deeds, 12.23.6, fr. 183 Olson.   **πολιτεύματος:** here quite close to πόλις, cf. e.g. 5.86.8.   **προαιρέσεως:** the conscious outlook behind the πράξεις. So at 1.64.5: in the First Punic War one would find the προαιρέσεις of both πολιτεύματα to be alike in μεγαλοψυχία and in τῆι περὶ τῶν πρωτείων φιλοτιμίαι.

**1.2** A big rhetorical question builds up the grandeur and ambition, with the stages marked by τηλικοῦτον μέν, οὐκ ἐλάττω δέ, ἀκμὴν δέ, ὅμως, ἀλλὰ καί. ἀκμὴν ... κινδύνους seems to immerse readers in the antagonists' psychological and practical state, until ὅμως disrupts: they go yet further.   **ἐπισημήναιτο** 'admire', or 'express admiration'; cf. e.g. 11.19.1 τίς οὐκ ἂν ἐπισημήναιτο τὴν ἡγεμονίαν (of Hannibal), *IMT* Kaikos 830.26 (I AD) 'approve, express approval'.   **συνεσταμένοι** 'having brought about'; cf. 2.1.1 (πόλεμον). The perfect middle/passive participle is used transitively, as often in P. οὐκ ἐλάττω: talk of this great war, and especially reading τὰς Ἰβηρικὰς πράξεις (2.3), more happily suit 214, in which there was much important action (Livy 24.41–2), than 213, during which *in Hispania nihil memorabile gestum* (Livy 24.49.7–8 – the exceptions involve no actual fighting). ἀκμήν 'still'; see Introduction §13 c. περὶ τούτων fits more closely with ἐλπίδας than with κινδύνους. ἐφαμίλλους 'equal', without the original sense of rivalry; cf. 1.57.6 (with ἀμφοτέρων), 28.17.11 (with ἑκατέρων). The word matches ἐπ' ἴσον. So κατὰ τὸ παρόν matches ὑπὲρ τοῦ μέλλοντος, though it is intensified by ἐνεστῶτας.

**1.3 Σαρδόνος**: despite T. Manlius' victory over Sardinians and Carthaginians in 215 (Livy 23.40–41.7), two legions are kept there for some years (214: Livy 24.11.2). Cf. Mastino (2005) 68–91. **πάντα περιελάμβανον**: they 'were encompassing' or 'taking possession' of all the places in question, or trying to, not just in hope, but practically. For this use of πάντα in relation to a context, cf. e.g. 5.9.1, and more explicitly ἅπαντα τὰ προειρημένα (2.9 below); 'all' relates to the whole sentence, not just Sardinia and Sicily. περι- suits πάντα; cf. 2.52.5 πᾶσαν ἤδη βεβαίως περιειληφὼς ταῖς ἐλπίσι τὴν Πελοποννησίων ἀρχήν, 5.33.5 πάσας ... περιειληφέναι πράξεις (cf. App. *Iber.* 56), 14.5.7 τὸ ... πῦρ περιελάμβανε πάντας τοὺς τόπους. Not 'they envisaged world-conquest' (Walbank). ταῖς χορηγίαις καὶ ταῖς παρασκευαῖς would not at this date suit 'all known parts of the world' (2.4 below), such as Asia. Cf. 1.3.6: the Romans first acted to acquire Greece and Asia after the Second Punic War. For discussion of when P. thinks the Romans aspired to rule the world see Petzold (1969) 175–6; Harris (1979) 107–9; Baronowski (2011) 71–2; Derow (2015) 128–31. His views are unlikely to have had much solid base in evidence. See also 2.6n.

**1.4 εἰς τὸ κατὰ μέρος ἐμβλέψας** 'looking at, considering the detail', i.e. in §§4–5 and then §6. This is connected with the impending historiographical discussion insofar as P. wishes to offer understanding of history both κατὰ μέρος and καθόλου (3.5.9); those who claim to write universal history without the detail are frauds (5.33.1–8). For ἐμβλέπω cf. 5.90.3 ὅταν μέν τις εἰς τὸν χρόνον ἐμβλέψῃ, *I.Erythrai* 1.122.20–1 (ii BC) ἐμβλέποντες εἰς τὰν σπουδὰν ἂμ ποιῇ ὁ δᾶμος. **δύο**: the consuls had two legions each, so two armies in all (Livy 24.11.2; P. 6.32.6). Marcellus clearly did not take two legions to Sicily (cf. Gelzer (1962–4) III 239); the *exercitus* at Livy 24.30.1 is the force which, or most of which, had already been in Sicily; cf. 35.1. **ὑπάτων:** Q. Fabius Maximus Verrucosus (cos. I 233; *RE* Fabius 116), the Cunctator; M. Claudius Marcellus (cos. I 222; *RE*

Claudius 220), the Marcellus of Plutarch's *Life*. Marcellus had been elected as suffect consul in 215, but was replaced for that year by Fabius (Livy 23.31.12–13). ἐντελῆ is given emphasis by its separation from στρατόπεδα. προεκάθητο: προ- does not always have a strong meaning in P.'s use of προκάθημαι, but it could suggest defence of Rome (*PL* 2αβ). In the light of 2.8, this would not seem so apt to Spain, but verbs are often less appropriate to a second object or phrase. δύο: there were two legions and then 8,000 soldiers – almost two legions – for the war in Spain (Livy 21.17.8, 22.22.1). The numbers, separate arrival and two commanders are enough for P. to speak of two armies, as with the consuls in Italy, and off Spain there are ships. Γνάϊος ... Πόπλιος: brothers: Cn. Cornelius Scipio Calvus (cos. 222), P. Cornelius Scipio (cos. 218), father of the Elder Africanus; *RE* Cornelius 345 and 330. Publius is sent with the ships at 3.97.2, but their operations seem more combined (3.97.4–8). In 212 or 211 both Cn. and P. Scipio were defeated and killed. Cf. esp. App. *Iber*. 54–64, and e.g. Richardson (1996) 23–30; Fernández Uriel (2006) 39; Varga (2015) 39–42. For these Scipios in Spain cf. Panzram (2002) 26–9; Torregaray Pagola (2003) 261–2.

**1.5 ὁμοίως:** the transmitted οἰκείως does not seem to be used in the sense of ὁμοίως. For the sense cf. 2.71.8 ὁμοίως δὲ καὶ περὶ Καρχηδονίους. For the separation of ὁμοίως from καί cf. 3.39.4, *IG* II².1006.78 (Athens, 122/1 BC). In this passage the order is caused by the addition of ταὐτά (Schweighaeuser; cf. §8, 6.35.10). Cf. Ammon. *in An. Pr. 1 CAG* IV 30.18–19 ὁμοίως δὲ τὸ αὐτὸ λέγει καὶ ἐπὶ τῶν πλεοναζόντων συλλογισμῶν. For the Carthaginians' forces in Spain, see 3.33.14–18; they have three commanders and armies, cf. Livy 24.41.5, 25.32.4, App. *Iber*. 60. In Italy Hanno has a force separate from Hannibal's; cf. Livy 24.14.1–2, 20.2; 23.41.10–12.

**1.6 καὶ μήν** 'and indeed'. This move east will make the point still more strikingly; cf. e.g. 5.10.8. **τοῖς κατὰ τὴν Ἑλλάδα τόποις:** often used instead of 'Greece' (5.10.8, etc.). **ἐφώρμει**, 'was moored off' and 'keeping watch on', suggests a purpose, mostly unfriendly: the different τοῖς κατὰ τὴν Ἑλλάδα τόποις and ταῖς ἐπιβολαῖς τοῦ Φιλίππου are effectively combined. M. Valerius Laevinus (cos. II 210; *RE* Valerius 211) is *intentus aduersus omnes motus Philippi Macedonum regis* even while at Brundisium (Livy 24.10.4, spring 214). The weighty στόλος 'fleet' appears after some time, with argumentative force. Involvement with Greece is particularly important for P.'s picture of συμπλοκή (cf. 2.12.7 ἐπιπλοκή ... εἰς τοὺς κατὰ τὴν Ἑλλάδα τόπους); Greece is here stressed more than Illyria or Roman anxiety (cf. 5.105.8). Philip was much concerned with the Illyrian coast as well as Greece (cf. e.g. 7.9.13); Valerius kept his fleet at Oricus in the winter of 214 (Livy 24.40.17), perhaps strictly Illyria rather than Greece (Dion. Perieg. 398), after the Romans had defended Apollonia in Illyria from Philip. In 213 Valerius was assigned Greece and Macedonia *cum legione et classe quam haberet* (Livy 24.44.5); in 211 he is looking after *Graeciae ... orae* (Livy 26.1.12). P. Sulpicius Galba Maximus (cos. 211, 200; *RE* Sulpicius 64), takes over from him in 210 (Livy 26.22.1, 26.4; *MRR* I 280). See also Introduction §12 e.   **τοῦ Φιλίππου:** ταῖς Φ. (FD) would be less normal than ταῖς τοῦ Φ.; but cf. 4.75.1.   **Πόπλιος ἐπέπλει Σουλπίκιος:** for P. an unusual substantial separation of *praenomen* from *nomen*.

**1.7 ἅμα δὲ τούτοις** ends the sequence climactically, as is indicated by §3; the actual subject of the narrative, Sicily, is made to form a climax. The restrained ἐφήδρευε links with ἐφώρμει and Greece (§6); but ἑκατὸν πεντηρικοῖς and πεζικὰς ... δυνάμεις connect with Spain (§4). The details highlight the naval force. As with Spain (§5), a brief sentence on the Carthaginians concludes.   **Μᾶρκος μὲν Κλαύδιος:** see 4n. above. The *a* is long; cf. *ILLRP* 376.1 (Argos, 67 BC) *Maarcium*, 3 Μαάρκιον.   **πεντηρικοῖς σκάφεσι:** see 4.1n.   **Ἄππιος:** Ap. Claudius Pulcher (cos. 212; *RE* Claudius 293), so not from Marcellus' branch of the Claudii. The names of Appius and Marcus in the MSS need to be swapped. This passage follows Marcus' arrival in Sicily, which comes later than the summary in 3.1; in P.'s clear division of responsibility, Appius should not be commanding the ships after the Senate's instructions (3.1) and Marcus' arrival. There are surprising divergences in the MSS over the roles of Appius and Marcus: see the apparatus at 3.1, 6, 4.1. Here in the MSS (FDG) Appius has the 100 quinqueremes, Marcus the land forces; at 5.4, Marcus is making an attack with 60 quinqueremes (FDGTVP$_1$). Appius is on land at 7.1 (FDGVP$_1$). At 6.6 the MSS (FDGVP$_1$) and Ath. 14.634b, citing P., make Marcus comment on 'his' ships (so too Plut. *Marc.* 17.1–2). It is not just that Marcus has overall command: we see confusion over the actual names; cf. 4.1, and Anon. *Obs.* p. 78.200–1 Van den Berg Ἄππιος δ' ἦν ἡγεμών.   **ἐφήδρευε** 'watched over', kept an eye on. ἐφεδρεύω is used with τοῖς τόποις καὶ καιροῖς at 3.90.2, with τοῖς ἐν τῆι Θράικηι ... πράγμασι at 5.34.8.

**1.8 Ἀμίλκας:** Livy calls him Himilco, a different name; see 24.35.3 *Himilco, qui ad Pachyni promunturium classem diu tenuerat* (cf. Geus (1994) 170–1). There is one Carthaginian name in §§6–8, six Roman names; P.'s predominant interest here is in Rome. The time precedes the Romans' initial acceptance of their failure (7.1, 9): around then, Hamilcar (or Himilco) takes more action and the resemblance with Romans ceases (Livy 24.34.16–35.8).   **ἐποίει:** the verbs from §3 to §8 are almost all imperfect (§4 προεκάθητο formally pluperfect). P.'s use of the imperfect is complex; but these efforts and holding actions continue in unresolved situations (§2), unlike the aorists of accomplishment in the next chapter. παρὰ Καρχηδονίοις is best deleted. The phrase works at §5 with the vague γίνεσθαι and the general subject of armies; but with 'did the very same thing', i.e. ἐφήδρευε τοῖς κατὰ τὴν Σικελίαν, 'among the Carthaginians' seems out of place. And since P. is alert to repetition (Introduction §5 b), it is unattractive to end a paragraph with the phrase that recently ended a sentence.

## 2 UNIVERSAL HISTORY IS BEST

**2.1 δι' ὧν** 'through these things'; a result, not a purpose; cf. 22.8.12, and likewise the more emphatic δι' αὐτῶν τῶν ἔργων. P. modestly stresses the facts rather than himself. ἡμῖν 'by me' is slipped in casually between ἐν ἀρχαῖς and τῆς πραγματείας 'the work', which go together; ἔργων on the other hand is stressed by αὐτῶν. For αὐτός in such a context cf. e.g. Cic. *ND* 2.10: (in 162 BC) *res ipsa probauit* augury and haruspicy. The proof is highlighted by ἀληθινήν and its separation from πίστιν. Cf. the more restrained 1.35.4: what Euripides seemed to have said well πάλαι, τότε (cf. νῦν here) δι' αὐτῶν τῶν ἔργων ἔλαβε τὴν πίστιν.

**2.2 τοῦτο δ' ἦν:** the fresh start for the explanation increases the impetus; a further τοῦτο δ' ἐστί at §4 leads into the final point, the wonder of Rome's sole rule. Less expansively at 39.8.7 (epilogue) ἐξ ὧν τὸ κάλλιστον ... τοῦτο δ' ἦν τὸ γνῶναι πῶς καὶ τίνι γένει πολιτείας κτλ. (with much similarity to §4 here). Cf. 16.7n. **οὐχ οἷόν τε κτλ.:** a shorter version of e.g. 1.4 (note 1.4.3, 5–6), shorter even than 9.44.2: 9.44.2 is very similar to §§1–2 here, but lacks ἐν ἀρχαῖς, and to συνθεάσασθαι adds τῆι ψυχῆι, τὸ κάλλιστον θέαμα τῶν γεγονότων and περιλαβεῖν. The focus now is less on the quasi-aesthetic experience. **τῶν τὰς κατὰ μέρος ἱστορίας γραφόντων:** a plurality contrasted with P. The same phrase comes at 1.4.6. The multitude are those who deal with just some part of the world and its events – save for mere pretences at universal history. Ephorus alone really wrote it, P. asserts (5.33.1–2), but before this united period. At e.g. 1.4.2–4 P. portrays the basic contrast between his type of history and that restricted in place and events. See further Introduction §3 a, and Sacks (1981) 96–121. **τὴν τῶν ὅλων οἰκονομίαν:** as if a deliberate arrangement. The phrase occurs at 9.44.2 and in Stoics: Cornut. 37 and, earlier, Chrys. *SVF* II 937, from Plut. *Stoic. Repugn.* 1049f–1050d, where there is a contrast between τὰ κατὰ μέρος and ἡ κοινὴ φύσις (1050a). P. is offering a vision stripped of philosophy and religion: his τύχη (§3) is given will and personhood only by his writing. Cf. Maier (2012) 210–48; Ferrary (2014) 265–73.

**2.3 ψιλῶς** goes with αὐτός, i.e. on its own, at 1.5.3, 2.39.11, 12.25b.2, etc. **τὰς Σικελικὰς ἢ τὰς Ἰβηρικάς:** now that the two are made parallel, they can be scornful alternative particulars; τὰς Σικελικάς alone would have been less effective rhetoric. **γνῶναι καὶ μαθεῖν:** a weightier version of 1.1.5 γνῶναι πῶς καὶ τίνι γένει πολιτείας κτλ.; cf. 6.2.3 τὸ γνῶναι καὶ μαθεῖν πῶς καὶ τίνι γένει πολιτείας κτλ., 3.32.8 on universal history. γνῶναι (Hermog. *Prog.* 27.3 Rabe) καὶ μαθεῖν comes weightily at Dem. 20.93. **μέγεθος:** an important consideration for historians, cf. e.g. 6.2.7, Thuc. 1.1.1, 2; but here the greatness is not visible from these events on their own. **τὸ συνέχον** 'the crucial matter'; cf. 10.45.5, 23.16.9 and LSJ συνέχω 3. **τίνι τρόπωι καὶ τίνι γένει πολιτείας:** rhetorically more resonant than P.'s usual πῶς καὶ τίνι γένει πολιτείας (1.1.5, 6.2.3 (both above), 39.8.7 (§2n.)). τίνι τρόπωι will be developed separately in §§5–6, with τίνι γένει πολιτείας to follow in §§7–8. For constitutions in P., see Introduction §1 c and §11 b. **παραδοξότατον:** an important consideration for P., as the book brings out (see 19.7, 20.9, 31.4nn., etc.). In cruder versions, P. indicates, it is pursued by other historians (cf. e.g. 3.47.6).

**2.4 δυναστείαν:** paired with ἀρχή on other occasions in P. (so 1.3.10, end of paragraph); for the world coming ὑπὸ μίαν ἀρχήν, the pair is used in the present version only (contrast 1.1.5, 6.2.3, 30.6.6, 39.8.7). The stylistic heightening here is evident. In this version, uniquely, τύχη leads the parts of the world rather than them falling ὑπὸ μίαν ἀρχήν: again stylistic enhancement. Here alone 'parts' of the world are so called, to bring out what is happening, and fit the argument on history κατὰ μέρος.

**2.5 πῶς μὲν κτλ:** a fair-sounding concession, even if made grudging by οὐκ ἀδύνατον and ἐπὶ ποσόν; the move is typical of P.'s rhetoric. **εἷλον Συρακούσας** and **Ἰβηρίαν κατέσχον** (chiasmus) look beyond this book; both will be harder tasks than the curt aorists make them sound. The difficulties with Syracuse will shortly be revealed. ἁπάντων (§6) contrasts with these limited names. **κατὰ μέρος:** emphasized by separation from συντάξεων 'works'. τῆς καθόλου τῶν πράξεων ἱστορίας makes a more imposing close to the second half of the sentence. **ἐπὶ ποσόν:** here 'to some extent'. On the phrase see Introduction §13 c n. 65.

**2.6 πῶς** is taken up – not as in the first half of the sentence – by a sequence of interrogatives, τί, τί πάλιν, τίνας, the last offering a further question within the second clause beginning τί. Understanding the course of this achievement is a detailed and elaborate business. **ἡγεμονίας:** a less brutal word than δυναστεία, though coupled with it at 1.63.9 οὐ μόνον ἐπεβάλοντο τῆι τῶν ὅλων ἡγεμονίαι καὶ δυναστείαι τολμηρῶς, ἀλλὰ καὶ καθίκοντο [cf. καθίκοντο here] τῆς προθέσεως; cf. 15.10.2 (Scipio before Zama). ἡγεῖσθαι is distinct from ἐπικρατεῖν καὶ δεσπόζειν at 6.50.3; ἡγεμονία commonly denotes 'leadership' of the Greeks sought by Spartans and others (e.g. 6.50.5). For P.'s use of ἡγεμονία cf. Edwell (2013) 49–51.    τί ... ἀντέπραξε 'which of the particular aspects worked against their total endeavours'.    ὁλοσχερεῖς links with ἁπάντων and is opposed to τῶν κατὰ μέρος. Its phrase is emphatically placed straight after τί; τῶν κατὰ μέρος is widely separated from the τί it goes with, and subordinated. τὰ κατὰ μέρος have a role defined by something larger.    ἐπιβολάς: universal leadership is now seen more as a plan; cf. 1.3.6, 1.63.9 above. But as often in comments on this plan, the chronological context is vague (so 9.10.11). The sentence §§5–6 hints at a relation with the capture of Syracuse, but this moment seems early for global aspirations (contrast esp. 3.2.6). The tricky idea of 'total attempts' is put safely in the middle (§§5–6), between Fortune's achievement (§§3–4) and the greatness of the events (§§7–9) – sound rhetorical strategy, as Libanius observes on Demosthenes (*Hypoth.* to *Cor.*, 6).    ἀντέπραξε ... συνήργησε: personifying language. Even at 15.16.6 (on Hannibal) note καί: ἔστι μὲν γὰρ ὅτε καὶ ταὐτόματον ἀντέπραξε [gnomic aorist] ταῖς ἐπιβολαῖς τῶν ἀγαθῶν ἀνδρῶν.    δυσχερές understates, wryly, and οὐ ... εὐμαρές (§7) still more so. We expected the converse of οὐκ ἀδύνατον (§5).

**2.7 οὐ μήν** rarely appears in P. after heavy punctuation without ἀλλά or γε (1.87.2, and 27.8.13, 28.3.9, 38.2.4 – the transmission may deteriorate). οὐ μὴν ἀλλά – so Bekker here – appears after heavy punctuation 120 times in P. Cf. Denniston (1954) 335, 338.    **τὴν τοῦ πολιτεύματος δύναμιν**: cf. 6.18.2 τὴν δύναμιν τοῦ πολιτεύματος, which becomes great in a crisis.    **κατανοῆσαι** after οὐ ... εὐμαρές matches καταλαβεῖν after δυσχερές (§6).

**2.8** This shorter sentence is pointedly dwarfed by the bigger construction §§9–10.    ἀντιποιήσασθαι 'seek to have'; cf. e.g. *IG* VII.188.10 (Pagae, 242–223 BC) τῶν τόπων ὧν ἀντεποιήσαντο Αἰ[τωλοί.    πάλιν 'on the other hand'; cf. *PL* 5.    πεζικαῖς ... δυνάμεσιν takes up 1.7 especially.    οὐκ ἄν εἴη θαυμαστόν: the same rhetorical move is seen at 18.40.3 τὸ μὲν ... ἴσως οὐ θαυμαστόν, τὸ δέ ..., [Dem.] 34.36 εἰ μὲν ..., οὐδὲν ἂν ἦν θαυμαστόν· νῦν δέ ...

**2.9–10** A heap of genitive absolutes is finally resumed in οὕτως ... μόνως and, with forceful repetition, μάλιστ' ... οὕτως. Events in different areas have accumulated: τούτων and πολλαπλασίων ἄλλων are joined together in τούτοις and then added to the pair περιστάσεων καὶ πολέμων – the latter a striking plural. The result of all this is not only the expected amazement (θαυμαστά; cf. §8) but also clarity (σαφῆ). The sentence closes soberly with the response needed from readers: an attention that is fitting in its intensity.

**2.9 ἐπιτελουμένων** 'being accomplished': the word suggests planning. It strongly points to ἀρχῆς meaning 'beginning' rather than 'rule' (cf. e.g. Arist. *An. Pr.* 1.26b30 πάντες [syllogisms] γὰρ ἐπιτελοῦνται διὰ τῶν ἐξ ἀρχῆς ληφθέντων). As 'starting point' for action ἀρχή forms a suitable pair with πολιτεία, especially in the sense of the political structure from which everything grows (cf. 6.50, with 2 τὸ τέλος ['purpose'] ... τῆς πολιτείας, for the Romans' domination).

**2.10 μόνως** (Schweighaeuser): so 7.12.3 οὕτως ... μόνως [Casaubon: μόνος MFDG] ἂν ὑποχείριον ἔχοις τὸν βοῦν. **ἂν ... τυγχάνοι τῆς ἁρμοζούσης ἐπιστάσεως:** for τυγχάνω ἐπιστάσεως cf. fr. 150 Olson; for requisite degrees of attention cf. Sext. *Math.* 7.22 (*SVF* II 44) βαθυτέρας δεῖται τῆς ἐπιστάσεως.

**2.11 ταῦτα μὲν οὖν ἡμῖν εἰρήσθω:** a common closing device in P., as in Aristotle (used by a speaker at P. 9.30.5). Commonly in P. it marks the end of an excursus, of which it often asserts the purpose. Here πρός indicates a reply to contrary views, as at 4.42.6, and the three instances of ταῦτα μὲν οὖν ἡμῖν εἰρήσθω in Diodorus, 2.5.7, 3.30.4, 20.70.4. **ἐμπειρίαν †ποιήσασθαι†:** ἐμπειρία 'experience, understanding' is not enough of an action noun (physical or mental) to go with ποιέομαι; cf. *PL* BI. τῆς τῶν κατὰ μέρος συντάξεως sounds like writers' activity rather than a work; cf. 1.4.2 μηδένα τῶν καθ' ἡμᾶς ἐπιβεβλῆσθαι τῶν καθόλου πραγμάτων συντάξει. So one might think of οἱ ὑπολαμβάνοντες as writers pleased at their own work (cf. §1 ὑπολαμβάνω) – writers rather than readers who are intending to peruse a limited history. In that case, something like πεπορίσθαι 'has been provided'; cf. the perfect φασὶ ... περιειληφέναι at 5.33.5 of would-be universal historians. <περι>ποιήσεσθαι (Naber) would be 'they will acquire'. **τῆς καθολικῆς καὶ κοινῆς ἱστορίας:** as at §6, P. closes with a resounding designation of his own sort of history. Only here and at §6 does he grandly combine καθολ- with ἱστορία; contrast e.g. 1.4.2 (above), 5.33.1, 2 τὰ καθόλου γράφειν. κοινή is used with ἱστορία at 4.28.4 for narration of events everywhere together in his eventual pattern (Introduction §1 c and §6 c). The phrase has more relation to subject matter at DH *AR* 1.2.1 τοῖς γε δὴ μὴ παντάπασιν ἀπείρως ἔχουσι τῆς κοινῆς ἱστορίας (Roman and other empires).

COMMENTARY: 3.1        105

## 3 THE SIEGE BEGINS

**3.1** The first sentence is likely to be the excerptor's summary of a much more elaborate narrative. It is improbable that P.'s account lacked the abundant non-Roman detail which Livy offers on events in Syracuse (24.23.5–29.12,

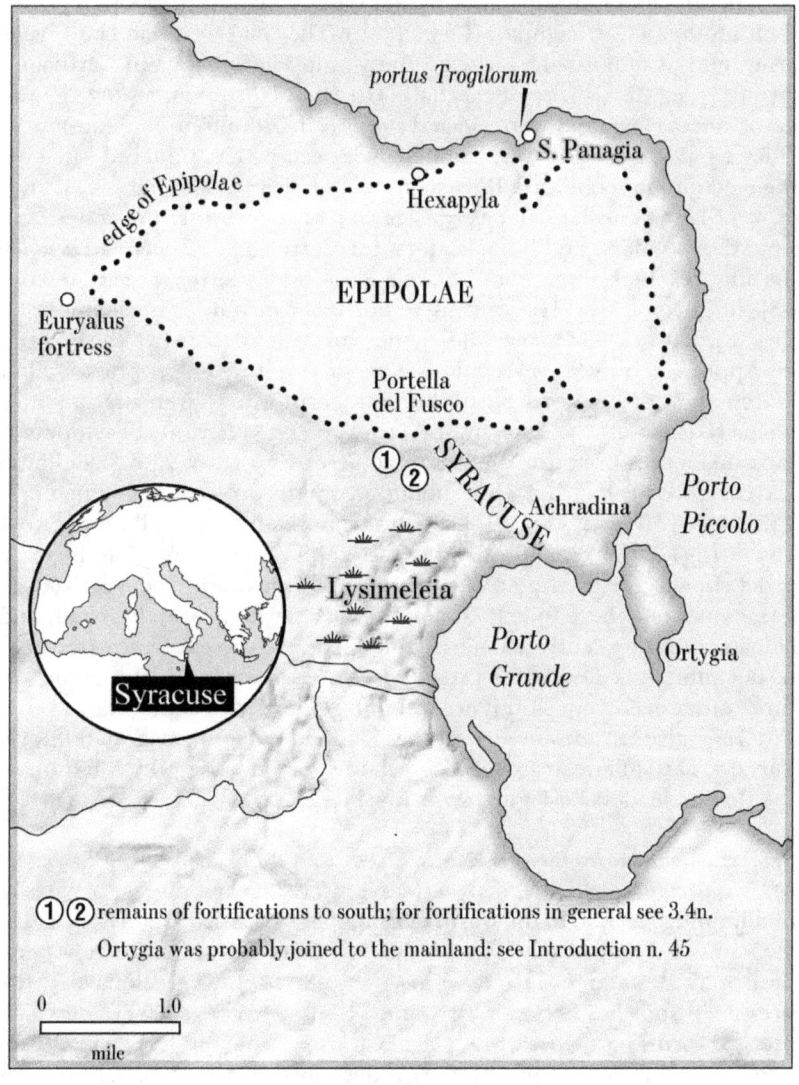

Map 2  Syracuse (Joe LeMonnier, https://mapartist.com/)

from re-entry of Hippocrates and Epicydes); P. is probably Livy's source. Elements in the language indicate that the excerptor is not simply using P.'s words. **Ἐπικύδης τε καὶ Ἱπποκράτης**: Epicydes is the younger brother (7.2.3); one might have expected the other order in P., as at 7.2.3 and 18 out of 20 times in Livy (26.30.3 comes for variety after 26.30.2). Hippocrates and Epicydes' grandfather was a Syracusan aristocrat (7.2.3), their mother a Carthaginian (Livy 24.6.2). They had served in Hannibal's army, and as ambassadors swayed the young Hieronymus in Carthage's favour (7.4.4–6, 5.5). See Lenschau (1913); S. Hornblower (2024) 146–7. **κατέλαβον**: they were elected *strategoi*, in tumultuous circumstances (Livy 24.32.9); but this verb sounds like 'occupied, conquered'. In Livy, the election happens after the assignation of Sicily to Marcellus (24.21.1; cf. 27.6). **ἑαυτοὺς ... ἀλλοτριώσαντες**: strange of Hippocrates and Epicydes, soldiers, and ambassadors, for Carthage. **προσπεπτωκυίας** 'having reached their ears'; cf. e.g. 3.20.1. **καταστροφῆς** 'death', LSJ II; 7.7.1–2 (of Hieronymus). For Hieronymus' assassination cf. Livy 24.7.4–7. **Μᾶρκον**: the names are muddled in T; this should be Appius. ἀντιστράτηγον could mean 'proconsul' or 'propraetor'; but Marcus cannot be a proconsul: he was consul when given the province of Sicily (Livy 24.21.1, Sil. It. 14.110–13, Plut. *Marc.* 13.1). Appius is most likely a propraetor; he was praetor in 215 (Livy 24.6.4; Bellomo (2019) 160–1). Livy does not mention Appius' prolonged command at 24.10.3–5 (*MRR* I 266 n. 6), probably from confusion (Bellomo (2019) 167 n. 104). **αὐτῶι** 'him', with some emphasis, like τούτωι, as the word order shows; cf. e.g. 21.27.9 αὐτῶν μέν. **νηίτην**: νηίτης, i.e. ναυτικός (cf. §2), comes only here in P. It comes once each, with στόλος, in Arrian and Appian; but the occurrence here could be due to the excerptor (see next n. but one). **αὐτοῖς** 'for them'. **ἐπετρόπευσε** 'took charge of'; its three other occurrences in P. are with the genitive, of a child (2.45.2 etc.). The narrative as presented here has skipped over the negotiation and warfare, particularly at Leontini north-west of Syracuse, which led up to the Roman leaders besieging Syracuse (Livy 24.27.6–33.8; cf. P. '7'.14b?).

**3.2 τὴν στρατοπεδείαν ἐβάλοντο** 'set up their camp' (*PL* βάλλω B). **Ἑξαπύλων**: the Hexapyla (Map 2) were an elaborate set of gates in or adjoining the wall to the north of Epipolae; cf. DS 14.8.3, Livy 25.24.1–7. Connected may be a large tower, the evidence for which has now been destroyed: Beste and Mertens (2015) 17, 24, 79. In their Beilage 1, the presumed spot lies between T7N and T8N. **τῆς Ἀχραδίνης**: of which the stoa forms part. κατὰ τῆς Ἀ., 'against', is possible but less elegant with κατά to follow. Achradina (Map 2) is described by Cic. *Verr.* 4.118–19 as one of several 'cities' within the city of Syracuse; it had its own walls (cf.

Beste and Mertens (2015) 248–9; Livy 24.33.9, 25.25.1). It contained a large agora, and Hieron's temple of Olympian Zeus. Cf. Lehmler (2005) 98–106, 145–50; Basile (2012). Pitassi (2009) 98 argues that Achradina was unsuitable for assault by sea, and thinks that the attack was on the west side of Ortygia.   **προσαγορευομένην:** T's order is preferable; cf. e.g. 2.21.7 τὴν Πικεντίνην προσαγορευομένην χώραν.   **στοάν:** Cic. *Verr.* 4.119 mentions *pulcherrimae porticus.* Cf. Bell (2012) for stoai in the large agora of Morgantina. The stoa here is not known; for the connection of its name with trade cf. Paus. 8.30.7 στοὰν δὲ ἥντινα καλοῦσι Μυρόπωλιν. As later at Tarentum (33.6, etc.), P. gives a precise place name.   **καθ' ἥν** 'by which'.   **κρηπῖδος:** probably a course of stone running beside the sea; cf. 5.37.8 ἐν τῶι λιμένι παρὰ τὴν κρηπῖδα περιπατοῦντας, Paus. 9.39.9 (not by the sea). Constraints of space here combine it with the defensive wall. This is better than making it part of the stoa. VP₁ add περιστοιχίσαντες 'having surrounded', since they do not have T's τὰς ... ποιεῖσθαι; but no surrounding is really in question. The word, for a common concept, is not Polybian.

**3.3 γέρρα** are standard items for sieges (16.11.2), probably wicker screens or sections; cf. 4.8 below, 21.28.4, Ath. Mech. 18.2; wicker shields *I.Lindos* 1.2 B.23–8 (99 BC).   **ἐν ἡμέραις πέντε** vividly conveys the generals' bravado; cf. the impressive 4.80.14 πᾶσαν ὑφ' ἑαυτὸν πεποιημένος τὴν Τριφυλίαν ἐν ἡμέραις ἕξ.   **< >:** for τοὔργον ἐπιτελέσαντες cf. 2.42.3. An addition is needed: 'they hoped to be quicker than the enemy in five days' does not make sense. ἤλπισε etc. are often slipped in between words that go together, e.g. 3.61.5 οὐδ' ἐπιβάλλεσθαι τῆι διὰ τῶν Ἄλπεων ἤλπισε πορείαι τὸν Ἀννίβαν, 90.5, 11.16.8 δι' αὐτῶν τῶν οὐραγούντων ἤλπισαν οἱ μὲν προτερήσειν κτλ.   **καταταχήσειν** appears in ironic sequences again at 3.16.4, 16.2.4. The Syracusans actually have everything ready (§5).   **οὐ λογισάμενοι** 'not considering *or* realizing'; for the latter cf. Plut. *Aem.* 16.1 μὴ λογιζομένωι τὸ γινόμενον. The clause comes better here (VP₁) than before ἐν ἡμέραις πέντε (T), where it ruins the ironic structure.   **τὴν Ἀρχιμήδους δύναμιν:** a striking phrase to use of the old man.   **προϊδόμενοι:** similarly used with the application of a general point at 3.81.12, 6.10.6.   **διότι:** the same as ὅτι, as at 1.49.1, 18.13.3, etc.   **ἁπάσης:** ἐστί is more likely to be added (TVP₁) than left out (*Suda*).   **πολυχειρίας,** heightened by ἁπάσης, takes up πολυχειρίαν; μία contrasts with πολυ- (and ἁπάσης), ψυχή with -χειρ-. Cf. 1.35.4–5 (Xanthippus) εἷς ... ἄνθρωπος καὶ μία γνώμη worsted Roman πλήθη. ψυχή suggests the total determined spirit rather than the intellect; cf. e.g. 24.10.11 ψυχῆι χρώμενοι λαμπρᾶι, and 7.7n.   **ἀνυστικωτέρα** 'achieves more'; cf. Aesop 46 (Boreas and Helios) πολλάκις τὸ πείθειν τοῦ βιάζεσθαι ἀνυστικώτερόν ἐστι. P.'s ἐν ἐνίοις καιροῖς tempers the enthusiasm with sobriety. ἀνυστικός comes only here in P.   **πλήν:** ἀλλά, the converse of their not having foreseen.   **ἔγνωσαν,** from the narrated time, is brought together with τὸ λεγόμενον from the narrator's: they realized the hard way a truth which P. sets before readers. Contrast e.g. 21.23.7 γνοίητε δ' ἂν τὸ λεγόμενον οὕτως (same time). More straightforwardly 1.71.7 διὸ καὶ τότε σαφῶς ἔγνωσαν ἡλίκην ἔχει διαφοράν κτλ.

**3.4 οὔσης γὰρ ὀχυρᾶς:** the two genitive absolutes, up to ὡρισμένους, show the particular circumstances (cf. §3 ἐν ἐνίοις καιροῖς) which enabled one man to be so effective; but they also show the Romans underestimating the fortifications.   **τὸ τεῖχος:** DS 15.13.5 τεῖχος περιέβαλε τῆι πόλει is separated from his description at 14.18.1–8 of Dionysius I's wall round the higher and non-urban land of Epipolae (see introduction to 37). But it is Epipolae that P. seems especially to have in mind with ὑπερδεξίων and ὀφρύος. He ignores, for example, the parts of the city wall that must have adjoined the low marshland of Lysimeleia; cf. Livy 24.34.3 *summissa quaedam*. By this stage, the circle of fortification runs round the coast on the east and north-east, then rises at Hexapyla to follow the edge of Epipolae, before descending at the Portella del Fusco in the south (see Map 2). Cf. Drögemüller (1969) 99–103; Karlsson (1992) 14 n. 5, 21; Ampolo (2011) 10, 185–9; Beste and Mertens (2015).   **ὀφρύος:** land jutting out like an eyebrow; cf. e.g. 10.38.8 τόπον ὀφρὺν προβεβλημένην ἔχοντα.   **καὶ μηδενὸς κωλύοντος:** the rhetoric highlights the problem for the Romans – even this easier situation would be difficult.   **κατὰ τινας τόπους ὡρισμένους:** the Romans' choices become predictable.

**3.5 ἡτοίμασε:** the verb is used of the Romans too, §3, 4.4; but Archimedes' preparation is made to seem less superficial, and specific to this siege; cf. 5.5, 8. The verb is taken up by ἐξ ἑτοίμου. It is used at 25.8, 30.7, 32.4 below of Hannibal and the Tarentines.   **ἐντὸς τῆς πόλεως:** as opposed to the outer fortifications of Dionysius and following rulers.   **< >:** <πρὸς τοὺς κατὰ γῆν> or the like is made necessary by ὁμοίως δὲ καί; devices within the city are not just to repel attacks by land, cf. e.g. 5.6 below.   **μηδέν,** though internal, is matched by πᾶν, ἐκ τοῦ καιροῦ by ἐξ ἑτοίμου. 'In no respect did they need to busy themselves on the spur of the moment.' Cf. e.g. 29.7.5 μηδὲν προκόπτειν. For ἐκ τοῦ καιροῦ cf. 10.43.9, 18.24.7, *I.Priene* B–M 68.22 (after 84 BC).   **δεῖν** gives a better sense of Archimedes' planning than just ἀσχολεῖσθαι; -δέν of μηδέν may have contributed to the omission in T.   **ἀσχολεῖσθαι:** cf. 5.98.3: the production of ὄργανα like ladders, μικρὰν ἔχοντα τὴν ἀσχολίαν.   **ποιεῖσθαι τὴν ἀπάντησιν:** cf. e.g. 3.95.4 ποιεῖσθαι τὴν ἀπάντησιν to Carthaginian attacks. Chh. 4–6 will show the pattern of attack and response on a large scale.

**3.6 πλήν:** despite this actually adverse situation. Appius' efforts (μέν) are only briefly mentioned, Marcus' (δέ) at great length (4.1–11). The narrative will return to Appius at 7.1. The irony in Appius' equipment is its obviousness, against Archimedes' cleverness. **ἀπὸ τῶν ἀνατολῶν:** the space does not seem abundant for an attack, if it is assumed the Hexapyla belong where usually thought. No numbers are given for the force.

## 4 THE ROMANS' SPECIAL DEVICE

**4.1 ἑξήκοντα:** the 68 ships (cf. §2) will be drawn from the 100 of 1.7. **σκάφεσι πεντηρικοῖς:** a variation found in P. and Diodorus for the commoner πεντήρης (as in §2, and e.g. *IG* II².1629.811, 325/4 BC). The 'five', harder to sink than the trireme, may have had three levels of oars, worked some by two men, some by one. Dionysius I is supposed to have begun it (DS 14.42.2), and the Romans to have adopted it in the First Punic War (P. 1.20.9–10, etc.). See Morrison (1996) 225, 285–91; Murray (2012) 261–8. **ἕκαστον πλῆρες:** the multitude of assailants is built up. **τόξα καὶ σφενδόνας καὶ γρόσφους:** the weapons are piled up in a trio; cf. 10.30.9 σφενδονητῶν κτλ. γρόσφοι are javelins, cf. 6.22.4. **ἀναστέλλειν** 'keep back'; cf. e.g. DS 18.70.4 ἀνέστελλε τοὺς ἐπὶ τῶν ἐπάλξεων ἀντιτεταγμένους, LSJ II.3.

**4.2 ἅμα δὲ τούτοις** creates anticipation. The sentence then accumulates a description of the ships, in the instrumental dative; the verb προσῆγον is followed by two prepositional phrases, and, after this effective delay, the object. The last word σαμβύκας is treated as a novelty for readers, since an explanation follows, and (§11) the name is elucidated; cf. λεγομένας here, Plut. *Marc.* 15.5, App. *Mith.* 103; contrast Ath. Mech. 27.7–9 πᾶσιν ... εὐγνώστους. The σαμβύκη which Biton describes is transported on land; that device suits the name less well. The sea version at least was thought Roman by the technical writer Moschus (Ath. 14.634b), and the invention of Heraclides of Tarentum, presumably for the Romans (cf. for Heraclides P. 13.4.1–5.6). This makes it recent. For P.'s account of it, see Landels (1966); Marsden (1971) 90–4; Lendle (1983) 167–76. **παραλελυμέναις τοὺς ταρσούς** 'which had detached their sets of oars'. A transitive middle-passive perfect participle; cf. e.g. 7.10.1 κατακεκληρουμένων τὰς τούτων οὐσίας, 11.15.3. The ships act; cf. 1.46.9 νῆες ... ἐπτερωκυῖαι, with 11 πτερώσας τὴν ναῦν. P., unlike App. *Mith.* 103 ἐπὶ δύο νεῶν φερόμενον, elaborately and elegantly describes how two ships are enabled to carry a σαμβύκη. Livy repeats the arrangement, without naming *sambucae* (24.34.6–7). For παραλύω see LSJ I.1, and 16.4.6 with ταρσούς (there a violent action); for ταρσός cf. e.g. *IG* II².1611.345–6

(357/6 BC) τῶν ξυλίνων ἔχουσι | ταρρόν.   σύνδυο 'in pairs', only here in P.; cf. e.g. *IG* VII.3073.76–7 (Lebadeia, ii BC) τοὺς | τέτταρας σύνδυο. The arrangement was standard with σαμβῦκαι: cf. Andreas *FGrHist* 571 F1, Appian above. It improved the balance required by the projection beyond the bows (§4).   τοίχους 'sides'; τῶν ἐκτὸς τοίχων denotes the other two sides.

**4.3 τὸ δὲ γένος τῶν εἰρημένων ὀργάνων:** so at 6.27.1 ἔστι δὴ τὸ γένος αὐτῶν τῆς στρατοπεδείας τοιόνδε is followed by a description of how the Romans set a camp up. FDG's τὸ δὲ γένος τῆς κατασκευῆς τῶν εἰρημένων ὀργάνων is too complicated; contrast 1.22.3 (so-called ravens) ὧν συνέβαινε τὴν κατασκευὴν εἶναι τοιαύτην. And there, as in Biton, there are numerous detailed measurements. With either reading, the description is at first in the past. ὄργανα are 'devices'.

**4.4 κλίμακα:** the Greek word ranges wider than 'ladder', which would not suit four-foot steps.   **ἀποβάσεως:** the interval between the foot of the κλῖμαξ and the wall (9.19.7 stipulates half the height of the ladder). When the κλῖμαξ is properly placed, it must match the wall in height.   **δρυφακτώσαντες** 'having provided with handrails', not 'having fortified'. δρύφακτος is 'handrail' in P. (1.22.6, 10); a duplication of σκεπάσαντες is not needed. The verb is found only here.   **σκεπάσαντες ὑπερπετέσι θωρακίοις** 'protecting the sides above the steps 'with high-reaching screens', like parapets. Men will keep ascending during the attack (§10); they could be assailed from the city.   **ἔθηκαν:** the account is naturally associated with Marcellus' forces; at §5 or §6, it spreads into generality. The relation of general and particular is often fluid in P.   **πλαγίαν** 'slanting'. Before the 'raising' (§6), the κλῖμαξ is laid onto the top of the inner sides of the ships; as the beaks (ἐμβόλων) on the prows rise, the κλῖμαξ which projects beyond them (προπίπτουσαν) will be somewhat slanting. The point is that it has not yet reached its raised position.

**4.5 ἱστοῖς:** the mainmasts of the two ships; any lesser masts would not be useful for the pulleys. This preparation is detailed separately; ἐνδεδεμένων κτλ. in §6 shows how it could have been put later.   **τροχιλεῖαι** 'pulleys', used too for the maritime 'ravens' at 1.22. 5, 8. For the spelling cf. e.g. *IG* XI.2.161.98 (Delos, 278 BC).   **προσήρτηνται:** the next sentence picks up on 'the' ropes and 'the' pulleys; the movement into the present works most smoothly with perfect here (as in T) rather than pluperfect (as in FDGVP₁).   **σὺν κάλοις** 'together with ropes'; κάλος = Att. κάλως, not καλός 'beautiful'.

**4.6 λοιπόν** 'so' shows what follows from this preparation; cf. e.g. 12.4.3.   **χρείας:** a military encounter; cf. e.g. 1.46.1 μετὰ τὴν χρείαν ταύτην. This word is used rather than, say, 'the wall'; it is the first hint of the difficulties.   **κορυφήν** 'top', cf. e.g. 1.22.5, as it will be after the raising. Presumably the ropes were attached before the 'top' was made to project beyond the ships (§4).   **ἕλκουσι:** the first present main verb is of vigorous and vivid action.   **τούτους:** the ropes.   **ἐν ταῖς πρύμναις** comes last; it is matched by ἐν ταῖς πρῴραις and underlined by παραπλησίως. The whole length of the ships is being used.   **πρῴραις:** for the spelling cf. e.g. SEG XXXIII.640.8 (Rhodes, ii–i BC).   **ἐξερείδοντες** 'supporting'; cf. Luc. Podagr. 54–7 (stick supporting invalid's steps).   **ἀντηρίσιν:** long pieces of wood (cf. e.g. I.Lindos I.2 D.61–5, 99 BC); they prevent wobbling (Apollod. Poliorc. 178.6 Schneider τὴν ἐφ' ἑκάτερα περίνευσιν). Since these ἀντηρίδες are held by the men, and are not pre-existing fixtures, ταῖς seems unwarranted; it repeats -τες.   **ἀσφαλίζονται:** cf. §8 ἠσφαλισμένον, §10 ἀσφαλῶς. As regards the machine, all is arranged securely.   **μηχανήματος** 'siege engine'; cf. e.g. Ath. Mech. 36.9.

**4.7 διὰ τῆς εἰρεσίας:** save that the object is here τὰς ναῦς, the participial clause transfers into a general statement what appeared as narrative in §2; the duplication shows this cannot be narrative in a historic present.   **πειράζουσι:** the challenge of the task appears now, despite §9 προσερείσαντες; cf. §8. This will be just the point at which the Romans actually fail, 5.10.   **προσερείδειν** 'lean against', as with ladders, 4.19.3.

**4.8 ὑπάρχει:** the placing has not been described.   **πέτευρον:** here a thin wooden platform, giving the four men more than a foot each (§3). The word is often used of an acrobat's springboard, *gracilis uias petauri* (Mart. 2.86.7).   **τὰς τρεῖς ἐπιφανείας** 'the three sides', not the side from which they come, facing away from the city. Cf. 4.70.9–10: the three sides of the city, and the remaining, north side.   **διαμαχόμενοι:** often used with πρός, like διαγωνίζομαι. The fighting that now appears is underlined by having both verb (ἀγωνίζονται) and participle, the participle focusing on the specific conflict.   **εἴργοντας** 'trying to prevent'; the reason for §7 πειράζουσι is now apparent. The lively εἰσρέοντας (T) would leave τὴν πρόσθεσιν stranded.   **ἀπὸ τῶν ἐπάλξεων:** the generalized account reaches the situation envisaged in the narrative of §1, striving against τοὺς ἀπὸ τῶν ἐπάλξεων μαχομένους.

**4.9 προσερείσαντες:** in this ideal general exposition, they eventually succeed.   **ὑπερδέξιοι** 'higher than', with genitive, as e.g. 11.15.3. The men at least stand above the wall, even if the κλῖμαξ is supposed to be just ἰσοϋψὴς τῶι τείχει (§4); but excessive height would prevent descent and bring disaster, cf. Ath. Mech. 27.10–28.3.   **οὗτοι μέν:** the four.   **τὰ πλάγια:** at either side; the screen in front of the πέτευρον remains, to protect the others as they come up.   **ἐξ ἑκατέρου τοῦ μέρους** goes better with ἐπιβαίνουσιν than with παραλύσαντες, where τὰ πλάγια makes it unnecessary. The men entering the city on both sides make the success vivid.   **τὰς ἐπάλξεις ἢ τοὺς πύργους** brings out the generality of what has become an engrossing narrative.

**4.10 οἱ δὲ λοιποί:** assumed to be a multitude.   **διὰ τῆς σαμβύκης ἕπονται:** the ascent of the four had not been mentioned; the ascent of the rest displays the whole machine in operation.   **ἀσφαλῶς and εἰς ἀμφοτέρας** show the plan and design working perfectly.   **τοῖς κάλοις** (§5n.) leads into the name: see §11n.

**4.11 εἰκότως:** P. finally comes to the name, a pleasing way to close a section. Cf. 1.85.7: the Saw (a place) ταύτης τετευχέναι τῆς προσηγορίας because of the similarity of its σχῆμα to a saw. The present close prepares for the joking close at 6.6.   **†ταύτης†:** a singular ship surprises, when both ships have just been said to bear the σαμβύκη (for 5.11 see n.); it cannot express Livy's *uelut una nauis* (24.34.7). The demonstrative in these circumstances is obscure, and will probably have come from ταύτης just before. V has τούτης (like P₁) with a sign of corruption in the margin; this will not indicate just an inability to emend to ταύτης. The word ταύτης has displaced is likely to be ἑκατέρας; for the word order, which varies that of §9 ἑκατέρου τοῦ μέρους, cf. 6.34.1 τὸ κέρας αὐτῶν ἑκάτερον, 7.11.3 ταῖς ὁρμαῖς ἑκατέραις after ἑκάτερον τὸ μέρος.   **ἐνοποιηθέν:** combined into one shape. ἐνοποιέω comes only here in P.; cf. Arist. *De An.* 1.410b11. Andreas *FGrHist* 571 F1 probably takes it from P.   **σαμβύκηι** ends the last sentence, neatly, as σαμβύκας ended the first (§2). The diagonally ascending κλῖμαξ, with ropes attached, resembles the highest part and the strings of the musical instrument σαμβύκη (Veget. 4.21.4 stresses the strings); the total ensemble resembles the whole (Andreas above). See Figure 1, instrument on left-hand side. On the instrument, see West (1992) 75–7.

## 5 ARCHIMEDES RESPONDS

**5.1 οὗτοι μὲν οὖν:** οὖν summarizes, with τὸν τρόπον τοῦτον; μέν, with οὗτοι, looks forward to δέ. It is a common pattern; cf. especially 1.22.11, after the explanation of the 'ravens': οὗτοι μὲν οὖν τοιαύτηι κεχρημένοι παρασκευῆι. FDGVP₁'s πλήν is much less appropriate; it may come from 3.3, 6. P. is

Fig 1 Musician with sambuca; wall-painting (detail), Museo Archeologico Nazionale di Napoli, inv. 9023 (AD 30–40); from Pompeii (Third Style), further provenance unknown. © Alamy

including the ordinary quinqueremes (4.1), and saves the σαμβῦκαι, effectively, for §§8–11 (8n.).   **διηρμοσμένοι** 'set up'. Cf. 25.5 below διαρμοσάμενοι, 32.10.3 πρέσβεις ... πρὸς ἑκατέραν τὴν ὑπόθεσιν ἡρμοσμένοι. The compound is very rare save in Plutarch; twice in *IG* II².1668 (347/6 BC).   **προσάγειν:** cf. 4.2, but here intransitive (LSJ A II), as at 1.46.9 – move to or against.   **διενοοῦντο** (FDGVP₁) underlines the original plan, and is paralleled at 3.43.4. On the other hand, τοῖς πύργοις (FDG) rather than τῶι τείχει (T) might come from 4.9; the meaning is either too narrow ('towers') or, if 'walls', a perhaps unwelcome change from the sense at 4.9. The ungrammatical τῶν πύργων in VP₁ may be a sign of trouble.

**5.2 ὁ δὲ προειρημένος ἀνήρ:** Archimedes, from 3.3.   **παρεσκευασμένος:** transitive, as at e.g. DS 3.37.3 παρεσκευασμένος τοξότας, Plut. *Marc.* 15.9.   **πρὸς ἅπαν ἐμβελὲς διάστημα** 'to suit every distance within reach of a missile'; cf. Plut. *Marc.* 15.9 ὀργάνων τε συμμέτρους πρὸς πᾶν διάστημα κινήσεις. P. structures the whole passage, until the σαμβῦκαι, around Archimedes' exact and complete planning for distance. διάσταμα, quite apart from its meaning 'radius', is a significant concept in Archimedes, so *Con.* I 300.9 Heiberg. See 3n. below. For ἐμβελής cf. DS 20.44.4 τοῦ τόπου παντὸς ἐμβελοῦς ὄντος.   **πόρρωθεν:** we know only that the Claudii set up camp μικρὸν ἀποσχόντες τῆς πόλεως (3.2).   **εὐτονωτέροις καὶ μείζοσι:** greater in size and in power.   **βέλεσι:** most likely a throwing-machine rather than things thrown; cf. 5.4.6 διαθεὶς τὰ βέλη καὶ τοὺς πετροβόλους, Whitehead (2016) 30–1. Livy, however, understands as *tela*: see 24.34.8 and Introduction §14 a.   **τιτρώσκων:** Archimedes himself is made to inflict the damage.   **εἰς ἀπορίαν ἐνέβαλε καὶ δυσχρηστίαν:** the pair occurs 10 other times in P. (e.g. 5.18.8), and so will be genuine here, despite VP₁. δυσχρηστία conveys distress as well as practical difficulty. A separate reaction here for the longer-range machines (cf. §3) suits the rhetorical structure rather than any plausible difference in feeling.

**5.3 ὅτε** with optative, 'whenever'.   **ὑπερπετῆ** 'flying over' (from πέτομαι), with too high an arc to hit a given ship; cf. 18.30.3.   **κατὰ λόγον ἀεί** 'always in proportion'. The same combination is used at 9.20.3, on camp design, where P. is urging generals to know some geometry.   **ἀπόστημα:** distance (of ship from wall). Distance appears most spectacularly in Archimedes' Ψαμμίτης, written for those concerned with the ἀποστάματα of the earth and heavenly bodies (II 258.1–10 Heiberg).   **τοιαύτην** marks a further stage than the simple ἀπορία καὶ δυσχρηστία (§2).   **ἤγαγε:** a decisive effect, despite the general ὅτε; so too ἐνέβαλε, contrast the imperfects in §§6–7.   **διατροπήν:** both emotional dismay and military turmoil; P. pairs it with κατάπληξις (so 1.42.11) and with κίνδυνος (3.53.4, followed by ὥστ' ἀναγκασθῆναι, like ἠναγκάσθη here). Cf. P. Tebt. I 27.104 (113 BC; practical confusion), Cic. *Att.* 9.13.7 (military calamity), *I.Egypte prose* 49.8 (Kôm Trouga, 5 BC; distress).   **αὐτῶν:** the Romans, as with οὗτοι (§1) – an effective contrast with the single individual Archimedes. The ἐπίπλους had been Marcus' at 4.1.

**5.4 Μᾶρκος:** P. turns to the proconsul for the shaming concrete decision. **δυσθετούμενος:** distressed and in difficulty. Cf. 33.17.2 δυσθετούμενοι τοῖς συμβαίνουσιν ἀποδυσπετεῖν ἀναγκάζονται, which suggests the word is authentic (despite T). **νυκτὸς ἔτι** 'while it was still night'; cf. Plut. *Marc.* 15.8 ἔτι νυκτός and e.g. 4.57.6, 9.7.7, Thuc. 4.110.1. Nocturnal secrecy is laudable cleverness in Philip (13.5 below), but ἠναγκάσθη suggests it is a humiliation forced on Marcellus. Plut. *Marc.* 15.8 elaborates it as a failed plan; Livy omits it. **ποιήσασθαι τὴν παραγωγήν:** of the ships to the wall; cf. App. *Mith.* 569: Pompey παρῆγεν ἐς μὲν τοὺς λιμένας ἑπτακοσίας ναῦς.

**5.5 γενομένων:** a new stage in the narrative, but continuing the diminution of distance. Livy continues it too, but without a marked new stage (24.34.9–10). **ἐντὸς βέλους:** too close for the missiles; cf. Eur. *Her.* 990–4: ὡς ἐντὸς ἔστη παῖς λυγροῦ τοξεύματος, Heracles killed him with his club. So Livy 24.34.10: some ships wanted to be *interiores ictibus tormentorum*. **πάλιν ἑτέραν ἡτοιμάκει** brings out Archimedes' advance inventiveness (pluperfect), without indicating preparation long ago, like Plut. *Marc.* 15.8 πάλαι παρεσκευασμένος.

**5.6 ἕως ἀνδρομήκους ὕψους** 'up to the height of a man' (locating the holes no higher). Cf. e.g. 3.37.10 ἕως Ἡρακλείων στηλῶν, P. Tebt. I 5.153 (118 BC) τὰ ἱερὰ ἀνοικοδομεῖν ἕως ὕψους π(ηχῶν) ι'. One would have expected a demonstrative in the sentence before the asyndeton; contrast 22.4.5 ἕτερον ἔγκλημα … ἔφη γάρ. Perhaps ὡς caused γάρ to be omitted. **κατεπύκνωσε** 'peppered' with holes; cf. DS 18.71.3 καταπυκνώσας doors with (abundant) nails. **ὡς παλαιστιαίοις** 'about a palm's breadth', roughly 3 inches; cf. 6.23.3, 9. *cubitalibus* [roughly 17 inches] *fere* says Livy (24.34.9), going somewhat astray. **κατὰ τὴν ἐκτὸς ἐπιφάνειαν** 'on the outer side'; cf. 4.8 above. More space could be allowed for weapons in the inside of the cavity. **σκορπίδια:** a small version of a small-scale catapult. Cf. Livy 24.34.9 *scorpionibus modicis*, Plut. *Marc.* 15.9 σκορπίοι βραχύτονοι; *1 Macc.* 6.51 σκορπίδια. σκορπίοι appear already at *IG* II².1627.333–4 (330/29 BC); cf. Vitr. 10.10.1–6. See Marsden (1969) 57–61. 'Scorpion slits' are probably not an innovation; cf. McNicoll (1997) 114–15, 214 (Philip V's wall at Iasus). **βάλλων**, omitted by the *Suda*, is parallel to §2 τιτρώσκων and so probably genuine; again the language makes Archimedes carry out the violent action himself (through others). **διὰ τούτων:** usage recommends 'by means of these' (people or things), not 'through' the holes. Since τοξότας καὶ σκορπίδια have just been brought in, τούτων should take them up. Cf. e.g. 4.60.5: to get mercenaries together καὶ διὰ τούτων ἀσφαλίζεσθαι τὴν χώραν. **ἀχρήστους:** out of action, of no use in war. Cf. §7, 5.47.2: all ἄχρηστοι, some perished; and e.g. *IG* II².1628.493–4 (326/5 BC): three triremes κατὰ πόλεμον ἀχρή|στους γεγονέναι.   ἐπιβάτας: fighting men on board ship; cf. §6 τοὺς ἀπομαχομένους ἀπὸ τῶν πλοίων and 4.1 above.

**5.7 ἐξ οὗ** 'so' draws all of §§1–6 together, with special reference to §§5–6, which connect to σύνεγγυς ὄντας. καὶ μακράν looks back to §2 πόρρωθεν; ἀφεστῶτας (FDGVP₁) produces more of a surprise than §2 ἐπιπλέοντας. ἀπόντας (T) ... ὄντας would not make an effective pair.   **οὐ μόνον ἀπράκτους** takes up §6 ἀχρήστους, but shows the outcome is much worse.   **παρεσκεύαζε** 'made', see LSJ I 3.   **τὰς ἰδίας ἐπιβολάς** 'their endeavours'. ἰδίας is not especially emphatic; cf. 3.41.2: the consuls ἑτοιμασάμενοι τὰ πρὸς τὰς ἰδίας ἐπιβολάς.   **καὶ διέφθειρε τοὺς πλείστους αὐτῶν:** brutally simple language ends §§1–7.

**5.8 σαμβύκας:** finally, after this devastating sequence, the account turns to what had dominated the depiction of Roman plans (4.2–11).   **ἐγχειρήσαιεν:** cf. 4.7 πειράζουσι προσερείδειν τῶι τείχει. But now we do not hear of success (cf. 4.6, 9) even in raising the σαμβῦκαι.   **παρ' ὅλον τὸ τεῖχος:** but presumably leaving space for the lighter artillery in §6, also against the wall. Wherever the four pairs of ships get to the walls, a machine can reach them.   **ἡτοιμάκει** sounds like a refrain after §5 ἡτοιμάκει. Unlike the machines in §§2–6, these are made to seem especially suitable for σαμβῦκαι.   **ἀφανῆ:** the contrast with the sudden appearance creates a startling visual impression; the word invites a Roman perspective.   **χρείας καιρόν:** the crucial time is now seen from a Syracusan perspective; cf. 4.6, where, assuming ἐγγίσωσι to be spatial, the χρεία falls slightly later (cf. §10 here).   **ἐκ τῶν ἔσω μερῶν ὑπὲρ τοῦ τείχους ἀνιστάμενα:** after ἀφανῆ, readers will see the sudden movement in part through Roman eyes. ἀνιστάμενα resembles the sudden fearsome rising up of men concealed in an ambush: cf. 5.13.6 διαναστάντων, 95.9 ἐξαναστάντων.   **προπίπτοντα πολύ** recalls the phrase used of the σαμβῦκαι before raising (4.4). This is a more alarming sight.   **κεραίαις:** here and in §10 not cranes, but their long arm. Cf. Marsden (1971) 92; Ath. Mech. 14.7–15.2 of another long beam.

**5.9 ὧν:** the ὄργανα (cranes).   **ἐβάσταζε** 'held'; lightly personifying. βαστάζω is used with stones at Hom. *Od.* 11.594, John 10:31.   **δέκα ταλάντων:** about 262 kg, on the Attic system; at Philo, *Pol.* C11 οἱ ταλαντιαῖοι λίθοι seem viewed as large.   **σηκώματα μολίβδινα:** lumps of lead. Cf. 21.27.4: onto the besiegers' battering rams διὰ κεραιῶν [i.e. cranes] ἐνιέντες σηκώματα μολιβδᾶ καὶ λίθους καὶ στύπη δρύϊνα.

**5.10 ὅτε ... τότε:** the cranes actually operate when the ships are close. **συνεγγίζοιεν** takes up the ἐγγίσαντες τῆι γῆι of 4.7, in the more ideal account; now the Romans do not get to set the σαμβῦκαι in action. **περιαγόμεναι:** more suitable to the arm of the crane than to the stationary crane. **καρχησίωι:** a swivel-joint, which allows turning horizontally and vertically at once. Cf. Hero, *Bel.* 88.1–9 for elaborate description, Ath. Mech. 35.4–37.2; Marsden (1971) 51, 102; Landels (2000) 96–7; Whitehead and Blyth (2004) 155. **διά τινος σχαστηρίας** goes with what follows. σχαστηρία is a release mechanism, or the long 'trigger' which forms part of one. See Apollod. *Poliorc.* 188.7–8 Schneider, Hero, *Bel.* 75.10–77.5, Vitr. 10.10.4; Marsden (1971) 48, 180–1, 219–20. **ἠφίεσαν:** imperfect of ἀφίημι. **κατασκεύασμα:** the designation of the ingenious device resumes and deflates 4.11. **τὸν λίθον** effectively ends the half-sentence, and contrasts with the longer and more pretentious κατασκεύασμα next to it.

**5.11 ἐξ οὗ:** see §7n. **μὴ μόνον ... ἀλλὰ καί:** the same rhetoric of destruction as in §7. **συνθραύεσθαι:** the resounding compound comes only here in P. **τοὔργανον:** the σαμβύκη. **τὴν ναῦν:** the plural is expected, as the one σαμβύκη is on two ships. **κινδυνεύειν ὁλοσχερῶς** 'to be in the gravest danger'. P. often uses ὁλοσχερ- with (-)κινδυν-, e.g. 4.46.2. The ships and men are not actually destroyed when the σαμβύκη is.

## 6 ARCHIMEDES PLAYS WITH SHIPS

**6.1 τινά τε:** P. continues with this kind of machine for dropping heavy objects, but turns in a different direction (πάλιν; cf. 5.5 πάλιν). He reverts to 5.5 and τοὺς ἀπομαχομένους ἐκ τῶν πλοίων. They are at the prow (§2) and attacking: they do not seem men climbing up a σαμβύκη (and only four machines may be needed for σαμβῦκαι). On §§1–4 see Landels (2000) 95–8. **ἐφορμῶντας** 'attacking', of the individuals, not of the Romans blockading. Hence not ἐφορμοῦντας (FDG), which Diggle (2020) 140–1 supports, on the grounds that ἐφορμάω is very rare in prose and found only here in P. (it comes e.g. three times in Plutarch). **προβεβλημένους:** the medio-passive is again used transitively. They have put wicker screens in front of themselves for protection. **διὰ τούτων ἠσφαλισμένους:** as at 4.8, γέρρα are thought to bring security. **πρὸς τὸ μηδὲν πάσχειν:** similarly of military safety 3.71.3 πρὸς τὸ μηδὲν παθεῖν. **διὰ τοῦ τείχους:** the men think they have outwitted Archimedes' plan of firing through the wall; cf. 5.6. Archimedes has an answer to their answer. ἐκ (T) is probably a simplification. ἠφίει: imperfects carry on until §6. καί matches καί in the next clause, as ἠφίει matches ἀφίει; each καί goes in effect with the whole phrase. συμμέτρους πρός: suitable in size to making them flee; cf. [Gal.] *Ther. Pis.* 13.16 (AD 198–211) μίσγε τὸ σύμμετρον πρὸς τὴν ἀνάπλασιν and 13.4 below. The phrase suggests careful calibration. φεύγειν ἐκ τῆς πρώιρας: the aim is not the obvious one of harming the men, but of clearing the space for the next stage.

**6.2 ἅμα:** not literally at the same moment as dropping the stone, but as part of the same connected scheme. χεῖρα σιδηρᾶν: the device is used for seizing hold of ships from the fifth century on (Thuc. 4.25.4, 7.62.3, 65.1–2), and dragging them. Cf. Whitehead (2016) 367. Here it is attached to the arm of the crane, but also joined to a chain so that it is not lost when removed from the arm (§3). ἧι δραξάμενος ... ὅτ' ἐπιλάβοιτο 'using this to grasp, whenever he got hold of the prow,' he would, etc.; cf. §3 ὅτε ... ποιήσειε. ὅτε is elided 11 times in P. E.g. οὗ 'wherever' (whichever bit of the prow) would have little point, with harsh hiatus. ὅθεν 'from where, because of which' makes little sense, and does not suit Polybian usage. δραξάμενος is from δράσσομαι, with πρώιρας as its implied genitive object. P.'s colourful verb shows the man who works the machine acting and thinking. P. uses it for certain only at 36.15.7 (metaphorical; fr. 54 Olson uncertain). οἰακίζων: P. uses the verb only here; cf. Ath. Mech. 26.4. More than one individual may actually have been involved. κατῆγε τὴν πτέρναν 'pulled down the back end' of the arm, and so raised the front end connected to the prow. For πτέρνα, lit. 'heel', the back of the foot, cf. e.g. Philo, *Bel.* 59.19, Hero, *Bel.* 91.8, Landels (2000) 117.

**6.3 κουφίζων** 'raising'; cf. LSJ II.1, *CGL* 6. ὀρθὸν ποιήσειε τὸ σκάφος ἐπὶ πρύμναν 'made the ship [cf. 4.1 above, etc.] stand upright on its stern': a spectacular and demeaning manoeuvre. Landels (2000) 96–7 plausibly finds the idea implausible. For ἐπὶ πρύμναν in this sense cf. Plut. *Marc.* 15.3 ὀρθὰς ἐπὶ πρύμναν, Ael. Arist. 48.12 Keil τὸ πλοῖον ἐκ πρώιρας ἀρθὲν ἐπὶ πρύμναν. τὰς μὲν πτέρνας τῶν ὀργάνων: P. moves temporarily into a plurality of machines, despite the single operator. εἰς ἀκίνητον καθῆπτε 'fixed so as to be immovable'; cf. 1.68.10 εἰς ἀδύνατον ἐκβάλλοντες τὴν διάλυσιν. τὴν δὲ χεῖρα: back to the singular. †ἐξέρεναι† should be something like ἐξερρίπτει. ἐξέρραινε (T), probably a conjecture, would be 'scattered out' or 'made ooze out', used of liquid substances (in prose Theophr. *HP* 3.13.2 συνεκραίνει καὶ τότε τὴν ὑγρότητα). Imagery would not suit the passage, nor would this image suit the crucial release from the 'hand'.

**6.4 οὗ γινομένου** could be right, despite DG's γενομένου; cf. 2.35.1 οὗ συμβαίνοντος of a prior event, and §6 below. **τινὰ μὲν ... τινὰ δέ** is now applied to the ships rather than the machines (5.9), in a scene of extravagant chaos. **πλάγια** 'on their side' is followed by καὶ κατεστρέφετο, 'were actually turned upside down'; cf. *CGL* καταστρέφω 2. **τὰ δὲ πλεῖστα**: most undergo a less extreme fate, one which leads into Marcus' mot. **ἀφ' ὕψους**: a still wilder picture – the ships are raised high up. Cf. e.g. Plut. *Comm. Not.* 1081b. **βαπτιζόμενα**: immersed in water, but not completely sunk, as ταραχῆς and §6 κυαθίζειν indicate. Cf. 3.72.4: βαπτιζόμενοι up to chest; 16.6.2: ship βαπτιζομένην but not underwater. The word also suggests filling up containers, in readiness for §6; cf. Philo, *Prob.* 97, Plut. *Soll. An.* 971b. **πλήρη**: P. often uses πλήρης with more than one noun in graphic scenes of confusion; cf. e.g. 1.37.2, 14.5.7, 30.5 below πλήρης ἡ πόλις κραυγῆς ἐγίνετο καὶ ταραχῆς. Here, still more than in 30.5 or §5 μετὰ βλάβης καὶ χλευασμοῦ, the nouns are on different planes.

**6.5 Μᾶρκος**, last seen at 5.4, returns for the finale; he is worsted by Archimedes, at the other end of the clause. **δυσχρηστούμενος** 'distressed', cf. 5.2, 4; here the emphasis is particularly on emotion, as ἐπί + dat. indicates (so too 3.107.4–5). **τοῖς ἀπαντωμένοις ὑπ' Ἀρχιμήδους** 'the things encountered at Archimedes' hands'; cf. 9.21.1 ἐκ τῶν ὑπὸ τῆς τύχης ἀπαντωμένων. **θεωρῶν** 'seeing' (that); cf. e.g. 10.4.3, *SEG* XII.306 (Demetrias, *c.*117 BC) θεωροῦντες τιμωμένους τοὺς τοιο[ύτους ἄνδρας]. **χλευασμοῦ** 'mockery'; cf. e.g. 38.20.6 μετὰ χλευασμοῦ καὶ λοιδορίας ἀσυροῦς καὶ δυσμενικῆς. **ἀποτριβομένους** 'repelling'; cf. 5.104.1 τὰς τῶν βαρβάρων ἐφόδους ἀποτριβόμενοι.

**6.6 δυσχερῶς μὲν ἔφερε** relates to the first of the two participial clauses, and, unlike the δέ-clause, gives Marcellus' actual feelings. **ἐπισκώπτων τὰς αὑτοῦ πράξεις**: he disarmingly turns the mockery seen in the second participial clause into self-mockery. At Plut. *Marc.* 17.1 he mocks his engineers instead. **ἔφη**: the dense imagistic wit of the utterance resembles, for example, Demetrius of Pharos' play on metaphorical bulls and horns at 7.12.3. In addition, the Roman shows himself moving dexterously amid different areas of Greek culture, military and symposiastic. **ταῖς μέν**: Athenaeus, although professing to quote P. verbatim, only does so from ταῖς onwards. **κυαθίζειν**: the ships are made like κύαθοι, vases which were dipped into mixing-bowls to transfer wine to cups. Cf. e.g. Athenian red-figure kyathos, Vienna, Kunsthistorisches Museum 4438, 475–425 BC, Beazley Archive 21370; Plut. *Alex.* 67.4 κυαθίζοντες (Madvig: βαπτίζοντες codd.) ἐκ πίθων μεγάλων καὶ κρατήρων. **Ἀρχιμήδην** ends a clause again; cf. §5. Ἀρχιμήδην is the commoner form; for compatibility with Ἀρχιμήδους, cf. Aeschin. 3.64 Δημοσθένους ... Δημοσθένην, *I.Pergamon Asklepieion* 133.1–2 (ii AD) Δημοσθένην Δημοσθένους. **σαμβύκας**: the exalted intellectual Archimedes is made to dismiss the instruments from his party, with a beating that corresponds to the damage inflicted on the machines. Plato's Agathon (really Eryximachus) τὸν αὐλὸν ἀπέπεμψεν ἐκ τοῦ συμποσίου (Plut. *Div.* 527b; cf. Plato, *Smp.* 176e6–9): he thought the words of those present would suffice. The σαμβύκη was foreign and many-stringed, its players decadent (see West (1992) 76–7): all the more reason for the σαμβῦκαι to go. σαμβύκη can be used of the performer (5.37.10, Plaut. *Stich.* 380–1); but here that is a secondary suggestion at most. **ῥαπιζομένας**: cf. Heracl. B 42 DK, D21 Laks–Most τόν τε Ὅμηρον ἔφασκεν ἄξιον ἐκ τῶν ἀγώνων ἐκβάλλεσθαι καὶ ῥαπίζεσθαι. **ἐκ πότου** 'from a party' (Athenaeus); cf. e.g. 16.21 πότους συνῆγε. ἐκσπόνδους (FDGVP₁) 'excluded from the treaty' would be obviously corrupt even if we had no other evidence. **ἐκπεπτωκέναι**: cf. e.g. Ar. *Plut.* 244 γυμνὸς θύραζ' ἐξέπεσον. Being hissed off the stage may be suggested too; cf. Dem. 18.265, LSJ 12.

**6.7 τοιοῦτον ἀπέβη τὸ τέλος:** the same form of closure and transition occurs at 18.27.7 and 25.2.15, preceded by καὶ τῆς/τοῦ μὲν ... μάχης/πολέμου. Cf. also Jos. *BJ* 4.235.

## 7 THE ROMANS GIVE SIEGECRAFT UP

**7.1 οἱ δὲ περὶ τὸν Ἄππιον:** 3.6–4.11 had described the Romans' equipment and machines, with 3.6 ὁ μὲν Ἄππιος, 4.1 ὁ δὲ Μᾶρκος. Appius' efforts had been treated briefly, Marcus' elaborately. Chh. 5–6 treated Archimedes' response to Marcus elaborately; 7.1–4 treat his response to Appius briefly. Μᾶρκος δέ at 6.5 and οἱ δὲ περὶ τὸν Ἄππιον here match the names at 3.6 and 4.1, and so underline the ABBA pattern. Archimedes' response to Appius had not been put first; it forms in 7.1–4 a brisk and explicit confirmation of the success seen against Marcus. P. does not attempt a detailed second bravura performance from himself and Archimedes; the sea had had more to offer. οἱ περὶ τόν sounds at first as if it means just 'Appius', cf. 6.5–6; but in §§2–4 it denotes his entire force, cf. e.g. 1.19.5, 21.7. The context only sometimes makes clear whether just the person or persons named are in question, or a group including them; modern 'people like X' can be similarly undefined. See S. L. Radt (1980, 2002), *PL* C2cα and 16.11, 28.12nn. **παραπλησίους**, emphasized by separation from δυσχερείας, begins the account with the similarity to Marcus' misfortunes. **ἀπέστησαν τῆς ἐπιβολῆς**: after the intricate and detailed account of Marcus' reaction (6.5–6) comes a simple and dramatic decision. §§5–6 spell it out, after §§2–4 give the causes. τῆς ἐπιβολῆς is more comprehensive than 6.5 τὰς ἐπιβολάς; cf. 5.7.

**7.2 ἔτι μὲν γὰρ ὄντες ἐν ἀποστήματι:** §§2–4 use the same structuring by distance as 5.1–7. Appius' men are treated as a single entity reaching successive stages; διεφθείροντο in §2 and §3 means only that some of them perished.       **τοῖς τε πετροβόλοις καὶ καταπέλταις:** τε belongs with πετροβόλοις but is attracted earlier. P. now uses words not found in 5–6; but πετροβόλος should be the heavier subset of λιθοβόλος in 5.2–3, cf. Whitehead (2016) 28. καταπέλται and πετροβόλοι are again separated at 1.53.11; contrast e.g. *IG* II².1487.84–5 (late iv BC) [κατα|πά]λτην πετροβόλον. At 5.99.7 πετροβόλοι are far fewer than καταπέλται, so probably larger and more valuable. καταπέλται may throw pointed missiles rather than rocks; cf. Whitehead (2016) 31.       **θαυμάσιον:** P. uses θαυμασι- in relation to objects only at 10.27.6 (fortifications). He is preparing for §7. His account turns immediately from specifics to Archimedes.       **ἐνέργειαν:** power, when in action. Cf. *PL* 2, and e.g. Apollod. *Poliorc.* 158.9 Schneider ἐνέργειαν καὶ βάρος of a battering ram.       **ὡς ἄν** 'inasmuch as, since', with no sense of unreality; cf. e.g. 38.15.10.       **Ἱέρωνος:** as at 6.5, the names ring the clause, and Archimedes' ends it. The wealthy Hieron II provided the money, but Archimedes conceived and executed the ideas. The creation of the machines goes back much further, it now appears, than the present siege. Hieron ruled from 275; Plut. *Marc.* 14.12 says Archimedes was his συγγενής and φίλος (his poverty, as at Sil. It. 14.343, may be doubted). Archimedes dedicates Ψαμμίτης to Hieron's son and co-regent Gelon (1, 20 (II 216, 258 Heiberg)); he is called ἐπόπτης but not ἀρχιτέκτων of Hieron's enormous ship (Moschion *FGrHist* 575 F1 Ath. and 2.2). Hieron's building and fortification at Syracuse were on a lavish scale: cf. Karlsson (1992) 112–13; Lehmler (2005) 120–55.       **ἀρχιτέκτονος:** of designers of siege machines Ath. Mech. 15.2–3, 32.4; but the genitive ἐπινοημάτων gives a more exalted sense, 'originator', cf. LSJ 2. Arist. *Pol.* 3.1282a3–4 separates, among doctors, the δημιουργός and the ἀρχιτεκτονικός. ἀρχιτέκτονος ... Ἀρχιμήδους could play on the name.

**7.3 συνεγγίζοντες** links ominously with 5.10 ὅτε συνεγγίζοιεν αἱ σαμβῦκαι. The men are approaching Epipolae (3.6).       **τοξότισιν:** a unique designation of holes for arrows, save for Anon. *Obs.* p. 51.3, 7, 9 Van den Berg, from this passage. Cf. Philo, *Par.* A22 τοξικαί (θυρίδες), with Whitehead. But 'continually harassed by the arrow-holes' is not a plausible use of passive and dative. Either one should supplement <ὑπὸ τῶν παρεστώτων>, cf. 5.6 οἷς τοξότας καὶ σκορπίδια παραστήσας, and for the word order e.g. 3.85.7, 30.4.11; such a phrase could have influenced the paraphrase of 5.6 διὰ τούτων at Anon. *Obs.* p. 51.9 ὑπὸ τῶν ἐν ταῖς τοξότισι καθημένων. Or, more neatly matching ταῖς ... ἐμβολαῖς, one could read τοξείαις 'bow-shots'; cf. e.g. Jos. *AJ* 5.205, DC 40.15.4 ἐντονωτάτας σφίσι τὰς τοξείας ... παρέχεται. **κακούμενοι:** P. uses κακόω only here, varying §4 ἐκακοποίουν; cf. 27.7.6 κακοποιεῖσθαι δὲ συνεχῶς. **προσόδου:** probably 'advance' rather than 'attack'. Cf. e.g. 9.27.6 (route of approach), Jos. *AJ* 17.292 (advance of army). **οἱ δέ:** these are protected against arrows and are pressing forward; cf. e.g. 10.14.12 βιασάμενοι πρὸς τὴν πύλην. **κατὰ κορυφήν:** on their heads; cf. 6.23.13, 18.30.3. The wicker screens are being used horizontally; and since machines are implied by the context, the weight will be too much for the wicker. **δοκῶν:** wooden beams (ἡ δοκός), a new element; defenders throw them down at 10.13.9. **διεφθείροντο** resumes the close in §2; disasters accumulate.

**7.4 οὐκ ὀλίγα δὲ καί:** one might have thought the 'hands' (6.2–4) useful only against ships. **ὡς καὶ πρότερον εἶπα** varies the commoner ὡς/ καθάπερ ἐπάνω προεῖπον/-α used in §3 (33 times in P.; similar phrases to the present 5.45.1, 58.3). The abbreviated rerun of 5.1–6.7 is emphasized. On εἶπα see Introduction §13 a. **ὅπλοις:** weapons, screens and the like, rather than body armour (which would not be worth saying). Another striking image of military futility is created. The brevity of the reversal in ἐξαιροῦντες ἐρρίπτουν is salient; 6.3–4 contrasts.

**7.5 τὸ δὲ πέρας** 'finally'; cf. e.g. 7.15.2. There is more sense of a decisive ending than in Marcus' reaction (6.5–6). **παρεμβολήν** 'camp'; cf. e.g. 6.32.2, Moretti, *ISE* II.114.B col. i.14 (Amphipolis, *c.*200 BC). The narrative brings the Romans back to square one (3.2 στρατοπεδείαν). **συνεδρεύσαντες:** Roman generals, like Greek monarchs, think councils essential. **χιλιάρχων:** military tribunes, the senior officers of each legion; cf. 6.19.1–9, Dobson (2008) 50–1. **οἱ περὶ τὸν Ἄππιον:** decision on the siege must actually have involved Marcellus (and his council) too; and §6 οὐδέποτε ... ἐθάρρησαν connects with §9 οὐκ ἐθάρρουν. But P. does not formally bring Marcus back until §8. **ὁμοθυμαδὸν ἐβουλεύσαντο:** a group decision, as at 27.8.7 ἔδοξεν αὐτοῖς ὁμοθυμαδόν, of a council convoked by the consul at war. **πάσης ἐλπίδος πεῖραν λαμβάνειν πλήν** resembles the phrasing (ἵνα) πάσας ἐξελέγχωσι τὰς σφετέρας ἐλπίδας πρότερον ἤ (2.35.6; cf. 50.12, 3.8.11); but here an actual assault will never be considered. **πολιορκίας:** πολιορκ- has various meanings in P., and elsewhere (cf. Garlan (1974) 3–6). So at 1.84.1–2 it conveys a long blockade. **Συρακούσας** rather than τὴν πόλιν underlines the daunting challenge of this particular city. **ὡς καὶ τέλος ἐποίησαν** refers to carrying out their intention rather than to capturing Syracuse; cf. §6 and e.g. 2.36.4 ὃ δὴ καὶ τέλος ἐποίησε.

**7.6 ὀκτὼ ... μῆνας:** the siege of Syracuse continues until late 212; so the eight months must run from the acknowledgement of failure to Appius' return, before the beginning of winter, to the consular elections for 212 (Livy 24.39.12–13). Livy 27.4.1 indicates that elections could happen at the end of summer, or beginning of autumn (Livy has an autumn too, 22.32.1, 28.37.5, 31.47.1). Cf. 25.2.3: the consuls are engaged in warfare at the *comitiorum consularium... tempus* for 212, so hardly January. The eight months need not be continuous: Marcellus himself seems to have a winter pause in 213 (Livy 24.39.13 [214 for Livy], 25.23.2). **στρατηγημάτων ἢ τολμημάτων:** a mockingly neat jingle; P. uses τόλμημα only one other time (9.24.7). **οὐδέποτε πεῖραν ἔτι λαβεῖν ἐθάρρησαν** 'never again dared try'; a contrast with the equally lavish οὐδενὸς ἀπέστησαν, and a humiliating close on Appius.

**7.7 οὕτως** 'so true is it that'; not 'therefore', as e.g. 30.5.3 shows. Especially similar to this climactic exclamation is 9.22.6 (Hannibal organized action globally) οὕτως μέγα τι φύεται χρῆμα καὶ θαυμάσιον ἀνὴρ καὶ ψυχὴ δεόντως ἁρμοσθεῖσα ... πρὸς ὅτι ἂν ὁρμήσηι τῶν ἀνθρωπίνων ἔργων. Cf. 1.35.4–5 (no οὕτω), 12.15.8 on Agathocles (no οὕτω) and 11.10.1 οὕτως εἷς λόγος εὐκαίρως ῥηθεὶς κτλ. Here and at 1.35.5 'one' is strengthened in ardent anaphora. The linked passages show the power of mental force. **ἔνια:** a judicious limitation, as at 3.3 above ἐν ἐνίοις καιροῖς. **μέγα τι χρῆμα:** of a person at 9.22.6 (see above), Charit. 5.3.4.

**7.8 ἐκεῖνοι:** Marcus and Appius; cf. καὶ κατὰ γῆν καὶ κατὰ θάλατταν. **γοῦν** 'at any rate'. The more general statement (§7) fits in this case at least; cf. 5.88.4, 9.23.6. **ἔχοντες** 'though they had'. **καὶ κατὰ γῆν καὶ κατὰ θάλατταν** brings together the division that has structured the section. On land there will have been two or three legions (infantry in theory 8,400–12,600 men). Cf. Gelzer (1962–4) III 239. **ἀφέλοι** 'were to remove', probably a remote possibility in the original thought; cf. 12.19.3 εἴ τις ἀφέλοι, 25g.2 εἰ ... ἐξέλοι τις. (ἐὰν ἀφέληι at 3.81.11 is a less remote chance.) **πρεσβύτην ἕνα:** the unusual word order picks out 'one' (cf. §7) and ironically underlines the defeat of the Roman consul and future consul by an old man. Archimedes was a contemporary of Eratosthenes (Procl. *in Eucl.* 68.17–20 Friedlein), so perhaps over 70. Cf. Heiberg (2013) 5–6. **Συρακοσίων:** governed by ἀφέλοι; cf. 3.81.11. Livy 24.34.1 *nisi unus homo Syracusis ea tempestate fuisset* confirms. The evidence for Συρακόσιον is not strong (P₁'s sentence imposes the change); it would implausibly suggest 'though a mere Syracusan'. For the absence of the article, cf. e.g. 7.5.7, 8.6. παραχρῆμα: if the imagined removal is now, as κυριεύσειν ἤλπιζον suggests, the Romans still seem too confident. The machines will remain, and Archimedes has already shown how to deploy them.

**7.9 οὐκ ἐθάρρουν οὐδ' ἐπιβαλέσθαι:** the close of §6 is now applied to Marcus too; 'not even' adds a sting. κατά γε τοῦτον τὸν τρόπον: the μέν-clause has already given a twist to the sentence, and this final γε-clause prepares to show the Romans in less abject spirits. VP₁ end before it, for a more resounding close. Ἀρχιμήδης: once again his name finishes, and marks out his supremacy.

**7.10 οὐ μὴν ἀλλά** 'but (instead)' shifts to the converse. τῶν ἀναγκαίων: especially but not only food; cf. 37.2 below, and 1.18.10 τῆι σιτοδείαι καὶ σπάνει τῶν ἀναγκαίων. πλῆθος: the great size and hence great population of Syracuse (37.12 below; Cic. *Verr.* 2.117–19, perhaps 5.93; Plut. *Marc.* 19.2) turn to its disadvantage. ταύτης: emphasized by separation from ἐλπίδος; §5 πάσης has indicated many possibilities. ἀντείχοντο 'held onto, maintained'; with ἐλπίδος 4.60.8, 31.18.15, DS 24.12.1. κατὰ θάλατταν ... κατὰ γῆν: they are doing better than in §8 (same phrase). αὐτῶν: objective genitive; cf. 34.13 below τὰς ἔξωθεν αὐτῶν ἐπικουρίας.

**7.11 ἄπρακτον** 'devoid of action'; conceiving of their blockade so shows Roman hyperactivity. προσεδρεύουσι 'encompass'; cf. DS 17.48.7 (Alexander at Gaza) δίμηνον προσεδρεύσας. The present shows the clause is part of their thought. ἅμα τι καὶ τῶν ἐκτὸς χρησίμων: for the phrasing cf. 9.4.7 (Hannibal at present in Capua) ἴσως μὲν ἂν καὶ περὶ τὴν πόλιν [Rome] ἀνύσασθαί τι τῶν χρησίμων. διεῖλον 'divided', as e.g. 6.26.9 τοὺς δὲ λοιποὺς διεῖλον εἰς δύο μέρη, *IG* XII.4.1.79–80 (Cos, *c*.300 BC) δια[ιρεῖν] | [κα]τὰ μέρη. δύναμιν will primarily denote the land army.

**7.12 δύο μέρη** 'two thirds'; cf. Livy 24.35.1 *cum tertia fere parte exercitus* (of Marcellus). The parts might, or might not, correspond to legions; cf. Gelzer (1962–4) III 239. τρίτον: a legion would have, in theory, 4,200 infantry, not counting the substantial losses (5.7). This would fit with Marcellus' feeling *nequaquam ... par* to Himilco's or Hamilcar's 25,000 infantry (Livy 24.35.3, 10). Marcellus surrounds *quod peditum fuit* of Hippocrates' Syracusan infantry of 10,000 (24.35.8); but since they are *dispersos ... et plerosque inermes* (24.36.1), that hardly fixes a lower limit. τὰ Καρχηδονίων αἱρουμένους: the Romans' prime concern emerges. Cf. Livy 24.35.1 *ad recipiendas urbes profectus quae in motu rerum ad Carthaginienses defecerant*, 6 *quae partis Carthaginiensium erant*; Plut. *Marc.* 18.1 πόλεις ἀπέστησε Καρχηδονίων. Similar phrases, mostly of individuals within a state, at P. 4.17.5, 53.7, 29.10.3, 30.30.3 τοὺς δὲ τὰ 'Ρωμαίων αἱρουμένους. **κατὰ τὴν Σικελίαν** at the end of the δέ-clause brings out the enlarged scope of this plan, as against ἐν τῆι πόλει at the end of the μέν-clause.

## 8–14b.2 PHILIP V AND PHILIP II

This very Polybian section moves unpredictably between particular and general, between narrative, metahistory and text-based polemic. It starts with negative narrative on one of P.'s main figures, the Macedonian king Philip V, in Messenia in 214/13 BC (8.1–2). The narrative quickly leads to digression on writers about Philip V and about monarchs (8.3–9); this takes P. to an extended treatment of the fourth-century historian Theopompus' wrongly negative handling of Philip II (d. 336 BC) and his official 'friends' (9.1–11.8). After only a small lacuna, if any, P. returns briefly to the Messenians (12.1); he proceeds to Philip's killing of another main figure, Aratus (12.1–8). Then, in a new excerpt, comes the much more positive account of Philip capturing Lissus in Illyria (13.1–14.11); the account will certainly have been read as part of the same section in the book. This section so far as preserved forms, as we shall see, a challenging and significant ensemble.

P.'s abundant polemic sharply separates him from Herodotus, Thucydides and Xenophon; see Introduction §3 d, §8 a. Polemic was apparent in Timaeus (iv–iii BC: *FGrHist* 566 F151–8; F117 on Theopompus). Timaeus himself is the victim of P.'s book-long polemic in book 12; but P. does not quote Timaeus directly at anything like the length of this citation (cf. 566 F31). Nearest is his approving quote of Demetrius of Phaleron at 29.21.2–6. The present prolonged quote helps capture Theopompus' excess – hinted at in Theopompus' own words (9.12) – and brings out P.'s good sense.

P. has much more to say about Ephorus, Theopompus, Callisthenes and Timaeus than about the earlier Herodotus, Thucydides and Xenophon. P. treats Ephorus very differently from Ephorus' contemporary Theopompus. Ephorus is P.'s exemplar for universal history (5.33.2). Theopompus, born in the late fifth or early fourth century, wrote first Ἑλληνικά, covering 411/10 to 395/4 BC, then Φιλιππικά on Philip II, covering 360/59 to 336. This narrowing, as P. presents it, from all Greeks to one monarch, strongly contrasts with P.'s universal perspective, and with his looking beyond individual figures.

It is unclear how closely Theopompus himself was connected with Philip II or with Alexander. Cf. *FGrHist* 115 T2 (Alexander restores Theopompus and others from exile; cf. *Syll.*³ 1 283, Chios, *c.*333/2 BC); T7, supposed letter of Speusippus (Bickermann and Sykutris (1928) 11.11–18: Theopompus at Philip's court); F250–4, writings of Theopompus to Philip and Alexander. Theopompus' narratives must have been extremely detailed: the *Hellenica* gave 12 books to 17 years, the *Philippica* 58 to 25; Thucydides had given 7 to 21. Theopompus interviewed extensively (T20a.3). But most fragments are from Athenaeus, and most describe censoriously the extravagance and depravity of particular peoples. This connects with the interest of Theopompus' reception in his harsh moral judgements (T20a.7–8, 25a, b); his style in such passages was thought vehement as well as exalted and daring (T20a.9–10, 28b, cf. 40 with 37, 39; 41). Theopompus' famed negativity makes him a suitable foil to P.'s ringing but reasoned praise of the Diadochi and Aratus. Theopompus' passage was climactically placed, in the prelude to one of the later books. It is perhaps the most remarkable quotation from him both in intensity and in style; it is cited by Athenaeus too, and Demetrius. P. makes from it one of his own most notable polemical passages. Theopompus assails Philip and his φίλοι; P. assails Theopompus – more judiciously, we are to think, but with matching energy. (On Theopompus, see Connor (1967); Shrimpton (1977, 1991); Flower (1994); Lane Fox (2011*c*) 350–2.)

P.'s treatment of Theopompus is cohesive; but his absorption in the particular instance leads the argument in unexpected directions: after 8.3–9, about monarchs, concentration on Philip was expected, not on the friends. The particular instance is not treated with scrupulous precision. P.'s rhetoric paints with as broad a brush as Theopompus'. He studiously omits the sentence (F225b.2.28–35) where Theopompus referred to the number of the ἑταῖροι as 800 (even if the number is corrupt it will still have been large; cf. Rzepka (2012)). P., despite his ἅπαντες ..., ὡς ἔπος εἰπεῖν (10.10), has a much smaller group in view: the chief figures, especially those who later called themselves kings (cf. 10.10). He does not, one may add, understand Theopompus' ἑταῖροι as the cavalry corps of that name (contrast 5.53.4, 30.25.7; possibly Hatzopoulos (1996) ii no. 79.4, Lete, second half of iv). See 10.5 τῶν ἐκείνου φίλων, 8 συνέργοις καὶ φίλοις, 11.8 τῶν φίλων. In Theopompus himself see 9.12 below τοὺς φίλους καὶ τοὺς ἑταίρους Φιλίππου προσαγορευθέντας; he does not once mention riding. (Otherwise on Theopompus Lane Fox (2011*d*) 373; Rzepka (2012).)

P. makes the friends a unitary group. They all acquire prolonged careers: perhaps first spotted by Philip, certainly expanding Macedon's dominion under him; his φίλοι, then Alexander's (10.10), then fighting with each other for large parts of the world, and winning glory and perhaps kingship. Those who began great deeds only under Alexander would not fit the reply to Theopompus. P.'s suggestion of a substantial and unified group is misleading. Few would qualify for it. Antigonus would, cf. Justin 16.1.12 *et Philippo regi et Alexandro Magno socium in omni militia*; and so perhaps would Antipater and Eumenes (cf. Nep. *Eum.* 1.3), though these did not declare themselves kings. P. also declines to differentiate among the Diadochi in behaviour and character, despite marked differentiations in parts of the historiographical tradition (so P. Oxy. LXXXVI 5535; Justin). (On the Diadochi, and on φίλοι, see Bengtson (1987); Strootman (2014) 111–35; Heckel (2016); Grainger (2017) 86–8, (2019) 1–128; Meeus (2022); 9.6n.)

The large metahistorical passage on Theopompus is linked to an exiguous piece of narrative on the Messenians; to that narrative the account of Aratus is explicitly linked too (12.1–2). P. contrasts Philip II and Philip V elsewhere; see 5.10.1–6, 9–11: Philip V failed to show himself a διάδοχος of Philip II's and Alexander's qualities. In the present passage, the antithesis is not spelled out: the friends of Philip II take centre stage. But 5.10 and e.g. 22.16.1–4 confirm that Philip II's magnanimity and help to his friends should be contrasted with Philip V's treachery and ingratitude. The contrast is implicit in the metahistorical train of thought. Both praise and blame of monarchs should be appropriate (8.7); P. wishes to blame Philip V appropriately (8.3–4), where others have praised him inappropriately (8.4), as Theopompus has inappropriately blamed Philip II and his friends (10.5, etc.).

The account of Philip V at Lissus (13–14) is subtler than simple encomium, but it is positive, and stands out. It has to be contrasted with P.'s negative comments on Philip V in Messenia: P. has heavily emphasized Messenia as the beginning of Philip's decline. He has also conspicuously warned that the same people will be praised and blamed in his work (1.14.7); he refers back to this principle at 16.28.3–8, precisely with regard to Philip V.

Unexpected moves keep readers reflecting: the moves to Theopompus' negative remarks (contrast 8.5–6, 8), and to P.'s own positive treatment of Lissus. P.'s responsiveness to change in a monarch, and to the specifics of events, emerges as sharply distinct from Theopompus' shocking inconsistency. (On P. and Philip V, see Introduction §6 b, d, §7 e, §11 b, §12 e, f; Nicholson (2018, 2023); Worthington (2023), esp. 76–8.)

Now for the Messenian events in the narrative; on Lissus see the introduction to 13–14. Philip V was held responsible, even at the time, for fomenting civil strife at Messene in 215 or 214; this led to the death of almost 200 citizens (7.12.9, 13.6–7, Plut. *Arat.* 49.3–5). P. sees here a breach of alliance (7.13.7): Philip had accepted the Messenians into his alliance, which ran across Greece (4.9.2–3, 16.1, 5.20.1; for his 'Hellenic League' cf. Scherberich (2009) 177–94). Philip had considered capturing Messene's citadel, a still more flagrant breach of the alliance (12.5, 7); but Aratus (12n.) had dissuaded him. P.'s ally and adviser Demetrius of Pharos made an unsuccessful attack on Messene, with Philip's alleged approval (3.19.11; cf. Paus. 4.29.1–5?). In 214 or 213 Philip's destruction of Messenian crops is an open breach of the alliance, if the Messenians still belong to it (as Plut. *Arat.* 51.2 suggests). Philip's conduct was disapproved of by Aratus (12.2 below, Plut. *Arat.* 51.3); at 9.30.2 and Livy 32.21.23, speakers attack ἡ περὶ τοὺς Μεσσηνίους ἀθεσία καὶ παρασπόνδησις and *caedes direptionesque bonorum Messenae*. Philip earned himself now or later the ferocious enmity of the Messenian poet Alcaeus (*AP* 9.519, 11.12; 7.247 and *APl.* (B) 5 are 197–196 BC). (On the events, see Introduction §12 f; Roebuck (1941) 71–84; Luraghi (2008) 258–61; Scherberich (2009) 160–1; Kralli (2017) 283–5, 300; Worthington (2023) 74–6.)

For P., Philip's actions in Messenia are central: they, not youthful misconduct in Thermus, are the real start of his decline from king to tyrant (5.12.5, 7.11.1, 13.3, 6–7). This decline is seen in Platonic terms (7.13.7), and has been given a larger theoretical context by book 6 (cf. 6.4.8, etc.). Book 7 treated the change at length, in a digression not completely preserved (11–13). It emphasized the role of Demetrius' advice in the killings (7.13.6), and of Aratus' in saving the Messenians' citadel – one good moment (7.12.1–10, 14.1–2; cf. 5.12.7–8, 9.23.9). The present passage returns to the treatment in book 7, but more to discuss and frame that treatment itself. By setting P. against Theopompus, the section brings out the balance and justice with which P. treats his Philip.

## 8 WRITING ON PHILIP V

**8.1 ὅτι:** the excerptor's start; see Introduction §14 g. From ἔφθειρε or earlier the wording will be P.'s. This seems to be the first action of the campaign in Messenia. After a single sentence or so, P. launches into extended justification of himself and related attack on others. **παραγενόμενος εἰς** 'arriving at'; cf. 23.5.2, etc. **ἔφθειρε τὴν χώραν:** an act treating Messenia as an enemy, despite 7.12.10; cf. 16.24.8 τὴν δ' Ἀλαβανδέων χώραν ὡς πολεμίαν κατέφθειρε. **δυσμενικῶς** conveys fierce ill-will, as θυμῶι suggests: cf. 15.3.1, 30.4.14. It is not just a legalistic 'like an enemy'. Only P. uses δυσμενικός; it is not found in inscriptions or papyri. **θυμῶι τὸ πλεῖον ἢ λογισμῶι χρώμενος:** cf. 2.35.3 (the Gauls decided everything θυμῶι μᾶλλον ἢ λογισμῶι), 6.6.12 (a mere monarch becomes a king through the dominance of λογισμός not θυμός) and the dialogue of Θυμός and Λογισμός in Cleanthes *SVF* I 570.

**8.2 ἤλπιζε** 'he expected'. The expectation shows his lack of λογισμός (γάρ). **ὡς ἐμοὶ δοκεῖ:** P. indicates, as often elsewhere, that he is reconstructing thought (20.10n.). **συνεχῶς οὐδέποτ':** forcefully juxtaposed. βλάπτων goes with ἤλπιζε rather than forming part of the alleged thought. Philip is taking things for granted; this is the cause of decline over generations too (6.7.6–7, 9.4–5). Contrast 7.11.7–12: Philip gains goodwill through good action. **μισήσειν:** by implication they will; contrast 7.11.8, Philip the ἐρώμενος of the Greeks.

**8.3 προήχθην:** P. uses this word in self-justification much oftener than others (8 times; Diodorus twice). **διά** 'in'; cf. 11.2.3, *PL* ICa1. **τῆς προτέρας βύβλου:** 7.10–14 give what remains about Messene. **σαφέστερον:** detailed, revealing exposition. Cf. 4.87.12: P. will treat the question σαφῶς later. **οὐ μόνον:** at 7.11.1, 10, 13.6 P. had presented Messene as the start of Philip's deterioration; the example was valuable for πραγματικοὶ ἄνδρες (7.11.2). Now the justification is the inadequacy of previous writers; cf. DS 13.35.5: I have been led to say this ἀκριβέστερον because of others' carelessness. **συγγραφέων:** Straton wrote at some time on the deeds (cf. §5) of Philip V and Perseus (*FGrHist* 168 T1); Heraclitus of Lesbos, who wrote a Macedonian history, might have been an ambassador of Philip's in 215 (*FGrHist* 167 T1–2). See also *FGrHist* IIA 190–1, B144, C825–6, D541–2, 595–6. Those who leave the events out altogether (τοὺς μέν) are probably not historians of Philip; cf. §§5–6.

**8.4 τοῖς δέ** 'for others, in others' view' (K–G I 421–2), not only is the ἀσέβεια not a fault (LSJ οἷος v 4), but they treat it as a subject of praise. The subject of the infinitive διασαφεῖν must be picked up from the context, as often (cf. 34.10 with n.); this is especially easy after τοὺς μὲν ὅλως παραλελοιπέναι. For τοὺς μὲν ... τοῖς δέ cf. e.g. 1.84.8 πολλοὺς ... τοὺς μὲν ... ἀνήιρει, τοῖς δ' ... ἐπιφαινόμενος ἐξέπληττεν (the understood object of the main verb is picked up from the context); 11.14.6, Thuc. 1.68.3, Lys. 2.14, Dem. 18.61 τοὺς μὲν ἐξαπατῶν, τοῖς δὲ διδούς. τοὺς (P) δὲ ... γεγονέναι τὴν ... ἀσέβειαν is not possible. Alternatively, one might read τοὺς ... τεθεικέναι; cf. 6.37.10 εἰς δ' ἀνανδρίαν τιθέασι καὶ στρατιωτικὴν αἰσχύνην τὰ τοιαῦτα. τεθεικέναι would then influence ἐν ἐπαίνωι; cf. Arist. *Rhet.* 1.1359a1–2 καὶ ἐν ἐπαίνωι τιθέασιν ὅτι, etc. **καθόλου** 'entirely': cf. καθόλου reinforcing ὅλος at 2.8.7, 31.3.3. **τοὺς μονάρχους:** the εὔνοια at least is not limited to Philip. **ἐν ἁμαρτίαι:** cf. Philo, *Vit. Mos.* 2.235 εἰ μὴ ἄρα ἐν ἁμαρτίαι θετέον τὸ γενεᾶς ἄρρενος ἀμοιρῆσαι (regard lack of sons as a failing); Xen. HG 4.3.5 νομίσαντες οὐκ ἐν καλῶι εἶναι πρὸς τοὺς ὁπλίτας ἱππομαχεῖν. **ἀσέβειαν Φιλίππου καὶ παρανομίαν:** ἀσεβ- and παρανομ- form a pair 9 times in P., much more than in other non-Christian writers (Plutarch 2, Josephus 2). **ἡμῖν:** adding an audience makes the absurd declaration more vivid.

**8.5 οὐ μόνον:** P. begins to spread out, first to historians on other deeds of Philip. **γράφοντας ... τὰς πράξεις** 'writing about the deeds'. πράξεις are for P. what history is about. γράφειν τὰς πράξεις comes 14 times in P., much oftener than elsewhere. Cf. DS 4.1.3 (of Ephorus); similar phrases with compounds, e.g. DS 4.57.1 (ἀναγράψαι), *I.Magnesia* 46.13–14 (late iii BC) τῶν ἱ[σ]|τορ[ι]αγράφων τῶν συγγεγραφότ[ων] τὰς Μαγνήτων πρ[άξ]ει[ς].

**8.6 αὐτοῖς:** governed by συμβαίνει. **διάθεσιν** 'character', with ἱστορίας. **συντάξεις** 'works'. **ἐγκωμίου δὲ μᾶλλον:** a pithy close. At 10.21.6–8, the strict demands of history for truthful and substantiated praise and blame are contrasted with the exaggeration suitable in the ἐγκωμιαστικός context of P.'s biography of Philopoemen. Cf. Anaximenes 3.1 p. 21.1–3 Fuhrmann on αὔξησις as essential to the ἐγκωμιαστικὸν εἶδος. Particularly relevant, and a preparation for what follows, are Theopompus' encomia of Philip II and of Alexander, the latter matched by a ψόγος (*FGrHist* 115 T48, F255–7). These encomia were especially famous, to judge from Fronto, *Caes.* 2.11.2 (contrast with present-day *encomiographi*). ἐγκώμια are commonly for display, competitions, school exercises: cf. e.g. Isocr. *Hel.* 14, *IG* VII.418.3 (Oropus, i BC), *P. Oxy.* XVII 2084 (iii AD; on the fig).

**8.7 ἐγὼ δ' ... φημι:** the author's opinion stands out from that of others, in a manner characteristic of Hellenistic intellectual prose; see Hutchinson (2014) 43–4. ἐγὼ δέ φημι *vel sim.* comes at P. 3.6.7, 9.5, 16.17.10, 22.18.6, twice with δεῖν. **λοιδορεῖν** prepares for the move to Theopompus. **ψευδῶς** goes with ἐγκωμιάζειν 'praise' too; P. would not censure praise in itself (1.14.7). See Introduction §7 d. **τοὺς μονάρχους:** a higher level of generality, prepared in §4 τοὺς μονάρχους. **ἀκόλουθον** 'in keeping with'; cf. e.g. 24.8.8 ἐντολὰς ἀκολούθους τοῖς προειρημένοις. προγεγραμμένοις prepares for the remarks on Theopompus' deviation from his opening (9.1–2, 11.2). **προαιρέσεσι:** the way someone chooses to live and act; more deliberate than 'character'. προαίρεσις is common in P. and Diodorus, Aristotle and the Stoics and documents, e.g. *SEG* XVI.255.3 (Argos, before 170 BC), *P. Tebt.* III.1 785.17 (*c.*138 BC).

**8.8 ἀλλ' ἴσως:** a rhetorically effective shift (cf. 30.31.5). It is attractively self-critical for P. suddenly to question his own speech act (i.e. §7). The contrast of easy assertion and difficult practice (5.33.6, 12.25c.5) here applies to P.'s own assertion and the practice of others. **διαθέσεις:** here 'conditions, positions' that one is in (cf. 1.12.9 διαθέσεις ἐν αἷς ὑπάρχουσι νῦν, 10.5.8); paired with περιστάσεις 'circumstances' at 10.21.2, and described as πολλὰς καὶ ποικίλας 3.27.8. For περίστασις with (πολύς καί) ποικίλος cf. e.g. P. 11.2.3, DS 17.13.1, P. Tebt. III.1 703.236 (late iii BC), *I.Egypte prose* 46.5 (Karnak, 39 BC). **εἴκοντες** does not imply a choice; cf. οὔτε ... δύνανται. ἄνθρωποι indicates human limits. **τὸ φαινόμενον** 'what they think'. Cf. 5.51.5, 7.12.5; Tac. *Hist.* 1.1.4 *rara temporum felicitate, ubi ... quae sentias dicere licet.*

**8.9 αὐτῶν:** historians. ἐνίοις varies τισί. **δοτέον ... οὐ δοτέον:** the succinct neatness conveys balanced intelligence. As at 35.2, συγγνώμη should not be awarded indiscriminately. At 2.7.3 failure through fortune earns pity and συγγνώμη, failure through folly, reproach – παρὰ τοῖς εὖ φρονοῦσιν.

## 9 THEOPOMPUS SPEAKS STRONGLY

**9.1 μάλιστα κτλ.:** after the short sentence 8.9 comes a massive period. The bulk is produced by, first, a rendering of Theopompus' fulsome praise (ὅς γ' ... Φίλιππον), then (ἀκρατέστατον ... §4 φίλοις) a mass of clauses which captures Theopompus' abuse, in Polybian language: four adjectival and participial groups, the first and last (ἀκρατέστατον κτλ., ἐκπαθῆ κτλ.) extended by ὥστε-clauses. The huge sentence builds Theopompus' mimicked excess into a structure of contradiction indicted by P. **περὶ τοῦτο τὸ μέρος** 'in this respect'; cf. e.g. 6.52.5. **Θεοπόμπωι:** readers are made to await the name with curiosity. This could have been Theopompus' first appearance in the work. He certainly does not appear amid οἱ λογιώτατοι τῶν ἀρχαίων συγγραφέων (6.45.1, on constitutions), a list beginning with Ephorus (cf. 6.46.10). **ἐν ἀρχῆι τῆς <περὶ> Φιλίππου συντάξεως:** similar phrases at 2.37.2, Ps.-Scymn. 109, but not of the actual proem as here (§2). The work is referred to as αἱ περὶ Φιλίππου ἱστορίαι at T17 (Diodorus), and τὰ περὶ Φιλίππου at F291 (Didymus). A bare genitive would suggest Philip was the author; contrast 11.4. **[διὰ τό]:** an anticipation of διὰ τό before μηδέποτε. P certainly does not have δι' αὐτό, as editors think. The impossible quasi-acute accent on α is probably a random mark like the quasi-grave on the τ of πρεσβύτιδος on fol. 96ᵛ 3rd line up; no accent for διά would in P be normal. δι' αὐτό makes little sense; δι' αὐτόν (Reiske) μάλιστα would be weak when the work was on

Philip; preparatory διὰ τοῦτο (Dindorf) is not Polybian. The *Suda*'s καί before μάλιστα could be right, cf. e.g. 3.26.2, 11.24a.2; but its καί in §7 is its own idea. **πραγματείας** varies συντάξεως; similarly 9.1.2, 11.1a.4–5, 'Euclid' 14 (Hypsicles) *pr.* (v.1.2.3–6 Heiberg). **Εὐρώπην:** cf. Isocr. *Phil.* 137 (to Philip II) τυγχάνεις τοσαύτην δύναμιν κεκτημένος ὅσην οὐδεὶς τῶν τὴν Εὐρώπην κατοικησάντων. This fragment of Theopompus is *FGrHist* 115 F27. **ἐνηνοχέναι** 'produce', of the earth or lands, cf. LSJ φέρω v; Virg. *G.* 2.167–72: Italy *extulit ... te, maxime Caesar.* **τοιοῦτον:** the surface meaning was obviously laudatory; cf. e.g. Soph. *OC* 694–701 (Athens' olive tree, such as never grew in Asia), Hor. *Odes* 4.2.37–8 (divinities have given the earth nothing greater than Augustus). Connor (1967) 136–9 maintains that Theopompus was being ironic; the adventurous presumption is that P. wholly misread and we can do better with no context. There is no force in the argument that 'such' in Theopompus' comments occurs in negative contexts: comments in Theopompus' fragments are usually negative. **παράπαν** 'at all', with μηδέποτε; cf. 3.26.4 μήτε γεγονότος μήθ' ὑπάρχοντος παράπαν ἐγγράφου τοιούτου μηδενός. **Ἀμύντου:** probably in Theopompus (P. has named Philip already); in the proem (§2), and probably in the first mention of Philip, for dignity not identification.

**9.2 παρὰ πόδας** 'immediately' (LSJ πούς 4b); a much commoner phrase in P. (23 times) than in other non-Christian authors. **δέ:** τε ... καὶ ... δέ not in Hellenistic prose or documents, but cf. Xen. *Cyr.* 5.3.43; 15.9 below πρός τε Νικόμαχον ... ὁμοίως δὲ καὶ πρὸς Μελαγκόμαν. **ἀκρατέστατον κτλ.:** P. depicts Scipio Africanus the Elder as φιλογύνης, but restrained on campaign (10.19.3–7). Appian calls Mithridates generally restrained; περὶ μόνας ἡττᾶτο τὰς τῶν γυναικῶν ἡδονάς (*Mith.* 550). **ἀποδείκνυσι:** commoner with a complement than δείκνυσι (*Suda*); cf. e.g. 6.58.11. **καὶ τὸν ἴδιον οἶκον ἐσφαλκέναι** 'brought disaster even to his own house', not just those of others. Particularly in view are his numerous and simultaneous marriages; with his final marriage, he ἅπαντα τὸν βίον τὸν ἑαυτοῦ συνέχεεν (Satyr. F25 Schorn, with Schorn's note). **τὸ καθ' αὑτόν** stresses that this was his doing, perhaps 'single-handedly'; cf. 1.52.2. **πρὸς τοῦτο τὸ μέρος** 'in this regard'; cf. e.g. 18.4.4. **παράστασιν** (Ernesti) 'wild eagerness'; it is paired with ὁρμή at 3.63.14, 5.48.7. προστασίαν (P, *Suda*) 'pomp, grandeur' does not relate to Philip's ἀκρασία, as the context demands. προπέτειαν (Reiske) 'rashness' gives a firmly negative word (3.16.4, etc.); Call. *Ep.* 42.2, 4 Pfeiffer, Heliod. 7.27.5 use it of lovers.

**9.3 κατασκευάς:** buildings, artworks, etc. (cf. e.g. 4.65.3, 73.6, 5.11.4, 16.6.6; *CGL* 14, 23). 'Construction', 'production' is not likely for friends and allies ('in his schemes for forming friendships and alliances', Loeb). The misdeeds will not be for friends and against allies. ἐξηνδραποδισμένον 'having enslaved'. Cf. Dem. Ol. 1.20 Φίλιππον δ' ἐᾶν πόλεις Ἑλληνίδας ἀνδραποδίζεσθαι. πεπραξικοπηκότα 'having taken through treachery'. For the word see Introduction §13 c, Wheeler (1988) 41–2. P. can apply it to the admired Elder and Younger Aratus, or Hannibal (2.57.3, 3.69.1, 9.17.1).

**9.4 ἐκπαθῆ** 'eager'; cf. e.g. 4.58.1. **ἀκρατοποσίας:** drinking wine unmixed (ἀ- + κεράννυμι) with water – a dangerous practice associated with Scythians and Thracians (Hdt. 6.84.3 ἀκρητοποσίη, Satyr. F20 Schorn). Alexander had a competition in it, with dire results (Plut. *Alex.* 70.1–2). Theop. *FGrHist* 115 F283b ascribes to it Dionysius II's poor sight. **καὶ μεθ' ἡμέραν:** drunkenness by day is particularly disapproved; cf. 27.1n. Worse is P.'s friend Demetrius I of Syria, drunk most of the day (33.19.1). Theop. *FGrHist* 115 F282 says Philip was often drunk in battle. **τοῖς φίλοις** at the end of the sentence leads into what follows.

**9.5 τὴν ἀρχὴν τῆς ἐνάτης καὶ τετταροκοστῆς αὐτῶι βύβλου:** P. proceeds from the work's beginning to the beginning of a book in its later part. The reference is relatively precise, as to the proem of Timaeus' sixth book (12.28.8); other book numbers come at 3.26.5, 12.25.7, etc. **παντάπασιν** strengthens P.'s standard amazement at other writers: 3.26.2 (Philinus), 12.25f.2 (Timaeus), etc. **ἀτοπίαν:** ἀτοπ- of other writers at 12.6a.1, 12.28.10 (both Timaeus), 39.1.7 (Postumius Albinus). **τοῦ συγγραφέως, ὅς γε** picks up and varies §1 Θεοπόμπωι, ὅς γ'. **χωρὶς τῶν ἄλλων τετόλμηκε καὶ ταῦτα λέγειν:** the indignant rhetoric relates especially to what P. omits after §6 and §12. **αὐταῖς γὰρ λέξεσιν** 'in his very words'. Dionysius as literary critic uses the same phrase at *Thuc.* 11, *Pomp.* 2.1. It is more unusual for a historian to make a long quote from a literary work. P.'s air of wrath leads him on from the possibility of someone looking the passage up (εἰ δέ τις ἀναγνῶναι βουληθείη). P.'s reproduction is not absolutely exact, as is seen from the independent citations in Ath. 4.166f–167c and 6.260d–261a (cf. §6 and §§7–12 here). **κατατετάχαμεν** sees from his readers' angle; contrast DH *Pomp.* 2.1 θήσω.

**9.6 γάρ** is P.'s join; cf. φησί. P.'s version is *FGrHist* 115 F225a. Ath. 4.167a–c (F224) gives the context: Philip and his ἑταῖροι spent extravagantly. They came from Macedonia, Thessaly, the rest of Greece; they were not picked for merit, ἀλλ' ('but rather') εἴ τις ἦν κτλ. **ἐν τοῖς Ἕλλησιν ἢ τοῖς βαρβάροις** has an Isocratean ring: τοῖς Ἕλλησιν καὶ τοῖς βαρβάροις *vel sim.* at *Call.* 27, *Hel.* 52, *Panath.* 213. Save in Isocrates, the phrase is uncommon with articles in other cases too (dative e.g. Ar. *Frogs* 724). **λάσταυρος:** a depraved person, obsessed with sex, passive or active. It appears in comedy and ordinary speech: so Men. *Sic.* 266, *SVF* III pp. 199–200. **ἢ βδελυρός** (see §8n.) P has omitted before ἢ θρασύς; most likely a scribal error, since the three items go better with οὗτοι πάντες. **τὸν τρόπον:** cf. §12, F236. **πάντες:** P. probably omits σχεδόν to play up Theopompus' extremity. **πρὸς Φίλιππον** is added to be clear without what preceded; τοῦ βασιλέως is then variation. **ἑταῖροι:** an official title, which at some unknown point changes to φίλοι. §13 below (see n.) might not mean φίλοι was an official title; it is not such at *I.Adramytteion* 34.6–8 (319–317 BC): φίλος (dear) to the kings, generals and all Macedonians. See further on the ἑταῖροι Savalli-Lestrade (1998) 254–8; Hatzopoulos (1996) I 458, (2020) 53–4, 58.

**9.7 καθόλου:** P. omits at least a passage (Ath. 4.167b–c) on how the better people were corrupted. He may well add καθόλου to help the transition (*Suda* α 2978 will come from P., not Theopompus). **κοσμίους:** κόσμιος and κοσμίως do not come elsewhere in P.; they come three times in this passage as known from Athenaeus. ζῆν μὴ κοσμίως and κοσμίως ζῆν are especially reminiscent of Isocrates, who has κοσμίως ζῆν 3 times (cf. also *Antid.* 228), twice with reference to kings (*Ad Nic.* 31, *Nic.* 38); the phrase is not common elsewhere. **βίων** 'property' (LSJ II); Philip and his companions were the world's worst οἰκονόμοι (F224). **ἀπεδοκίμαζε** 'spurned'. In F224.29–35 (Athenaeus), some decent people do come, but are corrupted. **ἐν μέθαις καὶ κύβοις:** slightly stronger than ἐν κύβοις καὶ πότοις (Athenaeus). Either variant suits Theopompus; cf. e.g. F133 τοὺς ἀποβάλλοντας τὰς οὐσίας εἰς μέθας καὶ κύβους κτλ.

**9.8 βδελυρίας:** loudly unsuitable and improper behaviour: see Theophr. *Char.* 11 (with Diggle's first note). βδελυρία and βδελυρός come 13 times in Aeschines 1; ἀθλητάς may develop Aeschin. 1.189 (depraved Timarchus' βδελυρία in comparison with γυμναζόμενοι), 192 (ὁ πρωτεύων βδελυρίαι). Theopompus takes Plato's metaphor ἀθληταὶ πολέμου (*Rep.* 3.416d9, etc.) in a sarcastic direction.

**9.9 τί γὰρ ... ἀπῆν** inverts Gorgias' praise of Athenian war dead (B6 DK, D28 Laks–Most): τί γὰρ ἀπῆν τοῖς ἀνδράσι τούτοις ὧν δεῖ ἀνδράσι προσεῖναι; τί δὲ καὶ προσῆν ὧν οὐ δεῖ προσεῖναι; The connection continues in ἄνδρες; ὄντες is 'though being', cf. Luc. *Salt.* 28 τὸ ἄνδρας ὄντας μιμεῖσθαι γυναῖκας. The phrase also evokes Isocr. *Paneg.* 111 τί τῶν αἰσχρῶν ἢ δεινῶν οὐ διεξῆλθον [3rd pers. pl.]; **ὧν:** οὐχ (Athenaeus) with a rhetorical question would make the transition to §10 καὶ περιήγοντο more awkward. **ξυρόμενοι**

καὶ λεαινόμενοι ('smoothed'): so making their appearance womanly; cf. Ar. *Thesm.* 191–2, 1042–3, Alexis fr. 266 K–A (with Arnott's note). Chrysippus alleges shaving was first introduced in Alexander's time (*SVF* III p. 198). ἐπανίστασθαι 'mount': graphic, but not vulgar. πώγωνας ἔχουσι matches the participial ἄνδρες ὄντες, and contrasts with the smooth faces at the start. These men look like men; for Theopompus, that makes their passivity and mutual attraction still more grotesque. Cf. Cat. 80.8, where, with Housman's *barba*, Gellius' beard exhibits his fellatio of a man.

9.10 περιήγοντο suggests campaigns. δύο καὶ τρεῖς: not an exclusive relationship. ἑταιρευομένους: the verb, which prepares for the play on ἑταῖροι, is used of male prostitution at DS 12.21.1 (law of Zaleucus). αὐτοὶ δὲ τὰς αὐτάς highlights the strange indifference to active or passive roles. ἐκείνοις: the same χρήσεις as (dative) the overt prostitutes. χρήσεις: wittily unspecific.

9.11 δικαίως 'rightly'; with a non-literal designation e.g. Isocr. *Antid.* 299. ἀλλ' ἑταίρας: in Athenaeus, despite Jacoby. The turn goes beyond the insulting feminine seen in e.g. Hom. *Il.* 2.235 Ἀχαιΐδες, οὐκέτ' Ἀχαιοί, to play on the title ἑταῖροι and the special meaning of ἑταίρα; cf. the play on (probably) ἑταίρων and ἑταιρῶν at Men. fr. 387 K–A. [οὐδὲ ... προσηγόρευσεν]: στρατιώτας and χαμαιτύπας/-ους 'prostitutes' cannot be the middle pair when ἑταίρους and ἑταίρας, ἀνδροφόνοι and ἀνδρόπορνοι match so neatly (φ is an aspirated *p*). A neat play is difficult to produce by conjecture, and Demetrius does not have the middle pair. That pair is also weak after the undoing of the title ἑταῖροι. Without it, §12 ἀνδροφόνοι does not have to imply 'they were no longer man-slaying' (a decline); φονεύειν ἐζήτουν in Athenaeus' next sentence supports the negative 'murderous'. They were ἀνδρόπορνοι despite being ἀνδροφόνοι; cf. §9 ἄνδρες ὄντες. χαμαιτύπη (later occasionally -τύπος) is a regular word in prose and comedy for 'whore, prostitute', whence χαμαιτυπεῖον 'brothel'; cf. e.g. *IOSPE* I².705.9–10 (ii AD). πόρνας was avoided before ἀνδρόπορνοι.

9.12 ἀνδρόπορνοι: the word is probably Theopompus' invention. ἀνδρο- means 'though notionally men'; cf. ἀνδρόγυνος at Aeschin. 2.127, Men. *Sam.* 69. This play with compounds goes further than Gorgias', e.g. *Hel.* 2 ὁμόφωνος καὶ ὁμόψυχος.

9.13 ἁπλῶς δ' εἰπεῖν: here 'to put it in a nutshell'. (ὡς) ἁπλῶς εἰπεῖν is found in oratory and philosophy, not historiography, save Plutarch. P. omits after §12 at least four sentences on drunkenness, cheating and greed. 'ἵνα παύσωμαι', φησί, 'μακρολογῶν': Theopompus' winning acknowledgement differs from the usual ἵνα μὴ μακρολογῶ/μακρηγορῶ, τί δεῖ μακρολογεῖν; etc. (e.g. Isocr. *Big.* 8). P.'s φησί makes clear who the first person is. **πραγμάτων:** matters to narrate, presumably at first related to the companions, so that τοσούτων and ἐπικεχυμένων contribute to the rhetoric. But not directly 'instances of badness', for which πρᾶγμα is too colourless. **ἐπικεχυμένων:** an expressive image. Livy 31.1.5, daunted by his material, speaks of walking into a sea; Theopompus depicts an overwhelming flood. **τοιαῦτα θηρία:** τοιούτους τὸν τρόπον is awkwardly redundant after this phrase; καὶ τοιοῦτον τρόπον could have been inserted to ease the grammar, for which cf. e.g. Gal. *Sem.* 2.3.17 (*CMG* v.3.1.170.20–2) τοιαῦτα ... οἵους. **φίλους:** for φίλοι as a Macedonian title, if so it is here, cf. e.g. Moretti, *ISE* II.114.A col. iii.4 (Amphipolis, *c.*200 BC) τούς φίλους τοῦ βασιλέως. **Κενταύρους:** drink drove them to assail the Lapith women, as on Parthenon metope S10; Ov. *Am.* 2.12.19–20. Mount Pelion is suitably close to Macedonia. **Λαιστρυγόνας:** Theopompus proceeds to a more extreme and distant example, the man-eating and rock-hurling Laestrygonians (Hom. *Od.* 10.114–24), located in the Leontine plain of Sicily (Sil. It. 14.125–6, *al.*). They are an ἔθνος θηριάνθρωπον (Herodian, *Epimer.* p. 76.4 Boissonade). **οὐδ' ὁποίους** 'any whatever'; cf. e.g. Plato, *Theaet.* 152d4 οὐδ' ὁποιονοῦν τι, P. 4.65.3.

## 10 POLYBIUS TO THE DEFENCE

**10.1 ταύτην κτλ.:** the demonstrative indignantly sums up Theopompus' passage; an opening rhetorical question leads into the structured demolition (§2 οὐ γάρ). Cf., after a quotation, DH *Dem.* 21.3 ταύτην τὴν διάλεκτον τίς οὐκ ἂν ὁμολογήσειε κτλ. (laudatory). **τε:** cf. 10.40.6 ἐπί τε [goes with διάληψιν] ταύτην κατενεχθῆναι τὴν διάληψιν καὶ τὴν ὀνομασίαν. **πικρίαν:** several times of Timaeus (§12, 12.14.1, etc.; cf. DS 13.90.6); this stem is used of Theopompus' writing or character at T20a (Dionysius), 28b (*Suda*), cf. 25b, 40 (Cicero; *asper, acer*). P. never uses the older πικρότης. **ἀθυρογλωττίαν:** speech unrestrained ('with no door') in content and length – Theopompus' μακρολογῶν is taken up (cf. T28b). ἀθυρογλωττία comes only here in pre-Christian writers. **ἀποδοκιμάσειεν:** Theopompus' verb is turned against him (9.7 above).

**10.2 οὐ γὰρ μόνον:** contradiction (cf. μαχόμενα) and falsity (cf. κατέψευσται) have been indicated at 9.1–4 and 8.7. The opening πικρία and ἀθυρογλωττία (10.1) emphasize expression now. The rhetoric amasses the charges, with οὐ μόνον, καὶ διότι and καὶ μάλιστα διότι. The sentence indicates, in reverse order, the structure of P.'s response, which glides from expression

(10.3–5) to falsity (10.5–12) to contradiction (11.1–6), before ending with the accent once more on expression (11.6). **μαχόμενα:** here not just inconsistent statements (16.28.4 μαχόμενα λέγειν ἑαυτοῖς) but violation of Theopompus' initial plan – for P. a crucial shortcoming (cf. e.g. 16.28.9; *I.Délos* 1520.8–10, *c.*150 BC). **ἐπιτιμήσεως** takes up ἐπιτιμήσειε (9.1). **κατέψευσται** 'has slandered'; καταψεύδομαι otherwise in P. only in book 12 (6 times). **τοῦ τε βασιλέως:** the king, who makes the friends important (9.7–8), is essential to the arguments on monarchy (8.7–8) and on contradiction (9.1, 11.1). But the friends are the foremost object of attack (9.6–13) and defence (10.5–12). **αἰσχρῶς καὶ ἀπρεπῶς:** not a common pair, but cf. Arist. *Rhet.* 3.1407b29, *al.* ἀπρεπ- is used of writing at P. 30.18.6; cf. e.g. Σ A Hom. *Il.* 1.29–31. **διατέθειται** 'has uttered', cf. 1.2.1 of writers; LSJ B 6.

**10.3 Σαρδαναπάλλου:** king of Assyria; cf. DS 2.21.8 (Ctes. *FGrHist* 688 F1.21.8), 23–7; 23.1–4 for his womanish luxury. The name may come from Ashurbanipal (reigned 669–631; cf. Faust (2021) 10–11). **ἤ** (P) could be right; but one could not envisage separate treatment of the companions, and the conjecture καί would neatly match §2 τοῦ τε βασιλέως καὶ τῶν φίλων, §5 περὶ δὲ Φιλίππου καὶ τῶν ἐκείνου φίλων. **μόλις ἂν ἐθάρρησε:** animatedly over-the-top language. **κακορρημοσύνηι:** only here. **οὖ:** singular, as the choice of lifestyle and the epitaph are the king's. **τεκμαιρόμεθα** 'deduce'; for διά cf. Philo, *Leg.* 261, Plut. *Them.* 18.1. Scepticism of narratives like Ctesias' need not be implied, if ἀσέλγειαν goes closely with προαίρεσιν. Cf. 36.15.6 Σαρδαναπάλλου δὲ βάρβαρον βίον ἔζη.

**10.4 [ἡ ἐπιγραφή]:** the phrase shows hiatus. Both it and Büttner-Wobst's ἡ γραφή are unwelcome; one would expect just λέγει γάρ; cf. e.g. Arist. *Cael.* 3.300b30, DS 20.41.6. **ταῦτ' ἔχω:** see *SH* 335. A long version of the epitaph, starting εὖ εἰδὼς ὅτι θνητὸς ἔφυς, was quoted by Chrysippus (*SVF* III p. 200). P. will have known it. It is not certain that there was a short version, starting ταῦτ' ἔχω and ending τέρπν' ἔπαθον· τὰ δὲ πολλὰ καὶ ὄλβια κεῖνα λέλειπται. P. is knowingly incomplete at the end and may be so at the start. See on the epitaph Rohland (2022) 38–75. P. makes the most of ἐφύβρισα and ἔπαθον (here taken to suggest unmanly sexual passivity). The underlying point in ἔχω 'I still possess' was variously regarded as outrageous or sensible; of sepulchral imitations cf. esp. *I.Kibyra* 1.362 b.4 (ii–iii AD) ἃ ἔφαγον ἔχω· ἃ κατέλιπον ἀπώλεσα.

**10.5 οὐχ οἷον** 'not only', in effect with all of περὶ … λέγειν (cf. 20.2n.; εὐλαβηθείη gives a sort of negative). Two main clauses contrast: μὴ ποτ' … οὐ δυνηθῆι (aor. subj.), 'will never be able to', replaces εὐλαβηθείη …

ἄν, 'would take care not to'. The neutral λέγειν makes the slide easier; compare the explicit 5.11.2 εἰς ἀσέλγειαν καὶ παρανομίαν ὠνείδιζε, Thuc. 5.75.3. **μαλακίαν καὶ ἀνανδρίαν:** a pair at e.g. Philo, *Spec. Leg.* 3.31. ἀναισχυντία then makes a trio; it is a strong word, cf. 35.4.7. The words can be used in military contexts, as at 3.79.4 μαλακίας καὶ φυγοπονίας. The trio neatly contrasts with τῆς ἀνδρείας καὶ φιλοπονίας καὶ συλλήβδην τῆς ἀρετῆς, and suggests that the sets are opposites. Womanishness is here an indivisible whole; manly fighting excludes womanish sexuality. **καταξίως εἰπεῖν:** the impossibility of adequate expression appears rhetorically at 1.37.1, 5.44.2. In §§6–12, P. is seen rising to a challenge.

**10.6 οἵ γε:** the opening of praise matches that of censure at 9.1 ὅς γε (Theopompus). **φιλοπονίαις καὶ τόλμαις:** similar to the singular, cf. 1.64.5, 6.52.10, Isocr. *Antid.* 291–2; but the Successors' plurality is underlined, by contrast with Philip, then Alexander. **βασιλείας ... ἀρχήν:** from a tiny kingdom they made the huge empire. Cf. Lane Fox (2011*b*) 269; but see also Borza (1990) 196–7. κατασκευάζω often denotes substantial political change ([Arist.] *Ath. Pol.* 37.1: oligarchy; DS 17.5.5: a new reign). For ἐκ cf. Theop. *FGrHist* 115 F122a: κατασκευασάμενοι their body of slaves ἐκ the former inhabitants. With <τὴν> before Μακεδόνων instead, κατεσκεύασαν would mean 'made' the empire glorious; but there was no empire before Philip, and βασιλείας prevents the sense 'made great instead of small', as in Cic. *Cael.* 39 (of Roman growth) *haec ex minimis tanta fecerunt*.

**10.7 χωρίς** 'apart from'. P. separates the friends from Philip by moving forward in time, and increases their achievement. **μετ' Ἀλεξάνδρου** is chiastically set against ἐπὶ Φιλίππου; 'with' rather than 'in the reign of' brings out their contribution, cf. §8. **πᾶσιν ὁμολογουμένην:** predicative, handed down so that it is acknowledged by all. **ἐπ' ἀρετῆι φημήν:** a grandiose phrase, used only by P., 6 times. **παραδεδώκασι:** the perspective is present, their fame is now.

**10.8 μεγάλην** seems to make a generous concession, but ἴσως undermines it; the rhetoric is adroit. The argument leads to an interesting perspective; until recently, historians have primarily stressed Alexander. **θετέον** 'one must assign' a great share. **καίπερ ὄντι νέωι παντελῶς:** usually, Alexander's youth increases his glory; here it undercuts his significance. Cf. e.g. 9.17.9 νέον ἀκμὴν ὄντα and hence inexperienced. εἶναι does not have a past participle, so ὤν can stand in; cf. e.g. 7.11.4. **οὐκ ἐλάττω** at the start answers μεγάλην, and leads onto the initial πολλαῖς and πολλούς. **συνεργοῖς καὶ φίλοις:** φίλοι is meaningfully expanded.

**10.9 οἵ:** an elaborately crafted panegyric now begins.   πολλαῖς μὲν καὶ παραδόξοις is matched by πολλοὺς δὲ καὶ παραβόλους, and action by endurance. A speech of Dinarchus began πολλῶν καὶ παραδόξων (fr. 35.1 Conomis); but P. strikingly applies the combination to battles which turn out unexpectedly. Cf. 2.4, 31.4nn.   **παραβόλους** 'perilous'. The separation heightens the trio of nouns (πόνους κτλ.). Trios joined by καί come much less often in P. than pairs: in book 5 pairs 174, trios 14. Here another trio follows shortly in §10.   **πλείστης ... πλείστης** might at first seem to continue πολλαῖς ... πολλούς; cf. e.g. DH *Dem.* 14 πολλὰ μὲν ... πολλὰ δ᾽ ... πλεῖστα δέ. But the sentence actually takes a twist from deeds to avoidance: despite all this opportunity, οὔτε ... οὔτε.   **περιουσίας:** more than is needed, which risks decline, cf. e.g. 6.7.7 (of kings), 18.55.7; but the friends pull through, like Hieron II, who lives to 90, with a βίος σώφρων, amid περιουσίαι καὶ τρυφῆι καὶ δαψιλείαι πλείστηι (7.8.7).   **εὐπορήσαντες ἀπολαύσεως** 'with abundant opportunity for enjoyment'; cf. for ἀπόλαυσις e.g. 5.48.1 (food and drink), 10.19.5 (sex and love).   **οὐδέποτε** indicates an extravagant claim, more so than in 7.8.7: Hieron kept every part of his body unharmed. Thus wine never overcame these men – despite Alexander's parties.   **ψυχικὰς ὁρμάς:** impulses to brawling and sexual violence. Alexander's drunken killing of Cleitus (Plut. *Alex.* 51.9–10, etc.) was famous; the friends could be contrasted with Alexander here, but that would harm the argument on Philip.

**10.10 ἅπαντες δ᾽, ὡς ἔπος εἰπεῖν** 'pretty well all'; so with πᾶς 1.1.2, 6.58.7. The slight modification masks big differences perceived among the Diadochi. Cf. P. Oxy. LXXXVI 5535: tyrannical Perdiccas, restrained Antipater.   **βασιλικοί:** while Philip and Alexander lived, they were already worthy of the kingship which Antigonus and others later claimed (306 BC on). Cf. 10.40.5: Scipio Africanus wishes to be called βασιλικός not βασιλεύς. True kingly qualities appear at 4.27.10: Philip V gives hope πραότητος καὶ μεγαλοψυχίας βασιλικῆς; cf. e.g. 16.28.3. Kingly and tyrannical behaviour are contrasted; cf. e.g. P. Oxy. LXXXVI 5535 col. i.5–8; P. 6.7.7, where as usual the tyrant is the reverse of σώφρων.   **ταῖς ... ταῖς ... ταῖς:** the repeated article intensifies the trio.   **μετ᾽:** adverbial, cf. 5.15.4 (unless interpolated from §7 μετ᾽ Ἀλεξάνδρου).   **ἀπέβησαν** 'emerged as'; cf. 7.13.7 τύραννος ἐκ βασιλέως ἀπέβη πικρός, LSJ II.4.   **Φιλίππωι:** taking in Philip's reign too, despite §§7–9. Nep. *Reg.* 3.1 just has *fuerunt praeterea magni reges ex amicis Alexandri Magni.*   **συμβιώσαντες:** simultaneous with ἀπέβησαν; §11 moves onto a new stage, after Alexander. συμβι- indicates, not sleeping in the same house, but shared activity, especially dining; cf. e.g. *IG* IX.1².2.248.6–15 (Thyrreion, ii BC), list of συμβιωταί, including cook.   **ἐπ᾽ ὀνόματος:** they are too well known to need naming; cf. §11.

But the brief sentence also papers rhetorically over historical cracks (see introduction to 8–14b.2).

**10.11 μετὰ δὲ τὸν Ἀλεξάνδρου θάνατον** marks a further stage, like §7 μετὰ τὸν ἐκείνου θάνατον. **οὕτω**: with παραδόσιμον. **τῶν πλείστων μερῶν τῆς οἰκουμένης**: the period goes beyond the initial disputes after Alexander's death; cf. e.g. 5.67.6–8 for later ones. The geographical scope increases the fame. **παραδόσιμον**: οὕτω and the context make a τοῖς ἐπιγινομένοις (6.54.2) unnecessary. An Aetolian speaker presents a hostile view of the Diadochi as known to all (9.29.1–2); P. will not have agreed with it, but will have been aware he is simplifying here. **ἐποίησαν**: their achievement, not the writers'. **πλείστοις ὑπομνήμασιν**: the discussion returns to writing. The Diadochi, like Alexander, were the subject of much biography and historiography – unlike the wars of the fifth century, where Herodotus and Thucydides discouraged imitators. Cf. *FGrHist* 154–5, 156 F1–11, Meeus (2022) 58–68, add P. Oxy. LXXXVI 5535.

**10.12 τὴν μὲν Τιμαίου**: with inexhaustible élan, P. suddenly brings in another author; as often in rhetoric, introducing a less bad instance makes the speaker seem reasonable and the person attacked extreme. Timaeus (*c*.350–260 BC) is criticized by DS 21.17.1–3 as well as P. 12.15 for his unremitting treatment of Agathocles, ruler of Syracuse *c*.317–289 BC. See de Lisle (2021) 48–52. **πικρίαν** takes up 10.1. **τοῦ Σικελίας δυνάστου**: from 306, Agathocles controlled most of Sicily, and claimed to be its king probably from 304. P. does not concede the title, but the claim at that date makes Agathocles an apt comparison to the Diadochi. **ἀνυπέρβλητον** 'unsurpassable', used by P. of the historian Zeno's shortcomings at 16.18.3. He talks at 12.15.4 of the ὑπερβολή of Timaeus' πικρία to Agathocles. **λόγον ἔχειν** 'is coherent, makes sense'; cf. e.g. Plato, *Ap*. 34b1–2. Timaeus' opinion of Agathocles, unlike Theopompus' of Philip (§11), fits his attack. **ἐχθροῦ καὶ πονηροῦ καὶ τυράννου**: another trio (§9n.). For Timaeus' personal enmity with Agathocles cf. 12.15.10 τῆς ἰδίας πικρίας, δυσμενικῶς, DS 21.17.1 τὴν πρὸς αὐτὸν ἔχθραν, φυγαδευθείς. **τὴν δέ**: *sc*. πικρίαν. **μηδ' ὑπὸ λόγον πίπτειν** 'does not even make sense'; cf. 4.15.11 ὥστε μηδ' ὑπὸ λόγον πίπτειν (the Aetolians' immoral incoherence over an alliance).

## 11 THE INCONSISTENCIES OF THEOPOMPUS

**11.1 προθέμενος**: opening and programmatic statements; cf. 9.1. **εὐφυεστάτου πρὸς ἀρετήν**: not necessarily Theopompus' words. They would be compatible with an aptness which was not actually realized (cf. Plut. *Sol.* 29.5, *Gracch.* 41.2); but P. does not make Theopompus present a decline, as P. does for Philip V's change ἐκ βασιλέως εὐφυοῦς to tyrant (4.77.4; cf. 10.26.8–9). Rather, Theopompus offers two inconsistent pictures; P. in praise and blame follows the truth. **αἰσχρῶν καὶ δεινῶν:** P. turns Theopompus' phrase against him (9.9), including the universality and the negative (τί ... οὐ προσῆν; cf. here οὐκ ἔστι ... ὃ παραλέλοιπε).

**11.2 λοιπόν**, 'hence', draws the conclusion from the contradiction; cf. 1.15.11; 38b.2n. **ἀνάγκη:** there are only two possibilities when Theopompus asserts both *p* (Philip was marvellous) and not-*p*. Either (i) he does not believe *p*, or (ii) he does not believe not-*p*. P. finds reasons for both; for (i), flattery (ψεύστην and κόλακα must be taken together). P. may suppose that the proem was circulated in Philip's lifetime; or the flattery could be aimed at his successors. For (ii), Theopompus is hoping to win credit for himself and belief for *p* by including negative comments: these will show he is not biased towards Philip. The mixture of positive and negative is different from that in P. on Philip V (10.26.7–10, 16.28.3–7): P. is treating each action as it deserves, Theopompus produces irrational abuse. **προέκθεσιν τῆς πραγματείας** 'proem of the work'; cf. 3.1.7. **τὸν ἱστοριογράφον** avoids repetition of the name, but also contrasts the profession and its obligations with ψεύστην καὶ κόλακα. **μειρακιώδη:** lack of mature judgement leads to ἀλογήματα (cf. 10.33.6); the word matches his want of stylistic perception, cf. 9.10–12 and e.g. DH *Isocr.* 12. **ἐπικλήτου:** called in from afar (cf. DH *AR* 6.53.1), so outlandish. **παραδοχῆς** 'acceptance'; cf. 1.5.5 παραδοχῆς ἀξιωθῆναι καὶ πίστεως. **ἐγκωμιαστικάς** looks back to 8.6 ἐγκωμίου δὲ μᾶλλον. Even Theopompus' positive remarks were over the top for history. The plural suggests Theopompus' praise was not just the phrase quoted at 9.1 – which he probably justified.

**11.3 καὶ μὴν οὐδέ** goes on to a fresh aspect, but the subject is related; cf. e.g. 6.47.7. The link is Theopompus' incoherence in relation to Philip. The laudatory view of Philip is now the starting point. **ὁλοσχερεῖς διαλήψεις** 'total views': total because relating to Theopompus' whole oeuvre. The views concern Philip and Greece as well as history-writing. **οὐδεὶς ἂν εὐδοκήσειε** 'no one would approve', matching 10.1 τίς οὐκ ἂν ἀποδοκιμάσειεν; P. is formally more restrained at 12.15.1 οὐδὲ ταῖς κατ' Ἀγαθοκλέους ἔγωγε λοιδορίαις ... εὐδοκῶ (of Timaeus). **ὅς γ':** the same construction as in 9.1 (one would criticize Theopompus, ὅς γ'). **ἐπιβαλόμενος** 'having undertaken'. **τὰς Ἑλληνικὰς πράξεις** is used by Diodorus for Theopompus' *Hellenica* (*FGrHist* 115 T13); they are an important subset of P.'s own work (3.1 18.11, 4.1.3). **ἀφ' ὧν Θουκυδίδης ἀπέλιπε:** Thucydides breaks off in 411; Xenophon, and perhaps others, had already started from this point: cf. *FGrHist* 115 T13, Marincola (1997) 289–90. **συνεγγίσας τοῖς Λευκτρικοῖς καιροῖς:** the Boeotian defeat of Sparta at Leuctra (371 BC) changed Greek history decisively. Yet Theopompus finished in 394 (T13–14). The looseness, characteristic of the passage, has a purpose: P. wishes to present the *Philippica* (beginning 360/59) as a sort of continuation of the *Hellenica*. **ἐπιφανεστάτοις** 'most famous'; P. so denotes the key events of his own history (3.5.9). **Ἑλλάδα:** P. makes mainland Greece the centre of 'Greek events'; so 5.105.9 dwells on τὰς κατὰ τὴν Ἑλλάδα πράξεις, despite 6 (islands and Asia). τὰς ταύτης ἐπιβολάς suggests P.'s usual distinction between Greeks and Macedonians; cf. e.g. 2.71.8, 38.5.2, contrast 7.9.3 (quoted treaty with Philip V) Μακεδονίαν καὶ τὴν ἄλλην Ἑλλάδα. **μεταξύ** 'in mid-narrative'; cf. 38.5.2 μεταξὺ ταύτην [siege] ἀπολιπόντες [in narrative]. ἀπέρριψε is more loaded than ἀπολιπόντες: it conveys suddenness and contempt. **μεταλαβών** 'changing'; cf. e.g. 4.74.1 μεταλαβεῖν τὰς ἀγωγὰς τῶν βίων. But a plural object is usual in this sense, and Valesius' μεταβαλών is tempting; §7 [καθὸ μετάβαλε τὴν ὑπόθεσιν] may indicate the original form of the phrase. **ὑπόθεσιν:** Theopompus changed his basic subject from Greece to Philip; P. will make a sort of new beginning after 168/7 (3.4.13), but keeps the same ὑπόθεσις (3.5.8–9). **προύθετο** 'proposed'; cf. e.g. 1.13.7. τὰς Φιλίππου πράξεις προύθετο γράφειν at the end of the half-sentence undoes ἐπιβαλόμενος γράφειν τὰς Ἑλληνικὰς πράξεις at the beginning.

**11.4 σεμνότερον ἦν καὶ δικαιότερον:** in effect 'would have been', but the alternative was an option at the time. Cf. 3.15.10, 11.28.7 δοκῶ γάρ, ἦν τοῦτο βέλτιον, K–G I 215–16. P. supposes that Theopompus could have continued with his *Hellenica* and included Philip's deeds; such an extension and the *Philippica* were alternative ways of covering the same years. For the pair cf. *IG* IV.597.4–5 (Argos, Roman period) σεμνῶς καὶ δικαίως. At Cic. *Att.* 2.1.3, Demosthenes aimed to seem σεμνότερος by moving from court speeches to *Philippics*; here Greece is a grander subject than one Macedonian king, however admirable. Justice often includes a recognition that one person deserves more than another: cf. e.g. *SVF* III 262.27–8 δικαιοσύνην δὲ ἐπιστήμην ἀπονεμητικὴν τῆς ἀξίας ἑκάστωι. **συμπεριλαβεῖν:** for including in a category, etc., cf. e.g. Theophr. *HP* 7.1.1. **Φιλίππου:** the topic is really Philip's deeds, but cf. §3 τὴν μὲν Ἑλλάδα (for the genitive with ὑπόθεσις cf. Plut. *Lyc.* 34.2); ἐν τῆι Φιλίππου τὰ τῆς Ἑλλάδος is neater without περί.

**11.5 οὐδὲ γὰρ προκαταληφθείς:** even if someone had been initially constrained to write of kings, before having the chance (ἐξουσίας) to treat Greece. Constraint, not 'devotion' (Loeb): cf. δυναστείας (2.39.7 ὑπὸ δὲ τῆς Διονυσίου Συρακοσίου δυναστείας ... ἐμποδισθέντες), ἐξουσίας (3.111.2 δοθείσης αὐτοῖς ἐξουσίας, *PL* 1, 2) and 8.8 above; 16.2.8 περικαταλαμβανόμενος τοῖς καιροῖς. The alternative of *Hellenica* with some Philip (§4) is recommended by asserting that anyone would have changed to it; no one would have changed as Theopompus did.   **ἐπέσχε** 'have hesitated to, held back from'. Cf. e.g. 7.12.4 τοῦ δ' ἐπισχόντος; 9.1.6, DC 285.19 for inf. (with sense 'restrain').   **σὺν καιρῶι** 'at this the opportune moment'; cf. e.g. 6.43.3, 18.13.8.   **ποιήσασθαι μετάβασιν:** more than changing the subject within a work (2.37.3 μεταβαίνειν to Greek affairs, Procl. *in Remp.* 1.12 ποιεῖσθαι τὴν μετάβασιν from soul to city); a little less than a total change of work. Cf. Suet. *Claud.* 41.2 *initium autem sumpsit historiae post caedem Caesaris dictatoris sed transiit ad inferiora tempora coepitque a pace ciuili*.   **πρόσωπον** 'character', as in a play or narrative; cf. Plut. *Sen. Rep.* 791e: Arrhidaeus ἦν ὄνομα βασιλέως καὶ πρόσωπον (there a sham). Greece replaces the king, so is treated as a person; cf. βίον below, and Dicaearchus' and Jason's Βίος [biography] τῆς Ἑλλάδος (see Verhasselt (2018) 7–11).   **ἐπὶ ποσόν** 'for a bit', let alone the substantial progress ascribed to Theopompus in §3. See Introduction §13 c n. 65.   **οὐδ' ὅλως οὐδείς:** in the idiom οὐδ' ὅλως, οὐδέ does not connect; cf. e.g. 6.3.3, 18.18.16. The strengthened negation gives emphasis beyond the previous οὐδείς; cf. e.g. 13.3.1 οὐδαμῶς οὐδείς. There is an aesthetic as well as a political implication: structures of works and oeuvres should not decline in grandeur.   **ἠλλάξατο** 'have taken in exchange', i.e. for Greece. Cf. e.g. Philem. fr. 77.3 K–A (if tears helped) ἠλλαττόμεσθ' ἂν δάκρυα δόντες χρυσίον.   **μονάρχου** returns to the general discussion of 8.7–9 above.   **πρόσχημα** 'grandeur', of kings and consuls 6.33.12, 30.18.2, DS 2.6.10; LSJ II. A negative 'façade' would be awkward for the earlier argument on Philip II.   **ἀκεραίωι:** not affected by some pre-existing constraint; cf. e.g. 9.31.1 μὴ προεισδεδεμένους, ἀλλ' ἐξ ἀκεραίου βουλευομένους. The clause at the end of the sentence matches οὐδὲ γὰρ προκαταληφθεὶς κτλ. at the beginning.

**11.6 τί δήποτ'** 'whatever?': a marvelling question, not a straight lead into a known answer, as can be seen from τί δήποτ' at 1.64.1, 18.40.1, and from εἰ μὴ νὴ Δί'; contrast e.g. Dem. *Phil.* 3.37 τί οὖν ἦν τοῦτο; §5 has shown that Theopompus went for the wrong alternative; but if absolutely no one would have gone for it unconstrained, whatever can have forced Theopompus?   **τὰς τηλικαύτας ἐναντιώσεις** 'such great discrepancies'; ἐναντίωσις comes only here in P. What follows shows the change to the *Philippica* is still in mind; but the contradictions within the *Philippica* are suggested too.   **εἰ μὴ νὴ Δί'** with lively rhetoric hits on a thought as if it were far-fetched, as it is at 3.20.4: '– unless' (εἰ μὴ νὴ Δία) Romans have wisdom from birth.   **τὸ καλόν** and τὸ συμφέρον appear as the two primary motives for action, hard to reconcile, at e.g. 21.32c.1–3, 24.12.2. **τῆς δὲ κατὰ Φίλιππον**: more specific than ἐκείνης, to highlight the possibility of concrete advantages. We do not know what P. believed about Theopompus' biography.

**11.7 οὐ μὴν ἀλλά** 'yet'. With mobile rhetoric, P. now changes to think the shift to the *Philippica* might be defensible. He will seem all the more reasonable when he returns to condemn the attack on the friends of Philip. **[καθὸ μετάβαλε τὴν ὑπόθεσιν]**: abundant usage shows that καθό, 'inasmuch as', would not spell out what the ἁμαρτία consisted of, as if it were ὅτι. The phrase is more likely a marginal explanation of ἁμαρτία; cf. e.g. Σ Aeschin. 2.51 (no. 113 Dilts) φθονερός] καθὸ κτλ., (they called him 'mean') 'because he' etc., Σ Dem. *Phil.* 1.8 (no. 43b Dilts) (he calls them sluggish) 'because they' etc. **ἴσως ἂν εἶχέ τι λέγειν**: cf. the more aggressive 3.8.9–10, 30.9.5 ὃν εἴ τις ἤρετο τί βούλεται, πέπεισμαι μηδ' ἂν αὐτὸν ἔχειν εἰπεῖν. These passages recall Platonic imaginings, cf. esp. *Rep.* 1.332c5–8 εἰ οὖν τις αὐτὸν (Simonides) ἤρετο ... 'what do you think he would have answered?' A plea of external pressure could be imagined: cf. 8.8–9 above.

**11.8 αἰσχρολογίαν**: unseemly language, false in this case, but reprehensible anyway. Cf. 12.13.3 (Timaeus), Arist. *EN* 4.1128a19–25 (Old Comedy), Epict. 4.3.2. **λόγον ... ἀποδοῦναι** 'offer a coherent explanation'; cf. the absence of λόγος in his abuse, 10.12 above. For the combination cf. e.g. 3.37.11 (a different sort of λόγος), Plato, *Phaedo* 63e9. **συγχωρῆσαι**: ἄν is understood. The hypothesized agreement of Theopompus produces a harmonious note to close the vehement passage. **διότι**: meaning ὅτι; see 3.3n. **παρέπεσε**: cf. 33.6.4 παραπίπτειν τοῦ καθήκοντος. The criticism returns in part to P.'s requirement τὸν πρέποντα ταῖς ἑκάστων προαιρέσεσι λόγον ἐφαρμόζειν (8.7 above).

## 12 DEATH OF ARATUS

The Elder Aratus (271–213 BC) was from a leading family in Sicyon (O'Neil (1984–6) 37–8). He was the dominating figure of the Achaean League, and responsible for its expansion beyond its base in the north Peloponnese. P. is very positive about Aratus, and positive notes in P. are not simply the reflection of a source; in an early assessment, though, he characteristically sees two sides to the same person (4.8.1–12; cf. Meadows (2013) 93–4). In P. Aratus appears predominantly (books 4–5, 7–8) in relation to Philip V, to whom he gives good advice; he is conspired against by rival advisers, but unsuccessfully. In the end, though, Philip chooses wrongly; the killing of Aratus is closely interwoven with the decline of Philip. Aratus had realized that kings measure friendships by expediency

(2.47.5) when he decided in 225 to negotiate with Philip's predecessor Antigonus Doson (2.47.1–6). He himself was reversing League policy in approaching Macedon, for practical reasons (the enmity of Cleomenes III of Sparta and the Aetolians). Earlier P. has used – and added to – Aratus' *Memoirs*, and perhaps other material by him (cf. 2.47.11, 4.2.1, Meadows (2013)). He has certainly stopped this before book 7 (cf. 7.13.2–7). Plutarch's *Aratus*, the fullest source for Aratus, largely uses P. for these last years, but has other sources too. (For Aratus, and his and the Achaean League's relations with the Macedonian kings, see Walbank (1933), (1967) 14–16, 24–67, 221, 272, 299–300; Urban (1979) 117–59; Hammond and Walbank (1988) 381–3; Scherberich (2009) 60–8, 110–22; Stadter (2015); Nicholson (2023) 42–58, 193–6.)

**12.1 Φίλιππος δέ:** one would expect more transition from the digression 8.3–12.8; so some lacuna is probable. The transition could have been like 5.13.1 ὁ δὲ Φίλιππος – ἀπὸ γὰρ τούτων παρεξέβην –; cf. 2.36.1. The content follows on well from 8.1–2. It is a twist, after the prolonged digression, that Philip's attacks on Messenia now did not amount to much; οὐδὲν ἄξιον λόγου justifies an absence of narration, cf. 1.24.8, 5.17.1.   **πολεμίους γεγονότας:** treacherous change from Philip; cf. 7.11.10, 12.5–7, Plut. *Arat.* 51.2 τοὺς Μεσσηνίους αὖθις ἐπιχειρήσας φενακίζειν καὶ μὴ λαθών, ἠδίκει φανερῶς καὶ τὴν χώραν ἐπόρθει. The Messenians' official alliance with the Aetolians (9.30.6) probably came later. Cf. Scherberich (2009) 160. A neat contrast is created between not harming enemies much and harming friends greatly; this generates the movement to Aratus (§2).   **οὐδὲν ... ἠδυνήθη** contrasts with ἐπιβαλόμενος; cf. 16.3.8 οὐκ ἐδύνατο χωρισθῆναι, καίπερ πολλάκις ἐπιβαλόμενος πρύμναν κρούειν. Philip's treachery is not even successful. Yet 8.2 above suggests significant damage.   **ἀναγκαιοτάτους** 'closest'; cf. e.g. Jos. *AJ* 10.229 τοῖς ἀναγκαιοτάτους τῶν φίλων, P. Oxy. LI 3643.17–18 (ii AD) ἀναγκαιο|τάτου μοι φίλου. ἀναγκαιοτάτους is effectively opposed to μεγίστην.   **ἀσέλγειαν** 'unrestrained behaviour'; it does not really suit poisoning. P. does not mention here Philip's seduction of Aratus' daughter-in-law (Livy 27.31.8, 32.21.4, Plut. *Arat.* 49.1–2, 51.3). For the conjecture ἀσέβειαν cf. e.g. 8.4 above (εἰς τοὺς Μεσσηνίους), 38.18.10 ἀποδείξασθαι τὴν αὑτῶν ἀσέβειαν εἰς ὁμοφύλους.

**12.2 πρεσβύτερον:** as at 4.85.4, the specification does not seem essential, but hints at Aratus' age. Aratus was about 57, Philip about 24.   **δυσαρεστηθέντα** 'displeased' (and making his disapprobation known; cf. μετ' οὐ πολύ). Not a particularly strong word; Philip's reaction is the more disproportionate.   **ἐν τῆι Μεσσήνηι:** omitted by P, but cf. app. at §6 and §7; the phrase may be genuine.   **μετ' οὐ πολύ** adds to the plausibility – not that P. has doubts. Taurion's alleged collaboration confirms that Philip had now left the Peloponnese. Aratus is in Aegium (Plut. *Arat.* 52.3), the central city for the Achaean League. **Ταυρίωνος:** already ὁ ἐπὶ τῶν ἐν Πελοποννήσωι βασιλικῶν πραγμάτων under Antigonus Doson (4.6.4); a permanent and official position, cf. 4.87.1 Ταυρίωνα τὸν ἐπὶ τῶν ἐν Πελοποννήσωι τεταγμένον, 2, 5.95.5. **ἐπανείλετο:** the agency is Philip's, as e.g. at 22.14.5 (Philip φαρμάκωι διέφθειρεν Cassander, at a distance); cf. Paus. 2.9.4 ἀπέκτεινεν Ἄρατον, οὐδὲν προϊδομένωι δούς οἱ φάρμακον. Philip's poisoning of ἑταῖροι is attacked by his contemporary Alcaeus of Messene, *AP* 11.12, 11.12*a*.5–6 (om. 9.519). G's ἐπανείλετο comes at least 8 times elsewhere in P., PFD's ἐπανείλατο never.

**12.3 παραυτίκα μέν:** it is not immediately apparent that Aratus is ill (cf. γάρ), let alone that he has been poisoned, and by Philip (cf. §4 ἐγένετο δὲ δῆλον). Cf. e.g. 3.68.1 παραυτίκα μὲν ... μετ' οὐ πολὺ δέ. **τοῖς ἐκτός:** those not involved in the deed, cf. 38.3.2; contrast τόν γε μὴν Ἄρατον αὐτόν. **ἡ δύναμις** is assigned the actions of the drug itself; cf. Gal. *Meth. Med.* 6 x 392.16–393.2 Kühn. **χρόνον ἔχουσα:** cf. Suet. *Tib.* 73.2 *uenenum ... lentum atque tabificum.* **διάθεσιν ἐργαζομένη** 'producing a condition' needs more so as to be specific, whether an adjective is added (e.g. νοσώδη) or an adverb (e.g. βραδέως), or both. For διάθεσιν ἐργάζεσθαι with adjective cf. e.g. Gal. *Praes. Puls.* 1 ix 251.3–5 Kühn.

**12.4 οὐκ ἐλάνθανε:** for the earlier stages of an illness, and the refusal of some to recognize it, cf. e.g. Pers. 3.88–99, Sen. *Ep.* 53.5–6. But τὸ κακόν includes the cause; cf. δῆλον. At 4.4.6 καὶ τοῦτ' οὐκ ἐλάνθανε τὸν Δωρίμαχον is similarly short; but there the effect is humorous, here Aratus' wisdom is conveyed.

**12.5 ἅπαντας γὰρ ἐπικρυπτόμενος τοὺς ἄλλους** 'concealing the matter from everyone else'; cf. 3.75.1: wishing ἐπικρύπτεσθαι τούς ἐν τῆι Ῥώμηι τὸ γεγονός. The clause prepares for μετριότης and ἠισχύνετο in §6. **συνήθειαν:** συνηθ- indicates friendship; cf. e.g. 23.5.2, 31.23.3 (φιλία mentioned in both), *IG* xii.3.91.3 (friend of Philip; Nisyrus, *c.*200 BC). Plutarch's retelling removes friendship with a slave (*Arat.* 52.4 ἑνός γε τῶν συνήθων). In P., the fidelity of one of Aratus' friends, a slave, is contrasted with the treachery of another, a king; cf. φιλίας below. **οὐκ ἔστεξε** 'did not hide', cf. 4.8.2; the brevity of the word contrasts effectively with ἐπικρυπτόμενος. **ἐπιμελῶς:** looking after a sick master is a slave's duty (cf. Eur. *Or.* 221), but carried out in exemplary fashion. **αὐτῶι** is Aratus, Cephalon τοῦ προειρημένου. **ἀρρωστίαν:** an undefined 'illness', seen from Cephalon's perspective. **τι τῶν:** Aratus is evidently spitting frequently. **τοίχωι:** presumably to keep the sputum away from the area of the bed. **δίαιμον:** δίαιμος is found predominantly in medical texts. A single instance of blood might not seem too alarming, or unique to poisoning (cf. e.g. Hipp. *Artic.* 50 II 185–8 Kühlewein); but Philo of Tarsus *SH* 690.7–8 thinks spitting blood life-threatening. **τἀπίχειρα** 'reward, payment', generally figurative. For the demonstrative and the relatively unusual sense of undeserved ill-treatment see 4.79.3 ταῦτα γὰρ ἐπίχειρα τότε τοῖς Αἰτωλῶν ἐγίνετο συμμάχοις. Cf. Soph. *Trach.* 540–2 τοιάδ'... οἰκούρι' ἀντέπεμψε τοῦ μακροῦ χρόνου. The narrative gives the word order force: the names contrast, and the separated τῆς πρὸς Φίλιππον points to a contrast with the friendship of Aratus and Cephalon. All this is lost in Plut. *Arat.* 52.4 'ταῦτ',' εἶπεν, 'ὦ Κεφάλων, τἀπίχειρα τῆς βασιλικῆς φιλίας.'

**12.6 οὕτως:** not here a sort of exclamation, cf. 7.7n., but leading on to ὥστε. See for μέγα χρῆμα 7.7n. and 12.15.8 (person); 9.14.5 (astronomy). As P.'s grandiose reworking of Aratus' utterance will show (εἰ κτλ.), P.'s manner here is in counterpoint with Aratus' character: μετριότης conceals, exalted praise reverses that concealment. μέτριος is used of expression too; cf. e.g. DH *Isocr.* 3, *Dem.* 18, 21. **ὁ παθών**, which P omits, is needed, as masc. κεκοινωνηκώς indicates; it creates pointed paradox. οἱ παθόντες and οἱ πράξαντες are similarly opposed at 36.4 above, cf. 36.8, and at 2.7.1. **ᾐσχύνετο:** for shame from the victim, with εἰ of what is actually the case, cf. Luc. *Prom.* 7 αἰσχύνομαι ὑπὲρ τοῦ Διὸς εἰ κτλ.; see also P. 3.33.17 (εἰ twice). **τοσούτων καὶ τηλικούτων** 'so many and so great'; also at 10.33.2, Isoc. *Pac.* 140, etc. In recasting Aratus' utterance, P. lays emphasis, not on the obligations of friendship, but on the benefits which Aratus conferred. The ἔργα will be especially those of the Social War (220–217), in which the Achaean League and Macedon fought the Aetolians and Sparta (Walbank (1933) 114–55; 153 for Philip's gains from the war). **κεκόμισται:** perfect, so from the present of Aratus' perspective then. **εὐνοίας:** close to friendship, cf. 5.37.2 εὔνοια καὶ συνήθεια; 7.9.4 (treaty) περὶ φιλίας καὶ εὐνοίας καλῆς, *BCH* 59 (1935), 66.16 (Larisa, 109/8 BC) φιλίαν καὶ εὔνοιαν. But εὔνοια stresses more the wish to benefit.

**12.7 μὲν οὖν:** P. introduces his own memorialization of Aratus' death. Cf. 5.39.6 Κλεομένης μὲν οὖν οὕτω μετήλλαξε τὸν βίον, followed by praise. P. speaks at 18.41.1 of his custom of obituaries (21.10n.); this is the grandest, though not the longest, example. **ἀρχῆς:** Aratus was elected the *strategos* of the Achaean League most alternate years from 245 to 213 (the office could not be held in consecutive years). See Plut. *Arat.* 24.5, Walbank (1933) 167–75. No one else approached this dominance (Buraselis (2019) 209). The magistracy was both military and political; cf. P. 2.43.1–5, Rizakis (2015) 123, 128. **διὰ τὸ πλῆθος καὶ διὰ τὸ μέγεθος** takes up τοσούτων καὶ τηλικούτων (§6): the Achaeans, unlike

Philip, rewarded Aratus fittingly. Through Aratus the League acquired more cities, and defeated their enemies the Aetolians, at the price of cooperation with Macedon. ἔθνος: this designation of the Achaeans as a group need not carry implications about origins. For the term cf. 2.37.7, 40.5, 44.5, etc., Beck and Funke (2015b) 14, 20, 25; Ager (2019) 175–6.    ἔτυχε: Aratus remains a person even after death; cf. §8.    καὶ παρὰ τῆι πατρίδι καὶ παρὰ τῶι κοινῶι: Plutarch tells of a dispute between Sicyon and the League as to where Aratus should be buried (*Arat.* 53.1); this version has been doubted (Hughes (2019)). P. includes no such disharmony. §8 implies the League contributed to the cult too.

**12.8** ἡρωϊκάς goes with θυσίας too; cf. *IG* ii².1035.27 (early i BC) τὰς τῶ]ν ἡρώων θυσίας καὶ τιμ[ά]ς. Plut. *Arat.* 53 gives far more detail on the burial and cult at Sicyon, no doubt from a historian, who may have used an inscription (so Hughes (2019)). P., though, is making an exception to his usual silence on heroic and divine cult for those who have just died (12.23.3–6 on Alexander, to make a point against Timaeus). Cf. Habicht (2017) 1 n. 3, 145–9. *IG* iv².622 (Epidaurus, ii BC?) is the base of a massive statue of Aratus, perhaps as hero: ] Ἀράτοιο πελώριον ω[ (1).    ὅσα πρὸς αἰώνιον ἀνῆκει μνήμην: 'belong to'; cf. 18.14.8 ὅσα πρὸς δόξαν καὶ τιμὴν ἀνῆκεν. The language is that of official commemoration; cf. *IGR* iv.292.20 (Pergamum, ii BC?) honours πρὸς αἰώνιον μνή[μην (ἀνηκούσαις?)], *TAM* ii.247.1 (W. Lycia, AD 146) τὸ ἡρῶιον κατεσκεύασεν εἰς αἰώνιον μνήμην.    εἴπερ καὶ περὶ τοὺς ἀποιχομένους ἔστι τις αἴσθησις: so far, solemnly conventional language – yet surprising in a history (Tac. *Agr.* 46.1 comes in the biography of Tacitus' father-in-law). Cf. e.g. Isocr. *Evag.* 2 ἡγησάμην Εὐαγόραν, εἴ τίς ἐστιν αἴσθησις τοῖς τετελευτηκόσιν ... χαίρειν [cf. εὐδοκεῖν] ὁρῶντα τήν τε περὶ αὐτὸν ἐπιμέλειαν κτλ., Hyper. 6.43 (εἰ, αἴσθησις, εἰκός), Cat. 96 (1 *si*, 6 *gaudet*).    καὶ ... καί: the pleasure is also, less obviously, in the sufferings of life, which forcefully conclude the obituary.    τῆι τῶν Ἀχαιῶν εὐχαριστίαι: the contrast with Philip is clear. The League matters more than Sicyon.    κακοπραγίαις καὶ κινδύνοις: Aratus is pleased not just because the trials have now passed (Hom. *Od.* 15.400 μετὰ γάρ τε καὶ ἄλγεσι τέρπεται ἀνήρ, etc.), but because of what that arduous life achieved.

## 13–14: LISSUS

Philip had for some years been engaged in Illyria: to the east Illyria bordered Macedonia; its west coast faced onto Italy, and the Romans controlled parts of it. Philip no doubt wished to reduce Rome's hold in that area (7.9.13, from Hannibal's treaty with Philip), and to combat the aggressive Illyrian ruler Scerdilaidas (5.108.1–3). In P.'s presentation, he hoped to master all Illyria (5.110.10), and cross to Italy and start conquering

(5.101.8–10, 108.4–5). Lissus, with Acrolissus on the adjoining larger hill, was an important place to capture: it was the first city close to the sea north of the Romans' area of control. The treaty of 228 BC, after the First Illyrian War, forbade Illyrian military ships to sail beyond Lissus (2.12.3, App. *Ill.* 21). It was most likely just an Illyrian city: the assertion that it was founded by Syracuse (DS 15.13.5) probably rests on a confusion with Issa (cf. Ps.-Scymn. 413–14, DS 15.14.2). P.'s close narrative of the capture is subtler than modern accounts which just portray Philip's strategic brilliance; it conveys the unlooked-for development of events. (On Lissus and Philip see Praschniker and Schober (1919) 13–26; Wilkes (1969) 9, 17–22, (1992) 130, 133, 135; Prendi and Zheku (1972); Pochmarski and Hoxha (2005) 245–8; Kleu (2017). For the events in wider perspectives, see Introduction §12 e, and May (1946); Walbank (1967) 68–82; Cabanes (1988) 297–8; Wilkes (1992) 156–68; Eckstein (2010) 230–2.)

## 13 PHILIP ATTACKS LISSUS

**13.1 πάλαι δέ:** a new extract starts here, as is shown by the title in F's margin, and by D's dicolon (:) and new paragraph. There is no indication of a new subject; so after 12.8 there must be a gap, probably considerable.

Fig 2 Lissus and Acrolissus; image (colour) by Shkelzen Rexha; licence https://creativecommons.org/licenses/by-sa/4.0/deed.en; see https://commons.wikimedia.org/wiki/File:Varri_i_Sk%C3%ABnderbeut_%26_Kalaja_-_Lezh%C3%AB.jpg

Philip had been concerned with Illyria since at least 219, and still more 217 (cf. 5.101.8–102.1); Roman successes on the coast in 214 will have intensified his interest (cf. May (1946) 50–1).   τῆι διανοίαι περὶ τὸν Λίσσον καὶ τὸν Ἀκρόλισσον ὤν 'his thoughts were on …'. Cf. 9.5.9 ἔτι τῶν ἐν Ῥώμηι ταῖς διανοίαις περὶ τὴν Καπύην καὶ τὰς ἐκεῖ πράξεις ὄντων. Lissus, rising above mod. Lezhë in Albania, had its own acropolis, and was physically separate from the higher hill beside it, which had Acrolissus on the top (see Figure 2). But §3 τῆς δὲ πόλεως confirms that Acrolissus was not a πόλις itself. See Strabo 7.5.8 (II 306.1 Radt), Steph. Byz. λ 79 Billerbeck Λίσσος· πόλις Ἰλλυρίας, καὶ Ἀκρόλισσος.   ἐγκρατής: Lissus will have been in the control of Scerdilaidas; cf. Vollmer (1990) 146.

**13.2 ποιησάμενος δὲ τὴν πορείαν** 'having marched'. The two days and the route leave the starting point mysterious to us; it will have appeared before §1.   κατέζευξε 'set up camp'; cf. e.g. 18.20.5. It is not clear whether Philip camps north or south of Lissus (cf. Walbank (1957–79) II 91–3).   Ἀρδάξανον: only here. The part of the Drin close to Lissus would be called Drilon (Call. fr. 744 Pfeiffer, Nic. *Ther.* 607, Strabo 7.5.7 (II 304.3 Radt)). The Mat at present is *c.*6 km from Lissus, quite far for οὐ μακράν and θεωρῶν (§3). The Ardaxanus is placed *c.*29 km from Lissus in *Barrington* 49 B2 (cf. Brizzi (1973)) – much too far.

**13.3 θεωρῶν** 'seeing that'; cf. e.g. 1.28.10, 3.103.7. Philip, as presented, has not had prior information.   τε … τε: the structure leads readers to think that Philip will despair of both; cf. 14.10 below παραδόξως.   περίβολον: for the fortifications of Lissus, see Prendi and Zheku (1972).   πρὸς θαλάττηι: idiomatic without the article, as in F; cf. 1.56.3, 12.21.5, etc. With it, P. offers only 18.1.5 πρὸς τὴν θάλατταν; the article is more likely to have been added than removed.   πρὸς τὴν μεσόγαιον: facing inland; cf. e.g. 13.4.6.   ἠσφαλισμένον διαφερόντως 'exceptionally well secured'. Cf. esp. 9.27.3 ὁ δὲ περίβολος αὐτῆς (Acragas) καὶ φύσει καὶ κατασκευῆι διαφερόντως ἠσφάλισται.   φύσει: the hill is particularly in mind.   κατασκευῆι: fortifications, as in 9.27.3 above.   αὐτῶι: Lissus; it goes with παρακείμενον.   τὴν εἰς ὕψος ἀνάτασιν 'its extension upwards'; the same phrase at 5.44.3, 10.13.8, cf. 9.26a.10 εἰς ὕψος ἀνατεταμένας, 18.22.9.   ἐρυμνότητα: P. uses ἐρυμν- especially of steep hills and mountains difficult to attack or climb up (3.47.9 τὰς ἐρυμνότητας of the Alps).   φαντασίαν: commonly of an imposing first impression, often misleading; cf. e.g. 11.3.7 φαντασίαν μὲν ἔχειν ἔφη (words contrasted with truth), 12.25d.4 τοιαύτην ἐφέλκεται (*sc.* medical theory) φαντασίαν ὥστε δοκεῖν μηδένα τῶν ἄλλων κρατεῖν τοῦ πράγματος (but practice exposes its uselessness). Here events are ironically prepared.   κατὰ κράτος 'by assault'.

## COMMENTARY: 13.3–13.6

For despairing of capture by assault cf. 7.1, 5–6 above; 7.15.4 (Sardis). ἀπέστη τελέως: more ironic preparation; cf. 14.9 below ἀνέλπιστον (with a twist). Philip does not foresee the capture of Acrolissus. οὐ λίαν 'not all that much'; cf. e.g. 12.25f.4 οὐ λίαν ἐκφανῆ 'not all that clear'. The turn in the sentence is gently understated; 'not at all' would have given crude heroics. Philip's πρᾶξις καὶ τόλμα πολεμική (4.77.3) quietly emerge.

**13.4 συνθεωρήσας** takes up θεωρῶν at the beginning of the previous sentence (§3): sight is now solving problems sight had perceived. συν- is for variation: συνθεωρήσας at 7.15.6 and 9 begins sentences after θεωρῶν/-ῆσαι in 4 and 7 (cf. also 7.17.7 and 6). τὸ μεταξὺ διάστημα 'the interval in between', with genitive; so too 3.37.4, 66.1. πρόποδος: the part of a hill or mountain that comes forward at the bottom, originally like the front foot of one striding (cf. Ptol. *Synt.* 7 (12.92.16 Heiberg)). So 3.17.2, Strabo 13.1.5 (III 532.13 Radt). σύμμετρον: spatially suitable, with διάστημα 33.6 below, 2.25.4. κατὰ τοῦτο goes with συστησάμενος ἀκροβολισμόν; the stratagem involves a different place (see §5). συστησάμενος ἀκροβολισμόν: an attack from light-armed troops (cf. §6) is a standard beginning to action; but even apart from the stratagem, things get more complicated (14.2). For συνίσταμαι of making ἀκροβολισμοί happen cf. 2.54.10. στρατηγήματι: curiosity is built up by πρὸς τὸ παρὸν οἰκείωι, and the following δέ (§5). γάρ and an immediate explanation would be expected: cf. 1.27.7, 3.18.9, 78.1, etc.

**13.5 δοὺς δὲ μίαν ἡμέραν:** Philip is not in a rush (contrast 5.7.3–6); readers are tantalized. παρακαλέσας ... τὰ πρέποντα τῶι καιρῶι: this phrase and variants, e.g. 5.53.6 παρεκάλει ... τὰ πρέποντα τοῖς καιροῖς, appear 14 times in P. and nowhere else. The speech is not even summarized. ἐν αὐτῆι: during the day. χρησιμώτατον: of the best soldiers at 11.24.6. εὐζώνων: light-armed forces, here needed to move swiftly in tricky terrain. ἔτι νυκτός: for secrecy. The Illyrians know Philip is about (§8), but are not observing closely. εἰς: with κρύπτω e.g. DS 4.12.2. φάραγγας ὑλώδεις 'wooded gullies', rather than the usual ὑλώδεις τόποι (3.40.12, 71.2, etc.): the double means of hiding is brought out (cf. 14.7 ἀφανῶς, and 3.18.10 κοίλους). κατὰ τὸν ἐπὶ τῆς μεσογαίου τόπον: as opposed to the side of Lissus facing the sea; cf. 14.7 ἐπὶ τῆς μεσογαίας. ὑπέρ: looking down onto rather than directly above; cf. e.g. 5.55.7 κατὰ τοὺς ὑπὲρ τὸν Φᾶσιν τόπους.

**13.6 δέ:** the μέν and δέ clauses correspond – forces, time, place. ἐπὶ θάτερα τῆς πόλεως and κατὰ θάλατταν answer κατὰ τὸν ἐπὶ τῆς μεσογαίου τόπον and ὑπὲρ τὸ προειρημένον διάστημα. πελταστάς: distinguished from the κοῦφοι in 14.2 below (cf. 5.7.11), and from φαλαγγῖται at 18.24.8 (cf. 1) and elsewhere. They are in σπεῖραι (14.5). They are obviously more suitable than φαλαγγῖται for this locale; they seem to be highly skilled fighters (cf. *SEG* XLIX.855 B.2–3, 8–12, Amphipolis, *c*.200 BC). It is not clear how exactly they were armed, in this period. See Hatzopoulos (2001) 66–73; Sekunda (2007) 339.   ἐπαύριον 'the next day'; see Introduction §13 c.

**13.7 περιελθών:** Lissus, on top of a hill, did not actually adjoin the sea (cf. Caes. *BC* 3.28.1); the main port may have been Nymphaeum (3.26.4, 27.1), a mile to the north.   ταύτηι stands out emphatically, straight after ὡς and before the elaborate phrase that follows (cf. 18.24.1; shorter 10.30.6).

**13.8 οὐκ ἀγνοουμένης:** usually the phrase is first-person in P. and elsewhere, οὐκ ἀγνοῶ *vel sim*. Here the dry manner suggests any hopes of escaping notice were unlikely to be realized.   **παρουσίας:** presence in the vicinity rather than now at this spot – the reinforcements must have taken a little while to arrive. Cf. 18.3n.   **ἦν ... ἠθροισμένον:** pluperfect; cf. e.g. 3.40.3 πρότερον ἦσαν ... προκεχειρισμένοι.   ἁπάσης suggests that Philip has not just taken, say, Scorda.

**13.9 διὰ τὴν ὀχυρότητα πιστεύοντες:** ironic preparation; cf. 14.1 below and 7.15.2 ὅταν πιστεύσαντες ταῖς ὀχυρότησι ... ἀφυλακτῶσι.   **μετρίαν τινα τελέως** 'extremely limited'; cf. 2.56.10 πάνυ μέτρια. The phrase is highlighted by separation from φυλακήν.

## 14 LISSUS AND ACROLISSUS CAPTURED

**14.1 διόπερ:** the connection with the previous sentence is underlined in the participial clause, where θαρροῦντες takes up πιστεύοντες, πλήθει πλῆθος and ὀχυρότησι ὀχυρότητα.   **ἅμα τῶι συνεγγίζειν ... εὐθέως ... ἐξεχέοντο** shows their confidence and their multitude; cf. e.g. 1.19.3 εὐθέως ... ἐξεχέοντο καὶ θρασέως ἐπέκειντο τοῖς Νομάσιν, Hom. *Il*. 16.259 αὐτίκα δὲ σφήκεσσιν ἐοικότες ἐξεχέοντο, Ap. Rhod. *Arg*. 1.879, 883 ἐκχύμεναι, προχέοντο (like bees).

**14.2 ἐν τοῖς ἐπιπέδοις ἐπέστησε:** the peltasts are evidently wearing armour, and so are less suited to running up the hill. Their firm and static position contrasts with both ἐξεχέοντο and προβαίνειν.   **τοὺς λόφους:** since no one is descending from the Acrolissus, Lissus must be mainly in question.   **συμπλέκεσθαι πρὸς τοὺς πολεμίους ἐρρωμένως:** similarly 16.2.8

COMMENTARY: 14.2–14.5

(of Philip's ships); for πρός cf. 4.11.7. Philip is using his εὔζωνοι in an innovative way; he is also demanding a lot of the less able and numerous group of them, as the armed enemy (cf. §4) come down the hill to them at speed.

**14.3 ποιούντων:** the subject is omitted; cf. e.g. 2.8.8 καταπαυσάντων δὲ τὸν λόγον. It is characteristic of P. to state explicitly that orders were obeyed; cf. e.g. 3.69.7 τῶν δὲ πραξάντων τὸ προσταχθέν.   **ἐπὶ ποσόν:** see 11.5n. above.   **κίνδυνος** 'conflict'. Cf. e.g. 1.51.2 τὸ μὲν πρῶτον ἰσόρροπος ἦν ὁ κίνδυνος, 5.69.8 ἡ μὲν ναυμαχία πάρισον εἶχε τὸν κίνδυνον; *I.Lindos* I.2 D.114–15 (99 BC) ὅπλα οἷς | αὐτὸ[ς ἐ]χ[ρ]εῖτο ἐν τοῖς κινδύ[ν]οι[ς] ('battles').   **πάρισος** 'equal' or 'roughly equal'; except as a rhetorical term, it is mostly used by P. and Strabo.   **δυσχωρίαις** takes up ὀχυρότησι (§1) from a different perspective; πλήθει takes up πλήθει (§1). The Illyrians' view seems confirmed.

**14.4 τούτων:** the εὔζωνοι.   **εἰς** draws on the more figurative sense of fleeing to a person for refuge; cf. e.g. Plato, *Laws* 2.669b7 καταφυγὴν αὑτοῖς εἰς αὑτοὺς μόνους εἶναι, Lys. 18.22 εἰς τίνας ... δικαστὰς καταφυγεῖν;, [Dem.] 47.14 καταφεύγειν δὲ εἰς τὴν ἄνθρωπον.   **καταφρονήσαντες:** absolute, not governing τούτων; cf. e.g. 3.90.3, 4.3.3. In this context, it further sets up the reversal, narratologically.   **προήιεσαν** (3rd pl. impf. of πρόειμι) matches the original προβαίνειν (§2) of the εὔζωνοι.   **ἐν τοῖς ἐπιπέδοις ... τοῖς πελτασταῖς** picks up §2 τοὺς μὲν οὖν πελταστὰς ... ἐν τοῖς ἐπιπέδοις. The Illyrians are showing further confidence; the εὔζωνοι are no longer of importance.

**14.5 θεωροῦντες:** they have a clearer view than those on the ground; but the retreat shows the narrative moving on in time from the οἱ μέν clause (§4).   **ἐκ διαδοχῆς:** one σπεῖρα after another. Cf. 3.116.8: attacking ἐκ διαδοχῆς ταῖς ἴλαις. The dative is not dependent on διαδοχῆς.   **ταῖς σπείραις ἐπὶ πόδα:** by units and facing the enemy, without turning (LSJ πούς 6b); cf. 2.33.7 τὴν ἐπὶ πόδα ταῖς σπείραις ἀναχώρησιν, where this orderly mode of retreat is called particular to Rome. Macedonian σπεῖραι have their own σπειράρχης: Moretti, *ISE* II.14.B col. i.12, 17 (Amphipolis, *c*.200 BC). But the relatively level ground does not seem to offer all that much room for forces, unless they extend beyond the διάστημα.   **τοῖς ὅλοις** 'completely'; cf. e.g. 3.112.8, 11.2.10 σφαλεὶς τοῖς ὅλοις.   **ἔλαθον ἐκκληθέντες** 'did not realize they were being lured out'; the aorist participle matches the aorist verb. Cf. 3.84.12 and LSJ λανθάνω A 2b for the implied ἑαυτούς; for ἐκκαλέω e.g. 18.22.9–10, Philip ἐκκληθῆναι πρὸς τὸν κίνδυνον, despite his initial judgement, through extreme εὐελπιστία.   **πιστεύειν:** cf. 13.9 πιστεύοντες.

**14.6 κατ' ὀλίγους:** to be contrasted with the masses moving together from Lissus (§1). It is not an organized movement; individuals wish to appropriate plunder. **ἐκλιπόντες τὸν Ἀκρόλισσον:** 'Acrolissus' applies only to the fortified area at the top, not the whole hill. **κατέρρεον:** a vivid verb, not of smoothly flowing movement; rather, an eagerly abrupt and tumbling descent. Cf. e.g. Thuc. 7.84.3 κατέρρεον ('they rushed down', Pelling ad loc.). §4 συγκαταβάντες is less colourful. **ἀνοδίαις:** no terrain for ordinary progress; cf. e.g. 4.58.10 τὸ δὲ κατὰ τῶν κρημνῶν φεῦγον ταῖς ἀνοδίαις, Livy 23.17.6 *per uias inuiaque ... perfugerunt*. **πεδινούς:** from πεδίον. ὁμαλοὺς καὶ πεδινούς captures the sensation of reaching manageable ground more graphically than §4 ἐπιπέδοις. **ἐκ <τῆς> τροπῆς:** ἐκ ($G^{mg}$) is better than καί (FDG). The rout has already happened, cf. §3 ἐτράπησαν, and 'booty and rout' is the wrong order. But the article is now needed, as in 1.9.5 τῆς ἐκείνων τροπῆς. For ἐκ with ὠφέλεια cf. 11.6.3.

**14.7 οἱ ... διειληφότες ... οἱ πελτασταί:** after the actions of two groups of Illyrians, οἱ ... οἱ (§4, §5), two groups of Macedonians seize the initiative. **ἐπὶ τῆς μεσογαίας:** cf. 13.5 above ἐπὶ [here too a conjecture] τῆς μεσογαίου. διειληφότες relates in tense to ἐξαναστάντες: they had divided up the places of their inland concealment. With ἐξαναστάντες the ambush ends; cf. §8 ὑπὸ τῶν ἐκ τῆς ἐνέδρας ἐξαναστάντων, 20.5 below. It makes little sense to have the men leave their original places (ἐκ FDG) and put fresh ambushes in the small gap between Lissus and Acrolissus (cf. *PL* διαλαμβάνω 1). In §8 they are not divided now: ὑπὸ τῶν κτλ., not ὑπό τινων τῶν κτλ. **ἀφανῶς** and ἀφανής come only three times in P. ἀφανῶς is set against ἐνεργόν: though emerging unseen, they move with vigorous speed. **τὴν πορείαν:** movement before the attack suits the topography; cf. 10.32.4 ἐξαναστάντες καὶ παρὰ πλάγια ποιησάμενοι τὴν πορείαν, 49.3 πορείαι χρώμενος ἐνεργῶι. Most likely the source of FDG skipped from τήν to τήν. **ἅμα δὲ τούτοις** matches κατὰ δὲ τὸν καιρὸν τοῦτον in an accumulation of surprises. **ἐκ μεταβολῆς:** in an unexpected reversal. Cf. e.g. 5.52.12, 22.9.12.

**14.8 οὗ συμβάντος:** both the events in §7. **διαταραχθέντες:** readers expect double disaster for the Illyrians; but, with a typical Polybian twist, the outcome is more complicated. **σποράδην ποιούμενοι τὴν ἀναχώρησιν:** contrast §5 ἐκ διαδοχῆς ταῖς σπείραις ἐπὶ πόδα ποιούμενον τὴν ἀναχώρησιν, Philip's orderly retreat – and that was feigned. Readers are being deceived as to the immediate outcome. **διεσώιζοντο** 'safely reached'; cf. 2.11.6, 15.15.3 (with εἰς). P. typically uses the verb of those who escape unexpectedly or with difficulty. The imperfect may hint that the outcome is not final. Cf. 3.116.1: Paullus ἔτι τότε διεσώιζετο; 9: Paullus dies. Contrast ἀπετμήθησαν.  πρὸς τὴν πόλιν neatly reverses ἐκ τοῦ Λίσσου at the start.  ἀπετμήθησαν: the run of the sentence suggests that they are cut off, not from the force now fleeing, but from the Acrolissus. At 10.32.4 (§7n.), those coming from an ambush ἀποτέμνονται the generals from their own camp; cf. also Hom. *Il.* 22.455–6 Ἕκτορα δῖος Ἀχιλλεύς | μοῦνον ἀποτμήξας πόλιος (as Andromache fears). There has been quick thinking by those in charge of the ambush.

**14.9 διὸ καὶ συνέβη** proceeds to a further stage, with a glance at §8 συμβάντος; cf. 15.25.7 συνέβη, 8 διὸ καὶ συνέβη.  ἀνέλπιστον: Philip captures both places παραδόξως (§10), but there is a more refined point here. The more daunting Acrolissus fell at once and with no battle, Lissus only the next day and μετὰ μεγάλων ἀγώνων. The narrative is elegantly shaped.  ἐνεργοὺς καὶ καταπληκτικάς: P. uses this combination 6 times, especially of attacks; otherwise, only at DS 17.24.3. ἐνεργούς here connects with §7 ἐνεργόν: all the army shows this vigour.

**14.10 Φίλιππος:** Philip returns to end the narrative. He has been absent since §3, and developments have not been entirely his work; but he now appears as their architect. He fulfils his initial aim ἐγκρατὴς γενέσθαι τῶν τόπων τούτων (13.1), cf. ἐγκρατὴς γενόμενος τῶν προειρημένων τόπων; he does so παραδόξως, thanks partly to events. But §11 shows that people attributed everything to him.  ἅπαντας τοὺς πέριξ: cf. 13.8 ἁπάσης τῆς πέριξ Ἰλλυρίδος. Lissus seems to have a dominating position in the area, in spite of nearby Scodra. ἅπαντας and ταύτης go strikingly together: this one deed is enough. πλείστους widens its impact still further. This passage suggests that Philip conquers Scodra too (numismatic evidence is indecisive: see Kleu (2017)). Philip seems to have acquired the territory to the south previously in Roman hands; cf. Livy 27.30.13, 29.12.3, 13, with P. 7.9.13. Zon. 9.6 p. 268 Dindorf has Philip sailing as far south as Corcyra, but that would not demonstrate possession of land. The poetic-looking πέριξ is common in P., but also Aristotle, and probably comes in *IG* VII.2712.33 (Acraephia, after AD 37).  ἐθελοντήν: this adverb comes much more often in P. than in other authors; it is not found in documents. As the γάρ-clause shows, the willingness means only avoidance of a siege rather than actual enthusiasm. Similarly e.g. 2.54.13.

**14.11 ὀχυρότης** and **ἀσφάλεια** take up 13.3 ἠσφαλισμένον and 9 ὀχυρότητα: if Lissus and Acrolissus were not safe, nowhere is. ὀχυρότης and ὀχυρωμάτων ring the sentence pointedly. The stem is repeated thus in P. only at 7.15.2–3 ὀχυρότησι, ὀχυρωτάτους, ὀχυρότητος (the first two generalizing, then Sardis).  τὴν Φιλίππου βίαν: such genitives with βία are not common in P. with individual people (sometimes of rivers and fire); but cf. 16.22a.5: safety seemed hopeless to those who fought πρὸς τὴν ὁρμὴν καὶ βίαν τὴν Ἀλεξάνδρου. βίαν is followed through with μετὰ βίας: cunning and luck are not dwelt on. **τῶν προειρημένων ὀχυρωμάτων:** the expression goes beyond §10 τῶν προειρημένων τόπων. Cf., for here and 13.3, the laudatory *I.Iasos* 612.19–20 (Bargylia, *c.*127 BC) τὰ ὀχυρώ|[ματα πάντα] δοκοῦντα εἶναι δυσάλωιτα [κατὰ] κράτος λαβόντος (M.' Aquilius (cos. 129)).

**14b.1 Δασσαρῆται:** this people, like the city Hyscana (14b.2), show Philip campaigning further east in Illyria. The Dassaretai are in the region of Lake Lychnidus (Lake Ohrid), as is seen from *IG* x.2.2.357, 362, 369, 371 (found in Ohrid, ii–iii AD), inscriptions of the Δασσαρήτιοι. See Papazoglu (1957) 224–30, 378, first map. Philip had already been concerned with this area (5.108.2, 8).

**14b.2 Ὕσκανα** (or smooth breathing?), neuter; *Vscana* (not *Huscana*) feminine in Livy. At 43.18.5 it is *maxima urbs* of the territory of the Penestae. See Papazoglu (1957) 217–18, (1988) 75–6, 293. The exact location is uncertain.

## 15–21 THE FALL OF ACHAEUS

The context is given in the Introduction §12 g; for the numerous characters besides Achaeus and Antiochus, a cast list may help (and sketch the story):

Sosibius: adviser to Ptolemy IV
Bolis: Cretan commissioned by Sosibius to rescue Achaeus
Arianus: messenger; Bolis' soldier
Cambylus: Cretan serving Antiochus III; helps Bolis capture Achaeus
Nicomachus and Melancomas: friends of Achaeus, exploited by Bolis
Laodice: Achaeus' wife
Aribazus: had commanded in main city of Sardis

The account is not just compelling narrative; it sustains a cohesive argument. The account also changes as it goes on. It proceeds from talk about action to action. The talk is accompanied by swift movements across a wide space, from Alexandria to Rhodes to Ephesus to Sardis, even, in imagination, from Sardis to Syria. (Cf. Hutchinson (2020).) These and lesser movements are given no specifics. The action itself is minutely planned and intensely imagined movement, across the small space from citadel to city – and then capture; space and physicality are graphically conveyed. Then comes a still moment, as Antiochus weeps over his bound enemy; horrendous judicial violence follows.

The impact of the narrative changes too. The earlier part has something amusing about it, thanks especially to P.'s wit in presenting the Cretans' change of plan, and to the character of these shameless tricksters. The last part offers something more tragic (detailed physical narrative near the end, like a messenger speech; final reflections) – but especially more Homeric. Andromache is recalled, and so are Hecuba, Priam and Achilles. In mind too are Croesus and Cyrus at Sardis (Hdt. 1.86.1–88.1; cf. P. 7.15.2–11 with Hdt. 1.84.1–4).

For all the emotional effect of the episode, emotion remains subject to judgement and practicality. The excursus which prepared the episode (35–6) says that Achaeus at the time won ἔλεος, Bolis hatred (36.9); emotional and moral responses are envisaged. But sympathy for Achaeus must depend, 35–6 imply, on seeing he has taken all possible care. The narrative itself demonstrates that he has (with some modifications). A larger point is drawn from this: anything can happen, humans cannot foresee everything (21.10). That conception underlies the episode and its impact. At every juncture, but especially the later stages, emotion is channelled to fit the thematic argument on unpredictability (19.7, 20.9, 21.6nn.).

The preview 36.7–9 means that, external knowledge apart, events are known to readers. The narrative shows the ironies that spring from what is to come; the early stages, in mimesis of events, do not openly indicate future treachery. The toing and froing of intermediaries is essential to the plot; Nicomachus, Melancomas and Arianus must not know Bolis' and Cambylus' plan. The whole plot turns on subtlety in human interaction, including the niceties of hierarchical behaviour. The narrative long delays the entry of the dynasts, Antiochus and especially Achaeus. Balance and interweaving are then crucial: their hopes and anxieties appear in parallel, until finally they are brought together in a moment of supreme inequality. The moment brings even Antiochus distress and reflection.

It has been supposed (i) that the episode adopts only Antiochus' perspective on events, and (ii) that this is because of P.'s source (so Schmitt (1964) 182; see Introduction §8 b, with Magnetto (2024)). To claim (i) ignores the balance of P.'s scenes and treatment. It is true P. never positively endorses Achaeus' claims to kingship; nor do many modern historians. But striking rather is P.'s moral and psychological sympathy for Achaeus, when he stresses Achaeus' fearsomeness elsewhere. The scene in Antiochus' tent (20.8–12) is said to prove (i) beyond doubt (Schmitt (1964) 182); but the narration is intensely engaged with Achaeus too, and both Antiochus' and Achaeus' feelings help P.'s argument. As to (ii),

35–6 well illustrate P.'s determination to think for himself. It is necessary to (ii) that Bolis should be an ultimate source for much of the account (Schmitt (1964) 182). He could well be; but if he is, that only shows how historians (P. or an antecedent) can escape the viewpoint of their source. Bolis and Cambylus are excoriated. With Antiochus' man Cambylus this is somewhat surprising.

One should add that P. had certainly visited Sardis, and interviewed someone there (21.38). Family there is conceivable (the name is relatively frequent there later). Whether or not he gained oral or documentary information, topography informs the narrative. Mention of a place name is significant (7.15.6). Sardis' detailed cityscape comes in less than does Tarentum's (24–34); but here movement inside city or acropolis is less relevant than movement between them.

In Fortune's big bang of recreation, 224–220 BC (4.2.4), Antiochus III acquires the Seleucid Empire, Ptolemy IV Egypt. Achaeus dominates in Western Asia (4.2.6); his family has intermarried with the Seleucid house. Achaeus initially stays loyal to Antiochus, despite his army's wishes and Molon's rebellion (4.48.9–10, 5.41.1). Soon, however, Achaeus declares himself king. P. sees pride, with fall to follow: Achaeus has successfully thwarted the ambitions of Attalus I in Western Asia (4.48.11). But Ptolemy at least encouraged Achaeus afterwards (cf. 5.57.2). P., unlike Antiochus, thinks Achaeus' earlier letter to Ptolemy IV (or III) spurious (5.42.7–9); certainly Ptolemy IV released Achaeus' father (4.51.1–7), and stood up for Achaeus' kingship in negotiations (5.67.12–13) before the battle of Raphia (217 BC). For Ptolemy, Achaeus in the west was a useful distraction to Antiochus in the east.

The years 222–213 BC display the uncertain order of Antiochus' to-do list. Antiochus crushed Molon immediately; the Fourth Syrian War postponed his subduing Achaeus. When defeated at Raphia, he went west (216) and forced Achaeus back into his capital Sardis. Achaeus himself, in P.'s account, had started an audacious move from Western Asia to Syria; his troops had stopped it (5.57.3–8).

Little remains of Achaeus' self-presentation; his letters to cities (5.57.5), unlike Antiochus', are lost. The main evidence is coinage. ΒΑΣΙΛΕΩΣ ΑΧΑΙΟΥ shows his claim, like the diadem (ribbon). See *SC* 953.1 and Meadows and Lorber (2010) (Figure 3). Seleucid Apollo and Ptolemaic eagle together proclaim importance and entitlement to rule (*SC* 955.1a, bronze, denomination B (b)). Bearded portrait and archaic Athena combined link him to the founding Macedonian power (Figure 3); see Gaebler (1935) 186, no. 3 (Athena: Antigonus Gonatas), 190, no. 16 (combination: Philip V; roughly contemporary). P.'s narrative indicates Achaeus' interest in grand appearance and honours (4.2.6, 51.6). The

Fig 3 Achaeus, silver tetradrachm, *CH* 2010.277 no. 74; image as in *Coin Hoards* 2010, by kind permission of Professor Andrew Meadows

Lydians had had two palaces; Achaeus probably inhabited at least one on the citadel.

P. studiously avoids pronouncing on Achaeus' claim to kingship rather than denying it like Antiochus. At 4.48.12 P. calls Achaeus the fiercest βασιλέων καὶ δυναστῶν: he declines to say which Achaeus is, straight after βασιλέα προσαγορεύσας αὐτόν. He admires Achaeus' initial refusal of kingship (4.48.9–10); but the present episode does not stress Achaeus' rebellion.

Archaeological evidence throws little light on the capture of Sardis (Rotroff and Oliver (2003) 11–13, 93). So far the remains of this Seleucid capital are less than might be expected. Hellenistic Sardis had seen much construction (Hanfmann (1983) 109–38; Berlin and Kosmin (2019)). The huge and elegant temple of Artemis may have been started soon after 281 and was still unfinished (Yegül (2020) I 7–11, 158–66). City and acropolis had been firmly divided from Lydian times; cf. Introduction §11 a. The citadel (Figure 4) was dauntingly inaccessible; the specifics of Achaeus' descent from it are unclear. The capture of the seemingly impregnable main city is narrated in 7.15–18. The bronze drachm *SC* 976, with a Seleucid elephant on the reverse, was probably minted by Antiochus in Sardis, during or just after the campaign (*SC* I p. 373). The end of the story is told by letters from Antiochus and his queen, the first about 5 March 213 (Gauthier (1989) 13–111; Ma (1999) 284–8; Petzl (2019) 10–13). Before the letters, Antiochus had imposed an extra 5 per cent tax and billeted troops extensively (*I.Sardis* II 307.5–6, 309.6–8); but his motivation may have been more financial and practical than vindictive.

Fig 4 Acropolis, Sardis, south side; ©Archaeological Exploration of Sardis/President and Fellows of Harvard College

He does not treat these measures as a unity: he alters them separately. Another burden too is removed, on grounds of fairness suggested by the Sardians (*I.Sardis* II 309.8–10). Quite different, in 209, is the Romans' treatment of Tarentum. (On events and episode: Meloni (1949–50); Schmitt (1964) 158–75, 181–8; Wörrle (1975); Huß (1976) 3–94, esp. 88–94; Ma (1999) 54–63; *SC* I pp. 347–50, 368–76; Capdetrey (2007) 294–7, 369–71; Ehling (2007); Miltsios (2009) 485–92; McGing (2010) 26–7; Ager (2012); D'Agostini (2014, 2018); Hutchinson (2014) 36–8; Chrubasik (2016) 87–9, 101–15; Richter (2017); Evans (2018) 13–14, 22, 55, 101; Saprykin (2020) 230–4.)

## 15 BOLIS TAKES ON THE RESCUE

**15.1 Βῶλις ἦν ἀνήρ ... §2 τοῦτον:** for the opening cf. 3.98.2 ἦν δέ τις ἀνὴρ Ἴβηρ ... οὗτος κτλ., 5.37.1 Νικαγόρας τις ἦν Μεσσήνιος· οὗτος κτλ. So e.g. Hom. *Il.* 2.811 'There is a hill'. The new person drives the action in 15–16 especially. His name rings the opening sequence (§§1, 8), and comes three times in between (§§3, 6). **Βῶλις:** *PP* VI 14750. The name will sound

COMMENTARY: 15.1-15.2    161

fitting; it appears only in the southern Aegean: Nisyrus (Ἀρχαιολογική Ἐφημερίς 1913 p. 7 l. 8, iii BC), Rhodes (*IG* XII.1.341).    **γένει μὲν Κρής, χρόνον δὲ πολὺν ... ἐλάττω** plays down Bolis' Cretan origins; the qualities after δοκῶν seem good. Cretans can escape bad Cretan characteristics (33.16.4–5). Later, though, Bolis will be seen to possess Cretan trickiness and treachery in full measure (16.4, 19.5nn.); and 36.9 has already alerted readers to villainy.    **Κρής:** there are many Cretans in Ptolemaic Egypt, 62 in La'da (2002) 128–35; cf. 125.    **βασιλείαι** 'kingdom'. P. has been speaking of Egypt or Ptolemy. This narrative opens in Egypt, not (as D'Agostini (2018) 69) with Sosibius and Bolis on the acropolis of Sardis. Sosibius, Ptolemy's foremost adviser, would not be so riskily located. At 19.1–3 Achaeus has clearly not met Bolis before, though Bolis has met Sosibius (15.3–4). Bolis tells Cambylus why he has left Alexandria (16.2).    **ἐν ἡγεμονικῆι προστασίαι** 'with the standing of a commander', cf. LSJ προστασία II.1a: a much lower place than Sosibius'.    **δοκῶν:** of reputation; cf. e.g. 18.3.1.    **ἔχειν ... τριβὴν ἐν τοῖς πολεμικοῖς οὐδενὸς ἐλάττω:** especially similar is 5.68.5; but here the phrase recalls Λαγόρας ὁ Κρής, τριβὴν ἔχων ἐν τοῖς πολεμικοῖς ἱκανήν. Lagoras devises the fall of Sardis (7.15.2). Bolis excels him in experience of war, and Cretan cunning.    **παράβολον** 'bold'; *PL* 1a.

**15.2 τοῦτον** points backward, so a connecting particle is unnecessary; cf. e.g. 2.24.6, 30.25.5.    **Σωσίβιος:** *PP* I 48, VI 17239. Prominent before, at and after Raphia (5.63.1, with Agathocles οἱ τότε προεστῶτες τῆς βασιλείας, 66.8–67.3, 85.9, 87.8). He seems active already under Ptolemy III (*IG* XI.4.649.3–4 ἀρετῆ[ς ἕνεκεν τῆς] | [εἰς τὸ]μ βασιλέα, Delos, 240s or 230s BC); he is perhaps the young Sosibius of Callimachus' epinician, fr. 384 Pfeiffer (Kampakoglou (2019) 21 n. 12). For him as adviser of Philopator see Huß (1976) 239–51.    **διὰ πλειόνων λόγων πιστωσάμενος** 'having secured his fidelity with elaborate words'. Cf. 24.5.7 τὰ ... φιλάνθρωπα διὰ πλειόνων λόγων ἀνενεώσαντο; Jos. *BJ* 4.214 ἐδόκει δὲ αὐτὸν ὅρκοις πιστώσασθαι πρὸς εὔνοιαν. πίστις will be a central theme of the episode.    **παρασκευάσας** 'having made'.    **ἀναδίδωσι:** a momentous decision; P.'s historic presents often mark fateful beginnings, e.g. 3.107.2 (Cannae enters the narrative), 15.2.4, 12 (plan and event bring renewal of war). So far this is an offer; cf. §4 ἀνεδέξατο.    **οὐδέν:** object of χαρίσαιτο, 'confer' a benefit; cf. e.g. 21.22.1, LSJ χαρίζομαι II.1a.    **τῶι βασιλεῖ:** the courtier stresses the king, cf. §8; for Ptolemy's direct collaboration with Achaeus and seeming concern for him cf. 5.57.1, 66.3, 67.12. Huß (2001) 405–6 underplays Philopator's role; but he rightly doubts P.'s picture of indifference to external affairs (5.34.10). Cf. Marasco (1979–80). Achaeus, as mentioned, stresses Ptolemaic connections in the eagle on *SC* 955, reverse;

Evans (2019) 105–6; Seaman (2020) 108. **συνεπινοήσας:** but the ideas will all be Bolis'. A causal chain runs from Ptolemy to Sosibius to Bolis. The word comes only here in P.; it is common in Galen. **πῶς καὶ τίνι τρόπωι:** essentially emphatic synonymy; cf. 1.32.2. Galen has πῶς καὶ τίνα τρόπον; or the like 8 times. **σῶσαι τὸν Ἀχαιόν:** finally Achaeus' name appears, still not the subject of action. The sentence began with Σωσίβιος; readers may see irony in the name, interpreted 'life-saver'. Cf. 26.1a.1: P. calls Antiochus IV Ἐπιμανῆ καὶ οὐκ Ἐπιφανῆ διὰ τὰς πράξεις.

**15.3 τότε μέν:** two-stage meetings are common, e.g. 38.7.12; but this short half-sentence shows Bolis' surprising independence. **διακούσας:** little different from ἀκούσας; the verb is especially common in P. and Diogenes Laertius. **ἐπισκέψεσθαι:** an easy change for -ασθαι (FDG), but of a sort that has to be made frequently, as at 2.64.5, 4.64.3. Cf. *SB* x 10272.8–9 (iii BC) οὐκ ἔφη ἐπ[ισκ]έ|ψεσθαι ἐὰν μὴ κτλ.

**15.4 δοὺς δὲ λόγον ἑαυτῶι:** the first of the episode's private reflections. **εἰς αὐτόν:** a distinctive phrase. Ironic meaning is reflected back by the selfish αὐτῶν and τοῦ σφίσιν αὐτοῖς συμφέροντος at 16.6. **φήσας ... αὐτῶι** corresponds to λέγων κτλ. in §2. Sosibius implied rewards, Bolis explains eagerly why he was a good choice (cf. §6 below): καὶ ... καί, οὐ μόνον ... ἀλλὰ καί, καὶ ... καί. Readers gain useful information through a scene rather than preliminary exposition. **πλείω χρόνον** (F, *Suda*): unlike Galen, who freely uses either πλείω χρόνον etc. or χρόνον πλείω etc., P. uses only πλείω χρόνον etc., e.g. 4.57.3, 9.4.3. **ἐμπειρεῖν:** unusual in literature (3.78.6, *Tobit* 5.6 Hanhart). It expresses a crucial expertise; cf. e.g. 14.3.7: Massinissa used as adviser διὰ τὴν τῶν τόπων ἐμπειρίαν. But Bolis will know less than Arianus (18.7). **Καμβύλον:** only instance of this name; distinctively Cretan, presumably. **ἡγεμόνα τῶν παρ' Ἀντιόχωι στρατευομένων Κρητῶν:** armies are typically organized by soldiers' origins; the Cretans are not subdivided by cities. Cf. e.g., at Raphia, 5.82.4 (Ptolemy), 10 ἐν μετώπωι τοὺς Κρῆτας ἔστησε (Antiochus). Outside Crete, 'Cretans' is an adequate category: cf. e.g. Moretti, *ISE* II.106.2 Κρής (Demetrias, 227–221 BC), a Cretan mercenary says of himself. Despite 15.1, the importance of being Cretan is emerging. **Ἀντιόχωι** (F?): cf. 5.68.5 τῶν παρὰ Πτολεμαίωι στρατευομένων, contrast e.g. 3.43.6 τοὺς παρ' αὐτοῦ στρατιώτας. **πολίτην ... συγγενῆ:** 'Cretan' is not now sufficient. It is hoped these city and family links will override loyalty to Antiochus.

**15.5 συνέβαινε:** the narrator indicates what Bolis conveyed (cf. §6). **πεπιστεῦσθαι:** they had been entrusted with a φυλακτήριον; see for the grammar LSJ II. **φυλακτηρίων:** fortified guards' buildings;

cf. e.g. *SEG* XXIV.154.13–14 (Rhamnus, *c*.264/3 BC). They seem close to the citadel; the path (18.7) to the citadel, difficult and needing time (18.11, 20.3), will not run from here.   ὄπισθε: not at the gates. If the 'Saw', the fortified ridge connecting city and citadel, led to the citadel gates, this is not part of it; cf. 7.15.6, Berlin and Kosmin (2019) 96 pl. 22.   κατασκευήν 'construction'. Elsewhere on its own only of defensive building rather than siegeworks (cf. e.g. 4.65.5, cf. 3; 9.27.3); possibly e.g. ἔργων has been lost. P. need not imply siegeworks at other parts of the acropolis wall.

**15.6 ἐπίνοιαν:** an incipient plan, cf. 7.15.6, but not yet set out for readers.   διειληφότος 'supposing', cf. 31.27.9, LSJ διαλαμβάνω III.6. P.'s ironic preparation is palpable.   ἢ μὴ δυνατὸν εἶναι: more doubtful than 36.8 above.   σωθῆναι τὸν Ἀχαιόν: after the climactic §2 σῶσαι τὸν Ἀχαιόν, the repetition conveys Sosibius' emotional involvement.   καθάπαξ: if it was 'at all' possible. More often it comes in negative clauses; cf. 20.2n., *PL* 2.   Βώλιδος: the close captures Sosibius' admiration.   τοιαύτης: cf. §4.   συνδραμούσης: coming together in time, cf. 6.48.4: these qualities ὁμοῦ συνδραμόντων κτλ.; but also with a metaphorical touch of enthusiastic running, cf. Alex. Aphr. *Anim.* 73.2 of βούλησις.   ταχέως κτλ.: after elaborate genitive absolutes, an expressively quick ending. For meaningful brevity cf. e.g. 4.75.5 ταχέως παρέδοσαν αὐτούς·, Pind. *Pyth.* 9.68, Call. *H.* 1.56 ὀξὺ δ' ἀνήβησας.   προκοπήν 'progress', usually grander or more philosophical (26 times in Plutarch's *Moralia*, never *Lives*); but cf., in a practical context, PSI V 502.26 (257/6 BC) οὐδὲ προκοπὴν ποιήσασθαι.

**15.7 ὅ τε γὰρ Σωσίβιος:** taken up by ὅ τε προειρημένος ἀνήρ (Bolis) at §9. This half-sentence starts Σωσίβιος and ends Βῶλιν; Sosibius makes Bolis act, Bolis goes to both Rhodes and Ephesus (§9 τε ... καί). Sosibius' generosity shows keenness; Bolis' motivation is financial. Large sums run through: μηδὲν ἐλλείπειν, πολλά, §8 ἐξ ὑπερβολῆς αὔξων εἰς μεγάλας ἐλπίδας ἦγε. χάριτας (§8) is now more clearly concrete than §2 χαρίσαιτο.   προεδίδου (Reiske): cf. 16.7 προδεδομένα.   τῶν χρημάτων: partitive; cf. 21.34.13 προσετίθει τῶν χρημάτων. No crude details yet; cf. 16.7.

**15.8 παρὰ τοῦ βασιλέως καὶ παρ' αὐτοῦ τοῦ σωιζομένου:** αὐτοῦ has point; Ptolemy's gifts are envisaged already (§2). For the participle with no name cf. e.g. 29.27.3 τοῦ δεξιουμένου. παρατου ... παραυτουτου misled a scribe. In the usual text παρ' αὐτοῦ τοῦ βασιλέως καὶ παρ' Ἀχαιοῦ τοῦ σωιζομένου, neither phrase convinces. The present σωιζομένου, 'now being saved', creates further irony.   ἦγε: imperfect for the mental state, set against ἐξέπλευσε (§9) for swift, effective action.

**15.9 τε:** for τε connecting sentences or half-sentences cf. e.g. 9.19.9, 23.3.7 (both with ὁ). **ἕτοιμος:** both 'ready' and 'keen'. **τὴν πρᾶξιν:** the focus of the action, not yet fully explained. **ἐπιμείνας:** better than ὑπομείνας for intransitive waiting over a specified time; cf. e.g. 21.41.9 (three days). **ἐξέπλευσε:** from Alexandria; cf. 16.2. **συνθήματα:** letters in code (*CGL* 3). The code was presumably agreed between Sosibius, Nicomachus and Melancomas when Ptolemy and Achaeus interacted; cf. §10. Perhaps the same code is used between Nicomachus, Melancomas and Achaeus (16.4). For code in letters see Aen. Tact. 31.2, 3, 30–1; Süß (1922); Liddel (2018) 135–8. **Νικόμαχον ... Μελαγκόμαν:** Nicomachus and Melancomas are probably Rhodian and Ephesian. Melancomas' name is especially attested in Ephesus (*LGPN* I 287); Nicomachus' is very common in Rhodes (*LGPN* I 336–7). P. does not indicate that Melancomas is Achaeus' commander at Ephesus. Nicomachus and Melancomas have been crucial intermediaries; they were not living at court in Sardis. They were probably effective with Ephesus and Rhodes, as citizens (cf. Boyxen (2018) 93 for citizens and Rhodes city); probably Nicomachus was involved when Rhodes got Ptolemy to restore Achaeus' father (4.50.10–51.6; cf. τά τε πρὸς τὸν Πτολεμαῖον, §10). The two add something new to Bolis' plan; Achaeus' trust in Ptolemy and Sosibius would not suffice (cf. 17.8, and 4.51.3). **Ῥόδον:** Bolis sails to Rhodes, then Ephesus, with soldiers (16.1); he sends one on to Sardis. **πατρὸς ἔχειν διάθεσιν** 'to have the position of a father' may suggest Nicomachus is substantially older than Achaeus. Achaeus' real father need not have died; cf. 6.39.7. The phrase and 4.50.10–51.6 suggest, on rereading, a significant sequence: Rhodes gives Achaeus' father σωτηρία, a Rhodian like a father to Achaeus will cause Achaeus' destruction. **εὔνοιαν καὶ πίστιν:** a common pair, first *IG* I³.113.17 (*c.*410 BC), cf. Welles, *RC* 66.11 (Pergamum, 135 BC), Sherk, *RDGE* 18.45 (81 BC); 6 times in P. (at 7.8.9 of sons towards fathers), once in Dionysius. πίστις is 'trustworthiness'. **Ἔφεσον:** for its close connection with Sardis cf. Ladstätter (2019); for its strategic importance, P. 18.41a.2.

**15.10 τὰς ἔξωθεν:** outside his dominion. For the repeated article cf. e.g. 28.2.7, Audollent, *Defixiones* 60.10–12 τού[ς] ἄλλο[υ]ς ἄπαν|τας τοὺς με[τὰ] Νερ[ε]ΐδ[ο]υ | κατηγόρους (Attica, iv BC).

## 16 BOLIS CHANGES TACK

**16.1 ἑτοίμους:** ἕτοιμος recurs, and creates onward momentum in the narrative; cf. 15.9, 16.3. **τὰ παρακαλούμενα:** still vague. **μετὰ ταῦτ'** marks a new stage, after three participles. **Ἀριανόν:** despite τινα, another important figure, sympathetically treated (17.6–7). The name is unusual;

in *TAM* IV.1.7.4, 256.1, 4 (Bithynia, imperial period) Ἀριανός could be Latin, cf. *AE* 2006.1767.5 (Thignica, AD 405). διαπέμπεται: historic presents for (-)πέμπω are common from Herodotus on, incl. Theop. *FGrHist* 115 F30a; they come 6 times in P. and often in Dionysius. διαπέμπεται highlights the significant juncture; contrast §3 ἀπέπεμψε.

**16.2 ξενολογήσων** 'to recruit mercenaries': not too lowly for Bolis' ἡγεμονικὴ προστασία (15.1). Cf. 15.25.16 (Scopas); Chaniotis (2005) 82–3. Bolis lies to his fellow Cretan (see §6n.). If the lie is plausible, Ptolemy is more warlike than P. suggests (cf. e.g. 5.87.3). **ὤιετο:** halfway between direct and indirect speech – not infinitive, but past. Cf. 18.5, 7nn. **μηδενὸς συνειδότος αὐτοῖς:** the weight falls on the participial phrase, within the relative purpose clause (a place to meet in). P. stresses secrecy is crucial to planning (9.13.1–5). Where trickery is involved, as it would be even if Cambylus deceived Antiochus, it is especially important to avoid a third person as witness (Gorg. B11a.7 DK, D25.7 Laks–Most).

**16.3 ταχύ** is not especially meaningful, but promotes the sense of swiftness in the narrative; ἑτοίμως (§1n.) begins the next clause. **ἐντολάς** 'instructions' to Arianus, not Cambylus. Cf. 22.12.7: Caecilius not showing Achaean magistrates the Senate's ἐντολὰς ἐγγράπτους to him. **ἑκατέρωι γνωστόν:** no guide would be needed, not even Arianus (cf. 17.7). **νυκτός** strengthens the atmosphere of intrigue.

**16.4 ὁ δὲ Βῶλις:** Arianus' name ringed the previous sentence; Bolis' now, directly after Arianus', spotlights the leading agent, in a short, weighty sentence. P. avoids the simple structure of a new idea from Cambylus persuading Bolis. **Κρής:** P. likes playing on Cretan qualities, usually immoral; he approved Cretan cunning at 7.15.2–16.2. ποικίλος could be approving (cf. 10.35.2) or disapproving (cf. 4.30.7); but πᾶν ... πρᾶγμα and πᾶσαν ἐπίνοιαν go beyond τὴν πρᾶξιν (15.2, 4) and τὴν ἐπίνοιαν (15.6), Bolis' plan with Sosibius. πᾶς suggest stopping at nothing, unlike the approving 7.15.5 πάντα τρόπον ἠρεύνα. For the anaphora of πᾶς cf. 1.31.8 (admiring), 18.14.11 (less admiring). **ἐβάσταζε** 'pondered'. The metaphorical use comes first in fifth-century drama (e.g. [Aesch.] *PV* 888); rarely in Hellenistic and later prose. **ἐψηλάφα:** literally 'felt around'; metaphorically again at 19.5, but this is unusual, cf. e.g. Sext. *Math.* 8.108. In P. the stem is extant only in book 8.

**16.5 τέλος:** the pace has slowed; cf. §3. **ἔδωκεν ἐπιστολὴν < >:** e.g. <παρὰ Σωσιβίου>; cf. 29.25.2 φέρων ἐπιστολὴν παρὰ Κοΐντου Μαρκίου, P. Cair. Zen. III 59499.73–4 (iii BC) εἰδοῦ | ἐπιστολὴ παρὰ Κλέωνος. A letter would be useful if it simply affirmed Sosibius' support for Bolis. τήν is unsatisfactory: P. has mentioned no letter; those to Achaeus (§9) are in a code unknown to Cambylus. ἐδήλωσε τὴν ἐπιβολήν (Bekker) would make εἰς τὸ μέσον awkward: two is too few for putting something metaphorically 'into the midst' for group discussion (seven even at Hdt. 3.83.1). **Κρητικήν**: Cretans are famous for being ἀεὶ ψεῦσται (Epimenid. B1 DK, Call. *H*. 1.8, Paul, *Tit*. 1:12). P. associates them with military tricks (4.8.11), since they are πλάγιοι ταῖς ψυχαῖς. Bolis goes further, and flagrantly breaches an undertaking. Cf. 28.14.1–4, a Cretan violation of a treaty even worse than usual. Κρητικήν is predicative: P. often adds a predicative adjective to ποιοῦμαι with article and verbal noun; cf. e.g. 1.28.9 (πελαγίαν), 38.5.1 (ἀτελῆ καὶ διερριμμένην).

**16.6 οὐ γὰρ ἐσκόπουν** continues §5 σκέψιν. P.'s narrating here is like Phylarch. *FGrHist* 81 F24 οὐδὲν τῶν προγεγενημένων φιλανθρώπων ἐπὶ νοῦν βαλομένη. **ὑπὲρ ... συμφέροντος**: in two respects, two distinct objects of neglect, Achaeus and Sosibius, oppose the undifferentiated Cretan pair (cf. αὐτῶν, σφίσιν αὐτοῖς). The weaker ἀσφαλείας matches σωτηρίας, the amoral τοῦ ... συμφέροντος the moral πίστεως.

**16.7 ἀμφότεροι** is taken up in τὴν αὐτήν. Κρῆτες ὄντες does not laboriously repeat §5 Κρητικήν, but explains their parallel thinking. Bolis' is now quick and decisive (contrast §4). Cambylus serves Antiochus; he would have had motives moral and prudential for changing Bolis' mind (cf. 17.6, where Cambylus worries Achaeus most). Yet P. prefers Cretan character operating independently. The tone differs from the last sentence: there is some amusement at a predictable surprise. **συντόμως** 'swiftly'. συντόμως is commonly positive: πρᾶσσε συντόμως is proverbial wisdom, *I.Miletupolis* 2.12 (iv–iii BC); Apollonius says he will send someone συντόμως, P. Cair. Zen. II 59201.2 (254 BC). Such connotations sharpen P.'s tone here. Plainer is the *statim* used at Cic. *Clu*. 69 of a similarly shameless about-turn. **κατηνέχθησαν** 'arrived at', aor. pass. of καταφέρομαι; cf. 30.19.4 ἐπὶ ταύτην κατηνέχθησαν τὴν γνώμην. **αὕτη δ' ἦν**: pause and new start increase anticipation and emphasis. Cf. e.g. 2.43.7–8: his efforts had one goal, τοῦτο δ' ἦν κτλ.; 21.24.4–5: all got the same answer, αὕτη δ' ἦν κτλ. Cf. Plut. *Quaest. Conv*. 1.4.3.621C; 2.2n. **δέκα τάλαντα**: a lot, but within the scope of non-royal individuals; cf. e.g. the 15 talents at *F.Delphes* III.4.283 col. E.6, 10, F.23, etc. (125 BC). The sum must be for bribery rather than travel. **προδεδομένα** resumes προεδίδου (15.7). They will get two lots of preliminary money; cf. §8 λαβόντας χρήματα. **διελέσθαι** 'divide among themselves'.

**16.8 τὴν δὲ πρᾶξιν** begins this part of the sentence; τῆς προειρημένης ἐπιβολῆς ends it (cf. for the phrase 14.2.1). The shaping underlines the extreme change in plan. **Ἀντιόχωι** clashes pointedly with §7 Σωσιβίου. **χρησαμένους:** better χρησομένους. For participles in different tenses joined by καί cf. e.g. 1.34.12, 16.33.5; for future helpers e.g. 3.31.5. δηλώσαντας and χρησαμένους do not combine well; δηλώσαντας comes before or at the time of the promise (ἐπαγγείλασθαι), while using Antiochus' help comes at a later stage. **εἰς τὸ μέλλον:** phrases emphasizing the connection of hope with the future are unusually common in P. Here the contrast with present gains is underlined. **ἐλπίδας** recalls forcefully Bolis' μεγάλας ἐλπίδας from the original plan (15.8). The addition of future to present money matches 15.7–8. **ἀξίας τῆς ... ἐπιβολῆς:** readers will think the phrase misapplied to an undertaking which deserves punishment, not reward. Cf. e.g. 6.14.6, Thuc. 3.39.6 κολασθέντων ... ἀξίως τῆς ἀδικίας.

**16.9 κυρωθέντων:** of adopting a plan at 5.49.6, 22.9.12 – more official contexts than this. Perhaps there is a sardonic touch in using κυροῦν for these machinations. **ἀνεδέξατο** meaningly echoes 15.4 ἀνεδέξατο τὴν πρᾶξιν [Sosibius' scheme] εἰς αὐτόν. The joint action (§8 δηλώσαντας) falls in practice to Cambylus. **μετά τινας ἡμέρας:** Arianus must visit Nicomachus and Melancomas first (17.4); this is not yet spelt out. **Μελαγκόμα:** seven names in one sentence conveys an intricate plot – the Cretans', and P.'s. **συνθηματικά** 'coded'; cf. 15.9. Before Damascius (v–vi AD), only P. uses the adjective (here) and adverb (17.4 below).

**16.10 ἐκεῖνον ἐκέλευε:** Bolis is subject, Cambylus object. Here the two strands of action intersect, despite §9 πέμψειν ... πρὸς τὸν Ἀχαιόν. Arianus had reached Cambylus unaided (16.1–3); only Cambylus can arrange passage to the citadel. κελεύω often means bidding equals do something; cf. *IG* I³.78 *a*.33 (V BC) μὴ ἐπιτάττοντας, κελεύοντας δέ. But Bolis still brusquely emphasizes limits on what he can and will do.

**16.11 τὴν ἐπιβολήν:** poised ambiguously between their actual attempt (cf. §8 ἐπιβολῆς) and Bolis' supposed attempt (cf. 15.7 ἐπιβολάς). **ἀντιφωνήσηι** 'reply'; of letters, like ἀντιφωνέω and ἀντιφώνησις in papyri, e.g. *BGU* IV 1204.4–5 (28 BC) τὴν οὖν ἁπάντων ἀντιφώνησιν | ἐν τάχει πέμψον. **τοῖς περί:** in this secret context clearly just those named. Cf. 7.1n. **οὕτως:** then and only then; cf. 1.59.3 (explicit), 11.16.5 (context indicates). Bolis is cautious, even with his fellow Cretan. δώσειν ... αὐτὸν 'dedicate himself'. Cf. 5.37.3 ἔδωκεν αὑτὸν εἰς τὰς διαποστολὰς κτλ. (eagerly arranging reconciliation), *SEG* xxxiv.558.59–60 (Larisa, *c*.150–130 BC) ἐπιδιδό[ν]|τες ἑαυτοὺς εἰς τὰ παρακαλούμενα προθύμως, *IG* xii.5(2).870.13–14 (Tenos, ii BC). συμμίξειν: cf. §5 συμμίξας τῶι Καμβύλωι. Bolis will not even meet Cambylus again unless things look promising.

**16.12** διατάξεως and συντεταγμένα, at opposite ends of the sentence, stress both the separate actions (cf. ἑκάτεροι) and the agreement. χωρισθέντες: χωρίζομαι commonly closes Polybian scenes of meeting (cf. 30.4 below, and e.g. 15.9.1, 38.7.12); more rarely in Diodorus (e.g. 28.12.1), rarely in later historians. διέτμαγεν closes scenes: Hom. *Il.* 1.534, *Od.* 13.439, Ap. Rhod. *Arg.* 3.1147.

## 17 THE RULERS ARE DRAWN IN

**17.1 καιρὸν πρῶτον** shows both eagerness and the necessity of choosing one's moment. Vitruvius fears interrupting Augustus inopportunely, then goes for *primum tempus* (1 *pr.* 1–2). προσφέρει: the present makes the vital moment livelier. The phrase recalls 7.5.11 προσφέρει τῶι βασιλεῖ τὸν περὶ τούτων λόγον, Lagoras on Sardis. τῶι βασιλεῖ need not imply Achaeus was no king: at 5.68.6 τοῦ βασιλέως is Antiochus, although Ptolemy has just been mentioned.

**17.2 †πρὸς τρόπον†**: with προσφάτου τ', Antiochus' initial reaction to an offer 'both new and surprising to him' mingles joy and doubt. Later (§3) he accepts. Newness to the mind makes feeling strong: cf. 3.34.7, *SVF* iii 391 (δόξα πρόσφατος needed for λύπη and ἡδονή). For αὐτῶι cf. P. 1.77.7 γενομένης δὲ τοῖς Καρχηδονίοις τῆς ... ἐπιστρατοπεδείας αἰφνιδίου. For τε cf. 13.3.8, 27.9.5, 28.3.10 ἀσπαστικήν τε καὶ παρακλητικήν, elision e.g. 1.4.8. τ' articulates the argument here. πρὸς τρόπον is impossible. πρὸς τρόπου (Schweighaeuser) produces serious hiatus (πρὸς τρόπου τ' would be doubtful word order). It would mean 'suiting his character, apt', possibly 'convenient' (cf. P. Cair. Zen. iii 59309.5, 250 BC). It would be too weak for ὑπερχαρής, as would προσφόρου 'useful'. τὰ μὲν ὑπερχαρὴς ὤν: 19.2 corresponds, (Achaeus) τὰ μὲν περιχαρὴς ἦν ..., τὰ δὲ κτλ. See Introduction §10 b. πάνθ' ὑπισχνεῖτο: all they wished (cf. 16.8), and everything possible. Sosibius made promises too (15.7). διαπιστῶν 'distrusting'; see Introduction §13 c n. 65. κατὰ μέρος 'detailed'. Their plans seem more elaborate than in 16.9. Achaeus likewise grills Arianus (§6, with κατὰ μέρος). αὐτῶν: perhaps P.'s viewpoint; in what follows Antiochus thinks Cambylus the agent.

**17.3 πιστεύσας:** set against διαπιστῶν; the aorist (contrast νομίζων and ἠξίου) marks a decisive moment. Achaeus does not simply abandon uncertainty (19.2–3). **ὡς ἂν εἰ** 'as it were' restrains theological assertion; cf. 11.11.1 νομίζων ὡς ἂν εἰ κατ' εὐχὴν αὐτῶι γίνεσθαι τὴν τῶν Ἀχαιῶν ὁρμήν. **σὺν θεῶι** or σὺν θεοῖς only here in P.; Antiochus is elated. The immorality of the scheme adds irony. Apart from the cautious σὺν θεῶι εἰπεῖν etc., historiography uses the phrase rarely: Plutarch's *Lives* twice and (all direct speech) Josephus three times, Appian once. **ἠξίου καὶ πολλάκις ἐδεῖτο:** a common pair; cf. 21.42.2 ἀξιῶν καὶ δεόμενος, Dem. 18.6, 54.2 ἀξιῶ καὶ δέομαι. πολλάκις gives further intensity. The monarch is reduced to entreaty. **συντελεῖν:** some way off in the narrative. **τὴν πρᾶξιν:** now the new plan, previously the original (15.4, 9, 16.6, 8). The change is pointed.

**17.4 τὸ δὲ παραπλήσιον ... ἐποίει** 'did the same' – although they were already convinced (16.1), Bolis is not present with both, or either, and the action happens in their two separate places. P. continues the symmetry of 16.9. The two plans make the neatness ironic. **πιστεύοντες** matches §3 πιστεύσας, but these men are being deceived. P. does not show that Melancomas joined the plot (so Mittag (2017) 362); that would undo the storyline. **ἀπὸ τοῦ κρατίστου** 'sincerely'; so at 24.10 below, but here with stronger narratorial condemnation. Only P. and Dionysius use the phrase. **γίνεσθαι τὴν ἐπιβολήν** takes up §3; but this ἐπιβολή is the original plan. **παραυτίκα** underlines innocent enthusiasm. P. greatly prefers παραυτίκα (75 times) to αὐτίκα (5); most historians (not Arrian) much prefer αὐτίκα. **συνθέντες** 'having given'. See Introduction §13 c. **τάς:** mentioned at 16.9. **συνθηματικῶς** picks up συνθηματικά from 16.9.

**17.5 πιστεύειν** looks back to §4 πιστεύοντες at the start of the sentence. The link highlights, not just trust as a theme, but chains of trust. The friends' advice should add to Achaeus' reasons for trusting (§8 below), but their own trust actually has no separate ground – they have seen Bolis. **τοῖς περί:** again just the individuals (all is secret). They have not met Cambylus. [οὕτως ... γεγραμμένων] is in the wrong place in FDG, which points to its origin in the margin. The *Suda* either had it in a different place or misses out intervening material; cf. e.g. the apparatus to 9.2. Even after §4 αὐτοῖς the superfluous insertion would clumsily delay the isolated main verb.

**17.6 ὁ δ' Ἀριανός:** a new subject again in the string of actions; cf. §§1, 2, 4: Cambylus, Antiochus, Bolis subjects, and Nicomachus and Melancomas (οἱ δέ). **διὰ τοῦ Καμβύλου:** as arranged (16.10). No spatial detail is given; contrast 18.8, 20.3.   τοῖς περὶ τὸν Ἀχαιόν: just Achaeus; cf. §5n.   συμπαρών: ἀπὸ τῆς ἀρχῆς makes a past participle unnecessary (εἶναι and compounds have none). As emerges, Arianus' continual presence had an important gap, Cambylus' and Bolis' meeting.   πολλάκις μὲν καὶ ποικίλως: a version of πολλοὶ καὶ ποικίλοι 'many and various', a phrase broadly applied, and popular with P., Diodorus, Appian, Cassius Dio. In §§6–7 the narrative spotlight is on Arianus, but Achaeus enters obliquely. His numerous inquiries (πολλάκις twice) help to show he tested the plan thoroughly.   Σωσίβιον: four names come in pairs – Sosibius, Bolis; Nicomachus, Melancomas. Cambylus is separated, with μάλιστα. Achaeus does not realize Bolis and Cambylus are a pair; he is particularly worried about Antiochus' officer and his motives.

**17.7 οὐ μὴν ἀλλ'** 'but'; a frequent combination in P., Aristotle, Diodorus and others. See 2.7n.   αὐτοπαθῶς 'naturally, spontaneously', ἐξ ἰδίας προαιρέσεως (Suda α 4515); cf. 3.12.1, 15.17.1–2 (reactions; opposed to 'contrived'). Not common; before P. Epicurus may have used it (1.137 Arrighetti).   γενναίως: often in P. of military courage and endurance (e.g. 1.17.12). Light falls on Arianus, and Achaeus, whose interrogation sounds fierce; cf. 4.48.12 βαρύτατος, φοβερώτατος.   μὴ γινώσκειν: secrecy works (16.3n.). This episode is interested in the subtleties of behaviour. Hellenistic drama plays on sincerity thought to be convincing pretence (Men. Sic. 343–60; cf. Plaut. Poen. 1106–10).   τὸ συνέχον 'essence, nub'. Cf. e.g. Philod. Rhet. 1 col. clxxvi.30–2 ὥ[σπερ] | ὂν τὸ πᾶν καὶ τὸ συ[νέ]|χον.

**17.8 Ἀχαιός:** he is finally the subject, at the start of the sentence, with Arianus as object at the end. Achaeus' reasons are probed; the language does not yet explore his mind (cf. 19.1–3).   καὶ ... καὶ μάλιστα stresses simultaneously that both factors were important and that one was so particularly; so elaborate is the plot. More ordinary is 6.11a.7 καὶ διὰ ... καὶ διὰ ... καὶ μάλιστα διὰ κτλ.   πιστεύσας parallels πιστεύσας of Antiochus (§3 above); but Achaeus remains more hesitant (§9; cf. §3n.).   ἀντεφώνησε: the crucial word ends the clause, without dative (contrast 16.11). Bolis needs only the fact of reply.   παραχρῆμα ... §9 τέλος: the sequence connects with 16.3–5: ἀπέπεμψε τὸν Ἀριανόν, pondering, τέλος. The pondering has moved to Achaeus. For παραχρῆμα see Introduction §13 c.

**17.9 ἑκατέρων** with a plural and a singular at 25.2.2. τοῖς περὶ τὸν Μελαγκόμαν at 19.4 suggests Melancomas is in view too, though the quasi-paternal Nicomachus (15.9) is naturally the one mentioned here.   ἐπέτρεψαν περὶ σφῶν: somewhat weaker than ἐγχειριοῦντες αὑτούς at the end of the sentence – a further, more physical stage. Cf. 14.6.4 ἐπέτρεψαν περὶ σφῶν αὐτῶν τοῖς Ῥωμαίοις, 21.4.13, Thuc. 4.54.2 Ἀθηναίοις ἐπιτρέψαι περὶ σφῶν αὐτῶν πλὴν θανάτου. **μηδεμιᾶς ἄλλης:** even trust in Nicomachus is not naïve. **σωτηρίαν:** the vital stem; cf. 15.2 σῶσαι, 6 σωθῆναι, 8 σωιζομένου, 16.6 σωτηρίας, 19.2 τὴν ἐλπίδα τῆς σωτηρίας. **πέμπειν ... ἅμα τῶι Ἀριανῶι τὸν Βῶλιν:** Achaeus views Nicomachus and Melancomas as controlling Bolis; they see it so too (18.2). **ἀσελήνου:** an advance on just νυκτός (16.3). Achaeus is prepared to wait; cf. 7.16.3, Thuc. 3.22.1 (waiting for moonless or partly moonless nights). Darkness will help Achaeus' eventual plans (20.2). Nicomachus, or even Melancomas in Ephesus, would presumably tell Bolis and Arianus to wait for such a night. **αὑτούς:** no dative is given; Achaeus could be thought to deliver himself to Nicomachus and Melancomas or Arianus and Bolis (cf. 19.3).

**17.10 ἦν γάρ τις ἐπίνοια:** P. now paints Achaeus' plans. He is unlikely to have evidence. Readers enter Achaeus' mind; his vast conception contrasts with his present confinement. In narrative structure the passage resembles App. *BC* 2.349–50, where the defeated Pompey plans going to the Parthian king ὡς δι' ἐκείνου πάντ' ἀναληψόμενος. But Pompey's folly is made clearer. **πρῶτον μέν:** escaping present danger (cf. 15.2, 16.6) is just the first stage, in a short clause. **διαφυγεῖν:** preverb and aorist imply decisive success. †**διὰ προόδου†:** better than the inane 'by means of an advance' would be δίχα περιόδου 'without taking a circuitous route', as might have seemed prudent; cf. Plut. *Cam.* 34.2 περιελθὼν δὲ μακρὰν περίοδον ... καὶ λαθὼν τοὺς πολεμίους. δίχα 'without' does not come elsewhere in P.; but it also appears only once in Appian (*BC* 5.358). Cf. e.g. DH *AR* 10.12.3 δίχα πάσης εὐλαβείας. For περίοδος cf. e.g. Plato, *Rep.* 6.503b2 ἄλλη μακροτέρα ... περίοδος, resuming 4.435d3 ἄλλη γὰρ μακροτέρα ... ὁδὸς ἡ ἐπὶ τοῦτο ἄγουσα. δίχα προόδου 'without any escort' (Loeb) would require a doubtful use of πρόοδος. διὰ περιόδου would not suit ὁρμήν, a swift onward movement, or the plan regarding Antiochus. **τοὺς κατὰ Συρίαν τόπους:** i.e. 'Syria'. Cf. 1.6.n.

**17.11 πάνυ ... μεγάλας ἐλπίδας:** Achaeus like Bolis has μεγάλαι ἐλπίδες (15.8, 18.2 – next sentence). But the phrase also joins with μέγα ... κίνημα καὶ μεγάλης ἀποδοχῆς. Great hopes for great things maximize irony: the 'tragic' irony of hopes which readers know are misplaced (cf. Colebrook (2004) 10–11). The emotion contrasts with §9 μηδεμιᾶς ἄλλης ἐλπίδος καταλειπομένης. For such complexity cf. 19.2. **ἄφνω καὶ παραδόξως:** a pair too at 3.43.9, 4.61.3, 5.6.6 (the last a plan); cf. DS 18.53.5. The dramatic entry envisaged suggests Ptolemy will equip Achaeus with troops. These would assist Achaeus' reception in Antioch – like Demetrius Poliorcetes' in Athens in 295 BC (Plut. *Demetr.* 34.4–7).   **ἔτι διατρίβοντος Ἀντιόχου περὶ τὰς Σάρδεις:** περί suggests Antiochus would still be engaged in operations (cf. 1.8.3, 10.38.7), unaware of Achaeus' escape.   **παρὰ ... Φοινίκην:** the phrase connects to ἀποδοχῆς only, not κίνημα; it stops the anaphora of μέγας seeming too pat.   **τε:** as often, attracted earlier in the phrase than logic requires; cf. 33.10n. It separates Antioch on the Orontes, a Seleucid city (Neumann (2021) 56–60), from regions Ptolemy controls (5.87.3, 6). Coele Syria at least is devoted to Ptolemy (5.86.10–11; cf. 5.67.10 for the pairing with Phoenicia). In this fantasy, Achaeus imagines himself popular both as Seleucid and as Ptolemy's ally; his coins support. (Walbank (1957–79) II 95 thinks P. has forgotten Ptolemy's control.)

## 18 BOLIS AND CAMBYLUS PLAN THE DETAIL

**18.1** Achaeus begins the paragraph, nominative but not in action; Βώλιδος ends the half-sentence. Others take over; Achaeus' possible actions are merely the object of planning and prevention.   **διαλογισμῶν:** thoughts, plans; cf. esp. 3.17.4–8 (διαλογισμοῖς 8).   **ἐκαραδόκει:** from Euripides on; popular with P. and Diodorus.

**18.2 Μελαγκόμαν:** Achaeus is to meet with Melancomas (19.4), so Melancomas' name appears now.   **διὰ πλειόνων** echoes 15.2 διὰ πλειόνων λόγων, and heightens Bolis' imperviousness.   **μεγάλας ἐλπίδας** echoes 15.8 εἰς μεγάλας ἐλπίδας; now Bolis has other hopes (16.8). See 17.11n.   **καθίκηται** 'achieve' (*CGL* 3); a peculiarly Polybian usage, with ἐπιβολή at 2.38.8, 55.6, 21.32c.3, etc.   **τῆς ἐπιβολῆς:** the shifting reference of ἡ ἐπιβολή brings out the shifts in Bolis' alliances. Cf. 16.8, 11, 17.3, 4.

**18.3 προδιαπεμψάμενος:** found only in P. (16.27.1, 21.4.7). διαπέμπεται came at 16.1, of Bolis sending Arianus to Cambylus; events have moved on.   **τῶι Καμβύλωι**, placed here not earlier, stresses that Bolis' fellow plotter, not Achaeus, is being granted Bolis' presence (§1). Here, though, παρουσία means just that Bolis is in the vicinity; cf. *IOSPE* I².32 A.85–6 (Olbia, iii BC) τήν τε πα|ρουσίαν ἐμφανισάντων τοῦ βασιλέως, 89–90.   **ἧκε:** imperfect of ἥκω, but 'he came', not 'he had come'.   **νυκτὸς ἐπὶ τὸν συντεθέντα τόπον** recalls arrangements for their earlier meeting (16.3), and the meeting with Achaeus (17.9). But now detailed planning takes up the next day (§4 μίαν ἡμέραν); Bolis' entry into the camp and meeting with Antiochus are kept for the secrecy of night (§9n.).

**18.4 ἐπὶ ταὐτό** 'in the same place'; cf. 1.82.4.      **συνταξάμενοι:** cf. §5 διάταξις and 16.12 above διατάξεως ... τὰ συντεταγμένα. Earlier, arrangements concerned messages and securing the plot; now they concern physical specifics. See §9n.      **μετὰ ταῦτα** separates the secret discussion from the environment of the camp; likewise ἐγεγόνει (§5) – arrangements had already been made.      **παρεμβολήν** 'camp' (7.5n.). Sardis is not yet accommodating Antiochus' army. Cf. *I.Sardis* II 309.6–8 (summer 213): half the houses in Sardis billeting soldiers.

**18.5 δεύτερον:** with someone else. Cf. 'Men.' *Monost.* 494 μόνος βάδιζ' ἢ δεύτερος, τρίτος δὲ μή. δεύτερον does not imply unimportance, i.e. anticipate Achaeus' plan; cf. LSJ αὐτός I.6. Two is significant: Bolis and Arianus could hold one person each while the ambushers emerged. Their own number cannot be increased, when all is so secret.      **εὐκαταφρόνητος, ἔτι δ' εὐχείρωτος:** εὐκαταφρόνητος 'not worth considering' comes 11 times in P., with τελέως again 2.35.3, 30.18.7. The figure with repeated εὐ- is not found elsewhere in P. It is kept from triteness by ἔτι δ' before the pragmatic εὐχείρωτος 'easy to overcome', which relates especially to τοῖς ἐνεδρεύουσιν. Such figures are widely diffused; cf. Arist. *Pol.* 5.1314b34–5 οὔτε γὰρ εὐεπίθετος οὔτε εὐκαταφρόνητος ὁ νήφων, *Gen. Corr.* 1.328b17; also e.g. Ap. Rhod. *Arg.* 3.1086, *F.Delphes* III.1.152.11 (*c*.150/49 BC) τᾶς τε ἐν τὰν πόλιν εὐεργεσίας καὶ εὐνοίας ἕνεκεν.      **ἔμελλε:** the explanation is almost like direct speech, but in the past.      **τοῖς ἐνεδρεύουσιν:** the first we have heard of them; cf. §8. P. concentrates on the battle of wits.

**18.6 δύσχρηστος** 'hard to handle', from χράομαι.      **πρόθεσις** 'purpose, plan'; can be quite specific, so 1.26.1. P. uses πρόθεσις far more than other writers; pre-set intentions are important to him. πρόθεσις appears in inscriptions, e.g. Welles, *RC* 52.46 (Miletus, 167/6 BC).      **ἀπέβαινε** 'was turning out' (on that hypothesis). This is difficult; one might suppose rather δύσχρηστος <ἂν> ... ἀποβαίνοι, as if in direct speech.      **τοῖς πεπιστευμένοις** designates Bolis authorially, or Bolis and Cambylus. They have ignored Sosibius' πίστις in entrusting the deed to them (16.6); Nicomachus and Melancomas urged Achaeus to trust Bolis (17.5 πιστεύειν). σπεύδουσι tells against referring the perfect to Achaeus' future entrusting of his body.      **ζωγρίαι** 'capturing alive', from ζωός + ἀγρέω (= αἱρέω). Separation from κυριεῦσαι emphasizes it further; similarly it ends §8 forcefully. ἐγχειρεῖν at 16.8 had suggested Achaeus would be alive, but the point now becomes a central issue. See 20.7n. on Molon. P. uses the noun much more than other writers, and often combines it, not with the standard (συλ)λαμβάνω, but with words and phrases of gaining control, like κυριεύω.  διὰ τό: this τό goes with κεῖσθαι; τὸ πλεῖστον governs τῆς ... χάριτος, the service done to Antiochus. Cf. for πρός 2.58.5 τὴν πρὸς τὸ ἔθνος χάριν καὶ φιλίαν.  ἐν τούτωι κεῖσθαι τῶι μέρει 'depended on this aspect'; separation stresses τούτωι. Cf. 3.4.8: the usefulness of my history ἐν τούτωι πλεῖστον κείσεται τῶι μέρει.

**18.7 ἔδει**: again from their perspective, as if in direct speech, but in the past.  ἡγεῖσθαι is the critical consideration; the important ἐξάγηι is subordinated.  διὰ τό: a relatively simple explanation on Arianus and the past; there is then much more detail on Bolis and the future.  γινώσκειν: the trickiness of the terrain starts to emerge. Sticking by a wall is not in question (15.5n.).  ἀτραπόν: the route is hard to reconstruct. Earthquakes have changed the acropolis in particular (hence the sheer cliff on the left side of Figure 4). The right side shows the start of one route possible now, towards, then downhill from, the Byzantine fortifications. That way is to the south. The other route that does not lead into the city would be west from the Byzantine 'Flying Towers', ringed in Figure 4 (see Berlin and Kosmin (2019) pl. 2 no. 22; Hanfmann and Waldbaum (1975) fig. 24). (Professors N. Cahill and B. Yıldırım have kindly helped here.)  πολλάκις advances on 17.9 πλεονάκις; καὶ τὴν εἴσοδον καὶ τὴν ἔξοδον doubles the advantage from each trip. P. has that phrase 4 times; cf. *I.Kios* 1.9 (iv BC) [εἴσο]δον καὶ ἔξοδον.

**18.8 κατόπιν** 'behind', following its genitive; cf. e.g. 30.25.6. ἀκολουθεῖν is 'accompanying' only in a loose sense, as at Ar. *Plut.* 13, 757. By being at the back rather than next to Achaeus, Bolis can observe unobserved: nothing will impede the capture.  παραγένωνται: cf. 20.3n., 20.5 ἐπεὶ δὲ παρεγένοντο πρὸς τὸν ... τόπον. It makes little sense to dwell on just Bolis getting there (παραγένηται FDG).  διὰ τοῦ Καμβύλου: as at 17.6; Cambylus handles this space.  τότ' picks up ἐπειδάν in a sudden moment. Control is underlined; contrast e.g. 15.27.5 τοὺς δὲ συλληψόμενοι.  μήτε ... μήθ': in these non-indicative ideas, scenes never realized present themselves vividly. θόρυβον, νυκτός, ὑλωδῶν show why Achaeus might escape, but also create landscape and confused action. The hillside was heavily wooded then; τινός suggests numerous crags. Suicide with a weapon, envisaged at 20.6, is not considered here. περιπαθής adds to the wild drama that never happens.  διαδραίη 'escape', aor. opt. of διαδιδράσκω.  ῥίψαι: opt., not ῥῖψαι inf.  κατὰ τὴν πρόθεσιν resumes §6 ἡ πρόθεσις, and returns to what will be actuality. But πέσοι ... ὑπὸ τὰς τῶν ἐχθρῶν χεῖρας, split by κατὰ τὴν πρόθεσιν, brings in Achaeus' perspective; cf.

36.8 above ἐγένετο τοῖς ἐχθροῖς ὑποχείριος, and 20.7, 12 below. The narrative again goes beyond just outlining the plan.

**18.9 παραγενομένου ... ὡς** 'having come to'. ὡς as preposition is not rare in P. (cf. e.g. 10.28.7); it here suggests seeing Cambylus in his official place. The perspective is different from §4 εἰσῆλθον εἰς τὴν παρεμβολήν, or more detail is indicated (they left the meeting-place separately). But both phrases must describe the pair's second night of joint action. In §4 they do not enter the camp on their first night (§3) but spend the day together before proceeding. In §10 they leave Antiochus for the camp, not the secret meeting-place; Bolis departs for the citadel ἔτι νυκτός (§11). So τὰ κατὰ μέρος (§4) are spelt out in §§5–8; they are not unexplained details, previously arranged. **παράγει:** historic present as Antiochus meets the chief agent. **Ἀντίοχον:** not in 'their' camp (§11); for a plurality of camps cf. e.g. 3.112.2–3, 10.38.6, 14.3.7. **μόνος πρὸς μόνον:** cf. Gorg. B11a.7 DK, D25.7 Laks–Most πότερα μόνος μόνωι; (secret meeting), Xen. *Cyr.* 6.1.36 μόνος μόνωι (unusual meeting with king). Cambylus evidently remains present; cf. §10 ἀμφοτέρους.

**18.10 ἀποδεξαμένου ... φιλοφρόνως** is standard in itself (cf. e.g. 3.67.4, 30.1.4, *SEG* XXVI.677.20 (Larisa, ii BC), XLI.330.6 (Messene, ii BC)); the three genitive absolute clauses build up Antiochus' enthusiasm. Then in §11 three main verbs deliver the pair's actions, with no feelings indicated. The scene shifts momentously to the ἄκρα. **ἐπαγγελιῶν** 'promises' (LSJ 3); πίστεις (here oaths, cf. 36.3) secure the promises of 17.2. Melancomas made no oaths (§2). **διὰ πλειόνων** recurs to bring out strong feelings in all; cf. 15.2 (Sosibius), §2 (Melancomas). Antiochus longs for completion, as at 17.3. **μηκέτι μέλλειν:** idiomatically eager, not suggesting real delay. Cf. Timoth. 791.189 (Xerxes) ἀλλ' ἴτε, μηκέτι μέλλετε, DS 19.6.5 παροξυνομένου δὲ τοῦ πλήθους καὶ βοῶντος μηκέτι μέλλειν, Virg. *G.* 3.42–3 *en age segnis | rumpe moras*.

**18.11 ὑπὸ ... τὴν ἑωθινήν:** this exact phrase comes 19 times in P., twice in Diodorus, not elsewhere. **Ἀριανοῦ:** sent ahead at §3 – P.'s plotting is meticulous. **παρεισῆλθεν:** Bolis matters most. **ἔτι νυκτός:** there has been no delay.

## 19 ACHAEUS DECIDES

**19.1 Ἀχαιὸς δέ:** the paragraph almost entirely concerns Achaeus' thoughts and actions. Its length advances on 17.8–11. Achaeus' mind should be central, in the light of 36.7–9; but readers have had to wait. **ἐκτενῶς**

καὶ φιλανθρώπως: cf. Moretti, *ISE* I.55.2 (Stymphalus, *c*.189 BC) ἐκτενεί[ας καὶ φιλανθρ]ωπίας, *TAM* v.1.514.10–12 (Maeonia, 61/0 BC) τὴν πρὸς πάντας | τοὺς πολίτας ἐκτένειαν καὶ φιλανθρωπί|αν. These indicate that φιλανθρώπως (*Suda*) is right; φιλοφρόνως (FDG) comes from 18.10 above. Achaeus receives Bolis more intensely than Antiochus; cf. 33.18.4 πασῶν αὐτὸν τῶν κατὰ τὴν Ἑλλάδα πόλεων ἐκτενῶς καὶ μεγαλοψύχως ἀποδεξαμένων. ἐκτενῶς, 'eagerly', shows fervour; cf. Cic. *Att.* 10.17.1 (about a letter) *quam in me incredibilem* ἐκτένειαν*!* ἀνέκρινε: Achaeus quizzes Bolis as he had Arianus (17.6–8), but presumably less fiercely (cf. §2 ὁμιλίαν); he spends his words on questions, cf. διὰ πλειόνων with 18.10 διὰ πλειόνων of Antiochus' exhortation. Antiochus examined τὰς κατὰ μέρος ἐπινοίας (17.2), but before he opted for trust (17.3). Less detail existed then; cf. 18.4.

**19.2 θεωρῶν** 'seeing'. **κατὰ τὴν ἐπιφάνειαν:** appearance and bearing can indicate character; cf. e.g. 27.12.1. But ἐπιφάνεια only takes one so far; cf. 33.4.1–3 – a false impression there, here incomplete. Readers again see Bolis' formidable qualities; cf. 15.1. **ἕλκοντα τὸ τῆς πράξεως στάσιμον:** his weight, i.e. worth, matched the weight, i.e. gravity, of the deed required – a striking phrase. Cf. 12.28.6 ἕλκων τὴν τοῦ συγγραφέως προστασίαν 'having the weight of an author's dignity'; Quint. *Inst.* 10.1.123: in philosophical writings *Brutus suffecit ponderi rerum*. στάσιμος here connects, unusually, with ἵστημι LSJ A IV 'weigh' (transitive); so Cephisod. fr. 12 K–A στάσιμα 'weights'. Cf. Nic. *Al.* 402 στάδιος, unusually. **τὰ μὲν … ἀποβησομένων:** what precedes makes one expect positive feelings; instead emotions conflict. A positive feeling is briefly described; less positive feelings, connected to τὸ τῆς πράξεως στάσιμον, receive more elaborate and arresting language. The whole vividly conveys interiority. Achaeus' thoughts cannot have been known; P. probably invents. **ἐλπίδα τῆς σωτηρίας:** the joy differs from earlier resignation (17.9); there no other hope was left πρὸς σωτηρίαν. **ἐπτοημένος:** scared, or agitated (cf. 31.11.4). Verb and compounds are first found in archaic poetry; P., Philo and Plutarch use them a good deal. **πλήρης ἀγωνίας** 'full of anxiety', a unique combination. ἀγωνία comes 5 times in P.; it denotes emotion from Dem. 18.33 onwards. **μέγεθος** develops what τὸ τῆς πράξεως στάσιμον suggests: not just life or death but those of a mighty ruler. For μέγεθος of significant events cf. e.g. 1.39.7; 3.4.13, of events in P.'s narrative. Here likewise P. suggests the impressiveness of his episode.

**19.3 οὐδενὸς ἥττων** recalls, significantly, Bolis' τριβὴν ἐν τοῖς πολεμικοῖς οὐδενὸς ἐλάττω (15.1). Achaeus matches all in διάνοια, but in practical τριβή is only ἱκανός. Such praise leaves scope for §5. For οὐδενὸς ἥττων cf. Plato, *Prot.* 316d10 (σοφιστής); cf. also P. 4.8.2 etc. οὐδενὸς δεύτερος. [ὅμως]: P.'s practice with ὅμως makes one expect this clause to clash with ὑπάρχων κτλ.; but that clause explains this. Not even the sentence before clashes with this clause; cf. τὰ δὲ κτλ. ὅμως may have entered the text as a gloss or amplification on ἀκμήν (cf. *Suda* α 906; Men. fr. 504 K–A, with apparatus). **ἀκμήν** 'still': see Introduction §13 c. Doubts persist. **πᾶσαν**: emphatically separated from πίστιν. Achaeus continues to withhold some πίστις, unlike even Antiochus (17.2–3). **ἀνακρεμάσαι** 'attach'. The verb stands out: not elsewhere in P. For the related sense 'let depend' cf. e.g. Philo, *Abr.* 59.

**19.4 ποιεῖται τοιούτους λόγους ..., ὅτι**: with ὅτι an unusual introduction. It accentuates this utterance; cf. 30.32.8–9 ἔγραψαν ἀπόκρισιν τοιαύτην, ὅτι 'ἡμεῖς κτλ.' The present tense highlights the moment. **κατὰ μὲν τὸ παρὸν οὐκ ἔστι δυνατόν**: at 20.9.4 the consul κατὰ μὲν τὸ παρὸν οὐκ ἔφασκεν εὐκαιρεῖν, but at least gives a reason; the king need not explain. **φίλων**: royal *philoi* are virtually official 'courtiers'; cf. Strootman (2014) 111–35, Savalli-Lestrade (2017). Whether they lived in Achaeus' palace or palaces is uncertain; cf. Weber (1997) 39 n. 51, and Antiochus' 'chosen friends in his palace', Raphia decree, hieroglyphics, Gauthier and Sottas (1925) 8 line 10. **τρεῖς ἢ τέτταρας**: P.'s narrative can be similarly vague (15.25.3, 36.10.4); but here Achaeus means to sound casual. Cf. the scornful 'three or four papyrus columns' at 5.33.3. Readers are to imagine Bolis' reaction: numbers matter to him. **ὧν συμμιξάντων**, 'when they have met', suggests experimenting with less valuable bodies. **ἕτοιμον αὐτὸν ἔφη παρασκευάσειν**: a relaxed pace; not 'he would come'.

**19.5 ὁ ... κρητίζων**: the narrator's short and witty sentence deflates Achaeus' affected nonchalance. There is some tension with the main idea that he did πάντα τὰ κατὰ λόγον (21.10). **ἐποίει τὰ δυνατά** 'was doing what he could', here implying it was not enough; cf. e.g. 18.33.1: Philip beaten τὰ δυνατὰ πεποιηκώς. The tone is indulgently condescending. **τοῦτο** sets up πρὸς Κρῆτα κρητίζων; cf. K–G I 659. **ἠγνόει**: i.e. he did not realize efforts were futile – he has suspicions. Differently Plut. *Lys.* 20.2 πρὸς Κρῆτα δὲ ἄρα, τὸ τοῦ λόγου, κρητίζων ἠγνόει τὸν Φαρνάβαζον. **τὸ δὴ λεγόμενον** comes elsewhere, e.g. Plato, *Phileb.* 46c9, P. Mich. I 77.10–11; but P. likes this allusive turn (13 times). **πρὸς Κρῆτα κρητίζων**: cf. Plut. *Lys.* 20.2 above, *Aem.* 23.10 with real Cretans, Bühler (1999) 242 (as proverbial). After 15.5, 16.7, etc., the play with the name has special force. **οὐθέν** takes up 16.4 πᾶσαν ἐπίνοιαν ἐψηλάφα. Bolis actually seems not quite prepared for this situation (20.1–2). P.'s tone and stance deliberately fluctuate. **ἀψηλάφητον**: only here until Christian writers. **ἐπινοηθέντων ἄν** 'which could have been thought up'. Cf. e.g. Arist. *Pol.* 2.1273a2 ἐπιτιμηθέντων ἄν ('which could be found fault with'). **εἰς τοῦτο τὸ μέρος** 'in this sphere'; cf. 10.1.10 πρὸς ταῖς εἰς τοῦτο τὸ μέρος ἦν ἐπινοίαις.

**19.6 πλήν** 'but', opposing Bolis' readiness with Achaeus' attempted deceit. **παραγενομένης τῆς νυκτός:** at least one daytime has passed since Bolis' arrival (18.11). **συνεξαποστελεῖν:** an easy correction. The compound appears 7 times in P., once in Diodorus (14.20.3) and a number of times in inscriptions, e.g. *I.Priene B–M* 108.23, 51 (early ii BC). συν- here, with no dative, is probably fossilized rather than meaning 'together with'; likewise 25.2.2. **προπέμψας:** he does not wish them to see the friends: they might know those four were not Achaeus. **συνεξορμᾶν:** the active (-)ορμάω often has the intransitive sense of the medio-passive; cf. e.g. 1.47.7 συνεξορμήσασαν.

**19.7 κοινωσάμενος** 'communicating with'. **παρ' αὐτὸν τὸν καιρόν:** 'at the crucial moment' of going. The phrase comes 11 times in P., once in Diodorus, occasionally in documents (e.g. P. Lond. I 44.25, 161 BC). **γυναικί** is put first, not the name. The communication is presented as personal, not information for the next in command (cf. 21.5n.). **διὰ τὸ παράδοξον:** the cause of emotion is made, not danger or fear, but P.'s theme of the unexpected; cf. 17.2, 21.6, etc. **τὴν Λαοδίκην ἔκφρονα:** see 20.11n. We have met Laodice at 5.74 (upbringing); her royal origin and status make her reaction the more startling. P. calls cowardice and wild reactions womanly and effeminate (36.15.1–2); but here Laodice is closer to the truth. ἔκφρων, mainly a prose word, comes only here in P. **λιπαρῶν** 'begging'. P. uses λιπαρεῖν mostly of women and womanish men (note 32.15.7, with γυναικιζόμενος). The grim ruler shows a tender lack of dignity. One may contrast the ideal restraint of wife and warrior on e.g. the white-ground lekythos Athens NM 1818 (attr. Achilles Painter, 440–435 BC?), J. H. Oakley (1997) 65–6, 144 no. 218. **καταπραΰνων:** only here and 5.52.14 in P. **ἐλπίσι:** Achaeus comforts Laodice with his earlier thoughts (17.10–11). The irony grows. Hector and even Priam are less upbeat in reconciling their wives to their departure; Laodice resembles Hecuba at Hom. *Il.* 24.200 more than Andromache at 6.405–6. For Andromache and Laodice cf. D'Agostini (2014). **προσεκαρτέρει** 'persisted': cf. *TAM* III.7.11–12 (Termessus, i BC), with τὸν πάντα | χρόνον, cf. χρόνον μέν τινα. Extending time within αὐτὸν τὸν καιρόν brings out the close description.

**19.8 πέμπτος αὐτός** 'with four others'; see LSJ αὐτός I.6. **μετρίας** 'quite reasonable' – the men must seem Achaeus' *philoi* (§4), cf. μέν and αὐτὸς δέ – but different from their present fine clothing, and suitable for rough terrain. Cf. Livy 45.32.5 (Macedonian *philoi*) *regius omnibus ... uestitus*. ἀναδούς: perhaps compressed for getting slaves to distribute. λιτήν 'simple': a largely Hellenistic and imperial word (but Atomists D329 Laks–Most (Democritus) λιτότης). Cf. e.g. 6.22.3 of helmet, likewise *IG* II².1478.16 (315/14 BC); Call. *Aet*. fr. 110.78 Harder: lower-grade unguents. At P. 21.34.10 the tyrant Moagetes, lowering himself, seems κατά τε τὴν ἐσθῆτα καὶ τὴν ἄλλην προστασίαν λιτὸς καὶ ταπεινός. At Plut. *Demetr.* 44.9 Demetrius, crushed, appears no king; he dons a grey *chlamys* ἀντὶ τῆς τραγικῆς ('grandiose') ἐκείνης. Kings usually wore purple *chlamys* and white διάδημα; cf. Plut. *Pyrrh*. 26.15; Smith (1988) 34–8; Virgilio (2003) 70, 79–82. On *SC* 952 obv. (gold stater), Achaeus wears diadem and *chlamys*. τὴν τυχοῦσαν 'any old'; cf. e.g. Plut. *Arat*. 45.1: they gave him Corinth ὥσπερ κώμην τὴν τυχοῦσαν. ταπεινὸν αὐτὸν ποιήσας: literally of clothing, cf. 14.1.13; symbolically, self-humiliation. Cf. DS 31.18.1–3: exiled Ptolemy VI refuses royal garb; τὸ τηλικοῦτο τῆς βασιλείας ἀξίωμα πρὸς ἰδιωτικὴν ταπεινότητα τύχης ἐπεπτώκει. προῆγε: after three participle-clauses, one short verb of fatal motion.

**19.9 συντάξας** 'having ordered'; see LSJ II.4. The king gives orders, cf. §6 προσέταξε, but to make someone else prominent. αὐτόν *ipsum*: no one else must answer. Odysseus' ragged disguise is endangered by Helen's questions; he *enters* Troy (Hom. *Od*. 4.244–51). [ἀεί] has been repeated from the following line; cf. DG's ἔφη in §6 from earlier in the sentence. ἀεί produces glaring hiatus. One cannot use ἀποκρίνασθαι to support it, as indicating a one-off answer each time: ἀποκρίνεσθαι matches πυνθάνεσθαι and is the better attested reading (editors misreport F). FDG's εἶεν may be a corruption of a scribe's αἰέν; but that exclusively poetic form cannot be attributed to P. here or at 5.74.9. τῶν περὶ τὸν Ἀριανόν: even if Bolis is included, Arianus, who knows the way, is likely to organize. πυνθάνεσθαι ... κατεπείγον 'ask Arianus whatever needed to be known at a given point'; cf. 6.34.6, *PL* κατεπείγω 1b. τῶν ἄλλων 'the other men'; cf. αὐτούς. Bolis and Arianus will find it natural that some *philoi* (§4) know no Greek. This runs counter to Strootman (2014) 128–35, where non-Greek *philoi* in Hellenistic courts are played down.

## 20 ACHAEUS IS BROUGHT TO ANTIOCHUS

**20.1 ἐπεὶ ... συμβαίνοντος**: Bolis' reaction is not given immediately. An artful half-sentence somewhat throws readers, like Bolis. The first part seems as expected. ἡγεῖτο, διὰ τὴν ἐμπειρίαν and κατόπιν ἐπέστη take up the plan (18.8); the explicit κατὰ τὴν ἐξ ἀρχῆς πρόθεσιν recalls κατὰ τὴν πρόθεσιν (18.8). But ἀπορῶν καὶ δυσχρηστούμενος abruptly follows. δυσχρηστούμενος looks back to δύσχρηστος ἡ πρόθεσις (18.6). The problem there, too many people, was met by this positioning; the new problem is not knowing about Achaeus. Bolis' position underlines failure: he is at the back but not in control. Characters' doubt spreads even to Bolis. **τοῖς περὶ τὸν Ἀριανόν** includes Bolis, cf. 19.6 αὐτοῖς; αὐτός singling Arianus out seems possible if unusual. Hultsch's οὗτος deserves consideration, though 5.35.7 would not parallel it well. Presumably Arianus knows the plan now. **ἐπέστη:** ἐφίσταμαι accompanies κατόπιν e.g. at 2.33.4, 3.74.3. **δυσχρηστούμενος:** P. uses δυσχρηστέω frequently, Diodorus 3 times; it is rare elsewhere (not found in documents). Here 'oppressed with difficulties'. For the pair cf. 5.18.11, 16.2.1 (Philip) ἠπορεῖτο καὶ δυσχρήστως διέκειτο περὶ τοῦ μέλλοντος, 5.2n.

**20.2 καίπερ γὰρ ὢν Κρής:** now even the Cretan is outwitted; cf. 19.5. **πᾶν ἄν τι κατὰ τοῦ πέλας ὑποπτεύσας** 'would have formed any suspicion, however extreme, against another'. πᾶν τι 3.12.1, 23.9.6; rare elsewhere. The idea is like Call. *Ep.* 43.6 Pfeiffer φωρὸς δ' ἴχνια φὼρ ἔμαθον. **ἠδύνατο:** lengthened augment for δύναμαι, as often from the fourth century on. **τὸν Ἀχαιόν** is the object of συννοῆσαι 'comprehend', but only to introduce the reported questions; so 5.81.2 συνειδὼς ... τὴν τοῦ βασιλέως αἵρεσιν ... ποία τις ἦν. **οὐχ οἷον ... πάρεστι:** not only did he not understand which was Achaeus, he had no idea if he was even there. For οὐχ οἷον see LSJ οἷος v.4; cf. e.g. 12.3.9. καθάπαξ heightens the negative; cf. e.g. 11.31.5 οὐδένα καθάπαξ, DH *Dem.* 6 οὐδὲν ἁμαρτάνει καθάπαξ. Bolis realizes Achaeus could be in disguise.

**20.3 τῆς ... §4 καιρόν:** a particularly prolonged sequence of absolutes captures the tricky descent; §4 ταχέως then abruptly restores Bolis' upper hand. **κρημνώδους μὲν καὶ δυσβάτου ... ἐπισφαλεῖς ... καὶ κινδυνώδεις:** paired adjectives paint scene and difficult motion; the darkness (§2) makes things worse. But the pairs are also opposed, with μέν, δέ and καὶ λίαν (for which cf. e.g. 2.40.4). Cf. 7.17.8 for descending from Sardis' citadel to the main city, διὰ στενῆς καὶ κρημνώδους, 7.18.1 ὑπερβάντες τοὺς κρημνούς. That descent was at the opposite side from the Prion (7.17.6); Achaeus knew it to some extent (7.17.7–8). This route seems quite unfamiliar (8.18.7–8). **καταφοράς:** downward slopes; cf., more abstractly, the inscription at Heisserer (1988) 121 A.17–18 (Mytilene, late iv BC) πρὸς τὴν καταφορὰν τοῦ τόπου 'fitting the downward slope of the terrain', *I.Délos* 500 A.31 (297 BC) πρὸς τὴν καταφορὰν τοῦ ἀετοῦ (pediment). **παραγένοιντο** (Reiske) is more attractive than παραγένοιτο (FDG), cf. §5 παραγένοντο; the five are close and collaborate.

COMMENTARY: 20.3–20.7    181

See 18.8n.    τῶν μὲν ... Ἀχαιόν: all assist, strictly two at the top, two at the bottom of each slope. πάλιν underlines the sequence. Devotion is vividly delineated.

**20.4 [γάρ]**: like [δέ], an attempt to start a new sentence; genitive absolute inside genitive absolute proved too much for a scribe. Perhaps both particles appeared above the line in the archetype. For interpolated γάρ cf. e.g. Hdt. 2.125.4. G's unusual parentheses show discomfort with its text.    συνηθείας: habit interests P.; cf. 30.8n. The clause is meant to show P.'s subtlety as well as Bolis' cunning.    καταξίωσιν 'respect, esteem': 4 times in P., only in him before the fourth century AD. Ironically, what brings the king low is his special standing in people's minds. The relation between monarch and *philoi* is memorably captured.    στέλλεσθαι 'conceal', not 'put aside' (Loeb) or 'repress' (LSJ IV.2). Cf. 3.85.7 στέλλεσθαι μὲν ἢ ταπεινοῦν τὸ συμβεβηκὸς ... ἠδυνάτουν, fr. 223 Olson ἐβουλεύετο [ἐβούλετο Hutchinson] μὲν στέλλεσθαι [Livy 44.35.2 *supprimere in occulto ... est conatus*]· οὐ μὴν ἐδύνατό γε κρύπτειν τὸ γεγενός.    ποῖος, insofar as distinct from τίς, underlines that Achaeus is precisely the worst dressed (cf. 19.8). His disguise distinguishes him: the *philoi* would hardly fuss over an inferior.

**20.5 Καμβύλωι**: present, cf. §9, but not named among οἱ διαναστάντες.    διατεταγμένον 'agreed', with a singular; so DS 13.46.3 with σύσσημον ('signal').    σύνθημα 'signal'. For the whistle in the darkness cf. 25.10n. The detail of whistling conjures up the moment more intensely.    διαναστάντες: διανίστημι is commoner from P. onwards (cf. P. Petr. II 18.2*b*.16, iii BC). Of ambushes, e.g. 3.74.1, 16.37.7.    ἐπελάβοντο: ἐπιλαμβάνομαι, just used of the *philoi* helping Achaeus (§3), now describes soldiers capturing them.

**20.6 τὸν δ' Ἀχαιὸν αὐτὸς ὁ Βῶλις**: word order joins them in forceful action.    ὁμοῦ τοῖς ἱματίοις, ἔνδον τὰς χεῖρας ἔχοντα: graphic, ingenious, not expected from 18.8. Touch and concrete physicality are conspicuous. ἱμάτια are any clothes, such as a cloak; so 13.7.2 (women's clothing). Clothes have been important from 19.8 on – protection, now all too protective.    συνήρπασε: more vigorous than ἐπιλαμβάνομαι (18.8 ἐπιλαβόμενος, 20.5).    συννοήσας: at §2 Bolis could not συννοῆσαι; he now fears Achaeus will.    μάχαιραν: a short sword or dagger, easily concealed, for a manly suicide.

**20.7 ταχύ** takes up §4 ταχέως: both start clauses. The next begins παραχρῆμα.    πανταχόθεν κυκλωθείς: the rebel Molon, συννοήσας τὸ γεγονὸς καὶ πανταχόθεν ἤδη κυκλούμενος, and visualizing his treatment ἐὰν ὑποχείριος γένηται, kills himself, probably with the sword (5.54.3). Here the circle is narrower, the participle past. The *philoi* are not said to be encircled. **ὑποχείριος … τοῖς ἐχθροῖς:** P. often has τοῖς ἐχθροῖς or τοῖς πολεμίοις with ὑποχείριος. While generally he prefers πολέμιοι, in this phrase he prefers ἐχθροῖς (in it Diodorus only has πολεμίοις). The phrase is important in the argument; cf. §12, 35.8, 36.8. The specific τὸν Ἀντίοχον at the end of the next clause effectively succeeds τοῖς ἐχθροῖς at the end of this.

**20.8 πάλαι:** as often of an interval felt as long. **μετέωρος** 'excited, in suspense', metaphorically in the air. Emotional μετέωρος and μετεωρίζω are popular with P. and Diodorus; cf. Thuc. 2.8.1, 6.10.5. Antiochus' impatience appeared at 17.3 and 18.10; this mental state corresponds to Achaeus' earlier agitation (17.9–18.1, 19.2). καραδοκῶν recalls ἐκαραδόκει of Achaeus' wait for Bolis (18.1); τὸ συμβησόμενον recalls τῶν ἀποβησομένων (19.2). **ἀπολύσας τοὺς ἐκ τῆς συνουσίας** 'dismissing those who had banqueted'; cf. LSJ συνουσία II. For dining in a royal σκηνή cf. 5.81.5. **μόνος:** as in Antiochus' meeting with Bolis at 18.9; but now the motive is less obvious. The monarch's loneliness, only accentuated by the 'two or three', creates a memorable picture; ἐγρηγορώς, which underlines the night-time, brings to mind Agamemnon's sleepless agitation at Hom. *Il.* 10.1–16, and Achilles' at 24.2–12. **σκηνῇ:** substantial spaces, with elaborate variations possible. Cf. 5.81.5, Callixenus *FGrHist* 627 F2 IIIC.165.30–167.29; Wallace (2017) 6–15; Morgan (2017) 47. **σωματοφυλάκων:** a key position under Alexander and later. Cf. *SEG* XXI.80.7 (Athens, late IV BC), Strootman (2014) 115–17; *IG* IV.1.5–6 (Attalus II, Aegina, 154–144 BC).

**20.9 παρεισελθόντων:** the dramatic entrance is syntactically subordinated to Antiochus' response. The significance of the event is seen through him. His reaction is unexpected, after his excitement (§8) and earlier enthusiasm. **τῶν περὶ τὸν Καμβύλον:** Cambylus, leader of the ambush, is the focal figure. Bolis is not mentioned again in what we have. **καθισάντων** 'having seated'; cf. §12 ἐκάθητο. **ἐπὶ τὴν γῆν:** repeated §12 ἐπὶ τῆς γῆς. A supreme humiliation for a ruler used to thrones; sitting on a seat embodies power. Cf. e.g. Livy 27.4.10 *sella eburnea* sent to Ptolemy IV, Wallace (2017) 11; Thomas on *Hymn. Hom. Merc.* 284. **ἀφασίαν:** only here in P.; not in Diodorus, in Dionysius only *AR* 12.2.4. Not a common word; first at Eur. *Her.* 515 ἀφασία δὲ κἄμ' ἔχει. At P. 15.28.1 what happened to Moeragenes ἄφατον ἦν καὶ παράλογον – the surprise of it makes one speechless. The weeping does not end the ἀφασία. Achilles' meeting with Priam is evoked through the time without speaking, the amazement, the tears, Antiochus sitting, Achaeus on the ground, Antiochus' *skene*, Antiochus' isolation. Cf. Hom. *Il.* 24.448, 472–3, 482–4, 507–15 (Σ A^a bT 24.452 σκηνήν). This is a darker version. **διὰ τὸ παράδοξον:** P. makes explicit the cause for behaviour and feeling, to mark out his theme. Cf. 19.7n. **πολὺν μὲν χρόνον:** the pace slows after §7 ταχύ. Cf. Plut. *Alex.* 21.2 συχνὸν οὖν ἐπισχὼν χρόνον Ἀλέξανδρος, καὶ ταῖς ἐκείνων [Darius' womenfolk] τύχαις μᾶλλον ἢ ταῖς ἑαυτοῦ συμπαθὴς γενόμενος. **συμπαθὴς γενέσθαι:** usage shows that the phrase implies feeling for Achaeus' distress and situation. Cf. with royal captives 10.18.7, DS 17.69.4 Ἀλέξανδρον συμπαθῆ γενέσθαι τοῖς ἠτυχηκόσι καὶ μὴ δύνασθαι κατασχεῖν τὰ δάκρυα, Plutarch above; see also P. 6.53.5, 27.9.5.

**20.10 ἔπαθεν:** something he cannot help. **ὡς ἔμοιγε δοκεῖ:** similar phrases of presumed motivation at 8.2 above, 3.23.2, 31.2.7, 32.3.11; here alone in P. with ἔμοιγε. The caution only adds plausibility. Antiochus' kinship with Achaeus (4.48.5) is not brought in. **δυσφύλακτον** 'hard to guard against'; used metaphorically by P. only here and 15.34.2: other historians portray τὸ ταύτης [Fortune] ἀβέβαιον καί δυσφύλακτον. **παράλογον:** contrary to reasonable expectation; cf. e.g. 15.28.1 (§9n.), 6 τὸ παράλογον τῆς σωτηρίας, 33.6.2 παραλόγωι συμφορᾶι. See 21.10 below. **τῶν ἐκ τῆς τύχης συμβαινόντων:** sympathy and reflection can coexist. At DS 17.36.2 the change in fortune and the greatness of the unexpected calamities reasonably makes those present συμπάσχειν τοῖς ἠτυχηκόσι. Diodorus too proceeds to the specifics of the change. But P., without inconsistency, subtly introduces a generalizing note, and reinforces his theme. In Appian Scipio at Carthage weeps ὑπὲρ πολεμίων, thinking of Carthage's history; he then reflects on empires including Rome (App. *Lib.* 628–30; no tears in P., see Németh (2023)). Antigonus Gonatas weeps on seeing Pyrrhus' head at Plut. *Pyrrh.* 34.8, remembering his own family; his anger shows sympathy for Pyrrhus too (cf. *Pomp.* 80.5, *Caes.* 48.2).

**20.11 Ἀχαιὸς ... πάσης:** an impressive statement of royal connections and imperial power. It builds up to the contrast in §12. Achaeus' family is closely connected with the Seleucids. Laodice 2 (Grainger (1997) 48) is wife of Seleucus II (246–225); cf. 4.51.4 ἦν γὰρ Ἀνδρόμαχος Ἀχαιοῦ μὲν πατήρ, ἀδελφὸς δὲ Λαοδίκης τῆς Σελεύκου γυναικός. In marrying Laodice 10 (Grainger (1997) 49) to Achaeus, Mithridates II of Pontus was linking his family with the Seleucids; he married another daughter to Antiochus (5.43.1–4), and wed the Elder Achaeus' daughter (Porph. *FGrHist* 260 F32.6: Armenian Eusebius). Laodice 10 when young was consigned to a friend of Antiochus Hierax, Seleucus' brother (5.74.4–5; at 5 τῆς Ἀχαιοῦ γενομένης γυναικός read γενησομένης?). Saprykin (2020) 233 dates

Achaeus' marriage after his revolt, but does not think Mithridates took sides. See also Olbrycht (2021) esp. 175–6, 180; D'Agostini (2021) 201–2.     **κύριος:** at 4.48.10–12 Achaeus regains τὴν ἐπὶ τάδε τοῦ Ταύρου πᾶσαν (i.e. in Asia) for Antiochus, then makes himself king. κύριος avoids any disputable term.     **ἐπὶ τάδε** 'this side' (north and west): standard phrasing. Cf. *OGIS* I.219.12 (Ilium, iii BC), *SEG* XXXVI.973.4–5 (Euromos, 197 BC); Ma (1999) 289 lines 29–30 (Balıkesir, 209 BC; this part Antiochus' letter) ἐν τῆι ἐ[πέ]||κεινα τοῦ Ταύρου. The Taurus Mountains separate Asia Minor from Syria, etc.; see Map 1.

**20.12 δοκῶν δὲ τότε:** P. does not immediately contrast the situation now, but adds a new strand. Achaeus was believed to be in a quite different situation; this too shows τὸ παράλογον.     **δυνάμεσι** 'forces, troops', as very often in P.; cf. e.g. *SEG* XIV.571.3 (Cyprus, 143/2 BC) [τῶν ἐν Κύπρ]ωι τασσομένων δυνάμ[εων].     **ὀχυρωτάτωι τόπωι τῆς οἰκουμένης:** similarly extravagant is 18.45.12 (visitors at Isthmian Games) σχεδὸν ἀπὸ πάσης τῆς οἰκουμένης. Achaeus' earlier safety seems overstated; cf. 15.6.     **ἐκάθητο δεδεμένος ἐπὶ τῆς γῆς, ὑποχείριος γενόμενος τοῖς ἐχθροῖς:** these elements are repeated (§§7, 9); the context gives new force.     **οὐθενὸς ἁπλῶς** 'no one at all'. Antiochus and his σωματοφύλακες do not count. Laodice knows only that Achaeus has left the citadel (21.4); the rhetoric is adroit.     **τῶν πραξάντων** resumes the scornful close διαβολὴν δὲ καὶ μῖσος τοῖς πράξασιν (36.9).

## 21 THE END OF ACHAEUS

**21.1 οὐ μὴν ἀλλ'** 'but', by contrast with nobody knowing.     **ἅμα τῶι φωτί:** apt for revelation; cf. 31.1.     **φίλων:** probably all are in the council (§2). Cf. 5.58.2; Moretti, *ISE* II.114.A col. iii.3–4 (Amphipolis, *c*.200 BC) κρ[ίνειν δὲ]| τοὺς φίλους τοῦ βασιλέως. Alternatively, the council is a subset; cf. Strootman (2014) 172.     **κατὰ τὸν ἐθισμόν** creates a contrast between routine and such astonishment. On campaign, a council evidently happens each morning, a dinner each night, in the royal σκηνή.     **ὑπὸ τὴν ὄψιν:** emphatic when used by P. with θεάομαι, θεωρέω, etc.     **τὸ παραπλήσιον τῶι βασιλεῖ:** only amazement is shared with Antiochus, not sympathy. Cyrus and his men are amazed at the sight of Croesus (Hdt. 1.88.1).     **ἠπίστουν τοῖς ὁρωμένοις:** more paradoxical than 20.9 (Antiochus). Cf. 5.18.10 ὥστε τοὺς πλείστους ὁρῶντας τὸ γεγονός μὴ πιστεύειν τοῖς συμβαίνουσιν, Luc. *Dial. Mar.* 4.3 τοῖς σεαυτοῦ ὀφθαλμοῖς ἀπιστῶν. Trust and belief are standardly applied to τοῖς λεγομένοις, etc. (so P. 3.52.6, 9.33.1, 16.11.6).

COMMENTARY: 21.2–21.4

**21.2 καθίσαντος δὲ τοῦ συνεδρίου:** as at 6.37.1, of a council of military tribunes. Sitting embodies the role; cf. e.g. *SEG* XII.87.14–15 (Athens, 336 BC) μηδὲ συνκα|θίζειν ἐν τῶι συνεδρίωι (Areopagus). **πολλοὶ μὲν ἐγίνοντο λόγοι:** the debate, not summarized, is to sound eager and cruel; views differ only on what punishment.

**21.3 ἔδοξε** suits a decision by the council. Cf. 28.19.2 ἔδοξε τῶι συνεδρίωι (convened by Ptolemy VI and advisers); *IG* XII.5.2.824.34 (early ii BC) ἔδοξεν τοῖς συνέδροις τῶν Νησιωτῶν. The council are the judges, Antigonus I merely the prosecutor, when Peithon is tried for planning rebellion (DS 19.46.1–4; 317/16 BC). Achaeus' kinship may have made Antiochus the keener to avoid formal responsibility. **πρῶτον ... σῶμα:** the punishments inflicted on Achaeus, living and dead, join pain with humiliation and display. Non-Greek elements appear. Assyrian connections are given by Van Proosdij (1934); but the combination of punishments especially recalls Darius' Behistun inscription Old Persian col. ii.71–8 (extremities, display, impalement) and 2 Samuel 4:12 (killing, extremities, display by pool). Cf. Ov. *Ib.* 299–300: Achaeus, *qui miser aurifera teste pependit aqua.* For conspicuous impalement see P. 1.86.4; 5.54.6–7 (Molon's corpse). Hermeias, from Caria, eagerly cuts off extremities (5.54.10–11; Antiochus restrains him). Athenians put Hyperbolus' corpse into an ἀσκός (Theop. *FGrHist* 115 F96a); the donkey's skin here must add to the humiliation. See also Fleischer (1972–5); Ehling (2007); Lincoln (2007) 8. **ἀκρωτηριάσαι:** ἀκρωτηριάζω can refer to any extremities; cf. e.g. DS 17.69.3. P. does not elaborate, unlike Hdt. 9.112. **τὸν ταλαίπωρον:** the punishment generates sympathy. Cf. 1.80.13 ἠκρωτηρίαζον τοὺς ταλαιπώρους, DS 17.69.4; Ov. *Ib.* 300 (above) *miser*. Here the narratorial comment, hard to imagine in Thucydides, stands in contrast to the council's and army's bloodthirstiness. Cf. ἔλεον at 36.9 above.

**21.4 ἐπιγνούσης τὸ συμβεβηκός** shows the killing is not public. τὸ συμβεβηκός includes both capture and punishment. **ἐνθουσιασμός ... καὶ παράστασις:** these words can be positive or negative. Cf. 11.12.2 παρίστημι and ἐνθουσιασμός positive, of an army; 10.33.6 μειρακιώδει παραστάσει. The cruelty makes the group exultation disturbing; so too the juxtaposition with the individual Laodice. **τὴν Λαοδίκην:** the papyrus confirms Scaliger's conjecture. Laodice appeared at 19.7, and was named at 20.11. Now she becomes crucial to events, after Achaeus' death (21.5, 9). The deduction from the noise recalls Andromache's fears on hearing lamentation for Hector (Hom. *Il.* 22.447–8; D'Agostini (2014)). But here everyone's οἰμωγή (§6) comes after Laodice's realization. Andromache is μαινάδι ἴση at this point (*Il.* 22.460); Laodice had been ἔκφρων (19.7, but here is shown only reasoning correctly. P.'s argument gets more from the laments of those whom the news totally surprises (§6). **ἐκ τῆς ἄκρας**: Laodice's standpoint for perception; cf. 7.17.4 τοῖς περὶ τὸν Ἀχαιὸν ἐκ τῆς ἄκρας ἀδήλους εἶναι τοὺς προσβαίνοντας. **μόνον**: she knows only his departure, not 'was alone aware' of it (Loeb; contrast 22.9.12 ὡς μόνος εἰδώς). **τεκμήρασθαι** 'infer'; cf. e.g. 9.16.1, Odysseus τεκμαιρόμενον ἐκ τῶν ἄστρων things nautical and terrestrial. **ταραχῆς καὶ κινήσεως**: not specific to rejoicing. Agitation in the camp presages disturbance in the citadel (§§8–9). P. uses the phrase of upheavals he will narrate, 3.4.12.

**21.5 ταχύ**: the narrative has reverted to speed; cf. 20.7 ταχὺ δέ.   [**τοῦ**] **κήρυκος**: no article is expected with κῆρυξ in such contexts. At 18.46.4, by contrast, ὁ κῆρυξ is a fixed part of the Games; cf. Σ Pind. *Pyth*. 1.58 ἀνεκήρυξε ... ὁ κῆρυξ. **πρὸς τὴν Λαοδίκην**: Laodice is treated as leader now; cf. §9. The Seleucids give queens increasing importance; cf. *I.Sardis* II 308 (June/July 213, with letter from Antiochus' wife); Widmer (2019); Jim (2021) 105–7. But here the male ruler's sudden death creates a special situation. **κελεύοντος τίθεσθαι τὰ πράγματα** 'urging her to make an arrangement with Antiochus'. Cf. *Suda* τ 572 (perhaps P.): 'he sent heralds, παρακαλῶν ἔτι καὶ νῦν τίθεσθαι τὰ πράγματα καὶ μὴ κινδυνεύειν τοῖς ὅλοις', ἀντὶ τοῦ συγκατατίθεσθαι.

**21.6 τὸ μὲν πρῶτον**: reaction changes, like Antiochus' (20.9). The message was evidently delivered in public. Laodice is not the real audience; despite politeness, Antiochus hopes to undermine her. Cf. §8 μάλιστα διὰ τῶν στρατιωτῶν. **†ἀναπόκριτος†**: perhaps ἦν ἄκριτος, 'there was confused' lamentation. For ἄκριτος of mass cries cf. 15.31.1, Plut. *Tim*. 27.2; of collective tumult *Dion* 34.5. For ἦν with οἰμωγή cf. DH *AR* 7.67.1, App. *Iber.* 316, *BC* 1.39. Less climactic would be <ἦν> ἀνυπόκριτος ('unfeigned'). 'Unanswered' or 'unanswering' makes little sense; τοὺς κτλ. are not Laodice, cf. τελέως ἀνέλπιστον. ἀδιάκριτος (Wunderer) would yield a dubious pair with θρῆνοι παράλογοι. **παράλογοι** 'beyond reason' rather than 'unexpected', though that shade might come in. **κατεῖχον** 'seized'. Cf. Heliod. 10.4.6 ἀκατάσχετος οὖν ὁρμὴ κατειλήφει τὴν πόλιν. **οὐχ οὕτως διὰ τὴν πρὸς τὸν Ἀχαιὸν εὔνοιαν**: cf. 15.25.10, on the lamentations at Arsinoe III's death, ταῦτα δ' ἦν τοῖς ὀρθῶς λογιζομένοις οὐχ οὕτω τῆς πρὸς Ἀρσινόην εὐνοίας τεκμήρια, rather of hatred for her killer. The construction of motive goes beyond the obvious. Readers recall 4.48.12 on the terrifying Achaeus. For 'not so much ... as' cf. e.g. 5.21.6, Dem. 21.205. **τὸ** governs φαίνεσθαι; παράδοξον is a complement of τὸ συμβεβηκός. **παράδοξον**: the effect is unlike Antiochus' initial silence at τὸ παράδοξον (20.9); but lament, tears, silence are all separated from normal speech. ἑκάστωι: not a united response, but individual perceptions.

**21.7 ἀπορία καὶ δυσχρηστία:** cf. 5.2n.; here 20.1 is recalled, ἀπορῶν καὶ δυσχρηστούμενος of Bolis perplexed. The main issue of the story is resolved; but further helplessness ensues. περί 'in'; cf. e.g. 2.39.8 ἦν ἀκρισία περὶ πάντας μὲν τοὺς Ἕλληνας.

**21.8 διακεχειρισμένος** 'having killed'; of kings not physically killing e.g. DH *AR* 1.81.6 (cf. 76.2), Jos. *AJ* 15.173. The word comes only here in P. Antiochus is now presented as responsible for the death, if not its specifics. **ἐπεῖχε τοῖς κατὰ τὴν ἄκραν ἀεί** suggests military pressure, not diplomatic, though the citadel is physically as before. τοῖς κατὰ τὴν ἄκραν varies §6 τοὺς περὶ τὴν ἀκρόπολιν; τοὺς ἔνδον (§7) and τῶν ἔνδον provide a further variant, but ἐκ τῶν ἔνδον here is also pointed. Cf. e.g. Dem. 19.299 ἔξωθεν οἱ ἐπιβουλεύοντες, ἔνδοθεν οἱ συμπράττοντες. **ἀφορμὴν ... παραδοθήσεσθαι:** παρέδοσαν αὑτοὺς swiftly follows (§9 ταχέως).

**21.9 ὃ καὶ τέλος ἐγένετο:** unique phrasing; 15 times P. has ὃ καὶ συνέβη γενέσθαι or, after generalizations, ὃ καὶ τότε συνέβη γενέσθαι. τέλος is added, as at 5.107.3 ὃ καὶ τέλος ἐποίησαν; here time stretches out, after intensely detailed narration. **πρὸς σφᾶς** 'among themselves'; cf. e.g. 1.82.4 διεστασίασαν πρὸς σφᾶς. **Ἀρίβαζον:** the other possible replacement leader; he was in charge of the main city during the siege (7.17.9, 18.4), before joining Achaeus (7.17.7) in the citadel (7.18.7). The name is Persian; cf. Launey (1987) I, 567–8; Strootman (2023) 24–5. It need not show the family's present identity. Cf. *FGrHist* 160 F1 col. ii.5 (on 246 BC) Ἀρίβαζος ὁ ἐν Κιλι<κί>αι στρατ[ηγός], 13; *IG* II².1939.14 (130–120 BC) Ἀρίβαζος Σελεύκου Πειραιεύς. **οὗ γενομένου:** P. uses this link more often than others do, but cf. e.g. DS 8.21.2, *Tit. Camirenses* 110.28 (after *c.*182 BC) οὗ γενομένου συνέβα κτλ. ταχέως means soon after this happening; cf. 2.67.6. **διαπιστήσαντες ἀλλήλοις:** the theme of trust and mistrust continues. **τὰς ἀκροπόλεις:** contrast §6 τοὺς περὶ τὴν ἀκρόπολιν. DS 17.21.7 has τὰς ἀκροπόλεις of Sardis. The plural is unlikely to include a hill other than the known acropolis (Professor Cahill confirms).

**21.10 Ἀχαιός:** P. here dwells only on this episode, not Achaeus' whole career, despite his 'custom' (18.41.1), especially for kings: so 18.41 (Attalus I), 36.16.1–10 (Massinissa), more briefly 5.39.6 (Cleomenes V); Pomeroy (1991) 85–109. Instead, he surveyed Achaeus' career at 20.11 above; the effect both there and here is more argumentative and more momentous. This sentence begins with two participles on what Achaeus did and had done to him before his execution; these emphasize P.'s argument and construction of events. A short main clause gives the death (κατεστρέψατο τὸν βίον); the sentence grows with a participle (γενόμενος) and dependent infinitives. These move into P.'s present and his readers' future. The final ἀνθρώπους ὄντας offers a universal present. The sentence advances in time, expands in scope and ends the episode solemnly. **πάντα τὰ κατὰ λόγον** were spelt out more fully at 36.8. Achaeus has briefly seemed outclassed in trickery; now he wins συγγνώμη, his vanquishers abhorrence. **πιστευθέντων:** cf. 16.6, their indifference to Sosibius' trust; 17.5, Achaeus urged to trust them; 18.6 τοῖς πεπιστευμένοις. Achaeus withheld complete trust at 18.3; the rhetoric is now simpler. **ἀθεσίας** 'faithlessness', from ἀθετέω, violating trust, etc. The main narrative has not employed such strong terms of moral condemnation. P. has ἀθεσία much more often than its other users, Diodorus and the Septuagint; cf. *IOSPE* I².352 col. i.15–16 (Taurian Chersonese, late ii BC?): Scythians manifesting their inborn ἀθεσία. **κατεστρέψατο τὸν βίον** 'ended his life'; 35.1n. **οὐκ ἀνωφελὲς ὑπόδειγμα γενόμενος τοῖς ἐσομένοις:** cf. 15.20.5 τοῖς δ' ἐπιγενομένοις [Fortune] ἐξέθηκε κάλλιστον ὑπόδειγμα πρὸς <ἐπ>ανόρθωσιν τὸν τῶν προειρημένων βασιλέων παραδειγματισμόν. ὑπόδειγμα is literally 'illustration', so an example. οὐκ ἀνωφελ- is rare; technical writing may tinge the expression. Apollonius of Citium (i BC) speaks of communicating the οὐκ ἀνωφελής/-έλητος consideration of limbs helped by ὑποδείγματα, drawings (*CMG* XI.1.1 pp. 38.6–11, 62.3–7). P. stresses his history is useful far more frequently than Thucydides. Often he employs the idea to justify himself and, relatedly, attack others (cf. e.g. 1.14.6, 57.3, 3.4.8, 31.12–13, 9.2.5–6). Here he is more intent on the argument of his episode. τοῖς ἐσομένοις is what prose says, e.g. DS 17.114.1, DH *AR* 1.6.4, *IG* XII.8.269.12–13 (Thasos, i BC); the poetic ἐπεσσόμενοι has probably led to F's ἐπεσομένοις.

**21.11 μηδενὶ πιστεύειν ῥαιδίως:** the episode suggests that even caution over trust does not secure one; but it certainly discourages facile trust. The message is moderate rather than cynical. **μὴ μεγαλαυχεῖν ἐν ταῖς εὐπραγίαις:** cf. 29.20.1: Paullus displays Perseus, and urges μήτε μεγαλαυχεῖν ἐπὶ τοῖς κατορθώμασι παρὰ τὸ δέον ... μήτε καθόλου πιστεύειν ταῖς παρούσαις εὐτυχίαις – one should visualize the opposite fortune (cf. 38.21.2–3). The point, then, is probably general, not censure of Achaeus' calling himself king. **πᾶν:** anything, however bad and inconceivable. **ἀνθρώπους ὄντας** is used in related contexts at 2.4.5 (allow for τὸ παράδοξον), 2.7.1, 23.12.4; ἄνθρωπον ὄντα closes Hasdrubal's speech, soon undermined, at 38.20.3. See too Hdt. 1.32.8 ἄνθρωπον ἐόντα (Solon to Croesus), 86.5 (Croesus), 6 ἄνθρωπος ἐών (Cyrus). Here P.'s close is resoundingly powerful. P. does not mention the gods, like Solon's speech at beginning and end (Hdt. 1.32.1, 33); there remains something religious or derived from religion.

The papyrus raises the question: did this episode and this sentence end the first of book 8's two years? The large initial θ or ε in col. ii would be an unusual way of beginning a new section of text; it seems like a sort of small-scale title, with larger letter size as is normal (Schironi (2010) 23) but with no extra space from the preceding line and no centring (for actual book titles without extra space or centring, see Schironi (2010) 23, 39). The mini-title could mark the fourth year of the Olympiad (ἔτος δ; the new year could not begin with Ἑλληνικά). But this could also be a book of extracts, with excerpts from book 9 to follow (θ, or ἐκ; papyri do not indicate numerals by strokes above the letter). In the same century as the papyrus, Brutus engaged in the parallel activity of summarizing P. (Plut. *Brut.* 4.8). The letter above θ/ε shows ink from a horizontal stroke above base height, cf. the α in col. i; so δ and especially λ are ruled out (for the hand cf. P. Berol. inv. 9775, i BC). α could fit ἀνθρώπους, if this is an extract. -ειδυῖαν ... ὄντας would mean 37–8 lines between col. i.4 and ii.2: easily possible from two columns less 7 lines. But if this is a complete text, one might expect at least a further sentence to conclude the *res Asiae*.

## 24–34 THE CAPTURE OF TARENTUM

P.'s account of this success greatly engages itself with the Tarentines as well as Hannibal. He sets the events in the context of Tarentine history from at least 283 BC (24.1); he includes references to Tarentine culture and history (28.2, 28.7–8, 9, 33.8, 9nn.). His account interweaves Hannibal's plans and actions, particularly on the military plane, with the plans and actions, largely non-military, of the young Greek aristocrats. We could call it a kind of συμπλοκή on a tiny scale. The sections up to victory concentrate the spotlight on Hannibal and the Tarentine conspirators, sometimes separately, sometimes together: 24 together, 25 Tarentines, 26 Hannibal, 27 Tarentines, 28 together (largely Tarentines), 29 together, 30 together, 31 together (largely Hannibal). Different levels of action and types of narrative come together: the military and political narrative of capturing a city and a narrative of small-scale intrigue. The latter is common in P.; cf. e.g. 31.11–15 on Demetrius' escape. This instance is akin to a conspiracy against a tyrant, by a group of daring young men; cf. esp. the account in Plutarch, *De Genio Socratis* and *Pel.* 7–11, perhaps from Callisthenes. Both types of action matter to P. Other participants in the events are significant too: the *praefectus* Livius, the other Romans, the Tarentines not involved in the conspiracy. These Tarentines become important in the narrative from 30 onwards; there attention fluctuates between them, the Romans and Hannibal.

The success of Hannibal's plans ties in with P.'s wider presentation of him (see Introduction §2 b, §5 c, §6 b, §7 c, §8 f, §10 b, §11 b, §12 a, b, c) – and of generalship: the following book will bring the point out (cf. 9.12–20, 9.22.1–6). In a still larger perspective, Hannibal and the conspirators together illustrate how meticulous and inventive planning can control what is going to happen. By contrast, the story of Achaeus' downfall, not far separated in the book, illustrates how the utmost care cannot exclude unpredictable and extraordinary events (15–21; cf. 35–6).

As usual, the wider arguments lead to some distortion. The general impression of impeccable success could easily have been modified. The young men and Carthaginians between them fail to stop first Livius, then the surviving Romans, then the pro-Roman Tarentines from getting to the 'acropolis' (30.6n., 31.1, 3; Map 3, Introduction §11 a). The young men had earlier been outside Livius' house (27.8n.); land access to the acropolis must have been over a bridge crossing a ditch, through a gate in the wall of the acropolis, next to the present Canale Navigabile (32.3, 32.5n., Cera (2019) 10, 27–8; for the sea see 30.6n.). Hannibal's attempt at taking the acropolis is marked as a failed intention – but not too heavily (33.1, 10, 34.2nn.). The failure is swallowed up in Hannibal's astounding plan to restore control of the sea to the city (34.2–12). Capturing the main city and the acropolis can be seen as separate projects (Introduction §11 a). This unit of narrative, probably marked off from what followed (34.13n.), enables a predominantly positive picture of Hannibal's planning, rather than suggesting a plan undercut by the continuing Roman presence in the acropolis.

Tarentum is important to P. from another perspective again. There is no suggestion that siding with Hannibal is a *defectio* from the Romans (24.3n., and Livy 25.11.20, 15.7), still less that the conspirators are traitors (24.4, 7, 26.1nn.). The conspirators see their action as freeing the city, a view which P. endorses (34.3–4n.). It may be doubtful quite how far Hannibal proved able to maintain the promised freedom; but P. contrives to play this down here (25.1–2n.). The patterning of the narrative shows the Tarentines, after losing their liberty to Pyrrhus through decadence (24.1n.), freeing themselves from the Romans, as befits Greeks akin with the Spartans (33.9n.); they are brought to a point where they can (allegedly) combat the Romans unaided (32.2, 4, 33.3, 34.8, 12nn.).

COMMENTARY: 24–34          191

The interaction between Romans and Tarentines is tinged with ethical and historical point. The Romans, keen imitators, are lured by a culture of drinking and dining into calamitous error (25.11, 27.1nn.); here the Tarentines pretend to fit their stereotype, but rise above it (27.4n.). Patterns of change in a people (the Tarentines) and of cross-cultural influence on a people (the Romans) complicate simple and static conceptions.

Such aspects do not in the least compromise the vivacity of the account, and its vivid specificity. Entertaining and humorous elements drive home pointedly the pragmatic and ethical ideas (25.6, 7, 29.6, 8nn.); the intensity of detail, arresting even in P., shows a practicality quite equal to the agents' own.

Taras' harbours had given it economic dominance in the region, though that dominance was affected when Brundisium became a Latin colony in 244 BC (P. 10.1.9; Poulter (2001) 219). The Museo Archeologico Nazionale di Taranto gives a sense of the city's material and cultural riches. It is debatable how far there was a decline in the third century (cf. Hyatt (2011) 91–9; Lippolis (1994*b*) 58, (1994*c*) 240; Masiello (1994) 319, tav. XVIII–XIX after p. 240). The Romans took the city from Pyrrhus in 272; the Tarentines became allies of the Romans (cf. Livy 22.61.12–13). The *foedus* may already have included an obligation to provide ships (P. 1.20.14; Livy 35.16.3, 8, cf. 26.39.5). The Romans put a legion into the city in the Gallic Wars of 225 (P. 2.24.13), and a garrison in 218 after the battle of the Trebia (3.75.4 – προφυλακαί). Livy seems to indicate there was at least no large garrison in the city when Livius hastily arrived with forces in 214 to stop the city accepting Hannibal and his army (24.10n.; Livy 24.20.12–13, with Weissenborn's *impigre*). Tarentum had in some sense entrusted itself to Hannibal after Cannae in 216 (P. 3.118.3, 5, not to be dismissed). Rome's taking of hostages had stopped further action; but a perception of broken *fides* would help to explain the Romans' brutal treatment of these hostages when they escaped (cf. Livy 27.25.1). Brutal indeed was the Romans' treatment of Tarentum when they captured it in 209; the city was thought to have lost its freedom (Strabo 6.3.4 (II 208.1–2 Radt); Livy 27.21.8, contrast *Per.* 15). At the time of these events, however (26.1n.), the *praefectus* was untroubled by popular anger at the killing of the hostages (24.3n.), and unaware of the conspirators' intentions (25.8, 27.5nn.), as were the Tarentines generally (24.10n.). He thought he was on friendly terms with these members of the elite (25.7, 27.4, 5nn.); hence an openly anti-Roman party is improbable.

The garrison, though, was particularly significant for the Tarentines' loss of freedom, as, of course, for the Romans' failure and success in defence. Though there was some force on the acropolis (31.1n.), P.'s account of 'the Romans' proceeding in arms to the acropolis according to custom (30.8n.) suggests that many of the garrison's soldiers, like the commander, were located in the main city.

P. shows a particularly detailed knowledge of Tarentum, including street names (29.1, 33.6nn.), and has a great deal of detail to offer on the conspirators. Research in Tarentum, and sources from there, seem plausible. Writers on the deeds of Hannibal are probable sources too, especially Silenus and, despite 3.20.5, Sosylus (cf. 3.6.1–2 etc.; *FGrHist* 175–80). Fabius Pictor may not have reached this year (Bispham and Cornell (2013) 166–7). It is now accepted that Livy's account is likely to be based on P.'s; complicated alternatives fade away when the two tellings are so close. Readers of P. will not easily believe that such a characteristic piece of Polybian narrative should all but transcribe a lost earlier account, and adhere to it in most sentences and the organization of all the material. Livy will be taking P. as his main source, and occasionally adding in details from elsewhere (25.1–2, 34.1, 9nn.; similarly Nicolet-Croizat (1992) xii–xix). Livy knows of a number of sources (25.11.20); Appian's version, *Hann.* 133–48, shows plainly that sources independent of P. remained available, and Livy seems at one point, at least, to be using a source also used by Appian (34.1n.; cf. 9n.). Livy's perceptive and resourceful version of P. is valuable both as a commentary and as a point of comparison, to bring out the particular nuances and emphases of P.'s remarkable account. (On Tarentum and events, see Introduction §11 a, §12 c; Wuilleumier (1939); Lazenby (1978) 110–12; Lo Porto (1992); Lomas (1993) 39–84; Seibert (1993*a*) 273–7; Le Bohec (1996) 215–18; Heftner (1997) 259–60; Lippolis (1997) 13–58; Poulter (2001); Chlup (2009); Fronda (2010) 188–233, 260–9, 337–9; Hyatt (2011); Grelle and Silvestrini (2013) 82–108, 161–70; MacDonald (2015) 161–5; Gallo (2018) 807–10; Cera (2019); Todaro (2021); S. Hornblower (2024) 148–9.)

## 24 HANNIBAL MEETS SOME TARENTINES

**24.0** See 34.3n. P.'s introduction not only placed the events in the context of Tarentum's history in the third century, but also set up the crucial points of topography (34.3). However, an account of Taras' harbours, location and economic success was left until book 10 (10.1). The stress was probably more on the politics. In P.'s main narrative, Tarentum's regional ambitions do not figure; internal change is the point. The structure of Tarentum can be seen from Map 3 (for more detail see Mastrocinque (2010) tav. II–III). In antiquity no channel separated the acropolis from the main city. Ships would have to go through a channel at the far end of the acropolis from the city to pass from the Mar Grande into the enclosed 'Mar' Piccolo and Tarentum's harbour. This channel was not in contact with the city; hence κρατούσης of the citadel.

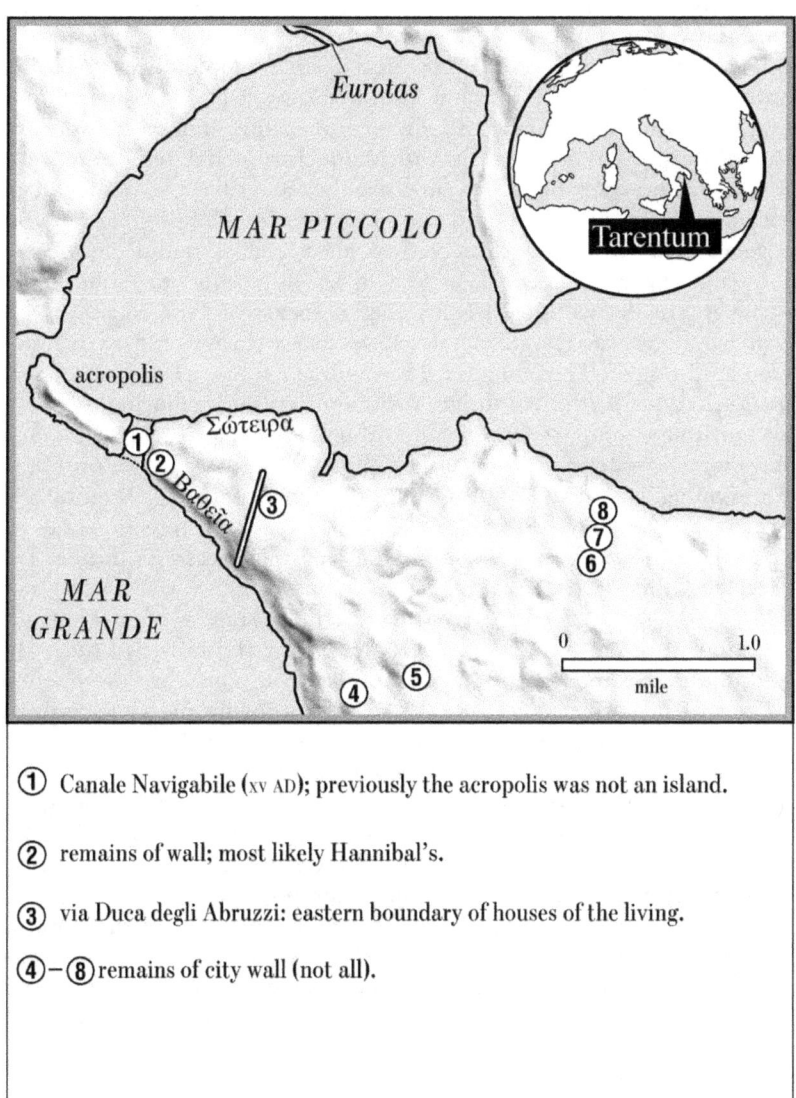

① Canale Navigabile (xv AD); previously the acropolis was not an island.

② remains of wall; most likely Hannibal's.

③ via Duca degli Abruzzi: eastern boundary of houses of the living.

④–⑧ remains of city wall (not all).

Map 3 Tarentum (Joe LeMonnier, https://mapartist.com/)

**24.1** The approximate location of the extract is assured because F has it in the margin. The first half-sentence, ὅτι ... Ἠπειρώτην, comes only in M, and may take words and phrases from P. rather than reproducing a half-sentence from him. P. gives the background to Hannibal taking Tarentum from the Romans in the hostilities between Rome and Tarentum, presumably from 283 if not earlier (Lomas (1993) 39–57). But here the emphasis is on Tarentum as an example of internal alteration. While in DH *AR* 19.8 and Plut. *Pyrrh.* 13.3–13 the domination of Pyrrhus is an unintended consequence of calling him to help against Rome, here internal boredom with democracy generates the move to monarchy, however figurative ζητεῖ may be. So at 6.9.5–9 democracy is too familiar to be valued, and the πλῆθος end up finding δεσπότην καὶ μόναρχον. The generality is marked by πᾶσα, φύσιν ἔχει and the present; the syntax ἐλευθερία ... ζητεῖ δεσπότην makes an abstract the subject, and so heightens the paradox. Decius Magius speaks of *Pyrrhi superbam dominationem miserabilemque Tarentinorum seruitutem* (Livy 23.7.5). On P. and constitutions, see Introduction §1 c and §11 a.   τὸ τῆς εὐδαιμονίας ὑπερήφανον: at 6.18.5, on Rome, P. presents citizens' enjoying εὐδαιμονία and turning to ὑπερηφανία as a standard process (ὃ δὴ φιλεῖ γίνεσθαι). Here the idea is condensed into a potent phrase. Cf. also 7.1.1–2 on Capua summoning Hannibal. For the luxury and prosperity of Tarentum cf. Strabo 6.3.4 (II 208.18–20 Radt). The particular connection was the ἀσέλγεια with which they had abused Roman ambassadors in 282; fear then led, thinks P., to the calling in of Pyrrhus (1.6.5; cf. DH *AR* 19.5.1–5, *MRR* I 189–90).   τὸν Ἠπειρώτην: Pyrrhus' name is often given this addition in other authors (e.g. DH *AR* 1.6.1); the only two times this addition comes in P., out of 22 mentions of his name, are the opening sentences of extracts (cf. 12.25k.2). It is probably the Constantinian excerptor's addition, as οἱ Ταραντῖνοι could well be.   ἐλευθερία: at Taras δημοκρατία ἐγένετο ἐκ πολιτείας after the loss of many aristocrats in a battle of 473 (Arist. *Pol.* 5.1303a2–6; cf. 1320b9–14).   ἐξουσίας: power, and here licence; applied to all three elements in the Roman constitution at 6.11.12.   πολυχρονίου fits P.'s conception of time affecting constitutions psychologically; the change in generations, as in 6.9.4–5, is here turned into a single quasi-mind. The prolongation contrasts ironically with the swift shift back, ταχὺ πάλιν μισεῖ.   φύσιν ἔχει: with infinitive, as at 29.22.1.   τὴν πρὸς τὸ χεῖρον μεταβολήν: similar phrases at 16.28.6, 18.33.6.   καὶ τότε: the καί underlines the connection with the generalization in a way that may seem superfluous; cf. 6.25.11.

**24.2** comes in M between §1 above and two passages from the proem of book 9. This dry piece of wisdom cannot be more precisely located in book 8.

**24.3** is very close to Livy 25.8.1 *huius atrocitas poenae duarum ... ciuitatium animos irritauit cum publice* ... The Romans have ceremoniously killed escaped hostages from Tarentum and Thurii (Livy 25.7.10–14). After the people of the two cities, P. probably went on in this or the next sentence to the Tarentine *nobiles iuuenes* (Livy 25.8.3), the subject of §4. Popular feeling is apparent: the young men are not isolated in their attitudes (cf. Livy 24.13.2–3). Livy says the *defectio* was looming anyway (25.7.10); but 27.4–5 below suggests that the Romans in Tarentum did not see it.   προσπεσόντων δὲ τούτων εἰς 'when news of this reached' Tarentum; cf. e.g. 3.85.7.   τοὺς Θουρίους: the place, not the people. Cf. 10.1.4, *IG* IV.1².95 col. i.43 (Epidaurus, iv BC).   ἠγανάκτει can be a strong word (38.9.3; *ira* Livy 25.15.7, of the people of Thurii).   τὰ πλήθη: here one πλῆθος in each city; cf. e.g. 10.25.6, 20.6.3.

**24.4** The young men do not send out an intermediary; the Romans trust them to go out on a raid themselves.   ἐξοδείαν: the word, before Middle Byzantine literature, only in P. (4.54.3, 8.25.4) and inscriptions from Egypt (so *OGIS* 1.56.60 (Tanis *et alibi*, 238 BC)). In the inscriptions 'procession', in P. a raid (cf. below 24.10, 25.4). Livy slips from *per speciem uenandi* (25.8.4) to *praedandi causa* (25.8.6).   παρεμβολῆι 'camp', 7.5n.   ἄλλοι: about eleven (Livy 25.8.3).   συγκαθέντες 'crouching down'.   εἴς τινα τόπον ὑλώδη παρὰ τὴν ὁδόν: *silua prope uiam* Livy 25.8.5. They hide by the road for a quick getaway, if necessary.   Φιλήμενος καὶ Νίκων: Philemenus seems from §§11–12 to be more the leading figure than Nicon (*Nico et Philemenus* Livy 25.8.3, 5; 27.16.3 *Philemenus, qui proditionis ad Hannibalem auctor fuerat*; contrast Nicon there and at 26.39.15 *eius factionis erat*). At least he is the keenest on expeditions. His name is unusual, with its Aeolic vocalism and accentuation (cf. Φιλουμενός). In this region, it is seen at *IG* IV.1².95 col. ii.50, cf. 49 Μεταπόντιον (Epidaurus, iv BC), and Ravel (1947) 99 nos 884, 886–7 (Tarentum, iii BC). Cononeus, the name given to this man at Front. *Strat.* 3.3.6, App. *Hann.* 133, is not attested at all elsewhere (*JHS* 12 (1891) 261 no. 38.5 (Lamos gorge, Christian) Κονωνει is Κόνωνι).

**24.5** τῶν ... Ἀννίβαν: Livy follows P. closely in these words, *progressi ad stationes* (guards) *comprehensique ... ad Hannibalem deducti sunt* (25.8.5); but his abbreviation *ultro id petentes* after *comprehensique* loses the dramatic mysteriousness towards the guards, built up by the structure οὐδὲν ... οὔτε ... οὔτε ... αὐτὸ δὲ μόνον τοῦτο.   πόθεν: not obvious; the camp is three days' journey away from Tarentum (26.2).

**24.6** ταχύ: the guards sense importance.   κατ᾽ ἰδίαν: more mystery. This effectively short sentence heightens the unfolding drama. Livy omits it.

**24.7 καί:** often strengthens λίαν in P. (cf. 20.3n.). Hannibal's enthusiasm animates the whole narrative; it is compatible with prudence (§10). **ἀπελογίζοντο** 'gave a λόγος'. **πολλὰς καὶ ποικίλας:** a common pair in P. (17.6n.); P. often uses it of utterances, and often separates it from the noun (cf. e.g. 18.43.8 for both). **χάριν τοῦ μὴ δοκεῖν:** P. characteristically sees cautious planning rather than simple indignation. His words do not show that the young men are concerned with power for themselves in Tarentum rather than with liberation of the city from Rome (thus Lomas (1993) 72). **ἀλόγως** 'without good reason'. Questions are raised by the apparently friendly relation of the elite to the Romans, which they will have to disclose (cf. 25.7). Hence both αὐτούς and πατρίδα, a carefully chosen word. The risk that they might seem to be 'traitors' acting for their own advantage is evidently beneath their consideration (Livy 25.9.8 *proditores*, 10.4, 26.39.11, cf. 23.43.3 of Nola; Front. *Strat.* 3.3.6). P. 18.13–15 discusses the difficulties of defining traitors; 18.14.9–10 opposes private ambition and the good of πατρίδες. **τὴν ὑποκειμένην πρᾶξιν:** the focus of their thought, not further spelt out; cf. §12. Livy has just *qui cum et causas consilii sui et quid pararent exposuissent* (25.8.6): he is less intent on the drama and the careful interaction.

**24.8 ἐπαινέσας ... ἐξέπεμψε:** the most important word is the short ἐξέπεμψε, 'sent out' of the camp (§9n.); Hannibal does nothing yet to make definite and binding agreements. There is no such word in Livy. ἐξέπεμψε follows an extended version of some standard phrasing for an appreciative and friendly response ('politeness' would be too weak). Cf. e.g. 1.49.11 ἐπαινέσας καὶ δεξάμενος τὴν ὁρμήν, 21.41.6 (πρεσβείας) ἐπαινέσας καὶ φιλανθρώπως ἀποδεξάμενος, Welles, *RC* 45 decree 15–16 (Seleucia Pieria, 186 BC) ἀποδεχομένην φιλοφρόνως τὴν τῶν | τοιούτων ἀνδρῶν προθυμίαν καὶ εὐεργεσίαν. φιλανθρωπ- 'warm' is common in inscriptions, e.g. *I.Milet* 306.5 (ii BC): your ψήφισμα καλὸν καὶ φιλάνθρωπον. Live exchange and inscriptions stand close in manner. **συμμιγνύναι ... αὐτῶι πάλιν** takes up their τῶι στρατηγῶι συμμῖξαι (§5); but the weight falls on the eager κατὰ τάχος.

**24.9 κατὰ δὲ τὸ παρόν:** a generous gesture follows, with the implication that this is only the start. Livy's *conlaudati oneratique promissis* spells it out (25.8.6; pre-set phrasing too: 10.14.3, Sall. *Jug.* 12.3). **τὰ πρῶτα:** the best; cf. 2.59.9 τοὺς πρώτους τῶν πολιτῶν. ἐπειδὰν κτλ. makes against 'the first' (Loeb). **ἐξελασθέντων πρωΐ:** animals for food and drink are kept in the camp at night (cf. 6.31.13). The young men will set off back in the morning. **ἄνδρας:** looking after the animals; not in Livy, but *sine certamine* (25.8.6) implies their presence. **ἱκανόν:** Hannibal does not want too many Carthaginians knowing his plan. **περιελασαμένους**

'round up'; apt only to the animals. **εὐθαρσῶς** 'without fear'; cf. *PL* εὐθαρσής 2b. **περὶ γὰρ τῆς ἀσφαλείας αὐτῶι μελήσειν** captures conversation. Cf. Arch. fr. 23.9–10 West ἀμφὶ δ' εὐφ[ρόνηι] | ἐμοὶ μελήσει, Ar. *Plut.* 229; Arr. *FGrHist* 156 F9.31 (less reassuring). Cf. also for the closing ἀσφάλεια P. Tebt. III.1 703 col. iii.256–7 (late iii BC).

**24.10 ἐποίει ... ἐξόδους:** the general's munificence is actually purposeful. The μέν-clause relates to §8 ἐξέπεμψε, the δέ-clause to §9. Perhaps it should be ταῦτα (cf. 5.108.5): ἐποίει δὲ τοῦτο should pick up what immediately precedes (2.66.9, 10.13.2). **ἀναστροφὴν ... πρός:** space of time for a purpose; cf. 5.7.3 σπουδάζοντες βραχεῖάν γε τοῖς Αἰτωλοῖς ἀναστροφὴν δοῦναι πρὸς τὴν βοήθειαν. **πολυπραγμονῆσαι** 'inquire into': neutral or commendable; cf. Leigh (2013) 100. **νεανίσκους** does not indicate age at all precisely; cf. 6.20.3, 35.8, etc. In 214, young aristocrats had interested Hannibal in Tarentum, and stressed the power of young men over the people at Tarentum (Livy 24.13.2–3). Roman forces had stopped anything happening (24.20.12–15). **πρὸς τοὺς πολίτας:** fellow citizens guessing the real purpose would be risky. Livy's *popularibus* (25.8.6) translates τοὺς πολίτας, cf. §12 τοὺς ἰδίους, *OLD² popularis²* 1a; it does not denote a faction of pro-Roman *populares* (so Walbank). **ἀπὸ τοῦ κρατίστου:** *bona fide*, cf. 17.4 above, with πιστεύοντες.

**24.11–12 τῶν περὶ τὸν Νίκωνα ... οἱ δὲ περὶ τὸν Φιλήμενον:** see 16.11n. The division between Nicon and Philemenus is ignored here by Livy. Nicon seems to organize the group's activities, here as later; Philemenus' concerns seem to be those of the leader (note αὐτοῖς), not just the top hunter (25.5). But ἀπέταξαν (25.5) suggests some group decisions.

**24.11 περιχαρὴς ἦν:** μόλις 'at long last' and perhaps τὴν προκειμένην ἐπιβολήν indicate a narrative contrast, though there need not have been an earlier depiction of gloom (cf. Livy's narrative, and P. 7.15.1, 16.1). The situation creates a pointed link with 17.2 ὑπερχαρὴς ὤν, 19.2 περιχαρὴς ἦν: see Introduction §10 b. **μόλις ἀφορμῆς ἐπειλῆφθαι** (perfect middle-passive inf. of ἐπιλαμβάνομαι): 'finally obtained an opportunity'; cf. 7.15.5. This phrase and ἔτι μᾶλλον παρώρμηντο (§12) show, with play on -ορμ-, the difference between Hannibal's elaborate thought and Philemenus' simple wishes. But Philemenus faces both Hannibal and his own people.

**24.12 δαψίλειαν** 'abundance'.

**24.13 †τότε†:** τὸ δὲ <πέρας> 'in the end' would give the final effect of the abundant booty – 'not just' πίστις, as in §12, but enthusiastic followers. Cf.

e.g. 1.48.9 (the final effect of the fire: it 'even' ruined the siegeworks). The asyndeton with τότε is unacceptable, and the meaning unattractive: 'at that time' or 'thereupon'. διόπερ 'hence' (Weil) would not fit the relation between booty producing πίστις and it producing enthusiasm. **τὰ μὲν ἀποδόμενοι, τὰ δ' εὐωχούμενοι:** the different tenses contrast immediate sale with continued feasting. Food and meals are crucial to political and practical influence in this episode: a reflection, in P., of Tarentum's decadence (§1; cf. 7.1.1–3), but a decadence particularly absorbed by the Romans. For εὐωχεῖσθαι with acc. 'feast on', cf. Xen. *Cyr.* 1.3.6, Eudox. fr. 283 Lasserre. **ἐπιστεύοντο παρὰ τοῖς Ταραντίνοις:** success is underlined in the combined repetition and variation; cf. §10 ἐκείνοις … πίστιν παρασκευάζειν πρὸς τοὺς πολίτας, §12 ἱκανὴν αὐτοῖς πίστιν παρεσκευακέναι πρὸς τοὺς ἰδίους. But οὐ μόνον and the change to the aorist mark an advance. The ζηλωταί will be enthusiastic adherents (*CGL* 4), rather than 'emulators' (Loeb) going on their own expeditions.

## 25 HUNTING AND GIFTS OF FOOD

**25.1–2** This time, by contrast with the first meeting, a formal arrangement is made: not a private deal for the young men, but in effect a treaty between cities, with the young men speaking for Tarentum, though without formal authority. ἔδοσαν … ἔλαβον displays the symmetry (cf. 22.9.9); but in the actual terms of the deal as reported the Tarentines' worries are more long-term than the Carthaginians'. Freedom and an absence of tribute often go together: so when Greece is 'freed', 18.46.5, 15; cf. 4.84.5, *I.Iasos* 1.2.6, 30–1 (text 309 BC, inscription 305–285/4 BC, Fabiani (2015) 14–15). Livy is more elaborate here (25.8.8), and includes specifications that the Tarentines are to keep their laws, and receive no *praesidium* unwillingly. Both laws and an absence of garrisons are standard elements in these contexts; cf. *I.Iasos* as above and 55, P. 15.24.1–4, DS 19.61.3, 28.13.1 (cf. Oliva (1993) 58–9). Hannibal does leave a garrison (34.13n.; cf. 33.8n.); the addition of 'unwillingly' in Livy (above) could represent exculpation after the event. The implication of ἐλευθερώσειν is that Tarentum has been subjected to tribute and orders by the Romans; cf. e.g. 36.17.13, the Macedonians' liberation from μοναρχικῶν ἐπιταγμάτων καὶ φόρων. The presentation of the Tarentines' actions in 280 (24.1) makes it the more important to preclude a new master now.

**25.1 χειρίσαντες τὰ κατὰ μέρος:** see 18.4, 18.9n.

**25.2 κατὰ μηδένα τρόπον:** emphatic legal language; cf. e.g. *F.Delphes* III.1.303.10 (i BC), also upbeat. **οἰκίας καὶ καταλύσεις** ('dwellings'): a legalistic fullness? The two seem the same at 31.4–6 below; Livius too dwells in a house at 27.6. Cf. 6.41.11, 15.32.10, Bechtel *et al.* (1913) 101 (καταλύσεις permanent).   διαρπάζειν: ends the sentence with force, long delayed after its object.

**25.3 ἐποιήσαντο:** plural – a shared plan.   **καί:** now shorter-term arrangements.   **σύνθημα:** with genitive as at 5.76.1. Here a password or the like, as in the obsessive procedures of Roman camps at 6.34.7–12.   **ὅτ' ἔλθοιεν** 'whenever they came' (optative). P. can still use the opt. in past sequence, cf. e.g. §10, 12.6.2, 32.5.7, *Syll.*³ II.559.24–5 (Megalopolis, iii–ii BC). See Introduction §13 a.

**25.4 ἔλαβον ἐξουσίαν** 'they gained the opportunity'. εἰς τό ... συμμιγνύναι is more than the bare infinitive with ἐξουσία at 5.56.8; cf. Isocr. *Nic.* 45 λαβὼν δ' ἐξουσίαν ὥστε ποιεῖν ... The phrasing καὶ πλεονάκις looks to the sequence of the first and second meetings (cf. 25.1), and of συμμῖξαι and συμμιγνύναι πάλιν (24.5, 8).   **ὡς ἐπ' ἐξοδείαν** takes up the same phrase from 24.4; then the new element of hunting is added in for the first time (contrast Livy 25.8.4). That element will be important to the episode. πάλιν is 'in turn', not 'again'.

**25.5 διαρμοσάμενοι** 'having arranged'; see 5.1n.   **ἐπετήρουν τοὺς καιρούς:** one might expect to hear more about both plundering and hunting; but instead the accent is on hunting. The agency, however, now passes from Philemenus (24.12) to the young men in general (cf. §7); it will presently pass to Hannibal. It would have been easy to make it all Hannibal's plan; cf. §8, Front. *Strat.* 3.3.6 and Livy 25.8.11 *tempus agendae rei Hannibali uisum est.* It could also have all been made Philemenus'; cf. App. *Hann.* 133. The imperfect contrasts with the definite ἀπέταξαν; ἀπέταξαν matches §11 ἐτάξαντο, after παρατηρήσαντες.   **Φιλήμενον:** a number of them hunting would be more suspicious, and he is the one with the reputation. But he will not actually have been hunting boar without assistants; cf. 29.6, 7 and e.g. Sen. *Phaedr.* 1–2, 29–30; Trinquier (2009) 107.

**25.6 μέρος:** see 19.5n.   **διάληψις** 'view', here in fact mistaken; see Introduction §13 c n. 65. τοῦ κυνηγετεῖν ends the sentence with force, and comes straight after βίον 'way of life'. Despite Xen. *Cyn.* 1 on mythological huntsmen, Demetrius I Soter of Syria (31.14.3) and P.'s own interest (ibid.), the supposed valuation is to sound entertainingly extreme. Contrast 29.26.2 on a constant attitude, μηδὲν τοῦ καλοῦ καὶ τοῦ δικαίου προυργιαίτερον τιθέμενον. Both extremity and pastime could be part of Philemenus' youth; cf. 31.29.5 on hunting for young men.

**25.7 ἐξιδιάσασθαι** 'win over'; cf. e.g. 31.18.5, DS 31.27a.1 (with bribery). **ἁλισκομένων**: present, since a repeated action; cf. App. *Hann.* 133 τὰ λαμβανόμενα. **Γάϊον Λίβιον**: C. or M. Livius (Macatus?), *RE* Livius 24, *MRR* 262 n. 7. M. is first attested later (Livy 26.39.1), and is easily explained as an error: M. is a particularly common *praenomen* for Livii, C. is found sometimes. In Livy's episode the *praefectus* is not named, perhaps to play down his role, or to conceal that he was called *Liuius*. See 27.1n. **πυλῶνα** 'gatehouse'; cf. 28.6n. At Call. *H.* 3.146–8 Heracles always stands before the gates of Olympus, hoping Artemis will give him πῖον ἔδεσμα. The scene is openly comic (laughter 148–9). That passage confirms there is something amusing and not wholly laudable in this keenness for food, especially in the duped prefect, but also in the guards, who must be Roman (§11n.). **[τὸν ὑπὸ τὰς Τεμενίδας προσαγορευομένας πύλας]**: if this phrase is deleted, τὸν πυλῶνα was employed without further specification, i.e. the πυλών at the gate Philemenus always used; similarly unspecified 2.9.3 τὴν πύλην (the gate they came to), 4.57.8 τοὺς ἐπὶ τοῦ πυλῶνος and probably 11.27.2 τῆς πύλης (the gate they were at). In the MSS' text, these gates, i.e. gate, are also those through which Hannibal enters: cf. 28.2 ὡς ἐπὶ [see 28.2n.] τὰς Τημενίδας προσαγορευομένας πύλας. But that cannot be. Livy confirms: the plan is that Philemenus should enter *portula adsueta ..., parte alia portam Temenitida adiret Hannibal* (25.9.9). Hannibal at 28.2 is approaching the Temenid gates, cf. 28.4 τὴν πύλην; the πύλη or πύλαι through which he enters in 28.10–13 has to be the same. Philemenus' gate, however, is τὴν παρακειμένην πύλην (29.4; see n.); and its πυλών (29.9) cannot be the πυλών of the Temenid gate (28.11–12), where there is a different killing of guards. The πυλών cannot be distant from its πύλη; cf. §10 (same people guarding), 2.9.3, etc. The phrase has been added from 28.2; cf. the interpolation of 22.13.7 from 22.13.11. Alternatively, Τεμενίδας (misspelt) could have displaced a different word; but ὑπό is suspiciously odd (cf. *PL* C1d).

**25.8 τὰ μὲν ... τῶν δ' ... τὰ μὲν ... τὰ δέ**: an intricate plan. In striking chiasmus δι' Ἀννίβου opposes αὐτός, ἑτοιμαζομένων opposes κυνηγετῶν. **τῶν θηρίων**: partitive. **τῶι Γαΐωι**: much less is said on Livius than on the guards. The point of gifts to Livius is not so obvious: presumably to create goodwill and avert suspicion. **τοῖς ἐπί** 'those in charge of'; cf. 29.9. **ῥινοπύλην**: a small gate, guarded by only one at a time; cf. 29.5–6. It is πυλίς at 29.8, *portula* at Livy 25.9.9; Hesych. ρ 338 glosses μικρὰ πύλη. The word is only extant in P.; cf. 15.31.10. A small entrance like a nose in comparison to a mouth? Cf. Soph. fr. 773.1 Radt πύλας ἑπταστόμους, etc.

**25.9 γάρ:** the implication is that the gates are shut only at night, although the enemy is not far away. Cf. e.g. Theocr. 14.47 λύκωι καὶ νυκτὸς ἀνῶικται. νυκτός is strongly placed; this is confirmed by the heavy anaphora in App. *Hann.* 133–4. **προφάσει:** ingenuity is stressed; contrast *credebant* Livy 25.8.10. **τῶι φόβωι τῶν πολεμίων:** the arrival of enemy raiders at 27.1–2 is evidently something new. More activity by the enemy is suggested in App. *Hann.* 133 and Front. *Strat.* 3.3.6 *quasi id per hostem interdiu non liceret*; that picture would offer a more coherent narrative here. **ἁρμοζόμενος δὲ πρός:** again a sense of cunning arrangement; cf. §5 above. **τὴν ὑποκειμένην πρόθεσιν:** still not entirely defined for P.'s curious readers; cf. 24.7.

**25.10 ἤδη δὲ κατασκευασμένου ..., (§11) τότε:** an elaborate genitive absolute structure subordinates Philemenus' specific plan to the larger scheme of the young Tarentines. **συνήθειαν:** likewise 29.5 κατὰ τὸν ἐθισμόν. ὥστε μὴ διαπορεῖν (the result of the familiar pattern was that they felt no uncertainty) ... ἀλλ' ... εὐθέως confirms that this is an informal set-up. It is unlike Bolis' whistle at 20.5 τὸ σύνθημα προσσυρίξας ... ἀπέδωκε, let alone the strict verbal συνθήματα of the Roman or Macedonian camp (6.34.7–12; cf. Moretti, *ISE* II.114.A col. iii.5–7 (Amphipolis, *c.*200 BC)). The set-up at the Carthaginian camp contrasts (§3). Livius has not made a formal arrangement with Philemenus, and the defences of the city are not tightly supervised.

**25.11 τὸν ἐπὶ τῆς πόλεως ἄρχοντα [τῶν Ῥωμαίων]:** a variation on §7 τὸν ἐπὶ τῆς πόλεως τεταγμένον; cf. 1.66.1 ὁ δ' ἐπὶ τῆς πόλεως στρατηγός. The somewhat unusual phrase is produced by the need for variation, and Livius' post of *praefectus* (the word *praifecti* comes only in book 6, as a type of ἄρχοντες; cf. 6.26.5). The phrase neatly matches τοὺς ἐπὶ τῆς πύλης, and continues the parallelism between magistrate and guards seen in §7 and §8. But τῶν Ῥωμαίων disrupts the neatness, and the specification is unneeded and unwelcome at this point. The guards will be Roman too; Romans would scarcely entrust security to Greeks. The unneeded double τῶν Ῥωμαίων at 21.37.1–2 comes from the excerptor. At e.g. 1.34.1, the *Excerpta Constantiniana* add ὁ στρατηγὸς Ῥωμαίων in a helpful way, as τῶν Ῥωμαίων is added here. **παρατηρήσαντες:** observing him, cf. DS 13.44.4; their observation brings knowledge of his plans. This vigilant patience links with §5 ἐπετήρουν. **ἀφ' ἡμέρας** 'from daytime on'. This drinking is beginning earlier than the usual evening start; for the phrase cf. 23.5.9, DS 29.32.1, Plut. *Sull.* 36.1. But the nature of Livius' activities is not yet given explicitly. In contrast to ἀφ' ἡμέρας, ταύτην ...

τὴν ἡμέραν, with forceful separation in the word order, shows the Greeks focused on serious matters. The Roman partying is not at a public festival, which the young men would know of anyway; the famous drunkenness of the Tarentines at their Dionysia (Plato, *Laws* 1.637b3–5) will be seen rather in the Romans, and without festal or Dionysiac context. A Tarentine public building will be used, in the heart of the city, but not the temple of Dionysus. (The temple was most likely in via Anfiteatro: cf. Lippolis, Garraffo and Nafissi (1995) 91–2; Pontrandolfo (2011) 396–7.) **Μουσείωι:** shrines, with porticoes, dedicated to the Muses are a widespread phenomenon in the Hellenistic period. Recurring features of Mouseia are the cult of the Muses, literary activity, members and dining; all were most extensive in the Museum at Alexandria (dining: *I.Portes du désert* 32.3–4 (Tentyris, i AD), *IGUR* I.241.4–5 (ii AD)). Cf. Fraser (1972) I 312–14. This Mouseion will have connections with Tarentum's cultural life, and perhaps philosophy. Evidently the occasion is to have an element of Greek culture. **τὸν Ἀννίβαν:** the name ends the sentence strongly; Hannibal is opposed to the *praefectus*. The organization of chh. 26 and 27 will bring out the point; cf. 27.1n.

## 26 HANNIBAL ADVANCES

**26.1 πάλαι:** P. puts these events in the second of this book's two Olympiad years, in 213/12. If these *res Italiae* were in 214/13, they would have to precede the *res Asiae* of that year (15–21); but they follow them, as is shown by FDG and M. The events should happen around the end of the season for campaigning, i.e. in late 213, and certainly not in February 213 (Fronda (2010) 337) or in March to April 212 (Lazenby (1978) 110). At 34.13 Hannibal passes τὸ λοιπὸν τοῦ χειμῶνος after this; cf. 4.82.1 τὸ λοιπὸν μέρος τοῦ χειμῶνος after the end of Philip's campaigning. Furthermore, wonder at Hannibal's staying put would no longer be appropriate if this was the end of winter (cf. e.g. Livy 24.20.15 – the *hiberna* in a fixed place). Livy probably thought that P., like some others, put these events late in the consular year which started in March 212 (25.11.20). He is no doubt in a tangle, as often, between consular years and Olympiads: cf. e.g. Dany (2000). For some discussions of the chronology see De Sanctis (1968) 322–3; Levene (2010) 57–8. Livy's *ager Sallentinus* (25.1.1) would indeed be three days' march from Tarentum (P. 8.26.2). Hannibal has had this camp for some time, cf. 34.13 τὸν ἐξ ἀρχῆς χάρακα; 24.11 suggests that he has been waiting for some while to achieve his design. The distance and the pretence indicate that he wished to keep his hope secret from the Romans in Tarentum (cf. τοὺς Ῥωμαίους here, *Romanis ... qui in praesidio Tarenti erant* Livy 25.8.13). It is implied here that Hannibal is normally expected to be in motion.   ὡς ἀρρωστῶν: feigning illness is part of the Polybian repertoire of tricks; cf. 5.56.6–14 (Antiochus III).   τότε: now that he is in league with the conspirators. πάλαι μέν and τότε δέ form a continuum, set against the καιρός (§3). The imperfect προσεποιεῖτο contrasts with the καιρός, and the aorist παρήγγειλε (§3).

**26.2 ἀπεῖχε:** the specifics, delivered in a short sentence, have evidently not been needed so far.   τῶι στρατοπέδωι 'with his army'; cf. 4.64.9 ἐπιδιαβάς [verb of motion, as is most common with these datives] τῶι στρατεύματι, Thuc. 3.96.1 αὐλισάμενος δὲ τῶι στρατῶι.

**26.3 καιροῦ:** the importance of καιρός in war is emphasized at 9.15.1, where the capture of cities is particularly in mind.   εὐκινησίαι: τόλμηι and other uses of εὐκίνητος point to skilful movement in the conflict rather than rapid movement before it. The cavalry evidently include those needed for the distracting raid (§4, 27.1–2).   μυρίους: Hannibal is countering a Roman garrison which is 5,000 in App. *Hann.* 137, after the loss of πολύ τι πλῆθος (30.9 below). The Roman *praesidium* at Puteoli was 6,000 (Livy 24.13.7), the Carthaginian at Arpi 5,000 (24.47.2). At least 2,000 of the 10,000 are cavalry (29.2); substantially over 2,000 of the 10,000 are Celts (30.1).   τεττάρων: despite συντόνως (§4) and the early start. The speed will vary (28.13), and what will await them at the city is uncertain. A siege is clearly not envisaged.

**26.4 ποιησάμενος ... συντόνως:** an expressively brief sentence. ἀναζυγήν: setting off; cf. 34.13 ἀνέζευξε. For the noun see Introduction §13 c n. 65.   Νομαδικῶν and Νομάδων ring the sentence. The locals are expected to be familiar with these formidable horsemen; cf. 27.1. The Numidians are often sent ahead of the rest of a force, as here, cf. e.g. 1.19.2 (προπορεύεσθαι), 3.68.1, Livy 21.48.5, Sen. *Ep.* 123.7; they are often used independently, as the locals are meant to think, cf. 3.71.10, 112.3. There had been raids by Numidians nearby (Livy 24.20.16). *ut praedonum magis quam exercitus accolis species esset*, says Livy 25.9.3, not quite on target.   τῆς δυνάμεως: governed by προ-.   εἰς 'about'.   τριάκοντα σταδίους: Fornaro (2005) 73 reckons P.'s stade as 211.4 m; in that case, 6.342 km here, 3.941 miles.   παρὰ τὴν ὁδόν: where viewers of the army are most likely to be.   ἐπιτρέχειν: running over the land, doing damage to crops and people (cf. 27.1).

**26.5 μηδεὶς κατοπτεύσηι:** i.e. no one should spy the whole force and report it. They will either be captured, or get away before seeing the whole force. The prime aim is put in the subjunctive; the constitutive possibilities are put in the more traditional optative. **διεμπιπτόντων**: running into them by mistake; with οἱ μέν. Cf. 1.21.11, 11.21.3 (ἐμπίπτω); the compound only at 38.9.11 (an error at Gal. xviiia 616 Kühn). **ἀναγγέλλοιεν**: as happens, 27.1.

**26.6 ἑκατὸν εἴκοσι**: on Fornaro's view (§4n.), 25.368 km, 15.763 miles, from Tarentum; the rest are 31.710 km, 19.704 miles away. The Numidians reach Tarentum at sunset (27.1), so the meal takes place several hours before; the pause lasts several hours (§10 κνέφατος). **ἐδειπνοποιήσατο**: the verb is generally used of army meals. **παρά τινα δυσσύνοπτον καὶ φαραγγώδη ποταμόν**: the adjectives include the environs of the river (τόπον Reiske, but παρὰ ποταμόν is normal Polybian idiom, παρὰ τόπον not). Hannibal is taking extra precautions that the full size of his force should not be seen; hence δυσσύνοπτον, 'hard to get a clear view of' (first in P.). The rough and wild setting contrasts with the Roman commander's meal in the Museum. And Carthaginians were imagined not to drink on campaign, Plato, *Laws* 2.674a3–7.

**26.7 τοὺς ἡγεμόνας**: the speech, though its first clause is the stuff of exhortations to the whole army (cf. e.g. 3.63.4, Plut. *Flamin.* 7.6), is addressed just to the leaders of units – less conspicuous, and more secret. Livy changes the address into a speech to all the soldiers (25.9.4). **κυρίως μὲν οὐ διεσάφει**: it is obvious that they are heading for Tarentum, but the details of the plan are kept hidden even in talking to the leaders. This discretion is generalized in the long passage in the next book on being a commander; see 9.13.1–6. **οὐδέποτε μειζόνων ... ἄθλων** ('prizes') seems surprising, as it is only the Romans' houses that will be plundered, 25.2, 31.6; but cf. 32.1. On booty in P., see Pinzone (1983) 139–47, Davies (2013) 325.

**26.8 συνέχειν ἕκαστον ... τοὺς ὑφ' αὑτὸν ταττομένους**: discipline works through a chain of command. In P., the present participle (1.84.3, etc.) is commoner in this phrase than the perfect (1.78.9); cf. *I.Pergamon* 1.13.58 (iii BC) ... τοῖς ὑφ' αὑτὸν τασσομένοις, Segre (1932) 447, line 8 (Rhodes, 184/3 BC) τῶν ὑφ' αὑτὸν τασσομένων. **πικρῶς ἐπιτιμᾶν** 'fiercely rebuke'; cf. 5.15.7 ἐπετίμα πικρῶς of Philip to leaders. Livy is less lively, 25.9.4 *nec ... paterentur*. Movement is tightly controlled; no punishment, though, is envisaged.

**26.9** The last injunction is that the leaders themselves should obey orders, and not act on their own initiative: ἰδιοπραγεῖν. See Introduction §13 c.

COMMENTARY: 26.10-27.1                                                    205

**26.10 κνέφατος**: only here in P. The noun is mainly found in poetry, but also in Xenophon and Arrian. Day and night are crucial in the narrative; a variation on σκότος γενέσθαι (27.3) is desired. **Φιλήμενον**: brought in at the end of the paragraph, whenever his guiding began. The position marks the separate strands in the plotting. The boar, which could have been kept for later, brings out the colourfulness of this particular strand, quite distinct from the military movements. **παρεσκευακώς**: Hannibal's personal involvement is conveyed more closely than in 25.8 ἑτοιμαζομένων αὐτῶι δι' Ἀννίβου. Fine meat is enjoyed by the guards and Livius; but Hannibal uses it strategically. **πρὸς τὴν διατεταγμένην χρείαν**: as at 24.12 πρὸς τὴν πρᾶξιν, and 25.9 πρὸς τὴν ὑποκειμένην πρόθεσιν, readers have a general idea, but are kept curious.

## 27 AN UNFORTUNATE PARTY

**27.1 τῶι δὲ Γαΐωι τῶι Λιβίωι**: the previous paragraph started from Hannibal, and was focused on his actions throughout. This paragraph starts with Livius, who is important throughout it; but it soon gets to actions taken by the young Greeks. Livy, who follows P. so closely in this episode, omits the whole paragraph on the *praefectus*' revelry. See 25.7n. For the nomen treated as an adjunct to the *praenomen* cf. e.g. 3.16.7 Λεύκιον τὸν Αἰμίλιον, 21.3.2 Γάϊον τὸν Οὐαλέριον. **μετὰ τῶν συνήθων**: 'friends', as at 31.11.6; more specific than 25.11 μετὰ πλειόνων. This does not sound an official duty. These friends conjure up the merrymaking of tyrants; cf. Plut. *Gen. Soc.* 594d. **ἀφ' ἡμέρας**: drinking, except in a festival, is not really supposed to happen during the day. Cf. Alc. fr. 346.1 Voigt πώνωμεν· τί τὰ λύχν' ὀμμένομεν; δάκτυλος ἀμέρα (only a sliver remains), Plato, *Laws* 2.674b3–6, P. 33.19; 25.11n. But the Tarentines had a reputation for drinking ἐξ ἑωθινοῦ (Ael. *VH* 12.30). For their excess with drink, even beyond festivals, cf. Theop. *FGrHist* 115 F100, 233. At 6.25.11 the Romans are thought especially good at changing their ἔθη and imitating what is better from others; here the imitation is less admirable. It is not just a matter of Livius' character: so rightly Chlup (2009) 9 n. 20. **πρόληψιν** 'thought in advance'. Even this soon in the paragraph, Livius is fitting into the young men's plan; they are more akin to Hannibal. **ἀκμαιοτάτην**: separated from διαθέσιν, 'condition', for emphasis. The response is related to the drunkenness, as is the case when the tyrant Archias learns something of the conspiracy against him, Plut. *Gen. Soc.* 595f–596c, *Pel.* 10.1–10. **προσαγγέλλεται περὶ δυσμὰς ἡλίου**: the scary moment fits a narrative of aristocratic plotting; but here Hannibal has planned it all (26.5). Readers as steeped in Demosthenes as P. is (18.14.1, etc.) are bound to think of the alarming news brought to Athens at Dem. 18.169: it is evening, people break off their dinner, summon generals, the city is in tumult. Livius is less worried.

**27.2 πρὸς μὲν αὐτὸ τοῦτο** contrasts with τῆς γε μὴν ὅλης πράξεως; cf. e.g. 21.5.9 χείρω μὲν ... βελτίω γε μήν. The μέν after τούς is probably interpolated; otherwise another half to the order would be expected. **καλέσας τινὰς τῶν ἡγεμόνων:** like Hannibal (26.7), but to less forceful effect. Only half the cavalry are to be sent out and, fatally, not until dawn. **τῶν πολεμίων:** partitive, with τούς ... χώραν. **καὶ μᾶλλον:** the trick has worked. καὶ μᾶλλον is used relatedly for Hannibal at 26.1: Hannibal heightens his pretence, Livius the more duped.

**27.3 Τραγίσκον:** a new figure is added to Nicon, cf. §7, 28.10; alone, 28.2. The name, 'little goat', is rare (Plut. *Arat.* 29.5). At Tarentum it may play jokily on the Tarentine children's game ἐξάγω χωλὸν τραγίσκον (Hesych. ε 3502 Latte). **ἅμα τῶι σκότος γενέσθαι:** not sooner, to avoid notice. **ἐτήρουν:** typical of their vigilance; cf. 25.11n. **ἐπάνοδον:** Livius has not been feasting his friends at his house.

**27.4 ταχέως:** fortunate, and possibly foreseen; certainly Hannibal's design of arriving in the middle of the night avoids all those returning from dinner (§9). **οἱ μὲν ἄλλοι:** once they are all assured Livius has left, the group is reduced. This is presumably for plausibility, though a wandering ὄχλος of inebriated young men is a standard feature in Menander (so *Epitr.* 169–71; πάμπολλ' *Perik.* 262). The original thirteen may have increased; cf. 24.13. **διακεχυμένοι** 'relaxed', by contrast, in appearance, with the others' tense waiting. Cf. διακεχυμένος of drunken bodies at Plato, *Laws* 6.775c5, and Plut. *Gen. Soc.* 596a συνεκλελυμένοι in soul as in body. **τι:** suggests meticulous imitation. The second καί (F) highlights the undignified behaviour. **ὑποκρινόμενοι:** used of pretence at 2.49.7, 3.31.7, like ὑπόκρισις. But the situation, and the theatrical tradition of tipsy choruses, make this particularly like real acting; they are adroitly playing the expected role of well-off Greek young men.

**27.5 ἔτι δὲ μᾶλλον:** than when Livius gave his orders (§2). **ἠλλοιωμένων:** similarly 3.81.5 ἀλλοιώσεως καὶ μέθης; cf. Sen. *Ep.* 85.24: not to fear impending evils is *dementis alienatique*. **γέλως ... καὶ παιδιά:** the constructed drunken merriment is again vividly conveyed. The Greek and Roman elites are as if on good terms. **πρόχειρος:** the fun flows easily;

cf. 23.5.7 of Deinocrates, εὔχαρις καὶ πρόχειρος in conversation. At Philod. *Poet.* 5 col. xviii.3, Mangoni (1993) 244 translates π[ρό]χειρος 'chiacchierone', 'over-chatty'.

**27.6 συνανακάμψαντες** 'accompanying his return home'. The compound comes only here and at Diog. Laert. 2.127. So fond youths (no longer boys?) and attentive young men take old men home (Call. *Aet.* fr. 41 Harder, Tib. 1.4.79–80): an affectionate act towards those with diminished mobility. **ἀποκατέστησαν** 'settled' or 'dropped off'; cf. P. Lond. VII (Zen.) 2067.15–16 (iii BC). **ἀνεπαύετο:** resting, not sleeping, as what follows shows; Livius is earlier than some diners (28.9), but he has started drinking earlier. **οὐδὲν ... ῥαιθυμίας:** Livius' mental state is elaborately evoked; the irony of events is obvious. ῥαιθυμίας is on the surface neutral, cf. 10.19.5; but from drunkenness there springs an undesirable ῥαιθυμία, cf. 4.57.3, 5.48.1, and the condemnation most common with the word is heard here too, cf. e.g. 3.81.4, 7.15.7. This is a small-scale exemplification of behaviour which P. disapproves; cf. Eckstein (1995) 73, 75.

**27.7 συνέμιξαν:** a proper meeting with their friends; contrast §5 συμμῖξαι. **διελόντες ... διαλαβόντες:** they are using their numbers with purpose. Dividing into μέρη has a military air. See 30.1 below of Hannibal, cf. 9.26.4; 6.24.3, 26.9, of the Roman army. **παρεφύλαττον:** probably εἰσβολάς is the object of both verb and participle. As ever, the young men are watching; but eventually they will act (28.10–12). **ἀγορᾶς:** Hannibal's whole plan is focused on securing the agora. The ways into the agora are evidently close enough both to the agora and to the gates; cf. ἔξωθεν. The location of the agora is disputed: cf. De Juliis (2000) 60–1. It was at any rate close to the harbour (in the Mar Piccolo), conveniently for a market-place. Cf. Albers (2018).

**27.8 ἐπέστησαν δὲ καί:** this seems like an addition to the three main groups. Livius' house seems to be between the agora and the gate leading to the harbour (30.6); it would not appear to have a guard of soldiers (cf. 30.6). **Γαΐου ... Λίβιον:** variations in naming him. ἐπὶ τὸν Λίβιον and ἀπ' ἐκείνου are emphatically placed, with contrasting prepositions. πρῶτον and ἀρχήν match at the end of the clauses. **ὑπόνοια τοῦ μέλλοντος:** relates especially to the events outside the city; πᾶν τὸ πραττόμενον relates to τῶν ἐν αὐτῆι τῆι πόλει γινομένων. The previous news to the city (26.5) went to Livius (§1), whether or not immediately. The young men do not think to continue keeping an eye on Livius (§9); it would only have needed one or two of them.

**27.9** An expressively constructed sentence begins with two pluperfect clauses, which present the change of time in concrete terms. The first, αἱ μὲν κτλ., conveys action and bustle, now ceasing; for ἐπάνοδοι cf. §§3–6 above and τοιοῦτος, i.e. the ἐπάνοδοι involve θόρυβος. The second clause, τῶν δὲ κτλ., positively conveys repose. The next two clauses, προύβαινε κτλ. and καὶ τὰ κτλ., present the progress of time as felt by the young men: the urgent movement of night and the continuation of hope. The imperfect verbs are in chiasmus; the pluperfect verbs had each ended their clauses. The τότε draws all together: 'then at last'. συναθροισθέντες reverses their earlier division (§§7, 8), and brings motion towards more definite action. Like the end of the previous paragraph πρὸς τὴν διατεταγμένην χρείαν (26.10), ἐπὶ τὴν προκειμένην χρείαν shows the agents proceeding to action still not entirely specified. Ap. Rhod. *Arg.* 3.744–51 depicts the fall of night and quiet, and Medea's separation from this large pattern; cf. also Hom. *Il.* 2.1.–7. The contrast with others adds intensity to the action here.    τὰ τῆς νυκτός is not very different in meaning from ἡ νύξ; cf. Charit. 2.4.3 προέκοπτε δὲ τὰ τῆς νυκτός.

## 28 THE YOUNG MEN LET HANNIBAL IN

**28.1** τάδε <δὲ τὰ>: introductory τάδε e.g. 3.25.7, Thuc. 4.118.4. The most satisfactory place for a demonstrative here is at the start, and τάδε <δὲ τὰ> would be easy palaeographically. An infinitive would be acceptable after τὰ συγκείμενα ἦν, but ἔδει is not. Some of the detail in 27.9 τὴν προκειμένην χρείαν will now be given.

**28.2** συνάψαντα 'on coming close'.    κατὰ ... πλευράν: Hannibal has come north-west from the *ager Sallentinus*, to the east side of Tarentum, which is reached from 'inland', i.e. further from the sea than is Tarentum. Cf. 13.3, 5 above.    ὡς ἐπί further specifies the goal. It is much the same as ἐπί; see *PL* ἐπί C2a. Cf. §4 (ὡς ἐπί of goal); §13, 17.10 (ἐπί of goal); 1.78.10 (ἐπί with συνάψαντες).    Τημενίδας: see 25.7n. The location of these gates is disputed (Cera (2019) 20–1). Their name connects them with the Peloponnese; Temenus, descended from Heracles, was in various accounts king of Argos (e.g. Plato, *Laws* 3.683d6).    τάφου: tombs are convenient landmarks for plans; cf. §9 below, and 9.17.2, 6. This special tomb outside the city may have been in an elevated location (cf. De Juliis (2000) 74). There may also be symbolic significance in the conspirators' choice. The tomb evokes Hyacinthus' tomb at Amyclae, a focus of the Spartan Hyacinthia (Paus. 3.1.3, 19.3; Polycr. *FGrHist* 588 F1); that connects the present liberation to Taras' Spartan foundation. In Antioch. *FGrHist* 555 F13 the foundation of Taras starts with a conspiracy at the Hyacinthia.  παρά μέν τισιν ... παρά δέ τισιν Ἀπόλλωνος Ὑακίνθου: whether these are books or informants (cf. *PL* παρά B5αβ–δ), P.'s learned researches interrupt and distance the narrative, and increase suspense. In the standard myth Apollo kills Hyacinthus by mistake; cf. e.g. Nic. *Ther.* 902–6. The combination Apollo Hyacinthus comes second here, as the more challenging expression, especially in connection with a tomb. Cf. Poseidon Erechtheus (Poseidon killed Erechtheus), *IG* I³.837.5–6 (*c*.450?), Eur. fr. 370.90–4 Kannicht, Kearns (1989) 210–11. The expression gains some support from the youth with lyre and flower on silver coins from Tarentum, 510–500 BC: Rutter (2001) 93 nos 824–5, Ravel (1947) 11, nos 70–2; cf. further Lippolis, Garraffo and Nafissi (1995) 56–8, 147, 224–6.

**28.3 Τραγίσκον:** Nicon in Livy (25.9.10), to simplify; both of them perform this action at 28.10 below.  ἀντιπυρσεῦσαι: the verb also at 10.46.1, in P.'s exposition of fire-signalling, his special subject. See Introduction §3 c.

**28.4 σβέσαι:** to avoid being seen, not least by guards at other gates.  βάδην: the pace of motion is important in this narrative; Hannibal's steady pace marks his cool deliberation.

**28.5 μέν:** eventually to some degree taken up by the genitive absolute on Hannibal at §10. But the account will be diverted in §§6–8.  ἐπὶ τοὺς τάφους: a surprising destination at the end of the sentence, until P. explains.

**28.6 πρὸς ἕω:** so Hannibal will not on first entering encounter houses and their inhabitants. The necropolis is to the east of the inhabited part of the main city, which is to the west of the acropolis. See Map 3.  μνημάτων ἐστὶ πλῆρες: visual, as if conveying the author's direct experience. Livy's *busta aliquantum intra moenia includunt* (25.9.10; text doubtful) may suggest less direct experience. The inhabited area of the main city seems to have ended at the via Duca degli Abruzzi; the necropolis was larger. Parts of it can be seen now at via Crispi (Tomba degli Atleti) and via Marche (less grand).  ἔτι καὶ νῦν rings the account, the second occurrence (§8) from the viewpoint of the storytellers. The storytellers' time and P.'s own, and an ἀρχαῖον oracle, remove readers from the intense sequence of time in 213/12.  πάντας ἐντὸς τῶν τειχῶν: it is unexpected that any tombs should be within the walls; ideas of pollution usually prevent this (Parker (1983) 70–3). Sparta was an exception (Plut. *Lyc.* 27.1, [Plut.] *Apophth. Lac.* 238d); but no link with Sparta is mentioned here, and the comparison is archaeologically questionable (Lippolis (1994*b*) 51). It is in the fifth century that the fortification of Taras expands and includes the necropolis: a problem for some arguments about the development of attitudes to the dead (Parker (1983) 71).

**28.7–8** P. varies forms and words notably in spelling out the phrase and explaining the custom: τοὺς τελευτήσαντας, τοὺς μετηλλαχότας ('the departed'), τοὺς μεταλλάξαντας; ἐντὸς τῶν τειχῶν, ἐντὸς τοῦ τείχους, ἐντὸς τῶν πυλῶν. There is also a change of angle between §7 and §8: from making one's dwelling with the more numerous to having them too with you.

**28.7 φασί:** more enticing storytelling by P. than naming a literary source.   **χρῆσαι:** no crisis is mentioned, as it would be in a full-blown aetiological tale.   **ἄμεινον καὶ λώϊον:** religious, evidently oracular language; cf. Plato, *Laws* 8.828a3. It is just ἄριστα in §8. For λώϊον cf. Parke and Wormell (1956) nos 55.3, 96.1, 379.4. On the other hand, ποιουμένοις τὴν οἴκησιν is ordinary Polybian language.   **τῶν πλειόνων:** familiar as a way of referring to the dead (e.g. Ar. *Eccl.* 1073); but also used in a joke by Callimachus (*Ep.* 4.2), and here meant as a puzzle. Cf. for the structure of the story Hdt. 7.141.3–144 (wooden wall), Ov. *Met.* 1.383–94 (mother's bones).

**28.8 [ἂν] οἰκήσειν:** ἂν οἰκῆσ᾽ (Büttner-Wobst) would introduce undesirable elision.

**28.9 οὐ μὴν ἀλλ᾽** can pick up after quite a pause; the combination often starts new paragraphs in P., so 16.30.1, after a substantial digression on Abydus and Sestus.   **τὸν τοῦ Πυθιονίκου τάφον:** the specific location did not necessitate the preceding digression. The conspirators' choice may convey pride in Taras' history. The date of the victory is unknown.   **ἐκαραδόκουν τὸ μέλλον:** more waiting for the young men. The verb comes often in P. and Diodorus; with τὸ μέλλον P. 2.52.6.

**28.10 συνεγγισάντων:** Hannibal is mentioned just in a short and colourless genitive absolute; the narrative persists with the Greek young men.   **ἀναθαρρήσαντες ταῖς ψυχαῖς** comes elsewhere (1.87.1; 34.1 below, with a pointed shift to the Romans); so does μετὰ δρόμου καὶ σπουδῆς (4.12.4; same pair twice in Plutarch). But the sentence still forcefully conveys the Greeks' excitement, and movement to action at last. ἀνα- ... ἀνα- for the two participles joins emotion and crucial action. μετὰ δρόμου καὶ σπουδῆς makes a contrast with the σχολῇ καὶ βάδην of the Carthaginians (§11); cf. just βάδην of Hannibal at 28.4.

**28.11 βουλόμενοι φθάσαι:** 'wishing' rather than just 'so as to'; cf. 3.66.1 σπεύδων φθάσαι. The eagerness is apparent as well as the plan; the quasi-heroic violence is what they want, more than cutting through the bolts (§12 οἱ μὲν ἐφόνευον ... οἱ δὲ διέκοπτον ...). **[καὶ] σχολῆι καὶ βάδην:** three times in Lucian. Reiske's deletion is probably right: καὶ ... καί in P. joins things emphatically different or distinct. For interpolated καί cf. 22.13.9. Again the paces of motion matter.

**28.12 εὐροήσαντος:** need not imply they were just lucky; cf. e.g. 3.15.1 εὔροιαν ... πραγμάτων. **προ-:** cf. φθάσαι. The guards of the πυλών at 29.9 are killed after some Libyans have entered, but the Tarentines here want to act quickly, on their own. **οἱ μέν ... οἱ δέ:** this indicates that οἱ περὶ τὸν Νίκωνα καὶ Τραγίσκον (§10) was more than just the two of them; cf. πάντες at 27.3.

**28.13 ταχὺ δὲ τῶν πυλῶν ἀνοιχθεισῶν:** in the last sentence of the paragraph, the Tarentine action is in a genitive absolute, and Hannibal comes to the fore. The speed again contrasts with the careful pace of Hannibal, through which all has come together. **πρὸς τὸν δέοντα καιρόν:** the same phrase at 9.14.9 (and elsewhere); there the importance of timing a march is stressed, at 9.15.1 it is universalized, in 9.18.3–4 it is seen in an attempt on taking a city by stealth. The present account leads up to that wider treatment. The worse temptation is to arrive too soon. **συμμέτρως:** suggests the moderate and the reasonable as well as a specific pace (cf. 10.49.2, with μετὰ τὸ δειπνῆσαι). **ἐπίστασιν** 'pause' rather than 'attention'; cf. Xen. *Anab.* 2.4.26, ἐπίστασις used of an army. If Hannibal had been going fast, he would have had to stop on the way so as to arrive late enough. An army would not escape attention on a road by moving σχολῆι. **ἐπὶ τὴν πόλιν** hangs onto παρ' ὁδόν awkwardly. For <τῆς> παρόδου <τῆς> ἐπὶ τὴν πόλιν cf. 5.23.5 ἐποιήσατο τὴν εἰς πόλιν πάροδον. Hultsch puts a comma before ἐπί, so that ἐπὶ τὴν πόλιν goes with ἧκον; but that would need εἰς τὴν πόλιν (cf. the opened gates and 29.1 εἰσόδου).

## 29 WILD BOAR DOES THE TRICK

**29.1 κατὰ τὴν πρόθεσιν:** a common and crucial phrase in P., most common in the form seen in §4 κατὰ τὴν ἐξ ἀρχῆς πρόθεσιν. Fulfilling one's original plan is much to be applauded. For expatiation on the subject, cf. e.g. 16.28.1–2, 9. **ἀσφαλοῦς:** a recurring strand; cf. §10, etc. **τελέως ἀθορύβου:** the killing of the guards (28.12) does not count as disturbance. **τὸ πλεῖστον:** a notable judgement, and sign of confidence. In fact, even after the killing of many Romans (30.12), the remainder do not prove easy to dislodge from the citadel. The phrase could be pressed ironically, but the emphasis on πρόθεσις suggests otherwise. **λοιπόν** moves onto the next stage in the sequence. **αὐτοὶ μέν:** Hannibal, but also his foot soldiers; §2 τούς γε μὴν ἱππεῖς is contrasted. **εὐθαρσῶς:** reflected in moving along a single road. **τὴν πλατεῖαν τὴν ἀπὸ τῆς Βαθείας ἀναφέρουσαν:** P. writes as if for those who know the topography. Hannibal's forces must be coming from the south: there is no space from the north. So the Βαθεῖα must run on the south-west side, as in Lippolis (2006) 212, not the north, as in De Juliis and Loiacono (1985) 492. See Map 3.

**29.2 δισχιλίων:** a large force, so ἐφεδρείαν indicates support as necessary rather than just keeping an eye. The nature of αἱ ἔξωθεν ἐπιφάνειαι is not clear; help from Metapontum would not arrive soon (cf. 34.1, Livy 25.11.10). **τὰ ... συμβαινόντων:** this episode, by contrast with that of Achaeus (20.10 above), shows an absence of surprises, for Hannibal. But he has them in mind, as at 15.15.5; τοιαύταις brings out the generality of the writer's perspective.

**29.3 ἐπέστησαν κατὰ πορείαν:** although thinking this the easy bit (§1), Hannibal stops his marching troops (contrast 28.13). He himself now waits, like the young Tarentines – ἐκαραδόκουν (28.9, 29.3). He feels fear – δεδιότες – as well as confidence – §1 εὐθαρσῶς. It not apparent why the Philemenus subplot still matters to him, now that entry has been achieved. Perhaps a further stream of entry might prevent insidious Roman movements. Livy mentions the double plan earlier (25.9.9). **<τὰ> κατά:** cf. 23.9.14 καραδοκοῦντες τὰ κατὰ τὴν Μεσσήνην, 17.6 above τῶν κατὰ τὸν Καμβύλον.

**29.4 ὅτε ... ὁρμᾶν** moves back to an earlier stage in the narrative (cf. 28.2), to display the elaborate scheme. **ἔχοντα τὸν ὗν ἐν φερέτρωι:** the article picks up the intriguing animal from 26.10; φερέτρωι adds a further intriguing detail. Philemenus actually has help (§7). **ὡς εἰς χιλίους:** cf. Xen. *HG* 4.1.19 ὡς εἰς ἑκατόν. ὡσεί (FDG) or ὡς εἰ is not easily justified. **τὴν παρακειμένην πύλην:** not the one Hannibal is about to enter; cf. 7.18.6. See 25.7n. **μὴ ψιλῶς ἐκ μιᾶς ἐλπίδος:** it was part of the original plan to have a backup. Related is the criticism of Aratus the Elder for not having double and side signals (9.17.9), and so failing to capture Cynaetha. It is traditional wisdom that just one anchor is not security enough: Eur. *Phaeth.* 124–6, Hdas. 1.41–2 with Headlam and Knox.

**29.5 κατὰ τὸν ἐθισμόν:** i.e. approaching with the procedure of whistling mentioned next (ἐπεί could not be postponed). The trick was the building up of an expected routine; cf. §6 ἀεί. **εὐθέως** goes with παρῆν, in a vividly organized clause. Cf. 5.50.12 παρῆν εὐθέως Ἄλεξις. By contrast with 25.10 above εὐθέως ἀνοίγεσθαι τὴν ῥινοπύλην αὐτῶι, the moment of opening will be dwelt on and prolonged. **καταβαίνων πρὸς τὴν ῥινοπύλην:** the small gate itself is not manned; guards are in the πυλών (cf. 25.7), which evidently rises considerably above ground level. *IG* II².1672.31–2 (329/8 BC, Eleusis) speaks of τῶι πύργωι τῶι παρὰ τὸν πυλῶνα.

**29.6 ὅτι βαρύνονται – φέρουσι γάρ:** with bold and lively syntax, the explanatory clause is put in the indicative, as if it were direct speech, not in the infinitive. All is governed by the genitive absolute, and the sentence picks up the thread afterwards. (This is different from the gliding into *oratio recta* common in P., e.g. 3.64.3–5, 18.5.3–4.) The plural points to the helpers, and an original 'we' in Philemenus' actual utterance; a plurality is not necessarily expected by the guard, but indicates a large load. Livy 25.9.13 is much more restrained: *dicenti uix sustineri grandis bestiae onus*. The pretended impatience is vivacious, and a cunning motivation to rush, not think. **ἀσμένως** forms a ring with μετὰ σπουδῆς; Livy gives a bare *portula aperitur* (25.9.13). **καὶ πρὸς αὐτόν τι διατείνειν** 'had some bearing on himself among others'; cf. 29.2.2 πρὸς αὐτήν (Senate) τι διατείνειν, LSJ A II.2. As καί and μερίτην indicate, Philemenus had hitherto divided the meat among all the guards of the πυλών (and other people too). **εὐαγρίαν:** skill at hunting, here as seen on a single occasion; cf. Luc. *Catapl.* 5.13. It is a choice word here: not common, but used in dedicatory epigram, Antip. Thess. *AP* 9.268.4, Alph. *AP* 6.187.5. Cf. also εὔαγρος in e.g. Rhian. *AP* 6.34.6, *I.Egypte métriques* 164.1 = *I.Ptolemaic* 563.1 Πανὶ … Εὐάγρωι (iii BC; S. Hornblower (2020) 214–15, 222–3).

**29.7 τὴν πρώτην:** separated from χώραν for emphasis; the person the guard recognizes is first. But the expression of the tactic distorts the arrangement: two at the front, holding either pole, two at the rear. For χώρα, 'position', see LSJ I.4. **νομαδικήν** 'herdsman's'. The disguise shows the elaborate charade devised for this moment. Philemenus has supposedly needed local help to carry this monstrous animal; in Livy he does not carry it at all (25.9.14). **ὡς εἷς τις ὢν τῶν ἀπὸ τῆς χώρας:** irony if these are more young aristocrats, as analogy with 28.11–12 suggests to readers. Livy has just *cum expedito uenatore*, 25.9.14. **[οἱ]:** the two at the back are not a foreknown or fixed arrangement. **τὸ θηρίον:** variation.

**29.8 ἐντός** 'on the inside of'; it need not imply that the ῥινοπύλη is an extended structure, cf. 28.9 above, the dead buried ἐντὸς τῶν πυλῶν,

1.40.3.    ἀκάκως 'without suspicion'. Cf. 7.17.9; Introduction §13 b.
ψηλαφῶντα: feeling to assess or explore; only here literally in P. The greedy enthusiasm of the guard is comic and ironic. Livy tones this down: *incautius miraculo magnitudinis in eos qui ferebant uersum* (25.9.14).    αὐτοῦ: they are still at the gate. Killing and being killed αὐτοῦ 'there and then' is elsewhere in P. applied to large numbers of people, especially on the battlefield (3.116.1, 14.8.11, etc.). There could be a sudden touch of grandeur here, or αὐτοῦ (FD) could be a correction to αὐτόν (G). If the original was, say, παραυτίκα, that would contrast effectively with σχολῆι καὶ μεθ' ἡσυχίας; cf. e.g. 3.51.11–12, 18.44.7.    πατάξαντες: P. need not have included this, and it is not a frequent turn of phrase in him (more detail at 11.18.4, fr. 204 Olson). It brings out the violence after the humour; the manual action contrasts with ψηλαφῶντα. Livy has a neat conception (25.9.14): Philemenus runs the guard through with a hunting-spear.    ἑπομένους: these men have been separated as a detachment in advance (cf. §9).    σχολῆι καὶ μεθ' ἡσυχίας: since all has been done so stealthily, a small number of the 1,000 Libyans can be let in through the little gate.

**29.9 κατὰ τὸ συνεχές:** the next stage for each after entering. Cf. 31.25.9, with 31.25.2; *CGL* συνεχής 5. For the position of οἱ μέν cf. 2.68.9, 7.18.6.    οἱ μὲν … ἐφόνευον: the parallelism to actions of the Tarentines in the first scheme is made apparent (28.12); but the two items are put the other way round, as are the constituents of the first item: 28.12 διέκοπτον τοὺς μοχλούς.    διὰ συνθημάτων: it is the middle of the night.

**29.10 εἰσελθόντων δὲ καὶ τούτων** takes up the start of the paragraph, §1 γενομένης δὲ τῆς εἰσόδου … ἀσφαλοῦς. προῆγον ὡς ἐπὶ τὴν ἀγοράν takes up §1 προῆγον ἐπὶ τὴν ἀγοράν. Convergence on the agora has obviously been arranged with the Tarentines in detail.

**29.11 συμμῖξαι καὶ τούτους:** τούτους is the subject (unless one read τούτοις). 'Meeting' is, despite καί, more suitable with this body than with the contingent Hannibal was leading; that is entirely natural.    περιχαρής picks up 24.11, and marks the progress of Hannibal's plan, not, as with other authors, an ironic ignorance (cf. e.g. Hdt. 1.119.2 of Harpagus, Virg. *Aen.* 1.685 of Dido; Lyne (1989) 181–5; Rutherford (2022) 359).    τὴν πρᾶξιν: again at the end of the next sentence (30.1); it has acquired more substance than at 24.7, 12.    τῶν προκειμένων: similar to the ending of the paragraph at 27.9 ἐπὶ τὴν προκειμένην χρείαν. The shaping underlines the onward momentum of proceeding through the plan.

## 30 ROMAN ESCAPE AND ROMAN DEATHS

**30.1 Κελτῶν:** one of the major elements in Hannibal's army, cf. e.g. 3.117.6; Κελτία, probably Cisalpine Gaul, comes in the treaty at 7.9.6, 7. The Celts are kept distinct, and have their own commanders (§§4, 9 below). The Carthaginian element (§§4, 9) is not explicitly mentioned here. Cf. further Ameling (1993) 217–18; Goldsworthy (2000) 34. συνέστησε τῶν νεανίσκων ... §2 ἀκολούθως δὲ καὶ ... συνεξαπέστειλε ... §3 τοῖς μὲν ἐγχωρίοις νεανίσκοις ... §4 τοῖς δὲ ... ἡγεμόσι: the division of function is clear. The Tarentines keep any Tarentines safe, Hannibal's leaders direct the troops (§3), and see that any Romans are killed (§4). P. could easily have made the Tarentine young men subordinate extras; but his arrangement gives them at least as much importance as the leaders. He has been following this group; a precise number of them is specified for each third of the 2,000 (6 in all, of those detailed off). P. is also concerned with the Tarentines in general, and Hannibal's careful treatment of them.

**30.2 ἀκολούθως** 'in the same fashion', i.e. dividing equally between μέρη. Cf. 28.2.7.    **διαλαβεῖν ... εὐκαιροτάτας:** cf. 27.7 διαλαβόντες τῆς ἀγορᾶς τὰς εὐκαιροτάτας εἰσβολάς. It is the same idea with some difference in phrasing. There are evidently three such roads (τρία μέρη 27.7, 30.1); Hannibal has appropriated the knowledge of the young men.

**30.3 ἐγχωρίοις:** not needed for clarity; cf. §1 τῶν νεανίσκων. τῶν Ταραντίνων could have been put instead of τῶν πολιτῶν; cf. §4 τοὺς ἐντυγχάνοντας τῶν Ῥωμαίων. But the relationship of the young men to their people is important.    **ἐξαιρεῖσθαι ... καὶ σώιζειν:** both verbs were not required, and one infinitive could have been made a participle: the action and its meaning are emphasized.    **ἀναβοῶντας ἐκ πολλοῦ** ('from a distance'; cf. LSJ πολύς IV.3). The young men will be heard as Tarentine by their accent, and hence trusted. Close contact with individuals is not envisaged, despite τοὺς ἐντυγχάνοντας. Contrast the friendlier approach in Livy, despite *procul*: 25.9.17 *ut ubi quem suorum procul uidissent, quiescere ac silere ac bono animo esse iuberent* (cf. Sen. *Ben.* 5.6.4).

**30.4 κτείνειν:** unusual in P., 3 times outside quotations, as against 49 times for ἀποκτείνω. See Introduction §13 c n. 64. The form evidently highlights the ferocity; cf. 10.5.3 παραγγείλας κτείνειν τὸν παρατυχόντα καὶ μηδενὸς φείδεσθαι.    **μέν:** the organized carrying out of commands is contrasted (§5 δέ) with the chaotic reaction of the people.

**30.5 τῶν πολεμίων εἰσόδου:** the phrase is taken up in §6 τῆς εἰσόδου τῶν πολεμίων. With notable embedded focalization, the alarmed Tarentines are made to share the Roman perspective (cf. 27.2), which Philemenus had pretended to share at 25.9. Hannibal will persuade most of the Tarentines to realign their approach (31.2–4). Livy makes the Tarentines think the Romans are ransacking the city (25.10.2) – evidently not impossible.    **πλήρης:** a favourite word for creating atmosphere from a space. Cf. 6.4 above: ships πλήρη θαλάττης ... καὶ ταραχῆς (with n.); 15.25.9: the city πλήρη ... στεναγμοῦ, δακρύων ...    **παρηλλαγμένης** 'quite extraordinary'; a strong word, cf. 5.48.9 τραγικὴν καὶ παρηλλαγμένην, 14.5.12 βοῆς ἀτάκτου, ψόφου παρηλλαγμένου ... πλήρης, *PL* I2b.

**30.6 συννοήσας ἀδύνατον αὐτὸν ὄντα διὰ τὴν μέθην** shows the success of the plan, but also the military thought of the commander; he is not just fleeing for his life. Greek writers are more inclined to see drunkenness as continuing than to distinguish sharply between drunkenness and hangover; but cf. e.g. [Arist.] *Prob.* 873b18–23.    **ἐξελθὼν ἐκ τῆς οἰκίας μετὰ τῶν οἰκετῶν:** the last phrase is repeated later in the sentence, superfluously; it comes only here in P. The domesticity of the ignominious escape is made apparent; the phrase is stingingly deployed of Leocrates' flight at Lycurg. 17, cf. 16. Livy leaves out such details, but does use the verb *effugit* (25.10.3).    **τὴν φέρουσαν ἐπὶ τὸν λιμένα:** the account could imply there was one particular route to the harbour, which might have been easy to block.    **τοῦ φύλακος ἀνοίξαντος αὐτῶι τὴν ῥινοπύλην:** it could seem obvious that the guard would let the *praefectus* out, but the moment ironically matches the guard letting Philemenus in through the ῥινοπύλη, 29.5–6 (cf. 25.8n.).    **διαδύς** suggests stealth; cf. 4.57.8, Thuc. 4.110.2.    **ἀκατίου:** a rather undignified exit for the commander; cf. e.g. Plut. *Dion* 14.7 (from Timaeus? Cf. *FGrHist* 566 F113). λαμβάνομαι typically takes the genitive, LSJ B.    **ἄκραν:** Livius is not fleeing Tarentum (contrast 4.58.11). He was laughed at by Fabius for losing the city, despite keeping the citadel until 209 (Plut. *Fab.* 23.3–4). Some later sought to have his initial *socordia* rebuked in a *senatus consultum*; others sought to reward his subsequent persistence (Livy 27.25.3–5).

**30.7 ἡτοιμασμένοι:** Philemenus, like Hannibal, has got things ready in advance (25.8 ἑτοιμαζομένων, 26.10 παρεσκευακώς) – a contrast with Livius' improvisation at the same moment (κατὰ δὲ τὸν καιρὸν τοῦτον).    **Ῥωμαϊκὰς ... συνήθειαν:** the contact of Romans and Greeks has led, not just to Romans imitating Greek revelry, but to Greeks acquiring Roman skills and instruments. The Romans had evidently not confined their military trumpets to members of their army. Livy 25.10.4

*inscienter a Graeco inflato* suggests a misapprehension, or an error in Livy's text of P. (*scienter* would not suit his sentence so well). The Roman trumpet was longer than the Greek; for an image cf. Trajan's Column, Scene VIII (Lepper and Frere (1988) plate x). On trumpets and their use cf. e.g. 14.3.6; Wille (1967) 84–90; West (1992) 118–21. **[καί]**: τις can begin clauses in P.; cf. e.g. 2.2.10 τινῶν δέ, 4.8.9, Introduction §13 b. The asyndeton between ἡτοιμασμένοι and στάντες is normal, as the participles relate to different times; cf. e.g. 2.34.7. But the structure becomes difficult if στάντες is preceded by a genitive absolute which is joined to the previous nominative participle by καί – itself an unsatisfactory arrangement. καί, τινῶν ..., στάντες would produce an awkward sequence. τινας τῶν (Casaubon) would oddly create a multitude of cross-cultural trumpeters. **ἐπὶ τὸ θέατρον:** a good place for the sound to carry from. The accusative suggests preceding movement; cf. 30.22.4 τούτους οὖν στήσας ἐπὶ τὸ προσκήνιον. On the theatre in Tarentum, see Lippolis, Garraffo and Nafissi (1995) 183–6.

**30.8 ἐν τοῖς ὅπλοις:** but Roman armour is not accompanied by Roman order (§9). **ἄκραν:** in fact those that get through will prove helpful to the successful defence; cf. App. *Hann.* 137. **ἐθισμόν:** unreflective habit is as damaging to them as the cunning exploitation of συνήθεια (§7) is useful to the Greeks and Carthaginians. κατὰ τὸν ἐθισμόν can be contrasted with κατὰ τὴν πρόθεσιν. See also 29.4, 5 above: κατὰ τὴν ἐξ ἀρχῆς πρόθεσιν, κατὰ τὸν ἐθισμόν. **Καρχηδονίοις:** not 'Hannibal', despite §4.

**30.9 πλατείαις:** the word was used recently of the orderly passages in Roman camps (6.31.7, 32.1, 33.4). **ἀτάκτως καὶ σποράδην:** the same emphatic pair as at 3.43.2 (βάρβαροι), 4.12.7. The Roman disorder contrasts with the strict Carthaginian organization at 26.8 (ταττομένους, τάξεως) and 31.6 (τάξει), and with the orderly plan, neatly narrated: οἱ μὲν εἰς τοὺς Καρχηδονίους ... οἱ δ' εἰς τοὺς Κελτούς takes up §4. At 38.6.4 ἀτάκτως is used of other historians' use of digression, while P. structures his changing narrative τεταγμένως. **πολύ τι πλῆθος:** no number is given; this is not a pitched battle. There is very similar phrasing at 3.53.3 (surprise attack); cf. 86.10 (killing *en route*).

**30.10 ἡμέρας:** the populace were mostly in bed at 27.9. They had had some perception of events (§11), but had not done much investigating. **οἰκήσεις:** houses provide safety for now (cf. 31.4–6), especially on the supposition that a hostile force has not taken the city. **†τάξασθαι†:** there is no parallel for the sense 'understand'. Something like e.g. <κα>ταλαβέσθαι could be imagined. Cf. 2.6 above (active); the middle comes in Dionysius, the New Testament, etc. For the Tarentines, by contrast with the Carthaginians, the events are at first impossible to work out; they then have a false theory (§11); finally they reach the truth (§12), which is confirmed (31.2–3); but the outlook from the situation surprises them (31.4). Planning from one perspective is opposed to handling the unexpected from another.

**30.11 σάλπιγγα:** another effect of the trick (30.7); now just one trumpet, cf. Livy 25.10.4.   **μηδὲν ἀδίκημα ... μηδ' ἁρπαγήν** fits the agreement (25.2), and is crucial to the Tarentines' acceptance of the Carthaginians.   **ἔδοξαν:** a settled conclusion, in the aorist, at that time (cf. γίνεσθαι); that conclusion will be disturbed, cf. §12 ὑπέτρεχε imperfect.   **ἐξ αὐτῶν τῶν Ῥωμαίων:** ironic; §12 πολλοὺς αὐτῶν ... πεφονευμένους picks the irony up.   **κίνημα:** a word for 'tumult', joined with ταραχή at 3.54.1, 7.17.3.

**30.12 τῶι** (Casaubon): τό [FDG] ... ὁρᾶν does not produce satisfactory syntax, with no main verb to govern or be governed by, and ὑπέτρεχέ τις ἔννοια to follow. It is easily changed to τῶι, 'because of'; cf. 5.97.6, 15.25.25.   **ἐν ταῖς πλατείαις:** a graphic addition, revisiting §9 in the daylight. The phrase is used for simpler horror at Plut. *Dion* 46.2.   **Γαλατῶν:** a more general ethnic term than Κελτοί, to capture the perception of the Greeks. The following insertion of τῶν Ῥωμαίων brings out the presence of the Romans' old enemies, incompatible with the Tarentines' original hypothesis. Cf. 2.23.5 (225 BC) Κελτούς, and 7: the Romans' old fear of Γαλάται. Perhaps Celts are doing this because they are less in awe of Hannibal's strictness than the Carthaginians (cf. 31.6); or P. may be selecting. Instead of the vivid despoiling, Livy has *Punica et Gallica arma* seen by the Romans (25.10.5).   **ὑπέτρεχε** 'occurred'. The word comes with ἔννοια at 9.6.2, 16.6.10; with a clause at 14.12.5, Epict. 4.2.2. It is not particularly elevated in register, as the passage in Epictetus confirms.   **Καρχηδονίων:** the crucial ethnic name at last.

## 31 HANNIBAL ADDRESSES THE TARENTINES

**31.1 τοῦ μὲν Ἀννίβου ... ὁ μὲν Ἀννίβας:** the triple genitive absolute makes it easy for Hannibal to reappear in the nominative. The internal contrasts take precedence over providing a δέ to answer 30.10 οἱ μὲν Ταραντῖνοι.   **παρεμβεβληκότος τὴν δύναμιν:** placing rather than encamping (Loeb, *PL*); cf. e.g. 10.12.2.   **εἰς τὴν ἀγοράν ... εἰς τὴν ἄκραν:** the opposition between the heart of the city and the separated citadel continues; cf. §1 ἀθροίζεσθαι πάντας εἰς τὴν ἀγοράν, §3 ἀπεχώρουν

COMMENTARY: 31.1–31.3      219

εἰς τὴν ἄκραν. Carthaginians no longer seem to be occupying the streets, to prevent pro-Roman Tarentines from leaving: cf. §3 ὅσοι; the Romans in §1, on the other hand, are those who got through. **προ-:** before the present events; cf. e.g. 5.51.7 προκαταληφθείσης. **εἰλικρινοῦς** goes beyond 30.10 τῆς δ' ἡμέρας ἐπιφαινομένης; a stronger word is employed than in Livy's *postquam lux certior erat* (25.10.6). It is used for bright, clear light at Philo, *Jos.* 145, Vett. Val. 6.3.8 (238.11–12 Pingree), Clem. Alex. *Ecl. Proph.* 32.3 (III 147.6 Stählin). The lighting suits the full public revelation of the position to the Tarentines; cf. Livy 23.10.7 *foro medio, luce clara*.

**31.2 ἐβόων ἐπὶ τὴν ἐλευθερίαν:** the all-important young men had previously shouted to their citizens not to move and assured them of safety (30.3); now they are calling them to go to the agora and participate in their own freedom. There are similar calls to freedom at 1.70.8, 5.39.3. Cf. 34.4 below. In Livy, Hannibal speaks against *dominationem superbam Romanorum* (25.10.8). Cf. P. 3.77.6: Hannibal says he will give Italians their freedom back; 3.85.4: he says he is fighting the Romans for the freedom of the Italians; Livy 23.10.7. **θαρρεῖν, ὡς ὑπὲρ ἐκείνων <ὁρῶντας> παρόντας τοὺς Καρχηδονίους:** previously the Tarentines saw (30.12 ὁρᾶν) that many Romans had been killed and suspected the presence of the Carthaginians (30.12 ὑπέτρεχέ τις ἔννοια τῆς τῶν Καρχηδονίων παρουσίας). Now they can see, or will when they reach the agora, that the Carthaginians are present; they know, the young men indicate, that the Carthaginians will fight against the Romans for them. So at 3.77.4 Hannibal tells the Italians he will fight the Romans ὑπὲρ ἐκείνων. The Carthaginians' claims will not be news (see above and cf. 3.118.3, Livy 24.13.2–3). τοὺς Καρχηδονίους could be the object of θαρρεῖν, 'have confidence in', as at Xen. *Cyr.* 5.5.42 and DC 73.2.6; but the result would be contorted. Furthermore, the idiomatic παρακαλεῖν θαρρεῖν would not have its usual absolute meaning 'tell not to worry' (at least 8 times in P.), and we would lose the idiomatic θαρρεῖν + ὡς and participle (genitive if participle goes with noun absent from main clause). There is no other grammatical justification for the accusative παρόντας.

**31.3 ὅσοι:** the pro-Roman contingent at least is firmly defined; contrast §4. **προκατείχοντο:** their minds were already made up; cf. 27.4.9 προκατεχόμενοι δὲ τῆι πρὸς Ῥωμαίους εὐνοίαι. **συνηθροίζοντο:** a variation on §1 ἀθροίζεσθαι, like χωρίς on §1 ἄνευ; the unifying motion is stressed. §4 ὁμοθυμαδόν takes it further. **φιλανθρώπους ... λόγους:** strategic kindness, as at 24.8, 3.77.4, Livy 23.10.1 *oratio perblanda ac benigna*. The adjective is emphasized by separation. There is no summary of this part of the speech as in Livy (25.10.8).

**31.4 ἐπισημηναμένων:** approving applause; cf. *I.Délos* 1517.34–5, 1518.13–14 (both c.154 BC) 'approving, appreciating'. ἕκαστα shows that everyone applauded everything.   **διὰ τὸ παράδοξον τῆς ἐλπίδος:** P. goes on to explain the reason – not so much love of the Carthaginians as delighted surprise. But the addition also shows Hannibal's assured psychology. He is planning; they are astonished. παραδοξ- is thematic throughout the book, and work (2.3n.); more unusual is this combination of surprise with thought about the future, cf. especially 1.44.5 τῶι παραδόξωι τῆς ἐλπίδος. Commonly (-)δοξ- and (-)ελπ- refer to expectation of the same thing; cf. e.g. 21.6 above τὸ παράδοξον καὶ τελέως ἀνέλπιστον, DS 16.93.2 παράδοξος καὶ παντελῶς ἀνέλπιστος.   **διαφῆκε** (Benseler) removes the MSS' hiatus.   **τοὺς πολλούς** does not contrast most Tarentines with the Tarentine collaborators, but rather the Tarentines, who form the majority of those present, with Hannibal's own army: both those men sent to sack (contrast §6 ἐφῆκε with διαφῆκε here) and the remainder kept in their ranks.   **τὴν ἰδίαν οἰκίαν:** back to safety (cf. 30.10 οἰκήσεις), but only if they hurry (μετὰ σπουδῆς) and follow the orders. The word they are to write, Ταραντίνου, is not just vivid detail but pointed. Any sign would have done; cf. 31.6 τὰς ἀνεπιγράφους, Livy 25.10.9 *quemque ... nomen suum inscribere*. But this choice displays to the Tarentines at the meeting Hannibal's attitude to their people (cf. Livy 24.20.10, 15); opposed to them are Romans and those who have fled to the Romans. Ταραντίνου forcefully ends a sentence that began τῶν δὲ Ταραντίνων. The standard -ου is employed in Ταραντίνου, not the local -ω (cf. *IG* XIV.668a, Tarentum).

**31.5 ἐπὶ [τὴν] Ῥωμαϊκὴν κατάλυσιν:** the article is odd; a generalizing singular seems improbable. Probably τὴν has crept in from ἐπὶ τήν just before; ἐπί τινα would not appeal.   **θάνατον:** put first in the phrase and separated from τὴν ζημίαν, somewhat as at 6.16.2 οἷς θάνατος ἀκολουθεῖ τὸ πρόστιμον. Hannibal's hatred of Romans is brought out. Safeguarding Romans' property would put a Tarentine in their number. Less drastic is Livy 25.10.9 *eum se pro hoste habiturum*.

**31.6 αὐτός:** selection is not delegated, as often in the Roman army (6.20.4–7, 25.1).   **τοὺς ἐπιτηδειοτάτους <τῶν> ἐπὶ τῶν πραγμάτων ... τοὺς δὲ λοιποὺς συνέχων ἐν τάξει:** a highly ordered and controlled version of sacking. Keeping soldiers in their τάξις recalls 26.8; with συνέχων cf. 26.8 συνέχειν. Such order is seen as distinctively Roman at 10.16.6–9. The rewards could be for the ἡγεμόνες in the first instance, as Hannibal suggested at 26.7 (but cf. 32.1n.). ἐπὶ τῶν πραγμάτων, however, sounds civilian (cf. e.g. 3.69.4, Welles, *RC* 31.26 (c.205 BC)), and τοὺς ἐπιτηδειοτάτους ἐκ τῶν ταγμάτων deserves consideration (Madvig (1871–84) I 482). **τὰς τῶν Ῥωμαίων οἰκίας:** Livy has *hospitia Romana* ('lodgings', 25.10.10, cf. 9); he is probably misinterpreting P.'s κατάλυσιν (§5), cf. 25.2n. He says the Romans were occupying houses that were empty (25.10.9); he is probably inventing in the Romans' favour. Cf. P. Hal. 1 col. viii.166–70 (iii BC), where soldiers forcibly eject people from their homes.

## 32 CITY VS CITADEL

**32.1 πολλῶν ... καὶ παντοδαπῶν:** similarly of plunder at 1.19.15 πολλῆς δὲ καὶ παντοδαπῆς ἐγένοντο κατασκευῆς ἐγκρατεῖς (Acragas). **κατασκευασμάτων:** precious objects, perhaps works of art, perhaps from temples, cf. 4.18.11, *LSCG Suppl.* 72 A.13 (Thasos, i BC), *I.Mylasa* I.102.15 (ii–i BC); if so, some were left (Plut. *Fab.* 22.7–8). The objects will be appropriated from Tarentum, or possibly elsewhere; in either case, Roman rapacity will not have endeared them to the Tarentines. (Romans taking art: 9.10.10; Scheer (1995), esp. 215–16.) Strabo 6.3.1 (II 202.13–14 Radt) has the Carthaginians doing great damage to Tarentine works of art. Livy indirectly plays down the Roman appropriations with his *et fuit praedae aliquantum* (25.10.10). **ὠφελείας** 'booty'; cf. e.g. 2.3.8, 2.22.5; Pinzone (1983) 141. **Καρχηδονίοις:** this may denote the whole force. Hannibal promised the leaders (26.7), but §2 ηὐλίσθησαν indicates the men generally.

**32.2 συνεδρεύσας ... ἔκρινε:** only a show of collaboration, but the action is in the Tarentines' supposed interest. **Ταραντίνων:** readers might expect these to be the conspirators; τοῖς Ταραντίνοις suggests a display of concern through chosen representatives. **διατειχίσαι:** hence not to make an immediate attack on the Romans in the citadel; site or defenders are thought difficult. Livy makes this inference about the site (25.11.1). **φόβος:** it is made clear that Hannibal does not intend to stay, or leave a large garrison. Fear and confidence run through the passage (§§4, 5, 33.3, etc.): Hannibal must ensure the right people have these feelings and cognitive states. **ἐπικάθηται:** with some connotations of besieging a city (LSJ ἐπικάθημαι II; 4.61.6 ἐπικαθίσαιεν τῆι πόλει). φόβος can περιστῆναι and ἐπιστῆναι (3.75.8, 6.18.2). **Ῥωμαίων:** the Tarentines are now in a state of enmity with the Romans.

**32.3 πρῶτον ... ἐπεβάλετο:** the palisade is only part of Hannibal's ἐπιβολή (33.1). This sentence is significantly short, the next one longer, for the further plan. **τάφρωι:** crucial planting for the narrative and the plan

(§§5, 7). Soldiers who had fallen into the ditch would be easily finished off (§7 below). The ditch is probably where the Canale Navigabile now separates off what was the acropolis: cf. Lippolis (1981) 89–91; see Map 3. *fossa ingenti*, says Livy (25.11.1), magnifying the scene.

**32.4 σαφῶς δὲ γινώσκων** stresses Hannibal's grasp of what will happen, but especially the resilience of the Romans. διαγινώσκων (G, cf. FD) would mean 'deciding'. **ἐναποδειξομένους** 'display' to impress, cf. e.g. 36.1.7; here with injured pride. **τῆιδέ πηι** 'in this way', more emphatic than indefinite. **χεῖρας** 'groups', bodies of soldiers; see LSJ v. As usual, selection and preparation are crucial (cf. e.g. 26.3–4 above; 31.6 τοὺς ἐπιτηδειοτάτους). **πρὸς τὸ μέλλον:** Hannibal characteristically thinks ahead, but now to a situation from which he and the Carthaginians are absent. Livy takes the point: *ut facile per se ipsi Tarentini urbem ab iis tueri possent* (25.11.3); but in him practicality is the concern, not morale. **καταπλήξασθαι:** in P. the general and statesman must often aim to produce an overwhelming reaction. Cf. 10.15.4–5 (Scipio and Romans), 11.9.1 (Philopoemen), 14.5.13 (Scipio); Seretaki and Tamiolaki (2018) 231–2. **εὐθαρσεῖς:** from the victory but also from the wall, cf. §2 φόβος; the fear must become the Romans', cf. 33.2.

**32.5 τὸν πρῶτον:** an immediate response. **θρασέως:** for now, it is the Romans who are εὐθαρσεῖς. The pairing with τετολμηκότως is emphatic; it recurs at 16.37.6. τετολμηκότως comes only in P. and Diodorus. **βραχύ:** contrast §6 ἰσχυρᾶς, and indeed ἐν βραχεῖ χώρωι. Hannibal handles the situation more discerningly than the Romans. **τὰς ὁρμὰς ... ἐκκαλεσάμενος:** typical tactics from the cunning; cf. 1.40.3: L. Caecilius Metellus θεωρῶν αὐτὸν (Hasdrubal) κατατεθαρρηκότα, καὶ σπουδάζων ἐκκαλεῖσθαι τὴν ὁρμὴν αὐτοῦ. See LSJ ἐκκαλέω II.2. **ἐπεί** 'when', 'as soon as'; the clause goes with what follows. **προέπεσον** 'were in front', in relation to the ditch; cf. e.g. 3.115.7 τοὺς Κελτοὺς ... πολὺ προπεπτωκέναι τῶν κεράτων, 4.4, 5.8nn. There must have been a bridge over the ditch. **δοὺς παράγγελμα** brings out the moment. **προσέβαλε:** a more decisive move than ἐπιχειρούντων.

**32.6 ἰσχυρᾶς ... τὸ πέρας** ('in the end', 7.5, 24.13nn.). It was no easy fight, but οἱ Ῥωμαῖοι at the end reverses their action near the start of §5. The effect is more climactic than at 10.12.8–9 τέλος ... ἐτράπησαν οἱ παρὰ τῶν Καρχηδονίων, καὶ πολλοὶ μὲν αὐτῶν κτλ. **ὡς ἄν:** more or less equivalent to ὡς; cf. e.g. 5.85.11. **ἐν βραχεῖ χώρωι καὶ περιτετειχισμένωι τῆς συμπλοκῆς ἐπιτελουμένης:** the phrase explains ἰσχυρᾶς, but also gives a

COMMENTARY: 32.6-33.3     223

memorable picture of the conditions. The picture is brought out by comparison with Livy, who looks only at the impediments to flight (25.11.5). συμπλοκή is close, intense fighting; cf. e.g. 3.51.8, *Syll.*³ II.567.11–12 (Calymna, *c*.204–201 BC).

**32.7 ἔπεσον:** a dignified word for death in battle, by contrast with the literal fall inflicted in συγκρημνιζόμενον. That verb, found only here until the Late Byzantine period, creates an undignified mass movement. The event is graphically and drastically conveyed; cf. 5.48.9 (Introduction §1 a) and 16.8.9.    **ἐν χειρῶν νόμωι:** proper battle, 'the use of hands'. A set phrase (first Hdt. 8.89.1), often contrasted with more humiliating and peculiar ends. Cf. e.g. 1.82.2 (throwing to beasts), DS 20.66.3 (κατεκρημνίζοντο, out of fear). The inglorious ἐν τῆι τάφρωι is contrasted.    **διεφθάρη** takes up the closing διεφθάρη at 30.9; this is even worse.

## 33 FORTIFICATIONS

**33.1 ἀσφαλῶς:** that is, after the Romans' attack has been dealt with. The idea runs through the passage: ἀσφάλειαν §§5, 7; cf. 29.1n.    **τὴν ἡσυχίαν ἔσχε:** Hannibal's control over his actions, as at 32.5, is opposed to the Romans' impetuous responses (32.4, 5). This still moment marks his success.    **ἐπιβολῆς** looks back to 32.3 ἐπεβάλετο and what follows.    **κατὰ νοῦν κεχωρηκυίας:** the same phrase used as at 29.11 above, κατὰ νοῦν αὐτῶι προχωρεῖν τὴν πρᾶξιν, where a plan is still in progress. But there is a contrast with the new and unsuccessful plan at the end of the paragraph (§10).

**33.2 συγκλείσας:** the citadel is now a place not of escape but of imprisonment.    **ἐντὸς τοῦ τείχους:** contrast 32.5 ἐκτὸς τοῦ τάφρου.    **δεδιότας ... §3 θάρσος:** the states of mind have now been reversed as intended (32.2, 4).    **καὶ περὶ τῆς ἄκρας:** one might have expected 'themselves' and 'the citadel' to come the other way round (cf. 1.65.4?); but the focus is now on the ἄκρα.

**33.3 πολιτικοῖς:** those living in the main city as opposed to the citadel. It means 'of the πόλις' at 1.9.4, etc.    **τοιοῦτο ... θάρσος:** the separation stresses τοιοῦτο.    **ἱκανοὺς ... τοῖς Ῥωμαίοις:** perhaps 'be a match for', as probably at Plato, *Prot.* 322c6–7; cf. P. 35.2.8 ὡς ἱκανοὶ γεγονότες ἀντίπαλοι Ῥωμαίοις. At any rate, the idea is more daringly put than in Livy, and is the Tarentines' own supposition; cf. Livy 25.11.7 *ut uel sine praesidio tueri se aduersus Romanos possent*. But Livy sees from P. that this is Hannibal's plan; cf. 34.8 below.

**33.4 μετὰ δὲ ταῦτα:** Hannibal now continues his aim διατειχίσαι τὴν πόλιν ἀπὸ τῆς ἄκρας (32.2). The first stage creates a sequence palisade – ditch – palisade, the second creates a τεῖχος (§6). Even the first sequence is almost as good as a τεῖχος (§5), and enables a security which goes beyond that achieved in the Tarentines' minds. ὥστε καὶ χωρὶς ἀνδρῶν ... ἱκανάς ... (§7) takes up and outdoes §3 ὥστε καὶ χωρὶς τῶν Καρχηδονίων ἱκανούς ... **μικρὸν ... ἀποστήσας:** set against §6 ἀπολιπὼν σύμμετρον διάστημα ('a reasonable interval'); the first set of defences is separated from the wall. **παράλληλον** takes up 32.3. The palisade and the wall of the acropolis make superfluous any mention of the pre-existing ditch by that wall; the ditch has served its narrative purpose. Livy's *fossa ingens* (a new one) ... *murum* (25.11.7) makes clearer the echo of what have become the citadel's defences against the city; cf. 25.11.1 *ab ipsa urbe muro et fossa ingenti saeptam*. τῶι τῆς ἄκρας τείχει varies 32.3 τῶι τείχει τῆς ἀκροπόλεως.

**33.5 ἐκ μεταβολῆς** 'in turn' often marks fairly mild contrasts or oppositions in P., cf. 4.10.5, 5.14.4; here perhaps of the heaping up as opposed to the digging down. That heap of earth makes it harder to escape from the ditch; προσέτι δὲ καί advances with a further palisade too. **τῶι:** the dative is more suitable than the accusative for the piling of dirt on the edge (χεῖλος) of the ditch; it is the location of the mass of earth (χοῦς) which matters. τῶι (FD) is more likely than τό (D$^{sl}$G) to be original: τό is a conjecture produced by τεῖχος. **τοῦ χοῦς:** the article appears since the mass of earth is an expected product of digging the ditch; cf. 4.41.3, 7 τὸν χοῦν. **ἀσφάλειαν ... ἀποτελεῖσθαι** sounds complete, but more is to come.

**33.6 τεῖχος:** near the Canale, at the junction of via T. N. D'Aquino and via Regina Margherita, were found remains of a wall hastily created from material including bits of houses. This is most plausibly identified with Hannibal's wall; cf. Dell'Aglio (2002–3) 227–9, (2015) 434, 436; Andreassi (2005) 229; Lippolis (2006) 212. **ἐπεβάλετο** ties up with 32.3 ἐπεβάλετο (of Hannibal's earlier fortification). **τῆς Σωτείρας ... τὴν Βαθεῖαν προσαγορευομένην:** the Σώτειρα should run along the north side of the city, by the Mar Piccolo: see 29.1n. and Map 3. τῆς Βαθείας has appeared in 29.1 without the suggestion in προσαγορευομένην that readers will not know it (but cf. Acts 9:11 πορεύθητι ἐπὶ τὴν ῥύμην τὴν καλουμένην Εὐθεῖαν). Probably only some streets had names; cf. e.g. P. Lond. VII 2191.37–45 (Pathyris, 116 BC), Pestman (1969).

**33.7 αὐτῶν** continues the emphasis of καὶ χωρὶς ἀνδρῶν. The idea contrasts with the notion that the men are the walls of the city (Alc. fr. 112.10

Voigt; cf. Thuc. 7.77.7). κατασκευασμάτων are here the wall, etc.; see *PL* 2. παρασκευάζειν at the end of the whole sentence reprises κατασκευάζειν at the end of the first part; but now the subject is the impersonal ὀχυρότητες rather than Hannibal, who is no longer needed.

**33.8 ἀπολιπὼν δὲ τοὺς ἱκανοὺς καὶ τοὺς ἐπιτηδείους:** the same phrase, including the repeated article, at 14.4.1 – but with no noun; contrast ἱππεῖς here. The men of Livy's *praesidium* are to help finishing the wall (25.8.11): so not just cavalry. (*praesidium* is 'garrison', as *reliquit* indicates.) τείχους <καὶ> would yield infantry too. ἱππεῖς cannot be governed by κατεστρατοπέδευσε: the verb is always intransitive in P. (88 times). **καὶ τὴν τοῦ τείχους:** the Romans, even if cowed, might be tempted to demonstrate their prowess on any new construction of Hannibal's (32.4, 34.1). **παρεφεδρεύσοντας** (Reiske): cf. esp. 10.6.7 ἀπέλιπε ... ἐφεδρεύσοντα. **περὶ τετταράκοντα:** 40, on Fornaro's view, would be 8.456 km, 5.254 miles (26.4n.). Hannibal is pointedly not taking the easy option of staying in the city. His main force stays in its camp, three days' march away (26.2). **παρὰ μέν τισι:** cf. 28.2; but here the divergence has more than just scholarly point. **Γάλαισον:** for the accent see Lobeck (1843) 409, on Theognost. *Can.* 407, Cramer, *Anecd. Gr.* II 73. *Galaesus* is the Roman name for the river by the first century BC (Livy 25.11.8, Virg. *G.* 4.126, etc.). **τοῖς πλείστοις:** the predominance of 'Eurotas' in the scholarly or other sources underlines the link with Sparta. §9 ὁμολογουμένην does the same. **Εὐρώτα:** one of the most famous features of Sparta's geography. Cf. e.g. Thgn. 785 Σπάρτην δ' Εὐρώτα δονακοτρόφου ἀγλαὸν ἄστυ (the river defines the city), Simon. fr. 11 + 13.29 Sider Εὐ]ρώταν κα[ὶ Σπάρτη]ς ἄστυ λιπόντ[ες. P. dwells on its size at 5.22.2.

**33.9 πολλά:** P. emphasizes the results of origin and kinship. This could be a neutral scholarly point, such as he elsewhere scorns (so 9.1.4); but συγγένεια carries implications on behaviour, as at 5.76.11, where the Selgeis did not disgrace freedom or their πρὸς Λακεδαιμονίους συγγένειαν (cf. *OGIS* I.234.12–13, 15–16 (Delphi, iii BC); *I.Selge* 6 (iii AD)). Here the Tarentines show vigorous enthusiasm for their freedom, cf. 31.2–4, 34.4, as is fitting for those akin to Spartans, cf. 6.10.11, 48.5, 50.1 (of course the Spartans' own history is more complicated; cf. e.g. 4.22.3–4, 81.12–13). συγγένεια, a major concern in Hellenistic inscriptions, is often renewed in friendly relations; cf. Moretti, *ISE* II.77.4 (Delphi, 256/5 BC?), *IG* IV.679.6–10 (Hermione, iii BC), *OGIS* I.233.35–6, cf. 11–12 (Magnesia on Maeander, iii–ii BC). In this passage an ethical and political aspect is renewed (cf. 34.3–4n.). The success of Hannibal's persuasion is seen too.

There is a lot of seventh-century Laconian pottery at Taras and Satyrion: see Pelagatti and Stibbe (2002), esp. 389. For subsequent 'Spartanness', see Poulter (2001) 20, 57–8, 137, 153–4, 161–3.

**33.10 λαμβάνοντος τὴν συντέλειαν** 'being completed'. The combination is seen esp. in P., e.g. 6.2.10, Diodorus, e.g. 13.47.5 (with ταχέως), and inscriptions, so *I.Priene B–M* 119.20 (ii BC). Here the present indicates that μετὰ ταῦτα refers to the sequence of achievements in Hannibal's mind: it goes with καὶ τὴν ἄκραν ἐξελεῖν. The thought does not come after the building. τε nudges closer to the start of the phrase, rather than following τήν as it logically should; cf. e.g. 4.11.8, and 7.2, 10.2, 17.11nn. **σπουδὴν καὶ προθυμίαν:** pairs with σπουδή are common and approving in inscriptions; cf. e.g. Moretti, *ISE* III.135.4 (Epidaurus, 111 BC) σπουδὰν καὶ ἐπιμέλειαν, Michel, *Recueil* no. 542.10–11 (Antandros, ii BC) τὴμ π[ᾶ|σαν] σπουδὴγ καὶ φιλοτιμίαν εἰσφερόμενος. **συνεργίαν** 'collaboration'; συνέργεια at 5.58.3. συνεργία is found in papyri of Philodemus, συνέργεια in documentary papyri. **Ἀννίβας** ends, and virtually began, the paragraph: see on §1.

## 34 A BRILLIANT IDEA

**34.1 ἤδη δ' ἐντελεῖς αὐτοῦ συνεσταμένου:** it sounds as if the finishing of the siegeworks (perfect) is more complete than the finishing of the wall (33.10). The parallel ἤδη τετελειωμένης for the wall comes later (§2). There is no mention, though, of the siege being begun; Livy plays it up more: *cum iam machinationum omni genere et operibus oppugnaretur* (25.11.10). Livy may have drawn on a source of the much more substantial account in Appian (*Hann.* 137–41; see below). P. does not give the same detail on the placing of the siegeworks as on the defences of the city (32.3, 33.4–7). He is playing this reverse down. **παρασκευάς:** at the end of the clause, reversed in the destruction of the κατασκευάς at the end of the sentence. Cf. 33.6–7 κατασκευάζειν, ... παρασκευάζειν, again with variation. **Μεταποντίου:** just across the water, about 38 km in a straight line. It was occupied by Romans, against the wishes of its people (cf. Livy 25.15.5–7, App. *Hann.* 148). The force is very substantial in Appian: half the garrison of Metapontum (137, 148). **κατὰ θάλατταν:** the crucial point, which might otherwise seem too obvious to mention; cf. §§2, 3. It is placed at the end of the clause. **βραχύ τι ... ἀναθαρρήσαντες:** now the loss of θάρσος is reversed (cf. 33.2–3), but only briefly: P. does not want to have Hannibal's success too much undone. **νυκτός:** a more cautious and cunning approach is suggested than the immediate attack at 32.5. **νυκτὸς ... κατασκευάς:** this part of the sentence, after the build-up of participles, is forcefully brief, with πάσας and no details. Livy develops the event, perhaps from a source of Appian's: *alia disiecerunt, alia igni corruperunt* (25.11.10; cf. App. *Hann.* 139–40).

**34.2 τὸ μὲν πολιορκεῖν τὴν ἄκραν:** the abandonment of this plan on the citadel is coupled with a new plan, which is also related to the citadel (§3) and is alleged to produce the same result (§5). A siege will resume, but with the Tarentines besieging (§12). Hannibal and P. take the defeat in their stride (cf. 9.9.2–5). The structure, and the drama of Hannibal's new idea, indicate that P. is only qualifying Hannibal's success a little, not thoroughly undermining it.   **τετελειωμένης:** the achievement of the wall is stressed again.   **ἀθροίσας:** P.'s use of the verb makes this seem more likely to be a meeting with all citizens, as at 31.1–3 (ἀθροίζεσθαι, συνηθροίζοντο), than a council meeting including selected Tarentines, as at 32.2 (συνεδρεύσας). General persuasion will prove crucial to the new staged scene.   **ἀπεδείκνυε** suggests the truth of what Hannibal says.   **τῆς θαλάττης ἀντιλαμβάνεσθαι:** a striking way to put it, not present in Livy; cf. §8 κρατῆσαι τῆς θαλάττης. But the phrase relates to specific action, not general dominance; cf. 1.39.14, Plut. *Per.* 25.4. There is no subject to the infinitive – this will turn into the Tarentines' job. θαλάττης forms an argumentative thread with κατὰ θάλατταν (§§1, 3, 5): Hannibal is continuing to deal with οἱ ἐνεστῶτες καιροί.

**34.3–4** This sentence is all in the narrator's voice, as προεῖπον emphasizes; it follows that ἐλευθερωθῆναι (§4) endorses the view of Hannibal and the Tarentine conspirators (cf. 25.2, 31.2). Embedded focalization seems implausible. Freedom at 25.2 is conceived in quite concrete terms; but it still forms part of the changes in the Tarentines: cf. 24.1, where prolonged freedom seeks a master. However pro-Roman one makes P. or P.'s work, the events are before Flamininus' 'liberation' of Greece; cf. Ferrary (2014) 40–3. One should not indeed suppose that P. thinks Hannibal to be pursuing an empire of multi-ethnic harmony (so Baronowski (2011) 127); and Hannibal is following a tradition in bestowing freedom, cf. e.g. Gruen (1984) I, 132–42; Oliva (1993). But freedom is an immensely important conception in P., not simply the object of cynicism; cf. e.g. 2.37.7–11, 4.30.5, 5.106.5, 10.22.3, 11.10.9, 13.9.4.

**34.3 κρατούσης:** cf. §8, but here the genitive object is much more limited. See 24.on. App. *Hann.* 142 gives more physical detail; the bridges over the channel which the Romans control are presumably earlier than the one big bridge at Strabo 6.3.1 (II 200.3–4 Radt).   **ὡς ἐπάνω προεῖπον:** with ὡς or καθάπερ a recurring phrase in P. (27 times, incl.

6.25.8 ὡς προεῖπον ἐπάνω); it is never used by any other author, even with εἶπον. Expression as well as content mark the utterance as P.'s. This is the first instance of the first person singular in this episode; its prominence varies even in P. (cf. Longley (2014) 200–3). **χρῆσθαι ταῖς ναυσὶν οὐδ' ἐκπλεῖν ἐκ τοῦ λιμένος:** the supplies from incoming ships are not dwelt on (App. *Hann.* 142–3, Livy 25.11.11). Perhaps they belong better at a later stage, as in Appian. In Appian Hannibal initially withdraws from Tarentum (141; cf. §13 below) before returning to suggest moving access (143). **ἀσφαλῶς:** the stem ἀσφαλ- had belonged to Hannibal and the Tarentines (33.1, 5, 7), and will return to the Tarentines (§12).

**34.5 ἃ συνορῶν:** Hannibal correctly perceives a situation already described by P. **ἐδίδασκε** does not necessarily imply the truth of what is said; cf. e.g. 5.63.3. **ἀποκλεισθῶσι τῆς κατὰ θάλατταν ἐλπίδος** effectively combines the physical and the mental; the mental is no less important to the argument. **παρὰ πόδας αὐτοὶ δι' αὐτῶν:** ironically at odds with Livius' keeping the acropolis for years until the Romans retook Tarentum (Plut. *Fab.* 23.3–4; note also Front. *Strat.* 3.17.3). But the emphasis in this passage is more on what follows from the agreed premise. **ταύτην ... τὸν τόπον:** this is more likely variation than the Romans giving over city and citadel; the city is not theirs to give.

**34.6 τοῖς μὲν λεγομένοις ... τοῦτο:** they agree that if *x* happened, *y* would happen, but cannot see how *x* could happen now, so see no point in mentioning it. The puzzlement sets up the revelation more satisfyingly than in Livy; there the coming of Carthaginian ships, from Sicily, is a serious possibility (25.11.15; cf. 26.20.7–11). The impossibility of the arrival now is not explained (κατὰ τοὺς τότε καιρούς takes up κατὰ τὸ παρόν from a different perspective); but οὐδαμῶς ἐδύναντο, ἀδύνατον, §7 ἠδυνάτουν, §8 οὐ δυνάμενοι lead up effectively to Hannibal's production of the solution. The exclusion of the naval possibility shows P.'s strategical thought constantly at work; but the point also suits the larger argument; see §8n. For the Carthaginian navy in these years see Steinby (2014) 121–55.

**34.7 ἐπὶ τί φερόμενος** 'with what aim in mind'; cf. 5.26.6 πᾶσιν ἄδηλος ἦν ἐπὶ τί φέρεται καὶ ἐπὶ ποίας ὑπάρχει γνώμης. As often, the question, and the weight, attach to the participle.

**34.8 φήσαντος ... αὐτοῦ:** subordinated to their reaction. **φανερόν:** Hannibal provokingly talks of clarity to the mystified Tarentines. **χωρὶς Καρχηδονίων αὐτοὺς δι' αὐτῶν** most immediately relates to the idea of a Carthaginian fleet, but looks back pointedly to 33.3 καὶ χωρὶς Καρχηδονίων ἱκανοὺς αὐτοὺς κτλ. Tarentine self-reliance must be built up. ὅσον ἤδη 'practically now', 'any moment'; cf. 2.4.4. More provocation, after §6 κατὰ τὸ παρόν. κρατῆσαι: aorist for a decisive moment of gaining mastery. μᾶλλον ἐκπλαγεῖς: the intensified reaction is now expressed in emotional terms.

**34.9 ὁ δέ:** the sentence explains Hannibal's mysterious ἐπίνοια (§8; cf. διενοεῖτο). The drama then resumes with revelation (§10 τὴν ἐπίνοιαν ἐπιδεῖξαι) and especially with the changed reaction of the Tarentines, on which the emphasis falls. Livy makes much more of Hannibal's exposition of his thought, with an *oratio* (25.11.18; cf. 16–17); the *oratio* excitingly presents the manoeuvre in direct speech, and begins, after the despairing reported question *quem ad modum ... euasuras?*, with an arresting *'euadent'*. In P. the road or street leads in between the new fortification (cf. 32.2 διατειχίσαι) and the original city wall; the ships are transported on vehicles (§§11, 12). At App. *Hann.* 143 the road goes through the middle of the city, and is dug through to create a second isthmus. This makes no sense topographically, and may result from combining two sources; Livy bears witness to, or less likely is, one of them. In him too the road goes *per mediam urbem* (25.11.17). He has probably taken the dubious phrase from a source which is not P. συνεωρακώς: cf. §5, συνορῶν again more or less beginning the sentence; Hannibal's perceptions run through. εὐδιακόσμητον: the word only here before Cyril of Alexandria (iv–v AD). It stresses ease (εὐ-), but the road needs adapting; cf. Livy 25.11.18 *munitumque iter*. Evidently the πλατεῖα has been created by Hannibal's own construction. But the present use is not depicted as part of the original plan. [παρὰ τὸ διατείχισμα]: the deletion avoids hiatus (or elision of a major word). After ἐντὸς τοῦ διατειχίσματος, the phrase seems laborious and unnecessary. τὴν ἔξω θάλατταν: the Mar Grande. ταύτηι: this word receives the weight of the structure. ἐκ τοῦ λιμένος: as at §3; but now sailing is not in question. The striking and substantial ὑπερβιβάζειν has force as well as νότιον, separated from its noun.

**34.10 ἅμα τῶι** 'as soon as', advanced on with the ἅμα τῶι of §11. The subject of the infinitive does not need to be expressed. συγκατέθεντο τοῖς λεγομένοις takes up and varies §6 τοῖς μὲν λεγομένοις συγκατετίθεντο (imperfect); but this is now the crucial moment (aorist). διαφερόντως 'exceedingly'; cf. 13.3n. ἐθαύμασαν: the word is used at 9.9.5 of an inevitable later response to Hannibal (cf. further e.g. 11.19.1). Taking the ships over the land at Tarentum appears commonplace in Strabo 6.3.1 (II 200.5–7 Radt); but cf. S. L. Radt (2002–11) VI 203–4. It had sometimes been done at the Isthmus of Corinth; cf. Thuc. 3.15.1, 8.7 with

S. Hornblower (and on 1.13.5), Ar. *Thesm.* 647–8 with Sommerstein and Austin and Olson, Strabo 8.2.1 (II 394.8–11 Radt).   **διέλαβον** implies the truth of ὡς οὐδὲν ἂν περιγένοιτο.   **ἀγχινοίας**: of Hannibal again at 2.36.3 (with τόλμα), 10.33.2, 18.28.6; both features are ascribed to Philip at 4.77.3. τόλμα is often 'courage', as e.g. at Moretti, *ISE* 1.49.2 (Epidaurus, 192 BC) τόλμας ... ἔργα; but here imaginative daring is more relevant. On the relation in P. of Hannibal's success and his qualities, esp. cognitive, cf. Krewet (2017) 102–3.

**34.11 ταχύ**: Livy elaborates a little on equipment, people, animals (25.11.18–19; cf. Sil. It. 12.437–48). P., however, seeks an impression of speed. His next clause would literally imply that this stage took no time at all; cf. Livy 25.11.19 *paucosque post dies*.   **πορείων** 'vehicles for transport', trolleys. The word comes only here in P. In inscriptions and papyri (e.g. *Syll.*³ II.581.23 (Hierapytna, *c*.200 BC)), it denotes various means of transport, animals included; it is rare in literature (e.g. Plato, *Laws* 3.678c6, DS 24.11.1).   **εἴληφει**: the tense heightens the effect of the hyperbole by looking back with the task already completed; so too at Hom. *Il.* 19.242 ἅμα μῦθος ἔην, τετέλεστο δὲ ἔργον. For συντέλειαν λαμβάνειν see 33.10n.   **ὁμοῦ** emphasizes the pair of nouns; cf. e.g. 6.26.10. Metonymy underlines them further, with the abstract nouns performing the action. προθυμία takes up 33.10; but now συνεργούσης, unlike συνεργίαν there, does not indicate help for the Tarentines. πολυχειρία, not common in P., may look back to 3.3; now numbers and the great individual cooperate.

**34.12 οἱ μὲν οὖν Ταραντῖνοι ... ἐπολιόρκουν**: not the Carthaginians too, despite Hannibal's φυλακή (§13). The emphasis is on the Tarentines' independence. At App. *Hann.* 141 the siege is passed to the Carthaginian Hanno; cf. 145 (but cf. Livy 25.15.8 for Hanno; Hasdrubal in Front. *Strat.* 3.17.3; Geus (1994) 123).   **ὑπερνεωλκήσαντες**: a rare word (twice in Strabo, once in Plutarch); P. is using a technical term. ὑπερβιβάζειν in §9 was more spectacular.   **ἀσφαλῶς** completes the series, cf. esp. 33.7, and shows things are sorted out for the Tarentines. As to the unexpected combination with ἐπολιόρκουν, cf. 1.73.3.   **ἀφῃρημένοι**: transitive; cf. e.g. 30.31.10.   **ἐπικουρίας**: the accent is on military assistance rather than supplies, cf. §1 βοηθείας, §5 ἐλπίδος; contrast App. *Hann.* 144 τὴν ἀγορὰν τὴν καταπλέουσαν αὐτοῖς ἀφῃροῦντο, cf. 145. Supplies do come in at §3, but P. is more concerned at the apparent solution of the military problem.

**34.13 φυλακήν**: Hannibal leaves μετὰ τῆς δυνάμεως, 'with his army', of 10,000 men; so the φυλακή sounds much less than the Roman garrison which after losses became 5,000. But Livy's *reliquit tamen modicum praesidium* (25.11.8) need not show that P. wrote φυλακὴν <ἱκανήν> (Naber (1857) 132, cf. 5.6.5); 25.11.8 comes at an earlier stage (33.8n.), and Livy frequently has *modicum* with *praesidium*. Later, rather than use up his original forces, Hannibal puts into Tarentum a *praesidium* of Bruttii, led by a Bruttian; cf. Livy 27.15.9, Plut. *Fab.* 21.2 τῶν τεταγμένων ὑπ' Ἀννίβου τὴν πόλιν φρουρεῖν. ἀνέζευξε 'set off'; cf. 26.4. τριταῖος: the camp has not moved; cf. 26.2. τὸ λοιπὸν τοῦ χειμῶνος: see 26.1n. ἔμενε κατὰ χώραν: not strange behaviour, as it had been before, 26.1–2. This seems a significant point of closure to the action. Cf. 3.94.7, 95.1, 105.11, 106.1, 33.10.13–14; introduction to 24–34, §§3–4n.

## 37 MARCELLUS CAPTURES EPIPOLAE

This brief account forms a decisive sequel to the long earlier narrative of Roman failure (chh. 3–7). The account was part of a longer sequence, including an earlier unsuccessful attempt at exploiting Syracusans who had joined the Romans (Livy 25.23.1–7). But, even allowing for the relative simplicity of capturing Epipolae, the process was not treated with the same opulence of detail as Hannibal capturing Tarentum, or (7.15–18) Antiochus capturing Sardis. This was not the final capture of Syracuse, which happened in P.'s next year (9.10.2).

None the less, the moment is treated as a crucial turning point (§13); it was probably enhanced by tears of mingled joy and sympathy from Marcellus (Livy 25.24.11; cf. Plut. *Marc.* 19.6), and perhaps by some evocation of Thucydides (§13n.). The Roman success will have followed not long in the book after Hannibal's success at Tarentum. For the likeness of Marcellus here to Hannibal there see Introduction §10 b. There is a little light irony on Romans lapsing into disorder (§8). But the Romans are now returning to a position where they can fulfil the grand vision of chh. 1–2. The oscillation is characteristic of history on the smaller scale in P.; the obstinacy is characteristic of his Romans (one might even wonder if they could have been more enterprising, §2n.). P.'s structure forcefully separates Roman success from Roman disaster (Epipolae from Archimedes); it forcefully conjoins Roman disaster and Roman success (Tarentum and Epipolae). P.'s shaping brings out the smaller surprises and the larger structures of history.

For references on the present events, see the introduction to 3a and 1–7. For Epipolae, see Map 2 and 3.2n. These fortified heights above the city proper are well seen in the maps and photographs of Beste and Mertens (2015), including Beilagen 1, 2a, 3a, 4 (cf. also Karlsson (1992) 21–8, Dreher (2008) inside back cover). Their work primarily concerns the defensive building at Euryalus (Map 2), which at the end of §11 Marcellus has yet to capture; cf. Livy 25.25.2–26.1.

**37.1** Livy 25.23.10–12, Plut. *Marc.* 18.3–4, Polyaen. 8.11 show where this quotation comes from. A Roman negotiator at the *portus Trogilorum* is secretly counting the lines of stone in the tower Galeagra, so that he can work out the height of the adjoining wall. ᾠκοδομημένος refers to the πύργος (περίβολος would not suit vertical measurement); but it is the τεῖχος which is scaled (§§2, 3, 7, 8). Livy and Plutarch are differently confused. The location is probably the cove of S. Panagia (see Map 2). Cf. Parke (1944); Beste and Mertens (2015) 250–1.    **δόμους:** courses of stone, 10.24.7, LSJ 3.    **συννόμων:** Strabo 17.1.48 (IV 488.10 Radt) has the singular συwόμωι λίθωι. Here the stones are not just finely dressed to fit together but, the argument implies, 'isodomic', with layers of equal height. Cf. Scranton (1941) 99–136 and McNicoll (1997) 86. The technique of the walls themselves varies; cf. e.g. Karlsson (1992) 101–3. P. is detailed; measuring ladders is something he cares about (9.18.5–9, 19.5–9, etc.).    **τῶν ἐπάλξεων:** these belong to the walls, not the tower; cf. 4.9 above τὰς ἐπάλξεις ἢ τοὺς πύργους.    **ἀπόστασιν** 'distance'; cf. LSJ B I.5.

**37.2 μετὰ δέ τινας ἡμέρας:** probably genuine. μετά/μετὰ δέ τινας ἡμέρας comes 25 times in P., far more than in other writers (Diodorus 4 times). Less probably it is a fill-in by T; μαθὼν δ' ἐξ of Suda λ 625 leads into an abbreviated sentence which is patently inauthentic (it ends ἐπολιόρκει). αὐτομόλου is part of a genitive absolute in VP₁ too. T's phrase prepares an elaborate structure of coincidence and recollection.    **αὐτομόλου:** the Romans had had other 'deserters' (so Livy 25.23.4), and could have discovered the dates of Syracusan festivals earlier; but this one brings further information.    **θυσίαν** 'festival'; cf. LSJ I.3. §9 διὰ τὴν θυσίαν and 31.26.7 πανδήμου θυσίας recommend θυσίαν rather than the *Suda*'s ἑορτήν; the *Suda* has ἑορτὴν πάνδημον elsewhere too, π 2564.    **ἤδη:** the festival has been going on for three days already; Livy 25.23.14 *per triduum agi* suggests a slip, or a text without ἤδη.    **Ἀρτέμιδι:** her cult is important at Syracuse; see Reichert-Südbeck (2000) 69–80. The attack happens in the spring (Livy 25.23.2, 8), so the festival is probably not the Lyaea, with its *omnium* (read *omni?*) *leguminum genere* and *frugibus* (Diom. *GLK* I 486.33, 487.3).    **σιτίοις λιτοῖς** 'simple food'; cf. 38.5.7 τὰ λιτὰ τῶν ἐδεσμάτων preferred as a novelty to τὰ πολυτελῆ (a recurring contrast). The opposition with δαψιλεῖ and πολύν suggests there is not that much of it either.    **δαψιλεῖ** 'abundant'; cf. *I.Stratonikeia* 1.256.10 (ii AD) οἶνον δαψιλῆ παρ<έ>σχον πᾶσι. The abundance spills over into πολὺν μὲν ... πολὺν δέ.    **Ἐπικύδους:** his brother Hippocrates had left him to look after the city (Livy 24.35.7). He acts as a munificent *strategos* (Livy 24.32.9), not a ruler; the city makes its own contribution.   τότε is the turning point of the sentence, as the penny drops.   προσαναλαβών 'calling to mind'; cf. ἀναλαμβάνω at Plut. *Lyc.* 21.3, Plato, *Polit.* 294d7–8 (with μνήμηι); *Tim.* 26a3, b2 'run over mentally'. Lamer, but possible, is the *Suda*'s προσανανεωσάμενος 'remembering'; cf. ἀνανέωσις at 12.6b.1, DS 5.67.3.   καθ' ὅ: best taken as a reported question; cf. LSJ ὅς в iv.6, *PL* ὅς C. In that case εἴη would be preferable to the past. 'Recalled the wall in the part where' seems unconvincing.   ταπεινότερον: cf. Livy 25.23.12 *humilioremque aliquanto pristina opinione sua*, of that particular part of the wall. ταπεινότητα of the wall in general (*Suda*) would be less to the point.   εἰκός: Marcellus is made to sound intelligent; in Livy the inference from the report (25.23.14) does not need to be spelt out.   μεθύειν: Philo, *Pol.* D2–4 advises bringing ladders secretly μεθυόντων τῶν πολεμίων ἔν τινι δημοτελεῖ ἑορτῆι (see Whitehead's notes). Predicted drunkenness had helped the Tarentine conspirators (25.11 above).   ἄνεσιν 'licence', not 'relaxation', in view of μεθύειν διά. At DS 17.112.6 ἅπαντες ὥρμησαν πρὸς ἄνεσιν καὶ τρυφήν, πολλῆς τῶν ἐπιτηδείων παρεσκευασμένης δαψιλείας.   τὴν ἔνδειαν τῆς ξηρᾶς τροφῆς: there is less to mop up the drink; the same effect at Parth. *Erot. Path.* 9.5, where Miletus is to be captured during a festival with much unmixed wine. The connection with the siege shows Marcellus' cleverness.   καταπειράζειν τῆς ἐλπίδος: cf. 7.5 above πάσης ἐλπίδος πεῖραν λαμβάνειν. But this one works.

**37.3 ταχύ**: the detail shows eagerness for this plan.   ἐγένετο περί 'concerned, busied himself with'; cf. e.g. 14.1.8.   τὰ συνεχῆ 'the next stages'; cf. 2.1.4 τὰ συνεχῆ τούτοις 'the events that followed'.   τοῖς μὲν ἐπιτηδείοις: throughout §§3–8, P. separates (i) those handling the ladders from (ii) those running up them; cf. §4 τοὺς δέ. Marcellus' contrasting treatment of these groups displays his generalship. P. mentions his selection (§4) of (i), but not of (ii): he dwells on what is less obvious. Contrast 10.35.5 ἐκλέξας τοὺς ἐπιτηδείους. For πρός with ἐπιτήδειος cf. 33.8 above, 6.26.6.   τὸν ἐπιφανέστατον καὶ πρῶτον κίνδυνον: similar language at 16.5.1 ἐπιφανέστατα δ' ἐκινδύνευσαν, 1.28.6 πρῶτοι <κινδυνεύσαντες>, 2.27.5: Atilius wanted πρῶτος κατάρξαι τοῦ κινδύνου, and so to gain most of the credit.   ἐκοινολογεῖτο 'discussed': more equal and extended talk (imperfect) than the brusque orders of §4. The verb suggests confidences not shared with all.   μεγάλας ἐλπίδας: especially of rewards; cf. §5, and 15.8 above μεγάλας ἐλπίδας (Bolis). At 6.39.5 a golden crown is given to the first men who climb a city's wall; cf. 10.11.6. But the phrase may suggest something beyond τὰς εἰθισμένας δωρεάς (10.11.6).

**37.4 ὑπουργήσοντας** puts these men hierarchically lower; it is followed by the more specific προσοίσοντας κλίμακας. **διασαφῶν** plays between the usual sense 'reveal, inform' (negated) and, with ἑτοίμους εἶναι, the unusual 'order' (affirmed); for 'order' cf. 3.106.4, 107.7. **πειθαρχησάντων:** they get the ladders ready to go. **λαβών:** two separate participial clauses are followed by the brief main clause ἤγειρε τοὺς πρώτους. **νυκτός:** the καιρός falls during the night (cf. 1.75.8–9); night is the time Philo envisages for attack during a festival (*Pol.* D4). The citizens will be drunk (§9, Philo) or in a drunken sleep (§9).

**37.5 προπέμψας:** sending ahead of himself; cf. 19.6 above. **τούτους** (C. Müller) is needed: 'those with the ladders' will not be offered rewards for valour, and οἱ ἅμα + dat. is an unlikely phrase. ἅμα ταῖς κλίμαξι after §4 suggests too: with the men carrying them. **σημείας:** a maniple, an entity usually of 60–120 men; cf. e.g. 6.29.4–5, Dobson (2008) 48. They are presumably to guard against any attack on the ground. **δωρεῶν:** the glory, as well as the value, is important, P. avers (6.39.9–10). But Marcellus does not appeal just to patriotism. **ἀνδραγαθήσασι:** so e.g. 10.11.6, rewards promised τοῖς ἐπιφανῶς ἀνδραγαθήσασι. **μετὰ [δὲ] ταῦτα:** after the two participles προπέμψας and προσαναμνήσας, P. moves onto a complex, introduced by μετὰ ταῦτα, of main clause with attendant participle; cf. e.g. 2.41.4–5, 5.87.6. This separation is essential to distinguish τοὺς πρώτους here from τοὺς πρώτους in §4. They are different people: contrast μετὰ σημείας with κατὰ σημείαν 'by maniple', i.e. a plurality; cf. 6.34.2. μετὰ δὲ ταῦτα would add a third participle to the previous two, as at 1.29.6 (δὲ del. Madvig (1871–84) I 481), 30.14; that structure seems unsatisfactory here. **ἐν διαστήμασι:** so 11.11.6 τὴν φάλαγγα κατὰ τέλη σπειρηδὸν ἐν διαστήμασιν ἐπέστησε, 15.9.7 (σημείας). κατὰ σημείαν recommends and requires understanding intervals among this group rather than an interval from the first climbers. There is a careful τάξις; cf. §8. **ἐξαποστέλλει:** historic present, as at 3.86.4, and with other verbs of sending (16.1n.).

**37.6 γενομένων δὲ τούτων εἰς χιλίους** 'there were about a thousand of them', i.e. the first part of the main force. Cf. e.g. 2.69.3, 3.102.6 ὄντας εἰς τετρακισχιλίους. **βραχὺ διαλιπών** 'leaving a short space' from the first part. Marcellus does not want a disorderly throng around the two ladders. **αὐτός:** Marcellus wishes to keep the bulk of the main force under strict control.

**37.7 οἱ φέροντες τὰς κλίμακας** are set at the other end of the sentence from the stars who close it, οἱ πρὸς τὴν ἀνάβασιν ἀποτεταγμένοι (as in

§§3–4). ἔλαθον: the Syracusans do not see them; the verb runs through the account, cf. §§8, 10. ἀσφαλῶς τῶι τείχει προσερείσαντες: their success recalls the ideal account of the σαμβῦκαι, which went so wrong in practice. Cf. esp. 4.7 προσερείδειν τῶι τείχει, 9 προσερείσαντες (they succeed), 10 ἀσφαλῶς (the κλῖμαξ secure in the ships). Now things go smoothly. ἐξ αὐτῆς 'immediately'; cf. e.g. 24.7.7 ἐξ αὐτῆς ὁ στρατηγὸς ὁρμήσας, *PL* αὐτός C1 (ἐξαυτῆς in LSJ). ἀπροφασίστως 'unhesitatingly', a rather exalted word to use of individual soldiers in a specific engagement. Contrast e.g. 21.20.9 εἰς πάντας δὲ τοὺς κινδύνους δεδώκαμεν αὐτοὺς ἀπροφασίστως (Eumenes II), *IG* II².1023.4–7 (late ii BC) ἐν ταῖς δὲ λοιπαῖς λει|τουργίαις ἁπάσαις ... ἐπιδίδωσιν | ἑαυτὸν ἀπροφασίστως.

**37.8 λαθόντων δὲ καὶ τούτων** underlines all continuing to go perfectly. **στάντων ἐπὶ τοῦ τείχους βεβαίως**: the next stage on from the assistants placing the ladders against the walls ἀσφαλῶς (§7). **οὐκέτι κατὰ τὴν ἐξ ἀρχῆς τάξιν**: the sentence takes an entertaining twist. Marcellus' careful choreography is abandoned in the general enthusiasm. Livy 25.23.17 has the more organized *secuti ordine alii*. **<ἀν>έβαινον** (Hultsch) is closer to T's ἔμελλον than is ἀνέθεον (Büttner-Wobst); and ἀναθέω is not found in P.

**37.9 κατὰ μὲν οὖν τὰς ἀρχάς**: while they are still walking along the top of the wall. **ἐφοδείαν**: the walkway along the wall. Similarly at 10.15.1–2 the Romans at New Carthage ἐπεπορεύοντο κατὰ τὴν ἐφοδείαν, but with more opposition, and descend at a gate; cf. §11 here. **ἔρημον**: ἔρημος is often used when the enemy is unexpectedly absent (*PL* 1cα), usually with κατέλαβε, etc., so 10.14.13 καταλαβόντες ἐρήμους τὰς ἐπάλξεις. εὕρισκον captures the extended surprise, and gives a different turn to §7 ἔλαθον, §8 λαθόντων, from a Roman viewpoint: it was not skill, there was no one there. **οἱ γάρ**: ἠθροισμένοι should be part of the explanation of ἔρημον εὕρισκον, not a definition of the group; e.g. φυλάττοντες could be missing (cf. 4.64.10, *al*.), omitted before ες, as T writes; cf. also οἱ ες μεν in the next line. The initial subject, after a participial clause, is split into οἱ μέν, οἱ δέ; cf. 3.43.10, 35.4.14 οἱ γὰρ πρότερον ἀποδειλιῶντες, ἐκτρεπόμενοι τὸν ἐκ παραθέσεως ἔλεγχον, οἱ μὲν κτλ. The *De obsidione* has altered the text (εἰς γὰρ VP₁) to throw emphasis onto the πύργοι; its previous sentence ends ἐγένοντο κύριοι τῶν πύργων. The absence of a defined subject is still awkward. **πύργους**: these structures allow social gathering. There are frequent towers along the Epipolae wall; cf. Beste and Mertens (2015). **ἀκμήν** 'still', 1.2n. Much the same division appears at 14.4.9 οἱ μὲν ἐκ τῶν ὕπνων, οἱ δ' ἀκμὴν ἔτι μεθυσκόμενοι καὶ πίνοντες, Enn. *Ann.* 288 Skutsch *nunc hostes uino domiti somnoque sepulti*. Military incapacitation through drink is mentioned less in Herodotus, Thucydides, Xenophon. πάλαι: with imperfect 5.26.6.

**37.10 διό:** accompanied by καί more often than not in P. τοῖς μὲν πρώτοις καὶ τοῖς ἑξῆς 'the first and indeed those that followed'. 'The first' are now Syracusans; cf. §§3–5. By contrast with Marcellus' careful ordering of Romans, most (οἱ πλεῖστοι) of the Syracusans are killed regardless of order: the earlier do not alert the later. μεθ' ἡσυχίας is used also of the parallel attack on Tarentum's fortifications (29.8 above). The phrase comes only two other times in P. ἔλαθον: now more of an accomplishment; cf. §§7–8.

**37.11 Ἑξαπύλοις:** where Appius vainly attacked the wall (3.6), Marcus now descends from it. ἐνῳκοδομημένην probably means 'built into' the structure of the Hexapyla; cf. e.g. Jos. *BJ* 3.174. τὴν πρώτην suggests this. Otherwise, 'built there'; cf. Livy 25.24.3 *prope Hexapylon est portula*, Thuc. 6.51.1 πυλίδα τινὰ ἐνῳκοδομημένην κακῶς ἔλαθον διελόντες (possibly alluded to here). διεῖλον 'broke open'. Cf. LSJ διαιρέω I; Livy 25.24.3 *magna ui refringi*. δι' ἧς: what follows in T is just rapid finishing off, perhaps with some borrowing from P. The little gate gives too small an opening for an army of thousands. Contrast Livy 25.24.7: after tricks with trumpets, *sub lucem Hexapylo effracto Marcellus omnibus copiis urbem ingressus*; Plut. *Marc.* 19.1 ἅμα φάει διὰ τῶν Ἑξαπύλων ὁ Μάρκελλος κατῄει. Syracuse is by no means captured yet; Achradina remains (Livy 25.26.1–2, Plut. *Marc.* 18.6). The final capture and sack of Syracuse come in P.'s next year (9.10.2).

**37.12** Livy 25.24.6, before the full entry of the army, indicates that the *Suda*'s sentence is an abridged version of P.: *magna pars tamen ignara tanti mali erat … in uastae magnitudinis urbe partium sensu non satis pertinente in omnia*. οὐδενὸς ἐπεγνωκότος τῶν πολιτῶν is the *Suda*'s simplification; cf. also Plut. *Marc.* 18.4. διὰ τὴν ἀπόστασιν 'because of the distance'; the same phrase comes at 1.86.8, of Hamilcar perceiving the attack only late. P. imagines the cityscape. μεγάλης: Cic. *Verr.* 4.117 (it is true) *urbem Syracusas maximam esse Graecarum*.

**37.13 θαρρεῖν:** 7.6 above οὐδέποτε … ἐθάρρησαν, 9 οὐκ ἐθάρρουν were limited to undertaking an assault; but the snippet shows the decisive reversal of the Romans' lack of confidence. τοῦ περὶ τὰς Ἐπιπολὰς τόπου: a periphrasis for 'Epipolae', though the singular τόπου is unusual. The Athenian expedition might have been mentioned hereabouts (cf. Livy 25.24.12). P.'s readers will in any case remember the importance of capturing Epipolae; cf. for κρατεῖν Thuc. 7.42.4 εἰ κρατήσειέ τις τῶν ... Ἐπιπολῶν τῆς ἀναβάσεως. The Athenians' failure forms a counterpoint to the Romans' success.

## 22 KING CAVARUS GOES DOWNHILL

There are only two short extracts from this episode. Athenaeus' comes explicitly from book 8. P's (*Exc. Const.* II.2.113.3–7) must come from book 8 too; see introduction to 23. P.'s account of Cavarus stretched back to 220 BC at least; the decline produced by a flatterer will have led towards the annihilation of Cavarus' kingdom (4.46.4). The narrative pattern shows thematic connections with the decline of Philip and with the downfall of Achaeus.

The move of Celts eastwards, and the battle of Lysimacheia (277 BC), had led to the establishment of a Celtic kingdom in south-eastern Thrace; its extent and exact whereabouts are disputed. Cavarus' coins show Greek deities and motifs; a relatively recent find combines Apollo and his lyre with a Celtic shield (Manov and Damyanov (2013)). P. suggests that it was only Cavarus' catastrophe which put an end to the 80 talents a year that Byzantium was forced to pay him and at least one predecessor (4.46.3–4). Cavarus' demand led in 220 to a war of Byzantium and (the Byzantines hoped) Achaeus with Rhodes and Prusias I of Bithynia (4.45.9–50.1). But P. does not see Cavarus' activity in a merely negative light. His negotiations led to peace (4.52.1–2); and the present passage indicates the help that he offered Byzantium against the Thracians. The location of Byzantium is seen as uniquely fortunate for controlling trade with the Pontus (4.38.1–10), but as unfortunate in exposing the city to Thracian attack (4.45.1–8; cf. 51.8); Byzantium also faced Bithynia across the strait. The war, and the sea route through Byzantium, had large implications for Greek trade. Cavarus' contribution is favourably viewed by P.; though often negative on Celts (Foulon (2000)), P. sees Cavarus as meeting the standards he looks for in Greek kings.

For Cavarus, his kingdom and the war, see Strobel (1996) 233–6; Gabrielsen (1997) 44–6; Jefremow (2005); Boteva (2010) 34–6; Manov (2010); Lazarov (2010); for the Galatians see Coşkun (2022).

**22.1 τῶν ἐν τῆι Θράικηι Γαλατῶν:** perhaps an oversimplification by the epitomator; cf. e.g. 5.77.2, 78.4–5, Foulon (2000) 332–5. **βασιλικός:** he had the qualities of the true king by nature; βασιλικὸς τῆι φύσει (an unusual phrase) again at 5.39.6, the obituary of Cleomenes III. βασιλικ- is paired with μεγαλοψυχ- and μεγαλοπρεπ- at e.g. 5.12.1, 43.3, 16.28.3. **μεγαλόφρων:** used of kings at 5.38.10 (Cleomenes III),

**31.12.2** (Demetrius I Soter, φύσει). At *I.Stratonikeia* III.1441.2 (Roman period) μεγαλοφρόνως is paired with φιλοτείμως, used by P. at 4.52.1 of Cavarus' efforts for peace.    πολλὴν μέν forms a laudatory sequence with μεγάλας δέ.    ἀσφάλειαν: 4.38.6–7 emphasizes the dangerous barbarians around the strait.    τοῖς προσπλέουσι: similar phrasing, with more obvious word order, at 4.50.3 τῶν εἰς τὸν Πόντον πλεόντων ἐμπόρων.

**22.2** μεγάλας is separated from χρείας for emphasis.    πρός + acc., like κατά + gen., is standard in these phrases; cf. e.g. 2.35.2 ὁ μὲν οὖν πρὸς τοὺς Κελτοὺς πόλεμος. At 4.45.1 P. says the Byzantines ἀΐδιον ἔχουσι πόλεμον with the Thracians; Cavarus' decline will produce the turn that the Thracians destroy his own kingdom (4.46.4 ἐκ μεταβολῆς). As to the Bithynians, the war with Prusias will be particularly in mind.

**22.3** Athenaeus' speaker is giving quotes on named κόλακες.    ὁ Γαλάτης could be Athenaeus' addition; cf. e.g. 251f, 252c; contrast P. 4.52.1 Καυάρου δὲ τοῦ τῶν Γαλατῶν βασιλέως.    τἄλλα 'in all other ways'. So e.g. 4.20.7 τἄλλα τοῖς βίοις ὄντας αὐστηροτάτους, DS 5.58.5 γενόμενος δὲ καὶ τἄλλα ἀνὴρ ἀγαθός. The hiatus after τἄλλα is suspicious whether ὢν or ἀγαθός or ἀνὴρ follows.    διεστρέφετο: was morally ruined. Cf. [Men.] *Monost.* 287 ἤθη πονηρὰ τὴν φύσιν διαστρέφει, Epict. 3.6.8 οἱ μὴ παντάπασιν διεστραμμένοι τῶν ἀνθρώπων.    Χαλκηδόνιος: Chalcedon is on the opposite shore of the Bosporus from Byzantium. A local Greek was important at Cavarus' court.

## 23 ANTIOCHUS AND THE YOUNG XERXES

This short episode shows Antiochus behaving with a regal munificence which contrasts with Philip V's cruel treachery and advances on Antiochus' earlier conduct with Achaeus. Rather than displace the son of a rebellious monarch, Antiochus restores his rule and marries his own sister to him. But a sting in the tail is to come, now or later. John of Antioch fr. 53 *FHG* IV 557 (vi–vii AD) reports that after this ἐκεῖνον μὲν διὰ τῆς ἀδελφῆς διεχρήσατο, τὴν δὲ Περσῶν βασιλείαν αὖθις ἀνεκτήσατο. Most likely this derives ultimately from P., or was known to him. (John does not seem to have used P. directly; cf. Sotiroudis (1989) 85–147.)

John puts the settlement in the time of Antiochus' war with Ptolemy (218–217); but it fits better Antiochus' campaign in the east after the conquest of Sardis (by spring 213). Probably, then, it is not a flashback in P.; the extract itself certainly comes from the second half of book 8, as the order in P shows (after Aratus and Cavarus; before 9.11, *res Hispaniae*, which should precede *res Asiae*). Antiochus' apparent change of plan will not have been immediate; John synchronizes it vaguely with the Second Punic War (218–201 BC).

In P.'s narrative, Antiochus is at enmity with the youthful Xerxes because Xerxes' father had not paid, or not paid all, his tribute (§4). It sounds as if Xerxes has just succeeded to the throne – or the debt would be his. Antiochus' ownership of Armenia will be more direct later, when his στρατηγοί take it over (Strabo 11.14.5 (III 390.21–5 Radt), 15 (III 398.30–2)). Xerxes is a formally independent king, no doubt claiming Achaemenid descent (cf. Strabo 11.14.15 (III 398.29–30)). There are coins of 'King Xerxes' (Bedoukian (1983) 74–7). John calls Xerxes τῶι Ἀρμενίων τυράννωι; Antiochus I of Commagene calls Arsames a king (Sanders (1996) 267–70; Brijder (2014) 324–32). Arsames was Armenian, and alive *c.*227 (Polyaen. 4.17); he 'founded' Arsameia on the Nymphaeus in Commagene (Dörner and Goell (1963) 40.13–16), and probably Arsamosata. This indicates a range beyond the kingdom of Sophene (Map 1). Strabo implies that Armenia, though small, was not split before Antiochus' στρατηγοί, and that Orontes was in charge of it immediately before them. The line between Arsames and Xerxes is unclear: the slot after Arsames is missing in Antiochus of Commagene's ancestral parade. (Some think Armenia was split already; one could also imagine competing claims and confused traditions.)

On this episode see Schmitt (1964) 28–30, 38, 88; Dörner (1975); Bedoukian (1983) esp. 74–7; Sherwin-White and Kuhrt (1993) 190–7; Messerschmidt (2000) 38–41; Facella (2006) 183–98; Taylor (2013) 73–4; Marciak (2017) 117–23.

**23.1** This opening sentence shows various signs that it has at the least been considerably changed from what was in P. μέσον is used as a preposition, 'between'; this is not found in P., Diodorus, Dionysius. Cf. *BDAG* μέσος 4 and e.g. Σ Theocr. 7.65c ἔστι δὲ ὁ τόπος μέσον Ἐφέσου καὶ Μιλήτου. P. occasionally calls Antiochus 'Antiochus the king' (13.9.5, 15.25.13); but it comes 7 times in the introduction of extracts, as at 31.9.1 ὅτι κατὰ τὴν Συρίαν Ἀντίοχος ὁ βασιλεὺς κτλ. Probably it is here orientating the reader of the excerpts. βασιλεύοντος πόλεως: the phrase may not be P.'s (cf. *PL* βασιλεύω 12). In any case, §2 βασιλείου implies he rules more. βασιλεύσαντα τῶν Συρακοσίων at 1.8.3 is consistent with Hieron's larger kingdom; cf. 7.8.1. Ἁρμόσατα should be Ἀρσαμοσάτων, named after Arsames; cf. Samosata, Artaxiasata. Pliny names it first of four cities in Armenia Maior (*NH* 6.26); for the spelling see Ptol. *Geog.* 5.13.19, Baumgartner (1895), for the gen. e.g. Strabo 14.2.29 (IV 84.2 Radt) Σαμοσάτων … ἣ κτλ. The probable citadel of Arsamosata overlooked the Elazığ (Harput) Plain: see Sinclair (1987–90) III 112–16. **πρός** 'by, adjoining'; cf. Strabo 11.14.6 (III 390.2–3 Radt) πρὸς τῶι Ἀραξηνῶι πεδίωι (Artaxata).

**23.2 παρασκευήν:** so Philip terrifies the Ambraciots with his siege παρασκευή (4.63.2; cf. 61.8). **τοῦ βασιλέως** does not deny Xerxes' own kingship; see 17.1n. **αὐτὸν ἐκποδὼν ἐποίησε** 'removed himself', more discreet and tactical than 'ran away'; similarly at 30.8.2. **βασιλείου** 'capital'; cf. e.g. 10.27.5 (Ecbatana). 'Palace' would be plural, and less relevant when the whole city is in question. **τἆλλα τὰ κατὰ τὴν ἀρχήν** is taken up at §5 τά τε κατὰ τὴν ἀρχὴν ἅπαντ' ἀ<πο>κατέστησε. That suggests territory he owns; cf. 7.11.4. **διατραπῆι** 'be dismayed, shocked' (so even at 10.12.7, of the whole πλῆθος; cf. στόμα, and DH *AR* 11.7.4). It seems rather weak in the circumstances, especially with καί, and does not match §5 ἅπαντ' ἀ<πο>κατέστησε. (Sext. *Pyrrh.* 2.166 διατρέπεται πᾶσα ἡ διαλεκτική 'is overturned' probably does not help.) One might consider διαρπαγῆι (aor. pass. subj.); διαρπάζω, διαρπαγή are not confined to cities, cf. e.g. DS 12.41.7 (ἅπασα ἡ χώρα), 17.104.6 (πᾶς τόπος, incl. farmland), DH *AR* 10.27.1 (γῆ i.e. farmland), 43.1 (χώρα i.e. farmland). διαστραφῆι 'be ravaged' would also be possible; cf. Σ bT Hom. *Il.* 1.1*b* τὰς ὁμορούσας πολίχνας ... διαστρέφοντες. **μετεμελήθη:** such instability was thought especially characteristic of the young (§§3–4). Cf. Fulkerson (2013) e.g. 11 n. 33. **συνελθεῖν:** a risky reversal of his earlier motion (αὐτὸν ἐκποδὼν ἐποίησε); cf. §3.

**23.3 πλεῖστοι** (Habicht): so 27.8.5 ταῦτα μὲν οὖν ἐδόκει τοῖς πλείοσι τῶν φίλων (of Perseus), 14 τῶν πλείστων φίλων. Achaemenid counsellors had the title οἱ πιστοί (Aesch. *Pers.* 1–2, 681, Xen. *Oec.* 4.6, 8); but there is no sign of such a title later, τῶν φίλων makes this not a title, and more would be needed for it to have point. **προϊέσθαι:** related advice at 4.4.3, fr. 231 Olson ὁ δ' ἔφασκε δεῖν μὴ προΐεσθαι τοὺς ἐχθροὺς ἐκ τῶν χειρῶν. **τὸν νεανίσκον** conveys (to Antiochus) Xerxes' naïveté, and (to readers) the counsellors' own heartlessness. Cf. 7.4.4 λαβόντες εἰς τὰς χεῖρας τὸ μειράκιον of cunning manipulators. **λαβόντ':** the acc. sing. (Reiske) is needed for advice to Antiochus; cf. κυριεύσαντα. For the elision cf. 12.16.3 (λαβόντ'); 3.11.8. **Μιθριδάτηι:** son of Antiochus' only known sister Antiochis or another sister; cf. Ogden (2010) 132; Olbrycht (2021) 176. The insertion of Antiochis' name in §5 could favour a different sister here. On the son's possible later role in Armenia see Coşkun (2016). For the name Mithridates in the family see *SEG* XXXVII.859 A.3 (Herakleia on Latmos, 196–193 BC). **δυναστείαν:** Mithridates would not necessarily be king. **κατὰ φύσιν** stresses, from the 'friends'' viewpoint, that this was his own sister; cf. 11.2.2 ἀδελφὸς ἦν Ἀννίβου κατὰ φύσιν, with Walbank on 1.64.1, and 33.18.9 for the word order. κατὰ φύσιν will not go with υἱός (thus Coşkun (2016) 853); that would suggest a woman could adopt.

**23.4 οὐδενί** suggests individual representations. Antiochus' independence from his advisers shows growing confidence; contrast 5.50.5 οὐκ ἦν αὐτοῦ κύριος, cf. 54.11. **τὸν νεανίσκον:** Antiochus is no longer a νεανίσκος himself, as e.g. at 5.45.7 (221 BC). He was perhaps around 30 (Schmitt (1964) 4–10). P. presents him showing indulgence as the older man. He needs more persuading by others to act similarly towards Euthydemus I of Bactria, but is won over by Euthydemus' son, a νεανίσκος (11.34.9); again age matters. **διελύσατο:** this verb governs τὰς ἔχθρας at 3.12.5; see LSJ I.4. The enmity, as seen by Antiochus, was inherited by Xerxes. This short clause and the next show the brisk simplicity of Antiochus' beneficence. **τὰ πλεῖστα** is made to sound generous, though Antiochus still exacts a significant recompense from Xerxes (§5). **φόρων** 'tribute': an essential part of the Seleucid system. See Capdetrey (2004) 107–15, (2007) 395–422. For having both τῶν χρημάτων and τῶν φόρων, cf. DC 57.17.7 χρήματα πολλὰ μὲν ἐκ τῶν φόρων ἀνείθη.

**23.5 παραχρῆμα:** there may be more to come. **τριακόσια τάλαντα:** the amount of a penalty inflicted on a Mithridates τῶι τῆς Ἀρμενίας σατράπηι (25.2.11; he governs only the lesser part of Armenia). **χιλίους ἵππους:** the mules and the tack suggest that the animals are needed now, rather than a symbolic gift; so too the elephants taken from Euthydemus (11.34.10). See Capdetrey (2007) 411. **τε,** like ἅπαντ', highlights Antiochus' munificence. **ἀ<πο>κατέστησε** 'gave back', as at 4.4.3 (cf. 1) ἐὰν μὴ τὰ ἀπολωλότα πάντα τοῖς Μεσσηνίοις ἀποκαταστήσηι. This can reasonably be said when Antiochus is at least in a position to seize the capital and Xerxes has removed himself. §2 δείσας μή indicates that the territory is not yet so damaged as to need restoration, as in SEG IX.166.23–5 (Cyrene, AD 71) τὸ Πτυλυμαῖ|ον ἀποκατέστη|σεν (= 11 *restituit*). κατέστησε 'arranged, established' would in this context require at least an adverb (cf. DS 17.2.1). πάντα is elided 14 times in P., ἅπαντα at 4.37.8. **Ἀντιοχίδα:** daughter of Seleucus II; see Schmitt (1964) 28, and §3n. above. Antiochus rejects the replacement of a local dynasty with his own family, and seeks rather to connect families by marriage. So he gives one of his daughters to Euthydemus' son (11.34.9). On Seleucid marriage strategies, cf. e.g. Wenghofer and Houle (2016) 202–3; D'Agostini (2021). **πάντας** recalls the good impression made on all by the young Philip, 4.27.10 πᾶσι τοῖς Ἕλλησι διὰ τοῦ προειρημένου ψηφίσματος καλὰς ἐλπίδας ὑποδεικνύων πραότητος καὶ μεγαλοψυχίας βασιλικῆς,

77.1-3.  **ἐψυχαγώγησε** 'entranced'; cf. e.g. 4.82.4 ἐψυχαγώγει καὶ παρεκάλει πρὸς τὴν ἑαυτοῦ φιλίαν.  **πρὸς ἑ<αυτὸν προε>καλέσατο** 'drew them to himself', as of Hannibal βουλόμενος προκαλεῖσθαι διὰ τοιούτου τρόπου πρὸς αὐτὸν τοὺς κατοικοῦντας τὴν Ἰταλίαν (3.77.7; cf. 60.9, 100.3, DS 16.71.1). προεκαλοῦντο comes at 24.9.13 and *IG* v.2.444.14 (Megalopolis, ii–i BC), and in general the spelling προε- rather than πρου- is not uncommon in P.'s MSS. At 12.26d.1 (προσ-, as P) cf. πείσειν.  **δόξας** 'having been judged'. It could be a pointed 'having seemed'. But at 4.31.7, 9.23.2 the contrast with what followed is apparent in the first clause; and perhaps if the later alleged deployment of Antiochis was mentioned now, the morally-minded excerptor would have included it.  **μεγαλοψύχως καὶ βασιλικῶς**: see 10.10n., 22.1n. and e.g. Cic. *Deiot.* 26: among *regiae laudes* is being called *magni animi*; Introduction §10 b.

# WORKS CITED

Adak, M., and Thonemann, P. (2022) *Teos and Abdera: two cities in peace and war*, Oxford.
Agati, X., Ciolfi, L. M., Monticini, F., Panoryia, M., and Vukašinović, M. (2017) 'Quand la *structure* détermine le *significat* : Dion Cassius, Georges le Moine et Polybe dans le prisme du *De Legationibus Romanorum ad Gentes* de l'empereur Constantin VII Porphyrogénète', in Delacenserie and Van Nuffelen: 221–49.
Ager, S. L. (2012) 'The alleged rapprochement between Achaios and Attalos I in 220 BC', *Historia* 61: 421–9.
— (2019) 'The limits of ethnicity: Sparta and the Achaian League', in Beck, Buraselis and McAuley: 175–92.
Albers, J. (2018) 'Die Häfen der Westgriechen: Hafenstrukturen in den griechischen Kolonien der Magna Graecia und auf Sizilien', in J. Daum and M. Seifert, eds, *North meets East 2: Aktuelle Forschungen zu antiken Häfen* (Aachen), 1–27.
Almagor, E. (2020) 'How to do things with Hellenistic historiography: Plutarch's intertextual use(s) of Polybius', in T. S. Schmidt, M. Vamvouri, R. Hirsch-Luipold, eds, *The dynamics of intertextuality in Plutarch* (Leiden), 161–72.
Ameling, W. (1993) *Karthago: Studien zu Militär, Staat und Gesellschaft*, Munich.
Ampolo, C. (ed.) (2011) *Siracusa: immagine e storia di una città*, Pisa.
Andreassi, G. (2005) 'L'attività archeologica in Puglia nel 2004', in *ACT* 44: 203–34.
— (ed.) (2009) *De la Grèce à Rome : Tarente et les lumières de la Méditerranée*, Saint-Maur-des-Fossés.
Asper, M. (2007) *Griechische Wissenschaftstexte: Formen, Funktionen, Differenzierungsgeschichten*, Stuttgart.
— (ed.) (2013) *Writing science: medical and mathematical authorship in ancient Greece*, collab. A.-M. Kanthak, Berlin.
Austin, M. M. (2006), *The Hellenistic world from Alexander to the Roman conquest: a selection of ancient sources in translation*, 2nd edn, Cambridge.
Avenarius, G. (1956) *Lukians Schrift zur Geschichtsschreibung*, Meisenheim am Glan.
Aversa, F., De Juliis, E. M., and Vitale, R. (2011) 'Taranto', in G. Nenci and G. Vallet, eds, *Bibliografia topografica della colonizzazione greca in Italia e nelle isole tirreniche*, 20 (Pisa), 113–234.

Baron, C. (2018) 'The historian's craft: narrative strategies and historical method in Polybius and Livy', in Miltsios and Tamiolaki: 203–21.
Baronowski, D. W. (2011) *Polybius and Roman imperialism*, London.
Basile, B. (2012) 'L'urbanistica di Siracusa greca: nuovi dati, vecchi problemi', *Archivio Storico Siracusano* 47: 177–224.
Baumgartner, A. (1895) 'Arsamosata', *RE* II 1271.
Bechtel, Fr., *et al.* (1913) *Dikaiomata: Auszüge aus alexandrinischen Gesetzen und Verordnungen in einem Papyrus des Philologischen Seminars der Universität Halle*, Berlin.
Beck, H., and Funke, P. (eds) (2015a) *Federalism in Greek antiquity*, Cambridge.
(2015b) 'An introduction to federalism in Greek antiquity', in Beck and Funke, eds: 1–29.
Beck, H., Buraselis, K., and McAuley, A. (eds) (2019) *Ethnos and koinon: studies in ancient Greek ethnicity and federalism*, Stuttgart.
Bedoukian, P. Z. (1983) 'Coinage of the Armenian kingdoms of Sophene and Commagene', *Museum Notes (American Numismatic Society)* 28: 71–88.
Beister, M. (1989) 'Hegemoniales Denken in Theben', in H. Beister and J. Buckler, eds, *Boiotika* (Munich), 131–53.
Bell, M., III (2012) 'Spazio e istituzioni nell'*agora* greca di Morgantina', in C. Ampolo, ed., *Agora greca e agorai di Sicilia* (Pisa), 111–18.
Bellomo, M. (2019) *Il commando militare a Roma nell'età delle guerre puniche (264–201 a. C.)* (Historia Einzelschriften 260), Stuttgart.
Bengtson, H. (1987) *Die Diadochen: Die Nachfolger Alexanders des Großen*, Munich.
Berardi, R. (2020) *The fragments of Hellenistic oratory: introduction, text, and commentary*, D.Phil. thesis, Oxford.
Berlin, A. M., and Kosmin, P. J. (eds) (2019) *Spear-won land: Sardis from the King's Peace to the Peace of Apamea*, Madison, Wis.
Beste, H.-J., and Mertens, D. (2015) *Die Mauern von Syrakus: Das Kastell Euryalos und die Befestigung der Epipolai*, Wiesbaden.
Bickermann, E., and Sykutris, J. (1928) *Speusipps Brief an König Philipp: Text, Übersetzung, Untersuchungen* (BSAW Ph.-h. 80.3), Leipzig.
Billerbeck, M., and Neumann-Hartmann, A. (2021) *Stephanos von Byzanz: Grammatiker und Lexikograph*, Berlin.
Bispham, E. H., and Cornell, T. J. (2013) '1. Q. Fabius Pictor', *FRHist* I 160–78.
Blomqvist, J. (1969) *Greek particles in Hellenistic prose*, Lund.
Boor, C. de (1912 and 1914–19) 'Suidas und die Konstantinsche Exzerptsammlung', *Byzantinische Zeitschrift* 21: 381–424; 23: 1–127.

Bortone, P. (2010) *Greek prepositions from antiquity to the present*, Oxford.
Borza, E. N. (1990) *In the shadow of Olympus: the emergence of Macedon*, Princeton.
Boteva, D. (2010) 'The ancient historians on the Celtic kingdom in south-eastern Thrace', in Vagalinski: 33–50.
Boyxen, B. (2018) *Fremde in der hellenistischen Polis Rhodos: Zwischen Nähe und Distanz*, Berlin.
Brief, S. (1907) 'Wie beeinflußt die Vermeidung des Hiatus den Stil des Polybius?', *Jahresbericht des k. k. deutschen Staats-Obergymnasiums in Ung.-Hradisch* 53, 1–20.
Brijder, H. A. G. (2014) *Nemrud Dağı: recent archaeological research and conservation activities in the tomb sanctuary on Mount Nemrud*, Boston.
Briscoe, J. (1978) review of Tränkle 1977, *CR* n.s. 28: 267–9.
—— (2008) *A commentary on Livy books 38–40*, Oxford.
Briscoe, J., and Hornblower, S. (2020) *Livy, Ab Vrbe condita book* XXII, Cambridge.
Brizzi, G. (1973), 'Ardaxanos fl.', *TIR* K34.17.
Browning, R. (1969) *Medieval and Modern Greek*, London.
Brun, P., Capdetrey, L., and Fröhlich, P. (eds) (2021) *L'Asie Mineure occidentale au III*ᵉ *siècle a.C.*, Bordeaux.
Buckler, J. (1980) *The Theban hegemony, 371–362 BC*, Cambridge, Mass.
Buckler, J., and Beck, H. (2008) *Central Greece and the politics of power in the fourth century BC*, Cambridge.
Bühler, W. (1999) *Zenobii Athoi proverbia* v (Göttingen).
Buraselis, K. (2019) 'Dissimilar brothers: similarities versus differences of the Achaian and Aitolian Leagues', in Beck, Buraselis and Auley: 205–17.
Burton, P. (2022) 'Polemic in Polybius', in T. Stevenson, ed., *Polemic in ancient historiography, literature, and culture* (Pretoria), 60–75.
Cabanes, P. (1988) *Les Illyriens de Bardylis à Genthios (IV*ᵉ*–II*ᵉ *siècles avant J.-C.)*, Paris.
Candau, J. M. (2003) 'Polibio como historiador helenístico: su actitud frente a la historiografía contemporánea', in Santos Yanguas and Torregaray Pagola (2003), 51–67.
Capdetrey, L. (2004) 'Le *basilikon* et les cités grecques dans le royaume séleucide : modalités de redistribution de la richesse royale et formes de dépendance des cités', in V. Chankowski and F. Duyrat, eds, *Le roi et l'économie : autonomies locales et structures royales dans l'économie de l'empire séleucide* (Lyons), 105–29.
—— (2007) *Le pouvoir séleucide : territoire, administration, finances d'un royaume hellénistique (312–129 avant J.-C.)*, Rennes.

Carney, E. D., and Müller, S. (eds) (2021) *The Routledge Companion to women and monarchy in the ancient Mediterranean world*, Abingdon.
Cartledge, P., and Spawforth, A. (2002) *Hellenistic and Roman Sparta: a tale of two cities*, 2nd ed., London.
Cavallaro, M. A. (2004) *Da Teuta a Epulo: interpretazione delle guerre illyriche e histriche tra 229 e 177 a. C.*, Bonn.
Cavallin, A. (1941) '(τὸ) λοιπόν: Eine bedeutungsgeschichtliche Untersuchung', *Eranos* 39: 121–44.
Cera, G. (2019) 'Osservazioni topografiche sulle mura di Taranto', *Atlante Tematico di Topografia Antica* 29: 7–32.
Champion, C. (2004) *Cultural politics in Polybius*, Berkeley.
Chaniotis, A. (2005) *War in the Hellenistic world: a social and cultural history*, Malden.
Chlup, J. T. (2009) '*Maior et clarior uictoria*: Hannibal and Tarentum in Livy', *CW* 103.1: 17–38.
Chrubasik, B. (2013) 'The Attalids and the Seleukid Kings, 281–175 BC', in Thonemann: 83–119.
(2016) *Kings and usurpers in the Seleukid Empire: the men who would be king*, Oxford.
Clarke, K. (2003) 'Polybius and the nature of late Hellenistic historiography', in Santos Yanguas and Torregaray Pagola: 69–87.
Colebrook, C. (2004) *Irony*, London.
Connor, W. R. (1967) 'History without heroes: Theopompus' treatment of Philip of Macedon', *GRBS* 8: 133–54.
(1968) *Theopompus and fifth-century Athens*, Washington, DC.
Coppola, A. (1993) *Demetrio di Faro: un protagonista dimenticato*, Rome.
Coşkun, A. (2016) 'Philologische, genealogische und politische Überlegungen zu Ardys und Mithradates, zwei Söhnen des Antiochos Megas (Liv. 33,19,9)', *Latomus* 75: 849–61.
(ed.) (2022) *Galatian victories*, Leuven.
Culham, P. (1992) 'Plutarch on the Roman siege of Syracuse: the primacy of science over technology', in I. Gallo, ed., *Plutarco e le scienze* (Genoa), 179–97.
D'Agostini, M. (2014) 'The shade of Andromache: Laodike of Sardis between Homer and Polybios', *Ancient History Bulletin* 28: 39–60.
(2018) 'Asia Minor and the many shades of a civil war: observations on Achaios the Younger and his claim to the kingdom of Anatolia', in Erickson: 59–81.
(2021) 'Seleukid marriage alliances', in Carney and Müller: 198–209.
Dany, O. P. (2000) 'Livy and the chronology of the years 168–167', *CQ* n.s. 50: 432–9.

Davies, J. K. (2013) 'Mediterranean economies through the text of Polybius', in Gibson and Harrison: 319–35.
De Juliis, E. M. (2000) *Taranto*, Bari.
De Juliis, E. M., and Loiacono, D. (1985) *Taranto: il Museo Archeologico*, Taranto.
de Lisle, C. M. (2021) *Agathokles of Syracuse: Sicilian tyrant and Hellenistic king*, Oxford.
De Sanctis, G. (1916) *Storia dei Romani* III.1, Rome.
— (1968) *Storia dei Romani:* III *L'età delle guerre puniche, Parte* II, 2nd edn, Florence.
De Sensi Sestito, G. (1976) *Gerone: un monarca ellenistico in Sicilia*, Palermo.
Delacenserie, E., and Van Nuffelen, P. (eds) (2017) 'Excerpta Constantiniana', *Byzantinoslavica* 75: 199–324.
Dell'Aglio, A. (2002–3) '50. Taranto: 2. Via D'Aquino ang. via Regina Margherita', *Taras* 23: 227–9.
— (2015) 'Taranto nel III secolo a.C.: nuovi dati', in *ACT* 52: 431–61.
Denniston, J. D. (1954) *Greek particles*, 2nd edn, Oxford.
Derow, P. (2015) *Rome, Polybius, and the East*, ed. A. Erskine and J. C. Quinn, Oxford.
Diggle, J. (2020) 'Polybiana', *Eikasmos* 31: 135–44.
Dijksterhuis, E. J. (1987) *Archimedes*, Princeton.
Dillery, J. (2018) 'Making *logoi*: Herodotus book 2 and Hecataeus of Miletus', in T. Harrison and E. Irwin, eds, *Interpreting Herodotus* (Oxford), 17–52.
Dobson, M. (2008) *The army of the Roman Republic: the second century BC, Polybius and the camps at Numantia, Spain*, Oxford.
Dörner, Fr. K. (1975) 'Die Ahnengalerie der kommagenischen Königsdynastie', *Antike Welt* 6, Sondernummer: 26–31.
Dörner, Fr. K., and Goell, Th. (1963) *Arsameia am Nymphaios: Die Ausgrabungen im Hierothesion des Mithradates Kallinikos von 1953–1956*, Berlin.
Dreher, M. (2008) *Das antike Sizilien*, Munich.
Dreyer, B. (2007) *Die römische Nobilitätsherrschaft und Antiochos III. (205 bis 188 v. Chr.)*, Hennef.
Drögemüller, H.-P. (1969) *Syrakus: Zur Topographie und Geschichte einer griechischen Stadt*, Heidelberg.
Dubuisson, M. (1985) *Le latin de Polybe : les implications historiques d'un cas de bilinguisme*, Paris.
Eckstein, A. M. (1995) *Moral vision in the* Histories *of Polybius*, Berkeley.
— (2006) *Mediterranean anarchy, interstate wars, and the rise of Rome*, Berkeley.

(2010) 'Macedonia and Rome, 221–146 BC', in J. Roisman and I. Worthington, eds, *A companion to ancient Macedonia* (Oxford), 225–50.

(2013) 'Polybius, Phylarchus, and historiographical criticism', *CP* 108: 314–38.

Edelstein, D. (2022) 'A "revolution" in political thought: translations of Polybius book 6 and the conceptual history of revolution', *Journal of the History of Ideas* 83: 17–40.

Edwell, P. (2013) 'Definitions of Roman imperialism', in D. Hoyos, ed., *A companion to Roman imperialism* (Leiden), 39–52.

Ehling, K. (2007) 'Der Tod des Usurpators Achaios', *Historia* 56: 497–501.

Erickson, K. (ed.) (2018) *The Seleukid Empire, 281–222 BC: war within the family*, Swansea.

Erskine, A., Llewellyn-Jones, Ll., and Wallace, S. (eds) (2017) *The Hellenistic court: monarchic power and elite society from Alexander to Cleopatra*, Swansea.

Evans, J. D. (2018) *Coins from the excavation at Sardis: their archaeological and economic contexts. Coins from the 1973 to 2013 excavations*, Cambridge, Mass.

(2019) 'The mint at Sardis', in Berlin and Kosmin: 97–113.

Fabiani, R. (2015) *I decreti onorari di Iasos: cronologia e storia*, Munich.

Facella, M. (2006) *La dinastia degli Orontidi nella Commagene ellenistico-romana*, Pisa.

Farrington, S. (2015) 'A likely story: rhetoric and the determination of truth in Polybius' *Histories*', *Histos* 9: 29–66.

Faust, A. (2021) *The Neo-Assyrian Empire in the southwest: imperial domination and its consequences*, Oxford.

Fendel, V. B. (2025) 'Taking stock of Greek support-verb constructions: synchronic and diachronic variability in the documentary papyri', in J. de la Villa (ed.), *Advances in ancient Greek linguistics* (Berlin), 295–311.

Fernández Uriel, P. (2006) 'The Roman conquest and organisation of the Iberian Peninsula', in Á. Morillo and J. Aurrecoechea, eds, *The Roman army in Hispania: an archaeological guide* (León), 37–52.

Ferrary, J.-L. (2003) 'Le jugement de Polybe sur la domination romaine : état de la question', in Santos Yanguas and Torregaray Pagola: 15–32.

(2014) *Philhellénisme et impérialisme : aspects idéologiques de la conquête romaine du monde hellénistique, de la seconde guerre de Macédoine à la guerre contre Mithridate*, 2nd edn, Rome.

Fitzgerald, W. (2016) *Variety: the life of a Roman concept*, Chicago.

Fleischer, R. (1972–5) 'Marsyas und Achaios', *Jahreshefte des Österreichischen Archäologischen Institutes in Wien* 50, Beiblatt: 103–22.

Flower, M. A. (1994) *Theopompus of Chius: history and rhetoric in the fourth century BC*, Oxford.
Fögen, Th. (ed.) (2005) *Antike Fachtexte / Ancient technical texts*, Berlin.
Formisano, M., and Eijk, P. van der (eds) (2017) *Knowledge, text and practice in ancient technical writing*, Cambridge.
Fornaro, A. (2005) *Problemi di metrologia nell'opera di Polibio*, Bari.
Foucault, J.-A. (1972) *Recherches sur la langue et le style de Polybe*, Paris.
Foulon, É. (2000) 'Polybe et les Celtes (I)', *Les Études Classiques* 68: 319–54.
Fowler, D. (2000) *Roman constructions: readings in postmodern Latin*, Oxford.
Fraser, P. M. (1972) *Ptolemaic Alexandria*, 3 vols, Oxford.
Fröhlich, P. (2008) 'Les tombeaux de la ville de Messène et les grandes familles de la cité à l'époque hellénistique', in C. Grandjean, ed., *Le Péloponnèse d'Épaminondas à Hadrien* (Bordeaux), 203–27.
Fronda, M. P. (2010) *Between Rome and Carthage: southern Italy during the Second Punic War*, Cambridge.
Fulkerson, L. (2013) *No regrets: remorse in classical antiquity*, Oxford.
Gabrielsen, V. (1997) *The naval aristocracy of Hellenistic Rhodes*, Aarhus.
Gaebler, H. (1935) *Die antiken Münzen von Makedonia und Paionia* II, Berlin.
Gallo, A. (2018) '"La punizione dei vinti": dibattiti e decreti senatori su Campani e Tarentini dopo la riconquista (211–208 a. C.)', *Klio* 100: 785–824.
Gans, H. (2006) 'Der antike Isthmos von Syrakus: Der topographische und städtebauliche Befund nach antiken, mittelalterlichen und neuzeitlichen Quellen', *Jahrbuch des deutschen archäologischen Instituts* 121: 227–67.
Garlan, Y. (1974) *Recherches de poliorcétique grecque*, Paris.
Gauthier, H., and Sottas, H. (1925) *Un décret trilingue en l'honneur de Ptolémée IV*, Cairo.
Gauthier, Ph. (1989) *Nouvelles inscriptions de Sardes* II, Geneva.
Gehrke, H.-J. (1985) *Stasis: Untersuchungen zu den inneren Kriegen in den griechischen Staaten des 5. und 4. Jahrhunderts v. Chr.*, Munich.
Gelzer, M. (1962–4) *Kleine Schriften*, 3 vols, Wiesbaden.
Geus, Kl. (1994) *Prosopographie der literarisch bezeugten Karthager*, Leuven.
Gibson, B. (2018) 'Praise in Polybius', in Miltsios and Tamiolaki: 75–101.
Gibson, B., and Harrison, T. (eds) (2013) *Polybius and his world: essays in memory of F. W. Walbank*, Oxford.
Goldsworthy, A. (2000) *The Punic Wars*, London.
Grainger, J. D. (1997) *A Seleukid prosopography and gazetteer* (*Mnemosyne* Suppl. 172), Leiden.

(2017) *Kings and kingship in the Hellenistic world 350–30 BC*, Barnsley.
(2019) *Antipater's dynasty*, Barnsley.
Grelle, F., and Silvestrini, M. (2013) *La Puglia nel mondo romano: storia di una periferia. Dalle guerre sannitiche alla guerra sociale*, Bari.
Grethlein, J., and Krebs, C. B. (2012) 'The historian's plupast: introductory remarks on its form and function', in J. Grethlein and C. B. Krebs, eds, *Time and narrative in ancient historiography: the 'plupast' from Herodotus to Appian* (Cambridge), 1–16.
Griffith, G. T. (1935) *Mercenaries of the Hellenistic world*, Cambridge.
Gruen, E. S. (1984) *The Hellenistic world and the coming of Rome*, 2 vols, Berkeley.
Guido, L. (2010) 'Encore à propos des débuts de l'administration romaine en Sicile : à mi-chemin entre idéalité et réalité', in D. Engels, L. Geis and M. Kleu, eds, *Zwischen Ideal und Wirklichkeit: Herrschaft auf Sizilien von der Antike bis zum Spätmittelalter* (Stuttgart), 121–36.
Haake, M. (2013) 'Writing down the king: the communicative function of treatises *On Kingship* in the Hellenistic period', in N. Luraghi, ed., *The splendors and miseries of ruling alone: encounters with monarchy from Archaic Greece to the Hellenistic Mediterranean* (Stuttgart), 165–206.
Habicht, Chr. (2006) *The Hellenistic monarchies: selected papers*, Ann Arbor.
(2017) *Divine honors for mortal men in Greek cities: the early cases*, transl. J. N. Dillon, Ann Arbor.
Hammond, N. G. L., and Walbank, F. W. (1988) *A history of Macedonia* III: *336–167 B.C.*, Oxford.
Hanfmann, G. M. A. (1983) assisted by W. E. Mierse, *Sardis from prehistoric to Roman times: results of the Archaeological Exploration of Sardis 1958–1975*, Cambridge, Mass.
Hanfmann, G. M. A. and Waldbaum, J. C. (1975) *A survey of Sardis and the major monuments outside the city walls*, Cambridge, Mass.
Harris, W. V. (1979) *War and imperialism in Republican Rome, 327–70 B.C.*, Oxford.
Hatzopoulos, M. B. (1996) *Macedonian institutions under the kings: a historical and epigraphical study*, 2 vols, Athens.
(2001) *L'Organisation de l'armée macédonienne sous les Antigonides : problèmes anciens et documents nouveaux*, Athens.
(2020) *Ancient Macedonia*, Berlin.
Hau, L. I. (2016) *Moral history from Herodotus to Diodorus Siculus*, Edinburgh.
(2021) 'The fragments of Polybius compared with those of the tragic historians Duris and Phylarchus', *Histos* 15: 238–82.
Heckel, W. (2016) *The marshals of Alexander's empire*, 2nd edn, London.

Heftner, H. (1997) *Der Aufstieg Roms: Vom Pyrrhoskrieg bis zum Fall von Karthago (280–146 v. Chr.)*, Regensburg.
Heiberg, J. L. (2013) *Quaestiones Archimedeae*, Cambridge.
Heisserer, A. J. (1988) 'Observations on *IG* XII 2, 10 and 11', *ZPE* 74: 111–32.
Hoffmann, G. (2014) '*Anaplèrôsis* et *agôgè* au temps des rois Agis IV (244–241) et Cléomène III (235–222)', in J. Christien and B. Legras, eds, *Sparte hellénistique* (Besançon), 111–27.
Hornblower, J. (1981) *Hieronymus of Cardia*, Oxford.
Hornblower, S. (1990) 'When was Megalopolis founded?', *ABSA* 85: 71–7.
(2020) 'The Corpus of Ptolemaic Inscriptions: the metrical texts', in A. Bowman and C. Crowther, eds, *The epigraphy of Ptolemaic Egypt* (Oxford), 208–25.
(2024) *Hannibal and Scipio: parallel lives*, Cambridge.
Hoyos, B. D. (1998) *Unplanned wars: the origins of the First and Second Punic Wars*, Berlin.
(ed.) (2011) *A companion to the Punic Wars*, Chichester.
Hughes, D. (2019) 'The cult of Aratus at Sicyon (Plutarch, *Aratus*, 53)', *Kernos* 32: 119–50.
Hultsch, Fr. (1859) 'Über den hiatus bei Polybius', *Philologus* 14: 288–319.
Huß, W. (1976) *Untersuchungen zur Außenpolitik Ptolemaios' IV.*, Munich.
(2001) *Ägypten in hellenistischer Zeit: 332–30 v. Chr.*, Munich.
Hutchinson, G. O. (2008) *Talking books: readings in Hellenistic and Roman books of poetry*, Oxford.
(2013) *Greek to Latin: frameworks and contexts for intertextuality*, Oxford.
(2014) 'Hellenistic poetry and Hellenistic prose', in R. Hunter, A. Rengakos and E. Sistakou, eds, *Hellenistic studies at a crossroads: exploring texts, contexts and metatexts* (Berlin), 31–51.
(2020) *Motion in classical literature: Homer, Parmenides, Sophocles, Ovid, Seneca, Tacitus, art*, Oxford.
Hyatt, A. P. (2011) *From Taras to Tarentum: the evolution of a Greek city in Roman Italy*, Ph.D. dissertation, Buffalo.
Ioannidou, G. (1996) *Catalogue of Greek and Latin literary papyri in Berlin (P. Berol. inv. 21101–21299, 21911)* (*BKT* IX), Mainz am Rhein.
Isayev, E. (2007) *Inside ancient Lucania: dialogues in history and archaeology* (*BICS* Suppl. 90), London.
Jefremow, N. (2005) 'Der rhodisch-byzantinische Krieg von 220 v. Chr.: Ein Handelskrieg im Hellenismus', *Münstersche Beiträge zur antiken Handelsgeschichte* 24: 51–98.
Jim, Th. S. F. (2021) 'Becoming a goddess: Hellenistic queens as protective goddesses', *ZPE* 219: 95–110.

Jiménez López, M. D. (2016) 'On support verb constructions in Ancient Greek', *Archivio Glottologico Italiano* 101: 180–204.
Jong, I. J. F. de (2004) *Narrators and focalizers: the presentation of the story in the* Iliad, 2nd edn, London.
——— (2014) *Narratology and classics: a practical guide*, Oxford.
Kaldellis, A. (2009) 'Classical scholarship in twelfth-century Byzantium', in A. Kaldellis, ed., *Medieval commentaries on the* Nicomachean Ethics (Leiden), 1–43.
Kampakoglou, A. (2019) *Studies in the reception of Pindar in Ptolemaic poetry*, Berlin.
Karlsson, L. (1992) *Fortification towers and masonry techniques in the hegemony of Syracuse, 405–211 B.C.*, Stockholm.
Kearns, E. (1989) *The heroes of Attica* (*BICS* Suppl. 57), London.
Khellaf, K. (2018) 'Incomplete and disconnected: Polybius, digression, and its historiographical afterlife', in Miltsios and Tamiolaki: 167–201.
Kleu, M. (2017) 'Philip V, the Selci hoard and the supposed building of a Macedonian fleet in Lissus', *The Ancient History Bulletin* 31: 112–19.
Kobes, J. (1996) *'Kleine Könige': Untersuchungen zu den Lokaldynasten im hellenistischen Kleinasien (323–188 v.Chr.)*, St. Katharinen.
Kosmin, P. J. (2014) *The land of the elephant kings: space, territory, and ideology in the Seleucid Empire*, Cambridge, Mass.
Kralli, I. (2017) *The Hellenistic Peloponnese: interstate relations. A narrative and analytic history from the fourth century to 146 BC*, Swansea.
Krewet, M. (2017) 'Polybios' Geschichtsbild: Hellenistische Prinzipien seiner Darstellungen menschlichen Handelns', *Wiener Studien* 130: 89–125.
Kritt, B. (2001) *Dynastic transitions in the coinage of Bactria: Antiochus – Diodotus – Euthydemus*, Lancaster, Penn.
——— (2016) *The Seleucid mint of Aï Khanoum*, Lancaster, Penn.
La'da, C. A. (2002) *Foreign ethnics in Hellenistic Egypt*, Leuven.
Ladstätter, S. (2019) 'Ephesus: Sardis's port to the Mediterranean in the Hellenistic period', in Berlin and Kosmin: 191–204.
Landels, J. G. (1966) 'Ship-shape and *sambuca*-fashion', *JHS* 86: 69–77.
——— (2000) *Engineering in the ancient world*, 2nd edn, Berkeley.
Lane Fox, R. (ed.) (2011a) *Brill's companion to ancient Macedon: studies in the archaeology and history of Macedon, 650 BC – 300 AD*, Leiden.
——— (2011b) 'The 360's', in Lane Fox, ed.: 257–69.
——— (2011c) 'Philip of Macedon: accession, ambitions, and self-presentation', in Lane Fox, ed.: 335–66.
——— (2011d) 'Philip and Alexander's Macedon', in Lane Fox, ed.: 367–91.

Langslow, D. R. (2012) 'The language of Polybius since Foucault and Dubuisson', in C. Smith and L. M. Yarrow, eds, *Imperialism, cultural politics, and Polybius* (Oxford), 85–110.
La-Roche, P. (1857) *Charakteristik des Polybius*, Leipzig.
Launey, M. (1987) *Recherches sur les armées hellénistiques*, 2nd edn, eds Y. Garlan, Ph. Gauthier and Cl. Orrieux, 2 vols, Paris.
Lauter, H. (2002) '"Polybios hat es geweiht ...": Stiftungsinschriften des Polybios und des Philopoimen aus dem neuen Zeus-Heiligtum zu Megalopolis (Griechenland)', *Antike Welt* 33: 375–86.
Lauter, H. (2005) 'Megalopolis: Ausgrabungen auf der Agora, 1991–2002', in Østby: 235–48.
Lazarov, L. (2010) 'The Celtic Tylite state in the time of Cavarus', in Vagalinski: 97–113.
Lazenby, J. F. (1978) *Hannibal's war: a military history of the Second Punic War*, Warminster.
Le Bohec, S. (1993) *Antigone Dôsôn, roi de Macédoine*, Nancy.
Le Bohec, Y. (1996) *Histoire militaire des guerres puniques*, Monaco.
Lehmler, C. (2005) *Syrakus unter Agathokles und Hieron II.: Die Verbindung von Kultur und Macht in einer hellenistischen Metropole*, Frankfurt am Main.
Leigh, M. (2013) *From* polypragmon *to* curiosus*: ancient concepts of curious and meddlesome behaviour*, Oxford.
Lendle, O. (1983) *Texte und Untersuchungen zum technischen Bereich der antiken Poliorketik*, Wiesbaden.
Lenschau, Th. (1913) 'Hippokrates 10', *RE* VIII 1779–80.
Lepper, F., and Frere, S. (1988) *Trajan's Column: a new edition of the Cichorius plates. Introduction, commentary and notes*, Gloucester.
Levathan, J. (2013) *Roman siege warfare*, Ann Arbor.
Levene, D. S. (2010) *Livy on the Hannibalic War*, Oxford.
Liddel, P. (2018) 'Writing and other forms of communication in Aineias' *Poliorketika*', in M. Pretzler and N. Barley, eds, *Brill's companion to Aineias Tacticus* (Leiden), 123–45.
Lincoln, B. (2007) *Religion, empire, and torture: the case of Achaemenian Persia*, Chicago.
Lippolis, E. (1981) 'Alcune considerazioni su Taranto romana', *Taras* 1: 77–114.
 (ed.) (1994a) *Catalogo del Museo Nazionale Archeologico di Taranto* III, 1. *Taranto, la necropoli: aspetti e problemi della documentazione archeologica tra VII e I sec. a.C.*, Taranto.
 (1994b) 'Il problema topografico', in Lippolis, ed.: 40–66.
 (1994c) 'La necropoli ellenistica: problemi di classificazione e cronologia dei materiali', in Lippolis, ed.: 238–81.

(1997) *Fra Taranto e Roma: società e cultura urbana in Puglia tra Annibale e l'età imperiale*, Taranto.

(2006) 'Ricostruzione e architettura a Taranto dopo Annibale', in M. Osanna and M. Torelli, eds, *Sicilia ellenistica, consuetudo italica: alle origini dell'architettura ellenistica d'Occidente* (Rome), 211–26.

Lippolis, E., Garraffo, S., and Nafissi, M. (1995) *Culti greci in Occidente: fonti scritte e documentazione archeologica* I: *Taranto*, Taranto.

Lo Porto, F. G. (1992) 'Ricerche sulle antiche mura di Taranto: gli scavi di Masseria del Carmine', *Taras* 12: 7–27.

Lobeck, Chr. A. (1843) *Pathologiae sermonis Graeci prolegomena*, Leipzig.

Loehr, R. M. (2017) *Emotions in Polybius' Histories*, Ph.D. thesis, UC Santa Barbara.

Lomas, K. (1993) *Rome and the western Greeks 350 BC–AD 200: conquest and acculturation in southern Italy*, London.

Longley, G. (2014) '"I, Polybius": self-conscious didacticism?', in A. Marmodoro and J. Hill, eds, *The author's voice in classical and late antiquity* (Oxford), 175–205.

Lorentzen, J. (2016) 'Pergamon', in S. Müth, P. I. Schneider, M. Schnelle and P. D. De Staebler, eds, *Ancient fortifications: a compendium of theory and practice* (Oxford), 303–9.

Luiselli, R. (2016) 'Un nuovo papiro di Polibio', in A. Casanova, G. Messeri and R. Pintaudi, eds, *'e sì d'amici pieno': omaggio di studiosi italiani a Guido Bastianini per il suo settantesimo compleanno*, 2 vols (Florence), 111–15.

Luraghi, M. (2008) *The ancient Messenians: constructions of ethnicity and memory*, Cambridge.

(2014) 'Ephorus in context: the return of the Heraclidae and fourth-century Peloponnesian politics', in Parmeggiani: 133–51.

Luraghi, N., and Magnetto, A. (2012) 'The controversy between Megalopolis and Messene in a new inscription from Messene', *Chiron* 42: 509–50.

Lyne, R. O. A. M. (1989) *Words and the poet: characteristic techniques of style in Vergil's* Aeneid, Oxford.

Ma, J. (1999) *Antiochos III and the cities of western Asia Minor*, Oxford.

MacDonald, E. (2015) *Hannibal: a Hellenistic life*, New Haven.

Madvig, J. N. (1871–84) *Adversaria critica ad scriptores Græcos et Latinos*, 3 vols, Copenhagen.

Magnetto, A. (2024) 'Kyme, Seleuco, gli Etoli: un nuovo documento da Kyme eolica e uno storico fra polis e corte', *Chiron* 54: 199–229.

Maier, F. K. (2012) *'Überall mit dem Unerwarteten rechnen': Die Kontingenz historischer Prozesse bei Polybios*, Munich.

(2016) 'Chronotopos: Erzählung, Zeit und Raum im Hellenismus', *Klio* 98: 465–94.
Mangoni, C. (1993) *Filodemo, il quinto libro della Poetica (PHerc. 1425 e 1538): edizione, traduzione e commento*, Naples.
Manov, M. (2010) 'In search of Tyle (Tylis): problems of localization', in Vagalinski: 89–96.
Manov, M., and Damyanov, V. (2013) 'The first mint of Cavarus, the last king of the Celtic Kingdom in Thrace', *American Journal of Numismatics* 25: 11–19.
Mantel, N. (1991) *Poeni foedifragi: Untersuchungen zur Darstellung römisch-karthagischer Verträge zwischen 241 und 201 v.Chr. durch die römische Historiographie*, Munich.
Marasco, G. (1979–80) 'La valutazione di Tolemeo IV Filopatore nella storiografia greca', *Sileno* 5–6: 159–82.
Marchand, J.-J. (ed.) (2001) *Edizione nazionale delle opere di Niccolò Machiavelli. Sezione 1: opere politiche*, 3 vols, Rome.
Marchetti, P. (1972) 'La deuxième guerre punique en Sicile : les années 215–214 et le récit de Tite-Live', *Bulletin de l'Institut Historique Belge* 42: 5–26.
Marciak, M. (2017) *Sophene, Gordyene, and Adiabene. Three regna minora of northern Mesopotamia: between East and West*, Leiden.
Mari, M., and Thornton, J. (eds) (2013) *Parole in movimento: linguaggio politico e lessico storiografico nel mondo ellenistico*, Pisa.
Marincola, J. (1997) *Authority and tradition in ancient historiography*, Cambridge.
(2003) 'Beyond pity and fear: the emotions of history', *Ancient Society* 33: 285–315.
(ed.) (2007a) *A companion to Greek and Roman historiography*, 2 vols, Malden.
(2007b) 'Universal history from Ephorus to Diodorus', in Marincola, ed.: 171–9.
(2013) 'Polybius, Phylarchus, and "tragic history": a reconsideration', in Gibson and Harrison: 73–90.
Marsden, E. W. (1969) *Greek and Roman artillery: historical development*, Oxford.
(1971) *Greek and Roman artillery: technical treatises*, Oxford.
Masiello, L. (1994) 'La necropoli ellenistica: le oreficerie', in Lippolis, ed.: 300–23.
Mastino, A. (2005) *Storia della Sardegna antica*, Nuoro.
Mastrocinque, G. (2010) *Taranto: il paesaggio urbano di età romana tra persistenza e innovazione*, Pozzuoli.

May, J. M. F. (1946) 'Macedonia and Illyria (217–167 B.C.)', *JRS* 36: 48–56.
Mayser, E. (1934–70) *Grammatik der griechischen Papyri aus der Ptolemäerzeit*, 2 vols, some parts in 2nd edn, Berlin.
McAuley, A. (2018) 'The House of Achaios: reconstructing an early client dynasty of Seleukid Anatolia', in Erickson: 37–58.
McGing, B. (2010) *Polybius'* Histories, Oxford.
McNicoll, A. W. (1997) *Hellenistic fortifications from the Aegean to the Euphrates*, Oxford.
McOsker, M. (forthcoming), 'Hiatus, style, and nominal chains in Plato's *Timaeus* (and *Critias*)', *Hermes*.
Meadows, A. R. (2013) 'Polybius, Aratus, and the history of the 140th Olympiad', in Harrison and Gibson: 91–116.
Meadows, A. R., and Lorber, C. C. (2010) 'Commerce ("Achaeus hoard"), 2002 (*CH* 10.277)', *Coin Hoards* 10: 115–27.
Meeus, A. (2022) *The history of the Diadochi in book XIX of Diodoros' Bibliotheke: a historical and historiographical commentary*, Berlin.
Meloni, P. (1949–50) 'L'usurpazione di Acheo sotto Antioco III di Siria', *Rend. Acc. Lincei* 346 ser. 8, 4: 535–53, and 5: 161–83.
Mercati, J., and De' Cavalieri, P. F. (1923) *Bybliothecae Apostolicae Vaticanae codices manu scripti recensiti* I [*Codices 1–329*], Rome.
Messerschmidt, W. (2000) 'Die Ahnengalerie des Antiochos I. von Kommagene: Ein Zeugnis für die Geschichte des östlichen Hellenismus', in J. Wagner, ed., *Gottkönige am Euphrat: Neue Ausgrabungen und Forschungen in Kommagene* (Mainz am Rhein), 37–43.
Miltsios, N. (2009) 'The perils of expectations: perceptions, suspense and surprise in Polybius' *Histories*', in J. Grethlein and A. Rengakos, eds, *Narratology and interpretation: the content of narrative form in ancient literature* (Berlin), 481–506.
(2013) *The shaping of narrative in Polybius*, Berlin.
Miltsios, N., and Tamiolaki, M. (2018) *Polybius and his legacy*, Berlin.
Mittag, P. F. (2017) 'Misconduct and disloyalty in the Seleucid Court', in Erskine, Llewellyn-Jones and Wallace: 359–72.
Momigliano, A. (1980) *Sesto contributo alla storia degli studi classici e del mondo antico*, Rome.
Mommsen, Th. (1906) *Gesammelte Schriften* IV, Berlin.
Moore, D. (2017) 'Proof through the night: representations of fire-signaling in Greek historiography', *Histos* 9: 108–27.
Moore, J. M. (1965) *The manuscript tradition of Polybius*, Cambridge.
(1971) 'Polybiana', *GRBS* 12: 411–49.
Morgan, J. (2017) 'At home with royalty: re-viewing the Hellenistic palace', in Erskine, Llewellyn-Jones and Wallace: 31–67.
Morrison, J. S. (1996) *Greek and Roman oared warships*, Oxford.

Münzer, Fr. (1923a) 'Sempronius (51)', *RE* IIA.1401–3.
— (1923b) 'Sempronius (96)', *RE* IIA.1443–5.
Murray, W. M. (2012) *The Age of Titans: the rise and fall of the great Hellenistic navies*, Oxford.
Musti, D., Mari, M., and Thornton, J. (2002) *Polibio, Storie* IV: *Libri VII–XI*, Milan.
Naber, S. A. (1857) 'Polybiana', *Mnemosyne* 6: 113–37, 225–58, 341–64.
Nederman, C. J. (2016) 'Polybius as monarchist? Receptions of *Histories* VI before Machiavelli, *c.*1490–*c.*1515', *History of Political Thought* 3: 461–79.
Németh, A. (2015) 'Layers of restorations: *Vat. gr.* 73 transformed in the tenth, fourteenth, and nineteenth centuries', in A. M. Piazzoni *et al.*, eds, *Miscellanea Bibliothecae Apostolicae Vaticanae* XXI (Vatican), 281–330.
— (2018) *The* Excerpta Constantiniana *and the Byzantine appropriation of the past*, Cambridge.
— (2022) 'The suicide of Hasdrubal's wife revisited in a new fragment of Polybius', in C. Pasini and F. D'Aiuto, eds, *Libri, scritture e testi greci* (Vatican), 87–104.
— (2023) 'Mismatching fragments from the *Excerpta Constantiniana*: a case study on the dialogue between Polybius and Scipio Aemilianus', *Vatican Library Review* 2: 185–212.
Netz, R. (2004) *The works of Archimedes* I: *the two books* On the sphere and the cylinder, Cambridge.
— (2009) *Ludic proof: Greek mathematics and the Alexandrian aesthetic*, Cambridge.
— (2013) 'Science in Syracuse: Archimedes in place', in C. L. Lyons, M. Bennett and C. Marconi, eds, *Sicily: art and invention between Greece and Rome* (Los Angeles), 124–33.
— (2022) *A new history of Greek mathematics*, Cambridge.
Netz, R., Noel, W., Tchernetska, N., and Wilson, W. (2011) *The Archimedes Palimpsest* II: *images and transcriptions*, Cambridge.
Neumann, K. M. (2021) *Antioch in Syria: a history from coins (300 BCE–450 CE)*, Cambridge.
Nicholson, E. (2018) 'Polybios, the laws of war, and Philip V of Macedon', *Historia* 67: 434–53.
— (2023) *Philip V of Macedon in Polybius' Histories: politics, history, and fiction*, Oxford.
Nicolai, R. (2018) 'Τὰ καιριώτατα καὶ πραγματικώτατα: a survey on the speeches in Polybius', in Miltsios and Tamiolaki, 117–30.
Nicolet-Croizat, F. (1992) *Tite-Live* : Histoire romaine. *Tome* XV. *Livre* XXV. *Texte établi et traduit*, Paris.
O'Neil, J. L. (1984–6) 'The political elites of the Achaian and Aitolian Leagues', *Ancient Society* 15–17: 33–61.

Oakley, J. H. (1997) *The Achilles Painter*, Mainz am Rhein.
Oakley, S. P. (2005) *A commentary on Livy books VI–X* IV: *book X*, Oxford.
 (2018) 'Livy on Cannae: a literary overview', in L. W. van Gils, I. J. F. de Jong, C. H. M. Kroon, eds, *Textual strategies in ancient war narrative: Thermopylae, Cannae and beyond* (Leiden), 157–90.
 (2019) 'Hannibal reaches the Alps: Livy 21, 32, 6 – 33, 1 and Polybius 3, 50, 1 – 51, 13', in G. Baldo and L. Beltramini, eds, A primordio urbis*: un itinerario per gli studi liviani* (Turnhout), 27–52.
Oetjen, R. (2010) 'Antigonid cleruchs in Thessaly and Greece: Philip V and Larisa', in G. Reger, F. X. Ryan and T. F. Winters, eds, *Studies in Greek epigraphy and history in honor of Stefen V. Tracy* (Pessac), 237–54.
Ogden, D. (2010) *Polygamy, prostitutes and death: the Hellenistic dynasties*, Swansea.
Olbrycht, M. J. (2021) 'Seleukid women', in Carney and Müller: 173–85.
Oliva, P. (1971) *Sparta and her social problems*, Amsterdam.
 (1993) 'Hellenistische Herrscher und die Freiheit der Griechen', *Eirene* 29: 43–60.
Østby, E. (ed.) (2005) *Ancient Arcadia*, Athens.
Panzram, S. (2002) *Stadtbild und Elite: Tarraco, Corduba und Augusta Emerita zwischen Republik und Spätantike* (Historia Einzelschriften 161), Stuttgart.
Papazoglu, F. (1957) *Македонски градови у римско доба*, Skopje.
 (1988) *Les villes de Macédoine à l'époque romaine*, Paris.
Parenty, H. (2009) *Isaac Casaubon, helléniste : des studia humanitatis à la philologie*, Geneva.
Pareti, L. (1997) *Storia della regione Lucano-Bruzzia nell'antichità*, Rome.
Parke, H. W. (1944) 'A note on the topography of Syracuse', *JHS* 64: 100–2.
Parke, H. W., and Wormell, D. E. W. (1956) *The Delphic Oracle* II: *the oracular responses*, Oxford.
Parker, R. C. T. (1983) *Miasma: pollution and purification in early Greek religion*, Oxford.
Parmeggiani, G. (ed.) (2014) *Between Thucydides and Polybius: the golden age of Greek historiography*, Cambridge, Mass.
 (2024) *Ephorus of Cyme and Greek historiography*, Cambridge.
Paton, W. R. (2011) *Polybius, The Histories* III: *Books V–VIII*, rev. F. W. Walbank and C. Habicht, Cambridge, Mass.
Pausch, D. (2011) *Livius und der Leser: Narrative Strukturen in* ab urbe condita, Munich.
Pédech, P. (1964) *La méthode historique de Polybe*, Paris.
 (1989) *Trois historiens méconnus : Théopompe, Duris, Phylarque*, Paris.

Pelagatti, P., and Stibbe, C. M. (2002) 'La ceramica laconica a Taranto e nella Puglia', in *ACT* 41: II 365–403.
Pernot, L. (2015) *Epideictic rhetoric: questioning the stakes of ancient praise*, Austin, Texas.
Perrin-Saminadayar, É. (1999) 'Les succès de la diplomatie athénienne de 229 à 168 av. J.-C.', *REG* 112: 444–62.
Pestman, P. W. (1969) 'A Greek testament from Pathyris (P. Lond. inv. 2850)', *Journal of Egyptian Archaeology* 55: 129–57.
Petzl, G. (2019) *Sardis: Greek and Latin inscriptions. Part II: finds from 1958 to 2017*, Cambridge, Mass.
Petzold, K.-E. (1969) *Studien zur Methode des Polybios und zu ihrer historischen Auswertung*, Munich.
Piérart, M. (2016) '"Le bien le plus grand et le plus précieux qui se puisse trouver" (Polybe XVIII 41, 5) ?', in A. Neumann-Hartmann and T. S. Schmidt, eds, *Munera Friburgensia: Festschrift zu Ehren von Margarethe Billerbeck* (Frankfurt am Main), 41–53.
Pinzone, A. (1983) *Storia ed etica in Polibio: ricerche sull'archeologia della prima punica*, Messina.
Piper, L. J. (1986) *Spartan twilight*, New Rochelle.
Pitassi, M. (2009) *The navies of Rome*, Woodbridge.
Pitcher, L. (2018) 'Polybius', in K. de Temmerman and E. van Emde Boas, eds, *Characterization in ancient Greek literature* (*Mnemosyne* Suppl. 411, Leiden), 221–35.
Pochmarski, E., and Hoxha, G. (2005) 'Lissus: Quellen und Stadtgeschichte', *Römisches Österreich* 28: 243–51.
Pomeroy, A. J. (1991) *The appropriate comment: death notices in the ancient historians*, Frankfurt am Main.
Pontrandolfo, A. (1994) 'Etnogenesi e emergenza politica di una comunità italica: i Lucani', in S. Settis, ed., *Storia della Calabria antica* (Rome), II 139–93.
(2011) 'Le evidenze archeologiche e iconografiche', in *ACT* 49: 393–428.
Poulter, A. (2001) *Transforming Tarantine horizons: a political, social and cultural history from the fourth to the first century B.C.*, D.Phil. thesis, Oxford.
Prandi, L. (2005) 'Polibio e Callistene: una polemica non personale?', in G. Schepens and J. Bollansée, eds, *The shadow of Polybius: intertextuality as a research tool in Greek historiography* (Leuven), 73–87.
Praschniker, C., and Schober, A. (1919) *Archäologische Forschungen in Albanien und Montenegro*, Vienna.
Prendi, F., and Zheku, K. (1972) 'Qyteti ilir i Lisit: origjina dhe sistemi i fortifikimit të tij', *Iliria* 2: 215–44.

Primo, A. (2009) *La storiografia sui Seleucidi: da Megastene a Eusebio di Cesarea*, Pisa.
Proosdij, B. A. van (1934) 'De morte Achaei', *Hermes* 69: 347–50.
Purcell, N. (1995) 'On the sacking of Carthage and Corinth', in D. Innes, H. Hine and C. Pelling, eds, *Ethics and rhetoric: classical essays for Donald Russell on his seventy-fifth birthday* (Oxford), 133–48.
Radt, S. L. (1980) 'Noch einmal Aischylos, Niobe Fr. 162 N.$^2$ (278 M.)', *ZPE* 38: 47–58.
— (2002) 'Οἱ περί τινα bei Strabon', *ZPE* 139: 46.
— (2002–11) *Strabons Geographika, mit Übersetzung und Kommentar herausgegeben*, 10 vols, Göttingen.
Radt, W. (2011) *Pergamon: Geschichte und Bauten einer antiken Metropole*, Darmstadt.
Ravel, M. P. (1947) *Descriptive catalogue of the collection of Tarentine coins formed by M. P. Vlasto*, London.
Reeve, M. D. (1971) 'Hiatus in the Greek novelists', *CQ* n.s. 21: 514–39.
Reichert-Südbeck, P. (2000) *Kulte von Korinth und Syrakus: Vergleich zwischen einer Metropolis und ihrer Apoikia*, Dettelbach.
Richardson, J. S. (1996) *The Romans in Spain*, Oxford.
Richer, N. (1998) *Les éphores : études sur l'histoire et sur l'image de Sparte*, Paris.
Richter, S. (2017) 'Antiochus III and the revolt of Molon', in Chr. Feyel and L. Graslin-Thomé, *Antiochos III et l'Orient* (Paris), 255–69.
Rix, H. (1963) *Das etruskische Cognomen*, Wiesbaden.
Rizakis, A. (2015) 'The Achaian League', in Beck and Funke, eds: 118–31.
Rodríguez Adrados, F. (2005) *A history of the Greek language from its origins to the present*, Leiden.
Roebuck, C. A. (1941) *A history of Messenia from 369 to 146 B.C.*, Ph.D. thesis, Chicago.
Rohland, R. A. (2022) *Carpe diem: the poetics of presence in Greek and Latin literature*, Cambridge.
Rollinger, R., Lang, M., and Barta, H. (eds) (2012) *Strafe und Strafrecht in den antiken Welten*, Wiesbaden.
Rood, T. (2007) 'Polybius', in I. J. F. de Jong and R. Nünlist, eds, *Time in ancient Greek literature* (*Mnemosyne* Suppl. 291, Leiden), 165–81.
— (2012) 'Polybius', in I. J. F. de Jong, ed., *Space in ancient Greek literature* (*Mnemosyne* Suppl. 339, Leiden), 179–97.
Rotroff, S. I., and Oliver, A., Jr. (2003) *The Hellenistic pottery from Sardis: the finds through 1994*, Cambridge, Mass.
Rutherford, R. B. (2007) 'Tragedy and history', in Marincola, ed.: II 504–14.

(2022) 'Herodotean emotions: some aspects', in M. de Bakker, J. Klooster, B. van den Berg, eds, *Emotions and narrative in ancient literature and beyond: studies in honour of Irene de Jong* (Leiden), 353–67.
Rutter, N. K. (ed.) (2001) *Historia numorum: Italy*, London.
Rzepka, J. (2012) 'How many companions did Philip II have?', *Electrum* 19: 131–5.
Sacks, K. (1981) *Polybius on the writing of history*, Berkeley.
Sanders, D. H. (ed.) (1996) *Nemrud Dağı: the hierothesion of Antiochus of Commagene*, 2 vols, Winona Lake, Ind.
Santos Yanguas, J., and Torregaray Pagola, E. (eds) (2003) *Polibio y la Península Ibérica*, Vitoria-Gasteiz.
Saprykin, S. (2020) 'The Pontic kingdom and the Seleucids', in R. Oetjen, ed., *New perspectives in Seleucid history, archaeology and numismatics: studies in honor of Getzel M. Cohen* (Berlin), 225–39.
Savalli-Lestrade, I. (1998) *Les* philoi *royaux dans l'Asie hellénistique*, Geneva.
(2017) 'βίος αὐλικός: the multiple ways of life of courtiers in the Hellenistic age', in Erskine, Llewellyn-Jones and Wallace: 101–20.
Schachter, A. (2016) *Boiotia in antiquity: selected papers*, Cambridge.
Scheer, T. S. (1995) '*Res Gestae Divi Augusti* 24: Die Restituierung göttlichen Eigentums in Kleinasien durch Augustus', in Schubert and Brodersen: 209–23.
Scherberich, Kl. (2009) *Koinè symmachía: Untersuchungen zum Hellenenbund Antigonos' III. Doson und Philipps V. (224–197 v. Chr.)* (Historia Einzelschriften 184), Stuttgart.
Schiefsky, M. (2005) 'Technical terminology in Greco-Roman treatises on artillery construction', in Fögen: 253–70.
Schironi, F. (2010) *Τὸ μέγα βιβλίον: book-ends, end-titles, and coronides in papyri with hexametric poetry*, Durham, NC.
Schmidt, T. (2019) 'Plutarch and the papyrological evidence', in S. Xenophontos and K. Oikonomopoulou, eds, *Brill's companion to the reception of Plutarch* (Leiden), 79–99.
Schmitt, H. H. (1964) *Untersuchungen zur Geschichte Antiochos' des Grossen und seiner Zeit* (Historia Einzelschriften 6), Wiesbaden.
Schorn, St. (2014) 'Historiographie, Biographie und Enkomion: Theorie der Biographie und Historiographie bei Diodor und Polybios', *Rivista Storica dell'Antichità* 44: 137–64.
Schubert, Ch., and Brodersen, K. (eds) (1995) *Rom und der Griechische Osten: Festschrift für Hatto H. Schmitt zum 65. Geburtstag* (Stuttgart).
Schweighaeuser, J. (1823) *Polybii Megalopolitani Historiarum quidquid superest* II, ed. nova, Oxford.
Sciacca, E. (2005) *Principati e repubbliche: Machiavelli, le forme politiche e il pensiero francese del Cinquecento*, Florence.

Scranton, R. L. (1941) *Greek walls*, Cambridge, Mass.
Seaman, K. (2020) *Rhetoric and innovation in Hellenistic art*, Cambridge.
Segre, M. (1932) 'Due nuovi testi storici', *RFIC* n.s. 10 = 60: 446–61.
Seibert, J. (1993*a*) *Hannibal*, Darmstadt.
  (1993*b*) *Forschungen zu Hannibal*, Darmstadt.
  (1995) 'Invasion aus dem Osten: Trauma, Propaganda oder Erfindung der Römer?', in Schubert and Brodersen: 237–48.
Sekunda, N. (2007) 'Military forces. Land forces', in P. Sabin, H. van Wees and M. Whitby, eds, *The Cambridge history of Greek and Roman warfare* I: *Greece, the Hellenistic world and the rise of Rome* (Cambridge), 325–57.
Seretaki, M., and Tamiolaki, M. (2018) 'Polybius and Xenophon: Hannibal and Cyrus the Great as model leaders', in Miltsios and Tamiolaki: 226–39.
Serrati, J. (2000*a*) 'The coming of the Romans: Sicily from the fourth to the first centuries BC', in Smith and Serrati: 109–14.
  (2000*b*) 'Garrisons and grain: Sicily between the Punic Wars', in Smith and Serrati: 115–33.
Sherwin-White, S., and Kuhrt, A. (1993) *From Samarkhand to Sardis: a new approach to the Seleucid Empire*, London.
Shipley, D. G. J. (2018) *The early Hellenistic Peloponnese: politics, economies, and networks 338–197 BC*, Cambridge.
Shrimpton, G. S. (1977) 'Theopompus' treatment of Philip in the *Philippica*', *Phoenix* 31: 123–44.
  (1991) *Theopompus the historian*, Montreal.
Sinclair, T. A. (1987–90) *Eastern Turkey: an architectural and archaeological survey*, 4 vols, London.
Smith, C., and Serrati, J. (eds) (2000) *Sicily from Aeneas to Augustus: new approaches in archaeology and history*, Edinburgh.
Smith, R. R. R. (1988) *Hellenistic royal portraits*, Oxford.
Sommer, M. (2013) 'Scipio Aemilianus, Polybius, and the quest for friendship in second-century Rome', in Gibson and Harrison: 307–18.
Soraci, C. (2016) *La Sicilia romana: secc. III a.C. – V d.C.*, Rome.
Sotiroudis, P. (1989) *Untersuchungen zum Geschichtswerk des Johannes von Antiocheia*, Thessaloniki.
Sprawki, S. (2006) 'Alexander of Pherae: *infelix* tyrant', in S. Lewis, ed., *Ancient tyranny* (Edinburgh), 135–47.
Stadter, P. (2015) '"The love of noble deeds": Plutarch's portrait of Aratus of Sicyon', in R. Ash, J. Mossman and F. B. Titchener, eds, *Fame and infamy: essays for Christopher Pelling on characterization in Greek and Roman biography and historiography* (Oxford), 161–75.
Steinby, C. (2014) *Rome versus Carthage: the war at sea*, Barnsley.

Stern, E. von (1915) 'Kleomenes III. und Archidamos', *Hermes* 50: 554–71.
Stramaglia, A. (2015) 'Temi "sommersi" e trasmissione dei testi nella declamazione antica (con un regesto di papiri declamatorî)', in L. Del Corso, F. De Vivo and A. Stramaglia, eds, *Nel segno del testo: edizioni, materiali e studi per Oronzo Pecere* (Florence), 147–71.
Strobel, K. (1996) *Die Galater: Geschichte und Eigenart der keltischen Staatenbildung auf dem Boden des hellenistischen Kleinasien* I, Berlin.
Strootman, R. (2014) *Courts and elites in the Hellenistic empires: the Near East after the Achaemenids, c. 330 to 30 BCE*, Edinburgh.
—— (2023) 'How Iranian was the Seleucid Empire?', in T. Daryaee, R. Rollinger and M. P. Canepa (eds), *Iran and the transformation of ancient Near Eastern history: the Seleucids (ca. 312–150 BCE)* (Wiesbaden), 11–35.
Stropp, J. W. F. (2023) *Pugna litterarum: Studien zur kompetitiven Geschichtsschreibung in der griechisch-römischen Literaturelite der Kaiserzeit*, Munich.
Sullivan, D. F. (2000) *Siegecraft: two instructional manuals by 'Heron of Byzantium'*, Washington, DC.
Süß, W. (1922) 'Ueber antike Geheimschreibenmethoden und ihr Nachleben', *Philologus* 78: 142–75.
Taylor, M. (2013) *Antiochus the Great*, Barnsley.
Thomas, R. (2019) *Polis histories, collective memories and the Greek world*, Cambridge.
Thonemann, P. (ed.) (2013) *Attalid Asia Minor: money, international relations, and the state*, Oxford.
Thornton, J. (2013*a*) 'Oratory in Polybius' *Histories*', in C. Kremmydas and K. Tempest, eds, *Hellenistic oratory: continuity and change* (Oxford), 20–42.
—— (2013*b*) 'Polybius in context: the political dimension of the *Histories*', in Gibson and Harrison: 213–29.
Todaro, G. (2021) 'Due letture della *defectio* di Taranto: Livio (25, 7–11) e Polibio (8, 24–31)', *La Biblioteca di ClassicoContemporaneo* 12: 207–36.
Torregaray Pagola, E. (2003) 'Estrategias gentilicias y simbolismo geopolítico en la narración polibiana de la conquista de la Península Ibérica', in Santos Yanguas and Torregaray Pagola: 245–78.
Tränkle, H. (1977) *Livius und Polybios*, Basel.
Trinquier, J. (2009) 'Les chasses serviles : aspects économiques et juridiques', in J. Trinquier and Chr. Vendries, eds, *Chasses antiques : pratiques et représentations dans le monde gréco-romain (III<sup>e</sup> siècle av.–IV<sup>e</sup> siècle apr. J.-C.)* (Rennes), 97–117.
Tully, J. (2014) 'Ephorus, Polybius, and τὰ καθόλου γράφειν', in Parmeggiani: 153–95.

Turyn, A. (1964) *Codices Graeci Vaticani saeculis XIII et XIV scripti annorumque notis instructi*, Vatican.
(1972) *Dated Greek manuscripts of the thirteenth and fourteenth centuries in the libraries of Italy*, 2 vols, Urbana.
Tuzi, G. (1891) 'Ricerche chronologiche sulla seconda guerra punica in Sicilia', in G. Beloch, ed., *Studi di Storia Antica* I (Rome), 81–97.
Urban, R. (1979) *Wachstum und Krise des achäischen Bundes: Quellenstudien zur Entwicklung des Bundes von 280 bis 222 v. Chr.* (Historia Einzelschriften 35), Wiesbaden.
Vagalinski, L. F. (ed.) (2010) *In search of Celtic Tylis in Thrace (III C BC)*, Sofia.
Varga, D. (2015) *The Roman wars in Spain: the military confrontation with guerilla warfare*, Barnsley.
Verhasselt, G. (2018) *Felix Jacoby, Die Fragmente der griechischen Historiker continued.* IV B 9: *Dikaiarchos of Messene*, Leiden.
Virgilio, B. (2003) *Lancia, diadema e porpora: il re e la regalità ellenistica*, Pisa.
Vollmer, D. (1990) *Symploke: Das Übergreifen der römischen Expansion auf den griechischen Osten* (Hermes Einzelschriften 54), Stuttgart.
Walbank, F. W. (1933) *Aratos of Sicyon*, Cambridge.
(1957–79) *A historical commentary on Polybius*, 3 vols, Oxford.
(1967) *Philip V of Macedon*, 2nd edn, Hamden, Conn.
Wallace, S. (2017) 'Court, kingship, and royal style in the early Hellenistic period', in Erskine, Llewellyn-Jones and Wallace: 1–30.
Wanlin, N. (2007) 'Remarques sur les problématiques actuelles de la théorie du descriptif : en relisant Philippe Hamon', *Polysèmes* 9: 177–85.
Weaire, G. (2021) 'Revisiting τὰ καθόλου and κατὰ μέρος in Polybius', *CP* 116: 26–44.
Weber, G. (1997) 'Interaktion, Repräsentation und Herrschaft: Der Königshof im Hellenismus', in A. Winterling, ed., *Zwischen 'Haus' und 'Staat': Antike Höfe im Vergleich* (Munich), 27–71.
Weil, R. (1982) *Polybe, Histoires: livres VII–VIII et IX. Texte établi et traduit*, Paris.
Welwei, K.-W. (1963) *Könige und Königtum im Urteil des Polybios*, diss. Köln.
Wenghofer, R., and Houle, D. J. (2016) 'Marriage diplomacy and the political role of royal women in the Seleukid far east', in A. Coşkun and A. McAuley, eds, *Seleukid royal women: creation, representation and distortion of Hellenistic queenship in the Seleukid Empire* (Historia Einzelschriften 240, Stuttgart), 191–207.
West, M. L. (1992) *Ancient Greek music*, Oxford.
Wheeler, E. L. (1988) *Stratagem and the Greek vocabulary of military trickery* (*Mnemosyne* Suppl. 108), Leiden.

(2022) 'Militärschriften', *DNP* Suppl. 12, 699–714.
Whitehead, D. (2016) *Philo Mechanicus:* On sieges. *Translated with introduction and commentary* (Historia Einzelschriften 243), Stuttgart.
(2022) *Isokrates: the forensic speeches (nos. 16–21). Introduction, text, translation and commentary,* 2 vols, Cambridge.
Whitehead, D., and Blyth, P. H. (2004) *Athenaeus Mechanicus,* On machines (Περὶ μηχανημάτων): *translated with introduction and commentary* (Historia Einzelschriften 182), Stuttgart.
Wiater, N. (2016) 'Shifting endings, ambiguity and deferred closure in Polybius' *Histories*', in A. Lianeri, ed., *Knowing future time in and through Greek historiography* (Berlin), 243–65.
(2020) 'From war-guilt to cause: Polybius' *aitia* in context', *Maia* n.s. 72: 491–514.
Widmer, M. (2019) 'Looking for the Seleucid couple', in A. Bielman Sánchez, ed., *Power couples in antiquity: transversal perspectives* (London), 32–41.
Wilamowitz-Moellendorff, U. von (1903) 'Philologie', in P. Hinneberg, ed., *Die Kultur der Gegenwart, ihre Entwickelung und ihre Ziele* (Berlin), I.2.1–29 (preliminary print: volume not actually published).
Wilcken, U. (1901) 'Ein Polybiustext auf Papyrus', *Archiv für Papyrusforschung* 1: 388–95.
Wilkes, J. J. (1969) *Dalmatia,* London.
(1992) *The Illyrians,* Oxford.
Wille, G. (1967) *Musica Romana: Die Bedeutung der Musik im Leben der Römer,* Amsterdam.
Wonder, J. W. (2018) 'The Lucanians', in G. D. Farney and G. Bradley, eds, *The peoples of ancient Italy* (Berlin), 369–84.
Wörrle, M. (1975) 'Antiochos I., Achaios der Ältere und die Galater: Eine neue Inschrift in Denizli', *Chiron* 5: 59–87.
Worthington, I. (2023) *The last kings of Macedonia and the triumph of Rome,* Oxford.
Wuilleumier, P. (1939) *Tarente : des origines à la conquête romaine,* 2 vols, Paris.
Yegül, F. K. (2020) *The temple of Artemis at Sardis,* 2 vols, Cambridge, Mass.
Ziegler, K. (1952) 'Polybios (1)', *RE* XXI.2.1440–578.

# INDEXES

References in the form '§1 a' are to sections of the Introduction, in the form '35.1' to notes in the commentary. The indexes of passages and of Greek words are much more selective for the commentary than for the Introduction.

## 1 PASSAGES

Aelian
  VH 12.30: 27.1
Aeneas Tacticus
  31.2, 3, 30–1: 15.9
Aeschines
  1.189, 192: 9.8
Agatharchides
  FGrHist 86 F6: §7 d n. 36
Alcaeus of Messene
  AP 9.518: §12 f n. 54
  9.519: 8–14b.2
  11.12: 8–14b.2, 12.2
Alexander of Aphrodisias
  Anim. 73.2: 15.6
Alexis
  fr. 2.3 K–A: §13 a
Ammonius
  in An. Pr. 1 CAG IV 30.18–19: 1.5
Anaximenes
  3.1 p. 21.1–3 Fuhrmann: 8.6
Andreas
  FGrHist 571 F1: 4.2, 11
Antiochus
  FGrHist 555 F13: 28.2
Apollodorus
  Poliorc. 178.6 Schneider: 4.6
Apollonius of Citium
  CMG XI.1.1 pp. 38.6–11, 62.3–7: 21.10
Apollonius Rhodius
  1.879, 883: 14.1
  3.744–51: 27.9
  3.1147: 16.12
Appian
  BC 2.349–50: 17.10
  Hann. 133: 24.4
  133–4: 25.9
  133–48: 24–34
  137: 26.3
  137–41: 34.1
  141: 34.12
  141–3: 34.4
  142: 34.3
  143: 34.9
  144: 34.12
  148: 34.1
  150–2: 35–6
  Iber. 54–64: 1.4
  Lib. 279: 36.2
  628–30: 20.10
  Mac. 1.3: §12 e
  Mith. 103: 4.2
  550: 9.2
  Sic. 2.6: §12 d
  3.1: §12 d n. 52
  3.2: §12 d
Archimedes
  Aren. II 258.1–10 Heiberg: 5.3
  Con. I 300.9 Heiberg: 5.2
  Sph. Cyl. pr., Netz et al. (2011) 191 col. ii.8–9 (I 4.18–19 Heiberg): 3a and 1–7
Aristotle
  EN 2.1109a33–5: 36.6
  4.1128a19–20: §1 b n. 3
  4.1128a19–25: 11.8
  8.1160a31–b9: §11 b
  HA 1.491b12–14: §13 a
  Pol. 3.1282a3–4: 7.2
  3.1284b25–34: §11 b
  5.1303a2–6: 24.1
  5.1314b34–5: 18.5
  Rhet. 3.1407b29: 10.2
[Aristotle]
  Prob. 873b18–23: 30.6
Arrian
  FGrHist 156 F9.31: 24.9
Athenaeus Deipnosophistes
  4.166f–167c: 9.5, 9.6, 9.7
  6.260d–261a: 9.5
Athenaeus Mechanicus
  15.2–3, 32.4: 7.2
  26.4: 6.2
  27.7–9: 4.2
  27.10–28.3: 4.9

266

Biton
  Marsden (1971) 72–4: 3a and 1–7

Caesar
  *BG* 6.11.1: 1.1
Callimachus
  *Aet.* fr. 41 Harder: 27.6
  *Ep.* 4.2 Pfeiffer: 28.7
    43.6: 20.2
  *H.* 1.56: 15.6
    3.146–9: 25.7
  fr. 384 Pfeiffer: 15.2
    744: 13.2
Callixenus
  *FGrHist* 627 F2 IIIC.165.30–167.29: 20.8
Catullus
  80.8: 9.9
  96: 12.8
Chrysippus
  *SVF* II 937: 2.2
  III p. 198: 9.9
  III p. 200: 10.4
Cicero
  *Att.* 2.1.3: 11.4
    10.17.1: 19.1
  *Cael.* 39: 10.6
  *Deiot.* 26: 23.5
  *Inv.* 1.2: §14 k n. 81
  *ND* 2.10: 2.1
  *Off.* 3.113: §14 a
  *Rep.* 1.34: §14 a, c
    2.27: §14 a
  *Verr.* 2.3: §12 d
    2.117–19: 7.10
    4.118–19: 3.2
Cleanthes
  *SVF* I 570: 8.1
Coins
  Bedoukian (1983) 74–7: 23
  *CH* 2010.277 no. 74: 15–21
  Gaebler (1935) 186, no. 3: 15–21
    190, no. 16: 15–21
  Manov and Damyanov (2013): 22
  Rutter (2001) 93 nos 824–5: 28.2
  *SC* 952: 19.8
    953.1: 15–21
    955: 15.2
    976: 15–21
Cornutus
  37: 2.2

Cratinus
  fr. 408 K–A: §13 c n. 66

Demetrius
  *De obsidione toleranda* 58–9: 37.9
  *Eloc.* 68: §5 a n. 22
    299: §5 a n. 22
Demosthenes
  *Ol.* 1.20: 9.3
  *Phil.* 3.36: §3 b
    3.37: 11.5
  *Cor.* 169: 27.1
    204: §3 b
    19.299: 21.8
    20.93: 2.3
    23.63: §3 b
[Demosthenes]
  34.36: 2.8
Dinarchus
  fr. 35.1 Conomis: 10.9
Diodorus Siculus
  1.2.1: §5 a
  1.16.1: §5 a
  1.27.3–5: §5 a n. 22
  1.36.1: §5 a n. 22
  1.37.5: §5 b n. 23
  1.56.1: §5 a n. 22
  12.21.1: 9.9
  13.35.5: 8.2
  14.7.3: §11 a n. 45
  14.18.1–8: 3.4
  15.13.5: 3.4, 13–14
  15.67.3: 35.7
  15.71.2: 35.6–8
  15.91: §13 c n. 64
  17.21.7: 21.9
  17.36.2: 20.10
  17.69.4: 20.9
  17.112.6: 13.2
  18.71.3: 5.6
  19.46.1–4: 21.3
  21.17.1–3: 10.12
  26.15.1–2: §12 d
  31.18.1–3: 19.8
  31.26.5: §7 a n. 34
Diomedes
  *GLK* I 486.33, 487.3: 37.2
Dionysius of Halicarnassus
  *AR* 1.2.1: 2.11
  1.6.1: §14 b
  1.7.1: §14 b
  1.16.4: §13 c n. 64

Dionysius (cont.)
  1.46–7: §5 a
  1.74.1: §14 b
  1.81.6: 21.8
  19.8: 24.1
  Comp. 4.14–15: §14 b
  Dem. 21.3: 10.1
  Pomp. 2.1: 9.5
  Thuc. 11: 9.5
  Vet. Or. 1.2–2.2: §14 b
Dionysius Periegetes
  398: 1.5
Duris
  FGrHist 76 F7: §5 a
  F10: §5 a

Ennius
  Ann. 288 Skutsch: 37.9
  401, 402, 403: §6 a n. 26
Ephorus
  FGrHist 70 F96: §5 a
  F191.37: §1 c n. 9
Epictetus
  4.2.2: 30.12
  4.3.2: 11.8
Epicurus
  Hdt. 76: §13 a
  Pyth. 113: §13 a

Frontinus
  Strat. 3.3.6: 24.7, 25.5, 9
Fronto
  Caes. 2.11.2: 8.6

Galen
  Meth. Med. 6 x 392.16–393.2 Kühn: 12.3
[Galen]
  Ur. Hipp. Gal. xviiia 616 Kühn: 26.5
Gellius, Aulus 19.9.7: §7 b
Gorgias
  B6 DK, D28 Laks–Most: 9.9
  B11a.7 DK, D25.7 Laks–Most (Pal.): 16.2, 18.9
  Hel. 2: 9.12

Hecataeus
  FGrHist 1 F301: §3 d n. 16
Heraclides
  FGrHist 1108 F1–2: 3a and 1–7
Heraclitus
  B 42 DK, D21 Laks–Most: 6.6
Heraclitus of Lesbos

  FGrHist 167 T1–2: 8.2
Hermogenes
  Prog. 27.3: 2.3
Hero
  Bel. 88.1–9: 5.10
Herodian
  Epimer. p. 76.4 Boissonade: 9.13
Herodotus
  1.32.1, 8: 21.11
  1.33: 21.11
  1.84.1–4: 15–21
  1.86.1–88.1: 15–21
  1.86.5–6: 21.11
  1.88.1: 21.1
  1.119.2: 29.11
  2.5.1: §3 d n. 16
  2.143.1–4: §3 d
  3.83.1: 16.5
  7.137.1: §1 c n. 9
  7.141.3–144: 28.7
  9.112: 21.3
Hesychius
  ε 3502 Latte: 27.3
Hippocrates
  Epid. 7.1.3: §13 c n. 65
Historians, anonymous
  FGrHist 148 fr. 44: §5 d n. 25
  FGrHist 154–5: 10.11
  FGrHist 156 F1–11: 10.11
  FGrHist 160 F1 col. ii.5: 21.9
    col. ii.12–13: §11 a n. 45
  FGrHist 255 col. v 18–23: §10 a n. 44
    col. vi 15–16: §6 d n. 28
  P. Berol. inv. 11632: §13 a n. 62, §13 c n. 64
  P. Köln vi 247 col. i.24–8: §6 b n. 27
    col. ii.28–30: §11 b n. 48
Homer
  Il. 1.534: 16.12
  2.1–7: 27.9
  6.405–6: 19.7
  10.1–16: 20.8
  19.242: 34.11
  22.447–8: 21.4
  22.460: 21.4
  24.2–13: 20.8
  24.200: 19.7
  24.507–15: 20.9
  Od. 4.244–51: 19.9
  13.439: 16.12
  15.400: 12.8
Horace
  Odes 4.2.37–8: 9.1

Inscriptions
Adak and Thonemann (2022): §13
  c n. 64
*BCH* 59 (1935), 66.16: 12.6
Behistun inscription Old Persian
  col. ii.71–8: 21.3
*CIL* I². 608: 3a and 1–7
  I².615–16: 3a and 1–7
*F.Delphes* III.1.303.10: 25.2
  III.4.283 col. E.6, 10: 16.7
Hatzopoulos (1996) ii no. 79.4:
  8–14b.2
Heisserer (1988) 121 A.17–18:
  20.3
*I.Adramytteion* 34.6–8: 9.6
*I.Délos* 500 A.31: 20.3
  1520.8–10: 10.2
*I.Egypte prose* 49.34: §13 c
*I.Erythrai* I.122.20–1: 1.4
*I.Iasos* I.2.6, 30–1: 25.1–2
  II.612.19–20: 14.11
*I.Kibyra* I.362 b.4: 10.4
*I.Kyme* 41: §5 a n. 22
*I.Lindos* I.2 B.23–8: 3.3
  I.2 D.114–15: 14.3
*I.Magnesia* 46.13–14: 8.5
*I.Milet* 306.5: 24.8
*I.Miletupolis* 2.12: 16.7
*I.Olympia* 52: §5 b n. 23
*I.Pessinous* 1–2.7: §13 c
*I.Portes du désert* 32.3–4: 25.11
*I.Priene* B–M 108.23, 51: 19.6
*I.Ptolemaic* 563.1: 29.6
*I.Sardis* II 307.5–6: 15–21
  309.6–10: 15–21, 18.4
*I.Stratonikeia* I.256.10: 37.2
  III.1441.2: 22.1
*IG* I³.113.17: 15.9
  I³.78 a.33: 16.10
  II².1023.4–7: 37.7
  II².1627.333–4: 5.6
  II².1628.493–4: 5.6
  II².1668: 5.1
  II².1672.31–2: 29.5
  II².1939.14: 21.9
  IV.1².95 col. ii.50: 24.4
  IV².622: 12.8
  VII.188.10: 2.8
  VII.2712.33: 14.10
  IX.1².2.241: §12 f
  IX.1².248.6–15: 10.10
  IX.2.517.3–9, 25–39: §12 f
  IX.2.517.29–34: §6 d n. 29
  X.2.2.357: 14.b.1
  XI.4.649.3–4: 15.2
  XII.3.91.3: 12.5
  XII.5.1.14: §5 a n. 22
  XII.5.2.824.34: 21.3
*IGR* IV.292.20: 12.8
*ILLRP* 376.1, 3: 1.7
*IMT* Kaikos 830.26: 1.2
*IOSPE* I².32 A.85–6: 18.3
  I².352 col. i.15–16: 21.10
Lauter (2002): §7 a
Ma (1999) 289 lines 29–30: 20.11
Magnetto (2024): §8 b n. 41
Michel, *Recueil* no. 542.11: 33.10
Moretti, *ISE* I.47.2: §12 f
  I.55.2: 19.1
  I.59.10–11: 35.1
  II.77.4: 33.9
  II.106.2: 15.4
  II.114.A col. iii.3–4: 21.1
  II.114.A col. iii.4: 9.13
  II.114.A col. iii.5–7: 25.10
  II.114.B col. i.14: 7.5
*OGIS* I.56.60: 24.4
Raphia decree, hieroglyphics,
  Gauthier and Sottas (1925) 8
  line 10: 19.4
*SEG* XII.87.14–15: 21.2
  XVI.255.3: 8.7
  XXIV.154.13–14: 15.5
  XXXIV.558.59–60: 16.11
  XXXVII.859 A.3: 23.3
  XLIX.855 B.2–3, 8–12: 13.6
Sherk, *RDGE* 18.45: 15.9
*Syll.*³ 1.283: 8–14b.2
  1.527: 36.2
  II.559.24–5: 25.3
  II.567.11–12: 32.6
*TAM* II.247.1: 12.8
  III.7.11–12: 19.7
  IV(1).7.6: 16.1
  IV(1).256.1, 4: 16.1
  V.1.514.10–12: 19.1
*Tit. Camirenses* 110.28: 21.9
Welles, *RC* 31.17–18: §13 c n. 65
  31.26: 31.6
  44.7–8: 35.8
  45 decree 15–16: 24.8
  66.11: 15.9
Isocrates
  *Antid.* 104: 1.1
  *Call.* 27: 9.6
  *Evag.* 2: 12.8

Isocrates (cont.)
   Paneg. 111: 9.9
   Phil. 137: 9.1

Jerome
   Dan. 3.11.10: §12 g n. 59
John of Antioch
   fr. 53 FHG IV 557: 23
Josephus
   BJ 4.214: 15.2
   4.235: 6.7
Justin
   Ep. Trog. 16.1.12: 8–14b.2

Libanius
   Or. 56.6: §1 b n. 3
   Hypoth. Dem. Cor. 6: 2.6
Livy 21.29.7–38.9: §14 a
   22.4, 7, 12: §11 a n. 45
   22.61.12–13: 24–34
   23.7.5: 24.1
   23.10.1: 31.3
   23.10.7: 31.1
   23.17.6: 14.6
   23.31.12–13: 1.4
   23.40–41.7: 1.3
   24.6.4, 6: §12 d n. 52
   24.8: §11 a n. 45
   24.8.14: §12 d
   24.10.3–5: 3.1
   24.10.4: 1.5
   24.13.2–3: 24.10
   24.20.12–13: 24–34
   24.20.12–15: 24.10
   24.21.1: §12 d, 3.1
   24.21.1–33.8: §14 f
   24.21.2–33.9: §12 d
   24.21.6, 11: §11 a n. 45
   24.27.1–4: 37.2
   24.27.6–33.8: 3.1
   24.29.4–5, 10: §12 d
   24.30.1: §12 d, 1.4
   24.32.9: 3.1, 37.2
   24.34.3: 3.4
   24.34.6–7: 3a and 1–7, 4.2, 11
   24.34.8: §14 a
   24.34.9–10: 5.5, 6
   24.34.13: 3a and 1–7
   24.35.1, 3: 7.12
   24.35.8: 7.12
   24.36.1: 7.12
   24.40.1–17: §12 e
   24.44.5: 1.5

   24.49.7–8: 1.2
   25.1.1: 26.1
   25.2.3: 7.6
   25.3–4: §11 a n. 45
   25.7.1–7: §12 d
   25.7.10–8.2: §12 c
   25.8.1: 24.3
   25.8.3: 26.4
   25.8.4: 25.4
   25.8.4–6: 24.4
   25.8.5: 24.5
   25.8.6: 24.7, 9, 10
   25.8.8: 25.1–2
   25.8.11: 25.5
   25.9.2: 26.5
   25.9.8: 24.7
   25.9.9: 25.7, 8, 29.3
   25.9.10: 28.6
   25.9.13: 29.6
   25.9.14: 29.7, 8
   25.9.17: 30.3
   25.10.4: 30.7, 11
   25.10.5: 30.12
   25.10.6: 31.1
   25.10.8: 31.2, 3
   25.10.9: 31.4, 5
   25.10.10: 31.6, 32.1
   25.11.1: 32.2
   25.11.3: 32.4
   25.11.5: 32.6
   25.11.7: 33.3, 4
   25.11.8: 34.13
   25.11.10: 29.2, 34.1
   25.11.11: 34.4
   25.11.15: 34.6
   25.11.16–18: 34.9
   25.11.18–19: 34.11
   25.11.20: 24–34, 26.1
   25.15.5–7: 34.1
   25.15.7: 24–34, 24.3
   25.15.20–17.7: 35–6
   25.16.6: 35–6
   25.17.1: 35–6
   25.23.10–12: 37.1
   25.23.12: 37.2
   25.23.14: 37.1, 2
   25.23.17: 37.8
   25.24.3, 7: 37.11
   25.24.6: 37.12
   25.24.8–10: §11 a n. 45
   25.24.12: 37.13
   25.32.2: §12 d
   26.1.12: 1.5

27.21.8: 24–34
27.25.3–5: 30.6
27.30.12: 14.10
27.31.8: 12.1
27.4.1: 7.6
27.4.10: 20.9
28.12.2–5: §14 k n. 81
30.45.5: §14 a
31.1.5: 9.13
32.21.4: 12.1
32.21.23: 8–14b.2
33.10.10: §14 a
35.16.3, 8: 24–34
39.52.1–6: §14 a n. 68
43.18.5: 14b.2
45.32.5: 19.8
*Per.* 15: 24–34
*Per.* 17: 35–9
Lucian
   *Dial. Mar.* 4.3: 21.1
Lucretius
   1.935–50: §4 b n. 21
Lycurgus
   17: 30.6

Martial
   2.86.7: 4.8
Menander
   *Epitr.* 169–71: 27.4
   *Sic.* 343.60: 17.7
   fr. 183 K-A: 36.6
   fr. 387 K-A: 9.11
   fr. 504 K-A: §13 c n. 66
Moschion
   *FGrHist* 575 F1.4.3: 3a and 1–7

Nepos
   *Epam.* 8.3: 35.6
   *Pel.* 5.1: 35.6–8
   *Reg.* 3.1: 10.10
Nicander
   *Al.* 402: 19.2
   *Ther.* 902–6: 28.2

Old Testament
   2 Samuel 4:12: 21.3
Ovid
   *Ib.* 299–300: 21.3
   *Met.* 1.383–94: 28.7

Papyri
   *BGU* IV 1204.4–5: 16.11
   Bechtel *et al.* (1913) 101: 25.2

P. Berol. inv. 9570 + P. Ryl. I 60:
   §14 c
P. Berol. inv. 9775: 21.11
   11632: §13 a n. 62
   21129 fr. 2: §14 c
P. Cair. Zen. II 59201.2: 16.7
   III 59499.73–4: 16.5
P. Hal. 1 col. viii.166–70: 31.6
P. Hamb. 91 *recto* 8: §13 c n. 65
P. Köln VI 247 col. i.24–8: §6
   b n. 27
   VI 247 col. ii.28–30: §11 b n. 48
P. Lille I 15.2: §13 c
P. Lond. I 44.25: 19.7
   VII 2067.15–16: 27.6
   VII 2191.37–45: 33.6
P. Oxy. I 12 col. vi 15–16: §6 d n. 28
   XV 1798: §5 d n. 25
   LXXI 4808: §14 c, §14 g n. 77
   LXXXI 5267: §14 c
   LXXXII 5300: §14 c
   LXXXVI 5535: 8–14b.2, 10.10, 11
PSI IV 377. 9: §13 c n. 65
   V 502.26: 15.6
   V 524.3–4: §13 c
P. Tebt. I 5.153: 5.6
   III.1 703.236: 8.8
   III.1 703.256–7: 24.9
   *SB* X 10272.8–9: 15.3
Pausanias
   2.9.4: 12.2
   4.29.1–5: 8–14b.2
   8.30.8: §8 a n. 40
Persius
   3.88–99: 12.4
Philemon
   fr. 77.3 K-A: 11.5
Philistus
   *FGrHist* 556 F51–6: 3a and 1–7
Philo of Alexandria
   *Vit. Mos.* 2.235: 8.4
Philo Mechanicus
   *Bel.* 50.14–51.7: §3 c n. 14
      50.25–6: §5 c n. 24
   *Pol.* C11: 5.9
      D2–4: 37.2, 4
Philo of Tarsus
   *SH* 690.7–8: 12.5
Philodemus
   *Poet.* 5 col. xviii.3: 27.5
   *Sign.* col. vii.5–xix.11: §3 d
Photius
   *Bibl.* 83.64b–65a: §14 b

Phylarchus
   *FGrHist* 81 F24: §5 a, 16.6
   F51: 35.3–5
Pindar
   *Pyth.* 9.68: 15.6
Plato
   *Laws* 1.637b3–5: 25.11
   2.674a3–7: 26.6
   *Polit.* 301b5–7: §11 b
   302e10–303b5: §11 b
   *Prot.* 322c6–7: 33.3
   *Rep.* 1.332c5–8: 11.7
   3.416d9: 9.8
   6.503b2: 17.10
Plautus
   *Poen.* 1106–10: 17.7
Pliny
   *NH* 6.26: 23.1
Plutarch
   *Aem.* 23.10: 19.5
   *Ag. Cl.* 22.1: 35.3–5
   *Alex.* 21.2: 20.9
   67.4: 6.6
   70.1–2: 9.4
   *Arat.* 24.5: 12.7
   49.1–2: 12.1
   49.3–5: §12 f, 8–14b.2
   51.2: 12.1
   51.2–3: 8–14b.2
   52.3: 12.2
   52.4: 12.5
   53: 12.8
   53.1: 12.7
   *Brut.* 4.8: §13 a n. 68, 21.11
   *Cam.* 34.2: 17.10
   *Demetr.* 34.4–7: 17.11
   44.9: 19.8
   *Dion* 14.7: 30.6
   *Fab.* 23.3–4: 30.6, 34.5
   *Lyc.* 27.1: 28.6
   *Lys.* 20.2: 19.5
   *Marc.* 13.2: 3a and 1–7
   14.7–15: 3a and 1–7
   15.4: §14 d
   15.5: 3a and 1–7, 4.2
   15.6: §14 d
   15.8: 5.4, 5
   15.9: 5.2, 6
   17.1: 6.6
   18.1: 7.12
   18.3–4: 37.1
   19.1: 37.11
   *Pel.* 7–11: 24–34

   10.1–10: 27.1
   27.6: 35.6–8
   *Pyrrh.* 13.3–13: 24.1
   34.8: 20.10
   *Gen. Soc.* 594d: 27.1
   595f–596c: 27.1
   596a: 27.4
   *Praec. ger. reip.* 814c–d: §14 d
   *Quaest. conv.* 4 *pr.* 659e–f: §14 d
   *Sen. Rep.* 791e: 11.5
   [Plutarch] *Apophth. Lac.* 238d: 28.6
Polyaenus 6.16.5: 35.9
Polybius
   1.1.5: 2.3, 4
   1.3.1: §1 c
   1.3.1–2: §12 a
   1.3.2: §1 c n. 6
   1.3.4: §6 a
   1.3.6: 2.6
   1.3.10: §1 b, 2.4
   1.4.2–4: 2.2
   1.4.4: §4 b
   1.4.6: §3 b n. 11, 2.2
   1.4.7–8, 11: §4 b
   1.5.1: §1 c n. 6
   1.5.5: §1 b
   1.8.3: 23.1
   1.14.1–3, 5: §7 d
   1.14.7: §7 e, 8.7, 8–14b.2
   1.14.7–8: §7 d
   1.15.1–12: §7 d
   1.19.3: 14.1
   1.21.4–22.1: 35.9
   1.22.3: 4.3
   1.22.11: 5.1
   1.32.2: 15.2
   1.34.1: 25.11
   1.35.4: 2.1
   1.35.4–5: 3.3
   1.35.5: 7.7
   1.37.5–10: §7 d
   1.40.3: 32.5
   1.46.9: 4.2
   1.48.9: 24.13
   1.57.6: 1.2
   1.63.9: 2.6
   1.64.5: 1.1
   1.71.7: 3.3
   1.80.13: 21.3
   1.85.7: 4.11
   2.1.7: 35.8
   2.2.1, 2: §6 d
   2.4.5: 21.11

# INDEXES

2.4.8: §7 d
2.7.1: 12.6, 36.4
2.7.1–3: 35–6
2.7.3: 8.9
2.8.12: §7 d
2.12.3: 13–14
2.12.7: §6 d, 1.6
2.14.2: §1 c
2.14.4–17.2: §1 c
2.23.5, 7: 30.12
2.24.1–17: §12 c
2.27.5: 37.3
2.33.2–6: §1 a
2.33.7: 14.5
2.35.3: 8.1
2.37.9: §11 b
2.38.6: §11 b
2.40.4: §8 b
2.41.11: §6 d n. 28
2.41.12: §8 e
2.43.1–5: 12.7
2.47.1–6, 11: 12
2.47.11: §8 b
2.52.5: 1.3
2.54.13: 14.10
2.55.1–63.6: §1 b
2.56–63: §8 b
2.56.2: §8 b
2.56.7: §1 b, §4 a n. 20
2.56.10–12: §1 b
2.61.11: §1 b
2.71.8: 1.5
3.1.4: §6 b n. 27
3.2.6: §1 c, 2.6
3.3.7: §6 a
3.4.2, 4–13: §6 a
3.5.7–8: §6 a n. 26
3.5.8–9: 11.3
3.5.9: 1.4
3.6.1–2: §7 b
3.6.14: §6 d n. 28
3.8.9–10: §7 b, 11.7
3.9.5: §1 b, §7 b
3.9.6–12.7: §12 b
3.10.1–6: §7 b
3.13.1: §12 b
3.15.9: §12 b
3.15.13: §12 c
3.16.6: §12 c
3.18.1–19.13: §12 e
3.19.11: §12 f
3.20.4: 11.6
3.20.5: 24–34

3.22: §5 a
3.22–7: §8 e
3.22.3: §8 e
3.23.2: 20.10
3.24–5: §5 a
3.26.1–2, 4: §8 e
3.27.3: §8 e
3.27.7–8: §12 b
3.28.5: §8 e
3.29: §8 e
3.29.4: §8 e
3.33.17–18: §8 e
3.34.2–3: 36.3
3.39.4: 1.5
3.47.6: 2.3
3.47.6–48.12: §3 d
3.48.10–12: §8 f
3.59.1–8: §6 b n. 27
3.61.5: 3.3
3.75.4: 24–34
3.77.4, 6: 31.2
3.77.6: §11 b
3.81: §2 b
3.82: §2 b
3.90.2: 1.7
3.97.2–4: 1–2
3.98.2: 15.1
3.107.2: 15.2
3.108.5: 35–6
3.116.1, 9: 14.8
3.116.8: 14.5
3.118.2–3: §12 c
3.118.3, 5: 24–34
3.118.4: §12 b, c
4.2.1: 12
4.2.4: §12 a
4.2.4–6: 15–21
4.2.4–11: §12 a
4.2.6: 15–21
4.4.6: 12.5
4.5.11: 10.12
4.6.4: 12.2
4.8.1, 5: §7 e
4.8.7: §7 e
4.8.10: §7 e
4.8.11: 16.5
4.8.12: §7 e
4.20.1–21.12: §1 c
4.21.10–11: §7 a
4.27.10: 10.10, 23.5
4.28.1–6: §1 c
4.28.2: §6 c
4.28.3, 5: §6 b

Polybius (cont.)
4.28.6: §1 b n. 3
4.31–3: 35–6
4.32.9, 10: §7 a
4.38.11–45.8: §1 c
4.45.1: 22.2
4.45.1–8: 22
4.46.3–4: 22
4.48.6, 7, 9–11, 12: §12 g
4.48.9–12: 15–21
4.48.10–12: 20.11
4.48.12: 21.6
4.50.10–51.6: 15.9
4.51.1–7: 15–21
4.51.3: §12 g
4.51.4: 20.11
4.51.6: 15–21
4.52.1–3: 22, 22.1
4.58.4: 12.2
4.63.2: 23.2
4.67.4: §7 d
4.75.5: 15.6
4.77.3: 13.3, 34.10
4.77.4: 11.1
4.79.3: 12.5
4.82.1: 26.1
4.87.1: 12.2
5.9.9: §11 b
5.10: 8–14b.2
5.11.2: 10.5
5.18.10: 21.1
5.22.2: 33.8
5.31.4: §6 b n. 27
5.31.4–5: §1 c, §6 c
5.31.8–57.8: §1 c
5.33.1, 2, 5: 2.11
5.33.1–2: 2.2
5.33.1–8: 1.4
5.33.2, 3: §3 a, 8–14b.2, 19.4
5.33.5: §3 a
5.34.8: 1.7
5.34.10: 15.2
5.37.1: 15.1
5.37.1–6: 35.3–5
5.37.3: 16.11, 35.3
5.39.6: 22.1
5.40.5–6, 7: §12 g
5.41.1: §12 g, 15–21
5.42.7–9: §12 g, 15–21
5.43.8–44.11: §1 c
5.48.7–9: §1 a
5.50.12: 29.5
5.54.3: 20.7
5.54.6–7, 10–11: 21.3
5.56.6–14: 26.1
5.57.1: 15.2
5.57.1–2: §12 g
5.57.3–8: §12 g, 15–21
5.63.1: 15.2
5.67.12–13: §12 g, 15–21
5.68.5: 15.1
5.72.2: 38b.2
5.74.4–5: 20.11
5.76.11: 33.9
5.77.1: §12 g
5.77.2–78.6: §12 g
5.81.5: 20.8
5.86.10–11: 17.11
5.87.3: 16.2
5.88–90: §1 c
5.91.1: §1 c
5.98.1–3: §3 c
5.98.2: 36.1
5.101.8–102.1: 13.1
5.101.9–102.1: §6 b
5.104.7: §12 e
5.105.6, 9: 11.3
5.105.8: 1.5
5.107.1–3: §6 e
5.107.4: §12 g
5.108.1–3: 13–14
5.108.4–5: §12 e
5.109.1–110.11: §12 e
5.110.10: 13–14
6.3.9: §11 b
6.4.2: §11 b
6.4.7–8: §11 b
6.6.12: 8.1
6.9.4–9: 24.1
6.11.3–8: §7 b
6.18.2: 2.7
6.18.5: 24.1
6.34.7–12: 25.2, 10
6.39.5: 37.3
6.45.1: §3 a, §4 b, 9.1
6.50.3: 2.6
6.54.2: §5 d
6.56.7: 3a
6.57.9: §11 b, 35.6
7.2.1–5.8: §12 d, 3a
7.3.4: §12 d n. 52
7.4.4: 23.3
7.5.1–7: §12 d n. 52
7.5.11: 17.1
7.7.1–2: 3a and 1–7
7.7.1–6: §8 a

7.8.1–9: §10 a n. 44
7.8.7: 10.9
7.9: §12 e
7.9.3: 11.3
7.9.6, 7: 30.1
7.9.9–15: §12 b
7.9.13: 13–14
7.11: §10 a, §14 f, 8.2
7.11–13: 8–14b.2
7.11–14: §10 a
7.12.3: 6.6
7.12.9: §12 f
7.12.10: 8.1
7.13–14: §10 a
7.13.2–7: 12
7.13.6: 8.2
7.13.6–7: §12 f
7.13.7: 8–14b.2
7.14.2–3: §12 f
7.15.1, 16.1: 24.11
7.15.2: 13.9, 15.1
7.15.2–11: 15–21
7.15.2–16.2: 16.4
7.15.6: 15–21, 15.5
7.15–18: §10 a
7.16.3: 17.9
7.17.4: 21.4
7.17.7–8: 20.3
7.18.1: 20.3
9.1.2, 5: §4 b
9.1.4: 33.9
9.2.1–3: §8 a n. 40
9.2.3–7: §1 c n. 8
9.2.4–6: §3 c
9.4.7: 7.11
9.8.1, 2–13: §7 c
9.9.1–9: §7 c
9.9.2–5: 34.2
9.9.5: 34.10
9.10.11: 2.6
9.11: 23
9.12–20: §3 c, 24–34
9.14.5: 12.6
9.19.5–9: §3 c
9.19.7: 4.4
9.20.3: 5.3
9.20.4: §3 c, 3a and 1–7
9.22.1–6: §6 b, 24–34
9.22.6: 7.7
9.22.9–10: §1 a, §2 a
9.22.10: §7 e
9.23.4: §7 e
9.23.5–8: §7 e

9.24.3–7: §2 a
9.24.7: 7.6
9.26a.1: 3a
9.27.3: 13.3
9.30.2: 8–14b.2
9.30.6: 12.1
9.44.2: 2.2
10.1.1–10: §12 c
10.1.9: 24–34
10.3.2: §8 c
10.5.3: 30.4
10.12.8–9: 32.6
10.15.1–2: 37.9
10.15.4–5: 32.4
10.17.1: 3a
10.18.7: 20.9
10.19.3–7: 9.2
10.21.8: §7 d n. 37
10.26.7–10: 11.1, 2
10.32.4: 14.7, 8
10.40.7: §6 b
10.43–7: §3 c
10.43.1–2: §3 c
10.44.1: §3 c
10.45.1: §3 c
10.47.12: §1 c
10.47.12–13: §3 c
11.1a: §6 e
11.5.9: §6 d
11.6.1–2, 3: §6 d
11.11.1: 17.3
11.18.4: 29.8
11.19.1–6: §7 c
11.19.3: §5 c, §14 k n. 81
11.19.6: §6 b
11.19.6–7: §12 b
11.34.1–10: §12 g n. 60
11.34.3: §11 b
11.34.9: §11 b, 15–21, 23.5
11.34.10: 23.5
12.4a.1–6: §3 d
12.6a.1: 9.5
12.9.2–3: §8 e
12.10.3–5, 7–9: §8 e
12.13.1–2: §3 d
12.13.3: 11.8
12.15: 10.12
12.15.1: 11.3
12.15.8: 12.6
12.15.10: 10.12
12.23.1–7: §8 a
12.23.7: §3a
12.25b.4: §5 c, 13.3

Polybius (*cont.*)
12.25f.4–5: §8 a
12.25g.2: §8 a
12.25h.3: §8 a
12.25i.5: §3 b n. 12
12.25k.8–11: §3 b
12.26.9: §3 b
12.26b.5: §3 b
12.26c: §3 b n. 12
12.26d.6: §5 c
12.27.1–4: §8 b
12.27.3: §8 d
12.27.3–6: §1 a
12.27.5: §8 a
12.28–28a: §3 d
12.28.5: §8 a
12.28.6: §8 a, 19.2
12.28.8: 9.5
12.28.10: §4 b, 9.5
12.28a.3–4: §8 d
12.28a.5: §8 d
12.28a.6: §3 b
12.28a.7: §8 e n. 43
12.28a.8, 9: §8 c
12.28a.10: §8 d
14.1a.1, 5: §6 e
14.4.9: 37.9
14.5.13: 32.4
14.12.1–5: §6 e
15.2.4, 12: 15.2
15.9.2–5: §6 b
15.10.2: §6 b
15.16.1–6: §7 c
15.16.6: 2.6
15.20.5: 21.10
15.24.4: §11 b
15.25.6: 16.2
15.25.9: 30.5
15.25.10: 21.6
15.27.7–28.4: §1 a
15.27.9, 10–11: §4 a
15.28.1: 20.9
15.28.4–6: §4 a
15.30.8: §4 a
15.31.13: §4 a
15.33.7–8, 12: §4 a
15.34–5: §4 a
15.34.2: 20.10
16.3.10: §6 b n. 27
16.14.5–10: §3 d
16.17.9, 10: §4 b
16.17.9–11: §3 d
16.18.3: 10.12
16.20.1: §8 a

16.20.5–7: §3 d
16.22a.5: 14.11
16.28.1–2, 9: 29.1
16.28.3–7: 11.2
16.28.3–8: 8–14b.2
16.28.4–7: §7 e
18.13–15: §2 a
18.14.1: §2 a, 21.10
18.24.8: 13.6
18.27.7: 6.7
18.40.3: 2.8
18.41: 21.10
18.45.12: 20.12
18.46.4: 21.5
18.46.5, 15: 25.1–2
20.9.4: 19.4
21.27.4: 5.9
21.34.10: 19.8
21.37.1–2: 25.11
21.38: 15–21
22.12.7: 16.3
22.20.4–7: §1 a
23.5.7: 27.5
23.14.12: §7 a n. 33
25.2.11: 23.5
25.2.15: 6.7
26.1a.1: 15.2
28.9.5–6: §3 b
28.14.1–4: 16.5
28.16.9: §6 c
28.19.2: 21.3
29.9.2–13: §3 b
29.20.1: 21.11
29.21.2–6: 8–14b.2
29.24.6–9: §3 b
29.26.2: 25.6
30.9.5: 11.7
31.2.7: 20.10
31.11–15: §7 a, 24–34
31.19.1: 23.1
31.22.8–10: §7 b
31.23.6–25.1: §7 a
31.23.9: §13 a
31.23.11: §3 b
31.24.3: §13 a, 25.6
31.24.5–8: §3 b
32.3.11: 20.10
33.16.4–5: 15.1
33.19.1: 9.4
36.3.9–4.4: §7 b n. 35
36.9.1–17: §7 b
36.9.13, 14–17: §7 b n. 35
36.11.2: §7 c
36.12.1–5: §7 a n. 34

36.12.2: §5 b
36.15.1–2: 19.7
36.15.7: 6.2
36.16.1–10: 21.10
38.1.1–3.13: §7 a
38.1.2–9: §7 c
38.1.5: §7 b n. 35
38.1.6: §5 d
38.1.7: §7 c
38.5.2: 11.3
38.5.4–6.6: §6 d
38.6.4: 30.9
38.18.7: §7 d
38.20.3: 21.11
38, new fragment: §1 b n. 3
38, new fragment: §7 b n. 35
39.2: §7 c
39.2.1: §1 b
39.5.2–3: §7 a
39.8.1: §7 a
39.8.6: §6 c
fr. 54 Olson: 6.2
fr. 204: 29.8
fr. 223: 20.4
fr. 231: 23.3
Polycrates
  FGrHist 588 F1: 28.2
Proclus
  in Eucl. 68.17–20 Friedlein: 7.8
  in Remp. 1.12: 11.5
Ptolemy
  Synt. 7 (I 2.92.16 Heiberg): 13.4

Quintilian
  Inst. 9.2.6–16: §3 b n. 13
    10.1.123: 19.2

Satyrus
  F25 Schorn: 9.2
Scholia in Aeschinem
  2.51: 11.7
Scholia in Pindarum
  Pyth. 1.58: 21.5
Sculpture
  Parthenon metope S10: 9.13
  Trajan's Column, Scene VIII: 30.7
Scylax
  FGrHist 709 T1: §14 b n. 69
Seneca
  Ep. 53.5–6: 12.4
    85.24: 27.5
    120.22: §7 e n. 38
Septuagint
  Tobit 5.6 Hanhart: 15.4

Sextus Empiricus
  Math. 7.22: 2.10
    7.30: 36.2
    8.108: 16.4
Silius Italicus
  12.473–82: 35–6
Simonides
  fr. 11 + 13.29 Sider: 33.8
Solinus
  5.1: §12 d
Sophocles
  Trach. 540–2: 12.5
Sosylus
  FGrHist 176 F1.31: §13 c
Stephanus of Byzantium
  λ 79 Billerbeck: 13.1
  μ 222: §14 e n. 73
Strabo
  1.1.1 (I 2.2–3bis Radt): §14 b
  2.4.2–3 (I 254.35–258.26 Radt):
    §14 b
  6.3.1 (II 200.3–4 Radt): 34.3
  6.3.1 (II 200.5–7 Radt): 34.10
  6.3.1 (II 202.13–14 Radt): 32.1
  6.3.4 (II 208.1–2 Radt): 24–34
  6.3.4 (II 208.18–20 Radt): 24.1
  7.5.7 (II 304.3 Radt): 13.2
  7.5.8 (II 306.1 Radt): 13.1
  8.6.23 (II 520.7–8 Radt): §1 b
  11.14.5 (III 390.21–5 Radt), 15 (III
    398.30–2): 23
Straton
  FGrHist 168 T1: 8.2
Suda
  τ 572: 21.5
Suetonius
  Tib. 73.2: 12.3
  Claud. 41.2: 11.5
SVF
  III 262.27–8: 11.4
  III 390: 17.2
  III pp. 199–200: 9.6

Tacitus
  Agr. 46.1: 12.8
  Hist. 1.1.4: 8.8
  Ann. 1.9.3–10.7: §7 b
    4.32.1, 2: §4 b
Theocritus
  14.47: 25.9
Theognis
  295: 3a
  785: 33.8
Theophrastus HP 8.10.1: §13 a

Theopompus
  FGrHist 115 F27: 9.1
  F30a: 16.1
  F96a: 21.3
  F100: 27.1
  F122a: 10.6
  F171: §5 a n. 22
  F224: 9.6, 9.7
  F225a: 9.6–13
  F225b.2.28–35: 8–14b.2
  F233: 27.1
  F248: §5 a n. 22
  F250–4: 8–14b.2
  F255–7: 8.6
  F282: 9.4
  F283b: 9.4
  F291: 9.1
  F409: 36.2
  T2: 8–14b.2
  T7: 8–14b.2
  T13–14: 11.3
  T17: 9.1
  T20a: 8–14b.2
  T48: 8.6
Thucydides
  1.97.2: §3 d
  3.15.1: 34.10
  3.22.1: 17.9
  4.25.4: 6.2
  5.26: §6 a n. 26
  5.75.3: 10.5
  6.51.1: 37.11

7.42.4: 37.13
7.65.1–2: 6.2
7.84.3: 14.6
Tibullus
  1.4.79–80: 27.6
Timaeus
  FGrHist 566 F117: 8–14b.2
  F151–8: 8–14b.2
  F158: §5 a n. 22
  T11, 16, 17, 25–7: §3 d n. 17
Timotheus 791.189: 18.10

Vases
  Beazley Archive 21370: 6.6
    213983: 19.7
Vegetius
  4.21.4: 4.11
Virgil
  G. 2.167–72: 9.1
    3.42–3: 18.10
  Aen. 1.685: 29.11
Vitruvius
  1 pr. 1–2: 17.1

Xenophon
  Anab. 4.3.26: §13 c n. 66
  Cyn. 1: 25.6
  Cyr. 6.1.36: 18.9
  Hell. 6.5.1: §1 c n. 9

Zonaras
  9.6 p. 268 Dindorf: 14.10

2 GREEK WORDS

ἀγανακτέω 24.3
Ἀγκαράτης 38b.1
ἀγνοέω §4 b, 13.8
ἀγχίνοια 34.10
ἀγωνία 19.2
ἀθεσία 21.10
ἀθλητής 9.8
ἀθροίζω 34.2
ἀκάκως §13 b
ἀκμήν §13 c, 1.2, 19.3, 37.9
ἀκόλουθος 8.7
ἀκολούθως 30.2
ἀκούω §1 b, 1.1
ἄκρα §11 a, 30.6, 8, 33.2, 4
ἀκρατοποσία 9.4
ἀκριβής §3 c
ἄκριτος 21.6

ἀκρόπολις §11 a n. 45, 21.9
ἀκρωτηριάζω 21.3
ἀλλάττω, ἀλλάττομαι 11.5
ἀλλοιόω 27.5
ἀλλότριος 1.1
ἀλόγως 24.7, 36.1
ἄν §3 b n. 12
ἀναγινώσκω §1 b
ἀναγκαῖος 12.1
ἀνάγκη 11.2
ἀναζεύγνυμι 34.10
ἀναζυγή §13 c n. 65, 26.4
ἀνακρεμάννυμι 19.3
ἀναστέλλω 4.1
ἀναστροφή 24.10
ἀνδρόπορνος 9.12
ἄνεσις 37.2

ἀνήκω 12.8
ἄνθρωπος 21.11
ἀνοδία 14.6
ἀντέχω, ἀντέχομαι 7.10
ἀντηρίς 4.6
ἀντιποιέω, ἀντιποιέομαι 2.8
ἀντιφωνέω §13 b, 16.11
ἀξία §6 e
ἄξιος §6 e, 16.8
ἀποβαίνω 10.10
ἀπόβασις 4.4
ἀποδείκνυμι §13 a
ἀποκαθίστημι 23.5, 27.6
ἀπολογίζομαι 24.7
ἀπόστασις 37.1
ἀποστάτης §12 g n. 60
ἀπόστημα 5.3
ἀποτέμνω 14.8
ἀπροφασίστως 37.7
ἀρχαῖος §3 a, §3 c n. 14, §4 b, §8 b n. 41
ἀρχιτέκτων 7.2
ἀσέβεια 12.1
ἀσέλγεια 12.1
ἀσκέπτως 36.1
ἀτοπία 9.5
αὐτόθεν 35.2
αὐτοπαθῶς 17.7
αὐτός 2.1, 19.8
ἐξ αὐτῆς 37.7
αὐτοῦ 29.8
ἀφασία 20.9
ἄχρηστος 5.6
ἀψυχαγώγητος §4 b

βαπτίζω 6.4
βασίλειον 23.2
βασιλεύς 15–21
βασιλικός 10.10, 22.1, 23.5
βαστάζω 5.9, 16.4
βδελυρία 9.8
βέλος 5.2
βία 14.11

Γάλαισος 33.8
Γαλάται 30.12
γενναίως 17.7
γέρρον 3.3
γίνομαι §13 a
γινώσκω §13 a

δαψίλεια 24.12
δαψιλής 37.2

δεῖ
δέον §12 g n. 60
δείκνυμι/δεικνύω §13 a
δειπνοποιέω, δειπνοποιέομαι 26.6
δεύτερος 18.5
δεύτερος πλοῦς 36.5
δημοκρατία 35.6
δῆμος §12 d
δήποτ' οὖν §4 a
διάβασις §6 c
διαδοχή 14.5
διάθεσις §6 e, §13 b, 8.8, 12.3, 15.9
δίαιμος 12.5
διαιρέω 7.11, 37.11
διακούω 15.3
διαλαμβάνω 15.6
διάληψις §13 c n. 65, 25.6
διαλογισμός §13 b, 18.1
διάνοια 13.1
διαπιστέω §13 c n. 65
διαρμόζω, διαρμόζομαι 5.1
διαρπάζω 23.2
διασαφέω 37.4
διάστημα 5.2
διαστρέφω 22.3, 23.2
διασώζω, διασώζομαι 14.8
διατάττω 20.5
διατείνω 29.6
διατρέπω 23.2
διατρέπομαι §13 b
διατροπή §13 b, 5.3
διαφερόντως §13 b, 13.3, 34.10
διαχειρίζω, διαχειρίζομαι 21.8
διαχέω 27.4
διδάσκω 34.5
δίδωμι 16.11
διεμπίπτω 26.5
διεξοδικός §5 c
διήγησις §6 a
διότι §13 b
δίχα 17.10
δοκέω 15.1
ἔδοξε 21.3
δόμος 37.1
δράσσομαι 6.2
δύναμις §13 b, 20.12
δυναστεία §11 b, 2.6, 23.3
δυνατός 19.5
δυσμενικός 8.1
δυσχρηστέω 20.1

ἐγκυρέω 35.5
ἐγκώμιον 8.6

ἐγώ
ἐμέ §3 b n. 12
ἐθελοντήν 14.10
ἐθισμός 30.8
ἔθνος 12.7
εἰ 12.6, 8
εἰλικρινής 31.1
εἶπον/εἶπα §13 a
εἰς 14.4, 26.4, 37.6
ἐκ 10.6
ἐκπλήττω §1 b n. 3
ἐκτενῶς 19.1
ἐκτροπή §1 c
ἐκχέω 14.1
ἐλευθερία §11 b, 35.6, 31.2
ἐλευθερόω 25.1-2, 34.3-4
ἕλκω 19.2
ἐλπίζω 3.3
ἐλπίς 31.4, 37.3
ἐμβλέπω 1.4
ἐμπειρέω 15.4
ἔμφασις §8 a
ἐν 8.4
ἐναλλάξ §6 c
ἐναποδείκνυμαι 32.4
ἐνδέχομαι
  ἐνδεχόμενος 36.1
ἐνέργεια 7.2
ἐνθουσιασμός 21.4
ἔνιοι §3 d
ἐνοικοδομέω 37.11
ἐνοποιέω 4.11
ἐντός 29.8
ἐντυγχάνω §1 b
ἐξιδιάζομαι 25.7
ἐξοδεία 24.4
ἐξουσία 24.1, 25.4
ἐπαγγελία §1 c, 18.10
ἐπαινέω 24.8
ἐπαύριον §13, 13.6
ἐπιβάλλω, ἐπιβάλλομαι §13 b
ἐπιβολή §13 b
ἐπικάθημαι 32.2
ἐπιπλέκω §6 c
ἐπισημαίνω, ἐπισημαίνομαι §13 b, 1.2, 31.4
ἐπίστασις 2.10
ἐπιτομή §14 e, f
ἐπιτρέπω 17.9
ἐπιφάνεια 4.8, 5.6, 19.2
ἐπίχειρα 12.5
ἕπομαι 29.8
ἔρημος 37.9
ἐρυμνότης 13.3

ἔσχατος §6 b n. 35
ἑταιρεύομαι 9.10
ἑταῖρος 8-14b.2, 9.6
εὐαγρία 29.6
εὐδαιμονία 24.1
εὐδιακόσμητος 34.9
εὐδοκέω 11.3
εὔζωνος 13.5, 14.2
εὐθαρσής §13 a
εὐθέως §13 c
εὐθύς §13 c
εὐκινησία 26.3
εὔνοια 12.6
εὐροέω 28.12
ἐφάμιλλος 1.2
ἐφεδρεύω 1.7
ἐφοδεία 37.9
ἐφορμάω 6.1
ἐφορμέω 1.6

Ζεύς
  εἰ μὴ νὴ Δία 11.6
ζηλωτής 24.13

ἡγεμονία 2.6
ἡγεμών §12 f
ἡμέρα
  ἀφ' ἡμέρας 25.11, 27.1

θαρρέω 31.2
θαυμάζω 34.10
θαυμάσιος 7.2
θαυμαστός 2.8
θεωρέω 6.5, 13.3
θυμός 8.1
θυσία 37.2

ἰδιοπραγέω §13 c
ἴδιος 5.7
ἱκανός 33.3

καθάπαξ 15.6, 20.2
καθό 11.7
καί 24.1, 7
καινοποιέω §12 a
καιρός 35-6, 17.1, 19.7, 26.3
καραδοκέω 18.1
καρχήσιον 5.10
καταζεύγνυμι 13.2
καταλαμβάνω 30.10
κατάλληλος §6 c
κατάλυσις 25.2
καταξίωσις 20.4

καταπέλτης 7.2
καταπληκτικός §1 b n. 3
καταπλήττω 32.4
καταπυκνόω 5.6
καταρρέω 14.6
κατασκευάζω 10.6
κατασκεύασμα 32.1
κατασκευή 9.3, 15.5
καταστρέφω 21.10
καταστροφή §13 b, 3.1
καταφέρω, καταφέρομαι 16.7
καταφορά 20.3
καταφρονέω 14.4
κατεπείγω 19.9
κατέχω 21.6
κατόπιν 18.8
κελεύω 16.10
Κελτία 30.1
Κελτοί 30.1, 12
κεραία 5.8
κῆρυξ 21.5
κίνδυνος 14.3
κινέω, κινέομαι §12 g n. 60
κίνημα 30.11
κλῖμαξ 4.4
κνέφας 26.10
κοινολογέομαι 37.3
κόσμιος 9.7
κράτιστος 17.4, 24.10
κρηπίς 3.2
κτείνω §13 c n. 64, 30.4
κυαθίζω 6.6
κύριος 20.11

λαμβάνω §13 b
λάσταυρος 9.6
λέγω §3 b
  τὸ λεγόμενον 19.5
λέξις §4 b
λίαν 13.3, 24.7
λιπαρέω 19.7
λιτός 19.8, 37.2
λογογράφος §8 a
λόγος §5 c
  κατὰ λόγον 5.3, 21.10
λοιπόν §13 b, 38b.2, 4.6, 11.2, 29.1
λῶΐων 28.7

μακρολογέω 9.13
Μᾶρκος 1.7
μάχαιρα 20.6
μεγαλεῖος 1.1
μεγαλόφρων 22.1

μέγας 7.7, 10.8, 17.11, 18.2, 37.3
  τὸ μέγιστον 36.3
μέγεθος 2.3, 19.2
μεθοδικός §3 c, §3 c
μειρακιώδης 11.2
μέλλω §5 d, 18.10
μέλω
  μέλει 24.9
μέρος 18.6, 19.5
  ἐν μέρει §1 b n. 3
  κατὰ μέρος §3 a n. 11, §10 b, 1.4, 2.2, 17.2, 25.1
  περὶ/πρὸς τοῦτο τὸ μέρος 9.1, 2
μέσον 23.1
μετάβασις 11.5
μεταβολή 14.7, 33.5
μεταξύ 11.3
μετέωρος 20.8
μέτριος 12.6, 19.8
μηκέτι 18.10
μήν 2.7
  οὐ μὴν ἀλλά 28.9
μηχάνημα 4.6
μνήμη 12.8
μονοειδής §4 b
μόνος 18.9, 20.8
Μουσεῖον 25.11

νεανίσκος 23.4, 24.10
νόμιμος §6 d

ὁ 8.4, 10.10, 36.6
ὅδε 28.1
  ἐπὶ τάδε 20.11
οἰκεῖος §5 c, §12 g n. 60, 3a and 1-7
οἰκέω
οἰκουμένη §6 b, §12 a
οἰκονομία 2.2
οἶκτος §1 b n. 3
οἷον 8.4, 10.5, 20.2
ὅλος §6 b, d, 2.2, 14.5
ὅλως
  οὐδ' ὅλως 11.5
ὁμοίως 1.5
ὅμως 19.3
ὁποῖος 9.13
ὅς §13 a, 21.9, 37.2
ὅτι 8.1
οὐ §5 c
οὖν
  μὲν οὖν 5.1
οὕτω 7.7
ὀφρύς 3.4

πάλαι 20.8, 37.9
παράβολος §13 b, 15.1
παραγίνομαι 8.1, 18.8
παράδοξος 2.3, 10.9, 19.7, 20.9, 21.6, 31.4
παραδόσιμος §5 d
παραδοχή 11.2
παραλλάττω
παρηλλαγμένος 30.5
παράστασις 9.2, 21.4
παρατηρέω 25.11
παραυτίκα 17.4
παραχρῆμα §13 c
παρεμβολή §13 b, 7.5, 24.4
παρουσία 13.8
πᾶς 16.4
πελταστής 13.6
πεντηρικός 4.1
πέρας 7.5, 24.13, 32.6
περί 21.7
  γίνομαι περί 37.3
  οἱ περί §13 b, 7.1, 16.11, 17.5, 6, 19.9, 20.1, 9, 24.11–12
περιλαμβάνω 1.3
πέριξ 14.10
περίοδος 17.10
περίστασις §13 b, 35.2
περιχαρής 29.11
πέτευρον 4.8
πετροβόλος 7.2
πικρία 10.1
πικρός §2 a
πίπτω 32.7
πίστις 15.9, 18.10
πλείων 28.7
πλῆθος 24.3
πλήν §13 b, 3.3, 6, 19.6
πλήρης 6.4, 30.5
ποιέω, ποιέομαι §13 b
ποικίλος 16.4
πολέμιος 35.6, 36.1
πόλις 13.1
πολίτευμα 1.1
πολιτικός §14 c, 33.3
πολυειδής §6 e
πολυμαθής §14 c
πολυπραγμονέω 24.10
πορεῖον 34.11
ποσός §13 c n. 65, 11.5, 14.3
πούς 9.2, 14.5
πραγματεία 9.1

πραξικοπέω §13 c, 9.3
πρᾶξις §3 c, §6 c, 8.5
προάγω §1 c, §6 a, 8.3
προαίρεσις §1 a, §6 e, 1.1, 8.7
προέκθεσις §6 e
πρόθεσις 18.6, 8, 29.1
προκάθημαι 1.4
προκαλέω, προκαλέομαι 23.5
προκοπή §13 b, 15.6
προκόπτω §13 b
προλέγω
  προειρημένος §5 b, 35.3
πρόληψις §13 b, 27.1
προπέτεια 9.2
προπίπτω 32.5
πρόπους 13.4
πρός 22.2, 23.1
προσάγω 5.1
προσαναλαμβάνω 37.2
προσανανεόομαι 37.2
προσεδρεύω 7.11
προσέχω §1 b n. 3
προσκαρτερέω 19.7
προσπίπτω §13 b, 3.1, 24.3
προστασία §13 b, 15.1
προστάτης §12 f
πρόσφατος 17.2
πρόσχημα 11.5
πρόσωπον 11.5
πρότερον 35.7
προτίθημι §12 b
πρόχειρος 27.5
πρῶτος 24.9
πτέρνα 6.2
πυλών 25.7, 29.5

ῥαιθυμία 27.6
ῥινοπύλη 25.8, 29.5

σαμβύκη 3a and 1–7, 4.11, 6.6
σαφής 8.3
σημεία 37.5
σκηνή 20.8
σκορπίδιον 5.6
σπεῖρα 14.5
στάδιος 19.2
στάσιμος 19.2
στέλλω, στέλλομαι 20.4
στρατηγός §7 a, §11 b, §12 d, f
συγγένεια 33.9
συγγενής 15.4

συγγνώμη 35-6
συγγραφεύς §3 a
συγκαθίημι 24.4
συγκεφαλαιόω §6 c
συγκρημνίζομαι 32.7
σύμμετρος 6.1, 13.4
συμμέτρως 28.13
συμμίγνυμι §13 a
συμπαθής 20.9
συμπεριλαμβάνω 11.4
συμπλοκή §3 a, §6 b–d, §12 a, 24–34
συνανακάμπτω 27.6
σύνδυο 4.2
συνέδριον 21.2
συνεξαποστέλλω 19.6
συνεργία, συνέργεια 33.10
συνεχής 29.9, 37.3
συνέχω
τὸ συνέχον §13 b, 2.3, 17.7
συνήθεια 12.5, 25.10, 30.7
σύνθημα 15.9, 20.5, 25.3
σύννομος 37.1
σύνοψις §6 e
σύνταξις 8.6, 9.1
συντάττω 19.9
συντέλεια 33.10
συντίθημι §13 c, 17.4
συντόμως 16.7
συντρέχω 15.6
σφέτερος §5 c
σχαστηρία 5.10
σωματοειδής §6 b
σωματοφύλαξ 20.8

ταλαίπωρος 21.3
τάξις 31.6
ταρσός §13 a
ταυτολογῶ §5 b
τε 10.1, 15.9, 17.2, 11, 33.10
τε ... καί §6 c, 28.11
τεκμαίρομαι 10.4, 21.4
τερπνός §4 b
τεταγμένως §6 d
τῆιδε 32.4
τις §13 a, 30.7
τίς §3 b
τοιοῦτος 9.1
τόλμα 34.10
τοξότις 7.3
τόπος §6 b n. 35, 1.6, 17.10, 37.13
τραγικός §1 a

τριβή 15.1
τρόπος 25.2
τροχιλεία 4.5
τυγχάνω
  ὁ τυχών 19.8
τύχη §4 b

ὑπεναντίος 36.1
ὑπέρ 13.5
ὑπερνεωλκέω 34.12
ὑπόδειγμα 21.10
ὑπόθεσις 35.5
ὑποκρίνομαι 27.4
ὑπόμνημα §1 c n. 6, §8 b n. 41
ὑποχείριος 20.7
ὕστερος §3 c n. 14

φαίνω
  φαινόμενος 8.8
φαντασία 13.3
φέρω 3a, 9.1
  φέρομαι 34.7
φημί 8.7
φιλανθρώπως 19.1
φιλία §12 b
φίλος §12 f, 8–14b.2, 9.6, 10.8, 13, 19.4, 21.1
φιλόσοφος §14 b
φράσις §4 b
φυλακτήριον 15.5
φύσις §6 e, 24.1
  κατὰ φύσιν 23.3

χαμαιτύπη 9.11
χαρίζομαι 15.2
χείρ 32.4
  ἐν χειρῶν νόμωι 32.7
χρεία 4.6
χρῆμα 7.7
χωρίζομαι 16.12

ψευδής §5 c
ψηλαφάω 16.4, 29.8
ψυχαγωγέω 23.5
ψυχή 3.3

ὡς 18.9
ὡς ἄν 7.2, 32.6
ὡς ἄν εἰ 17.3
ὡς ἐπί 28.2
ὠφέλεια 32.1

## 3 GENERAL

Achaean League §8 e, §11 b, §12 f,
    §13 a, 1, 12.2, 5, 7
Achaemenids §11 a, 23, 23.3
Achaeus §1 b, §9, §10 a, b, §11 b, §12
    g, §14 f, 35–6, 36.8, 15–21–
    21.11 *passim*, 24–34, 22
Achilles 15–21, 20.9
Achradina 3.2
Acrolissus §11 a, 13–14–14b.2 *passim*
acropoleis §11 a, 13.1, 15–21, 18.7,
    21.9, 24.0, 24–34, 32.2, 3, 33.2,
    3, 4, 34.2, 23.1
acting 27.4
Adranodorus 3a
Aegium 12.2
Aetolians §7 d, 12.1, 5
    and Romans §12 e, f
Agamemnon 20.8
Agathocleia §4 a
Agathocles (Alexandria) §1 a, §4 a
Agathocles (Syracuse) 10.12
age and interactions 23.4
Agis IV 35.3–5
agorai 3.2, 27.7, 31.1
Alcaeus of Messene 8–14b.2
Alexander the Great §6 b n. 27, §6 d
    n. 28, §11 b, §12 g, 8–14b.2–
    11.8 *passim*
Alexander brother of Molon §12 g
Alexander (Pherae) §11 b, 35.6–8
Alexandria 15–21, 15.1, 9, 25.11
Alps §12 c
analepsis §1 c
Ancari, Etruscan name 38b.1
Andromache 15–21, 21.4
animals
    in camp 24.9
    requisitioned 23.5
Antigonus I 8–14b.2, 21.3
Antigonus Doson §11 b, §12 f n. 55, 12
Antigonus Gonatas 20.10
Antioch on Orontes 17.11
Antiochis daughter of Seleucus II 23.3, 5
Antiochus I of Commagene 23
Antiochus III §1 c, §6 d, §9, §10 a, b,
    §11 b, §12 a, g, 15–21–21.11
    *passim*, 37, 23–23.5 *passim*
    and P.'s sources §8 b
Antiochus Hierax 20.11
Antipater 8–14b.2, 10.10
Antisthenes of Rhodes §3 d

aorist
    participle and verb 14.5
    participle set against present 17.3
    set against imperfect 15.8, 26.2,
        34.10
Apollonis §1 a
Apollonius of Citium §3 d
Appian
    has sources independent of P. 24–34
    language §13 c
    sources 34.1, 9
    transmission of §14 j
Aratus (Elder) §1 c n. 6, §7 e, §8 b,
    §11 b, §12 f, §14 f, §9, 8–14b.2,
    12–12.8 *passim*, 29.4
Aratus (poet) §3 d
Arcadia §1 c, §7 a
Archidamus brother of Agis IV §11 b,
    35–6, 35.3–5, 35.3, 4
Archimedes §9, §12 d, §14 d, 3a and
    1–7, 1.1–7.12 *passim*, 37
    emblem for power of knowledge 3a
    and 1–7
    and Hieron II 7.2
    life 7.2, 8
    planning 5.2, 4
    and P. 7.1
    readers 3a and 1–7
Ardaxanus 13.2
argument §2 a, b
    distorts events 1–2, 24–34
    distorts groups of people 8–14b.2,
        10.10
    and events 21.10
    and narrative 15–21, 21.10
Arianus 15–21–21.11 *passim*
Ariarathes IV §12 a
Aribazus 15–21, 21.9
Aristotle §3 d, §11 b
Armenia 23–23.5 *passim*
armies, consular 1.4
Arpi 26.3
Arsameia on Nymphaeus 23
Arsames 23
Arsamosata 23, 23.1
Arsinoe III 21.6
Artemis
    cult at Syracuse 37.2
    temple at Sardis 15–21
Asia §12 g
asyndeton §5 c, 36.2

Athenaeus Deipnosophistes §14 e,
    8–14b.2, 22.3
  quoting practice 6.6
Athenians 37.13
Athens §2 b, 17.11
atmosphere 16.3, 30.5
Attalus I §12 g
attention, degrees of 2.10
Attic §13 a
Atticism §13 c
Augustus §7 b, 17.1
author in Hellenistic prose 8.7

barbarians §7 d
beauty and historiography §4 b
biography §1 c, §7 e n. 37
Bithynia 22
Bithynians 22.2
Biton 3a and 1–7, 4.2, 3
boar §10 b, 25.5, 26.1, 29.4
Bolis §9, §10 b, 15–21–21.11 *passim*
books
  connections between §10 a
  connections within §10 b, §11 a, b
  as entities §10 a
  of P., earlier read more §14 b, e, j
  precise references 9.5
booty 26.7, 32.1
Bosporus 22.3
brevity
  effective 24.6
  expressive 15.6, 26.3
bridges 24–34, 32.5, 34.3
Brundisium 24–34
Bruni, Leonardo §14 k
Bruttii 34.13
Brutus *see* Iunius
Büttner-Wobst, Th. §14 l
Byzantium §1 c, §12 g, 22, 22.2, 3

Caecilius Metellus, L. (cos. 251) 32.5
Callimachus §4 b
Callisthenes §3 a, §4 b, 8–14b.2, 24–34
Cambylus 15–21–21.11 *passim*
camps 18.9, 24.9
  Roman 25.3
Cannae, battle of §12 c, 24–34
Capua 24.1
Carthage §1 c, §5 d, §7 b, §9, §10 b,
    §12 d, 3a and 1–7
Carthaginians §5 d, 7.12, 24–34–34.13
    *passim*
Casaubon, I. §14 l

Cassius Dio §13 c, §14 g
cavalry 26.3, 33.8
Cavarus §9, §11 b, 22–22.3 *passim*
Celts 26.3, 30.1, 12, 22
Centaurs 9.13
Cephalon 12.4
Chalcedon 22.3
character §2 a, §7 e
characters
  compared §10 b, 19.1
  doubts of 20.1
  focus in paragraph 19.1, 27.1
  internal reflection 15.4, 17.10, 19.1
chronology 3a and 1–7, 26.1
Cicero §14 a
citadels §11 a; *see* acropoleis
cities
  in book 8 §11 a
cityscape 15–21
Claudius Marcellus, M. (cos. I 222)
    §10 b, §11 b, §12 d, 3a and
    1–7–7.12 *passim*, 37–37.13
    *passim*
  and Hannibal §10 b
Claudius Pulcher, Ap. (cos. 212) §11
    b, 3a and 1–7, 1.1–7.12 *passim*,
    37.11
  his post 3.1
Cleomenes III §8 b, §11 b, 35.3–5,
    22.1
close
  of section 4.11, 6.7
  within section 5.7
closure desired by character 18.10
clothing §4 a, 19.8, 20.4, 6
code in letters 15.9
commentaries, Hellenistic §3 d
consistency 35.8
  value in P. 10.2
*consol* 3a and 1–7
Constantine VII Porphyrogenitus §14
    g, j
constitutions §11 b
  change between 24–34
  and psychology §11 b, 24.1
consular elections, when? 7.6
conversation mimicked 24.9
Corcyra 14.10
Corinth §1 b, c, §5 d n. 25, §7 c
Cornelius Scipio, P. (cos. 218) 1.
Cornelius Scipio, P. (cos. I 205),
    Africanus the Elder §6 b, §7 c,
    e, §8 c, 32.4

Cornelius Scipio Aemilianus, P. (cos. I 147), Africanus the Younger §7 a, b n. 35, e, §13 a, §14 d, 20.10
Cornelius Scipio Asina, Cn. (cos. I 260) 35–6, 35.9, 36.3
Cornelius Scipio Calvus, Cn. (cos. 222) 1.4
council
 of Antiochus §11 a
 of generals 7.5
 of kings 21.1, 2, 3, 23.3, 4
courts, Hellenistic 19.9, 22.3
Cretans §7 d, 15.1, 16.4, 5, 7, 19.5, 20.2
Crete §12 f
Croesus 15–21, 21.1, 11
crossing §6 d
Crusade, Fourth §14 j n. 80
Ctesibius 3a and 1–7
cult, heroic and divine 12.8
cultures interact §11 a, 24–34, 24.13, 27.1, 30.7, 22
Cynaetha §7 a, 29.4
Cynoscephalae, battle of §6 d
Cyrus the Great 15–21, 21.1, 11

Darius I 21.3
Darius III 20.9
Dassaretai 14.b.1
dawn and revelation 21.2, 31.1
*De obsidione toleranda* §14 h
death, consciousness in 12.8
Decius Magius 24.1
decline 8–14b.2, 8.2, 11.1, 12, 22
*defectio* 24–34, 24.3
Demetrius of Phaleron 8–14b.2
Demetrius of Pharos §6 b, §12 f, 8–14b.2
Demetrius I Poliorcetes 17.11, 19.8
Demetrius I of Syria §7 a, 9.4, 24–34, 25.6, 22.1
Demochares §3 d
democracy §11 b, 24.1
Demosthenes §2 a, §3 b, §5 c, 2.6, 11.4, 27.1
detail
 pointed §4a
 vivid 20.5
Diadochi §6 b n. 27, 8–14b.2–11.8 *passim*
 writing on 10.11
dialect §13 a, 31.4
 accent 30.3

Dicaearchus 11.5
digressions 12.1, §1 c
 pre-Hellenistic §1 c n. 9
 in Timaeus §1 c
Dimale §12 e
dining 10.10, 20.8, 24–34, 25.11
Dio Cassius *see* Cassius Dio
Diodorus Siculus §5 a, §13 c
Dionysius I §11 a, 3.4, 5, 4.1
Dionysius II 9.4
Dionysius of Halicarnassus §4 b, §5 a
 language §13 c
 papyri of §13 c
 and P. §14 b
 transmission of §14 j
Dionysus, cult at Tarentum 25.11
drama, Hellenistic 17.7
Drilon, Drin 13.2
drinking 9.4, 24–34, 25.11, 26.6, 27.1, 4, 5, 30.6, 37.2, 4, 9
Duris §5 a

education §3 b
Egyptians §6 e
elision §5 a n. 22, 28.8, 34.9, 23.5
emotion
 and argument 15–21
 and newness 17.2
 and practicality 15–21
emotions, distribution of 32.2, 4, 5, 33.2
empire
 Macedonian 10.6
 Roman 10.6
 Seleucid 23.4
encomium 8.6
Ennius §6 a n. 26
Epaminondas 35.6
Ephesus 15–21, 15.9, 18.2
Ephorus §3 a, d, §4 b, §5 a, §8 a, 2.2, 8–14b.2, 9.1
Epicydes §12 d, 3.1
epideictic §3 b
Epipolae §10 b, §11 a, 3.2, 4, 7.3, 37–37.13 *passim*
epitomes §14 f
Eumenes II §3 b
Eumenes of Cardia 8–14b.2
Eurotas 33.8
Euthydemus I of Bactria §12 g n. 60, 23.4, 5
examples, manipulated for argument 35.8, 9

*Excerpta Antiqua* §14 f, j, 35–6
*Excerpta Constantiniana* §14 g, h, i, 35–6, 24.1, 23.1
excerptor: initial summary 3.1
excursus
　end of marked 2.11
　justified 1.1
　extracts of P. in papyrus? 21.11
　eyewitnesses §8 c

Fabius Maximus Aemilianus, Q. (cos. 145) §13 a
Fabius Maximus Verrucosus, Q. (cos. I 233) 1.4, 30.6
Fabius Pictor §7 d, 24–34
fathers, real and figurative 15.9, 17.9
first person plural for tact 36.6
Flamininus *see* Quinctius
Flaminius, C. (cos. I 223) §2 b
Flavus (Lucania) 35–6
Florence §14 k
focalization 5.8, 20.9
　embedded 30.5
　embedded unlikely 34.3–4
　spatial 21.4, 5, 6
food §10 b, 24.13, 25.7, 37.2
Fortune §4 b, §12 a, 2.2
freedom §11 b, 24–34, 25.1–2, 31.2, 33.9, 34.3–4

Galaesus 33.8
garrisons §12 c, 24–34, 25.1–2, 26.3, 34.1, 13
Gaul §6 a
Gauls §1 a, 30.12
Gelon son of Hieron §12 d
gender 9.9, 10.5
　sexual roles 9.9, 10, 10.4
general and particular §2a, b, 8–14b.2
generalization, sweeping avoided 35.1
generalship 24–34, 24.10, 26.7, 37.3
genitive absolutes, accumulated 2.9–10, 18.10, 20.3
Gracchus *see* Sempronius
Greece §10 b, §12 a, f, 11.3, 4, 5
　Romans enter §6 d
　and συμπλοκή 1.6
Greeks §5 d
　fate of §7 c
　guards Roman 25.11

habit 29.5, 30.8
Hamilcar (no. 9 in Geus (1994)) §12 b

Hamilcar (Himilco no. 10 Geus) 1.8, 7.12
Hannibal §2 a, b, §6 b, §7 c, §8 e, f, §9, §10 b, §11 b, §12 a, b, c, e, §14 a, 3.1, 13–14, 24–34–34.13 *passim*, 37
　alleged plans §6 b, §12 b
　and Marcellus §10 b
　and P. parallel §8 f
　P.'s portrayal of §7 c, §12 b, c
Hanno (no. 22) 1.5
Hasdrubal (no. 4) 32.5
Hasdrubal (no. 5) §12 b
Hasdrubal (no. 14) §1 b n. 3
Hecataeus §3 d
Hecuba 15–21
Hellanicus §3 d
Henna 3a and 1–7
Heraclides of Tarentum 4.2
Heraclitus of Lesbos 8.2
Hermeias 21.3
Hero 3a and 1–7
Herodotus §3 a, d, §7 d, §13 c, §14 l, 8–14b.2, 10.11, 37.9
Hexapyla 3.2, 4, 6, 37.11
hiatus §5 a
hierarchy
　and behaviour 15–21
　of command 26.8
　inverted 7.8
　military 37.4
Hieron II §12 d, 3a and 1–7, 7.2, 10.9
Hieronymus §8 a, §10 a n. 44, §11 b, §12 d, 3a and 1–7, 3.1
Hipparchus §3 d
Hippocrates §3 d
Hippocrates (Syracuse) §12 d, 3.1, 7.12
historians, anonymous §13 c
　rivals of P. §3 d, §8 a
history
　change of subject in 11.5
　particular 2.2
　quotation in 9.5
　universal §3 a, §4 b, 2.2, 3, 11
　useful 21.10
Homer 15–21, 20.9
hope 38b.2, 15–21, 16.8, 17.11, 31.4, 37.3
house of *praefectus* 25.2, 27.4, 8
houses
　in captured city 31.6
　deconstructed 33.6

Hultsch, Fr. O. §14 l
humour 24–34
  amusing elements 25.7, 37.8
  change from 29.8
hunting 25.5, 6, 29.6
Hyacinthia 28.1
hyperbaton *see* word order
hyperbole 34.11
Hyscana 14b.1, 2

illness, feigned 26.1
Illyria §12 e, g, 1.6
Illyrians §11 a, 13–14–14b.2 *passim*
image of futility 7.4
imagery 9.13
impalement 21.3
individual
  against plurality 5.3
  importance of 7.7, 8
individuals and συμπλοκή §6 b, §12 a–g
infinitive, subject not given 8.4, 34.2
inscriptions
  and actual exchanges 24.8
  language of §13 c
  in P. §8 e
  in Timaeus §8 e
intentions, pre-set 18.6
interiority 19.2
irony 15.2, 4, 17.3, 29.7, 8, 30.6, 34.5, 37
  and hope 17.11
  ironic preparation 13.3, 9
  and neatness 17.4
  tragic 17.11
Isocrates §5 a n. 22, c n. 24
Italy in Second Punic War §12 c
Iunius Brutus, M. (praetor 44) §14 a n. 68, 21.11

jingle of words 7.6
John of Antioch 23
Josephus, language §13 c
justice 11.4

kindness, tactical 31.3
kings
  clothing 19.8
  and freedom §11 b
kingship, P.'s ideal of §11 b, 10.10, 22, 22.1, 23.5
knowledge, local
  shown by P. 24–34, 29.1
  used by Hannibal 30.2
koine §13 a

Laelius, C. (cos. 190) §8 c
Laestrygonians 9.13
Lagoras §10 b, 15.1, 17.1
Laodice wife of Achaeus 15–21, 19.7, 20.11, 21.4
Laodice wife of Seleucus II 20.11
Larisa §12 f
Latin and P. §8 e
learning 28.1
legions 7.8, 12
Leonidas II 35.3–5
Leontini §12 d, 3.1
Leuctra, battle of 35.6, 11.3
light-armed troops 13.4, 14.2
Lissus §9, §11 a, §12 e, 8–14b.2, 13–14–14b.2 *passim*
Livius, C. §11 b, 24–34–34.13 *passim*
Livy
  chronology 35–6, 26.1
  commentary on §14 l
  omits embarrassing material 27.1, 30.6
  and P. §8 a, §14 a, 3a and 1–7, 3.1, 24–34
  simplifies cast 28.3
  sources 34.1, 9
  use of P. 24–34
long and short words contrasted 5.10
Lucan §1 c
Lychnidus, Lake 14b.1
Lycortas §7 a
Lycurgus, king from *c*.219 §12 a
Lydians §11 a, 15–21
Lysimacheia, battle of 22
Lysimeleia 3.4

Macedon §12 f, g, 1.6, 12, 12.5, 7
Machiavelli §14 k, l n. 82
Magnesia, battle of §6 d
maniple 37.5
Manlius Torquatus, T. (cos. I 235) 1.3
manuscripts of P.
  D §14 f
  F §14 f
  G §14 f
  M §14 g
  P §14 g
  T §14 h
manuscripts of siege literature §14 h
Mar Grande 24.0, 34.9
Mar Piccolo 24.0, 27.7
Marcellus *see* Claudius
married couple 19.7
Mat, River 13.2

Megalopolis §7 a, §13 a
Melancomas 15-21-21.11 *passim*
mercenaries, recruiting 16.2
Messene §7 a, §10 a, §12 f, 35-6, 8-14b.2
Messenia §9, 8.1, 12.1
Messenians 8-14b.2
metahistory 8-14b.2
Metapontum 29.2, 34.1
metonymy 34.11
mind
  of characters 17.10, 19.1, 20.8
  power of 7.7
Mithridates II 20.11
Mithridates nephew of Antiochus III 23.3
Moagetes 19.8
Moeragenes §1 a, §4 a
Molon §12 g, 15-21, 18.6, 20.6, 21.3
monarchy §11 b, 8-14b.2, 10.2, 24-34
money 15.7, 16.7
moon 17.9
Moschus 4.2
motion §12a, 15-21, 26.1, 3, 8, 28.4, 10, 11, 12, 23.2
Mouseia 25.11
Museo Archeologico Nazionale di Taranto 24-34

nakedness §4 a
name of thing as close 4.11
names
  numerous 16.9
  in pairs 17.6
  of places, precise 3.2, 29.1
  play on? 15.2
  of streets 24-34, 29.1, 33.6
narrative
  and argument §2 a, b, 15-21
  change in 15-21
  elegant shaping 14.9
  and generalized account 4.8
  homodiegetic §7 a
  manipulates sense of chronology 3a and 1-7
  rhythm §4 a
narratology §1 b, §4 a, §7 a
Naupactus, Peace of §12 f
navy, Carthaginian 34.6
necropolis 28.6
Nicagoras 35.3-5
Nicomachus 15-21-21.11 *passim*
Nicon 24.4, 11-12, 27.3, 28.3

Nicostratus §4 a
night 5.4, 16.3, 17.9, 18.4, 11, 20.8, 25.9, 26.10, 27.9, 37.4
non-Greek
  courtiers 19.9
  punishments 21.3
numerals and bravado 3.3
Numidians 26.4

obituaries 21.10, 22.1
Odysseus 19.9
Olympiads §6 e, §10a, 21.11, 26.1
*onero* 24.9
optative §13 a, 25.3
oracles, language of 28.8
Orontes (ruler) 23
Ortygia §11 a n. 45

Panaetius §13 c
panegyric 10.9
papyri
  of Appian, Dio, Dionysius §14 c
  language of §13 c
  of Plutarch §14 c
  of P. §14 c
paradox 12.5, 21.1, 38b.2
participle
  with article and no name 15.8
  weight on 34.7
participles and asyndeton 30.7
parties 6.6
Pelopidas 35-6, 35.6-8, 35.6, 8, 36.3
Peloponnese §2 a, §7 a, 12.2
Penestae 14b.2
Perdiccas son of Orontes 10.10
perfect middle/passive participle transitive 1.2
Pergamum §11 a n. 45, §12 g
Perotti, Niccolò §14 k
Perseus §3 b
perspectives 30.10
Pharos §12 e
Philemenus 24.4-30.7 *passim*
Philinus §7 d, §8 e
Philip II §2 a, §9, §11 b, §14 f, 8-14b.2-11.8 *passim*
Philip V §2 a, §3 c, §6 b, d, §7 e, §9, §10 a, §11 b, §12 a, e, f, §14 f, 1.6, 8-14b.2-14b.2 *passim*, 22, 23, 29.2, 5
  and Achaeans §12 f
  alleged plans §6 c, d, §12 e
Philistus 3a and 1-7
Philo Mechanicus 3a and 1-7

*philoi see* Index 2 φίλος
Philodemus §3 d
Philopoemen 32.4
philosophy §3 b n. 12
Photius §14 j
Phylarchus §1 b, §4 a n. 20, §5 a, §8 b, §14 e, 35.3-5
pity 8.9
planning 24-34
Plato 11.7
  and constitutions §11 b
play on senses 37.4
plot
  in P. §4 a, 18.11. 21.7
  of P. §1 c
  P.'s and characters' entwined 16.9, 17.8
Plutarch §1 c, 35.3-5, 35.3
  language §13 c
  papyri of §14 c
  and P. §14 d, 3a and 1-7
poisoning 12.3
polemic 8-14b.2, 9.5
politeness 21.5
Poliziano §14 f
Polybius
  alleged to misread Theopompus 9.1
  books 1-5, 6-40, 1-2, 4, 6, 12: §1 c
  contrasts self with Theopompus 8-14b.2, 11.2
  detailed local knowledge 24-34
  displays balance 3a and 1-7, 8-14b.2
  distinctions in 35-6
  dryness 13.8
  earlier books read more §14 b, e, j
  extension of work §6 a
  extravagance 20.12
  first person singular in 34.4
  life §1 c, §7 a, c
  not undermining Hannibal 34.2
  parallel to characters §8 f, 1.1
  quotation in 9.5
  relation of language to documents §13 c
  shows reasonableness §2 a, b, §3 b, d, 10.12
  subtlety 20.4
  sympathy for characters 15-21
*popularis* 24.10
Portella del Fusco, Syracuse 3.4
pottery, Laconian 33.9

*praefectus* §11 b, 25.11
*praesidium* 34.13
praise §2 a, §7 d, 8.7, 10.9, 11.2
present tense
  historic 15.2, 16.1, 18.9, 19.4
  not historic 4.6, 7
Priam 15-21, 20.9
printing of P. §14 k
Prion, Sardis 20.3
Prusias I §12 g, 22, 22.2
Ptolemy III §12 g, 15-21, 15.2
Ptolemy IV §1 c, §6 e, §12 a, g, 15-21-21.11 *passim*, 23
Ptolemy VI 19.8
punishment 21.3
Puteoli 26.3
Pyrrhus 20.10, 24-34, 24.1

queens 15-21, 21.5
questions
  rhetorical §3 b, 1.2
  in rhetoric 11.6
Quinctius Flamininus, T. (cos. 198) 34.3-5
quotation
  in Dionysius 9.5
  in history 9.5

Raphia, battle of 15-21
readers §1 b, §4 a, 35-6, 2.8
  advance knowledge of 15-21
  deceived 14.8
  emotions §1 b
  future of 21.10
  given information through scene 15.4
  Greek and Roman §7 b
  how far bound by author §10 b
  kept curious 25.9
  surprised 14.7, 8
  tantalized 13.5
  thrown 20.1
reception of visitors 19.1, 24.8
Reiske, J. J. §14 l
relative pronoun joining sentences 21.9
religion
  near-religious sense of limits 36.8, 21.11
  restraint on gods 17.3
repetition §5 b
  avoided *see* variation
  effective 15.6
  of formation 18.5

revolution (word) §14 k n. 81
rhetoric §3 b
  in P. §3 b, 1.2, 10.8, 10, 12, 11.6, 7,
    20.12, 21.10
  broad-brush 8–14b.2
  concession 10.8
  fairness 2.5
  purposeful organization 2.6
  self-critical note 8.8
  structure 10.2
Rhodes §1 c, §12 g, 15–21, 9, 18.2, 22
Romans §1 c, §6 a–d, §7 a–d, §11
    b, §12 a–d, 3a and 1–7–7.12,
    24–34–37.13 *passim*
  and Aetolians §12 e, f
  brutality 24–34
  Carthaginians outwit §7 c
  disordered 30.9, 27, 37.8
  and Greek culture §11 a, 6.6, 24–34,
    25.11
  Greeks outwit §7 c
  keep trying §7 d
  ordered 31.6
  plunder 32.1
  resilience 32.3
  too confident 3a and 1–7
  when planned world-empire
    1.3, 2.6
  worsted 7.8
Rome §9, 3a and 1–7
  domination §6 a
  P.'s approach to §7 b, c
  and P.'s structure §1 c

sambuca *see Index* 2 σαμβύκη
  instrument 4.11, 6.6
Sardanapallus §11 b, 10.3
Sardinia 1–2, 1.3
Sardis §8 f, §9, §10 a, b, §11 a,
    15–21–21.11 *passim*, 37, 23
Scepticism 36.2
Scerdilaidas §12 e, 13–14, 13.1
Schweighaeuser, J. §14 l
Scipio Africanus, Elder and Younger
    *see* Cornelius
Scorda 13.8, 14.10
scorpion slits 5.6
Scylax §14 b n. 69
Seleucid Empire §12 g, 15–21
Seleucids 15–21, 20.11, 23.4, 5
  non-Greek elements 19.9, 21.3, 9
  queens 21.5

Seleucus III §12 g
self-mockery, Marcellus' 6.6
semantic changes, fifth to third
    century §13 b
Sempronius Gracchus, Ti. (cos. I 215)
    35–6
Sempronius Tuditanus, P. (cos. 204)
    38b.1
sentence
  beginning and end 34.1
  size expressive 9.1
sentences, contrasting size 2.8
shaping 14.9, 37
shaving 9.9
ships
  as agents 4.2
  'five' 4.1
  taken over land 34.10
Sicily §3 a, §8 a, §10 b, §12 c, d, 3a
    and 1–7–7.12 *passim*, 10.12,
    34.6
Sicyon 12.7, 8
siege literature, Byzantine §14 h
Silenus 24–34
simple and intricate language contrast-
    ed 7.1
simplicity of language 5.7, 7.1
sitting 20.9, 21.2
slave, friendship with 12.4
Solon 21.11
Sophene 23
Sosibius 15–21–21.11 *passim*
Sosylus 24–34
sources §8 b, 1–2, 3a and 1–7, 15–21,
    24–34
Spain §6 b, §10 b, 1–2, 1.2, 4
Sparta §11 a, 35–6, 12.5, 33.8
Spartans 24–34, 28.1, 6, 33.9
spectacle with machines 6.3
speech, direct and indirect blurred
    16.2, 18.5, 29.6
speeches in Timaeus §5 c
Speusippus 8–14b.2
spontaneity, apparent §1 c, §6 a
stade 26.4, 6, 33.8
Stephanus of Byzantium §14 e–5
stoai 3.2
Strabo §14 f
  and P. §14 b
Straton 8.3
style and history §4 b
*Suda* §14 b n. 69, §14 i

suicide 18.8, 20.6
Sulpicius Galba Maximus, P. (cos. I
    211) 1.6
support verbs §13 b
sympathy in narrator 21.3
syntax, boldness with 29.6
Syracuse §9, §10 a, b, §11 a, b, §12
    d, §14 f, h, 3a and 1–7–7.12
    *passim*, 13–14, 37–37.13 *passim*
    size 7.10
Syria 15–21, 17.10
Syria, Coele 17.11

Tacitus §4 b
tactics §3 c
talent (money) 16.7
Tarentine young men 24–34–34.13
    *passim*
Tarentines 24–34–34.13 *passim*
Tarentum §8 f, §9, §10 b, §11 a, §12 c,
    24–34–34.13 *passim*, 37
Taurion 12.2
Taurus Mountains §12 g, 20.11
tears 11.5, 20.9, 10, 21.6, 37
technical writing
    Hellenistic §3 c, 3a and 1–7
    and P. §3 c, 3a and 1–7, 4.3
Temenus 28.1
temples 15.21, 25.11
texts, other, P. engaging with §3 d,
    8–14b.2
theatre in Tarentum 30.7
Thebes 35.8
Theopompus §3 d, §5 a, *§9*, §14 f,
    8–14b.2–11.8 *passim*
Thracians 22
Thucydides §1 c, §3 a, d, §7 d,
    §13 c, §14 l, 3a and 1–7,
    8–14b.2, 10.11, 11.3, 21.3, 37,
    37.9, 11
Thurii 24.3
Timaeus §1 a, c, §3 a, d, §5 a, c, §8
    a, d, e, §14 b, 3a and 1–7,
    8–14b.2, 10.1, 12
time: sense of evoked 27.9
Timoleon §8 a
titles in papyri 21.11
tombs 28.1
tone fluctuates 19.5
touch 20.6
towers 37.9
tragedy §1 b

Tragiscus 27.3, 28.3
traitors §2 a, 24.7
transmission of P. §1 c, §14 c, f–j
Trasimene, battle of Lake §12 c
Trebia, battle of the §12 c, 24–34
tribute 23.4
trumpets 30.7, 11
trust 17.5, 21.9; *see Index 2* πίστις
tyrants, narratives of conspiracy against
    24–34, 27.1

understatement 2.6, 13.3
unpredictability 15–21; *see Index 2*
    παράδοξος

Valerius Laevinus, M. (cos. II 210) §12
    e, 1–2, 1.6
variation §5 b, §13 c, 35.6, 36.1, 3.1,
    7.3, 4, 8.9, 9.5, 13.3, 28.7–8,
    29.7
variety
    and nature §6 e
    and P. §6 e
verb, colourful 6.2
vividness 24–34, 4.6, 9
    depiction of devotion 20.3
    detail 20.5
    of unrealized ideas 18.8

Walbank, F. W. §14 l
wall, Hannibal's? 33.6
walls 37.1
    and men 33.7
    isodomic 37.1
war, causes §8 e
War
    First Punic §1 c, §7 d, §12 b, c, 1.1,
        3a and 1–7, 4.1
    Fourth Syrian §1 c, §12 a, 15–21
    Second Punic §3 a, §6 b, §7 b, §12 a
        causes §12 b
    Social §1 c, §12 a, f, 12.5
    Third Punic §7 b
    wars §6 b, §12 a
Weil, R. §14 l
wicker screens 3.3, 6.1, 7.3
wit 3a, 6.4, 6, 19.5
    imagistic 6.6
wittiness 35.4, 9.13
women in P. §7 d, 19.7, 21.4
word order §5 c, 12.5
    hyperbaton §5 c, 36.5, 2.1, 29.7, 22.2

interrogative delayed 35.5
names clash 16.8

Xenophon §13 c, 8–14b.2, 11.3, 37.9
Xerxes (Armenia) §9, §10 a, §11 b,
    §12 g n. 60, 23–23.5 *passim*

year in P. §6 e, 35–6, 21.11
young people, instability in 23.2

Zama, battle of §6 b, e, §7 c
Zeno of Rhodes §3 d, §4 b, 10.12
Zeno of Sidon §3 d

For EU product safety concerns, contact us at Calle de José Abascal, 56-1°,
28003 Madrid, Spain or eugpsr@cambridge.org.